D1606360

GEORGE
PALMER
PUTNAM

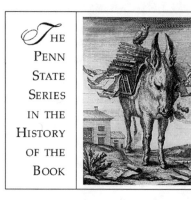

THE
PENN
STATE
SERIES
IN THE
HISTORY
OF THE
BOOK

James L. W. West III, General Editor

The series publishes books that employ a mixture of approaches: historical,
archival, biographical, critical, sociological, and economic. Projected topics
include professional authorship and the literary marketplace, the history of
reading and book distribution, book-trade studies and publishing-house
histories, and examinations of copyright and literary property.

Peter Burke, The Fortunes of the *Courtier:*
The European Reception of Castiglione's *Cortegiano*

James M. Hutchisson, The Rise of Sinclair Lewis, 1920–1930

Julie Bates Dock, ed., Charlotte Perkins Gilman's
"The Yellow Wall-Paper" and the History of Its Publication and Reception:
A Critical Edition and Documentary Casebook

John Williams, ed., Imaging the Early Medieval Bible

James G. Nelson, Publisher to the Decadents:
Leonard Smithers in the Careers of Beardsley, Wilde, Dowson

Penn State Reprints in Book History

James L. W. West III and Samuel S. Vaughan, Editors

Roger Burlingame, Of Making Many Books:
A Hundred Years of Reading,
Writing, and Publishing

Ezra Greenspan

GEORGE PALMER PUTNAM

Representative American Publisher

The Pennsylvania State University Press
University Park, Pennsylvania

Library of Congress Cataloging-in-Publication Data

Greenspan, Ezra.
    George Palmer Putnam : representative American publisher / Ezra
Greenspan.

        p.   cm.—(Penn State series in the history of the book)
    Includes bibliographical references (p.   ) and index.
    ISBN 0-271-02005-9 (cloth : alk. paper)
    1. Putnam, George Palmer, 1814–1872.   2. Publishers and
publishing—United States Biography.   3. G.P. Putnam & Sons
—History.   4. Publishers and publishing—United States
—History—19th century.   I. Title.   II. Series.
Z473.P95G74   2000
070.5′092—dc21
[B]   99-36895
                                                              CIP

Copyright © 2000 The Pennsylvania State University
All rights reserved
Printed in the United States of America
Published by The Pennsylvania State University Press,
University Park, PA 16802–1003

It is the policy of The Pennsylvania State University Press to use acid-free
paper for the first printing of all clothbound books. Publications on uncoated
stock satisfy the minimum requirements of American National Standard for
Information Sciences—Permanence of Paper for Printed Library Materials,
ANSI Z39.48-1992.

Contents

List of Illustrations

———•·•———

Acknowledgments

————

This book—I can now see—was written under the sign of the palmetto. Its research began when I first came to the University of South Carolina; little did I then appreciate that I would be working in the country's premier English Department of historians, collectors, and connoisseurs of the book or foresee how much or in how many ways their expertise would aid my own work. After seven pleasant years more of work than of labor, I would like to express my thanks to them collectively.

I would particularly like to thank those colleagues who have been especially helpful in expediting my work. Bert Dillon and Robert Newman generously put the resources of the department behind me early and late and in so doing facilitated the timely composition of this book. Paula Feldman, Trevor Howard-Hill, and Patrick Scott answered many questions about British publication practices and led me to sources vital to an understanding of the transatlantic aspect of this study. Matthew J. Bruccoli provided a model of professionalism, as well as filled the hallways outside my office with much of the best book talk, academic gossip, and show music to be found in Columbia. Joel Myerson served as a bibliography of information, as well as an all-around ideal colleague. To my thousand questions he gave a thousand answers and posed a number of queries that I would never have thought to ask.

The years in which I have worked on this book have been years of fine professional companionship with literary, cultural, and print historians in this country and overseas. I would like to thank them collectively for answering my many questions and steering me in productive directions. Among them I would like to single out for appreciation Kathleen Diffley, Robert Scholnick, James L. W. West III, and Michael Winship for reading the work in manuscript and giving advice that has helped me to improve its content and focus. I would also like to express my appreciation to the current generation of Wileys (especially Deborah Wiley and Bradford Wiley, as well as Charles Ellis) and of Murrays (especially Virginia Murray) for their hospitality in allowing me to read through their company archives and for their interest in this project.

Finally, I owe thanks to my copyeditor, Eliza Childs, for streamlining the prose and to Cherene Holland and Peter Potter at Penn State University Press for expediting the passage of the manuscript into print.

Grants from a number of funding agencies have made possible the research and composition of this book: externally, the National Endowment for the Humanities and the American Philosophical Society; and internally, the Provost's Office, the English Department, and the Office of Sponsored Program and Research of the University of South Carolina.

I have drawn heavily on countless libraries in this country and Great Britain, beginning with Thomas Cooper Library at the University of South Carolina, whose reference, special collections, and interlibrary loan librarians kept me well provided. I would like to thank the following libraries and institutions for permission to quote from their holdings of primary materials: American Antiquarian Society; Boston Public Library; Bowdoin College; Century Association; Columbia University; Cornell University; Curtis Memorial Library (Brunswick, Maine); Dartmouth College; Duke University; Essex Institute; Flint Memorial Library (North Reading, Massachusetts); Harvard University; Historical Commission of North Reading, Massachusetts; Huntington Library; Library of Congress; Massachusetts Historical Society; John Murray, Publishers; Pejepscot Historical Society (Brunswick, Maine); Pierpont Morgan Library; Princeton University; New-York Historical Society; New York Public Library; Radcliffe College; Smithsonian Institute; Union League Club of New York; University of California at Los Angeles; University of Michigan; University of South Carolina; University of Vermont; University of Virginia; Vassar College; Vermont Historical Society, and Wesleyan University.

Several parts of this book have previously appeared in print. A version of chapter 1 appeared as "George Palmer Putnam: Historical and Cultural Antecedents of an Ex-Yankee Publisher," *New England Quarterly* 69 (December 1996): 605–26. Part of the discussion of the Wiley and Putnam Library of American Books in chapter 6 appeared as "Evert Duyckinck and the Editorship of Wiley and Putnam's Library of American Books, 1845–47," *American Literature* 64 (December 1992): 677–93. Part of the discussion in chapters 6 and 7 of the Putnam–Henry Stevens connection appeared as "The Battle of the Yankee Booksellers in Europe: George Palmer Putnam, Henry Stevens, and the Fight for Dominance in the International Rare Book Market," *Biblion* 5 (spring 1997): 148–70. And a small portion of the discussion of Edmund Quincy's *Wensley* in chapter 9 appeared as "Addressing or Redressing the Magazine Audience: Edmund Quincy's *Wensley*," in *Periodical Literature in Nineteenth-Century America,* ed. Kenneth M. Price and Susan Belasco Smith (Charlottesville: University Press of Virginia, 1995), pp. 133–49. I appreciate the permission of the publishers to reuse those materials.

Lastly, I would like to thank Riki, Yoni, Noam, and Tamar for tolerating the intrusion of the Putnam family into our own and for never asking the question: Who invited them, anyway?

Introduction

When he died in 1872 at age fifty-eight, George Palmer Putnam was eulogized by the recently founded publishing trade journal as not only one of the outstanding men of his generation of Americans but also "one of its most trusty representative men."[1] That designation was probably truer than the writer knew, for Putnam, as I have assumed all along in writing this book, was in several reciprocally related senses the representative publisher of nineteenth-century America. But as I have also assumed, his ability to function as his generation's representative was, as Pierre Bourdieu states generally of publishers in their mediating position between writers and the reading public, "equivocal."[2] Indeed, as I will show, his ability to represent his profession not only to itself but to authors and the public was always more limited than he believed.

A life of Putnam, about whom there is little modern scholarship of serious or reliable import, is long overdue.[3] He was, simply, one of the most centrally situated, broadly and multiply involved, and professionally and patriotically dedicated figures of his time in the world of American arts and letters. That his period of professional activity spanned the formative era that gave rise to the institutionalization of modern print culture in the United States makes his life story all the more significant. His roles were many: he was leader of the American publishing industry during the formative period in which it became an industry and primary organizer of its New York Book Publishers' Association. He was also founder of the house of G. P. Putnam and Company, operator of *Putnam's Monthly,* authorized publisher to the New York Crystal Palace, publisher to many of the leading authors of his time and patron generally to the idea and practice of American authorship, pioneer American in the transatlantic book trade, leading proponent of international copyright and prime mover behind the formation of the International Copyright Association, and founding honorary superintendent of the Metropolitan Museum of Art. Furthermore, he had a literary stature unmatched by any other publisher of his time as the author of travelogues, reminiscences, journalistic correspondence, reference works, and statistical compilations and as the unofficial annalist of the American publishing industry. All in all, as publisher, author, editor, trade organizer, and copyright advocate, Putnam was as involved as any other nineteenth-century literary professional in the emergence of modern publishing in the United States and in the institutionalization of its print culture.

With these activities and accomplishments in mind, I gradually came to see the most promising approach to writing Putnam's life as being that of cultural biography, the method that permitted the most comprehensive correspondence between his life and the life of his society. In taking this approach, I have been particularly intent to locate his life as fully as possible in and against that of his family. To do so was, in part, to follow his own inclination to see family as the basic social unit. Putnam led very much a family-centered existence, a life devoted to his wife, ten children, and extended relations and imbued with a vivid sense of his descent through his mother and father to two historically prominent New England families. What makes that connection especially significant for me is the fact that he was tightly connected at both ends of his family lineage to the world of American letters. On one end, he was the son of parents who were local and regional figures in the fields of education and amateur authorship; on the other, he was the father of a multitalented brood of children who in the decades following his death distinguished themselves as national leaders in such print-related fields as publishing, book selling, book manufacturing, academia, librarianship, and medical research. To focus on his family life, therefore, allowed me a means to demarcate not only his life but that of the entire Putnam family as a specific register of the social, educational, cultural, economic, and technological developments transforming life in nineteenth-century America.

Notes

1. "George Palmer Putnam," *Publishers Weekly* 1 (26 December 1872): 697.
2. Pierre Bourdieu, "The Field of Cultural Production, or: The Economic World Reversed/Pierre Bourdieu," in *The Field of Cultural Production: Essays on Art and Literature,* ed. Randal Johnson (New York: Columbia University Press, 1993), 39–40.
3. The chief source for virtually everyone who has written about GPP had been his

son's turn-of-the-century biography, which was the most comprehensive publishing annal/biography of its sort written in its era but which is one that must today be used with caution. Although GHP was one of the most scholarly and knowledgeable publishers of his generation, he worked in a slipshod fashion and his book does not meet modern scholarship's overriding test of reliability. It is, however, a tremendously useful, informative source, which I have attended to closely, if with what I think of as an attitude of respectful skepticism; GHP, *A Memoir of George Palmer Putnam,* 2 vols. (New York: G. P. Putnam's Sons, 1903). He also published for a broader audience a slightly amended, less detailed edition of this work as *George Palmer Putnam: A Memoir* (New York: G. P. Putnam's Sons, 1912). My references are exclusively to the earlier version.

I have also paid serious regard to the various memoirs written by members of the family, a family that inherited from GPP a faith and proficiency in print discourse. They include the following: GHP, *Memories of My Youth, 1844–1865* (New York: G. P. Putnam's Sons, 1914); GHP, *Memories of a Publisher, 1865–1915* (New York: G. P. Putnam's Sons, 1915); Ruth Putnam, ed., *Life and Letters of Mary Putnam Jacobi* (New York: G. P. Putnam's Sons, 1925); Corinna Smith Lindon, *Interesting People: Eighty Years with the Great and Near-Great* (Norman: University of Oklahoma Press, 1962)—not to mention the numerous autobiographical pieces written by GPP over three decades for the newspapers and magazines.

List of Abbreviations Used in the Notes

Family Members

GPP   (George Palmer Putnam)
GHP   (George Haven Putnam, son)

Collections

BT-C   Bayard Taylor Collection, Special Collections, Cornell University Library

D-NYPL   Duyckinck Family Collection, Manuscripts and Archives Division, New York Public Library

GHP-C   George Haven Putnam Collection, Special Collections, Butler Library, Columbia University

GPP-NYPL   George Palmer Putnam Collection, Manuscripts and Archives Division, New York Public Library

GPP-P   George Palmer Putnam Collection, Special Collections, Firestone Library, Princeton University

HP-LC   Herbert Putnam Collection, Manuscript Division, Library of Congress

JL-NYPL   James Lenox Collection, Manuscripts and Archives Division, New York Public Library

Family Antecedents:
The Palmers and Putnams of New England

"Of making many books there is no end"—these, the first words ever to pass out of the mind of George Palmer Putnam and onto the printed page, were surely the most ironic he was to write during his long involvement in the culture of nineteenth-century print. An awareness of their irony, however, would hardly have registered on the earnest nineteen-year-old, all-purpose bookstore clerk then making his first foray into publication.[1] In naively citing the biblical warning, he could not have foreseen that the central story of his own life would be the making of many books or that that activity would be one increasingly integral to the life of his own society. But within several years of writing these words, Putnam was to become deeply involved in the rapidly expanding print culture of his time, and, once involved, he was to play a leading role in its evolution during one of the most dynamic periods in the history of American letters.

The boy who left home and school in small-town Maine in 1825 at age eleven to enter the working world, first in Boston and then four years later in New York City, where he arrived with no visible contacts or prospects, was hardly as unprepared as one might think to begin working his way into and up through the culture of book reading, writing, and making. In fact, his family, on both sides, was a distinguished one in the social, political, and cultural life of colonial and early republican New England, as it would continue to be on a national level through the nineteenth century; and Putnam's life and career make best sense when understood in the larger context of his family. This is so not only because he had a keen sense of family connectedness and loyalty but also because his earliest experience of letters came in the family home as the son of a teacher and an amateur man of letters. Indeed, his family home was one that would have put him in intimate touch with the changing atmosphere of letters in his society, since the Putnams and Palmers had been immersed for generations in their surrounding culture.

George Palmer Putnam was descended on his father's side from a well-established, middle-class New England family of farmers, ministers, physicians, and ship captains (roughly similar to that of Nathaniel Hawthorne, whose distant ancestor had married a Putnam and who himself married George Palmer Putnam's first cousin Sophia Peabody). His earliest New World ancestor, John Putnam, arrived in Massachusetts in 1642 and settled and prospered in Salem, the family seat for numerous generations.[2] John Putnam's grandson Benjamin was a sea captain, who was presumably otherwise occupied when other members of the extended family played a leading role in agitating for the punishment of witches.[3] Benjamin Putnam died in 1715 and left a will stipulating, among other things, that his son Daniel be provided for in order to continue his education at Harvard.[4]

Daniel Putnam graduated in 1717 and married his first cousin Rebecca Putnam the following year in Salem. Shortly thereafter, he answered the call of the people of Reading, Massachusetts, a village about twenty miles north of Boston, to become the minister of the church they planned to organize in the newly declared parish on the north side of town. Promised by the community a meetinghouse and parsonage and an annual salary of £66 and fifteen cords of wood, he accepted their call. He began to preach in 1718 but was ordained only in 1720 as minister of the settlement later incorporated as North Reading. There, on the main street, his grateful parishioners built him a two-and-a-half story house of plank construction that remained the Putnam family home into the early-twentieth century.[5] His early years there could not have been easy; in 1722 a collection was taken up by the town to help its minister, who "is represented to be in great straits."

That act of charity brought him whatever short-term relief £5, 17 shillings, could purchase. With time, though, he managed to establish his presence and that of his family in the community and lived out his long life there, preaching for nearly four decades and acquiring a reputation for piety and dedication.[6] He also managed to accumulate for his use and that of his children a fairly distinguished ministerial library, if one as remote from the interests of his nineteenth-century descendant as was the library of the Puritan occupants of the Old Manse from the interests of their nineteenth-century "follower."[7] One other legacy Rev. Putnam deeded his family was land; at some point in his tenure, the community voted to give him twenty acres of land and to plant him an orchard, which he gratefully accepted as given "to me my heirs and asines forever."[8] That land became the basis of his family's growing estate during the following generations, as the Putnams prospered and became one of the village's leading families even before the American Revolution.

His eldest son, also named Daniel (1721–73), was a respected church deacon and doctor who made his mark in local affairs, serving as selectman in 1763, 1768, and 1771 and as Reading's representative to the General Court in the year of his death.[9] He developed a substantial medical practice in the village, which provided him the wherewithal to enlarge the family's already considerable holdings in land, the primary basis of its wealth. When Daniel's two eldest sons died, probably in the same epidemic that carried him away several weeks subsequently in late 1773, the court awarded the entirety of his real estate to his eldest surviving son, Henry (1755–1806), only eighteen at the time.

That first Henry Putnam was to answer the call to arms on 19 April 1775. He served in a regiment commanded by his townsman Captain John Flint, but otherwise, in contrast to his Connecticut cousin General Israel Putnam, he saw little action during the war. Rather, he followed largely in his father's and grandfather's footsteps, distinguishing himself as a prominent citizen of the town and, from 1778, as the elected deacon of the church to which his grandfather had ministered.[10] He also served North Reading, as was by then virtually a family tradition, as selectman and representative to the General Court. A hard-working farmer like his father, he increased the family estate, which by now expanded beyond the large family farm to include land holdings elsewhere in Massachusetts and in New Hampshire and part interests in local saw and grist mills. By the time he died in 1806, he was one of the most substantial landowners and a leading citizen in the town.

If the first Henry Putnam witnessed the birth of a new country, his eldest son, also Henry (1778–1827), represented the first generation of Putnams to experience the broadened opportunities that came with nationhood. Not much is known about his early years other than the facts that he was raised in the paternal homestead in North Reading and that he went on to Boston Grammar School. He then matriculated at Harvard College, one of the eldest among the seventy students in the class of 1802, which also included three other young men from North Reading.[11] Although he was the first member of his immediate family to attend Harvard since Rev. Daniel Putnam nearly a century before, Henry pursued his studies with little of his great grandfather's religious zeal. In fact, his name appears conspicuously in tallies of students caught missing prayers in the chapel.[12] Like many of his classmates, he took off a few weeks during several winters of his academic career, with college permission, to teach school in the area. An intelligent, creative young man, Henry Putnam distinguished himself at school chiefly by his literary talent. He contributed a long English poem to exercises held at the chapel in July 1800; then two years later he was the English-language poet at his class's commencement.[13] But taken all in all, his years at Harvard seem to have been unexceptional. He graduated with his class in 1802 with an eye toward the practice of law and subsequently gained admission to the Suffolk County bar. Three years later, he received his master's degree, one of about half of the class of 1802 to do so.

These are the bare facts about the father of George Palmer Putnam. From them one can readily infer that, in many ways, Henry Putnam belonged to a new generation of Putnams, one less bound to the family home and ways. The first eldest son in generations not to serve the local Congregational church as deacon, he was not only less rigid in his own faith, eventually passing completely out of the ranks of Congregationalists, but less able or perhaps simply less inclined to bind his wife and children to the ancestral religion. Moreover, he had less tie to the geographical area where the family had lived since its arrival in the New World. While his brother Joshua remained at home and inherited the family homestead and the bulk of their father's estate, Henry chose soon after his marriage to Catherine Hunt Palmer in 1807 at Jamaica Plains to move away from Massachusetts.[14] He was not to return there for any length of time until the last year of his life, when he retreated alone and probably in destitution to the family home, where he died on 12 January 1827.

On the Palmer side of the family, the New World line of descent was shorter but more distinguished.[15] George Palmer Putnam's mother, Catherine Hunt Palmer, was the granddaughter of General Joseph Palmer, the first member of his family to emigrate to America. Born in Devonshire in 1716 of a prosperous, middle-class family and well educated in his youth, he emigrated to New England in 1746 with his wife and brother-in-law, Richard Cranch, early his business partner and later a judge in Massachusetts. A man of means, Palmer bought a large tract of land in Braintree, Massachusetts, which he named Germantown after the large number of immigrant German workers he employed. During the three decades preceding the Revolutionary War, he established a variety of manufactories, which came to include a spermaceti candle factory, a chocolate mill, a glass factory, and salt works. In 1752, the colonial legislature granted him a fifteen-year monopoly on the manufacture of glass, a skill in which he excelled.[16] To complement his stature as the leading entrepreneur of the community, he built a fine, three-story residence called Friendship Hall, where he lived like a country gentleman, entertaining his neighbors, who included the Adamses and the Quincys; tending to his several acres of orchards and gardens; and overseeing the growth of his library, one of the finest in colonial Massachusetts.

As hostilities intensified between the colonies and Britain, Palmer was gradually moved to play a leading role on the colonial side. So did his eldest son, Joseph Pearse (later father of Catherine Hunt Palmer), a leader of the Boston Tea Party. During 1774 and early 1775, Joseph Palmer became a central figure in political gatherings on both the colonial and the national level. Shortly before the outbreak of fighting, he was elected to represent Germantown (or Braintree) at the Continental Congress. John Adams, who was passed over for the position, approved of the choice, calling Palmer "as good a Hand as they can employ, and having been for sometime in the Center of all their Business, in the County, Town and Province, [he] is the best man they have."[17] He responded to the call to arms on 19 April 1775, and the following month he represented Suffolk County at the second Continental Congress, where he was chosen secretary. During the war, he rose to the rank of brigadier general and was charged with various responsibilities, including the fortification of Boston and the attack on British forces in Rhode Island. That latter expedition ended in disaster. Palmer was charged with irresponsibility and tried by court martial, before being cleared by the Continental Congress.

He emerged from the war with his finances considerably weakened, having given generously to the cause and been repaid in large part in colonial currency, whose depreciation was so severe as to make it virtually worthless. One immediate consequence was the loss of Friendship Hall to Palmer's creditor and one-time friend John Hancock, who, at least according to family legend, actually had the family forced out of its doors.[18] Always resourceful and untiring, Palmer resettled his family in Roxbury and tried to recoup his fortune in the last years of his life by starting a salt works in Boston. He died, however, in 1788 before seeing his plans through to completion. Although not left in debt, the Palmer children and grandchildren never again experienced the easy days of affluence and comfort enjoyed during the General's lifetime. Over the decades leading up to George Palmer Putnam's childhood, stories about that earlier era of Palmer affluence continued to circulate widely among the general's descendants but only as family legend. Joseph Palmer's more direct legacy to his descendants was the gift of pride and gentility, but stripped of the financial resources needed to sustain that attitude.

General Putnam's only son, Joseph Pearse, inherited something of his father's entrepreneurial spirit but little of his talent for execution. A 1771 graduate of Harvard, he married the following year Elizabeth Hunt, the attractive seventeen-year-old daughter of a successful distiller from Watertown. Her education had been limited by her father's disbelief in female learning, and Palmer sought to teach her from the books in his father's library. Since the completion of his own studies he had been in business with his father, who had set up a retail store and import-export business in Boston that the two men stocked with products, including those manufactured in the various family works back in Germantown. Amid growing tension between the local authorities and citizenry, the young couple settled in Boston, where the first of their nine children (Mary, the future wife of the lawyer-playwright Royall Tyler) was born the next summer. Three months later came Joseph Pearse Palmer's participation in the Boston Tea Party (or, in the family vernacular, the making of "salt water tea"). His role an open secret in town, word soon reached the ears of the royal governor, who ordered him expelled from Boston and the family's store and warehouses on Long Wharf burned to the ground.[19] Under duress, the young family lived for a short time with Elizabeth Palmer's wealthy father, then, thinking it unsafe to return to Boston, moved into their own house in Watertown.

Like his father, Joseph Pearse was increasingly drawn during the early 1770s into enthusiastic involvement in current affairs on the patriot side, as were many of his Harvard classmates and friends. On the night of 18–19 April 1775, he and his father rode together to Lexington to answer the call to arms; his father returned so drained that he had to be helped off his horse. Several weeks later, the younger Palmer was appointed quartermaster general of the gathering Continental Army, a position he maintained until relieved of his responsibilities when George Washington arrived in Cambridge to assume control of the army.[20] He served for a short period in 1777 as his father's brigade major, but during most of the rest of the war he was engaged with his father primarily in the manufacture of salt from sea water on the Palmer farm, as well as in other business operations. In 1778, the General invited him and his family to move into the large farmhouse on the Germantown estate, where they lived several years in Palmer-style opulence with servants and grooms to attend the needs of the growing family.

After the end of fighting, he opened a store in Cornhill, Boston, with his father as silent partner. But the store failed, as, on a larger scale, did the far-flung enterprises of his father. Following the loss of the family estate and the transferal of the family's home and business to Boston, Joseph Pearse Palmer joined his father in his ambitious new project of salt works on Boston Neck, into which the two men sank the remainder of the family's assets as well as funds raised from investors. But soon after the General died, their creditors, lacking faith in the still incomplete project and in the younger Palmer, withdrew their funds, undermining the works and leaving Palmer, for the first time, on his own and without a source of capital for executing future projects. Even in the months before his father died, he was describing his situation as "truely [sic] distressing—destitute of necessaires, in my family, and void of any means of providing" and appealed to an acquaintance for employment, no matter how "trifling" the work.[21]

From the time of his father's death and the loss of the salt works to the end of his life, Joseph Pearse experienced little but frustration and failure. Despite financial assistance from his wealthy in-laws, he had little success in various enterprises carried out in various localities, and his family was forced to adapt itself to living far below its previous station in life. Their reduced circumstances did not come easily to the proud Palmers: the family was forced to take in boarders and to do its own manual chores, yet it continued to receive company elaborately and to live beyond its means. Forced to reduce the size of his family, Joseph Pearse Palmer chose to forestall the education of his oldest son (also Joseph) and to send him to sea as a cabin boy. Likewise, he allowed his oldest daughter Mary to go to New York in 1789 as a companion to the children of Elbridge Gerry, a signer of the Declaration of Independence who had recently been appointed a representative in the newly constituted Congress.[22]

Matters only deteriorated, however, in the following decade. Having exhausted opportunities in Boston, Palmer gladly accepted the offer of his Hunt brothers-in-law in 1790 to take possession of a farm in Framingham that had been deeded to them. Just a few years removed from the genteel pleasures of the General's country seat, the family now gave itself over to the common chores of manual labor in and out of the house (living, in effect, a reversal of the plots of such favorite recent British novels as *Tom Jones,* which Joseph Pearse once enjoyed reading out loud to family and friends in his father's library). With a growing number of children at home (their ninth and last child, Catherine Hunt, having been born in Framingham in 1791) and few of the financial resources their parents had had in raising them, Elizabeth and Joseph Pearse Palmer had no recourse but to take upon themselves the task of educating their children at home. During winters, Palmer turned his own schooling to profit by opening a private school for boys. Preferring such work to farming but failing to attract enough students in the Framingham area, he accepted the invitation in 1794 of his son-in-law Royall Tyler, who had himself recently moved to Vermont to practice law, to try his fortune as a tutor in the family of wealthy Vermont acquaintances, a gambit that required that he leave his family behind on the Framingham farm. As matters turned out, Palmer had scarcely better fortune during the three years he spent in Vermont, which was too sparsely populated to provide him enough students to generate much income to send back to the family at Framingham. So matters continued until one day in 1797 when Palmer, while inspecting a new bridge being built over the Connecticut River at Woodstock, fell through a plank and was killed on the rocks below (as, by chance, just a week later his son Edward, an apprentice printer living down river in Brattleboro, met his death by drowning in the same river).

By that time, the family home had ceased to exist. Most of the children were already off the farm and beyond the supervision of Elizabeth Hunt Palmer, who had abandoned the farm before her husband's death and moved to Watertown to be near her own family. She still had three children with her, including Catherine Hunt, whom she raised in proximity to the locale of her own childhood. Assisted by a loan from a Mr. Smith and offered the use of a building owned by her brother William, Elizabeth Hunt Palmer joined forces with her sister Kate Hunt in opening up a small store dealing in English goods in the center of Watertown. After a few years, the store provided her with a steady income, but the time and attention required for its management made it impossible for her to attend as fully as she wished to her three children.[23] Worried that they were being neglected and left to imitate the behavior of the local children, she worked frantically to place them with relatives. In 1798, a family arrangement was made to have the eldest of the three, Elizabeth, sent off to live with the Peabody family of Atkinson, New Hampshire (whose mother was a Cranch, the family with which the Palmers were intermarried at the generations of both Joseph Palmer and Joseph Pearse Palmer). Four years later, Elizabeth married the Peabodys' son Nathaniel, with whom she was to have, among her seven children, three gifted and, in time, famous daughters: Elizabeth Palmer Peabody, Mary Peabody Mann, and Sophia Peabody Hawthorne. Months after the departure of her daughter Elizabeth, Elizabeth Hunt Palmer was able to send her youngest son George (for whom George Palmer Putnam would be named) to Mary Cranch in Quincy, who had briefly housed Elizabeth until arrangements for her live-in situation with the Peabodys could be finalized.

Mrs. Palmer continued to worry, however, about the education and welfare of her bright, youngest child. Watertown, so a refrain of her letters went, was no place to raise children. In April 1799, she was hoping to send Catherine to live with her aunt Elizabeth Cranch at West Point, but nothing came of that scheme. By year's end, she was frantic to find a better situation for Catherine and enlisted her daughter Elizabeth to help her persuade Mary Cranch of Quincy to invite Catherine to live with her.[24] That effort apparently came to fruition the following year when Mrs. Cranch did take Catherine into her house. By this circuitous route, the young girl wound up in the vicinity of the home in which her father had grown up. She lived with her aunt in relative comfort and was even able to attend for a time the Young Ladies' Academy run by Susanna Rowson, who was as well known in her own day as the preceptress of that school as she was as the author of her best-selling novel, *Charlotte Temple* (1791). How many terms Catherine spent at Rowson's school is unknown, but it seems clear that the time she spent there not only provided her with her highest level of formal education but served her in later years as the basis of her own career as a private school mistress.

Catherine Hunt Palmer presumably met Henry Putnam, her senior by thirteen years, somewhere in the Boston area, although virtually nothing else is definitively known about their early history other than the fact of their marriage in 1807. Their union must have seemed, at the time, a godsend to Mrs. Palmer, who had fretted for years over her inability to provide for her unmarried children. In time, though, she came to regret deeply her youngest daughter's marriage to Putnam. Even at the time of their wedding, things could not have been going well professionally for Putnam, who was then practicing law in Suffolk County, because shortly afterward the couple decided to move to the relative outpost of Brunswick, Maine. They took Mrs. Palmer along with them, who used her savings to help finance provisions for their new home. Why they moved specifically to Brunswick is not clear; the most likely reason is that, lacking an economically secure base in Massachusetts, they accepted the advice of Catherine's school friend Narcissa Stone, herself a member of one of Brunswick's leading families, to try the small but growing town as the site of a private school.

Brunswick was little more than a handsome New England village at the time, its population of about three thousand people living in a narrow range of white-painted, two-story homes and stores stretching neatly along one broad main street and a few narrower cross streets. The commons set aside by the town fathers was still not drained and was widely used for the pasturing of cows, and much of the town's land was as yet "unimproved." Blueberry bushes, whose picking was a favorite late-summer activity, grew wild in many places; first-growth forests surrounded the town; vegetable gardens grew widely and served not only villagers' practical needs but also as a source of pride;

and favorite recreational activities, such as pigeon shooting, sledding, and swimming, reflected how closely life in Brunswick corresponded to the natural cycle of the year. The general tenor of life in the village can be gauged by some of the regulations passed by the town council in 1830, which forbade children from sliding down streets on vehicles not drawn by animals and from grabbing on to moving vehicles and which fined citizens for allowing geese to wander off their property ($.06 per goose).[25] Throughout the period of the Putnams' residence in Brunswick, the sight of Indians passing through the town or traveling up and down the adjacent Androscoggin River was common; the senior Putnam even claimed to be acquainted with members of the Penobscot tribe.[26] In fact, for a period of time an Indian woman named Molly Suctomer lived in the one-story building adjoining the Putnams' house.[27]

Although it might have been fanciful to advertise early-nineteenth-century Brunswick as being, in Henry Putnam's words, of "so singular a combination of the beautiful and the sublime," the town certainly had its charm and character.[28] More important, it had ambitions that clearly distinguished it from the average New England village of the time. Its primary source of pride lay in Bowdoin College, Maine's first school of higher education, which was founded in 1794 and grew considerably over the course of the next few decades. During the period of the Putnams' residence, the college was situated on a six-acre campus surrounded by a fence; the three buildings within formed an incomplete square. The college library, though originally meager, soon grew considerably as a result of the bequest of James Bowdoin, son of the Massachusetts governor for whom the school was named, of his books and paintings. By the 1820s the student body had expanded to 120 young men; among those present simultaneously during the early 1820s were such men of future prominence as Franklin Pierce, Nathaniel Hawthorne, and Henry Wadsworth Longfellow—the latter two became professional authors whom George Palmer Putnam, a boy growing up just blocks down Main Street during their residence at the college, would publish.

Boosts to the ambitions not only of the college but of the town and state were given by the move to independence from Massachusetts, which culminated in Maine's statehood in 1820. That same year Brunswick became the home of one of Maine's first printing offices. Six years later, a group of local men (including Bowdoin President William Allen; the Putnams' friend, Bowdoin professor Parker Cleaveland; and

Stephen Longfellow) petitioned Congress to establish an "astronomical observatory in the town of Brunswick, and state of Maine; a state of great commercial facilities, and having a large and growing commerce"; their primary desire, they declared, was to promote "American genius."[29] In short, the town came to aspire to the status of a regional center for education and culture.

It had even stronger aspirations to commercial and industrial development. By the 1820s, Brunswick was beginning to show early signs of industrialism. The largest employer by far was a sizable factory overlooking the Androscoggin River in which cotton and woolen textiles were spun on machinery operated by a workforce of nearly one hundred people. Other new factories were set up along the river to take advantage of the ready supply of waterpower: grist mills (one of which was reportedly managed by Henry Putnam around 1820), saw mills, and shipbuilding facilities. Stages connecting the town to points east, west, and north arrived daily, although there was no rail connection until 1849. Despite these developments, agriculture remained a major source of livelihood in and around the town, with grains, vegetables, and apples the primary crops of choice.

Such was the town in which the Putnams relocated in 1807 and in which their five children were born in biennial succession: Henry in 1808 (died in 1815), Catherine in 1810, Anna in 1812, George Palmer in 1814, and Elizabeth in 1816. The first generation of Putnams raised outside of eastern Massachusetts, the Putnam children developed a quick affection for the out-of-door life style of northern New England. Although George Palmer Putnam never wrote publicly about his Maine years, he did reminisce to his son about the pleasures he took winters skating on the Androscoggin and summers boating up river to Bath.[30] No doubt, he also took part in the activities typical of children in the town: swimming in the river; foraging the fields for blueberries, raspberries, and blackberries; playing ball; ice skating and sledding; and exploring along the river and in the surrounding woods. At the same time, as the only son in the family, he was called upon to help his parents indoors and out with the daily chores. With his father often away from home on field trips through Maine in the early 1820s, George must have been expected early on to assume a large share of family responsibility, a trait that would be one of the most fully developed in the mature man. One early sign of his sense of responsibility has survived:

while walking by Bowdoin one day, he spotted a fire on the roof of one of the college buildings and ran back into town, shouting the alarm.[31] Such action would have been quickly appreciated by the townspeople; in a more serious outbreak of fire in 1822, one of the original college buildings had burned to the ground.

Provincial though Brunswick was and precarious as was the financial situation of the family, with Henry Putnam unable or unwilling to work as a full-time lawyer, the young Putnams had the good fortune to grow up in one of the town's most cultured families. Although far removed from the luxury of the fine private library owned by General Palmer, where his children found the latest English and Continental imports side-by-side with handsomely bound rare volumes and first editions, the children of Catherine and Henry Putnam did not lack for books or intellectual stimulation. Their father was one of a small number of college graduates in the town and was widely recognized in the community as a man of learning and varied abilities. He is listed, in fact, among the honorary degree recipients at Bowdoin for 1807, the year he arrived in town, even if in all likelihood he received that degree ad eundem rather than as an honor.[32] No less esteemed was their mother, the steadier and more focused of the parents, a well-read woman with strong ideas and powerful convictions. Aided in her earlier years by her friend Narcissa Stone, who returned to Brunswick and, after her father's death, established herself as one of the most active, influential people in the community, Mrs. Putnam ran a string of private schools in town from 1807 until 1825 and quickly made her presence known as the town's foremost private schoolmistress. On the most practical level, she took this initiative in large part of necessity as the main provider of the family's livelihood, even though the schools also served her own children, all of whom, boys and girls alike, eventually attended their mother's classes. On the larger historical level, she was participating, like her father and several of her elder sisters, in the broad educational movement sweeping across post-Revolutionary New England, as children from all classes sought to acquire the basic skills offered through primary and secondary schooling. "Rich and poor have an equal privilege of schools in Maine," as her husband was to write in 1820, "every attention is paid to the education of children by all classes."[33] Indeed, that new reality of expanding education in which the Putnam parents found themselves, as it gave rise to an accompanying increase in literary-based skills matched to a proliferation of books, magazines, and newspapers, became the basis in the next generation of their son's career as a nationally minded publisher.

Like her parents before her, who removed the rug from the parlor that became her father's classroom, Catherine Hunt Putnam typically turned the parlor of the family home into her classroom. The Putnams' first home in Brunswick was a two-story structure on Main Street built by Captain John Dunlap (whose son Robert, a future governor of Maine and United States Congressman, was to become an important professional contact for George Palmer Putnam at several times in his career). By the time the Putnams arrived in Brunswick, Dunlap, who had prospered from the fur trade, lumber operations, and shipping interests, was not only a community leader but reputedly the richest man in Maine. In 1799 he had headed up the building committee for Bowdoin's Massachusetts Hall; at about the same time, he began the construction of the finest house in town for himself, a handsome mansion that was completed by 1800.[34] His old house he rented out. The Putnams, his second set of tenants, lived in it from 1807 until 1820, at which time Dunlap apparently chose to give the house to his recently married daughter and her husband, Dr. Isaac Lincoln. Mrs. Putnam then moved her school next door to the Forsaith House and, several years later, to the home of Narcissa Stone's uncle, on the corner of Main and Mill streets.[35]

The sole surviving document from any of her Brunswick schools is a printed examination sheet, dated 16 October 1824. It indicates a fourteen-week term and lists the various grades, with a possible range from "perfect" to "irregular," she gave this particular student for recitations.[36] Although Mrs. Putnam was regarded by her family as a demanding woman, this girl received grades exclusively of either "perfect" or "well." In addition, it is clear from a letter sent to her grandson by one of Mrs. Putnam's former students that in 1821 the school had forty-five girls and three boys in attendance (one of whom, she mentioned, was seven-year-old George), that it was housed in a large hall of the family residence, and that Mrs. Putnam managed the house and school with no help except that given by her eldest daughter Catherine. That correspondent thought enough of Mrs. Putnam to visit her at several unspecified dates in New York City; it is not hard to imagine that a number of her other former students also carried away a vivid memory of her and her school that remained with them through adulthood.[37]

1.   Dunlap-Lincoln House, Brunswick, Maine. The Putnams' first residence after moving to Maine and Putnam's home from birth to age six. (Courtesy Pejepscot Historical Society)

Her exertions were hardly limited to the sphere of education, the field to which other Palmer women of that generation and the next were attracted. An unusually strong-minded individual, she also arrogated to herself the role of activist in the affairs of the Baptist church in Brunswick. Although a town, like others throughout New England, that had long been a bastion of Congregationalism, the parent faith of both the Palmers and the Putnams, Brunswick had been no more able than other early-nineteenth-century communities to prevent inroads by competing sects. Mrs. Putnam had herself been admitted to the First Congregational Church of Brunswick in 1813, to which she was preceded by her husband; but three years later she left that church and joined the town's First Baptist Church.[38] The reason for her break was stated in a letter to her brethren, in which she explained her motivation as owing to the discrepancy she perceived between the organization of the First Congregational Church and her God-enlightened views on "the order and foundation of God's lower house."[39] By the 1820s her new church was to have the unusual distinction of having in its small congregation both the first printer in Maine (its minister, Benjamin Titcomb) and the first printer in Brunswick (Joseph Griffin). In fact, for a time she even wrote articles for Griffin's *Baptist Herald*, the first Baptist paper issued in the United States.[40] But even before Griffin set up shop in Brunswick, Mrs. Putnam had quarreled theologically with the congregation of the First Baptist Church and had taken steps, along with Narcissa Stone and a group of other congregants, to form Brunswick's Second Baptist Church. In this latter church she played a leading role during her remaining years in Brunswick, a pattern of devotion and service that she maintained during the rest of her long, active life. Remembered by her granddaughter as a woman "whose whole life was absorbed in a vivid militant theology," Catherine Hunt Putnam continued to devote herself to the Baptist cause during the last decades of her life in New York.[41] There she directed the Baptist Female Bethel Union and helped found and direct the First Baptist Mariners' Church, a missionary organization dedicated to spreading their gospel among sailors who, they hoped, would carry it in turn to the four corners of the globe.[42]

A more elusive figure is Henry Putnam, a man of many talents and few accomplishments who strayed far from the parental faith and home but who seems never to have found either himself or his place. Whatever role he played in the family was certainly less forceful than that of his wife, whose affairs apparently dictated the family's move to Brunswick as well as its removal from the village in 1826. In a similar pattern, he was presumably following the lead of his stronger-minded spouse when he gave up his membership in the Congregational Church in 1821. During the two decades he lived in Brunswick, his role in the community never equaled his abilities. His name, always trailed by the honorific "Esq.," does appear from time to time in the ledgers of community organizations (the Congregational Church, the town council) but seldom with consistency or authority. Perhaps his finest moment came when he was appointed to a five-man local committee charged with drafting a report outlining how New England industry had suffered as a result of the federal embargo against England. The report concluded with an affirmation of the rights of free speech and freedom of the press, and a copy of the protest was then sent to President Jefferson.[43] The following year Putnam is listed as a representative to the Maine legislature. In addition, for nearly a decade he handled many of the legal affairs of his Congregational Church, a period of service that continued until (and presumably ended with) his wife's break with the church.

All in all, though, among the hard-working, hard-driving Yankees of Brunswick, Putnam must have seemed to others (and perhaps to himself) comparatively like a failure. He served consistently in no roles of authority, he accomplished so little during nearly two decades in town that his name appears only infrequently in early histories of Brunswick, and, except for the extraneous remark that he was the ancestor of the New York publishers and "loved the sport [of pigeon shooting] better than the law ... he was noted for his pigeon stand and booth of brush, and his game," he went unmentioned in the primary nineteenth-century history of Bowdoin.[44] Nor is he mentioned except in passing in a nineteenth-century chronicle of early Maine lawyers and law courts.[45] Whatever his initial expectations, he never developed much of a legal practice in Maine, nor is it certain that he ever worked very hard at doing so. Perhaps his poor health played a role in impeding his career—such, at least, is the explanation repeatedly advanced in the memoirs of later generations of Putnams. Their mentions of his life, though, are so few and guarded and their omission of accounts of his death so complete as to make the public explanation sound suspiciously like a deliberate family attempt to hide what must have been his true affliction: alcoholism.

The strongest evidence of Putnam's alcoholism comes in a letter written by his mother-in-law, who lived with the Putnams for a time in Brunswick, to her eldest daughter. In it, Mrs. Palmer expressed her conviction that his intemperance and irresponsibility made him unfit for family life:

> Our dear Catherine is now without a school for 8 months—And you have no more idea of her sufferings on his account than a Child unborn—I *myself have witnessed* the most *Christian* patience and forbearance in her deportment to him—and I will venture to say there is not one of you that could have borne what she has for 7 years—etc before it was *publicly* known how he squandered his time and his *substance* with *low br[ed][[?]* or dissolute companions. My sufferings while with him, and before she could be *convinced* of it were *inexpressible*. I have

preached—and done everything I could before Sophia [Mrs. Palmer's daughter] was married to convince him it wd end in *ruin*—And now his mind is entirely inebriated that he is a great brute and he ought to be in an almshouse where he might have [a con]stant guardian—he needs it.[46]

Although an angry letter from an unsympathetic mother-in-law may not provide a firm basis for conclusion, the evidence does fit the explanation.[47] To judge her from her letters and from other sources, Mrs. Palmer was anything but a vindictive woman; furthermore, her portrait of Henry Putnam does help to explain the lopsided nature of parental responsibilities in the family and the early exit of George Palmer Putnam from their Brunswick home.

One of Henry Putnam's few surviving letters exposes him in a situation of powerlessness he probably knew many times. He had just returned home, he wrote a fellow lawyer, only to find that in his absence Captain Dunlap, his landlord, had thrown all his papers in the street, "crammed into barrels and boxes and jammed together as they screw tobacco." At the time, his finances seem hardly to have been in much better condition; he mentioned that he had recently paid off all his major debts and would have been all clear with his remaining creditors had his own debtors paid him even one-fifth of the money they owed him. He closed the letter with the vague hope of starting business "*de novo* up the Androscoggin, where it is said they sometimes obtain bills of cost in cash, whereas here the best fortune is green pine slabs."[48]

A man who had tried on many vocations, Putnam experimented with a new one in 1820. Always the alert observer and recorder of the natural and human history of New England, Putnam decided to compose a series of descriptive letters about his adopted town. The letters were printed and published in 1820 by Joseph Griffin, the young printer whom President Appleton of Bowdoin had recruited from the printing office of Flagg and Gould of Andover, Massachusetts, just months before to operate a press on behalf of the growing school.[49] One of the first issues off his press, which in time became the most distinguished in Maine, was Putnam's anonymously penned *A Description of Brunswick, (Maine),* the parentheses indicating the state's then-provisional status. Actually nothing more than a pamphlet, the work might today be of little interest to anyone but antiquarians except for one then-unforeseeable eventuality: its author was the father of a man who was to play a major role in the transformation of the terms of authorship and letters in nineteenth-century America. One therefore wonders what the six-year-old boy learned at the time or took away in later years from his father's early adventure in authorship, a matter unfortunately about which (as about any aspect of his relations with his father) no record has survived.

Written in the fictionalized form of a series of five letters addressed by one South Carolinian planter, educated at Harvard but nevertheless untutored in Yankee ways, to another, Putnam's *Description* contains fine sketches of the conditions and character of life in early Brunswick—of its topography, history, demographics, economy, climate, and ethos. Its prevailing view is of a small, isolated community striving to overcome its rural, provincial origins; and its main theme, perhaps the reason for its pretentious format, the spirited energy and initiative of this particular group of Yankee settlers in turning the waters of the bordering Androscoggin to power and industry, the woods to lumber, and the soil to food for both local and external consumption. Putnam played the fictional game of assumed identity with zest, injecting into it the sectional rivalry between New England and the South, particularly strong after the recent Missouri Compromise: "You know I came into New England, especially into Maine, with deep prejudices against the northern character. The term *Yankee* we were taught to consider odious: but I now confess it a title, I should be proud to bear."[50] In actuality, Putnam's own Yankee character was so strong as to give the book the tone of local boosterism, the effect of which was to undermine its claims to authenticity by overstating the superiority of life in Brunswick and Maine generally to that in Charleston and the South.

Putnam's little book was as manifestly a New England publication in its production and distribution as in its content. Its market, like its subject, was strictly regional, a pattern common among books printed at this time in New England. Following the Revolution, the press had spread widely beyond incipient East Coast centers in Boston, New York, and Philadelphia into the hinterland; nowhere did the pattern of local and regional publishing take stronger root than in the towns and small cities of early-nineteenth-century New England. In attracting to itself one of the first presses in the state, Brunswick was fortunate to open a channel of communication with the region. But given the nature of local publishing and the situation of Griffin, who had only recently finished his apprenticeship and invested what little money he had in outfitting his one-man, one-press shop, prospective authors could expect only a tight geographical circle of readers, and thus at best only uncertain profits, for works issuing from his shop.

Such limited prospects might have discouraged a professional writer of the next generation, but they did not disturb Henry Putnam, who adhered to a set of still-amateur expectations that included official authorial anonymity and gentlemanly rules of conduct. The publication of the book, he states near the end, was urged upon him by a group of local "gentlemen"; under these circumstances, the unnamed author responds as any gentleman might by merely "yield[ing] to their solicitation."[51] But was this simply a case of amateur authorship, New England style, of a man of polite letters and learning doing his duty on behalf of his fellows? Certainly Putnam took a kind of authorial pleasure in assuming the false identity of a Southern planter of means and leisure writing for his like, knowing full well that local readers would read the transposition of the Southern gentleman onto the middle-class New Englander as an act of irony in which a Yankee author and Yankee readers could take common pleasure.[52] Furthermore, his sense of obligation to the community is clear throughout.

But there is more to the matter than Putnam's simply responding to the wishes and playing on the expectations and prejudices of his local audience. For one thing, he must have had a financial stake in the book; it is implausible that Griffin would have agreed to publish it had not Putnam paid at least part of the production costs of the volume. But this seems not to have been the primary consideration with Putnam, who did not even bother to take out a copyright for the book. What mattered more to him was the pleasure he took (or, more likely, discovered) in writing it—in assembling facts and statistics, interviewing local dignitaries and functionaries, researching the town's history, and making his own experiments in New England living. In a larger sense, however, Putnam was not only satisfying his and his local audience's expectations but also participating in the expanding circles of print discourse that by 1820 encompassed rural northern New England. Whatever his personal relations at home, he was discovering a potential audience not previously within his reach.

Once he discovered the possibilities for expression in print that were developing around him in Maine, he soon passed to further acts of public writing. Shortly after the founding of the *New England Farmer* in 1822, a weekly journal whose editor, Thomas Green Fessenden, was committed to publicizing the "science of agriculture" to the citizens of New England, Putnam became an occasional contributor, sending in articles filled with pieces of learned advice. Published in Boston but containing news and information suitable for all of New England, the journal was an ideal place for Putnam's submissions; its general philosophy of enlightened agriculture according closely with his own. In fact, as a weekly vehicle of agricultural information and miscellaneous news and entertainment to the readers of the region, the *New England Farmer,* under Fessenden's able control, represented a step toward early editorial professionalism that in some ways paralleled Putnam's own authorial direction, although Fessenden displayed the virtues of professionalism—systematization, regularity, and punctuality—as clearly as Putnam flouted them.

The following year Putnam self-published a second edition of *A Description,* bringing it up to date by adding two letters dated 1823 that discussed recent developments in the town and college. At the end of that edition, and in partial violation of its epistolary pose of the South Carolina gentleman that Putnam continued to affect, he placed a blurb indicating how strong the writing habit had become with him: "Note.—The Author's travels in Maine will shortly appear." No such book ever appeared, but the next year Putnam did publish a related book, *Touches on Agriculture,* which incorporated some of the extensive information he had acquired about Maine agricultural practices from his travels around the state and region.

Once again, his stated purpose in writing the book was a sense of public service: "The little essays, I venture to throw before a discriminating public, go, from a sense of duty; believing, that much is now doing and ought to be done for the rising, interesting and important state of Maine."[53] Although he did not print his name on the title page, he did identify himself on it as "the author of the Description of Brunswick." That, presumably, was all his readers needed to know, for this book, like everything he wrote for publication, was manifestly a local affair. Written in a chatty, genial tone, it had the sound of a friendly voice engaged in conversation with its neighbors, a conversation as personal, specific, and local as that of the previous book. Putnam spoke often of himself, but virtually always within the sphere of a strictly local referentiality. The book is filled with the record of his own agricultural experiments, climatic and meteorological observations, pest-control suggestions, and home remedies and recipes, all guided by his philosophy of applied science for Mainers and New Englanders: that farmers study the book of local nature rather than the almanacs of their ancestors.

All points of contact between author and audience were made on local grounds—the weather in recent years, the results of the 1823 fire in Brunswick, the extremes of temperature he saw registered on Professor Cleaveland's thermometer, the success of farmers (some of them named) observed in their fields, the relative prospects of growing specific crops in Maine or farther south, even the rocks and logs on which he jotted down the thoughts and observations that became the basis of the book's content. The degree of self-referentiality was carried yet another degree further the following year, when he brought out a second edition of the book, this time with his name on the title page and a reference made to the criticism of the first edition by the *New England Farmer* as being unsystematic.[54] As had been his practice with *A Description,* he took the opportunity of a second edition to update his book, bringing its chronology up to 1825 and mentioning near the end the fact of his presence in Salem, Massachusetts, where the book was printed and where Putnams had lived ever since the arrival of their earliest ancestor in the New World.

The year 1825 was a decisive one for the Putnam family. At some point during that year, his parents decided to send eleven-year-old George to Boston to do an apprenticeship in the carpet store of John Gulliver, husband of Henry Putnam's sister Sally. They no doubt saw the Gullivers' invitation as an opportunity for George to gain a background in business, even though the act preempted for him the possibility of higher education. That fact does not seem to have bothered Henry Putnam, who continued to follow the unremunerative path of authorship right through 1825. The course of his own life and that of his family, however, was abruptly altered in December when Brunswick experienced the worst fire in its history. Originating in a factory, the "great fire" of 1825 destroyed much of the downtown area, throwing dozens of families, including the Putnams, into the streets. Ironically, Henry Putnam had anticipated two years before that Brunswick might be susceptible to such a catastrophe. Noting that a pump had been built near the large textile factory to bring water to Main Street, he complained that the city had been too lazy to complete a full-scale water system: "This [pipe] has been carried but a little way and might easily be carried through the village. But mankind is selfish, and while this little village has suffered much by fire, another may be necessary to awaken them to a sense of their own interest. No reservoirs of water have been provided."[55]

The family did not remain in Brunswick long enough to see the problem corrected. Having lost her home and, with it, the source of her livelihood, Catherine Hunt Putnam made a prompt decision to start over elsewhere with her daughters, in all likelihood without their father and quite possibly even deliberately at a distance from him.[56] Her destination was New York City, where she had a sister, Amelia Palmer Curtis, and, perhaps more urgently, the acquaintance of a leading Baptist minister, Spencer Houghton Cone, in whose Broome Street church she would be active for the rest of her life.[57] She arrived in New York by March 1826 and, aided quite possibly by a loan from Narcissa Stone and strong letters of reference, quickly set about the business of finding a location and recruiting students for her planned school.[58] By May she was able to write back to an old family friend in Brunswick that her new school was already underway "in a very pleasant part of the City, with very eligible accommodations, but that the commencement of any establishment in N. Y. must be necessarily slow in its operations." She had opened the school, she wrote, with only seven students but had fair prospects, she believed, for attracting others soon.[59] Two of those original students were the daughters of one of her earliest friends in the city, Dr. Samuel Latham Mitchill, known throughout the city for his polymathic learning and encyclopedic interests (as well as quirks, which included the proposal that the country be renamed Fredonia and its citizens Fredes).[60]

In time, her professional prospects would improve, as the schools she ran on Broome Street, then Bleecker, toward the northern limits of the then heavily settled sections of Manhattan, took hold and her reputation spread. But beginning over in a new location was undoubtedly a trial for a woman who had previously known life only in New England, and 1827 proved to be a particularly difficult year for her. First her husband died in Reading; whether she and her children attended the funeral there is unknown. Then her oldest daughter Catherine died. Meanwhile, she remained separated from her son, still in Boston. She could take consolation, at least, in the fact that he was comfortably situated among relatives there. They included not only the Gullivers but also, given George's sociable nature, the many family members and friends who lived in town or within easy traveling distance of it. He particularly liked to visit his favorite cousins, the Peabodys, whose father, for a fee, cleaned his teeth, and he also got to see aunts and uncles from both sides of the family when they passed through town, as did Narcissa Stone. Furthermore, he would have participated in the network of correspondence as letters passed regularly through the various branches of the family, which was experiencing the growing pains typical of nineteenth-century families that increasingly kept in touch through correspondence as its individual members moved around the region and country.

George Palmer Putnam was to spend a total of four years in Boston. Had he been able to follow his own will in the matter, he would probably have left his situation there a good while earlier. Despite his family's hopes and wishes, his work in his uncle's store did not engage his intelligence or direct him toward a desirable career goal. Although he liked his Aunt Sally and got along well with his cousin John Putnam Gulliver, one of his favorite first cousins for the rest of his life, Putnam found the work in the store menial and unfulfilling. Sweeping the floors, keeping the racks orderly, delivering packages, and doing various odds and ends around the shop were not activities capable of satisfying a bright, curious teenager.[61] But even if he had been given a degree of responsibility more in proportion to his ambition or roles more demanding of his mind, I suspect that Putnam would inevitably have drifted into dissatisfaction with the work. In truth, he never was—even after he had found and settled down to his true vocation—strictly speaking a businessman. It was not simply that he had little patience for bookkeeping and accounts, or little talent for the system they required; it was that he sought a field of professional activity that connected his own personal good to that of society. In this regard, he was very much his mother's son.

   One of his chief complaints during his four years with the Gullivers, a refrain of the letters he sent back home, was what he later called "literary starvation."[62] It is a shame that no information has survived about the nature or extent of the family library back in Brunswick or about reading habits in the family, but one thing is certain: even with barely a primary school education, young George Palmer Putnam had developed early on an irresistible taste for books and ideas. With a mother who not only valued books and learning but communicated her ideas to her children in ways both formal and informal and a father who pursued the lure of authorship (even if that pursuit took him for long stretches out of the family home), Putnam could only have found his intellectual predisposition strengthened. Even though his formal schooling ended at the age of eleven, and he never returned to institutionalized learning, except for occasional rudimentary lessons in a hodgepodge of subjects such as writing and French, Putnam's desire for intellectual growth knew no bounds. In fact, in the years immediately following his departure from Boston, he displayed an appetite for learning so intense that one can understand it, at least in part, only as a measure of the degree of intellectual inanition he had been feeling at the Gullivers. But if he knew during those years that he was dissatisfied with his life as a shop clerk, he could not yet have recognized the fact that the one commodity he would ever hold in his hand and find pleasure in selling was a printed text.

Besides his repressed intellectuality and curiosity, the other trait that comes through in Putnam in this period is his general precocity. In a letter to his mother written when he was fifteen, he is already the man of the family: "For my part I do not think you ought to provide any more clothes for me, I feel as if I was old enough not only to support myself but to help you instead of being any tax upon you."[63] With an ineffective and often absent father in his earlier years and neither father nor mother in adolescence, Putnam had no alternative but to grow up quickly. Having soured on the idea of providing "a footing for the understanding" of Bostonians in the carpet business, he gradually came to the realization during his life with the Gullivers that he needed to start life over—not only in a new locality but also in a new vocation. With his mother and sisters Elizabeth and Anna settled in New York, which was rapidly emerging as the city of greatest economic opportunity, he grew determined to try his fortune there.[64] It is not clear whether he had ever been formally apprenticed to his uncle, that arrangement having lost some of its authority in the increasingly capitalistic terms of employment and trade of the 1820s; whatever the nature of the family agreement, he was able to secure his uncle's permission in 1829 to break off his employment and to go off on his own.

That decision was the most formative one he had yet made. Booking passage on a schooner for the week-long cruise around Cape Cod

and down the coast, the fifteen-year-old Putnam embarked on the trip
that was to prove the most important of his life: his destination was
what he later called "the remote El Dorado of New York"; his fate, to
become a New York publisher during the great take-off era of American
publishing and letters.[65]

Notes

1. GPP, *Chronology: or, An Introduction and Index to Universal History, Biography,
and Useful Knowledge* (New York: Leavitt and Appleton, 1833), 1.

2. Eben Putnam, the distinguished Putnam family and New England genealogist,
was still living and publishing his books in Salem into the early twentieth century. He
was consulted by GHP, another Putnam with a lively interest in his Old and New England forebears, for information about the family history.

3. On the leading role played by Putnams in the witch craze, see Paul Boyer and
Stephen Nissenbaum, *Salem Possessed: The Social Origins of Witchcraft* (Cambridge:
Harvard University Press, 1974), 110–52.

4. Clifford K. Shipton, comp., *Sibley's Harvard Graduates,* vol. 6 (Boston: Massachusetts Historical Society, 1942), 211.

5. Information about Rev. Putnam's early career comes primarily from *Two Hundred Fiftieth Memorial Volume of Ancient Redding* (1896), 236. For information about the
Putnam homestead and the family history, I am indebted to Mary C. Rubenstein, of Flint
Memorial Library, North Reading, Massachusetts, who pored through her library's town
files for information about the Putnams. In compiling the following sketch of the generations leading up to that of GPP's father, I have relied particularly on the typescript of a
historical overview of the Putnam family that comes from the files of the library's Local
History Room.

The Putnam family home recently entered the National Register of Historic Places
and currently serves as a museum and headquarters of the North Reading Historical
Society.

6. Much of this information comes from Lilley Eaton, *Genealogical History of the
Town of Reading, Mass.* (Boston: Alfred Mudge and Son, 1874), 136, 141, 154, 212–13.

7. A catalogue of Rev. Putnam's library is in the collections of the American Antiquarian Society.

8. Quoted in Helen M. McDonald, "Putnam Homestead Built in 1722 Was First
Parsonage in North Reading," *Middlesex County Bulletin of Agriculture and Home Eco-
nomics* (June 1930). (A clipping is in the Local History Room files of Flint Memorial
Library, North Reading.)

9. Eaton, 290; see also Eben Putnam, *The Putnam Lineage* (Salem, Mass.: Salem
Press, 1907), 212–13.

10. Eben Putnam, *A History of the Putnam Family In England and America* (Salem,
Mass.: Salem Press, 1891), 364–65.

11. This information comes from an 1811 clipping from an unidentified newspaper,
probably of Maine origin, about the incoming class in 1798. One of those North Reading classmates, Isaac Gates, would also become a lawyer in Brunswick, Maine. The

newspaper clipping is in the Henry Putnam alumni file in the Harvard University Archives, Harvard University.

12. *Faculty Records,* vol. 7 (1797–1806), Harvard University Archives, Harvard University.

13. Ibid.

14. His father all but excluded Henry, his eldest son, from his will. The main clause in which he is mentioned states simply: "I give to my son Henry Putnam Twenty Dollars He having had his portion in my life time." In a related gesture suggesting bad father-son relations, his father passed over Henry, though trained in the law, as his executor, appointing younger brother Joshua to that role and rewarding him with the bulk of the estate.

A copy of the probated will is in the Historical Commission of North Reading, Mass. I am indebted to Barbara O'Brien for reproducing it for me.

15. For the history of the Palmer family, I rely chiefly on the following sources: "Biographical Sketch of Gen. Joseph Palmer," *New Englander* 3 (January 1845): 1–23; Frederick Tupper and Helen Tyler Brown, eds., *Grandmother Tyler's Book: The Recollections of Mary Palmer Tyler* (New York: G. P. Putnam's Sons, 1925); and James R. Cameron, *Calendar of the Papers of General Joseph Palmer 1716–1788* (Quincy, Mass.: Quincy Historical Society, 1978).

16. Cameron, *Calendar,* 2.

17. Adams to James Warren, 15 March 1775; in Robert J. Taylor, Mary-Jo Kline, and Gregg L. Lint, eds., *Papers of John Adams,* vol. 2 (Cambridge: Harvard University Press, 1977), 404–5.

18. Louise Hall Tharp, *The Peabody Sisters of Salem* (Boston: Little, Brown, 1950), 14.

19. Tupper and Brown, eds. *Grandmother Tyler's Book,* 32–33, 34–35.

20. Clifford K. Shipton, comp., *Sibley's Harvard Graduates,* vol. 17 (Boston: Massachusetts Historical Society, 1975), 586–87. Washington wrote to Joseph Palmer on 7 August 1776 to explain, among other things, that he preferred a quartermaster general for the army who came from some other area than Massachusetts, lest other sections of the country charge him with local favoritism; John C. Fitzpatrick, ed., *The Writings of George Washington,* vol. 3 (Washington, D.C.: United States Printing Office, 1931), 405. Interestingly, the original of this letter came into the possession of GHP, the great-great-grandson of General Palmer.

21. Palmer to Alexander Hodgdon, 13 January 1788; Emmet Collection, New York Public Library.

22. That summer, Gerry, who was later to become a governor of Massachusetts and vice president of the United States, introduced a motion to Congress "that a committee be appointed to report a catalogue of books necessary for the use of Congress, with an estimate of the expense, and the best mode of procuring them." That act set into motion a complicated chain of events resulting in the founding of the Library of Congress, an institution that a century later GPP's youngest son Herbert would serve as librarian. On the early history of the Library of Congress, see David C. Mearns, *The Story up to Now: The Library of Congress, 1800–1946* (Washington, D.C., 1947), 1–6.

23. The best source of information on the family during the years immediately following the death of Joseph Pearse Palmer is the Peabody Family Papers at the Massachusetts Historical Society, which include a series of letters filled with personal and family matters written by Elizabeth Hunt Palmer to various members of her family.

24. Elizabeth Hunt Palmer (mother) to Elizabeth Palmer (daughter), 13 December 1799; Peabody Family Papers, Massachusetts Historical Society.

25. *By-laws of the Town of Brunswick* (Brunswick, Maine: J. Griffin, 1831).

26. [Henry Putnam], *Touches on Agriculture* (Portland, Maine: W. Thayer, 1824), 35. He spoke of the tribe as exhibiting "noble, generous, elevated traits of mind" and expressed his appreciation of their tragic history in romantic terms similar to those of such contemporary men of letters as Freneau, Cooper, and Bryant: "I seated myself one pleasant evening on the delightful interval of Canton, Maine. I was on the Indians' sacred burying-ground. The remnants of the tribes of the Androscoggin, where are they? No more. Destroyed by encroaching whites, or driven from their native soil toward the setting sun, by those who *pretend* to cherish the blessed doctrine of 'peace on earth, and good will to men'" (35).

27. This information comes from a typescript of an 1889 newspaper extract in the collections of the Pejepscot Historical Society, Brunswick, Maine.

28. [Henry Putnam], *A Description of Brunswick, (Maine) in letters by a gentleman from South Carolina to a friend in that state* (Brunswick, Maine: Joseph Griffin, 1820), 4.

29. Memorial of Sundry Inhabitants of the State of Maine, 6 January 1826, in House Document 35, 19th Congress (Washington, D.C.: Gales and Seaton, 1826).

30. GHP, *George Palmer Putnam,* 1:12–13.

31. Ibid., 1:13.

32. According to a bylaw of the college approved in 1806, "Persons, who have received a Degree in any other University or College, may, upon proper application, be admitted *ad eundem,* upon payment of the customary fee to the President. But honorary Degrees, conferred by the Trustees, with consent of the Overseers, on account of distinguished merit, shall be free from all charge." Laws of Bowdoin College (Hallowell, Maine: E. Goodale, 1817), 27. I am indebted for this information to Dianne M. Gutscher, special collections curator of Hawthorne-Longfellow Library, Bowdoin College.

33. [Henry Putnam], *Description of Brunswick, (Maine),* 10.

34. William D. Shipman, *The Early Architecture of Bowdoin College and Brunswick, Maine* (Brunswick, Maine: Brunswick Publishing, 1973), 14.

35. This information comes from several sources but chiefly from Thompson Eldridge Ashby, *A History of the First Parish Church in Brunswick, Maine,* ed. Louise R. Helmreich (Brunswick, Maine: J. H. French and Son, 1969), 110.

36. The sheet survives in the archives room of Curtis Memorial Library, the public library of Brunswick.

37. Despite the gap of time, her report, published in GHP's *George Palmer Putnam* (1:14–15), has the sound of authenticity. This woman also recollected a trip made by Henry Putnam to her home area of Paris, Maine, where he had gone, as he often did to locations throughout the state, to collect information for an agricultural journal he occasionally wrote for.

On the other hand, Catherine Hunt Putnam probably did not normally enjoy the luxury of having so many students. A letter written by her niece in 1824, presumably based on information received directly from Mrs. Putnam, spoke of her as having fourteen "scholars" for that winter term; Mary Peabody to Mary W. Tyler, January 1824; Royall Tyler Collection, Vermont Historical Society.

38. Henry Putnam's name appears among those of the original signers of a proposal to build a new Congregational meeting house in Brunswick; see Ashby, *First Parish Church in Brunswick,* 90–91. The dates for Catherine Hunt Putnam's membership in the Congregational Church and departure from it to join the Baptists are given in *Manual of the Congregational Church, Brunswick, Maine* (Brunswick, Maine: Joseph Griffin, 1872), 33; and *The First Parish Calendar, Brunswick, Maine* (14 November 1937).

39. Her letter is excerpted in Ashby, *First Parish Church in Brunswick,* 111, and in *The First Parish Calendar, Brunswick, Maine* (14 November 1937).

40. Joseph Griffin, *History of the Press of Maine* (Brunswick, Maine: J. Griffin, 1872), 76.

41. Ruth Putnam, ed., *Life and Letters of Mary Putnam Jacobi* (New York: G. P. Putnam's Sons, 1925), 4.

42. See Catherine Hunt Putnam, *A Concise History of the Origin, Organization, and Progress of the First Baptist Mariners' Church, New York* (New York: T. Holman, 1868).

43. George Augustus Wheeler and Henry Warren Wheeler, *History of Brunswick, Topsham, and Harpswell, Maine* (Boston: Alfred Mudge and Son, 1878), 138.

44. Nehemiah Cleaveland and Alpheas Spring Packard, *History of Bowdoin College* (Boston: James Ripley Osgood and Company, 1882), 97.

45. Putnam is mentioned only within the context of a sketch of a better-established local lawyer, Peter Alden: "Henry Putnam, Isaac Gates, and Ebenezer Everett, all graduates of Harvard, established themselves by his side, and divided a business that was not more than sufficient for one." William Willis, *A History of the Law, the Courts, and the Lawyers of Maine* (Portland: Bailey and Noyes, 1863), 231.

46. Elizabeth Palmer to Mary Tyler, 15 February 1822; Royall Tyler Collection, Vermont Historical Society.

47. Using a different (and, to me, unknown and unlocatable) source of evidence, Clifford Shipton came to a similar conclusion. His remarks on Putnam's intemperance are quoted in a typescript of a biographical sketch about Putnam compiled by an unnamed twentieth-century descendant of the Dunlap family of Brunswick. The author of that sketch wrote to Shipton to learn more about the mysterious "South Carolinian" who had anonymously written *A Description of Brunswick, (Maine).* That latter-day Dunlap then proceeded to take Shipton's response to the query and draw the totally unfounded conclusion that Catherine Hunt Putnam was responsible for driving her husband to drink, a presumption as unexamined as it is boorish. The unsigned typescript is in the Henry Putnam alumni file, Harvard University Archives, Harvard University.

48. Henry Putnam to Jacob Smith, 7 March 1821; Hawthorne-Longfellow Library, Bowdoin College.

49. Clement Robinson, *Joseph Griffin, Printer, and the Juvenile Key* (14 January 1957), 2 (pamphlet). Flagg and Gould was a highly reputed printing firm that trained a number of fine printers. One of them was John Trow, a native of Andover, who was to become one of New York's leading printers for two generations and GPP's printer of choice and long-term friend.

50. [Henry Putnam], *Description of Brunswick, (Maine),* 3.

51. Ibid., 28.

52. Putnam enjoyed the fiction so much that he continued to use it as basic plot device of the two letters he incorporated into the second edition of *Description.*

53. [Henry Putnam], *Touches on Agriculture,* 4.

54. Henry Putnam, *Touches on Agriculture,* 2d ed. (Salem, Mass.: John D. Cushing, 1825), 4.

55. Henry Putnam, *A Description of Brunswick, Maine* (Brunswick, 1823), Letter 6 (p. 18 of typescript copies at South Caroliniana Library and American Antiquarian Society).

56. I make this inference on admittedly slight evidence: the fact of his death in January 1827 in Reading, Massachusetts, the ancestral Putnam family home; the lack of any mention of him in New York directories, other print sources, or in the New York correspondence of his wife; and the statement in a mid-nineteenth-century New England

journal that Putnam returned to live in Massachusetts before the end of his life ("Notes—Cumberland Bar, Maine," *American Quarterly Register* 12 [February 1840]: 284).

57. GHP, *George Palmer Putnam,* 1:44–5.

58. Ibid., 1:45. One person who agreed to help her in her effort to get started was Robert Dunlap of Brunswick, son of her old landlord, whose letter testifying to her excellence as a teacher eventually wound up in the hands of her grandson GHP, who printed it in *George Palmer Putnam,* 2:409.

59. Catherine Hunt Putnam to Parker Cleaveland, 26 May 1826; Hawthorne-Longfellow Library, Bowdoin College.

60. For a good sketch of Mitchill, see Martha J. Lamb, *History of the City of New York,* 3 vols. (New York: Valentine's Manual, 1921), 3:512–14.

61. He was not alone in feeling constrained; John Putnam Gulliver was also destined for a career outside his father's store. An outstanding student, he studied for the ministry and became in time a well-known professor of religion at Andover Theological Seminary.

62. GHP, *George Palmer Putnam,* 1:18.

63. Ibid., 1:21–22.

64. Little is known about either of GPP's surviving sisters. Elizabeth lived most of her life in New York City. She married local businessman Isaac Smith in 1842, and the Smith and Putnam families subsequently remained in close contact (first from across the Atlantic, then, following the Putnams' return in 1847 to the New York City area, from across the city). GPP had a high opinion of his sister and brother-in-law, whom he esteemed, in part, for their generosity in housing Catherine Hunt Putnam after her retirement in the early 1840s.

GPP seems to have had a more distant relationship with Anna, a woman of literary ability who married the talented journalist, daguerreotypist, and inventor Henry Hunt Snelling in New York City in 1837 and subsequently moved with him to Detroit, where he edited a series of small journals. They moved to Boston for a period of months from late 1839 to 1840, then settled in New York City in 1841. They were intellectually active both individually and collectively during their nearly thirty-year marriage. Anna coauthored several plays with Snelling and also published a novel *Kabaosa; or The Warriors of the West* (1842). Snelling was best known for his work in daguerreotypy and photography. He wrote a well-regarded *The History and Practice of the Art of Photography,* which GPP published in 1849 and brought out in updated editions through the early 1850s (and which was reissued in a facsimile edition in 1970 introduced by Beaumont Newhall). The fourth edition (1853) included Anna Snelling's translation of Alphonse de Brebisson's photography manual *The Collodion Process in Photography for the Production of Instantaneous Proofs.* Snelling also edited and published *The Photographic Art Journal* in New York in the early 1850s. Although I have located no surviving letters between the two men (or between GPP and Anna), it seems quite plausible that GPP consulted with Snelling at various times, especially in the 1850s, about the latest techniques of reproducing daguerreotypes and photographs for print.

I am grateful to Leon Jackson, who informed me about Anna Putnam's marriage to Snelling and plied me with sources about them. Much of the preceding information about Snelling's accomplishments comes from Newhall's introduction to *The History and Practice of the Art of Photography* (Hastings-on-Hudson, N.Y.: Morgan and Morgan, 1970).

65. GPP, "Rough Notes on the Book Trade," *American Publishers' Circular and Literary Gazette* 1, octavo series (15 July 1863): 242.

CHAPTER 2

Early Years in New York City and the Book Trade

Decades after his initial debarkation at the foot of Manhattan Island, the place from which natives and immigrants alike stood face-to-face with the sight of America's busiest port and emporium, Putnam gave a charming account of his arrival in his new home. His portrayal of his distance from his earlier self (and of 1860s New York from its own earlier self) imbued it with something of the character of Benjamin Franklin's retrospective description of his own initial entrance into eighteenth-century Philadelphia as a provincial Yankee boy lacking contacts and means in an unknown city. Although the adolescent Putnam presumably had relatives waiting to greet him upon his arrival and a place to stay, they make no appearance in his self-portrait; the impression he gives there is of a boy footloose in the big city:

> It was in 1829 that the book-trade and I were introduced to each other. . . . Two or three times a week the stages would start off hours before daylight to take passengers to "the splendid steamer Washington" at Providence—a longer and more tiresome journey than it is now to New York, six times the distance. Not, however, by the swift luxury of stage-coach, or railway, or

steamer was my momentous journey to be performed, but by a week's voyage in Capt. Nickerson's "fast schooner" round Cape Cod, varied by a morning's call at Holmes' Hole and Hyannis, and by reiterated calms in the Sound. Coenties Slip and the wonder of Pearl Street were approached with suitable deference and awe, as one might now arrive at Moscow or Timbuctoo.

Thus, at the age of fifteen, afloat in the great metropolis, expected to make my own way in the world, my first studies consisted of paragraphs in the papers beginning "Boy wanted." With one of these cut from the "Courier" I promptly presented myself, as required, at the counting-room of the great mercantile house of Phelps, Peck, and Co., on the corner of Fulton and Cliff Streets.[1]

As Franklin took to eighteenth-century Philadelphia, so Putnam quickly made nineteenth-century New York his home and the center of his far-flung activities. By the time he became established as a leading member of the book trade and citizen of the city, commentators typically referred to him not only as a publisher but specifically as a New York publisher. That distinction was one that he must have heard many times during his travels around the country and that in time he internalized himself, and it is one still worth drawing in speaking of his career. Whether considered specifically or generically in terms of the evolution of American letters and publishing, Putnam's career was shaped and defined by the professional opportunities and dynamics present in mid-century New York City no less than Franklin's was by those in eighteenth-century Philadelphia. In arriving in New York on the eve of its transformation into the first metropolitan center in the United States and of the growth of its print sector to national primacy, the unattached teenager, still in search of a career, was unwittingly tying his fortunes to a complex of developments that over the course of the next generation would remake the professions of letters and, with them, the face of the rising modern city and nation.

In 1859, the talented New York engraver John Bachmann published a bird's-eye, circular cut of Manhattan and its surroundings that presented the city to the observer's eye as spreading north up the island and east and west across the water to adjacent slivers of Brooklyn and New Jersey, as well as rimming a more distant circumference of

2.   "New York and Environs," 1859 lithography from engraving by John
Bachmann. (Courtesy Eno Collection, New York Public Library)

localities stretching off to the horizon.[2] Even then, neither its perspective nor its implied message of pride in spreading power and influence
was unique to Bachmann, who simply gave definitive expression to a
kind of engraving then popular in the city. By that time, a brassy pride
in the city's rapid growth and emergence into the center of American
economic power was already commonplace among New Yorkers. One
has to think no further than to Whitman to appreciate how powerful
was the impulse to glorify the fast-paced growth and activity of the

city at mid-century. At nearly the same time Bachmann was pictur-
ing the city his way, Whitman was creating his own paean to New York
in a poem that operated through the semiotic linkage of the "word"
and "Mannahatta." The result was a verbal sketch of a new modern
city whose scenes and rhythms seemed far more than one or two generations removed from the genteel, urbane spaces and measures of
Knickerbocker local color:

I see that the word of my city, is that word up there,
Because I see that word nested in nests of water-bays, superb,
    with tall and wonderful spires,
Rich, hemmed thick all around with sailships and
    steamships—an island sixteen miles long, solid-founded,
Numberless crowded streets—high growths of iron, slender,
    strong, light, splendidly uprising toward clear skies;
Tide swift and ample, well-loved by me, toward sundown,
The flowing sea-currents, the little islands, the larger adjoin-
    ing islands, the heights, the villas,
The countless masts, the white shore-steamers, the lighters,
    the ferry-boats, the black sea-steamers, well-model'd;
The down-town streets, the jobbers' houses of business—the
    houses of business of the ship-merchants, and money-
    brokers—the river-streets,
Immigrants arriving, fifteen or twenty thousand in a week,
The carts hauling goods—the manly race of drivers of
    horses—the brown-faced sailors,
The summer-air, the bright sun shining, and the sailing clouds
    aloft,
The winter snows, the sleigh-bells—the broken ice in the river,
    passing along, up or down, with the flood-tide or ebb-tide;
The mechanics of the city, the masters, well-formed, beautiful-
    faced, looking you straight in the eyes;
Trottoirs thronged—vehicles—Broadway—the women—the
    shops and shows,
The parades, processions, bugles playing, flags flying, drums
    beating;
A million people—manners free and superb—open voices—
    hospitality—the most courageous and friendly young
    men;

The free city! no slaves! no owners of slaves!
The beautiful city! the city of hurried and sparkling waters!
the city of spires and masts![3]

Such magisterial visions as those held by Bachmann and Whitman of the Empire City, as some commentators had taken to calling the city, were a relatively recent phenomenon. To take one example of how compressed was the time period in which the city was expanding—not until the second decade of the nineteenth century did New York City even have a plan for the layout of streets across Manhattan. Only in 1811 did a city commission set forth a master plan for the largely uninhabited part of the island north of Houston Street, laying it out in today's familiar gridiron configuration of east-west streets intersecting north-south avenues at right angles.[4]

The fast-paced expansion of old New York was just beginning when Putnam arrived in the city in 1829. But to one accustomed to Brunswick and Boston, New York presented a bigger, denser urban experience. In this regard, he might have compared impressions with his future professional neighbors, the Harper brothers, who left their parents' Long Island farm to apprentice, then to start their own printing/publishing business, in New York. According to a company legend, in their early days of business the brothers got some of the power needed to run their presses from a horse they had transferred from the family farm. The sense of dislocation experienced by newcomers like Putnam and the Harpers was also well known to old-time New Yorkers, who could remember the city in its quieter, more intimate Knickerbocker days. In some quarters, that feeling lingered to the end of Putnam's life. A few years after his death, for example, his sons published a volume of engravings of historic buildings in the city, many of which had not survived even the early decades of the nineteenth century.[5] By no coincidence, that volume was introduced by Putnam's old friend and fellow New England transplant, William Cullen Bryant, who like Putnam had seen "old New York" pass before his eyes during his half century in the city.

The city that could attract such future literary professionals to it—indeed, that made it possible for them to become the first generation of modern literary professionals—had been ravaged physically, economically, and even demographically during the Revolutionary War. Even with its fast recovery, New York continued to lag behind Philadelphia and in some regards even Boston, although that situation changed dramatically by the middle decades of the century. To the teenage Putnam, it was already clear by 1830 that New York City would outdistance its rivals and grow into the commercial and cultural center of the country, even if he could not yet foresee its emergence as the first true metropolis of the United States. Whether he had yet read the federal census returns, as he soon would, he had already developed the habit of mind in common with many other people of his generation of paying a patriotic heed to statistics. Had he consulted the latest federal census returns, he would have learned that the population of New York City doubled between 1790 and 1800, to 60,000 people, then doubled again by 1820 to 123,000. He certainly did consult census statistics in subsequent decades and therefore knew that the city's population doubled one more time by 1835, when New York became the first city in the Americas to reach the quarter-million mark; and yet again by 1850, when the city had more than half a million inhabitants.[6]

To one who had spent his first decade in a small town in northern New England and then moved mostly among a middle-class population in Boston, the people of New York must have seemed unfamiliarly diverse, as the city attracted to itself heavy migration not only from other parts of the state and country but also from Europe.[7] Immigration into early-nineteenth-century New York consistently surpassed that into not only any other American city but the rest of the nation as a whole. Once the annual rate of immigration passed the ten thousand mark in the 1820s and began its rapid rise to the hundred thousand mark of the 1840s, when economic and political instability drove Irish and German nationals away from their homelands by the tens of thousands, the fact of immigration dramatically changed the look and character of the city, which increasingly bore less resemblance to the Knickerbocker community limned by Washington Irving in the 1810s than to Whitman's urban mass of heterogeneity. The cumulative influx into the city was so great that by 1850 New York had fewer native-born inhabitants than did Philadelphia, even though its total population was 20 percent larger.[8] Not even the city authorities were able to forecast the pace of growth. In supervising the planning and construction of their handsome new city hall on Broadway south of Chamber Street early in the century, they had all sides of the building except the north built of white marble, believing that that side "would be out of sight to all the world."[9] Within several decades, however, continued population growth was pushing an increasing number of inhabitants, including Putnam's mother in the 1820s and Putnam in the 1830s, uptown toward Greenwich Village, a process of northward expansion that accelerated over the last two-thirds of the century.

The economic expansion of the city during this period was equally dramatic. The second quarter of the century saw the rise of New York City for the first time to a position of unrivaled commercial ascendancy over Boston and Philadelphia. While Philadelphia continued to rival New York as a manufacturing and retail center, New York left every city in the country completely in its wake as a trade emporium of national, even international, importance. According to the 1840 census, New York not only outperformed Boston and Philadelphia together in terms of foreign and domestic trade but garnered for itself a large percentage of the nation's total trade. This performance was facilitated as New York took full advantage of its favorable geographical location, but it did not occur until the coming of the Black Ball Line, established in New York in 1818, which gave the United States a full fleet of ships making the transatlantic crossing at regular intervals, regardless of season and capacity.[10] That line of packet ships was successful enough to encourage newly founded lines to follow its lead in the 1820s, a pattern of development that in the next generation was carried into the age of steam. By the 1840s, two to three steamships on the average per week were leaving New York for Europe (as well as heading back to New York) and were able to make that eastbound crossing in about half the time required a generation earlier. Once he became active in the transatlantic book trade in the late 1830s, Putnam was to acquire a firsthand expertise in the transportation revolution.

No event brought home to New Yorkers the potentiality of their city more forcefully than did the completion of the Erie Canal in 1825, which opened up trade between the city, the state, and the great expanse of territory extending to the west—this, at the time that New York was clearly emerging as the main American port of trade to the east. At the ceremonies marking the arrival of the first ships in New York harbor by way of the canal, De Witt Clinton symbolically poured a keg of Lake Erie water, transported for the occasion by the fleet, into the Atlantic, as Dr. Mitchill (the same one whose acquaintance Catherine Hunt Putnam would make several months later) did likewise with vials containing samples he kept of the major world rivers. That nexus, which Clinton called at the time "the navigable communication ... between

our mediterranean seas and the Atlantic Ocean," was a great source
of hope to New Yorkers of all classes and backgrounds, who turned out
that day in masses along the harbor and in the streets in one of New
York's greatest celebrations.[11] A large parade passed from the Battery
up the west side of town to the northern limits and then across and
back down the east side to the Battery, then finally up Broadway to
its final destination at the new city hall. Various kinds of groups,
accompanied by bands, joined in the march—military groups, trade
organizations, benevolent societies, literary and scientific societies, fire
companies, members of the higher professions, as well as private citizens. Various of the trade groups passed by with models mounted on
carts and wagons displaying their professions, the most impressive of
which, to one bystander, was that of the city's printers, which featured
a printing press in constant operation running off the words of an ode
written for the occasion.[12]

The high expectations harbored by the farsighted architects of
the canal quickly met with material results, as the canal facilitated
New York's advantage over other cities in the rapidly growing trade
with the West. Although the Manhattan skyline of the antebellum era
was still dominated by the spires of its many churches, a better gauge of
its character was the forest of mastheads rising above South Street on
the East River side of the harbor, a token of the scope of the city's river
and ocean traffic.[13] Meanwhile, along the Hudson River side of the harbor, New Yorkers could see the new steamers that were revolutionizing
travel and trade between their city and the rest of North America,
Europe, and the world. For that matter, the look of the city proper had
also begun to change substantially. By the 1830s and 1840s, stately residences in several neighborhoods of lower Manhattan were rapidly
being converted to places of business. Through the center of them ran
Broadway, quickly emerging as the leading retail thoroughfare of the
nation. When John Jacob Astor set out in 1834 to build the city's most
lavish hotel on the avenue, he had the entire block of houses on Broadway between Vesey and Barclay leveled. Former mayor Philip Hone,
who owned a house on the next block, was one of many homeowners
there who chose to sell their homes on the avenue, take their profits,
and move further north in advance of the rising commercial tide. In
1836, he sold his home at 235 Broadway to Elijah Boardman for
$60,000 (after having bought it fifteen years before for $25,000), who
meant to convert the ground floor to shops.[14] Within a decade, that area

of the avenue would be home to dozens of shops, including many of New York's best bookstores (among which was that of G. P. Putnam and Company in the early 1850s). The process of the transformation of the avenue and the city into a finance-driven commercial center was cleverly captured in a pair of cartoons published in 1848 on adjacent pages of Cornelius Mathews's short-lived humor magazine, the *Elephant:* one showed a line of ministers, each one holding in his hand a miniature church on a stake, skulking away up the street; the other pictured a preacher lecturing a congregation above the caption, "1850! Dow, Jr., the only preacher left down town!"[15] Those pictures would have been immediately familiar to New Yorkers, who had grown accustomed to the annual ritual of the first of May, the city's "moving day," on which New York presented the image of a city on wheels.

The increasingly commercial nature of life in antebellum New York was a frequent subject of conversation and commentary among contemporary New Yorkers. One symbol of it was the new Merchants' Exchange opened on Wall Street in 1841, after its predecessor had been destroyed along with much of the commercial section of lower Manhattan in the unprecedentedly destructive fire of 1835. The city struggled to rebuild after the fire, whose effects were intensified by the deep national recession that soon followed; but the overall effect was to allow the city, as it has since done many times, to engage in a process of urban renewal. The rebuilding of the Merchants' Exchange was a conspicuous part of this process; whereas the old building had been one of the landmarks of the city back in the 1820s and 1830s, the new one dwarfed it in size. A monumental neoclassical structure surmounted by a gold dome, the new exchange occupied an entire city block. It was followed a year later by the opening of the city's splendid new custom house, a building necessitated by the rapid expansion of the city's commercial sector. Philip Hone, who like many patrician old-timers was discontented with the course of developments in the city but who nevertheless owned stock in the new exchange, derided it as "a costly temple of mercantile pride" and made fun of the "congregat[ion]" that would fill its rotunda.[16] He fancifully imagined the confusion of a traveler visiting the new New York of the 1840s: "With his back to 'New Trinity,' the most beautiful structure of stone in America (and I know of none more beautiful anywhere), he passes the Custom House, which cost a million; eight or ten banks, each a palace for the worship of mammon; and the new Exchange, with a portico of granite columns such as Sir Christopher Wren had no notion of; worthy, indeed, of Palladio or Michelangelo—an edifice the cost of which sunk all the money of myself and other fools who subscribed for it, besides contracting a debt of which nothing but the interest will ever be paid out of the income."[17] For that matter, he lagged no further behind changing times than did the architecture of the period, which still called up Greek Revival designs to house the commercial activities carried out in banks and other business workplaces.

With the transformation of the city's economic life came corresponding changes in its cultural life. This would inevitably have been the case in any city, but it was particularly so in a city like New York whose traffic in ideas and products had not recently been dominated by any one well-established group. By comparison with Boston or Philadelphia, New York was a more decentralized city, and accordingly one more open and receptive to the new forces remaking it both internally and externally. The rapid increase in the city's economic and commercial activity, population, and wealth pushed New York into a leading position in the various fields of the arts and sciences, even though a full-fledged institutional infrastructure of libraries and museums did not emerge until after the Civil War. When it did, Putnam would play a leading role in their planning.

Putnam's activist career during the middle decades of the century as a publisher, promoter of American authors and works, and benefactor of the arts would bring him into direct contact with the upsurge of cultural life in New York, but his most immediate personal experience of the city's cultural opportunities dated from his earliest days there. Shortly after arriving in town and still lacking any formal means of achieving his intellectual aspirations, Putnam took to the newly founded Mercantile Library as his center of home instruction. The library, which was situated just a few blocks from his employer's bookstore, had been founded as an institution to serve the fast growing clerical and working classes of the city. The year after his arrival, Putnam saw ex-mayor Hone lay the cornerstone of the library in its new, enlarged quarters at Clinton Hall. There Putnam would sit at night after finishing his long day's work and, like thousands of other young men and women after him in similar facilities, read his way into a knowledge of the world around him. One night in the library he heard Edward Everett give a lecture on society in the Middle Ages, a talk so graphic that it helped spark Putnam's own interest in reading and writing about history.[18] Putnam never forgot the debt he owed such public institutions, a debt he would repay in later years by using his book and periodical agency in England and his overseas connections to supply libraries and historical societies throughout the United States with books, manuscripts, and documents.

As New York's general cultural life experienced a period of rapid growth and vitality, one of the most immediate beneficiaries was the publishing industry. Properly understood, it grew up in combination with attendant changes in transportation, communication, labor, and entertainment. One person who appreciated the sweep of these changes was the anonymous author of the lead article in the 1856 *Harper's Monthly,* who drew a science fiction sketch of the current age of miracles from the perspective of the year 3000. Addressing himself to an audience of readers presumed to be alert to their age as one radically transformed by advances in technology, he depicted a variety of radical developments, including those that turned the antebellum era into "the golden age of ancient literature," and he singled out the Harpers' participation by calling them the most learned family of their time (a tongue-in-cheek misinterpretation of the voluminous Harper's Family Library series as authored rather than published by them).[19] Other contemporary commentators focused exclusively on the expansion of the print sector, and with good reason: it had grown by mid-century into one of the largest sectors of the city's economy. This was a matter not simply of an exponential growth in the number of new publications, the aggregate of their dollar value, the output of new presses, and the size of readership, but of the centrality, even integrality, of print in people's lives. In his recent study of print and the public sphere in antebellum New York City, David M. Henkin has smartly labeled this new reality "city reading"—tens of thousands of people waking up each morning to view the world that day through the pages of their daily newspapers or reading the public writing around town on billboards and the exteriors of buildings.[20]

The best example, to my mind, of the omnipresence of print in the society and of its pervasive role in mapping the changing contours of the city during this era of rapid, uncontrolled growth is the daily newspapers that became popular in New York by the early 1840s. Priced at one or two pennies per copy, they were inexpensive enough to be affordable to most people and, more important, written in a way that addressed a relatively broad (if still primarily male) cross section of the population. Combined circulation rose from a copy of one paper for every 16 residents in 1830 to a copy for every 4.5 residents twenty years later (and one newspaper for slightly more than every 2 residents on Sunday).[21] A typical issue, for example, of Horace Greeley's influential New York *Daily Tribune* in the 1840s transmitted the following array of information: general news from the city, state, nation, and world (with the latest national news communicated through "telegraphic dispatches"); editorials on various current affairs; series on matters of local or national interest; commercial and financial reports; obituaries and marriages; reports of upcoming political and cultural events and commentaries or reviews of those recently transpired; marine journals; book and periodical reviews or notices; corporation and legal notices; advertisements for a wide range of businesses and products; real estates listings; and original or reprinted fiction and poetry. Issued on a daily basis six days a week and supplemented by a popular weekend issue for the country, the *Tribune* reached a broad, fairly diverse readership. While newspapers of this sort were clearly addressing themselves to the wide-ranging interests and concerns of a newly centralizing, relatively heterogeneous middle-class audience, they were also the product of the technological improvements in transportation, communication, and manufacturing remaking the very nature of life in the city. The best editors, such as Greeley, James Gordon Bennett, and William Cullen Bryant, recognized that their papers constituted new centers of public information in an increasingly impersonal, capitalistic society and were more than casually aware of their status as a new kind of public servant operating in the emergent antebellum public sphere of print. But so, for that matter, was the rising generation of book publishers, who in the early 1840s were only one step behind and who would eventually be led to a comparable position of cultural arbitrage in the midcentury decades by George Palmer Putnam.

Having arrived in New York when this process of wholesale urban and cultural transformation was already underway, Putnam began his career in the city in the most symbolically appropriate way: by following a print trail from a local newspaper to his first place of work. Whereas in Boston he had found his situation in the traditional manner of family arrangements, in New York, where his family had fewer personal and professional connections, he had no such option. In this regard, his situation was typical of an increasing number of New Yorkers; as the city grew rapidly in the early decades of the century and its business relations became more commercial, employers and employees alike found themselves increasingly dependent on impersonal means of mediacy, such as newspaper print, for aligning their interests. The fifteen-year-old Putnam still had no clear idea of his vocation when he followed the advertisement in the New York *Courier and Enquirer,* a commercial daily whose publisher he would come to know and to which he would occasionally send contributions from Europe, to a mercantile house on the corner of Fulton and Cliff streets, where he was briefly interviewed before being rejected. His second application was at a book-shop on lower Broadway near Maiden Lane. Its owner, George Bleecker, was looking for a "boy" to do all-purpose menial work around his book-store and accepted Putnam, although he might have been a bit old for the position. Putnam boarded with Bleecker above the store and earned the petty annual sum of $25—an indication, no doubt, of how hard-pressed and limited in alternative prospects he then found himself.

As matters turned out, this initial job afforded the teenage Put-nam a good elementary education in the profession from the bottom up. For two years he worked as a low-level clerk in Bleecker's store, which sold a variety of educational and theological books, as well as stationery and sundries. That education broadened in April 1830 when Bleecker, afflicted with the ambition common among booksellers and printers of his time, began publishing a semimonthly magazine, the *Euterpeiad: An Album of Music, Poetry and Prose,* which he or his editor character-ized as having been inspired by their ambition "to supply what has long been wanted in this country—a paper devoted to the interests of music."[22] A miscellany typical of periodicals of its time, the magazine published a hodgepodge of articles on music and the arts, commented on performances in the arts in New York and elsewhere, transcribed musical scores, offered occasional serials and original poems, and transmitted the latest news and gossip. Operating with presumably exaggerated expectations, the journal's publisher foresaw "a vast field of useful and profitable exertion opened before us; we discern a certain prospect of doing 'some service to the state,' and of reaping for ourselves an ample harvest of honest reputation and honest emolument."[23] Dur-ing the fourteen months in which he controlled it, Bleecker employed the services of several different print shops in town, hoping to cut expenses and increase his circulation. He also sent his young clerk, whose reliability he implicitly trusted, up the river to such towns as Hudson and Poughkeepsie soliciting subscriptions.

The expenses of the journal proving beyond his means, Bleecker was forced to transfer it in July 1831 to its printer, James Robinson. By that time, Putnam had moved on to a better position as general clerk to Jonathan Leavitt, the operator of a much larger and more broadly supplied bookstore just a block or so away from Bleecker's at the corner of Broadway and John Street. Trained in Massachusetts as a bookbinder, Leavitt had been induced by his brother-in-law, Daniel Appleton, to join him in the retail business in New York, with Appleton putting up the capital and Leavitt handling the store's large book department. In 1830, the partners dissolved the agreement and Leavitt took his half-share of the stock and went into business for himself.[24] He had begun to prosper while still in partnership with Appleton, and once on his own he soon looked to expand his business by branching out into publishing. His specialty in both roles was religious books, still a major component of the book trade, and he solidified his status as a seller and publisher of religious and theological books by establishing a connection with the Boston firm of Crocker and Brewster, a leading house in the field. As a retailer, he also dealt in imported works in related fields from England and Germany; Putnam was to remember them as so numerous as to force Leavitt to rent a room simply for their storage.[25]

It was in Leavitt's shop that Putnam received his secondary education in the book trade. Paid a weekly salary of $2, which doubled after the first few months, Putnam worked initially as a clerk behind the counter of Leavitt's store, besides doing the various kinds of menial work required in a shop and running errands for his employer. He soon won Leavitt's respect and gradually earned additional responsibilities, such as copying letters and eventually the important task of cataloguing the store inventory.[26] By the time that he assigned Putnam that last task, one requiring expertise as well as responsibility, Leavitt must have understood that in hiring him he had gotten more than the simple clerk and bookkeeper he had been looking for; he also got an extraordinarily energetic, visionary young man who would one day leave his mark on the trade. In fact, during the five years he worked for Leavitt, Putnam was already embarking on two major projects that foreshadowed the core ideology and character of his mature publishing career.

Although he did not get off work evenings until 9:00 or sometimes 10:00, Putnam began an intensive, continuous course of self-instruction about the time he went to work for Leavitt. For years he had been reading for

pleasure in a more or less haphazard manner, but by 1831 he determined to widen his intellectual horizons beyond the limits of his experience and to do so in a way that systematized his grasp of the world.
Drawing primarily on sources available to him at the Mercantile
Library in Clinton Hall, he began a course of reading in world history,
working his way forward from the classical historians through the
moderns. To facilitate his absorption of so much information, he developed a system of note-taking that evolved from hundreds of pages of
notations to organized tables of dates and events convenient for the
kind of handy reference that Putnam intended. Altogether he would
remember himself as having spent three years working away at his
tables, chiefly late at night and sometimes into the early morning after
finishing work in the store.[27]

At some advanced point in his work, it occurred to him that a manual that was useful to him might also be useful to others. Excited by
the thought of publication, he took his idea to Leavitt, whose judgment
he trusted. Leavitt apparently took his young clerk seriously enough
not to reject the idea out of hand but wished for professional assurance
about the project's intellectual authenticity before considering it seriously for possible publication. Much later in life, Putnam recalled with
ironic detachment the spectacle he presented of a pretentious aspirant
author with an elementary school education approaching, first, one of
New York's most learned churchmen and scholars, John McVickar, who
had been valedictorian in his class at Columbia College and graduated
at age seventeen (Putnam's age roughly at the time of their meeting)
before becoming an Episcopalian minister and professor of moral philosophy at his alma mater.[28] Known for his grim bearing, which might
have prevented his ascension to the college presidency, he looked over
the manuscript and its author quickly and dismissed the project summarily. But when Putnam next approached John Frederick Schroeder,
also a learned Episcopalian minister, he received an entirely different
reception and was able to carry back to Leavitt an enthusiastic endorsement of his manuscript.[29] Leavitt then made arrangements with his
former partner Appleton in New York and his current trading partners
Crocker and Brewster of Boston for the joint publication of the book,
which was brought out 1833.

Leavitt's decision to publish the work had nothing to do with sentiment. He made his decision strictly as a business calculation, knowing
that he could count on Putnam for little or no investment in production

expenses but seeing in the work the basis for a wide, popular reception. That judgment soon proved correct, as the first edition of one thousand copies quickly sold out. In fact, the book, originally titled *Chronology; or, An Introduction and Index to Universal History, Biography, and Useful Knowledge,* was to run through twenty issues or editions in Putnam's lifetime and through many more during the following half century, with Putnam (and, after his death, editors selected by G. P. Putnam's Sons) periodically updating and expanding it to meet changing times. In retrospect, it is not hard to see the reason for the book's success: what originated as an attempt by Putnam to educate himself struck a receptive chord in his generation of American readers. The key to Putnam's manual, to invoke a term employed in the preface of editions right into the twentieth century, was its appeal to "the general reader." Already displaying the audience-savvy instincts of an experienced publisher, Putnam addressed that general readership as though it were himself, which in some fundamental sense it was. His unspoken strategy was to systematize and simplify knowledge of the world in a way that appealed to an audience eager to broaden its horizons but unable to afford formal education on a secondary or postsecondary level. Seen in a wider perspective, Putnam's *Chronology* was hardly an isolated success; manuals of self-instruction were already becoming one of the most popular publishing niches in the Anglo-American publishing world of the second generation of the century, which saw large successes scored by publishers intent on packaging and selling "useful knowledge" to a broadening reading public.

While Putnam was waiting for the appearance of his *Chronology,* he was weighing a different kind of publishing venture. During his several years of clerking for Leavitt, he came into close contact not only with the world of books but also with their makers. Listening to the talk of the authors, publishers, and printers who passed through Leavitt's store and grasping the chaotic situation of the trade, Putnam gradually came to see the need for a formal publication that would contribute an organizing voice to the decentralized world of New York book publishing. His decision in 1834 to undertake a book trade journal on his own was as pioneering as it was ambitious; the early book trade historian Adolph Growoll correctly stated that "before 1834 the book trade of the United States was without a journal devoted exclusively to its interests."[30] The nearest American model was William Leggett's *The Critic: A Weekly Review of Literature, Fine Arts, and the Drama,* which had had but a half-year's run, ending about the time that Putnam arrived in the city. Leggett attempted to manage his weekly virtually single-handedly, soliciting subscriptions and running the office by day and writing his copy by night; but he gave up when he concluded that all his efforts were succeeding only in pushing him further into debt.[31] Furthermore, *The Critic* was only remotely concerned with the book trade; it was really a general cultural review with a single article each issue devoted to a miscellany of trade news.

Putnam's projected journal was a far different matter; its primary intended audience was members of the book trade, not the readers of polite letters.[32] Lacking the capital to finance the undertaking, Putnam persuaded the printing firm of West and Trow to issue the work at its expense, thus limiting his own role to that of editor/compiler.[33] Just the same, doing so meant, in effect, writing or compiling the entire text of the journal himself, a task complicated by the fact that he had to perform it, as he had the *Chronology,* during his scant free time from work. Altogether Putnam kept his *Booksellers' Advertiser and Monthly Register of New Publications* going on a monthly basis through the entirety of 1834, before claiming overwork as his excuse for discontinuing it.[34] One year later, citing "the frequent inquiries that are made for it, and the many regrets that have been expressed by the Trade, here and in Europe, at its discontinuance," Putnam resumed publication in March 1836, announcing his intent to bring the journal out on a quarterly basis and to expand its contents.[35] When an unanticipated career opportunity intervened, however, that issue proved to be its last.

The *Booksellers' Advertiser* demonstrated compellingly how quickly and thoroughly Putnam, not quite twenty at the time of its initial appearance, had mastered the situation of letters and bookmaking in the United States. Limited to a format of eight pages per issue, Putnam nevertheless made the most serious attempt to date to put into circulation a centralized organ of communication for the publishers and booksellers of the United States.[36] Just as he had tried to systematize knowledge in his *Chronology,* so in the *Booksellers' Advertiser* he tried to present a streamlined compendium of current information essential to the concerns of the American book trade. Poring through foreign and domestic publications and soliciting information from members of the trade, he supplied each issue with a list of new publications in the United States and England (and also, occasionally, in France or Germany), as well as with a miscellany of items about publishers,

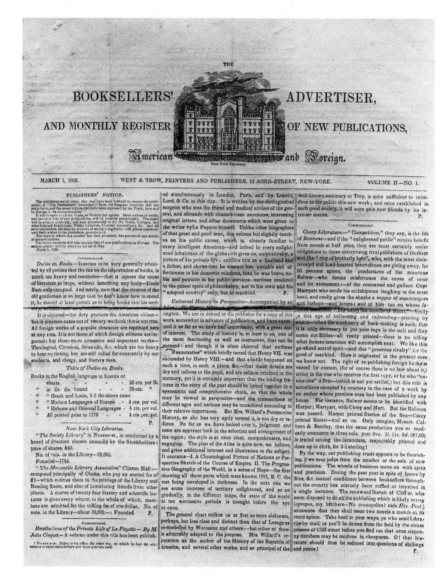

3.   Front page of Putnam's *Booksellers' Advertiser and Monthly Register of New Publications* (1 March 1836), the first trade paper in American publishing history. (Courtesy American Antiquarian Society)

booksellers, bookstores, authors, libraries, colleges, and periodicals. His unspoken self-assurance in his ability to reach his intended audience of fellow professionals was clear from the first issue, in which he listed agencies for subscriptions in Boston, Philadelphia, Raleigh, Cincinnati, and London; solicited advertisements from members of the trade; and announced an (undoubtedly exaggerated) inaugural printing of 13,000 copies.

The venture turned out to be more a visionary leap than the practically useful innovation that its young editor had hoped for. Although it was favorably noticed in various places and unquestionably offered an important service to booksellers, publishers, and editors, the *Booksellers' Advertiser* failed to attract the most basic testimony of patronage: the advertisements of the trade. Of the few advertisements it did attract, a fair number came from Putnam's employer, Jonathan Leavitt. Why this lack of success? The most fundamental explanation is that Putnam was ahead of his time in trying to centralize a trade that had not yet developed beyond its historic provincialism. Putnam would later remember the *Booksellers' Advertiser* as "the grandfather of the present *Publishers' Circular* [itself the forerunner of *Publishers' Weekly*]," an assessment that was essentially correct: the journal (and the publishing vision it entertained) ran well in advance of the development of the American book trade.[37] Only one decade removed from the world of his father, Putnam was already articulating in the *Booksellers' Advertiser* a nationalist vision of society in which the "progress" of literary culture worked to the good of the entire society. Unnostalgic about the past and dismissive of any form of provincialism or regionalism, Putnam saw his role and that of his comrades in the trade as that of public servants attending to the good of the entire country.

He also had a fairly clear idea of how they might realize their potential strength. As early as the mid-1830s, Putnam was equating the ability of publishers to fulfill their role as public servants with their mastery in setting the new steam-based technology to do for the printing/publishing function what it was already doing for the rest of the economy. He made this point best in an article in the final issue of *Booksellers' Advertiser* in which he linked early signs of the cheap literature phenomenon in the United States to the new print technology that helped to make it possible: "Verily in this age of ballooning and railroading—printing by steam—when the machinery of book-making is such, that it is only necessary to put your rags in the mill and they come out all Bibles—all ready printed—there is no telling what human invention will accomplish next."[38] For Putnam, the implications of this process were clear and immediate: a country that would be putting its rags to mill in massive quantities needed a more fully coordinated, centralized publishing mechanism to effect the passage of print products from authors through publishers to the reading public. Moreover, beyond a faith in steam power lay a broader faith in the technological powers of the nineteenth century—such as they already were and such as his imagination foresaw they would soon be—to transform society for the better.

One can discern in the *Booksellers' Advertiser* the unswerving optimism about the trade and the nation, and the activistic ideology of the profession that underlay Putnam's entire career. That ideology hardly changed over the course of his life. Never a man whose thinking was overly troubled by complexities or ambiguities, Putnam entered his maturity driven by a sense of service to profession and nation that, whether traced back to a source in family, region, or nation (or, as I tend to think, to a congruence of all three), powered his career in the trade from its beginning to its end. If not yet able to see what lay on the other side of the rising swell that the trade and the country were then riding, the young Putnam was keenly optimistic about the future of publishing and letters in the United States. He considered the rapid increase of print production in the country—and the technological improvements that were making it possible—to be an unmixed blessing, and he proudly compiled lists of statistics in his journal, in large part, to document what he would presumably have considered "the progress of progress."

Then again, the lists he compiled or reprinted of the numbers of books produced, sold, and read were a simple demonstration of the basic principle he expressed time and again in the journal: the absolute good of conveying a maximum amount of print at a minimal price to a democratic readership. Appropriately enough, the first advertisement printed by the journal was a full page ad for the new *Penny Magazine* that Charles Knight published in London, accompanied by a promotional text that defended the undertaking as a good to the people. Although that publishing rationale endeared Knight to him then and later, Putnam made it clear that he believed that logic to be much better suited to the more democratic conditions of American print culture.

Idealistic to a fault in his editorial handling of the journal, Putnam stated in one of his brief remarks, "To talk of literature as an article of traffic, is an ungrateful task," and in general adopted a bookman's version of utilitarianism that allowed him to apologize for the policies of American pirates (such as the Harpers) as acts of patriotism.[39] Those positions he soon outgrew, but he never outgrew his unyielding faith in the books that got published and the responsibility of publishers to ensure that they were "good" books.

Why did Putnam give up the journal in early 1836 so soon after having resumed it on an expanded basis? The most likely answer is that about the time of its publication he received an enticing offer to join the young New York publishing house of Wiley and Long as a junior partner. The key figure in the house was John Wiley, whom Putnam knew to be one of New York's most aggressive young publishers-booksellers and the son of the important Knickerbocker publisher Charles Wiley.[40] In joining Wiley, Putnam would complete the final stage in his publishing education and move into a world of books and bookmakers far beyond the horizons of the untrained teenager who had entered the city just seven years earlier. He would also be coming into contact with a man who would remain his professional colleague, directly or indirectly, for the rest of his life.

The elder Wiley, the publisher of James Fenimore Cooper, Richard Henry Dana, and other literary and nonliterary figures of the 1820s, had been well known throughout the trade as one of its most dynamic figures. The younger Wiley got his initiation into the book trade in his father's shop, where he worked until his father's death in 1826. During the decade between his father's death and the time he employed Putnam, John Wiley tried various schemes and arrangements, none very successful, to get himself established in the book trade.[41] He worked variously during these years both in retail bookselling and in publishing, the latter both on his own and in partnerships. Relatively early in this period, Wiley became the New York agent for Thomas Wardle and for Carey and Lea, both Philadelphia firms involved heavily in the import of European books into the United States, Wardle as a retailer and Carey and Lea primarily as reprinters.[42] His first partnership, destined to be a short-lived one, was with the New York printer-publisher Andrew Goodrich, which ended some time in 1834. Early that year, they put their imprint on an issue of Timothy Dwight's *Travels,* but that seems to have come at the end of their partnership. Later that same year Wiley proudly followed his father's example by publishing under his own name (without Goodrich's) a work by Cooper. But that work, *A Letter to His Countrymen,* was a relatively minor one not calculated for popularity; and Cooper, in any case, was hardly intent on returning to a Wiley imprint after nearly a decade of successful relations with the Careys of Philadelphia. When he did leave them in the following decade, one of the publishers he settled into relations with would be Putnam.

One of Wiley's most ambitious publications of 1834, begun during his partnership with Goodrich but continuing after its termination, was a monthly periodical, the *Father's Magazine* (which became the *Fathers' and Young Men's Magazine* before it ceased publication in November of that year).[43] Its brand of moralistic instruction, rooted in the teachings of the church and Bible and directed to the maintenance of the nuclear family, was clearly compatible with Wiley's temperament and character. But the decision to launch it was first and foremost a business initiative. He and his editor saw the field of domestic instruction as ripe territory for a new journal, one likely to do for fathers and sons what the already established *Mother's Magazine* and various juvenile periodicals were doing for women and girls. Its prospectus declared the age as one characterized by plans "for doing good," a goal all the more pleasant for Wiley when it could be paired with the likelihood of doing himself some financial good. A nine-month trial period, however, convinced him that he could not accomplish both.

Before the year was out, Wiley entered into a partnership with another local bookdealer, George Long. By chance (or perhaps not by chance), their fathers had had professional dealings back in the early 1820s, when they were among the group of New York booksellers (which also included the father of John Wiley's later editor, Evert Duyckinck) who jointly published a new eight-volume edition of *Plutarch's Lives.* Wiley and Long set up partnership at 161 Broadway, an address that would be patronized in the next decade by such people as Melville, Poe, and Fuller when, reconstituted as Wiley and Putnam, it earned a reputation as one of New York City's finest bookstores. In the mid-1830s, though, the store was not easily distinguishable from its competition, nor had the partners yet found their particular niche in the trade.

Ambitious to expand but short of capital, Wiley and Long engaged in occasional joint publication projects, whether with local colleagues or with out-of-town partners. One of their first issues was the *Fathers' and Young Men's Magazine.* They also issued a second edition of Charles Davies's *A Treatise on Shades and Shadows, and Linear Perspective,* which they brought out as New York representatives of a transnational team of publishers from Boston, Hartford, Philadelphia, Charleston, and Cincinnati. Joint publications of this sort, hardly unknown to their fathers either, allowed them to lower their risk and to improve the work's chances of widespread distribution.

Such titles as they were bringing out, few in number and diverse in subject and genre, indicate a lack of publishing specialization not uncommon for the time. But even with a list that was undistinguished and that included no renowned author, such as his father had had, on whom to build the firm's reputation, Wiley was a resourceful businessman, and he did develop an idea about how to increase the size of its operations. His plan was to bring his firm more directly into the fast growing transatlantic traffic in books, always an important but now potentially an extraordinarily profitable component of the American book trade. Although it is likely that the reason Wiley decided to employ Putnam was simply to bring into the business one of the brightest, most energetic young professionals in New York, it is also plausible that his ulterior intent was to maneuver his business into leadership in this expanding field and to use Putnam to help put it there. By the time Wiley offered and Putnam accepted a junior partnership, the two men would have discovered that they were of one mind about the possibilities for expansion into transatlantic trade. Putnam had not only been watching the growing transatlantic commerce with keen interest but had recently heard the glowing report of Jonathan Leavitt, who had traveled to Europe in late 1835 to establish overseas agencies for his company. In fact, in the last issue of the *Booksellers' Advertiser,* Putnam gave a puff for the new American Library and Newsroom opened in London by Richard J. Kennett and expressed his approval of the "growing mutual confidence and intercourse between the dealers in literature on both sides of the Atlantic."[44] Little could he have foreseen that within a few years his own firm of Wiley and Putnam would be positioning itself side by side with Kennett, before supplanting him entirely, in the transatlantic book trade.

After joining Wiley and Long as a junior partner at a capital investment of $150 (probably all the savings he then had), Putnam carried out a thorough inventory of the firm's stock of books and periodicals, a job for which he was well prepared by his editorship of the *Booksellers' Advertiser* and his years with Leavitt, for whom he had just finished a 116-page book catalogue. His new store's inventory taken and assessed, Putnam then embarked on the real mission of the firm: an extended tour of the professional book markets and makers of Britain and the Continent.[45] That Wiley entrusted a trip of such importance and expense to a young man not simply a new partner but a relative novice in the profession might seem like a foolhardy decision, but the man later known as "cautious John" was neither then nor at any other stage of his career one to take unnecessary or ill-considered gambles. Clearly, he had confidence right from the start in Putnam and trusted his ability to scout the territory and establish relations between their house and British and Continental publishers. Forward-looking as was Wiley's wish to extend his firm's scope of operation to wider, transcontinental markets, by the mid-thirties it was hardly visionary. By then Wiley knew that he was facing competition from other New York publishers who were also casting eager eyes over the Atlantic. Just the previous year, tours of the leading European book trade centers had been made by William Appleton and, as mentioned, by Jonathan Leavitt. In fact, Putnam's itinerary of 1836 so nearly replicated that of Leavitt just months before that he must have modeled his journey at least in part on his former employer's.[46]

Whatever the precise reason for his decision, Wiley made one of the best choices of his publishing career in sending Putnam overseas on behalf of the firm. Endowed with an unusually comprehensive grasp of books foreign and domestic, boundless energy, and a winning personality, Putnam was ideally suited for the mission. And so, in March 1836, George Palmer Putnam boarded the packet ship *England* and embarked on a crossing of the Atlantic Ocean that was to have a significance for him of both a personal and a professional nature—personal, as the first civilian passage made by a member of his immediate family since the initial generation of Putnams and Palmers had arrived in eastern Massachusetts in the mid-seventeenth and mid-eighteenth centuries; and professional, as a career-launching expedition that would leave his and his firm's imprint on the internationalization of books and the book trade in the mid-nineteenth century.

Notes

1. GPP, "Rough Notes of Thirty Years in the Trade," *American Publishers' Circular and Literary Gazette* 1, octavo series (1 August 1863): 242.

2. The original print is in the Eno Collection, Division of Prints and Photographs, New York Public Library; a reprint appears in John A Kouwenhoven, *The Columbia Historical Portrait of New York* (Garden City, N.Y.: Doubleday, 1953), 287.

3. "Mannahatta" was first published in the 1860 edition of *Leaves of Grass,* from which I quote; Roy Harvey Pearce, ed., *Leaves of Grass, 1860* (Ithaca: Cornell University Press, 1961), 404–05.

4. Martha J. Lamb, *History of the City of New York,* 3 vols. (New York: Valentine's Manual, 1921), 3:571–73.

5. Eliza Greatorex, *Old New York; The Battery to Bloomingdale* (New York: G. P. Putnam's Sons, 1875).

6. These figures come from a convenient source for early urban population statistics, Riley Moffat, *Population History of Eastern U.S. Cities and Towns, 1790–1860* (Metuchen, N.J.: Scarecrow Press, 1992).

7. The number of non-native inhabitants who made contributions to publishing in antebellum New York City was so considerable as to have constituted a significant historical pattern. GPP's early employer Jonathan Leavitt was from Haverhill, Massachusetts, as was Daniel Appleton, the founder of New York's second largest nineteenth-century publishing house. Alfred Smith Barnes, a major textbook publisher, came from New Haven; Edward Payson Dutton, founder of E. P. Dutton, came from Keene, New Hampshire; and Charles B. Norton, a principle figure in the early organization of the trade, came from Connecticut. New York was also the chief magnet, as Philadelphia had been in previous generations, for foreign book professionals looking to set themselves up in the United States. Robert Carter, a leading religious publisher, came to the city from Scotland; Robert Bonner, the immensely successful publisher of the New York *Ledger,* from Ireland; and Frank Leslie, one of the most flamboyant publishers of the era who built a profitable network of newspaper and magazine publications chiefly through the innovation of lavish illustrations, from England.

A similar pattern of migration typified New York's antebellum journalistic press, whose rapid growth matched that of book publishing. Benjamin Day, proprietor of the first of the city's penny papers, the *Sun,* came to New York from Springfield, Massachusetts, at age twenty. Horace Greeley of the *Tribune* was born on a farm in New Hampshire and raised there and in Vermont. His coeditors, Charles Dana and George Ripley, who both had distinguished careers in journalism, were likewise New Englanders. Henry Raymond, founder of the *Times,* was from western New York and a graduate of the University of Vermont. James Gordon Bennett, one of the founders of the penny press, did not arrive in New York from his native Scotland until the age of twenty-four. William Cullen Bryant, longtime proprietor of the *Evening Post,* grew up in the Berkshires region of Massachusetts; William Trotter Porter, founder of the weekly sporting paper *Spirit of the Times,* in Vermont and New Hampshire.

It also typified New York magazine publishing. Nathaniel Parker Willis of the *Mirror* and the *Home Journal* was from Portland, Maine. Rufus Porter, founder of *Scientific America,* grew up in Massachusetts and Maine. Park Benjamin, the editor of a variety of magazines and story papers (and at an early period in his city residence a boarder with Mrs. Putnam), was born in Guiana and raised primarily in Connecticut. John L. O'Sullivan, the flamboyant publisher of the *Democratic Review,* had grown up in a number of foreign locations before attending Columbia College. Even Putnam's coeditors of *Putnam's*

Monthly, Charles Frederick Briggs, George William Curtis, and Frederick Beecher Perkins were natives, respectively, of Nantucket, Providence, and Hartford.

8. This calculation is based on the immigration and nativity charts complied by Robert Greenhalgh Albion, *The Rise of New York Port* (Newton Abbot: David and Charles, 1970), 418–19.

9. Lamb, *History,* 3:486.

10. Albion, *Rise of New York Port,* 40–44.

11. Lamb, *History,* 3:699.

12. Benson J. Lossing, *History of New York* (New York: George E. Perine, 1884), 74.

13. Edward K. Spann, *The New Metropolis: New York City, 1840–1857* (New York: Columbia University Press, 1981), 2.

14. Allan Nevins, ed., *The Diary of Philip Hone, 1828–1851,* 2 vols. (New York: Arno Press, 1970), 1:201–2.

15. *Elephant* 1 (12 February 1848): 28–9.

16. Nevins, ed., *Diary of Philip Hone,* 573–74.

17. Ibid., 611.

18. GPP still recalled the power of that lecture fifteen years later; *American Facts* (London: Wiley and Putnam, 1845), 72–73.

19. "January First, A.D., 3000," *Harper's Monthly* 12 (January 1856): 156. I owe thanks to Barbara Brannon for turning my attention to this wonderfully rich, prescient sketch.

20. *City Reading: Written Words and Public Spaces in Antebellum New York* (New York: Columbia University Press, 1998). A major reevaluation of the new contexts of reading and writing in early nineteenth-century America has been evident in the last fifteen years. Within this expanding critical literature the works of William J. Gilmore and Richard D. Brown stand out as explications of the degree to which print culture had by this time become a primary factor in both rural and urban life; see Gilmore, *Reading Becomes a Necessity of Life: Material and Cultural Life in Rural New England, 1780–1835* (Knoxville: University of Tennessee Press, 1988); and Brown, *Knowledge Is Power: The Diffusion of Information in Early America, 1700–1865* (New York: Oxford University Press, 1989).

21. Statistics given in Edwin G. Burrows and Mike Wallace, *Gotham: A History of New York City to 1898* (New York: Oxford University Press, 1999), 677.

22. *Euterpeiad* 1 (15 April 1830): 1.

23. Ibid., 3.

24. J. C. Derby, *Fifty Years among Authors, Books and Publishers* (New York: G. W. Carleton, 1884), 174.

25. GPP, "Rough Notes," 248. Putnam remembered the responsibility for the room taken at Clinton Hall and for filling orders with the trade as having been assigned to Daniel Appleton, an account that conflicts with most other published accounts of Appleton's career and the earlier dating of the split between the partners. See, e.g., Samuel C. Chew, *Fruit among the Leaves* (New York: Appleton-Century-Crofts, 1950), 4; and Gerard R. Wolfe, *The House of Appleton* (Metuchen, N.J.: Scarecrow Press, 1981), 7.

26. GHP, *George Palmer Putnam,* 1:37–38.

27. This information, and that which follows on the publication of GPP's first book, comes from his "Rough Notes," 244.

28. For a sketch of McVickar, see the entry in *Dictionary of American Biography* (New York: Charles Scribner's Sons, 1933), 12:172–73.

29. The only letter I have seen in GPP's hand during this period is an undated note he wrote to Schroeder in which he explained his manner of compilation and commented on his general situation:

I shall feel sincerely grateful for any assistance you may have leisure to afford me, by examining my compilation, noting any errors you may discover, or suggesting improvements.— If the book should be of any benefit to me I think it will not be mis-applied. I have had few advantages—not even common school instruction—but I try to make the best use of the little leisure time I can call my own. My mother is a widow, and I, her only son. She teaches a young ladies school 495 Broome st.—

Mr. Leavitt is willing to publish the volume I have compiled as soon as he is satisfied that it will be acceptable with the public.— Trusting your kindness, sir, I have ventured to take this liberty which I hope you will excuse—and if you can consistently give a fair opinion of the plan and filling up (so far as you may have examined it) on paper, I shall be under great obligation.

The letter is in the Berg Collection, New York Public Library.

30. *Book-Trade Bibliography in the United States in the Nineteenth Century* (1898; repr. New York: Burt Franklin, 1939), xli–xlii.

31. See his unusually candid farewell editorial, "To the Patrons of the Critic," *Critic* 2 (13 June 1829): 89.

32. I have been frustrated in my attempts to locate a full run of this important journal. The *Union List of Serials* gives the Library of Congress and Harvard University as the only repositories of nearly complete runs of the *Booksellers' Advertiser,* but both sets have been lost for years. The only other confirmed full run is at the University of Michigan, but whereas the time I requested a photocopy of it and the execution of my request it was misplaced and has not since been located. I have therefore been forced to base my analysis of the *Booksellers' Advertiser* on the incomplete microfilm file at the University of Minnesota that was shot from the print copy at Harvard, which consists of vol. 1, nos. 1–7 and 12; and volume 2, no. 1.

33. This was the first professional connection between GPP and his future printer, John Trow, who had apprenticed (like Joseph Griffin a few years before him) at the shop of Flagg and Gould in Andover. Trow left his partnership with John T. West in 1836 to go out on his own, before entering in 1840 into partnership with GPP's former employer Jonathan Leavitt. For a sketch of Trow, see John Clyde Oswald, *Printing in the Americas* (1937; repr. New York: Hacker Art Books, 1968), 215–16.

34. GPP revealed his name only in the "Valedictory" of the supposed last issue, December 1834, in which he wrote: "I resign it [the journal] because it cannot be properly attended to without interfering with more legitimate duties, or infringing on midnight hours." Quoted in "Rough Notes," 244–45.

35. *Booksellers' Advertiser* 2 (1 March 1836): 1.

36. His conduct of the journal expressed a nationalistic pride in what he considered the superiority of American bookmaking practices to those of Europe. One basis of that pride was his belief that printed works were more widely dispersed and did broader good in the United States than in Europe. After reprinting an item about the spirit of sectarianism and the practice of partial journalism in Germany, where publishing houses, institutions, and associations routinely issued their own in-house papers, he boasted of his own journal as a counterstatement of American consensus: "In the United States they do things more correctly: the booksellers having a general 'Advertiser,' for the equal benefit of all"; *Booksellers' Advertiser* 1 (April 1834): 28.

37. GPP, "Rough Notes," 244.

38. "Cheap Literature," *Booksellers' Advertiser* 2 (1 March 1836): 1.

39. *Booksellers' Advertiser* 1 (April 1834): 25.

40. Relatively little is known about John Wiley, the senior figure in Wiley and

Putnam and the founder of John Wiley and Sons. On Wiley's early career, the best source is John Hammond Moore, *Wiley: One Hundred and Seventy-five Years of Publishing* (New York: John Wiley and Sons, 1982), 33–34.

41. His frequent changes of address and of partnership during this period were symptomatic not only of his own difficulties but of the general precariousness of business affairs among his peers.

42. This information comes from an unidentified clipping contained in a folder in the small company archive kept at the present-day John Wiley and Sons.

43. The only documented run of the journal is at the American Antiquarian Society.

44. *Booksellers' Advertiser* 2 (1 March 1836): 2.

45. GPP, "Rough Notes," 258.

46. GPP was the compiler of the thick catalogue of domestic and foreign books, dated February 1836, advertised for sale by Leavitt, Lord, and Company. Placed near the end of that catalogue was a blurb publicizing the firm's intent to increase its book importing operations: "Mr. Leavitt having very recently returned from a tour in England, Scotland, France, and Germany, and having established a regular correspondence with the principal publishing houses in London, Oxford, Edinburgh, Glasgow, Paris, Leipsic, Halle, etc., the subscribers are enabled to furnish all the important works published in those places, in any quantity, and at much lower prices than heretofore" (109).

CHAPTER 3

————•·•————

Wiley and Putnam,
New York and London

Putnam crossed the Atlantic more than a dozen times during his three and a half decades as a publisher. Having made so many crossings and made them in ships that spanned the ages of sails and steam, he gradually came to think of himself as an amateur authority on the subject—the various lines in competition with one another and their respective captains and crews, the capacities of the different ships on which he traveled, the speed of passages, even the changing physical environment that improved technology brought to the trip. He also displayed a different kind of nautical expertise: while his wife or friends were down in the cabin riding out migraines or seasickness, he preferred to take the trip up above, immune to those ailments and fond of the motion. Travel was an adventure Putnam enjoyed; his appetite for it remained keen to the end of his life.

His maiden voyage in 1836, though, was special. For a young man of his background, this was an opportunity to stretch his muscles on a transatlantic scale. Free to combine the grand tour with a beginning professional's dream chance to meet the leading men of letters and their professional bookmakers, Putnam found in Europe a playing field wide enough to test his ambitions and ideals. Typically "improving his time" on the crossing in order to be prepared to transact business directly on his arrival in London, he read through London book catalogues while his fellow passengers socialized over whiskey. At the same time, Putnam had the knack, then and always, for mixing business with pleasure: as a publisher, his business often was his pleasure. He therefore looked forward with a young man's pent-up enthusiasm to seeing through his own eyes the scenes and places known to him chiefly through the pages of Scott, Irving, Wordsworth, and other favorite writers. That process was already underway during the transit; shortly after reaching port, he described the crossing in a letter to his mother as being "very like others which have been 'written of in books' by Geoffrey Crayon and his numerous successors."[1]

The crossing was an unusually quick one, nineteen days from New York to Liverpool, his jumping-off point for what grew into a six-month, experience-rich tour of England, Scotland, France, Switzerland, Germany, and Belgium. His mind was initially not turned exclusively to business. He spent the first few days in Liverpool, where he saw the sites and took in a performance by Charles Kean as Hamlet, then he traveled by train to Manchester. From there he proceeded by stage, stopping whenever possible to see the tourist attractions, via Birmingham, Stratford (where, in an ironic anticipation of his own career, he stayed at an inn favored by Americans ever since Washington Irving mentioned it as a place where he composed scenes of the *Sketch-Book*), and Oxford before finally reaching London. Putnam's arrival in London, a city sprawling on a scale surpassing even his expectations, registered immediately as a special event; it marked, he later wrote, "an epoch in my life."[2] He soon came to know the city well and to use it as his base of operations for the remainder of his stay. He spent about half of his time in the city; the other half on short trips into the surrounding countryside, a longer trip to Scotland, and an extended tour of the Continent. The priority he gave London accorded with its status as the world capital of English-language publishing. Even though Wiley and Long had not yet decided to establish a branch office in the city, they might have wished Putnam to explore that possibility, and they certainly expected him to make the rounds of London's publishers and to arrange for the importation of their works or, where possible, the exchange of their printed works for those of Wiley and Long. But, above all, they hoped that he would make arrangements with European publishers that would allow Wiley and Long to gain an advantage over their competitors in the profitable business of reprinting works for the American market.

The seriousness with which an unknown American publisher was received in London and elsewhere in the mid-1830s was testimony less to Putnam's ability and charm than to the rising status of the American market and to the growing regard of the international trade generally among European publishers. Even though the battle over American reprints was largely still a few years away, British publishers were well aware of the commercial success of such American writers as Cooper and Irving in their markets and began reprinting their works, as well as an increasing number of works in nonfictional and scholarly genres in which British publishing condescension to American books had been strongest. At the same time, they were even more conscious of the sales potential for their own works in the large, fast-growing American market. Perhaps the most significant sign of the new seriousness with which English publishers regarded the American market was the departure for New York, at the same time Putnam was arriving in London, of Frederick Saunders, son of the head of the London house of Saunders and Otley, with instructions to open an American branch office.[3] Saunders's task was the mirror image of Putnam's long-term mission in London: to establish a two-coast presence in the international trade in books; to forestall local pirating of the firm's popular works, such as Edward Bulwer's *Rienzi;* and, at a higher level, to stir up support in America for an international copyright as a means of pre-empting the widespread practice of literary piracy carried out on both shores.[4] But where Saunders met with immediate resistance from such leading American publishers as the Harpers, who considered him an interloper on their profitable territory, Putnam was perceived less as a threat to domestic publishers than as a possible partner and was generally given a warm reception.[5] So, for that matter, were other American publishers who came to Britain during the mid-1830s with similar ambitions, such as the New Yorkers James Harper of Harper and Brothers, William Appleton of Appleton's, Jonathan Leavitt of Leavitt, Lord, and Company; and the Bostonian Nahum Capen of Marsh, Capen and Lyon.

Directly after arriving in the city, Putnam moved to make the acquaintance of the trade. Furnished with letters of introduction from Wiley and others and well read in English trade lists, Putnam made the rounds of London's leading houses: John Murray, whom he admired for his successful and generous relations with authors and whose famous offices at 50 Albemarle Street he had longed to see; the Longmans, his future neighbors in Paternoster Row with whom he went to dinner several times; Edward Moxon, whose book of sonnets was handled by Wiley and Long in New York and whose penchant for the belles lettres issued in attractive fashion accorded with Putnam's own publishing taste; William Pickering, an unusually learned, innovative publisher/bookseller and a force in the trade; quite possibly Richard Bentley, already showing signs of becoming a serious publisher of American literature; and various other publishers, large and small. After Putnam returned to London on a more permanent basis in 1838, some of those preliminary contacts developed into long-lasting professional relationships, such as the one with the Murrays that involved cordial business dealings between the two families and their firms for nearly a century. Similarly, while in Oxford, Putnam made the acquaintance of the local publisher D. A. Talboys, whose scholarship he held in high regard and contrasted with the lack of learning typical of his American colleagues. He also saw and in some cases made the acquaintance of a number of England's literati, including Anna Jameson; G. P. R. James, whose works were experiencing a vogue of popularity in America; and Wordsworth, whom he spotted in his publisher's counting house. Of his conversations with writers, he particularly enjoyed his long talk with Thomas Hartwell Horne, a leading bibliographer who had worked extensively as a cataloguer of collections in the British Museum and whose highly regarded *An Introduction to the Critical Study and Knowledge of the Holy Scriptures* Putnam knew from his days with Jonathan Leavitt.[6]

Because Scotland was also an important center of book and periodical publication, Putnam made Edinburgh the secondary focal point of his trip, journeying north in June and staying on for several weeks until called back to London by business. Edinburgh was home to such leading publishers as the Blackwoods, the Chambers, and John Constable, and although we have no particulars concerning his dealings there, it is hard to imagine that Putnam did not attempt to meet as many publishers as possible and try to make arrangements for handling their books and magazines in New York. He also made the acquaintance of David Brewster, editor of the *Edinburgh Encyclopedia,* and hoped to but did not make that of Francis Jeffrey, the influential critic who had edited the *Edinburgh Review* in its days of glory. Putnam's presence in the country, though, was a matter of sentiment as well as of business, and he spent as much time as possible touring the countryside, especially Abbottsford, a fixed point in his literary sensibility. While there, he made it a point to seat himself in Scott's study and pore through his artifacts, which he described, as he did everything relating to favorite authors and books, in detail to his mother (who obviously shared his passion for the romances of Scott and his imitators). One other favorite stop in Scotland was at Dundee, where he looked up Thomas Dick, author of *The Christian Philosopher,* and engaged him in a long conversation.[7]

In August, he began his journey across the Continent, taking the ferry ("a pygmy affair") across the Channel to Boulogne and finding himself, for the first time in his life, in a country where English was not spoken. With an overseas American's knack for finding his own kind, he generally managed to choose English-speaking traveling partners on the journey to Paris, where he stayed cheaply near the Luxembourg Gardens while transacting his business. Mornings he spent primarily in the bookstore of Jean Antoine and Guillaume Galignani, the leading address for English-language publishing and book retailing in Paris. Although British publishers feared the brothers as reprinters, Putnam found them charming and genial men and conducted business with them amicably for more than a decade.[8] He also learned from their retail and promotional expertise; at the height of his operations in London in the next decade, he modeled his own publishing offices in part after theirs, which featured the well-known *cabinets de lecture* that the brothers kept stocked with the latest journals and books in English and other languages.[9] Among their various publications, they issued their own excellent English tour guides to Paris and France, as well as their widely read newspaper *Galignani's Messenger* and other journals of their own compilation.[10] During this trip Putnam might also have made the acquaintance of Hector Bossange, a leading Parisian publisher and literary agent who conducted business widely across European national and linguistic boundaries.

From France, Putnam continued across the Continent, stopping to make the acquaintance of librarians and publishers in major population centers, to fill book and journal orders for clients, and to visit the local attractions. Perhaps he carried a list of names and addresses assembled for him back in New York; if so, by this time he would certainly have been able to add to that list from the network of contacts he had formed during his trip. The only publisher he mentioned specifically as having met in the German states was the young Christian Bernhard Tauchnitz, who had recently founded a publishing house separate from his uncle's which he soon built into one of the greatest houses in Europe and one chiefly renowned in the English-speaking world for its Collection of British and American Authors. A fluent English speaker several years younger than Putnam, Tauchnitz proved himself a cordial host, showing Putnam through his facilities, especially his pioneering stereotype vaults, and escorting him around Leipzig and out to the site of the Napoleonic battlefield.[11] Putnam was particularly impressed by Leipzig's new Booksellers' Exchange, where members of the trade gathered twice each year at one of Europe's greatest book fairs. Even in England he had not witnessed the degree of organization or the scale of operations that he saw in the Prussian book trade, which he was quick to point out produced more new works annually than did the English and French combined.[12] To Putnam, it was the Germans—not the English—who deserved the label of "a nation of book-makers," and it was probably from them as much as from the English that he got ideas for improving the organization of the book trade in the United States.[13]

After passing through Switzerland and Germany, Putnam rounded his circle and headed back toward England via Belgium, crossing the Channel from Ostend and reaching London in late September. He had had a chance by then to gauge the possibilities for his firm in the European book market, as well as to gain a full enough set of personal impressions to fill a book of travels (although it is not clear whether he had as yet formulated any plans to write and publish one). Those impressions, taken in total, were deeply and, for an American tourist in Europe, characteristically ambivalent, the touchstone of his sentiments and observations naturally being his own national identity. Like many of his compatriots, Putnam could not separate what he had seen in Europe from his native associations: the air in Abbottsford from the atmosphere in Brattleboro, Vermont; the falls of the Rhine from those of his own native Androscoggin or even Niagara. More generally his mind was fixed on practical considerations; he came to grasp the cost of living, accessibility of books and education, class structures, political systems, and national manners of European countries primarily in terms of and by comparison with those of America. When it came time to put these impressions to paper and then to print, Putnam would resemble his father, if on a broader scale, in easily falling into the pattern of insider-outsider explication made always with a patriotic sense of where his own loyalties lay.

As a popularizer, defender, and merchant of American letters, Putnam was particularly interested in seeing and evaluating the state of European culture. He spent a good portion of his free time visiting the museums, libraries, churches, and historical artifacts of the cities he toured, studiously keeping notes and marking up his copies of their guidebooks for future reference. No Sunday transpired without his open-eared attendance at church (or sometimes churches), regardless of denomination or creed; and no opportunity passed him by to see the local sites or meet local dignitaries. An amateur enthusiast of the fine arts, he was particularly impressed by the extent of their public display in Paris: "And then to expose those valuable and exquisite works of art so freely and publicly to all classes and conditions of the populace, and yet no mutilation or injury to them, is even thought of. Americans and Britons may well wonder at it, and do likewise. It is perhaps this very liberality in the display of the fine arts to 'the common people,' which creates and promotes among them such instinctive politeness, as well as taste and refinement."[14] But when it came to assessing the public accessibility of books and book culture, he came away convinced that the United States had the clear advantage over Europe (and especially England): "How many of the thousands among us who get the last novel of Bulwer, James, or Marryat, for the trifling sum of fifty cents, could make the purchase, if they had to pay one pound eleven shillings and sixpence, or seven dollars, as in London? New novels can only be afforded there by the librarian, the nobility, or the millionaire. But with us, all classes have books; and the mechanic's apprentice, with the penny paper in his hand, may discuss the politics of the day as wisely, perhaps, as his master, or the president himself."[15] Such remarks made clear Putnam's commitment to judging a culture in large part by the degree to which it made the fine arts and print accessible to the general public; that tenet underlay not only his observations on Europe during his tour but the operating philosophy on which he eventually established his own publishing house.

He returned to New York in October or November 1836, about the time that Martin Van Buren was elected to the White House, succeeding Andrew Jackson. That continued line of Democratic succession presumably did not please Putnam or his business partners, but Wiley and

Long were no doubt more immediately interested in hearing the report of Putnam's travels and discussions in Europe than in current events in Washington. They must have been heartened by what they heard; the firm subsequently entered the international market more aggressively than ever before. In fact, it handled a number of books that dealt directly with the international theme, including several of James Fenimore Cooper's European travel books, and soon afterward published Putnam's own *The Tourist in Europe*. Furthermore, as the New York agents of Carey, Lea and Blanchard, the largest publishing house in Philadelphia and one attempting to go head-to-head with the Harpers in the fight to retain leadership of the European reprint business, Wiley and Long was handling through its retail operations an increasing number of reprinted titles, a field in which the firm did not have to contend with the Harpers, who avoided the retail trade.

Some time in February or early March 1837, the title of the firm was changed to Wiley and Putnam, Long having left or retired from the business and Putnam been promoted in his stead to a full-fledged position as partner, if still the junior financially. The edition of Scott's *The Lady of the Lake* that had been published under the Wiley and Long imprint the year of Putnam's trip (and possibly as a result of it) was reissued in 1837 under the Wiley and Putnam imprint. Drawing upon arrangements made by Putnam, the firm advertised its services early that year in the local media as an importer of books from Europe. In March, the *Knickerbocker* announced Putnam as "recently returned from a bibliographical tour through Great Britain, France, and Germany, during which he made arrangements for executing orders for public libraries, as well as for universities and literary institutions, which receive their importations free of duty."[16] The two places mentioned specifically by the magazine were Columbia College Library and the Mercantile Library, the latter the place where only a few years before Putnam had done his own reading. But these were only two libraries on a long list; Wiley and Putnam pursued the institutional book business in the coming years as aggressively as any other firm in the country and did so on a national basis, exploiting its geographic and transportation advantages to buy for institutions in less accessible regions of the country. These libraries' exemption from the stiff import duties on books might have been a strong inducement to them to import books through firms, such as Wiley and Putnam, engaged in the international trade, but that consideration was hardly the primary one that the firm was counting on. More central to its calculations was the expansion of institutional and private book buying in the country generally. Once Putnam was more permanently installed in England, able to oversee the placing of orders in that country and through his network of agents on the Continent, the firm was ready to press its advantage even more aggressively over its competition.

Shortly after Putnam's status rose within his company, he gained more prominence in the book trade citywide. He was a member of the committee of local publishers who made the arrangements for a lavish dinner given on 30 March by the Booksellers' Association of New York in honor of the city's authors. Held at the City Hotel and attended by nearly three hundred people, the dinner celebrated the achievements of authorship and publishing on a scale not previously seen in New York City or, for that matter, in any other American city (Philip Hone, who knew the subject well, declared it "the greatest dinner I was ever at, with the exception perhaps of that given to Washington Irving on his return from Europe").[17] Putnam was one of the book and periodical publishers called upon to give a toast at the dinner, the trade also being represented by, among others, the Harpers, William Stone of the city's *Commercial Advertiser,* Charles King of the *American,* William Cullen Bryant of the *Evening Post,* Lewis Gaylord Clark of the *Knickerbocker,* and George Morris of the *Mirror.* The real dignitaries of the evening, though, were the writers, such as Washington Irving, James Kent, Edgar Allan Poe, and James Kirke Paulding, all of whom were called upon to offer toasts. Also in attendance that evening were Putnam's two examiners of about four years before, John McVickar and John Frederick Schroeder, who might (or might not) have been surprised to see their former supplicant occupying a position of responsibility in the world of books. More important for the future of his career was his chance to make an initial acquaintance with Irving, whom he persuaded to send a transcript of his dinner remarks to the local newspapers.[18]

Just weeks after the dinner, the financial markets of the country were convulsed by one of the most severe bank panics of the century, which swept through the entire economy, attacking capital-poor industries, such as publishing, with particular severity. Even Harper and Brothers, the most successful publishing house in the city, was severely affected by the contraction of credit, which left it hard pressed to pay its bills.[19] Smaller firms, like Wiley and Putnam, were left treading water, at best, hoping that no deluge would follow. Perhaps less extended than most of their competitors, the young partners somehow weathered the storm and continued to pursue their publishing and retail operations. Among the titles they handled that year were the first edition of Hawthorne's *Twice Told Tales,* published in Boston by the Stationers' Company, and Cooper's *Gleanings in Europe.* Under their own imprint, they issued *Elements of Moral Philosophy* by Jasper Adams, president of the College of Charleston. This work was published in Cambridge by the Harvard University printers but carried Wiley and Putnam on the title page of copies sold in New York (as Carey and Hart put its imprint on copies sold in Philadelphia). Also on the firm's list that year were the artist Seth Eastman's *Treatise on Topographical Drawing;* and various previously published works now kept in print, such as Victor Cousin's *Report on the State of Public Instruction in Prussia,* Thomas Moore's *Lalla Rookh,* and the complete poems of Thomas Campbell.

But a list comparatively small and unremarkable could hardly have been the primary basis of the firm's operations. Wiley had been more active in recent years as an agent of other firm's works and general distributor to the trade, a role he presumably retained after Putnam became his partner and the reconstituted firm continuing to do a sizable percentage of its business out of its retail operations at 161 Broadway. That status quo was not to last long, however: Wiley and Putnam decided to follow up on the momentum established by Putnam's European trip by attempting to make itself the leading literary agency in New York for the purchase of foreign books.

Far from being discouraged by the existing financial conditions, the firm went ahead with ambitious plans to expand operations. Some time in late 1837 the firm decided to open a branch office in London, the first American publisher to do so, and to install Putnam there on a permanent basis as its director as well as as its point man in the international book trade. According to a circular dated 1 January 1838, Putnam was due to sail in mid-March, a date that proved premature by several months while orders were still being taken and final preparations being made for the venture.[20] In the hope of attracting new clients, the circular advertised a long list of current Wiley and Putnam customers, including Charles Anthon, Francis Hawks, Evert Duyckinck, James Kent, and John Frederick Schroeder, as well as representatives of Columbia College, New York University, New York Mercantile Library, West Point, and the University of Louisiana. It also offered the best terms available: orders of all sizes for books and journals to be shipped regularly on the packets out of Liverpool; an established correspondence with the leading booksellers in London, Oxford, Edinburgh, Glasgow, Paris, and Leipzig (cities all covered in Putnam's 1836 itinerary); the lowest possible commission, usually 10 percent, which would be charged to the purchase price paid by Wiley and Putnam; and the expertise to procure even the rarest volumes.

Just weeks before Putnam finalized his preparations, New York City celebrated the arrival of the first steamships from England, the *Sirius* and the *Great Western*. Though launched by rival groups days apart, they arrived within hours of each other on 22 April, the latter having cut the duration of the transatlantic passage to two weeks.[21] Their arrival created a stir throughout the city and was of more than passing interest to the firm, which capitalized on the event by issuing Ithiel Town's small book on steam navigation in the weeks immediately following their arrival in port.[22] Steam power, as Wiley and Putnam well understood, would help to expedite the passage of books as well as people across the ocean. One of the more notable commentaries on his era's perception of shrinking global geography was that registered by Thomas Carlyle, who several years after this event responded to the reception of a transatlantic letter posted by Ralph Waldo Emerson two weeks before by predicting to his friend, "By and by we shall visibly be, what I always say we virtually are, members of neighbouring Parishes; paying continual visits to one another."[23] Wiley and Putnam was, of course, hardly the only publisher in town to recognize the benefits that steam-powered transportation would bring publishing operations. An equally adventurous reaction came from James Gordon Bennett, the brash publisher of the New York *Herald,* who took a berth on the return voyage of the *Sirius* with the intent of arranging a foreign correspondence for his newspaper with the principal political and commercial centers in Europe of a sort that no other American paper then had.[24]

In the midst of these events, Putnam sailed on the same packet that had taken him to England two years before, arriving in London in July or early August. His first major task was to hunt up offices convenient to the book district, which he had come to know well during his previous trip. The earliest sign of his success in doing so was an advertisement for the Wiley and Putnam London office at 67 Paternoster Row that appeared in the 15 August issue of *Publishers' Circular,* the semiofficial organ of the London trade, followed three days later by a related notice in the *Athenaeum*. Both advertisements identified the firm as "American Publishers," gave its addresses in London and New York, and announced its services as importers of books to London. *Publishers' Circular* also listed the American journals the company had on hand, including the *North American Review, Knickerbocker, American Monthly Magazine,* and *New York Review*.

Putnam's primary responsibility during his first year in London was to get his firm established and recognized in the trade. His previous period of residence in the city undoubtedly expedited this task, as did the fact that he occupied a unique status in the London trade. Although Obadiah Rich and Richard J. Kennett, both American bookdealers living in London, were active in the sale and trade of American works, as were a small number of English sellers, Putnam alone had the benefit of a home office in New York that allowed for a relatively smooth coordination of operations between London and New York. The range of Putnam's activities and responsibilities can be inferred from a circular that the firm issued back in New York in late 1838 or early 1839, advertising the advantages of their two-coast facilities as importers of foreign books and periodicals, whether British publications shipped from Liverpool or Continental publications from Le Havre or Hamburgh.[25] The circular announced that all orders would be "personally and carefully attended to by one of the firm, who is well acquainted with the British and Continental Book Market" and that they would be filled on cheaper terms than could be offered by either local or foreign competitors. Where possible, the circular promised, large orders and rare books would be purchased at library auction sales, a means of book purchase that was to become increasingly important for the firm in the 1840s. And since most of its business was done with the trade back home or with institutional customers, Wiley and Putnam claimed that it could "usually deliver English Books in New York at prices as low, and sometimes much less, than those of London Publishers" and make them available for delivery in New York normally within seventy days of the receipt of orders. So, too, with respect to a wide variety of British magazines and reviews, for which the London office offered its services in sending them off by packet on the first day of every month for purchase back in the States. In addition, the firm also indicated its desire to be part of the growing international trafficking in books, whose network reached from the United States to Continental Europe, by importing European catalogues to American customers and handling the purchase of European books on the same terms it offered for English books.

What all these functions added up to for Putnam was a many-sided immersion in the business of importing and exporting books and magazines. It brought him into contact with a wide range of literary professionals besides publishers, including binders, printers, booksellers, shipping clerks, customs officers, librarians, collectors, and authors. When the order required, as not infrequently happened, the purchase of Continental works, Putnam was responsible for filling them in the various book centers of Western and Central Europe. Usually he conducted that business through the mails, but occasionally, when such orders individually or collectively warranted his direct supervision, he oversaw them in person (a practice that began in autumn 1838 and became more common in the 1840s). Furthermore, because the London office was inadequately staffed, especially in its early years, Putnam was forced personally to supervise much of the requisite work, beginning with the actual purchase of books and magazines, whether from storekeepers, publishers, or auctioneers, and ending with their final preparation for shipping. Another of his responsibilities—probably the most time-consuming one of all—was the task of conducting the office's correspondence. Not surprisingly, the vast majority of the letters from the London office that have survived are in Putnam's hand.

At the same time, Putnam handled a considerable return traffic of incoming packages from America. Although the firm had anticipated a much heavier volume of traffic entering than exiting America, Putnam was eager to promote a large and growing return traffic in American print products into London, whether to be sold by prior order to specific customers, retailed from his Paternoster Row store, or exchanged with British publishers for their works. Although both John Wiley and Putnam had initially seen the supervision of that return traffic as one of his responsibilities in London, Putnam put more emphasis on it than did his partner, who was more concerned that the New York office remain the center of the firm's operations. The size of that traffic, which grew with time, was due, in part, to Putnam's effectiveness and creativity as a literary professional. Stationed at the crossroads of this transcontinental traffic in printed products, Putnam worked a position initially advantageous so well that he eventually elevated it to one of genuine professional and cultural significance (about which, more later).

In short, Putnam quickly found himself as busy as he could have wished in the minutiae of the international book trade. As busy as he soon became, he could boast, as he did in an 1840 letter to his fiancée, that, endowed with his work habits and native energy, "I can accomplish as much as 5 common persons in the same time—especially if they're not Yankees."[26] In all likelihood he needed that capacity simply to keep up with his daily responsibilities, which only increased in time with the volume of the firm's business. Furthermore, once the branch office was firmly established, he gradually allowed himself to merge the more mundane aspects of his job with his loftier ideal of promoting American culture in Europe. Using both his home and office as a base, he gradually made himself the most effective promoter of American books and culture in England and his office and store the central repository of such works in London.

As tirelessly energetic and wholeheartedly devoted as Putnam was, he could not have been so effective in promoting American books and in wielding his influence had there not already been a strong and growing interest among Europeans in America and its culture. In truth, his timing in coming to London was decidedly advantageous: he was the right person arrived at the right place for enacting his program of American cultural salesmanship. Although Putnam frequently complained about English insularity and close-mindedness and experienced his fair share of them during his years in London, he was actually the beneficiary of a renewed interest there, as well as on the Continent, in the character and affairs of his own country. The most obvious sign that the interest between America and Europe was becoming a mutual affair during the 1830s and 1840s was the growing size and popularity of the travel literature that writers from each hemisphere wrote about the culture and society of the other. While Putnam had made his own contribution to that literature and had relied on James Fenimore Cooper's recent European travel book in doing so, such highly regarded European women and men of letters as Frances Trollope, Harriet Martineau, Alexis de Tocqueville, Frederick Marryat, Charles Lyell, and Charles Dickens had all journeyed or would soon travel to America and published their accounts in books read and issued on both sides of the Atlantic.

But if many of those first-hand, first-person portraits of America became popular works in the United States, they were hardly part of a mutual admiration society. This was so not only because of their sometimes judgmental commentary or portrayal but also because of the uneven currents roiling the fast-growing transatlantic traffic in books and magazines. As early as 1837, one of those travel authors, Frederick Marryat, had come to Washington, D.C., to argue for the adoption of copyright protection for British authors against American pirates. Although not immediately successful, he helped to establish a precedent followed five years later by his better-known contemporary Dickens. In fact, no work was more fully incorporated as both cause and effect into this transatlantic exchange than Dickens's *American Notes,* an account of his 1842 trip to America that he made in part to protest the piracy of his works. During his stay Dickens had repeatedly used the public platform afforded by his American popularity to make the case for the necessity of authorial protection. But no sooner was *American Notes* published than it became the latest work sucked into the transatlantic maelstrom, a work more widely appropriated than were many others bobbing alongside it in the North Atlantic by coming in for unauthorized reprinting not only by American book publishers but also by their new domestic competitors, magazine publishers who rushed the latest popular European works into print as cheap "extras" and sold them for a fraction of their normal book prices.[27]

The logic of the growing international trade in books and of his own situation at the crosscurrents of the Anglo-American waterway might well have pushed Putnam early on to take a role in the inchoate American movement for international copyright legislation. There is no clear evidence, however, that Putnam became actively involved before his return home in 1840.[28] With most of his time spent arranging for the import/export of books and magazines, he also directed little of his attention in 1838–39 to playing his favorite role of publisher. But one work—it was probably the first—on which he put his London imprint, just several months after his establishment there, was the first overseas edition of Edgar Allan Poe's *Narrative of Arthur Gordon Pym,* which had been published in July by Harper and Brothers in New York. The book probably came out in New York shortly after Putnam had sailed, a fact that would at least partly confirm his recollection a generation later that he had received a copy of the Harper edition in his London office and decided to reprint it in a joint venture with Daniel Appleton, then located in London.[29] They unilaterally excised the crucial last paragraph of the novel, with its vision of the white specter, and added an introductory note of their own—or, more likely, of Putnam's—

composing: "It will be seen by a note at the end of the volume, that Mr. Pym's sudden death (of which we have no particulars) occurred while these sheets were passing through the press; and that the narrative consequently breaks off abruptly in its most important part. But the exciting interest of the story, and the intrinsic evidence of its truth and general accuracy, induce us to give it to the public as it is, without further comment."[30] That note was signed simply, "The Publishers. 67 Paternoster-row, London, Oct. 1838."

Although the London edition of *Pym* has long been regarded as an act of piracy, that claim seems misinformed.[31] Because no publisher in Britain had as yet staked a legal claim on the work, there was no copyright for Putnam to violate. In fact, he presumably filed for his own; the title page of his edition indicated that the work had been "entered at Stationers' Hall." The real question is whether his edition did or did not result from an arrangement between Wiley or Putnam and the Harpers. Although there is no report that he made a payment to the Harpers prior or subsequent to publication, it is quite possible that he did. At this point in his career, he enjoyed good relations with them and within a few years would be serving them as their London representative. A further question is why he undertook its publication as a joint venture. If he possibly included Appleton in the publication, he certainly did include two British firms, Whitaker and Company and Charles Tilt, whose names appeared beneath his own on the title page (as Appleton's did not). The most likely explanation is that, still new to publishing arrangements in Britain, he felt the necessity of aligning himself with publishers who had existing distributional networks. Tilt, in particular, would have been well situated to play this role; just the year before he had advised Chapman and Hall on the distribution of *The Pickwick Papers* to country booksellers.[32]

The publication of the London *Pym* was an aberration from the general activity of the English office, which did little publishing in its first year and not much for a few more years, even after it was firmly established. Most of Wiley and Putnam's publishing activity was carried out in New York, where its publication list remained nearly as undefined and directionless as it had been during Wiley's early career. Wiley clearly had less ardent a penchant than his father (and, as matters would turn out, than his partner) for the belles lettres. For that matter, his list reflected a course directed, if by anything, more by expediency than by any particular taste or conviction. If Wiley did exhibit any tendency at all, it was toward a mild attraction to works of religion and conduct, one that reflected his personal conservatism and orthodoxy. He had exhibited this taste early on in publishing works such as the *Father's Magazine,* and that preference for the moral and the pragmatic changed little over the course of his long career. Wiley was already at the time of the partnership the publisher of the great Biblical scholar Edward Robinson, who in the 1840s would become the editor of the firm's theological journal, the *Bibliotheca Sacra and Theological Review,* and in 1839 Wiley was advertising his firm as the agent for the publications of the Andover Theological Seminary, as well as of its theological enemy, the *Christian Examiner.*

In the initial years of their partnership, the tone and content of the firm's publishing activity seem to have been dominated by Wiley's taste and views. Although the list of publications remained eclectic, it carried a preponderance of titles of a theological, moralistic, or educational character. At the time Putnam left for England, the typical profile of Wiley and Putnam authorship remained a throwback to the past: a learned man (though seldom a professional author) connected to the churches, universities, or legal or medical professions, mostly in New York, who wrote serious works addressed to a relatively learned audience—the author, in William Charvat's phrase, as "gentleman-lawyer-minister-scholar-poet."[33] The firm had never published many works by women or in the area of the belles lettres, and that pattern persisted into the new decade.

Once Putnam became a partner, the publication list began to grow, slowly at first, then faster, during the decade of the partnership. The expansion of the list was due not only to Putnam's growing influence in the company and his spreading network of relations in the United States and Britain but also to market conditions. As the United States emerged from the recession of the late 1830s and early 1840s, its economy entered a period of sustained expansion, one that was experienced with particular dynamism in the publishing sector, still a relatively immature area of economic activity before it began its development in the 1840s into a modern industry. As early as the late 1830s, Wiley and Putnam began a cautious move into such areas as travel literature, fiction, and poetry, one consistent with the turn taken by various other American publishers who increasingly saw the belles lettres as a central area of popular taste and consumption and redirected their resources and publishing strategies accordingly. By the mid-1840s, that trend had progressed so far with Wiley and Putnam that the center of their publishing operations and the basis of their reputation as publishers had shifted to the field of letters.

It would be hard to say unequivocally whether either Putnam from his perch in London or Wiley from his in New York was able to foresee such developments in the late 1830s. Whatever the case, to Putnam especially this reorientation of publishing strategies would have come as a welcome prospect, one aligned with his views on American publishing and cultural nationalism. He had been attracted immediately on his arrival in London to the city's great literary publishers, John Murray and Edward Moxon, who remained models to him for years to come of what a publisher should be; and he harbored visions of one day being able to translate their practices into American cultural terms. Although that day was still far beyond his reach, he was able to increase his firm's activities in literary publishing. Moxon, in fact, became a Wiley and Putnam author in 1838 when an edition of his *Sonnets* was published by the firm in New York—in all likelihood, through Putnam's mediation.[34] Another author whom he probably persuaded to publish with his firm was his mother's old favorite, Anna Jameson, whom Putnam had called "one of the most graceful and elegant female writers of the age."[35] Her *Winter Studies and Summer Rambles in Canada,* came out in New York under the Wiley and Putnam imprint in 1839. At the same time, Putnam was also selling and/or distributing the works of other literary writers, such as Poe, Washington Irving, and James Fenimore Cooper, from his Paternoster Row store, while Wiley handled editions of Scott, Campbell, Dickens, Shakespeare, and other popular British authors, classic and contemporary, from the Broadway store.[36]

Which titles they actually published and which they only distributed cannot always readily be determined today, what with their operations crisscrossing along both structural and geographical lines during these years. One thing, however, is clear: by the time Putnam got established in London, the company had entered full scale into the multidimensional workings of the international book trade. With hundreds of titles new and old coming into their New York and London offices through various arrangements or agencies with publishers on both sides of the ocean, with their publishing and retail lists intersecting, and with a patronage base that spanned not only the country but an ocean and that required a complex delivery system linking transatlantic steamship lines and postal service to local stores in New York and London, Wiley and Putnam had quickly evolved into a many-sided business concern offering a complex horizontal and vertical tier of services and responsibilities.[37] Whereas one may explain this phenomenon in terms specific to Wiley and Putnam, one may alternately see it as an outgrowth of the increasing complexity of the publishing industry as it entered an early modern stage of development. The terms on which Wiley and Putnam was operating by the late 1830s were far removed not only from the locally based, small-time terms on which Henry Putnam had dealt with Joseph Griffin in Brunswick less than two decades earlier but also from the small-scale world of publishing and retailing that Putnam himself had encountered when he first came to New York City in 1829. A man with a strong historical sensibility, Putnam could not have been unmindful of the historical leap he and his contemporaries were making.

Even with a publishing list that was beginning to expand and diversify, the firm still saw its bookselling operations, both retail and trade, as the central component of its activities. This was typically the way Putnam chose to present his company in the fairly regular stream of advertisements that he placed in the appropriate London journals during his first year and a half in London, advertisements that portrayed the firm primarily as importers/retailers of American works. A small number of those works were the firm's own publications; most, those of rival American publishers. He also consistently advertised his store as keeping on hand a stock of the leading American journals. A typical advertisement, placed in the *Athenaeum,* presented Wiley and Putnam as "having now completed their arrangements for supplying Books and Periodicals published in every part of the United States, on short notice, and a moderate commission. Those not already imported they can obtain, for special orders, in sixty to seventy days, or, by the steamers, in about forty days. The collection of W. and P. in New York is choice and extensive, and being in direct correspondence with all the other American Publishers, they have facilities for executing orders more promptly and on lower terms than usual."[38]

Putnam remained in England through the end of 1839, overseeing his firm's gradual expansion into the local bookselling market. Although sales and account figures for the firm are entirely lacking, there is good reason to believe that the firm was growing both in London and in New York even before Putnam's return to America and the sustained expansion of the firm and the industry in the 1840s. As early as April 1838, even as Wiley and Putnam were still planning and working out the details of Putnam's London operations, the two men had moved beyond simple newspaper advertisements and were systematically issuing advertising catalogues of the company's stock in books and journals, which they sold from their store on Broadway and mailed out to regular customers. The two men continued to do so until the breakup of the partnership in 1848, but the actual work in most cases seems to have been done by Putnam (who had most of them printed in London by his favorite local printers, Manning and Mason).[39] Putnam was an old hand at compiling such catalogues, as well as bibliographic lists generally, which he had compiled on behalf of the industry generally in the pages of the *Booksellers' Advertiser* and even for a short while before his departure for England in the *New York Review*.[40] Not just a personal talent or interest, his bibliographic expertise reflected important developments in the book trade throughout the United States: the systemization such brochures exemplified was becoming increasingly common and necessary with the growth and maturation of the industry. But where in the *Booksellers' Advertiser* Putnam had attempted to bring greater order to his profession and to help it reach a clearer sense of self-definition, the brochures for his own company had a more limited and self-serving goal: to advertise the commercial possibilities arising out of his firm's international situation in such a way as to broadcast its advantages to the book-buying public in Britain and America.

The catalogues continued to advertise the firm as being primarily a dealer in American books and magazines in both New York and London. Whether calling itself an "agency for the sale of American books" or the "American publication office," Wiley and Putnam's London office offered to import any American print product to order in Britain, just as the New York branch ordered British and Continental print products for American customers. The firm made an effort to import a wide variety of print products, whether journals or books, rare books or regular commercial items. The London office regularly imported copies of such leading American journals as the *Democratic Review, North American Review, Knickerbocker,* and *New York Review,* hoping to find or create a local market for American journals, while the New York office pursued an already established market for a variety of British periodicals. This practice escalated in the early 1840s, although competition and high prices eventually proved an insurmountable obstacle to its success, both for Wiley and Putnam and for others who either imported against them or simply reprinted cheaper versions in America from British sheets.[41] Ultimately, the firm lost out to cheaper editions of periodicals brought out by reprinters, which brought prices down to unparalleled levels, just as book publishers during the early 1840s found themselves losing out to periodical reprinters issuing pirated texts in periodical formats printed at minimal standards and priced well below prevailing book rates. One of the reprinters, Jonas Winchester, who was active in both book and periodical selling, was ironically the publisher of the journal (the *New World*) in which Wiley and Putnam did much of their advertising for their English periodical agency and for which Putnam served in the early 1840s as an occasional London correspondent.

Far more successful was the main field of the firm's business, which throughout its brief history remained in books. The catalogues issued by the firm during 1838–39 list a wide variety of titles, numbering in the hundreds (and growing into the thousands in the catalogues issued in the 1840s), in all the established genres of the day. One catalogue boasts of their imports to New York as comprising "the richest [collection of English books] ever imported" into the United States.[42] Their New York store quickly gained a reputation as carrying one of the finest general inventories in the city, as well as an outstanding assortment of imported and specialty works. Its proprietors also knew how to exploit their London connections; early in the period of Bozomania that swept the city in the late 1830s, they featured in one of their Broadway-facing windows the first portrait of Dickens to appear in the United States.[43] For his part, Putnam used both his catalogues and his newspaper advertisements to invite the British public to visit his Paternoster Row store and employ his services. The earliest of the catalogues prepared in London, for example, called "the attention of Scientific, Theological, and Literary men generally to their exclusive and choice stock of Foreign and American books" and to the favorable terms on which these items, as well as those not already in stock, could be procured.

At the same time, Putnam, no doubt impressed by the social facilities offered by Murray, Galignani, and other well-established publishers of his acquaintance, also sought to turn his business offices into a gathering place for Americans abroad: "American Gentlemen visiting London," he advertised, "will find at above, No. 67 Paternoster-Row, the various New York Newspapers, etc., a Register of Names, References to Lodgings, etc.; and Mr. Putnam will be happy to furnish any information at his command."[44] Putnam, in fact, did more than that; with some visitors he played local tour guide, initiating American tourists to London life and sharing the pleasures of English culture with them. One of those tourists was Evert Duyckinck, one of Wiley and Putnam's most frequent customers who was making the grand tour in 1838 after completing college when Putnam happened upon him between acts at the theater in Paris.[45] He gave a rapt Duyckinck a brief rundown of theaters and literary life in London, which he was able to demonstrate first hand when Duyckinck arrived in the city the following spring for a period of several months. Putnam not only showed Duyckinck around town and introduced him to leading writers, editors, and publishers, including Edward Moxon, but even housed him in the same boarding house where he was then living on the Strand.[46] Putnam never lacked for a publisher's social charm and generosity, and taking visitors such as Duyckinck around town drew out much of what was most special in his personality as well as reinforced in him what, like many Americans abroad, he sometimes needed to be reassured about: his own Americanness. Six years later, his relationship with Duyckinck, which had continued through the mails as book agent, took on another dimension when Duyckinck, already an investor in the firm, became Wiley and Putnam's literary advisor and led the firm into its most active years in literary publishing.

As 1839 neared its close, Putnam prepared for his first trip home since his departure for England in summer 1838. That year and a half had put considerable distance between his current self and the one he left behind in New York, but by the same token he had been traveling so fast through both his personal development and his professional career that this was just another chapter in the continuing story of his early manhood. A decade that had begun with him as an adolescent learning the carpet business in Boston was ending with him a respected American bookman installed on Paternoster Row and dealing with the leading literary professionals in both America and England. That fact was brought home to him upon his return to London in summer 1840, when he was partly bemused, partly gratified, to hear that a meeting of London publishers to discuss the American trade had been postponed until his return.[47] But as matters were to turn out, those first years in England were but a prelude to a career whose most creative and dynamic years were still ahead of him.

Notes

1. The primary source for GPP's 1836 journey to Europe is the diary he kept and the letters he wrote to family and friends (especially to his mother), which he adapted for publication as *Memoranda during a Tour of Eight Months in Great Britain and on the Continent, in 1836.* That work was bound together with and issued at the conclusion of his tour guide, *The Tourist in Europe.* A great deal of the former was published first in the pages of the *Knickerbocker Magazine* as "Random Leaves from a Journal of Travels in England, Scotland, France, and Germany," which appeared in eight installments: *Knickerbocker* 9 (April 1837): 398–404; (June 1837): 563–72; *Knickerbocker* 10 (July 1837): 41–50; (August 1837): 147–61; (September 1837): 240–51; (October 1837): 330–41; (November 1837): 387–405; (December 1837): 527–37. Even before deciding to publish that work serially, the editor had printed an earlier selection while GPP was still in England, in the "Editors' Table," *Knickerbocker* 8 (July 1836): 117–19.

The quotation comes from *The Tourist in Europe* (New York: Wiley and Putnam, 1838), 73.

2. These details, prefaced by the description of GPP as "a young and enthusiastic American, of fine parts—who has seen every portion of his own country, and whose heart is replete with all good impulses—now on a tour through Europe, which he visits for the first time," come from a letter written by GPP and published in the "Editors' Table" of the *Knickerbocker* 8 (July 1836): 117.

3. Arno L. Bader, "Frederick Saunders and the Early History of the International Copyright Movement in America," *Library Quarterly* 8 (January 1938): 37.

Their paths would cross again after Putnam established his own publishing house in New York, in which Saunders had a position of responsibility in the early 1850s.

4. For a good sketch of Saunders and Otley, see *Dictionary of Literary Biography,* 106; Patricia J. Anderson and Jonathan Rose, eds. *British Literary Publishing Houses, 1820–1880* (Detroit: Gale, 1991), 271–74.

5. The Harpers, for example, issued their own edition of Bulwer's *Rienzi* and reacted with anger when other houses in the United States did likewise. They had contracted with Bulwer in 1835 to pay him a lump sum per volume in exchange for printing rights to his new works, but in the absence of an international copyright protection their competitors were not required by law to respect that agreement. Not surprisingly, Bulwer became a prized catch for literary pirates in the years following the Harpers' initial agreement with him. In truth, the Harpers practiced selective righteousness; when situated on the opposite side, they were not slow to reprint on publishers holding similar kinds of contracts with foreign authors.

The main provision of the memorandum of agreement between Harper and Brothers and Bulwer is printed in James J. Barnes, *Authors, Publishers and Politicians: The Quest for an Anglo-American Copyright Agreement, 1815–1854* (London: Routledge and Kegan Paul, 1974), 53. Barnes also gives an excellent discussion of the cutthroat competition between American publishers over Bulwer (53–60).

6. It was one of three books by Horne listed in a Leavitt trade catalogue dated February 1836 that was compiled by GPP.

7. Dick was a popular writer in America, a fact recognized by the Harpers, who included his *Celestial Scenery* in their popular Family Library. He was also a contributor to the *Knickerbocker,* whose editor, Lewis Gaylord Clarke, was a friend of GPP's and might have written him a letter of introduction.

8. The leading English-language pirates in Paris, the Galignanis reprinted without payment the works of, among others, GPP's future author, James Fenimore Cooper,

who as though in revenge was constitutionally unable to spell their family name correctly.

9. One of the fullest, if not the most objective, descriptions of their reading rooms appears in their own local guidebook, under the entry of "reading-rooms and circulating libraries":

> There are many establishments of this kind in Paris; but the most distinguished and most frequented by Frenchmen and foreigners, particularly Englishmen and Americans, is that of Messrs. Galignani and Co., No. 18, rue Vivienne (bottom of the courtyard), which is conducted on a most extensive scale. The reading-rooms are spacious and handsome, well lighted and aired. The tables are covered with all the European newspapers and periodical publications worthy of notice, and there are upwards of 20,000 volumes in all languages. Contiguous to the rooms is a garden, for the use of the subscribers. The philosopher, the politician, and the student, may here enjoy their favourite pursuits, whilst the victims of ennui may pass their hours with pleasure and advantage. The terms of subscription are—per day, 10 sous; a fortnight, 5 francs; a month, 8 fr. The *Circulating Library* of Messrs. Galignani is conspicuous among all others for its excellent selection and great number of volumes. The subscription is by the fortnight or month.

New Paris Guide (Paris: A. and W. Galignani, 1846), 18.

10. On the Galignanis and their operations during this period, see Giles Barber, "Galignani's and the Publication of English Books in France from 1800 to 1852," *Library* 16 (December 1961): 267–86. Barber mentions that in the late nineteenth century G. P. Putnam's Sons, then under the direction of GHP, handled the sale of Galignani's *Paris Guide* in New York (269).

11. An ambitious, resourceful publisher, Tauchnitz was already eyeing the growing international market in cheap English-language books, and in the young American he probably saw someone well able to assess that market from a different perspective. The previous year he had similarly hosted young William Appleton, the son of Daniel and GPP's future colleague in attempts to organize New York publishers, who was also making the commercial tour of the Continent on behalf of his firm. On Tauchnitz, see the chapter "Continental: Mainly Tauchnitz," in Simon Nowell-Smith, *International Copyright Law and the Publisher in the Reign of Queen Victoria* (Oxford: Oxford University Press, 1968), 41–63; and the superb compilation of William B. Todd and Ann Bowden, *Tauchnitz International Editions in English, 1841–1955: A Bibliographical History* (New York: Bibliographical Society of America, 1988).

12. GPP, *Tourist in Europe,* 247.

13. Ibid., 247.

14. Ibid., 184.

15. Ibid., 172.

16. "Editors' Table," *Knickerbocker* 9 (March 1837): 316.

17. Allan Nevins, ed., *The Diary of Philip Hone, 1828–1851,* 2 vols. (New York: Arno Press, 1970), 1:251.

18. GPP, "Recollections of Irving," *Atlantic Monthly* 6 (November 1860): 602–3.

19. Eugene Exman, *The Brothers Harper* (New York: Harper and Row, 1965), 93–94, 395–96.

20. A copy of that circular is in the Wilbur Fisk Papers, Wesleyan University, Middletown, Conn. Wesleyan was presumably one of the firm's institutional clients; Middletown was one of GPP's destinations during his business trip through New England in June 1840; GPP to Victorine Haven, 18 June [1840], HP-LC.

21. Robert Greenhalgh Albion, *The Rise of New York Port* (Newton Abbot: David and Charles, 1970), 318–19.

22. *Atlantic Steam-Ships* (New York: Wiley and Putnam, 1838).

23. Joseph Slater, ed., *The Correspondence of Emerson and Carlyle* (New York: Columbia University Press, 1964), 305.

24. Benson J. Lossing, *History of New York* (New York: George E. Perine, 1884), 368.

25. The circular is in the Wilbur Fisk Papers, Wesleyan University.

26. GPP to [Victorine Haven,] 20 August 1840, HP-LC.

27. The size and enthusiasm of the public gatherings organized in American cities during Dickens's 1842 trip represented a cultural phenomenon whose significance did not escape Charles Lyell, himself then touring America. "There may be no precedent in Great Britain for a whole people thus unreservedly indulging their feelings of admiration for a favorite author," he wrote, even though he noted that his more skeptical friends considered Dickens's reception as being "more akin to lion-hunting than hero-worship." *Travels in North America,* 2 vols. (New York: Wiley and Putnam, 1845), 1:159.

28. The subject of GPP and international copyright has proven a vexed one to twentieth-century scholars. As Heyward Ehrlich has persuasively shown, GHP, who succeeded his father as head of the family firm and as a leader of the American copyright movement, exaggerated and misstated his father's actual role, a mistake that was uncritically accepted by subsequent commentators and incorporated into the early scholarly record. Ehrlich helps to set that record straight, even though he goes too far in the opposite direction in underestimating the role that GPP actually did play; "The Putnams on Copyright: The Father, the Son, and a Ghost," *Papers of the Bibliographical Society of America* 63 (1969): 15–22.

If it is clear that GPP was not, as his son claimed, the first proponent of the international copyright movement in the United States or the author of the first pamphlet advocating it, his actual role in the movement was one of long-term commitment and exemplary leadership, as subsequent chapters will show. One can only speculate when his active championship of the movement began. It seems likely that he was already well informed and opinionated about the issue during his early years in the New York trade and that he had discussed the situation with leading writers and publishers from both continents in the late 1830s. There is no evidence, however, that his active role began until his return visit to the United States in 1840. From that point on, he remained involved and committed until the end of his life—even if his understanding of the issues was sometimes reductive and his appreciation of the tough political bargaining limited.

29. GHP, *George Palmer Putnam,* 2:258.

30. It was signed simply, "The Publishers. 67 Paternoster-row, London, Oct. 1838."

31. For an instance of this charge, see Burton R. Pollin, ed., *Edgar Allan Poe: The Imaginary Voyages* (New York: Gordian Press, 1994), 43. I owe thanks to Richard Kopley for turning my attention to this text.

32. Anderson and Rose, eds., *British Literary Publishing Houses,* 297.

33. *The Profession of Authorship in America, 1800–1870,* ed. Matthew J. Bruccoli (Columbus: Ohio State University Press, 1968), 10.

34. It seems likely that Moxon was also a personal friend of GPP's. GHP named Moxon as one of the people belonging to the social circle, drawn primarily from the ranks of the literati, formed by his parents in London in the 1840s; GHP, *George Palmer Putnam,* 1:73.

35. GPP, "Literary Intelligence," *New York Review* 2 (April 1838): 518.

36. Jacob Blanck has claimed on the basis of Wiley and Putnam's advertisement for Cooper's *The American Democrat* in the 15 August 1838 *Publishers' Circular* that it was

the London distributor of the book, but that claim seems unlikely (Jacob Blanck and Michael Winship, comps., *Bibliography of American Literature,* 9 vols. [New Haven: Yale University Press, 1955–91], 2:289). The firm's advertisements listed numerous American books and journals that it sold from its store and for which it served as presumably the primary but not the exclusive retailer in London, works that must have numbered in the dozens. But advertisements in *Publishers' Circular* and other advertising sites for the trade make it clear that Wiley and Putnam had competition from a small number of local stores for the sale of American works. Furthermore, as decisions in British courts between the mid-1830 and mid-1850s made copyright protection conditionally available to foreign authors, Wiley and Putnam would have played a secondary role in retailing some of the more attractive American works published locally by such firms as those of Richard Bentley and John Murray that took a commercial interest in American books.

37. Two generations later, the firm of G. P. Putnam's Sons, under the direction of GHP, became a leader in binational publishing and bookselling activities, but by that time improvements in communication and technology and increased industrywide centralization made such operations far simpler than they had been in the early days of his father's activity in London.

38. *Athenaeum,* no. 593 (9 March 1839): 178.

39. The best collection of these catalogues is at Houghton Library, Harvard University. They were sent to Harvard on a regular basis, Harvard being one of the firm's most valued customers (and Jared Sparks, head of Harvard College Library's purchases, by 1840 a friend and client of GPP's).

40. He compiled a long list of new publications in America and Europe for this fine journal; "Literary Intelligence," *New York Review* 2 (April 1838): 511–24.

41. For a fuller discussion of the competition among American publishers and booksellers for the British periodical market, see Barnes, *Authors, Publishers and Politicians,* 30–48.

42. This catalogue, now at Houghton Library, Harvard University, unfortunately has no date or printer's imprint, but it presumably dates from late 1839 or 1840.

43. The matter was reported approvingly in the "Editors' Table" of the *Knickerbocker* 12 (October 1838): 377.

44. This information comes from the catalogue dated 1 October 1838 and printed in London by Manning and Mason, who that same month printed the London edition of *The Narrative of Arthur Gordon Pym.*

45. This information comes from a late 1838 entry in Duyckinck's unpublished diaries; D-NYPL.

46. Entries for April and May 1839 in Duyckinck diaries; D-NYPL.

47. GPP to [Victorine Haven], 20 August 1840; in HP-LC.

--- •· ---

Home and Office, Privacy and Professionalism, 1840–1841

Putnam would return to New York on nearly a yearly basis during his decade-long residence in London in order to confer and coordinate matters with Wiley, attend to clients new and old, and take care of a variety of arrangements not easily managed through the mails. In returning to New York early in 1840, though, he found that what had been intended as a professional trip quickly became complicated by personal considerations he had long deferred. A bachelor now twenty-six years old, Putnam entered into a whirlwind romance shortly after his arrival in New York City, a two-chapter story that played itself out around a short visit, probably his first, to Washington to consult with members of Congress. That was only one of multiple trips that he would make to the capital during that decade, as well as in subsequent ones, on book- and copyright-related business. The chief evidence concerning both matters, in fact, exists in the courtship letters he wrote from Washington to his soon-to-be-fiancée in New York.[1]

Victorine Haven was only sixteen when they became engaged immediately upon his return from Washington. Orphaned in girlhood and raised in large part by her elder sister Corinna and their aunt and uncle, she moved in 1836 from the family home in Dorchester, Massachusetts, to New York City to live with Corinna and her husband, John Bishop, a retired sea captain. Responsible for her sister's upbringing and education, Corinna decided to send Victorine to the nearby Bleecker Street school of Catherine Hunt Putnam. It was there, presumably, that Putnam and Victorine first made each other's acquaintance, possibly even before his removal to London but more likely shortly after he returned to New York in winter 1840.[2] A sheltered but strikingly attractive young woman, Victorine had already caught the eye of Putnam's Boston cousin, John Putnam Gulliver, who occasionally stayed at his Aunt Catherine's home during vacations from his ministerial studies at Yale; and she soon caught Putnam's.[3] It is not hard to imagine that the handsome, well-dressed, and disarmingly charming Putnam must have caught hers as well. Their relationship progressed so quickly during Putnam's first months in New York that by June he secured her agreement to a correspondence while he made a week-long trip to Washington to transact business with leaders of Congress.

What exactly that business was, Putnam never specified in his letters to her or in any other known place, nor was the subject ever discussed in print by his descendants. But one can be reasonably certain that it concerned some aspect of the international book trade, a subject that had preoccupied him for some time and that was now also attracting the attention of Congress. For both of them the issue had become inescapable. Why this was so for Putnam is not hard to explain: situated at the intersection of the transatlantic traffic in books, he needed to be alert not only to the mechanics of the traffic but also to the rules that governed its conduct. For that matter, his concern with one of the central rules of conduct, the free-wheeling policies of reprinting foreign works permitted by the lack of an international copyright agreement, dated back to his editorship of the *Booksellers' Advertiser*. Whereas the trade had by and large governed itself in the first phase of his career by the self-regulatory practice of "courtesy of the trade," whereby publishers agreed to respect their colleagues' "rights" to particular works or authors that they had been the first to announce and print, that system had fallen into general neglect following the Panic of 1837 and would remain largely dysfunctional for nearly a half-dozen years.[4] Given his commitment not only to what he considered fair play between the United States and Great Britain as equal trading partners but also to the vulnerable situation of American authors within the larger workings of the international system, Putnam was particularly intent to see trade regularized in ways that protected both American authors and publishers.

Congress, which was preoccupied in the mid-1830s with more urgent domestic economic problems, came to the issue only in 1837 when a group of British authors appealed to it for relief from the unfair practice common among American publishers of reprinting foreign fiction for the American market without authorial permission or compensation.[5] In presenting their memorial to his colleagues in the Senate, Henry Clay added his own peremptory appeal for Anglo-American literary accord: "When we reflect what important parts of the great republic of letters the United States and Great Britain are, and consider their common origin, common language, and similarity of institutions, and of habits of reading, there seems to me to be every motive for reciprocating between the two countries the security of copyrights. Indeed, I do not see any ground of just objection, either in the Constitution or in sound policy, to the passage of a law tendering to all foreign nations reciprocal security for literary property."[6] His colleagues, it turned out, would operate on very different ideological principles, principles predicated less on Clay's vision of an amicable international republic of letters than on a notion of separate spheres of fiercely capitalistic competition both within and between individual nations. The battle in Congress was soon joined, with opponents of international copyright quickly gaining the advantage in the political maneuvering, an advantage they aggressively maintained for decades. So divisive did the issue become and so irreconcilable the positions that the debate continued without resolution until nearly the end of the century.

Why did the issue of international copyright become an issue in the United States in the late-1830s, when it had not previously been a matter of overriding importance even to the majority of American authors, publishers, editors, printers, and bookbinders? The immediate reason was the rapidly growing size and importance of both the domestic and the international book trade. As one commentator wrote in 1839 in a review article on literary property, "The prodigious increase, within the last ten years, of republications in this country of the works of British authors, and their sale at an incomparably cheaper rate than the English originals—are topics of common remark among those who pay any attention to matters of literature."[7] Although the statistics the writer cited regarding the workforce employed and the capital invested in reprinting were grossly exaggerated, the person's central contention was accurate: reprinting had by then become a common topic of discussion in the contemporary press, between authors, and even in Congress.[8] The debate within the United States was not unrelated to the one taking place concurrently in England, where intense discussion was underway about the damage being done to British authors and publishers by the unrestricted reprinting of their works on both sides of the Atlantic. As though that were not already irritating enough, British publishers, in a not so distant echo of the American debate, soon were complaining about the effect that the cheap reprinting of American works was having on the distribution of their works within Britain.[9] Although the British were able to reach a copyright agreement with the French in the early 1850s, a parallel accord with Washington was not to be signed until 1891.

On a broader scale, the emergence of the issue of international copyright can be understood not simply as a solitary issue but rather as part of a larger complex of issues resulting from the rapid expansion, commercialization, and internationalization of the printmaking industry, a complex of developments that was being experienced on both sides of the Atlantic. With the increasing professionalization and commercialization of the spheres of literary professional activity and the growing identification of literary property with monetary value, a commodity inviting the give and take of competition and protection, literary professionals in the United States, acting both on and across group lines, moved to define rules of conduct advantageous to their perceived interests. Within a year of the British authors' initiation of the international copyright debate, American literary professionals of all sorts took their cases to Congress, lobbying congressmen and presenting petitions in the hope of either reforming or preserving the status quo.

From the beginning, the debates in Congress, no less than those taking place simultaneously among literary professionals, approximated anything but the high-minded, if outdated, republican ideals originally enunciated by Clay for a concord of fair-minded nations dealing equitably with one another. As the participants in the debates soon found out, the issues at stake and the interests involved in protecting them occupied anything but consensually accepted grounds. The fight over copyright was no simple or clear-cut battle between the "good" defenders and the "bad" opponents of copyright, although that is the way it has uncritically been described by generations of commentators going back to Putnam and other cultural progressives of the nineteenth century. It was, rather, a many-sided, many-handed contest between competing interests to determine the definition of the territory on which literary professionalism was to take place in modern America. Little wonder, then, that the battle dragged on for decades, since neither the issues under discussion nor the contexts for their resolution were unequivocal. Those issues were basic to the development of professional authorship, publishing, and letters: Where did the rights of authors, publishers, and readers fall on a scale ranging from the mutually inclusive to the mutually exclusive? How were competing definitions of authorship (and, by implication, reading) as a public or a private activity and of literary property to be mapped out? What was the public realm of letters and what body, if any, was to stand guard over it? And how was the United States to weigh not only the interests of its literary professionals against those of foreign nations but also of its own national body of letters against that of European nations?

Whether or not Putnam came down to Washington in June 1840, as he unquestionably did in autumn 1843, with the intention of influencing members of Congress to vote in favor of international copyright is not clear.[10] Several months earlier his New York office had been approached by Francis Lieber, a young, German-born professor at South Carolina College and a prolific author seeking an international readership, with the request to publish his pro-copyright polemic.[11] Written in the form of a public letter to Senator William Preston of South Carolina, Lieber's piece was filled with arguments that Preston, a recent convert to the cause, could use in turn to sway his colleagues. But men like Lieber, though eloquent and learned in their arguments, spoke a language of abstractions and ideals often far removed from the language of tough political realities spoken by members of Congress, many of whom owed loyalty to special interests, especially manufacturers, a group whose principals were already outspokenly opposed to limitations on their economic freedom. By 1840, Clay himself had come to understand the strength of the forces against which he was contending and thereafter was far more tempered in his expectations and circumspect in his political strategy.

The firm did agree to publish Lieber's pamphlet, if at his expense.[12] In all likelihood, the partners would have been in general agreement with his position, an interpretation supported by the fact that they were to become the chief publisher of pro-international copyright pamphlets in the United States during the next several years.[13] It is not clear if Putnam was in New York at the time Lieber approached the house or that, even if he was, Lieber's work had any direct influence on his Washington trip, since international copyright was not on the Congressional agenda during the week of his stay in the capital. In early 1840 Clay had renewed his effort to persuade his colleagues to pass his copyright bill but quickly backed away when it came up for debate on 15 April, choosing first to postpone the debate and then not to call for the debate at all. As a result the bill was eventually tabled shortly before Congress recessed in July.

An alternative explanation for Putnam's trip was a different item on the Senate agenda during the week of his stay that also related to the international book trade. That matter was the initiative of Alexandre Vattemare, a French national who had come to Washington some months before to urge the United States, as he had already lobbied other Western countries, to enter into an international system of exchange between national libraries of duplicate books, documents, and scientific specimens.[14] His memorial was presented to the Senate officially by Senator Preston, by this time an advocate of international copyright and a member of the Library Committee. Besides issuing a report on Vattemare's petition, Preston also submitted an accompanying bill authorizing the librarian of Congress to receive three copies of all publications priced under ten dollars in return for copyright protection.[15] These were measures with which Putnam would have quickly sympathized as a patron both of letters and of literary institutions. He would himself soon serve intermittently as a book agent for both the British Museum and the Smithsonian Institution, and he would also work to introduce American books and the names of their authors into European circulation (the latter, a prospect that Vattemare had mentioned specifically as one of the likely outcomes of his proposal).[16] Vattemare made a strong case in his memorial for the various advantages that would accrue to the United States, whose public libraries then lagged far behind those of Europe and which stood to receive a large infusion of books much needed to broaden and deepen their holdings. In many ways, though, Vattemare's ideas were ahead of their time in the United States, where not only library collections but the entire public realm of print—whether defined in terms of the capacity of public libraries; copyright enforcement, storage, and organization; or the status of the "national library" as either a concept or a physical reality— lagged far behind their counterparts in Europe. But whether Putnam had previously met Vattemare in Europe or was anything more than a spectator of the debate over his proposal is unclear. He was present, at least, when Preston's committee returned a favorable report on Vattemare's memorial; a bill was signed into law the following month authorizing Congress to enter into an international exchange of its documents.[17]

Putnam also had time during his week in town to tour the city, visiting the White House and the Capitol (from whose library balcony he wrote his first letter to Victorine Haven) and meeting a variety of people, including Senators Preston, Webster, and Talmage (who represented New York and to whose house he was invited).[18] Perhaps the most interesting man he met during the trip was the artist Charles Bird King, a longtime resident of the city who kept a studio and gallery in his fine house on Twelfth Street.[19] At a time when art museums and galleries in the United States were still few, people eager to view works of art often had no alternative but to visit the studios of contemporary painters. King's, as Putnam no doubt had heard, was widely reputed the best in Washington, one of the few cultivated spots on the generally barren social and cultural map of antebellum Washington. So Putnam, who passed up few chances to visit interesting people in the arts and letters, filled an otherwise unoccupied part of a morning by walking over to King's house.

Strolling with his host through the upper gallery, which occupied the whole of the second story, Putnam was broadly impressed by the display of King's work, which included many of the more than one hundred Native American portraits he had painted during the previous two decades. Taking advantage of his reputation as the leading painter in the city, King was well situated to take the portraits of the various Native American leaders who came to the capital on political business. At a time when private patronage was hard to attract in the United States, he not only had the advantage of unparalleled access to Congress but also enjoyed an unmatched success among Native American portraitists of his time in placing many of his paintings in official Washington. Their original home was in the Indian Gallery housed in the War Department building not far from King's residence and superintended by Thomas McKenney, chief of the Bureau of Indian Affairs.[20] From there they were moved to Renwick's Smithsonian Institution in 1858, but were unfortunately lost when virtually the entire Gallery of Art was destroyed in the fire of 1865.[21] By chance, Putnam was to confer shortly after his return to London in summer 1840 with the greatest painter of Native Americans of his generation, George Catlin, and to serve as one of the many intermediaries employed by Catlin in his unsuccessful attempts to persuade the American government to purchase his nonpareil collection of Native American paintings and memorabilia. Ironically, Catlin's nonrecognition allowed his paintings to survive, as King's did not.

After finishing his business in Washington, Putnam returned to New York, ostensibly to make final arrangements with Wiley before returning to London but actually to propose to Victorine Haven. Her acceptance came more unconditionally than did the consent of her sister, who took some time before responding to Putnam's proposal for a wedding early the next month followed by a brief honeymoon in Niagara and the couple's departure out of New York harbor on 25 July. Worried principally about Victorine's age, Corinna accepted Putnam himself but insisted on a year's delay before the marriage. Having no other recourse, the couple reluctantly agreed.

While awaiting Corinna's response, Putnam took a trip to New England to finish up business affairs. Traveling up the Connecticut River valley and then east to Boston, he stopped at various places to meet current clients and engage new ones, drum up orders to take back with him to England, and renew acquaintances with family and friends. That quick northern swing proved to be a highly successful one. In New Haven, he spent much of his time at Yale College, where he met with Benjamin Silliman, a noted scientist and future Putnam author, and other members of the faculty and presumably took orders both for them and for the college library.[22] That evening, he went to the college chapel with his cousin George Tyler before continuing the next morning up the valley by train to Meriden, then by horse and gig to Middletown, probably stopping to do business at Wesleyan before going on to Hartford. His primary business in Hartford was with the president and faculty of Washington College (renamed Trinity College in 1845), one more fast growing antebellum college whose business he was seeking. He also had time to visit with old friends and to make a new one, Lydia Sigourney, with whom he passed a pleasant hour that, as matters transpired, was soon to be renewed in Europe.[23] The next day, he passed through Springfield on his way to Boston, his final destination, arriving at the Tremont House in the evening to find waiting for him the letter conveying Corinna's decision. He spent the weekend in

Boston, Cambridge, and Salem, interspersing business with family visits. On Saturday, he met three of the most respected, scholarly authors in the country—George Ticknor, George Bancroft, and William Prescott—all of whom were dependent on European sources for their scholarship and writing and who could therefore profit from Putnam's services. Later that day, he drove out to Cambridge to meet Jared Sparks, a prolific historian and the librarian at Harvard College. Besides soliciting business from Sparks for his firm, Putnam also offered to host him later that summer during Sparks's visit in London. The next morning he attended services at Trinity Church, then drove out to Salem to see his Peabody cousins.

Throughout the trip, Putnam traveled in a state of heightened emotions. Perhaps it was his inner excitement, perhaps his reacquaintance with the special look and feel of his native New England, that inspired him to describe the towns he saw along the river valley as "unrivalled in beauty and neatness by any in the world.... If there is any thing which may give just pride to an American," he wrote Victorine, "it is the evidence of taste, comfort, general competency (if not independence) and contentment, which is so apparent throughout New England particularly, in contrast to the extremes of wealth and grandeur of the few, and the degradation of the many, as seen in Europe."[24] Those good feelings also accompanied him during the trip that he and Victorine made, chaperoned by the Bishops, to Niagara Falls. If not the honeymoon the couple had hoped it would be, the trip at least gave them a chance to enjoy time together and deepen their acquaintance. Upon their return to New York, they made final plans for the coming months of separation, and Putnam encouraged Victorine to prepare herself for her new life and home—the latter, in part, by reading books of travel and fiction about the places she would soon see, such as Abbotsford, to which he promised her a trip. Their separation was to be a fairly long one; having been away from London for nearly a half-year, Putnam did not foresee returning to America before the beginning of 1841.

Putnam sailed out of New York port, as originally planned, on 25 July on board the *Roscius*. Wondering "at my own stoicism in so quietly and coldly consenting to such a separation," he passed away his time on the crossing by socializing with a traveling companion (a Col. Johnson from Missouri) and others among the thirty-odd passengers on the boat, playing shuffleboard, and reading novels by James and Cooper. The crossing was a slow one, taking twenty-one days from New York to Liverpool. After paying their way through customs, Putnam and his friend quickly completed the trip, this time being able to make the journey down to London entirely by train. They took up residence for a week or two at 7 St. James Street in luxurious quarters, Putnam proudly reported back, which had previously been "occupied by Prince Louis Napoleon and Suite just before they made their insane attempt to overturn my friend Prince Louis Philippe!!"—an event about which Putnam meant to get more information during his next trip to Paris.[25] Marveling at having passed from Liverpool to London in half a day and having been able to show up the next morning bright and early at the office, he was sorry to hear that he had missed the well-regarded New England novelist Catharine Maria Sedgwick and her family, whose outbound ship had apparently crossed his own. Once readjusted to his work routine in the office, he quickly went about catching up with the pile of correspondence and orders that had accumulated in his absence, filling orders from Yale, Dartmouth, Hamilton, and other colleges and answering letters or orders of individuals scattered from Boston to Charlotte. The backlog was such that he spent a nonstop week answering correspondence and filling orders around town for books, but Putnam confessed to enjoying the arduous schedule. Then, as during all but the last few years of his career, he was to thrive on a breakneck pace.

By the end of August, he had moved to quieter, less expensive residential quarters on Cecil Street, off the Strand. There he lived for a short while with Augustus Wiley, his partner's brother, who was temporarily helping to relieve Putnam of the burden of running the London office until a clerk from the New York office could be sent. Just the same, Putnam remained "tremendously" busy through much of the year, his work often keeping him at his writing desk late into the night. Calls on his time and attention were never ending, and his day-to-day duties were numerous: answering letters from Britain, the Continent, and America; writing circulars and advertisements; filling orders with books he searched for in stores all around London or tracked down in Europe through the mail; preparing invoices; picking up incoming packages at the port and clearing them through customs; and examining and collating materials for outgoing shipments. Meanwhile, he needed to superintend the general workings of the office and cultivate its position in the London book world. His ability to do all these things well was a source of pride: "I can accomplish as much in a given time as at least three ordinary persons—I might say six."[26] With a mixture of pride and a sense of historical novelty, he mentioned one particular set of incoming orders that he was able to fill and send back to New York within several days, confident that the orders would be in the homes of his clients within a month of their dispatch from North America.

By this time, he was becoming comfortable with his own position and that of his firm in London: "Every body seems particularly pleased with our agency here, and our plans for making known American literature,—and without joking, I think we shall be the means thereby, of great and mutual benefit to both countries."[27] Other publishers and booksellers deferred to him, he noted, on matters concerning the American trade. A sure sign of success, his business began to draw imitators, as in the case of his old acquaintance Daniel Appleton, who came to London in 1840 to establish his own firm's overseas connection and who copied Putnam's advertisements and some of his promotional methods. But Putnam was often generous to a fault with people he liked, such as Appleton, with whom he continued to enjoy good personal and professional relations. Other Americans, tourists and professionals alike, also drew on his seemingly unlimited generosity for favors and services. Although too busy for weeks after his return to London to visit his American friends around town, he made time to host American visitors. Two whom he saw on the same day within a month of his own arrival were his new Harvard acquaintance Jared Sparks ("a very nice man indeed and one I am proud to know") and the renowned biblical scholar Edward Robinson ("probably the most learned American living"), a valued Wiley and Putnam author who passed through London on the home leg of a trip to Palestine.

Once the pace of affairs eased, he had more time to socialize with friends and visitors. One evening in October, he went over to the West End to see George Catlin, who charmed him with stories about his adventures out West. The visit went so well that Putnam resolved to see him and his wife many more times, "for they are the nicest people I have met with here."[28] Soon after, he lived up to that resolution, going with Col. Johnson to hear Catlin lecture at his gallery about his collection of native robes, which were modeled in a kind of mock-fashion show up on a platform by some of the guests as Catlin gave particulars to the audience. Afterwards, Catlin's "Indians" staged "a man-dance with all the whoops and yells and scalps etc."[29] Johnson joined the participants, but the undemonstrative Putnam, grandson of a leader in the most famous American instance of "playing Indian," kept his seat.[30] By that time

Putnam was mixing professional and personal relations with Catlin, who was seeking a publisher for the lavish, illustrated volume he wished to bring out on the North American Indians, a project so expensive as to have driven him, like Audubon earlier in the century, to Europe in the hope of finding a publisher and audience able to patronize a venture too rich, commercially speaking, for American taste. Having failed to persuade Congress to buy his nonpareil collection of Native American artifacts and six hundred paintings of Native Americans for a price of sixty thousand dollars, in frustration he had packed up his family, collection, assorted possessions, and two grizzly bears and sailed to London.[31] A fine showman, he quickly succeeded in attracting attention to his work and discussed his publication plans with various publishers in town, among them Putnam, whose firm announced in September that it was bringing out a two-volume edition of *The Manners, Customs, and Condition of the North American Indians.*[32] When the work was published later that year, however, it came out through Catlin's own agency, although it is likely that Wiley and Putnam helped with its distribution, as it did with later self-published works by Catlin.[33]

From time to time, Putnam interspersed the routine of affairs with trips out of town. He journeyed to Oxford for a couple of days in September, where he made the acquaintance of John Henry Parker, publisher to the university. Although Parker was one of the most learned publishers in England, Putnam was amused to find him ignorant about even the most elementary facts about the United States and enjoyed debating with him the relative merits of democracy and aristocracy. No trace of that discussion or their later dealings has survived, but it seems likely that Putnam was looking not only to deal directly with Parker but also to offer the university services similar to those he was successfully offering American colleges. He also hoped to go to Brussels, as he did from time to time, for a few days to transact business but was too busy to get away. Putnam did make a trip to Paris, however, later that fall, where he worked time into his schedule to follow up his curiosity about the aborted coup by Louis Napoleon, an account of which he sent to the New York *Commercial Advertiser* but which arrived too late to be printed in its entirety.[34] Some of his information seems to have come through his Parisian correspondent, François Guizot, formerly the French ambassador in London and recently installed as prime minister under Louis Philippe.[35]

Putnam spent most of that November week in Paris transacting business, but he also left time to visit with old friends and see something of the city. By chance, two American acquaintances were staying in his hotel: Lydia Sigourney, ostensibly in Europe traveling for her health but also getting a reprieve from an unhappy marriage; and Reverend Leonard Woods, making a tour of Europe before assuming his appointment as president of Bowdoin College. Putnam's primary business was with his old contacts in town, the Galignani brothers and Hector Bossange, both extensive dealers in the international book trade and the latter, the Paris agent for Wiley and Putnam.[36] As usual, he mixed business with pleasure in his dealings with them, enjoying in particular a dinner party at the Galignanis' house. That evening was a genuine cultural experience for Putnam, who appreciated the skill with which the Galignanis made "even an ignorant foreigner who knows only his mother tongue" feel welcome in their house and among their guests.[37] Fond of Paris but aware of how limited he was by his barely rudimentary French, Putnam self-mockingly described to Victorine what happened when he stopped at a store to buy her a present. Unable to make his wishes known to the salesperson, Putnam needed the mediation of a twelve-year-old English girl to express his wishes to the salesperson. He could take consolation, at least, in knowing that he was not alone in his communication problems, not when there were numbers of what he thought of as his fellow "Barbarians in Paris," as there always seemed to be. One evening that week, Putnam took Wood with him to dinner at the home of Bossange ("one of the best men in the world") and witnessed the spectacle of an American in Paris even more provincial than himself. Also aware of Wood's bewilderment was Bossange's clever daughter, who was amused by the clergyman's slow manner of speech and habit of expressing his opinions in the form of sermons.

The return trip across the Channel turned out to be a rougher crossing than normal, but it did not stop Putnam from taking his supper with the captain, the only passenger with enough stomach to enjoy that ritual of sea travel. On arriving safely in London, he was pleased to find that the clerk from New York, Mr. Danforth, had arrived and was installed in the office. He was already anticipating that Danforth, once properly initiated, would free him from various office duties and allow him to put more distance between his personal life and the office, a consideration that weighed on his mind with his marriage impending. But if he really believed that a possibility, he misconstrued his own temperament.

Since leaving New York, his mind had been on his return there and the prospect of his wedding. He arrived back in London from Paris more impatient than ever. At the time, he anticipated sailing home on the *President,* scheduled to leave on 1 February, and to return to London as early as 15 March with or without Victorine, the press of business not allowing for a longer celebration. One important matter he took care of in the weeks before his departure was the perpetual problem of insufficient office space. By early January, he supervised Wiley and Putnam's move to its third location in London's book publishing center, this time at Amen Corner, Stationers' Court. The following month Putnam sailed as planned on the *President,* reputed to be one of the finest steamers in transatlantic service since its introduction in 1829 and just recently remodeled; but he was unable to keep to his intended schedule. The departure from Liverpool had to be put back to the tenth, and, once launched, the ship encountered an unusually rough crossing because of persistent head winds and strong gales, even pausing for several days at Halifax before completing the last leg of its trip. With reports of shipwrecks already common news items on both sides of the Atlantic, anxious rumors about the *President* began to circulate in the New York press weeks before her arrival, but the ship arrived safely in port on 3 March. The night before, a group of grateful passengers, among them Putnam, composed an open letter to the captain in tribute to his skill in delivering them safely, which was printed in the New York *Herald* and the *Commercial Advertiser* the day after their arrival.[38] That same day, William Henry Harrison was inaugurated in Washington in one of the most jubilant celebrations the capital had ever witnessed, an event that gave Putnam a further reason to rejoice, since he saw in Harrison's election a sign of better things to come for the American economy after the turbulent financial years of three consecutive Democratic administrations.

Putnam's wedding took place at the Bishops' home at 41 Charlton Street in New York on Saturday, 13 March. A family of liberal Unitarians, the Bishops would have had less trouble in persuading the nondoctrinal Putnam than his conservative mother to accept their choice of Orville Dewey, one of the country's leading Unitarian clergymen, to perform the ceremony.[39] Putnam's best man was John Sargent, one of his earliest New York friends and at the time a staff member of James Watson Webb's New York *Courier and Enquirer.* Shortly afterward, the young couple traveled down to Washington, where they joined the multitude of well-wishers and job seekers who greeted the new president. Harrison, for his part, found it difficult to reject the overtures of the hundreds of people eager to meet him and seek his patronage. As one observer reported of him during those hectic initial weeks, which turned out to be the only ones he survived of his presidency, "Whoever called to pay him a visit was sure to be asked to dinner; whoever asked for a place was sure to get a promise; whoever hinted at a want of money was sure to receive a draft."[40] The attractive young couple were among the many whom Harrison agreed to receive; according to the family story, Harrison looked at the teenage bride, chucked her under the chin, and asked her her age.[41]

Perhaps Putnam also had business to attend to in Washington and acquaintanceships to renew, but he and Victorine did not remain there long. Putnam was anxious about the press of business awaiting him back in England and intended to sail back as soon as possible after the wedding, reserving the true honeymoon for the other side of the Atlantic. He was in New York long enough to do little more than consult with Wiley, drop a good word for the firm's large new catalogue of imports with the editor of the *Knickerbocker* and leave with him the latest British magazines, and speak to a few professional acquaintances.[42] More urgent than anything else was the need to work out final details for the return trip and the establishment of a real household in London. The couple had discussed the possibility that Victorine, still only seventeen, would be accompanied in the voyage by her sister and that, if necessary, she would postpone her own departure until a date convenient for her sister. But Corinna Bishop declined the invitation to join them, then or later, so on 1 April the couple sailed together from Boston on the *Caledonia,* ready to begin their new life together on foreign soil.[43]

Notes

1. These letters, which form part of the largest surviving collection of the Putnam family papers, are in HP-LC. They apparently passed through the hands of various of the siblings, some of whom used them in writing family memoirs, before passing on to the Library of Congress via the children of Herbert Putnam, the youngest son of Victorine and GPP and the longtime librarian of Congress (1899–1939).

2. GHP, *George Palmer Putnam,* 1:49–51. GHP misdates his father's initial return

to the United States to 1841, a logical consequence of the mistake he makes in misdating his father's establishment of the London office to 1840.

3. Ibid., 1:62–63. There is at least indirect confirmation of Gulliver's strong feelings for Victorine in a letter he wrote GPP shortly after the wedding. It expresses his strong regard for Victorine and offers the newlyweds his sentiment, "May your honey moon never set." 4 June 1841; GPP-P.

4. For a cogent discussion of these issues, see James J. Barnes, *Authors, Publishers and Politicians: The Quest for an Anglo-American Copyright Agreement, 1815–1854* (London: Routledge and Kegan Paul, 1974), 84–86.

5. For a good overview of the tangled course taken by international copyright through the American Congress, see Thorvald Solberg, "International Copyright in Congress, 1837–1886," in *Copyright Miscellany,* no. 18 (Boston: John W. Luce, 1939).

6. Ibid., 4.

7. This was an anonymous review article on two new publications, one arguing for and the other against international copyright, the latter of which had been extensively cited in the negative committee report during the 1838 Congressional debate on copyright; "Literary Property," *New York Review* 4 (April 1839): 273.

8. For a sound estimate of the figures involved in the reprinting business, see Barnes, *Authors, Publishers and Politicians,* 69–70.

9. On the latter point, see James J. Barnes, *Free Trade in Books: A Study of the London Book Trade since 1800* (Oxford: Oxford University Press, 1964), 104, 106–8.

10. GPP traveled up and down the eastern seaboard in autumn 1843 collecting names for a memorial advocating international copyright, which was presented to Congress in December. The nearly one hundred signatories included his cousin Elizabeth Peabody, his favorite printer John Trow, his early employer Jonathan Leavitt, and his longtime coworkers the Appletons. He also sent an advance copy of the memorial to England, where it was published (introduced by the editor's snide remarks) in the *Athenaeum,* no. 835 (28 October 1843): 963.

11. Francis Lieber, *On International Copyright* (New York: Wiley and Putnam, 1840).

12. On Lieber and his work on behalf of international copyright in 1839–40, see Frank Freidel, "Lieber's Contribution to the International Copyright Movement," *Huntington Library Quarterly* 8 (February 1945): 203–4.

13. Other pamphlets issued by Wiley and Putnam propounding the pro-international copyright position were Cornelius Mathews, *An Appeal to American Authors and the American Press in Behalf of International Copyright* (New York: Wiley and Putnam, 1842); and Cornelius Mathews, *The Better Interests of the Country, in Connexion with International Copyright* (New York and London: Wiley and Putnam, 1843).

14. On Vattemare's mission, see Carol Armbruster, "The Origins of International Literary Exchanges: Alexandre Vattemare's Adventures in America," *Biblion* 5 (spring 1997): 128–47.

15. See *Senate Documents,* 26th Cong., 1st sess., 5 June 1840, Report no. 521; Senate Bill 365, 26th Cong., 1st sess., 5 June 1840.

16. Vattemare predicted that should American copyrighted books, then simply rotting in a government basement in Washington, be worked into his international exchange system, "a demand would infallibly arise for American books now unknown, except within narrow limits, or confined in circulation in the United States alone." *Executive Documents,* 26th Cong., 1st sess., House Document 50.

17. Armbruster, "Origins of International Literary Exchange," 142.

18. The originals of the letters in which he described his impressions of Washington

are in HP-LC. Two of the three letters are reprinted in GHP, *George Palmer Putnam,* 1:57–62.

19. Information on King comes primarily from Andrew J. Cosentino, *The Paintings of Charles Bird King (1785–1862)* (Washington, D.C.: Smithsonian Institute, 1977).

20. It was the same McKenney, a man of that time unusually sympathetic to Native Americans' rights, who was chiefly responsible for one of the most interesting American imprints of the antebellum years, *The Indian Tribes of North America,* a superb three-volume folio set issued between 1837 and 1844 with color lithographic reproductions of 120 portraits made after copies of the originals painted by King and others.

21. Cosentino, *Paintings of Charles Bird King,* 59–60.

22. In a pattern that repeated itself many times over, Silliman became not only GPP's client but also his friend. He so valued their relationship that he went up to Boston the next year in the hope of congratulating GPP and his bride and seeing them off at the port for their trip to London but somehow miscalculated his timing and missed them; Silliman to GPP, 19 May 1841, GPP-P.

23. Perhaps he shared his personal news with her, since she was to adopt Victorine at the time of their wedding as one of her favorites and in future years to make concerned inquiries about their children.

24. GPP to Victorine Haven, 18 June [1840]; HP-LC.

25. GPP to [Victorine Haven], 20 August 1840; HP-LC. The attempt by Louis Napoleon to overthrow Louis Philippe ended, as GPP had foreseen, in a debacle, one final act of which GPP expected to witness in person: "The young prince [Louis Napoleon] is to be tried by the Chamber of Peers at Paris in a few weeks—and as I shall probably have to go there on business I may see the trial"; in ibid.

26. Ibid.

27. GPP to Victorine Haven, 23 September 1840; HP-LC.

28. GPP to Victorine Haven, 18 October 1840; HP-LC.

29. GPP to Victorine Haven, 1 November 1840; HP-LC.

30. I take this term from the fine study of Native American–European American cultural interaction by Philip J. Deloria, *Playing Indian* (New Haven: Yale University Press, 1998).

31. Marjorie Catlin Roehm, ed., *The Letters of George Catlin and His Family* (Berkeley: University of California Press, 1966), 146–49.

32. The firm made that announcement in its new, in-house trade journal, *Wiley and Putnam's Literary News-Letter and Monthly Register of New Books, Foreign and American* 1 (September 1841): 2.

33. In 1845 Wiley and Putnam advertised that it was importing to New York an edition of Catlin's stunning *North American Indian Portfolio,* which Catlin had self-published in London in 1844. Fearing the competition of a pirated edition in New York (presumably that of J. Ackerman) against their own enormously expensive one, the firm warned prospective purchasers that additional volumes were to follow and that they were to be copyrighted, as the original was not. That threat, however, proved empty: no further volumes followed; *Wiley and Putnam's Literary News-Letter* 4 (September 1845): 364.

34. GPP to Victorine Haven, 1 November 1840; HP-LC.

35. How and where GPP made Guizot's acquaintance is not certain. He might have met him during Guizot's official period of service as ambassador in London in 1840. GPP socialized with the members of the American legation and no doubt met many members of other legations as well. One other possible point of contact between them was Guizot's *Essay on the Character and Influence of Washington,* which was issued by James Munroe

in Boston that June, the same month in which GPP visited in Boston and met with Munroe. While there, GPP sent Guizot some books via Munroe's office that apparently were lost, along with many of Guizot's other possessions, on the *Phoenix* when it collided with another ship and sank. That ship was well known to GPP; he had once crossed from Le Havre on it; GPP to Victorine Haven, 1 November 1840, HP-LC.

36. This last point comes on the authority of GHP, *George Palmer Putnam,* 1:180.

37. GPP to Victorine Haven, 17 November 1840; HP-LC.

38. In the *Commercial Advertiser* of 3 March there is also printed a news-filled letter from an unnamed "friend" among the ship's passengers, presumably GPP.

39. Ruth Putnam, ed., *Life and Letters of Mary Putnam Jacobi* (New York: G. P. Putnam's Sons, 1925), 12.

40. The observer was Thomas Colley Grattan, British consul in Boston; quoted in Allen Nevins, ed. and comp., *American Social History* (New York: Henry Holt, 1923), 261.

41. As told by GHP, who presumably heard it from his parents; *George Palmer Putnam,* 1:66.

42. "Literary Record," *Knickerbocker* 17 (March 1841): 269.

43. GHP misstates the facts when he claims that his father sailed back to England alone, to be joined by his mother in the fall (*George Palmer Putnam,* 1:72). The Boston *Daily Advertiser* of 2 April 1841 lists "Geo. P. Putnam and lady" on the passenger list for the *Caledonia.*

CHAPTER 5

——•◦•——

Life and Business in London

Soon after the Putnams arrived in Liverpool, accounts began to circulate of two events of considerable interest to them: news of the death of
President Harrison and mounting concerns about the fate of the *President,* the transatlantic steamer that had brought Putnam over from
England just several months before.[1] That ship had preceded their own
out of port by three weeks but had not been seen or heard from since.
As additional weeks went by with no report from or sighting of the
ship, concerns for her safety gradually turned into certainty that the
President was lost. In his letters to the popular American magazine
New World, for which he was then serving as an occasional foreign correspondent, Putnam dutifully reported back to the United States the
latest news and rumors reaching London about its likely end. As early
as his letter dated 1 May, with memories still fresh in his mind about
his own hard crossing, he held out little hope for its salvation: "The
President steamer is still missing, and nearly all hope of her safety is
now extinguished. It is possible, certainly, that she may yet be afloat,
but there is but little reasonable probability that she could be so, and
yet be out till this time—50 days—unseen and unheard of."[2] No authoritative word was ever heard about the *President,* only one of a number
of ships to sink early that year.

After completing their long-anticipated honeymoon excursion to the north of England and Scotland, the young couple settled down to the task of setting up their household. They were commencing their married life in London under difficult circumstances, far from relatives or any organized support system and all but unguided by personal experience about the practical necessities of home economics. Putnam had never lived in anything but bachelor quarters since his establishment in London, and Victorine had never lived on her own. As they went about organizing their lives, they not surprisingly followed the model of interpersonal relations and family life most immediately available to a middle-class couple of their time, a model they might have found especially appropriate given the disparity in their ages and ranges of experience: the external sphere generally occupied by the husband, the domestic by the wife. Even their correspondence back home to New York followed this pattern. Although Putnam typically wrote dozens of letters each week back to clients and colleagues in the United States as part of his business routine, he corresponded only infrequently with relatives. His typical letter consisted of a straightforward business account written in an abrupt, factual style and manifestly indited with speed on office stationery. He had his own name for it: "male writing."[3] Victorine, by contrast, handled the majority of the family correspondence, even that with his mother and sister, and typically occupied herself primarily with domestic concerns that she detailed to her correspondents at considerable length. When she had no choice once but to write home on Wiley and Putnam office stationery, she apologized for the fact and mentioned that she was waiting for Putnam to resupply her with personal paper.[4]

This division of roles had been established even before the wedding, as in their transatlantic correspondence Putnam typically took upon himself the role of general instructor and guide to Victorine's willing pupil. The role came easily to him, as to all appearances did that of listener to Victorine. As one might expect of a middle-class Victorian family situated squarely in the sphere of letters, one of the areas about which he was most eager to share his views (and about which Victorine seems to have been most interested in listening) was that of authorship and letters. She had written to him early on in their relationship to indicate her desire to "improve" herself, and both agreed that a suitable way of doing so was an intensive regimen of reading.[5] Even before he separated from her in spring 1840, he had suggested various titles for improving her mind; prominent among them were the works of Scott, with the added inducement of a promise to guide her through Scott's home territory after they began their residence overseas.

Victorine took her readings so seriously that one of the most interesting exchanges between her and her publisher-fiancé in 1840 concerned her intense reaction to the work of his new friend and client Catharine Maria Sedgwick. In response to Victorine's lament about not having Sedgwick's literary talent, Putnam tried to set his and, he hoped, her priorities straight: "Miss Sedgwick is known and justly respected as a writer—an authoress—but in my opinion she is even far more worthy of esteem as a woman—and a freind [sic]. Talent may exist, and shine, in its proper sphere as well as through books—and especially when united with good sense, benevolence and amiability such talent is as respectable and more loveable than all the fame of authorship."[6] Coming from a man who was encountering the recent phenomenon of female authorship in his professional life, such advice was certainly prudent, though perhaps prudish as well. It was also clearly the advice of a man who had paid greater heed to Sedgwick in her role as older friend and mentor than to the complicating views about culture and domesticity she expressed as author of *Hope Leslie,* a work that Putnam would unquestioningly bring out a decade later in a revised edition. Undoubtedly, a major reason for his early attraction to female writers, such as Sedgwick and Sigourney, was the smooth way he perceived them as reconciling the dual demands of home and letters in their lives and works. Given his views on such matters, he was well able to appreciate the sentiment that Sigourney expressed to him several years later when, after the birth of the Putnams' second child, she kindly inquired the names and ages of their children, a curiosity she justified as being for her "a sort of introduction to the domestic circle of distant friends, or at least a glossary of passages in their history,—as the bookmakers say."[7] That conflation of the literary and the domestic, a pattern of discourse that characterized not only Sigourney's writing but that of numerous other women writers of the antebellum generation, agreed with both Putnam and Victorine because in effect it reinforced the forms and ideology of their household. Each of them, for his or her own reasons, seems to have accepted the unspoken premises on which such domestic literary sentiments were based, but they were to find them tested in the years to come as not only the society changed but their children grew into maturity.

Whereas in previous years Putnam had served visiting Americans by helping them to familiarize themselves with the city and find lodgings, he now took responsibility for doing the same for his own family, exerting himself in particular to expedite Victorine's acclimation to life in London. Their first residence was in rooms in Euston Square, where the family began the practice of renting rooms or small houses that would characterize its living arrangements throughout its years in London. Sociable by nature and already well connected to various social and professional circles, Putnam attempted to work his wife quickly into relationships with both Americans and Britons of his acquaintance. Victorine soon proved herself to be as socially adept as her husband. Their oldest son mentions that she was able to build a social life for herself relatively quickly, although neither she nor Putnam ever lost the habit of referring to New York as "home." Among the friends and acquaintances they entertained were publishers, such as Edward Moxon and Nicholas Trubner, as well as a small number of local friends and Americans resident in or visiting London. As time went on and circumstances permitted, the Putnams began to entertain formally at home, a function for which they shared a pleasure and for which they would develop a reputation as leading literary hosts in New York in the early fifties. Many of their friends were connected to the arts and letters as creators or manufacturers, but their home of the mid-forties was also frequented by a variety of political exiles, including Mazzini, Louis Blanc, and Louis Napoleon, as well as by the successive American ministers and their staffs.[8] In addition, Victorine, who all her life preferred the countryside and beaches to the city, showed a streak of independence early in their London residence by taking her fledgling family for summer trips to Brighton and Ramsgate.

The primary domestic story of the Putnams during their London years was the growth and development of their family. During what they would later look back on as a generally happy seven years' residence, the Putnams celebrated the births of three of their eventual ten children (Mary, George Haven, and Edith). But with each new arrival, Victorine naturally found her responsibilities multiplied. Although the couple eventually hired a nurse to help with the children and an occasional servant or two for the house, their long-term practice of in-home education and close nurturing was established early on, with the primary responsibility, as was typical in middle-class Victorian homes, falling on the mother. How Victorine managed during these years one can only infer; her surviving letters rarely transcend the minutiae of daily family life: the health of the children, her chores, the house, her husband's (over)work. No doubt, those details accurately reflect the way she spent most of her day before her husband's return from the office.

At the same time, she must often have had her mind on the domestic sphere back in New York. The arrival of each transatlantic steamer was accompanied by the expectation of letters from America. As soon as they were brought home from the office, those letters were devotedly read and formed the staple of evening conversation. From time to time, steamers also delivered treats from New York, such as Catherine Hunt Putnam's preserves and pickles or presents from the Bishops.[9] If to visitors to their home, then and later, the Putnams generally appeared a model Victorian family, it seems unlikely that during her early years in London, a city she and Putnam alike considered thousands of miles from home, Victorine even remotely thought of this as an idyllic period. However deeply attached the young couple were to each other and to their children, she must often have been left with stretches of loneliness and boredom.

The strain of domestic living was presumably much less for Putnam, who was routinely out of the house for the entire day, his work schedule monopolizing his time until supper and often even after his return home well into the night. A work day seldom went by in which he was home before 7:30 P.M. Furthermore, his trips to the Continent or the United States, generally made alone during these years, often took him away from home for weeks at a time. One of his trips to Paris, in spring 1844, he actually made at Victorine's insistence that he remove himself from the swirl of activity and complications at home following the birth of their second child.[10] This new disruptive presence in his parents' lives was their first son, George Haven, one of the three sons who would eventually join their father in operating the family publishing house. Although Putnam might not have contemplated or even desired any such eventuality, the growth of his family during this period eventually proved to be a blessing for him in his professional as well as in his private life: in the years following the Civil War his firm would follow the line of evolution common among publishing houses and developed into a family-owned and -managed operation. In fact, Putnam had, in his later years, the good fortune of being able to share

PUTNAM FAMILY ALBUM

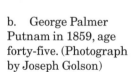

a.   George Palmer Putnam as a young man. (Courtesy Prints and Photographs Division, Library of Congress)

b.   George Palmer Putnam in 1859, age forty-five. (Photograph by Joseph Golson)

c.   George Palmer Putnam, studio pose taken late in life. (Courtesy Prints and Photographs Division, Library of Congress)

d. Catherine Hunt Putnam, late in life. (Courtesy Prints and Photographs Division, Library of Congress)

e. Victorine Haven Putnam. (Courtesy Prints and Photographs Division, Library of Congress)

f.   George Haven Putnam in 1864, age twenty, lieutenant in the Union Army. (Photo by Joseph Golson)

g.   Mary Corinna Putnam in 1866, age twenty-three or -four, shortly before leaving New York to study medicine in Paris. (Photo by Joseph Golson)

h.   Edith and John Bishop Putnam in the early or mid-1850s. (Courtesy Prints and Photographs Division, Library of Congress)

i.   Herbert Putnam around 1867, age five or six. (Courtesy Prints and Photographs Division, Library of Congress)

responsibilities for running the firm with sons whose publishing talents complemented and, especially in the case of George Haven, in some ways surpassed his own.

Along with a growing family, Putnam enjoyed the prospects of a growing business during his remaining London years, a period in which Wiley and Putnam became one of the leading publishing and retailing companies in the American book trade. The operations of the New York and London branches grew both separately and in tandem during these years. The Broadway office, located in the center of the city's bookselling district, developed by the mid-forties into one of New York's finest bookstores, offering a supply of imported titles matched perhaps only by Appleton's up the street. At the same time, Wiley and Putnam gradually expanded its publishing operation until it emerged in 1845 as one of New York's leading publishing houses, with a list of high-quality books matched by few other houses in the country. Meanwhile, the London office grew from its tenuous beginnings in the late 1830s into a well-known address in the bookmaking district of London, and Putnam from relative obscurity to solid reputation among London publishers. The demands of handling the rising volume of transatlantic business that emanated from both the New York office and the American book trade generally caused the firm repeatedly to outgrow its quarters and Putnam to search for competent help with the intensifying demands upon his time and attention. Not until 1844–45, when he moved the business a third time, this time completely out of the Paternoster Row neighborhood into more spacious quarters at Waterloo Place and secured additional clerical assistants, was he to feel himself and the London office well prepared to handle the rising volume of business.

Befitting its status as one of the leading American houses in the transatlantic book trade, the firm began issuing in September 1841 a monthly trade sheet, *Wiley and Putnam's Literary News-Letter and Monthly Register of New Books, Foreign and American,* which attempted to serve simultaneously the interests of the house and those of the industry. Although issued through the New York office and addressed to an American readership, the *Wiley and Putnam News-Letter* was presumably the initiative of Putnam, who no doubt saw the chance to align the strategic position and self-interest of his firm with some of the broader purposes of his earlier *Booksellers' Advertiser.* The *Wiley and Putnam News-Letter* clearly bore the impress not only of Putnam's bibliographic skill and wide knowledge of current activities and developments in the bookmaking world but also of his sense of service to his fellow publishers and book-buying clientele. Sent gratis to colleges, public libraries, and book collectors throughout the United States, the *Wiley and Putnam News-Letter* communicated information about the most recent publications in Europe and America and the latest news in authorial and publishing circles. In the process, it naturally paid special attention to the publication list of Wiley and Putnam. The more the firm's publishing list grew, the more strategically valuable the journal became. Although the firm had for several years been issuing catalogues to advertise its growing stock in books available for retail or mail order sale, the *News-Letter* allowed it for the first time to advertise its publishing operations on a timely and regular basis.

Beginning in 1840, Wiley and Putnam attempted to expand its retail operations by moving more aggressively into the periodical market. Although the firm was already the leading seller of American periodicals in London, that market was still a severely restricted one; American journals had to overcome not only superior local products but also a firm British prejudice against American publications. A more realistic target for expansion lay in the much larger market for British journals in America. The partners moved into this market on the assumption that with demand on the rise for periodicals generally in the United States, the advantages they enjoyed in supplying imported books might also serve them in supplying imported periodicals to the domestic market: lower prices, swifter delivery, and superior connections with the originating publishers. That year Putnam began making arrangements with British publishers to buy early issues of their journals for sale in the United States. In the fall he reached an initial arrangement with John Murray, who agreed to provide Wiley and Putnam copies of his *Quarterly Review* at two shillings each, provided that the firm take a minimum of 250 copies.[11] During the next two years, Putnam made similar arrangements with other leading periodical publishers in London, Edinburgh, and Dublin. In its first issue of the *News-Letter,* Wiley and Putnam advertised that it had made arrangements to supply "at greatly reduced prices" copies of *Blackwood's, Fraser's,* the *Monthly Magazine, Dublin University Magazine,* and *Engineer's and Architect's Journal.*[12] The following year it was advertising more than twice as many journals and still claiming that it could undersell its competition.[13]

But, if superior economy was their trump card in the game of foreign magazine sales, Wiley and Putnam failed to take sufficient account of changes in the general rules of the game and of the ruthlessness of their fellow players. Although Putnam succeeded in making special deals at his end with Blackwood, Fraser, Murray, and other British periodical publishers to receive favorable terms for the sale of their journals in New York, Wiley proved unable to match the distributional resourcefulness of his competitors in New York. Wiley and Putnam soon found itself coming up against reprinters able to undersell its "greatly reduced prices" by running off unauthorized cheap paper editions printed from early copies. One reprinter was the firm's sometimes printer Robert Craighead, who joined with Leonard Scott in forming one of New York City's premier magazine reprint businesses.[14] Another pair were Jonas Winchester and Park Benjamin, publisher and editor of the popular literary weekly the *New World,* who by 1843 were using the same price-cutting strategy against other magazine publishers that they had used against book publishers by reprinting popular British fiction as serials in their inexpensive periodical. So volatile were the conditions of the literary marketplace that, just a few months after Wiley and Putnam advertised its periodical agency in the pages of the *New World,* Winchester and Benjamin turned on them and began reprinting Wiley and Putnam's most popular magazine import, *Blackwood's.* Perhaps Wiley and Putnam were surprised—although as literary professionals they should not have been—by the ethically questionable but legally permissible practice of New York reprinters of underselling the firm's authorized editions of British periodicals. Undoubtedly the two men resented it, but in truth they were themselves guilty of overestimating the ease with which they could move down the high road to profitability in the periodical market when faced with publishers who typically took the more direct low road to competitive superiority. By the mid-1840s they reconsidered their initiative and began to retreat from the periodical market in favor of the safer policy of concentrating on their bookselling and publishing operations.[15]

Then again, Wiley and Putnam could not have kept itself entirely free from the widespread shadiness that characterized operations in the book trade during the cheap publication wars of the early 1840s. Interestingly enough, Putnam had had an amicable relationship dating back at least to 1838 with Park Benjamin, editor of the *New World* and soon to emerge as one of the most aggressive of the American "book-aneers"—to use the term of Thomas Hood, the chief wit of the phenomenon—patrolling the North Atlantic. At that time Benjamin was editing New York's *American Monthly Magazine,* a competitor to the *Knickerbocker.* Putnam supplied occasional bibliographical listings of new works published in the United States and England to both periodicals,[16] and after setting up his London office, he served both magazines as English agent and even attempted to secure Charles Dickens's agreement to write for them—no small irony in view of the unmitigated spite that Dickens would develop in the early 1840s for Benjamin, whom he kept squarely in his sites as one of the most flagrant American wavers of "the Black Flag of Literature."[17] Although a loose advocate of international copyright while editing the *American Monthly,* Benjamin abandoned that position after becoming editor of the *New World.* Once installed in that role, he defended the *New World*'s brazen stance of piracy-as-democratic-good, virtually the only position an editor of that periodical could have taken without embarrassment. He had already made that transformation when he met with Putnam in spring 1841 just before or after the latter's wedding to discuss possible "arrangements" between them.[18] The two men agreed that Putnam was not only to write occasional letters for the *New World* filled with the latest social, political, and cultural news from London but also to perform various services there for the journal and its operators, the most important of which was to procure early sheets of novels from their British publishers for reprinting in the magazine. That he was successful in doing so is attested to by the fact that the three works (the best known of which was *Barnaby Rudge*) that Benjamin mentioned in his one surviving letter from this time to Putnam were among the most popular serials to appear in the *New World* in 1841.

How purely theirs was a partnership of convenience one can only wonder. If that was all it was, it might seem like one of the strangest imaginable, a literary hawk and dove nesting amicably for a time in the former's perch. But their positions were probably far from diametrically opposed, since the day-to-day circumstances of their profession no doubt tended to bear out the sagacity underlying Mrs. Thrale's famous quip about "Business disqualif[ying] a Man for heaven more than Pleasure does."[19] Whatever their actual ideologies, literary professionals with sharply differing views regarding publishers' versus authors' rights and other issues routinely did business together. Putnam was no exception; during his London years he often represented people and firms with whose policies he was in strong, even vocal, disagreement. One such client was Harper and Brothers, a firm whose pirating practices increasingly irritated his sensibility at this time and later shrank his profit margin. Another was Benjamin, who for his part might have been willing to compromise his policies to suit Putnam. That Benjamin mentioned Putnam's effecting "arrangements" might imply his willingness to make payments to British proprietors, although there is no record that Putnam offered to make or actually transacted any such payments. Whatever the nature of such arrangements, Putnam's agency for the *New World* ended by October, when the journal announced that it had hired its own agents in London, Bremen, and Mexico (Donald MacLeod, Francis Grund, and Brantz Mayer, respectively).[20]

One also wonders into which pocket Putnam deposited the fees that he received from clients like Benjamin whom he served personally: the one marked "Wiley and Putnam" or the one marked "Putnam." For a man who operated at the opposite extreme from Dickens's Mr. Wemmick, firm distinctions between London expenses and profits assignable to the company and expenses and profits assignable to his family, or even clear boundaries between clients and friends could not be easily drawn. Even on the level of daily routine he was continually obscuring such distinctions, spending a considerable amount of office and after-office hours entertaining actual and potential clients; he even used the family home at times for such purposes. Doing so, of course, obliged Victorine's cooperation, which as a rule she gave graciously. She must occasionally, however, have had her patience stretched thin by his professional demands on her and their home, and there must have been specific instances when she vocally protested. One such moment came when her husband brought home James Kingsley of Yale College, one of Wiley and Putnam's more important accounts: "I am sure there is not much pleasure in having stupid old people like Professor Kingsley, and lots of others whom I could name, that George asks because they have it in their power to give large book orders for colleges and so forth, and George thinks if these old codgers see what a nice, pretty, little wife he has, they cannot help giving him the orders."[21] In general, though, Victorine seems to have liked most of the clients Putnam brought to the house, even befriending some (or, just as often, their spouses), although she generally kept her distance from the affairs of the office and business. When she did come to the store, it was normally to see her husband or to hunt for reading material.

The loosely regulated trade conditions that undermined Wiley's attempts to sell British periodicals in New York also complicated Putnam's attempts to arrange for the publications of British authors in the United States. Even with the best intentions to honor authorship in the abstract and the concrete, Putnam sometimes found himself wading neck deep in transatlantic mud. One good example of how murky conditions were for transatlantic publishing and of how seriously Putnam's wishful assumptions were tested by local circumstances was the case of George Borrow, whose first book made its initial American appearance in a Wiley and Putnam edition.

That book was *The Zincali; or, an Account of the Gypsies of Spain,* which Wiley and Putnam published in 1842 when Borrow was at the beginning of his successful career. Inexpensively priced and brought out both in cloth and in paper wrappers, the firm's edition followed the text of the fancier, two-volume London edition published the previous year by John Murray, the house that would publish Borrow's works through the century. Although leading Borrow scholars have claimed that Wiley and Putnam's was a pirated edition, that charge seems unfounded.[22] Strictly speaking, what was true of the London *Pym* was also true of the New York *Zincali:* Wiley and Putnam was the first firm to put the work into circulation in a secondary market and did so when there was no prior claim to copyright. With courtesy of the trade at the time frequently violated, however, the attractiveness of the work soon proved to be its undoing; the following year the New York reprinters Winchester and Benjamin pirated the Wiley and Putnam edition (and its text) as a *New World* "extra" printed in double columns and priced at $.25 (compared to the $.50 Wiley and Putnam paperback edition), and other reprinters in town and out quickly followed suit.[23] This was fairly standard operating procedure for Benjamin, who was by then committed to reprinting promising works of rising authors like Borrow in whom he saw an usually attractive—and, due to its foreign authorship, unprotected—resource to exploit to increase sales of his journal. Knowing a good thing when he saw it, Benjamin followed his cheap edition of *The Zincali* the next year with a $.25 edition of Borrow's next work, *The Bible in Spain,* an act that he defended as part of the ongoing "great revolution in the literary world" in which "friends of the people," at whose head he positioned himself as a democrat and literary utilitarian, set out "to do the greatest good to the greatest number" by supplying them with cheap reading matter.[24]

But even if the Wiley and Putnam edition of *The Zincali* was indisputably the first to appear on the American market, it is by no means clear on what basis Putnam got hold of the work. It seems plausible that, given his close business relations with and open admiration for Murray, Putnam made some kind of arrangement with him for American publication. This was the argument that George Haven Putnam made a half century later in defending his father's reputation against charges of unauthorized appropriation of *The Zincali.*[25] But as he learned, that argument was unprovable; his demand that the Murrays check their files for confirmation of a Putnam-Murray arrangement produced no evidence. Whatever the exact facts, Putnam continued to do business uninterruptedly with the Murrays (both father and son, the elder John Murray dying in June 1843). If anything, the level of their cooperation rose during the last five years of Putnam's London residence. In fact, in 1843 Murray, anticipating that *The Bible in Spain* would also be pirated and operating on the principle that some foreign revenue was better than none, acted quickly to salvage at least a minimum of profit by selling Putnam copies of the work for distribution in the United States.[26]

Given the problematic circumstances enveloping transatlantic publishing, clashes between Putnam and Murray, whether of nationalist ideology or of book publishing practices (or a combination of the two), were virtually inevitable. One that did occur, in 1846, involved the charge that Putnam's firm was not making adequate compensation to Murray's for rights to various works reprinted in the United States. Putnam responded with equal parts ingenuity and ingenuousness by dressing himself in Murray's own colors: "You are quite in error about our *liberality.* We are the *Murrays* of the New World—and always ready to meet our prototype in the spirit of his own enlightened views. We are content to give all the usual sphere of profit, as on copyright books, whenever you will enable us to publish *simultaneously,* anything suited to our market. What could be fairer or more liberal?"[27] He would be happy, he continued, to make Murray handsome payments in return for the reception of American rights to his books, but circumstances often intervened between his wish and his ability to pay liberally. Not all the books he received turned out to be suitable to American taste, which Putnam considered less "dry" than the British. Furthermore, even when they did appeal to American taste, local retail conditions did not always permit his firm full freedom of operation. To maximize that possibility he insisted to Murray here, as he would later, on the necessity of near simultaneity of publication, since he needed to beat possible reprinters in the race to the press (a condition to which Murray often responded with his own demand for timely reciprocity, since copyright protection in England, when available at all to foreign writers or their publishers, required priority of publication in England). Just the same, Putnam preferred, as was typically his way, to look at the bright side of things and to encourage Murray that it was in their mutual interest to continue their dealings: "It is desirable that [our] arrangements should be made early;—but I think that when they are once matured, and you give us good and popular books you will find it worth while to do so."[28] Murray seemed satisfied with Putnam's explanation; that same day he responded to Putnam's letter by offering him a variety of books from his list "*at low prices* for the American market," including several editions of Byron and Boswell's *Life of Johnson*.[29] In subsequent years he continued to engage with Putnam in a variety of cooperative transatlantic publications, including Borrow's *Lavengro*.

Truth as to the charges and countercharges of "illiberality" and "liberality," in all likelihood, lay somewhere between their positions, but absolute righteousness in business dealings was seldom found during these free-wheeling, free-trading years in the transatlantic book trade. With reprinters from both book and periodical publishing companies crowding the docks of New York, Boston, and Philadelphia and steam-driven presses waiting at their order for putting words to paper quickly and cheaply, a publisher like Putnam intent on protecting the rights and profits of both authors and publishers was left little time or room for maneuvering. To publish the works of a popular author, such as Borrow, was predictably to attract reprinters, no matter whether he himself had paid for exclusive rights to issue those works in the United States. Just as his edition of *The Zincali* was reprinted in turn by Winchester and Benjamin, so a decade later his authorized edition of *Lavengro* was followed to market by a cheaper edition from Harper and Brothers, the firm he regarded from the 1840s to the end of his life as his particular adversary in the fight for an international copyright. But unscrupulous publishers were not the only complicating factor. Putnam was clearly guilty of overestimating the degree of mutuality in the interests of authors and publishers. Despite the good will he harbored toward each and the public advocacy he engaged in toward reconciliation of their interests, he was hardly in a position to do justice to either group, no less to both. What he generally wound up attempting to do, consciously or unconsciously, was to chart a middle course of pragmatic idealism, a course whose rationale was perhaps best defined by Ralph Waldo Emerson from a writer's angle of vision in an essay reflecting the literary professional facts of this time: "Whilst the debate goes forward on the equity of commerce, and will not be closed for a century or two, New and Old England may keep shop. Law of copyright and international copyright is to be discussed, and, in the interim, we will sell our books for the most we can."[30]

Borrow was only one popular British author of this period whose publication set Wiley and Putnam to navigate a course through the narrow straits of international publishing. Another was Thomas Carlyle, who, like Borrow, was by the early 1840s a desirable British literary prospect attracting the attention of American publishers from Philadelphia to Boston. Unlike the unprotected Borrow, Carlyle at least had the watchful eye of his friend Ralph Waldo Emerson to look after his interests in the United States. This role Emerson took upon himself for a number of Carlyle's works, whose production in the United States he not only supervised but in some instances also financed. With Emerson as his dutiful agent, Carlyle was surprised and delighted to discover in the mid-1830s that the New World offered him an unanticipatedly large market for his writings that seemed to rival in size and potential profitability the more familiar one back home. During the early years of their dealings, Emerson was able to make arrangements for the publication of Carlyle's books in Boston that earned the British author fairly sizable profits. But as his popularity grew in the early 1840s simultaneously with the increased competitiveness among pirates, Carlyle suffered the fate of a growing number of his contemporaries of seeing profits he considered his own going into the pockets of foreign publishers. So when Wiley and Putnam offered him a deal in mid-1846 to become the American publisher of many of his books and to pay him 10-percent royalties (the sum they offered many of their American authors) for the exclusive right to publish them in the United States, he was distinctly interested.[31]

Putnam seems not to have met Carlyle during his early years in London. If he did not then know the man, however, he was certainly well acquainted with Carlyle's attractiveness as an author for the American market. He was also well acquainted with his local publishers, first James Fraser and then, after Fraser's death in 1841, Chapman and Hall. The initial connection between Carlyle and Wiley and Putnam was made in autumn 1845 when Chapman and Hall approached Putnam with a proposition to authorize his firm to bring out an American edition of *Oliver Cromwell's Letters and Speeches,* an initiative the firm took without informing Carlyle. Putnam quickly accepted and made Chapman and Hall the small but standard payment of £10 in exchange.

What must have looked to him like a good, straightforward transaction rapidly devolved into a publishing imbroglio. In accordance with the agreement, Putnam received a bound copy of the English sheets shortly before its local publication, which he sent on to Wiley for printing by the firm in New York. Wiley was therefore surprised when Emerson, who had mistakenly been led by Carlyle to believe that a press-ready copy of the work was being sent to him via Wiley and Putnam for sale to an American publisher of his choice, deputed Horace Greeley to stop by the Broadway office to pick up the volume and, given the amount of time already lost since its London publication, to put it into print himself on his newspaper's presses. Greeley was surprised to be rebuffed and quickly wrote to Emerson to inform him that Wiley and Putnam "decline delivering the book as they were reprinting it, having bought it in London of Chapman and Hall, and would deliver my copy as soon as they could safely do so."[32] Emerson, who knew nothing of the deal made between Chapman and Hall and Wiley and Putnam, considered the latter's response "cool enough" and reacted by seeking the intervention of his New York lawyer-brother William (who, by a quirk of circumstances, would become Putnam's Staten Island neighbor and friend later in the decade). By that time, though, Emerson knew that Wiley and Putnam had already published the work and that he had scant recourse to take against what he considered a particularly blatant act of unethical conduct.

The denouement of this publishing farce occurred when an embarrassed Carlyle, having learned that a misunderstanding about his desires for the book had led Chapman and Hall to make its initial agreement with Putnam without his authorization, hastened to write Emerson in early January 1846 to explain what had happened.[33] Not that Carlyle was himself satisfied with this turn of affairs. His hopes raised by the recent reception of a £50 payment from Carey and Hart of Philadelphia for rights to their authorized American edition of *Critical and Miscellaneous Essays* and by a (rather implausible) proposal from a minor New York publisher to bring out *Cromwell* in return for either half profits or 10 percent of the retail sales, Carlyle accounted himself shortchanged by nearly £100 between the deal that was already made and the deal that should have been made for *Cromwell*—a lost opportunity that he complained was due to a "trick of the Wilies."[34] Within weeks, however, he was busy preparing for press an expanded version of his unexpectedly successful *Cromwell,* which upon its completion gave him his chance to renegotiate the terms of both its English and its American publication. Emerson explored various possible arrangements for him in the United States but was unable finally to come up with a satisfactory alternative to Wiley and Putnam.

In the meantime, the negotiations over *Cromwell* became subsumed within larger considerations when Putnam came to Carlyle's house one day in late April 1846 and made an offer that Carlyle found too tempting to reject:

> Mr Putnam, really a very intelligent, modest, and reputable-looking little fellow, got at last to sight of me about a week ago;—explained with much earnestness how the whole origin of the *mistake* about the first edition of *Cromwell* had lain with Chapman my own Bookseller (which in fact I had already perceived to be the case); and farther set forth, what was more important, that he and his Partner were, and had been, ready and desirous to *make good* said mistake, in the amplest most satisfactory manner,—by the ready method of paying me *now* ten percent on the selling-price of all the copies of Cromwell sent into the market by them; and had (as I knew already) covenanted with you to do so, in a clear, *bona-fide,* and to you satisfactory manner, in regard to that First Edition: in consequence of which you had made a bargain with them of like tenor in regard to the Second.[35]

That was not all that Putnam came prepared to offer: he also proposed that Wiley and Putnam be given the status of authorized publisher of three earlier works, *The French Revolution, Sartor Resartus,* and *Heroes and Hero-Worship,* all to be reissued under its imprint and paid for at the rate of 10 percent royalties. In addition, he acceded to Carlyle's request that E. P. Clark, a "Lynx-eyed" bank clerk recommended by Emerson, be permitted to check Wiley and Putnam's account books for verification of the number of copies of Carlyle's works printed and sold.[36] In return, Putnam expected to receive from Carlyle a statement of authorization to be prefaced to each book published by his firm. The conversation went so well that Putnam wished to formalize its content with a letter of intent signed on the spot, but Carlyle demurred, perhaps not yet willing to suspend his initial skepticism about a firm he had previously relegated to the animal kingdom as wolves and foxes and renamed "the *Wily and Put-on-him Firm.*"[37] Meanwhile, he wrote to seek Emerson's advice.[38]

There followed a six-week-long flurry of letters between publishers, author, and agent in which details of the deal were worked out. By this point, Putnam's original offer of 10-percent royalties had been amended to a half profits arrangement shared between author and publisher, following the return of manufacturing and promotional expenses. On 15 June 1846 Putnam received the authorizing statement from Carlyle that he considered minimum insurance for his firm against American pirates and that he planned to print at the head of each Carlyle book.[39] Two days later he went to Carlyle's home to finalize the terms of their agreement, and the next day the two men met in Putnam's office on Waterloo Place to sign a contract. Thus Wiley and Putnam became, for the time, Carlyle's main publisher in the United States. In addition to the titles already mentioned, it also brought out editions of *Chartism* and *Past and Present,* which it issued bound together in its Library of Choice Reading. The editions of *Sartor Resartus, The French Revolution, Past and Present,* and *Heroes and Hero-Worship* all carried Carlyle's 18 June 1846 imprimatur in place of copyright notice unvaryingly declaring: "This Book ... I have read over and revised into a correct state for Messrs. Wiley and Putnam, of New York, who are hereby authorised, they and only they, so far as I can authorise them, to print and vend the same in the United States."[40] Equivocal as it was, that statement was as much as Carlyle (or, for that matter, any foreign author) could do to protect himself and his publishers from American pirates. With his books brought up-to-date and issued by a centralized source in New York and Clark authorized to oversee a fair accounting of royalties, Carlyle settled back with the satisfaction of knowing that affairs were in good hands (Clark's and Emerson's) and waited in high expectations for the Wiley and Putnam edition to bring him returns. He would have had good reason to feel confident: he had signed one of the most favorable contracts to date between a British author and an American publisher.

The venture proved, however, to be another embittering disappointment for Carlyle, whose relations with Wiley and Putnam ended on a note of acrimony similar to the one on which they had commenced several years before. As late as spring 1847, Carlyle remained confident that all was well, even though he probably wrote a letter early that spring to Putnam, who at the time was traveling on the Continent with Victorine, to ask for an accounting of their affairs. That request must have been simply precautionary because Carlyle shortly after making it allowed himself in a letter to his sister to call his books "a kind of *landed property* to me [that] yield a certain rent more or less considerable, every year."[41] Putnam promptly responded that he was sailing the following week to New York and would contact Clark about the sum owing to Carlyle for *Cromwell.* Clearly eager to market that work in such a way as to appeal to multiple strata of the market, the New York office had printed the work in 1845–46 in two formats: a handsomely gotten up, two-volume cloth text, and an inexpensive four-part, two-volume text, each number of which was wrapped in simple brown paper, priced at $.50, and included as one part in Wiley and Putnam's Library of Choice Books (series nos. 29–32).[42] As to the other books, Putnam regretfully reported that they had not yet been in print long enough to accumulate royalties but hoped to be able to send him a check after the next accounting period (which the firm typically set for July).[43]

The firm sent a royalty payment on *Cromwell* to Carlyle that summer, but he belittled the "magnificent sum" of £73.4.9, complaining that it was a mere tenth of what he deserved and vowing to "write to W. and P. today, indicating that I have got the Bill; and, in polite language, that they are 'd——d swingla's' for sending no more."[44] His outrage, however, was unfounded, owing to his misguided expectation that royalties in the United States would approximate those in Britain, where he was reported to have received an estimated payment of £1,000.[45] In American terms, royalties amounting to £73.4.9 (roughly, $365) on a foreign-authored book was considerable. Because Wiley and Putnam sold the book in its different formats at variable prices and allowed a discount to the trade of approximately 25 percent, one can only estimate the number of copies sold. Whatever the exact computation, the firm was clearly paying royalties on sales in the unit of thousands—a healthy figure.

Carlyle clearly did not understand the dynamics of contemporaneous publishing conditions in the United States, which—the mirror image of those in Britain—militated against profits for either authors or publishers on foreign works comparable to those earned in the home market. But Wiley and Putnam also entered the deal with unjustifiably optimistic expectations. Unlike Chapman and Hall, the firm had reprinters nipping at its heels as it put *Cromwell* and Carlyle's earlier works to press, with the result that competing editions must have reduced sales of its own substantially. The most unyielding reprinter was the New Yorker William Colyer, who had already issued a cheap ($.12 ½) unauthorized edition of *Past and Present* shortly after its initial English publication in 1843 and kept it in print for at least several years.[46] He then followed the two-volume, $2 edition of *Cromwell* issued in the Wiley and Putnam Library of Cheap Reading with his own one-volume, double-columned $.50 edition, an act that forced Wiley and Putnam to relinquish its marketing strategy for the Library and to drop the price of its edition to $.50.[47] Evert Duyckinck believed that Colyer had been set up to this act by the Harpers, his brothers-in-law, in retaliation against Wiley and Putnam as an aggressive new rival attempting to push its way into the market the Harpers had long dominated.[48] This might have been so, but the cold logic of literary economics and simple cognizance of the shortest path to a profit would have been a sufficient inducement for Colyer's edition even without the incitement of the Harpers.[49]

Whether Wiley and Putnam made subsequent payments to Carlyle is unknown. Carlyle's letter of 29 April 1848 to Clarke suggests that none had been made in the intervening year; indeed, he charged Clarke to pursue those *"Privateers,"* if he thought the act might result in some good.[50] Doing so would not have been easy; by the beginning of 1848 Wiley and Putnam had split up, with Wiley receiving most of Carlyle's works in his share of the company assets and, with them, the responsibility of his account. Clarke followed Carlyle's request by contacting Putnam, who was surprised to hear that Wiley had not paid off the account and wrote back in June to say that Wiley would do so after the July accounting was completed, adding his regret that the sum owed Carlyle was likely to be small: "The publication of [Carlyle's works] has been far less profitable than we could have expected." To his knowledge about three hundred copies of both *Cromwell* and *Past and Present* remained on hand. He added that he was so discouraged about the prospects for new editions that he had sold the stereotype plates of the Carlyle editions, which he had purchased at the auction of some of the firm's assets, far below cost to Harper and Brothers, who he hoped would stand behind Carlyle: "Of course as there was no legal copyright, I could not transfer any,—but I have urged upon Messrs. Harper, as a matter of courtesy, to render to Mr. Carlyle the same returns which are agreed upon—especially as they have arranged with him for the publication of his new work—or about to do so."[51]

Such news, passed on to Carlyle, could hardly have come as reassurance. With "courtesy" as a final line of defense for his literary property, little wonder that he, like many writers of his generation newly alert to the developing opportunities for professional authorship, came to see foreign dealings as the ultimate frustration in his hopes of making the pen the basis of his livelihood. His final comment on his dealings with Wiley and Putnam, jotted down several decades after the fact onto the sheet of an 1846 letter to his brother in which he had allowed himself to hope for "some considerable money" from the publication plans then under discussion with Putnam, was terse and bitter: "There never came one sixpence, Putnm a mere plundering Fox (May 1869)."[52]

Although not strictly accurate, his assertion expressed the dissatisfaction that writers frequently experienced in the mid-century international literary market. In the largest sense, though, Carlyle's dissatisfaction was not merely with Wiley and Putnam and various other American publishers but with the new system of "mechanism," one of the ominous signs of the times that Carlyle saw industrial capitalism as introducing to publishing: "Literature, too, has its Paternoster-row mechanism, its Trade-dinners, its Editorial conclaves, and huge subterranean, puffing bellows so that books are not only printed, but, in a great measure, written and sold, by machinery."[53] Neither at home with that arrangement nor able to hold himself or his texts aloof from it, Carlyle would not have been unambivalently happy with any publishing arrangement available to a mid-century author, even had he gotten his just financial due from North America.

Putnam not only had no such ambivalence but was decidedly whiggish about modern print culture. Although he could not have been pleased with the sour conclusion to his dealings with Carlyle, such dealings were a relatively minor part of his many-sided activity as a bookman in the 1840s. During these years, he performed a wide variety of professional functions, some with a sense of purpose. His clients were numerous, and his work for them ranged widely, from matters in which he represented the firm to those in which he acted strictly on his own authority. But for virtually all the people and institutions he assisted professionally, the work he did, the services he performed, and the favors he executed related chiefly to his role of literary professional as international mediator. His services rivaled in number and variety those of a concierge at a major international hotel; there were few book-related functions he did not perform, and most he executed with pleasure. For American authors looking for British publishers or needing related services in the British market, he served as agent. For both individual and institutional buyers, he purchased books and journals, contemporary and rare, domestic and foreign. For university and municipal libraries, he filled subscriptions to professional literature and periodicals; for historical societies, he purchased manuscripts and rare editions. For fellow American publishers, he made arrangements with British and Continental publishers and authors for sale or republication of particularly desirable works in the United States. For individuals back home unable to find stationery of comparable quality, he purchased British paper. For both American and British friends and clients, he opened his firm's mail pouches for the surest transatlantic delivery then available. For those in need of international monetary conversion, he occasionally (and usually reluctantly) served as a surrogate banker. For book collectors, he looked through the catalogues of libraries and auctions in Europe to locate choice volumes. For autograph collectors, he gave from (and sometimes added to) his growing stock in well-known names. And for friends, such as Catharine Maria Sedgwick, he was willing to draw on his "good nature" by doing such special favors as locating lost or misdirected letters or finding lodgings.[54]

As if these many functions did not occupy enough of his time and energy, Putnam also took on the ideologically charged task of promoting American writers and books in London. During his decade-long residence in England, he served as the chief American importer not only of American books but of the cultural nationalism then on the rise in the United States, which he introduced in various ways and forms into the bookmaking district of London. This was for him nothing less than a mission, which he performed energetically throughout his London years but especially in the mid-1840s. He often sat at his writing desk late into the evening, dashing off letters soliciting information on American book production and drawing up charts with the results of his research, which were usable on two fronts: in Britain, to inform a foreign audience about the achievements of American print culture; in the United States, to inform members of Congress as well as the trade about the depredations made by foreign reprinters against American authors and publishers. This work culminated in 1845 with publication of *American Facts,* a volume of national self-explanation designed to educate Europeans about the politics, history, and culture of the New World. That volume's compilation and publication emanated from the same cultural and economic impulse that prompted the firm to bring out Wiley and Putnam's Library of American Books, whose first title appeared within several weeks of *American Facts.*

That important book had a private as well as public history. Ever since setting up shop in London in 1838, Putnam had been working to promote American letters in England, an unremunerated task of little economic importance to the firm but of great personal value to Putnam. By 1843, he was investing more time and energy than in past years in marketing and promoting American books (a fair number, naturally, from his own firm). The reason for this reapportionment of his time had less to do with a change in his personal views than with the rapid growth of the American bookmaking industry and American letters— and of his own firm's share in both. Drawing on his extensive personal familiarity and correspondence with American authors, he began in summer 1843 to send out a circular to writers in the United States soliciting information about the number and sales of their individual works.[55] There was little information then in the public realm about the extent of American authorship or publishing, and Putnam hoped to supply some much-needed knowledge about subjects he took to be vital not only to the national reputation but also to the national interest. Besides such inquiries he made an investigation into the few sources then available to a researcher on the American publishing sector: publishers' lists, the 1840 census, articles in the contemporary press, letters from knowledgeable correspondents, word-of-mouth from other publishers, and the file of his own *Booksellers' Advertiser.* These early efforts did not go unacknowledged; he received more than a dozen letters from the United States supporting his efforts and thanking him for his initiative even before the publication of *American Facts.*

In his first extended statement on the situation of American letters, called "A Few Preliminary Notes and Statistics," Putnam addressed himself simultaneously to Britons and Americans. This work was printed as an introduction to his firm's 1843 *American Book Circular,* a sixty-four-page booklet giving a detailed listing of recent American publications.[56] Taking aim at the presumption of American culture inferiority prevalent in Britain and in much of the United States, a view that had recently gained renewed currency with the publication of Archibald Alison's influential *History of Europe,* Putnam set out to marshall the evidence and draft a script in defense of American claims to genuine culture—culture, I might add, that except for its accessibility to the many and its openness to American authorship he defined very much in terms of a European model. Putnam's point of departure was a statement by Alison predictably suited to goad a patriotic American's sense of inferiority/superiority toward Europe; in fact, its phrasing was especially bound to irritate a professional American bookman like Putnam: "Literature and intellectual ability of the highest class meet with little encouragement in America. The names of Cooper, Channing, and Washington Irving, indeed, amply demonstrate that the American soil is not wanting in genius of the most elevated and fascinating character; but their works are almost all published in London— a decisive proof that European habits and ideas are necessary to their due development."[57]

Putnam, of course, knew as well as anyone else the ignorance and misinformation about the production and consumption of American letters on which claims like Alison's lay (he also knew of the four-volume edition of Alison's *History* brought out in New York that year by the Harpers at a fraction the price of the Blackwoods' ten-volume British edition).[58] Two years later, still angry at the injustice of Alison's claim, he effectively parodied it by reversing its inference: "The works of Byron, Scott, and Dickens, are all published at Boston; a decisive proof that American habits and ideas are necessary for their due development."[59] Although stung by the standard views of Alison and other detractors of Americans culture, Putnam was concerned primarily with demonstrating the vitality of authorship, publishing, and reading in the United States. Interestingly, the argument he presented for American cultural vitality was one that paralleled from a publisher's perspective the argument made more idiosyncratically from an author's perspective by Emerson, Melville, Whitman, and others during the course of the next dozen years.

Putnam's views were hardly original for the 1840s; what made them significant was the breadth of perspective he commanded from his transatlantic perch. That perch afforded an authority to his observations that perhaps no other American publisher of that decade commanded. Although the argument of his essay was thinly and schematically developed, he grasped immediately the necessity of conceiving of modern commercial publishing as a fast-evolving complex involving the makers, producers, and consumers of letters both separately and inter-relatedly. In addition, he understood that to talk about it intelligently he also needed to address the developing infrastructure of cultural production and consumption in the United States, including the growth of libraries, schools, and transportation systems. In drawing a picture of a robust American book trade, he knowingly took the controversial step of discussing reprinting as a practice that took place on both sides of the Atlantic, specifying numerous instances in which texts by American writers were reprinted overseas without the permission, compensation, or acknowledgment of their authors. This last aspect of his argument, which violated the conventional wisdom of unrivaled English cultural superiority, was bound to upset English writers, editors, and publishers alike. To Putnam, however, it was merely a matter of reciprocal justice to communicate information long known to him to the general Anglo-American audience for letters. He began this act as early as 1841, publicizing the injustice done to Richard Henry Dana, whose *Two Years Before the Mast* was a best-seller in England but a work for which the author received no compensation. Putnam's information was impeccable; Edward Moxon had informed him that year that he had sold 7,000 copies of the book, and an unnamed reprinter from Fleet Street disclosed to him that he had sold another 5,000 copies of the work in his own one-shilling edition.[60] Aware that American authors like Dana had been treated as poorly on the international market as their British peers, Putnam was determined to use his essay as a medium through which to redress the international balance of authorial victimization.

His stated position, however, typically turned out to be far less balanced than Putnam self-righteously considered it to be. Far from attempting to arrive at an integrated, transnational view of reprinting and modern literary culture, Putnam insisted on taking a stridently America-first position. Even though he closed his article with the wish that "the courteous liberality which the writer, as an American, has received in England, induces the hope that these few remarks, although rather oddly introduced, may not give any cause of offense," he should have known that the cultural act in which he was engaged was neither innocuous nor likely to be interpreted as such. His article had taken special aim at Charles Dickens, whose aspersions against American cultural dealings during the several previous years had clearly irritated Putnam. Putnam now singled out Dickens for criticism as not only a cultural crank but a party to an act of piracy against the American writer Joseph Neal, whose *Charcoal Sketches* was reprinted without permission in a magazine edited by Dickens. Dickens reacted, predictably, with fury to the claims made in Putnam's article, expressing his opinion privately to Carlyle later in 1843 (several years before Carlyle reached a similar conclusion) that Wiley and Putnam "lie consumedly—after the true American fashion of smartness."[61]

Criticism from a writer like Dickens was one thing for Putnam; from his fellow publishers in London, whom he thought of as peers and on whose good will he was dependent, a more immediate threat. When he published in London a book called *Change for the American Notes* "by an American Lady" (actually, the English journalist Henry Wood), a rejoinder to Dickens's *American Notes* as critical of English society as was *American Notes* of American, Putnam soon found himself scrambling for cover and justifying his behavior in publishing it to the younger John Murray: "Ever since the publication of that book (which I have always regretted) I have been anxious that it should be understood that we as publishers do not endorse the sentiments—much less that I should return the many courtesies and the liberal confidence which has been extended to me in England, by *writing* such a book."[62] In his next breath, however, he returned to his typical posture of American defense, a Putnam's last stand from which he budged neither then nor later: "It is folly to suppose that 'Men and Manners' in America do not present in some respects, fair marks to criticism, censure and ridicule—and so far as Mr. Dickens' 'Notes' are concerned I think there was nothing to object to, though much more might have been expected. Travellers magnify the sins, and leave the virtues to take care of themselves."

The article in the *American Book Circular* was for Putnam a warm-up to the full-length defense of America he worked on intermittently for the next two years. Talk about his "seventh wonder" must have filled the household during the many months Putnam gathered and processed information culled from sources near and far.[63] Carefully titling the resultant book *American Facts* and putting it to press in London in 1845, Putnam offered it to the public with a disarmingly modest remark: "It does not aim at a display of fine writing; it is merely a collection of plain, unadorned notes, relative to the progress and present condition of the United States."[64] In truth, that compilation of "plain unadorned notes" and statistics, overwritten throughout with a stridently nationalistic argument, might more accurately have been called an American polemic, a mode of discourse into which Putnam, like many of his fellow cultural nationalists of the 1840s, easily fell. As a token of American enterprise applied to the printing process, he had his book illustrated with portraits of distinguished American men via the new process of anastatic printing.[65] With so much of Putnam's personal and national pride invested in the book, it is not surprising that Victorine reported back to the family in New York his high hopes for it, tempered by her mock-seriousness: "He is writing a book that is going to create a wonderful sensation, and will spread his fame to the uttermost bounds of creation."[66]

The views put forth in the book were the same culturally nationalistic views that Putnam had expressed two years before and that he would continue to express throughout his publishing career. They were presented in the bibliographical mode in which Putnam felt most comfortable. Essentially a work of compilation limited in its grace and sophistication rather than a work of critical acumen, *American Facts* nevertheless made a serious contribution to current thinking about the size, nature, and status of literary culture in the United States. It did so by assembling a wider variety of facts and statistics about the geo-political structure of the country and about American productivity in the useful and fine arts than was then available outside the Census returns and by disseminating such information to the general reading public. More important, it not only centralized a great deal of information not previously easily accessible to the public but attached it to a narrative of American material and cultural productivity that became a central component of the developing American self-image at mid-century. In future years, the progressivist views and nationalistic rhetoric of antebellum books like *American Facts* would provide an attractive ideological narrative that supported and guided the activity of mid-nineteenth-century American writers and publishers (as they would underwrite the nationalistically minded, meliorist historiography of twentieth-century literary and cultural historians).

It was this talent for popularizing information rather than for sophisticated critical thinking and writing that was always Putnam's strength as a writer and publisher. In *American Facts,* he employed it in documenting the achievements made by Americans of recent years. Although much of the general statistical information he used came from published sources (such as the 1840 census returns and the annual volumes of the *American Almanac,* whose London edition he published), a sizable amount of the information he gave on book production and authorship came from his own investigation. The range of Putnam's knowledge of the writers and artists of his generation, much of it made on the basis of personal acquaintanceship, was impressive, even though the taste it expressed was hardly original and in certain regards strikingly conservative. Although he was well aware of the talent of Emerson and Hawthorne, the example he gave of a poem that "will live as American poetry" was Longfellow's "Psalm of Life."[67] Even the operative definition of culture he worked with was conservative, a definition that assumed culture to be Anglo-American in nature and most available first and foremost to people of that heritage. Of immigrants, then arriving in America in unprecedented numbers, he was generally suspicious, as he was of the ability of people of non-English blood to absorb and contribute to Anglo-American culture.[68] But overriding these specific limitations was his firm belief in the value of print, the underlying subject of the project itself.

Putnam correctly anticipated that his vehement defense of America would give offense to many Europeans. The mixed reviews the book got were probably the best reception he could have expected in London, where one journal referred to Putnam as "the crack American publisher in England" and another to his book as "the best collection of American Facts that has yet been made." To the level-headed critic in the *Athenaeum,* the book presented a powerful case for "a progress in national prosperity unexampled in the history of the world," but he doubted that such was the case of the individual American citizen and remained unpersuaded that the cultural level of the country was up to that of England.[69] To the right of the *Athenaeum,* the criticism was tougher. But the familiar chorus of smug condescension from the conservative press did less to upset Putnam than did the positive remarks of American correspondents like Charles Sumner, George Hillard, Edward Everett (then American minister to England), and others to sustain his faith in his project. More important, he would live to see much of his public rhetoric became part of the conventional wisdom of his society.

Putnam was not at all prepared, however, for the attack that came from where he least expected it—not only from back home but from his old friend and new colleague Evert Duyckinck. Recently hired by Wiley to oversee the firm's foray into literary publishing, Duyckinck had written privately to Putnam to state his disapproval of the book and to forewarn him that he was coming out with a review in the *Democratic Review*. In the review Duyckinck objected, in the first place, to the book as arguing a self-defeating proposition that no self-possessed nation of Western Europe would ever think to adopt and, in the second place, to its author as being a man "out of his element as a critic."[70] Putnam was so outraged by Duyckinck's charges and so hurt by what he considered the violation of their friendship that, after protesting to Duyckinck that "any one who 'makes a book' must be very weak if he considers himself annihilated by every harsh word which may be said or written about it," he proceeded to defend himself and his work with a four-page refutation.[71] He readily admitted to Duyckinck his limitations: "I know my station and am conscious fully that I am no 'Edinburgh reviewer' and cannot boast of graduating even at a grammar school." He stood firm, however, on his knowledge of European cultural condescension and on the need to defend American integrity. That stance might have been a justifiable one for a person to make after living more than a half-dozen years overseas in close quarters with Europeans and European bookmakers, but Putnam was apparently unaware that much of the anger he felt was at his own vulnerability—the vulnerability, ironically, of the author to tough and, in this case, perceptive criticism. His dignity, he clearly felt, was at stake: "You have abused and rather made fun of me in print before some thousands."[72] This was hardly Duyckinck's point or intention, but his criticism of Putnam was sharp: Putnam not only knew the terms of publishing much better than he did those of authorship but felt personally more comfortable playing the role of the former.

Fortunately for both men, their disagreement over the worth of *American Facts* did not damage their working relationship, which was just then entering a stage of close collaboration resulting from the firm's recent decision to launch itself aggressively into literary publishing.[73] With Duyckinck managing editorial affairs from the Broadway office and Putnam working the field from London to Paris, that partnership was to yield more gratifying professional rewards than either man had yet known in his career. For Putnam, the work he did during his final years in London, 1845–47, marked the culmination of his activity in the international book trade and of his decade-long partnership in Wiley and Putnam.

Notes

1. It is quite possible that GPP had considered returning to England on the ship. GHP reported his father as having told him that he had booked return passage on the *President* but was forced by business complications to cancel at the last moment; *George Palmer Putnam,* 1:104.

2. The letter was printed in the *New World* 2 (22 May 1841): 336.

3. GPP to Victorine Haven, 1 February 1841; HP-LC.

4. Victorine Haven Putnam to Catherine Hunt Putnam and Elizabeth Putnam Smith, 3 November 1844; HP-LC.

5. Her letters of this period do not survive, but her sentiments can be inferred from GPP's responses; GPP to Victorine Haven, n.d. [June 1840]; HP-LC.

6. GPP to Victorine Haven, 1 November 1840; HP-LC.

7. Lydia Sigourney to GPP, 17 October 1845; GPP-P.

8. Though vaguely liberal in his politics and democratic in his sympathies, GPP was not a worldly or politically driven man. He brought the same broad curiosity to relations with emigrés that he did to all his relations. As early as his 1836 tour through the Continent, he made contact with the exiled Polish leader Adam Jerzy Czartoryski, whom he looked up in Paris and with whom he discussed the abandonment of Poland by the Western European powers and the situation of the Polish immigrant community in America. GPP, "Random Passages," *Knickerbocker* 10 (September 1837): 250–51.

His son guesses that it might have been his father's ignorance of foreign languages and his broadly sympathetic views that drew emigrés to him and his home; they might well have seen it as a safe house for them and their discussions; GHP, *George Palmer Putnam,* 1:73–77.

9. Catherine Hunt Putnam to GPP, 5 August 1844; HP-LC.

10. Victorine Haven Putnam to Catherine Hunt Putnam, 2 May 1844; HP-LC.

11. Entry in letter book, note from John Murray to Wiley and Putnam, 3 October 1840; archive of John Murray Ltd. I am indebted to James J. Barnes for alerting me to the presence of this item in the Murray archive.

12. *Wiley and Putnam's Literary News-Letter* 1 (September 1841): 8.

13. Occasional advertisements were printed in the *New World*.

14. See James J. Barnes, *Authors, Publishers and Politicians: The Quest for an Anglo-American Copyright Agreement, 1815–1854* (London: Routledge and Kegan Paul, 1974), 34–35. Wiley and Putnam's competition with Craighead did not prevent the firm from continuing to use his fine printing and stereotyping facilities for some of its books.

Among the books that Craighead manufactured for the firm were Poe's *Tales* in 1845 and Melville's *Typee* in 1846.

15. As late as 1846 the firm continued to advertise its ability to import original editions of English periodicals into New York a week to ten days in advance of reprinted editions and to do so at the relatively cheap annual prices of $3.50 for quarterlies and $4.50 for monthlies. These terms were offered in a Wiley and Putnam circular dated February 1846, at Houghton Library, Harvard University.

16. Benjamin even did GPP the kindness to insert a favorable blurb in his journal for *The Tourist in Europe; American Monthly Magazine* 5 (April 1838): 384.

17. See the letter from Dickens to Wiley and Putnam (or Putnam) of 31 August 1838 printed in GHP, *George Palmer Putnam,* 2:271. The original letter, from which GHP printed this excerpted version, is not extant in GPP-P.

18. A 10 April 1841 letter from Benjamin to GPP followed him across the Atlantic only a week or two after his departure. The original is in GPP-P; its text is printed in GHP, *George Palmer Putnam,* 1:111–12.

There is good reason to believe that GPP and Benjamin had a personal relationship, going back to the 1830s, that antedated their professional dealings. GHP mentions Benjamin as having been a boarder at Catherine Hunt Putnam's house on McDougal Street in New York (1:46), where the two young literary men presumably met. Furthermore, according to one source, Benjamin's first wife was Catherine Hunt Putnam's niece, whose mother, Amelia Curtis, was the only immediate family member Mrs. Putnam had living in New York at the time of her own move; see the family tree printed as an appendix to Frederick Tupper and Helen Tyler Brown, eds., *Grandmother Tyler's Book: The Recollections of Mary Palmer Tyler* (New York: G. P. Putnam's Sons, 1925), 329.

19. Journal entry of 14 July 1780; in Katharine C. Balderston, ed., *Thraliana: The Diary of Hester Lynch Thrale,* 2 vols. (Oxford: Clarendon Press, 1951), 1:446n4.

20. See *New World* 3 (25 September 1841): 204; 3 (30 October 1841): 284; and 3 (4 December 1841): 368.

21. Victorine Haven Putnam to Catherine Hunt Putnam, n.d. [c. February 1846]; HP-LC.

22. On pirated American editions of Borrow, see Michael Collie and Angus Fraser, *George Borrow: A Bibliographical Study* (Winchester, Eng.: St. Paul's Bibliographies, 1984), 29–34.

23. Ibid., 32–34.

24. Park Benjamin, "Cheap Publications, Trash, etc.," *New World* 6 (20 May 1843): 598.

25. The issue arose when GHP agreed in the late 1890s to issue new editions of Borrow's works and a new biography of Borrow by the American academic William I. Knapp jointly in New York and London with the new generation of John Murray. The negotiations between the two publishers and Knapp proved to be protracted and frustrating, continuing over three years and stretching GHP's patience with "this rather 'difficult' author" to the breaking point. The main source of friction between Knapp and GHP, it turned out, was, ironically, the author's late insistence that the New York edition be typeset separately in the United States in order to protect his copyright in both countries—this for a book that GHP, himself an important player in the events culminating in the international copyright treaty signed by the two countries in 1891, considered not likely to attract pirates. The negotiations finally ended in 1898 with an agreement roughly satisfactory to all three parties—or so GHP believed until he saw in the just-issued London edition of Knapp's *Life, Writings and Correspondence of George Borrow* a reference to Wiley and Putnam's American edition of *The Zincali* as having been pirated.

Calling that charge "a reflection on the good faith of my father's publishing concern," GHP could not let it pass unchallenged, going so far as to issue a counterclaim that neither Wiley and Putnam nor its successor, G. P. Putnam, had ever issued an unauthorized edition of an English work. Apparently lacking business records of his own going back to that period, GHP asked Murray to look through his, firmly expecting that Murray would find corroborating evidence for that claim. Murray did honor that request but found no information either to confirm or to deny GHP's assertion. In the meantime, GHP unilaterally altered the text of Knapp's biography for the New York edition in such a way as to redirect Knapp's original charge of piracy from "Wiley and Putnam" to "W." and urged Murray to do likewise in his firm's London edition. After putting the matter to Knapp, who resolutely defended his assertion, Murray declined to accept GHP's suggestion.

So the matter remained until early 1900, when GHP, still irked by the imputation made by Knapp against his father, raised the matter a second time. He had recently checked through his father's correspondence books and found an angry exchange of letters between GPP and Harper and Brothers in 1851 concerning his father's charge against them of reprinting his authorized edition of Borrow's *Lavengro,* the Harpers' countercharge that they did so only in retaliation for GPP's reprinting against several of their books, and GPP's response that he had published the works in question with the permission of their author. Using these letters as blanket proof of his father's innocence, GHP concluded that "all the business that [GPP] had done in the publication of English books had been done under arrangements which were proposed or were made satisfactory to the English authors and publishers."

The file of letters concerning the Putnam-Murray joint republication of Borrow and their publication of Knapp's *Life,* which is as illuminating on late-nineteenth-century transatlantic publishing as it is on the specific case of Borrow, is in the John Murray Ltd. archive. Especially revealing are the following letters: GHP to Murray, 4 December 1894; GHP to Murray, 29 August 1898; GHP to Murray, 7 October 1898; GHP to Murray, 14 October 1898; GHP to Murray, 19 December 1898; W. I. Knapp to Murray, 5 January 1899; GHP to Murray, 30 January 1900.

26. Michael Collie, *George Borrow: Eccentric* (Cambridge: Cambridge University Press, 1982): 183.

27. GPP to Robert Cooke (of John Murray), 24 April 1846; John Murray Ltd. archive.

28. Ibid.

29. A record of his note to GPP was written into Murray's copybook, at the back of which is the list of books he offered to GPP and the terms on which he offered them; John Murray Ltd. archive.

30. The essay was "Experience," published in *Essays: Second Series* (Boston: James Munroe and Company, 1844), 70.

Even Charles Dickens, one of the most victimized objects of international piracy and consequently most outspoken English advocates of international copyright, opined at times that a compromise between literary ideals and market realities had to be reached. This was the essence of the advice, for example, that he gave in late 1842 to the American writer and copyright proponent Cornelius Mathews, who had sought his advice at a time when he was negotiating to purchase *Brother Jonathan,* a magazine whose publishing niche was as a reprinter of European works: "As to your using the works of British Authors, there can be no doubt that you would be justified in doing so, while matters remain as they are; and that the best return you could make, would be the advocacy of an honorable and honest change." But such an editorial policy, he added, would probably limit the journal's circulation in its competition with journals unregulated by similar scruples. Madeline House, Graham Storey, W. J. Carlton, Philip Collins, K. J. Fielding, and Kathleen Tillotson, eds., *The Letters of Charles Dickens,* 10 vols. (Oxford: Clarendon Press, 1965–), 3:406.

31. The best source for reconstructing Carlyle's relations with Wiley and Putnam is in the correspondence between him and Emerson and in GPP's correspondence. The following account relies in particular on the following: Charles Richard Sanders, Kenneth J. Fielding, Clyde de L. Ryals, et al., eds., *The Collected Letters of Thomas and Jane Welsh Carlyle,* 26 vols. (Durham: Duke University Press, 1970–); Ralph L. Rusk and Eleanor M. Tilton, eds., *The Letters of Ralph Waldo Emerson,* 10 vols. (New York: Columbia University Press, 1939, 1990–95); and Joseph Slater, ed., *The Correspondence of Emerson and Carlyle* (New York: Columbia University Press, 1964).

32. These details are stated in Emerson's letter to Carlyle, 15 December 1845; Slater, ed., *Emerson and Carlyle,* 386.

33. Sanders, Fielding, Ryals, et al., eds., *Collected Letters,* 20:93–94.

34. Ibid., 20:93.

35. Slater, ed., *Emerson and Carlyle,* 397.

36. Carlyle gave these details of their conversation in letters to Emerson on 30 April 1846 and to his brother John on 3 May 1846; Sanders, Fielding, Ryals, et al., eds., *Collected Letters,* 20:183–84, 186.

Clark was not only a sharp-eyed clerk but also a Carlyle devoté; he inserted more than one thousand plates and portraits into his leather rebound copy of *Sartor Resartus;* Leon Jackson, "The Reader Retailored: Thomas Carlyle, His American Audiences, and the Politics of Evidence," *Book History* 2 (1999): 156.

37. Sanders, Fielding, Ryals, et al., eds., *Collected Letters,* 20:115.

38. Even before receiving Carlyle's letter, Emerson had made up his mind about the advantageousness of making an inclusive deal for Carlyle's books with a single publisher rather than the catch-as-catch-can individual deals he had been making for years. Somewhat reluctantly, he decided that the publisher best situated to do justice to Carlyle was Wiley and Putnam and informed Wiley (of whom he had a lower estimation than of GPP, "[who] seems eager to stand well and rightly with his fellow men") of this decision in a letter dated 9 April 1846 that offered his firm the right to print "a correct and uniform" edition of Carlyle's works, subject to Carlyle's approval. The original of this letter is not in GPP-P, but its text is given in GHP, *George Palmer Putnam,* 1:164–65. On Emerson's opinions of Wiley and GPP, see his letter to Carlyle of 15 July 1846 in Slater, ed., *Emerson and Carlyle,* 403.

39. The text of that statement was inscribed in Carlyle's letter of 15 June 1846 to GPP; Sanders, Fielding, Ryals, et al., eds., *Collected Letters,* 20:203.

40. For bibliographical details of these editions, see Rodger L. Tarr, *Thomas Carlyle: A Descriptive Bibliography* (Pittsburgh: University of Pittsburgh Press, 1989).

41. Sanders, Fielding, Ryals, et al., eds., *Collected Letters,* 21:206.

42. Taking as his source the 16 December 1845 advertisement in the New York *Tribune,* Rodger Tarr lists the price for the work as $1. Actually, that advertisement covered only the first volume; Tarr, *Thomas Carlyle,* 113.

Although Tarr lists the priority of the two issues as "undetermined" (112), I think it clear that Wiley and Putnam followed the usual procedure of publishing the more expensive clothbound issue first. Wiley and Putnam advertisements inserted into the paperbound issue of *Cromwell* for published and forthcoming titles in the Library of Choice Reading include several titles not listed in the advertisements inserted into the clothbound issue of *Cromwell.*

43. GPP to Carlyle, 15 May 1847; Houghton Library, Harvard University.

44. Sanders, Fielding, Ryals, et al., eds., *Collected Letters,* 22:79–80.

45. Tarr, *Thomas Carlyle,* 110.

46. Ibid., 105–6.

47. A squib in the February 1846 issue of *Appleton's Literary Bulletin* indicated that Colyer had reprinted on the Wiley and Putnam edition, an act that presumably forced Wiley and Putnam, in turn, to issue a $.50 version of its original edition.

48. The Harper brothers, Duyckinck wrote GPP, had warned Wiley of imminent retaliation against the firm for "the wrongs and injustices inflicted by you [Putnam] as their confidential agent in sending new books to Wiley and Putnam." Their anger, he claimed, led not only to the reprinting of Wiley and Putnam books by Colyer and by the Harpers but to the end of GPP's overseas agency for the Harpers; Duyckinck to GPP, 7 February 1846; GPP-P.

In truth, the Harpers had good reason for their growing distrust of GPP, who was diverting books that might otherwise have gone to them to his own firm. One case in point was *Sketches from Life* by the recently deceased Laman Blanchard. GPP had obtained a copy of the sheets from its publisher Henry Colburn with the Harpers in mind but admitted to Evert Duyckinck: "I am strongly tempted to *appropriate* the book.... I shall not decide 'till the last moment which parcel recieves [sic] the book." *Sketches from Life* was published the following year by Wiley and Putnam as part of its Library of Choice Reading. GPP to Duyckinck, 3 December 1845; D-NYPL.

Sure enough, the Harpers broke their agreement with GPP and hired as their new agent Sampson Low, a well-placed London publisher who was the proprietor of *Publishers' Circular;* see James L. W. West III, "Book Publishing 1835–1900: The Anglo-American Connection," *Papers of the Bibliographical Society of America* 84 (December 1990): 363.

49. This was hardly the only time that Wiley and Putnam would cross paths with Colyer and the Harpers in competition for the reprint market. Another important book the company squabbled over with Colyer, and no doubt with other New York publishers as well, was Robert Chambers's *Vestiges of the Natural History of Creation,* which was originally published in 1844 in London by John Churchill. Although no documentation survives, it seems likely that Putnam heard of the book in London and, thinking it a worthwhile publication for his firm to issue in New York, followed his customary pattern and arranged with the publisher for American rights to the work. But the 1845 Wiley and Putnam edition of *Vestiges,* the first American printing of this important predecessor to the work of Darwin, did not monopolize the American market for long; Colyer came out with a pirated edition by 1846 and the Harpers in 1847 with their own $.37 ½ edition, both undoubtedly designed to undersell the Wiley and Putnam edition. I am indebted to Robert Scholnick for turning my attention to the competition for *Vestiges.*

50. Sanders, Fielding, Ryals, et al., eds., *Collected Letters,* 23:25–26. The likelihood exists, however, that Carlyle did receive payment from Wiley and Putnam after the semi-annual accounting done on 1 January and 1 July 1848. The firm's accounts for those periods show a balance owed to Carlyle, after expenses, of $123.88 and $233.77, respectively, although they do not indicate whether payment ensued. A copy of the account sheets, apparently sent from Carlyle to Clark and from Clark to Emerson, was deposited in the Ralph Waldo Emerson Memorial Association papers now at Houghton Library, Harvard University. I owe thanks to Leon Jackson for turning my attention to them.

51. GPP to E. P. Clark, 19 June 1848; Houghton Library, Harvard University. It is unknown whether GPP paid any royalties to Carlyle (directly or indirectly through Wiley) on the remaindered copies of the Wiley and Putnam clothbound edition of *Cromwell* that he sold that year under his own imprint. It is also unknown whether the Harpers ever

paid royalties on their editions of *Cromwell,* which they printed from the Wiley and Putnam stereotype plates, beginning with their 1851 edition of *Cromwell.* A plainer one than GPP's in typography, the Harper edition differed textually from GPP's primarily in the engraving of Cromwell that the Harpers substituted for the Chapman and Hall engraving used by GPP as the frontispiece to volume 1 and in the inclusion of the Supplement, which had been printed independently in England, at the end of volume 2.

52. Sanders, Fielding, Ryals, et al., eds., *Collected Letters,* 20:186n.

53. In "Signs of the Times," which was originally published in the *Edinburgh Review* of 1829 and republished in Carlyle's *Critical and Miscellaneous Essays.* I am indebted to my colleague Patrick Scott for turning my attention to this citation.

54. Sedgwick to GPP, 1 July 1839; Berkshire Athenaeum, Pittsfield, Mass.

55. He stated as its goal: "The object is simply to collect such facts as may show the progress of American literature and the tastes of the people, as indicated by the supply of different branches of reading and knowledge: in short, to make up a chapter of the statistics of Book-making in the United States, for no invidious purpose, but as a contribution to the 'Curiosities of Literature.'" The copy of the circular sent to Jared Sparks, dated 2 August 1843, is at Houghton Library, Harvard University.

56. The article is dated "London, March 31, 1843," and was printed by Manning and Mason, the firm's favorite London printers. Although unsigned and unidentified except as being the research of an American, it is clearly the work of GPP.

57. *History of Europe, from the Commencement of the French Revolution to the Restoration of the Bourbons,* 10 vols. (Edinburgh and London: W. Blackwood and Sons, 1842), 10:624. GPP printed this passage as the epigraph to his essay.

58. The much cheaper price of the Harper edition was construed by some commentators as a proof of the desirability of the current system of copyright-unregulated transatlantic trade. See Eugene Exman, *The Brothers Harper* (New York: Harper and Row, 1965), 161–62.

59. GPP, *American Facts* (London: Wiley and Putnam, 1845), 76.

60. He published this information in his letter of 1 May 1841 to the *New World* 2 (29 May 1841): 352. Moxon's regard for the work was genuine; he was eager to discuss the work in 1850 when Herman Melville came calling at his London office; Lynn Horth, ed., *Correspondence,* vol. 14 of *The Writings of Herman Melville* (Evanston: Northwestern University Press, 1993), 161–62.

61. Dickens to Carlyle, 18 April 1843; House, Storey, et al., eds., *Letters of Charles Dickens,* 3:473–74.

62. GPP to Murray, 11 January 1844; John Murray Ltd. archive.

63. Victorine, who had recently complained to her mother-in-law that GPP "is so awfully busy that there is no getting a word from him that does not savor of Shop," wrote her again near the end of the process: "George is still engaged correcting the proof-sheets of his seventh wonder; I shall be almost glad when it is published, then he will be a little more sociable." Victorine Haven Putnam to Catherine Hunt Putnam, 2 December 1844 and 23 February 1845; HP-LC.

64. *American Facts,* v.

65. GPP (and a small number of his contemporaries, including Poe) considered anastatic printing a historical breakthrough in the reproduction in print of facsimiles taken from engravings or letter press. In his monthly letter (dated 1 February 1845) of literary intelligence printed in *Wiley and Putnam's Literary News-Letter,* GPP raved about the technological leap the new process introduced: "The importance of this great discovery can scarcely be over-rated; it is next to that of printing itself. Stereotyping will now be entirely suspended"; *Wiley and Putnam's Literary News-Letter* 4 (March 1845): 297. This

did not happen in GPP's lifetime, but his prediction proved prophetic: our own time has seen the widespread adoption of offset photo-lithography in book printing.

66. Victorine Haven Putnam to Catherine Hunt Putnam, 26 January 1845; HP-LC.

67. *American Facts,* 101.

68. Ibid., 153–54. GPP did, however, publish that year *Wiley and Putnam's Emigrant Guide,* a pocket-sized volume of useful information addressed to prospective immigrants to the New World and designed to educate them about American society and to facilitate their crossing.

69. *Athenaeum,* no. 915 (10 May 1845): 459.

70. [Duyckinck], "Notices of New Books," *United States Magazine and Democratic Review* 16 (May 1845): 507–9.

71. GPP to Duyckinck, 27 June 1845; D-NYPL. He was still simmering over the review two months later when he next wrote Duyckinck, protesting that the review was "inconsistent, untrue, unjust and uncalled for." GPP to Duyckinck, 18 August 1845; D-NYPL.

72. GPP to Duyckinck, 18 August 1845; D-NYPL.

73. Duyckinck attempted to smooth the waters between them by replying to GPP's letter that he had not volunteered to write the review for the *Democratic Review* and that, in any case, he continued to feel only the warmest sentiments toward GPP: "If I have wounded your self love I apologize for I would not offend one with whom my relations have been and always ought to be agreeable." At the same time, he stood firmly by his critique of *American Facts.* Duyckinck to GPP, 29 July 1845; D-NYPL.

CHAPTER 6

International Dealings in American Books, 1845–1847

The last several years of his partnership with Wiley involved Putnam in the most exciting, satisfying work he was to do in the international book trade. Years of hard work now resulted in expanded social and professional ties in England and allowed him to entertain both at home and at work on a scale previously beyond his means. In March 1844 he moved his business from Paternoster Row to more spacious, expensive quarters at Waterloo Place and named his new offices the American Literary Agency.[1] Stocking one of its rooms with American newspapers, magazines, and books in imitation of the *cabinets de lecture* he frequented on his trips to Paris and putting on exhibit paintings lent to him by leading artists (such as Catlin and Asher B. Durand), he proudly oversaw his early outpost of American culture.[2] As usual, Putnam had no lack of visitors to show around, his office by then a well-known address to visiting Americans as well as residents of the city. Among the stream of visitors to the agency during 1845–46 were three men with whom he would have important professional dealings: Bayard Taylor, to whom he gave temporary work at the store; Gansvoort Melville, the older brother and literary agent of Herman; and Washington Irving, later in the decade to become his most valuable author. The presence of all three visitors testified to the risen status of Putnam's position as a public figure, but the circumstances of Taylor's acquaintance with his future publisher are particularly revealing. Then an aspirant writer with high ambitions, Taylor was on the return leg of a literary-inspired tour of Europe, which had been financed primarily by the letters he sent back to American newspapers. Finding himself nearly penniless while waiting for a check from New York and unable to get employment in London, he remembered having heard of the existence of a London branch of an American publishing house. Inquiring the address at a local bookseller, he walked over to the American Literary Agency and made the acquaintance of "Mr. Putnam," as he called him in his popular account of his travels through Europe published later that year by Wiley and Putnam.[3] By that time, "Putnam" was a name familiar enough to have been recognizable to many of the readers of the firm's books.

A year after Putnam moved his offices, he moved his family to a house on Mornington Road near Regents Park. Buying their own furniture for the first time and patriotically naming their house Knickerbocker Cottage, the Putnams were now able to live more comfortably and entertain more freely than when they had occupied rented rooms. Once the family was installed in its new home, Putnam renewed his earlier hope and invited his mother to come live with them and help educate a new generation of Putnams, but she again declined to leave New York. Intensely sociable people who still had not overcame their feelings of strangeness in England and remoteness from family back home, the Putnams welcomed this opportunity to fashion a social life more congenial to themselves. Occasionally they gave large, formal parties for the American community and local friends, but more typically they hosted small gatherings of friends and clients over dinner, as, for example, when they invited Washington Irving, William Beattie, and William Howitt to the house in 1846 to help celebrate Putnam's thirty-second birthday. He also enjoyed inviting American travelers passing through the city, many of whom frequented the American Literary Agency. On one occasion, he delighted his daughter Mary, probably only three or four at the time, by inviting Tom Thumb for a summer tea party; the memory of the young man seated in her child's chair along with the other guests around the family's mahogany serving table remained with her through life. Putnam also liked to bring home prospective clients for dinner, perhaps calculating the effect that Victorine's charm and beauty would have in helping him to win their accounts. Because Putnam worked such extended hours, their opportunities to go out evenings were few, although they had live-in help and frequent access to free tickets through such visitors as the actor Edwin Forrest. But they did see occasional shows; in the case of the Hutchinsons, a touring American family of singers, they made it a point to see all four of their shows in London.

With more room for living and entertaining and easy access to Regents Park, which Putnam considered the most beautiful in London, the family settled into a more expansive style of life. On Sundays, Putnam enjoyed taking Mary on walks through the park and its zoological gardens, although she and her increasingly mobile brother could also play in the small garden off the drawing room outside their house. The relatively spacious interior provided the parents ample room not only for themselves but also for their live-in helpers. Their main room was the sitting room on the ground floor, where Putnam liked to sit at night in a rocking chair and read while Victorine sat in an easy chair opposite her work table. Across the room was the sideboard where Putnam proudly kept, under lock and key, his growing autograph and portrait collection. Victorine had her own library in her bedroom, as well as a writing table and piano. Several months after they took possession of the cottage, they were able to adorn the walls of one of its rooms with three paintings left in their care by the landscape artist Thomas Doughty, an acquaintance of Putnam's.[4]

Their new scale of living was not without its price. Putnam had not only his business operation in London and his growing family to finance but also his recently retired mother, to whom he regularly sent checks (usually via his cousin Elizabeth Palmer Peabody in Boston). A number of the letters he and Victorine sent home to family in the mid-1840s contain his postscripts lamenting the high cost of living and doing business in London. He clearly felt pressed to justify himself to a disgruntled John Wiley, who complained about the mounting expenses and perhaps requested an accounting. Much as his complaint stung both Putnam and Victorine, it quite possibly was justified. As would be the case in later phases of his life, Putnam was pushing his expenses right up to the limits of his income.

During these years Putnam continued to travel to Paris with some frequency, where he made arrangements for the sale of French books and periodicals to American buyers. During some of these trips, he ventured beyond Paris on book-buying expeditions that took him as far as Italy and Germany. Well provided with letters of introduction, he was able to gain access to some of the leading libraries and collections of Europe and bought heavily for his main private client, James Lenox of New York, and his major institutional clients, college libraries such as Harvard, Yale, and South Carolina College.[5] Whereas American bookbuyers historically had had little choice but to do most of their purchasing in Europe, there was something new about the trips that agents like Putnam made on their behalf in the 1840s. In a period of rising wealth and commercialism, Americans with more money to spend found an increasing number of European fine book collections making their way to the market and becoming available for American dollars converted to pounds.

On those fast-paced trips to public and private libraries, Putnam must have presented himself as a type of the American businessman increasingly familiar to European eyes. The type would certainly be recognizable as such to the young Henry James from his early travels on the Continent. In his postbellum *The American,* he created a version of the mythic American of his time in Christopher Newman, a California businessman arrived in Paris in the 1860s with deep pockets and the ambition to possess "the best article in the market." In the novel's delightfully perceptive opening scene, James situated Newman in the Louvre with a one-word French vocabulary ("combien") and the desire to purchase a copyist's rendering of one of the museum's paintings, a forerunner of the flesh and blood French woman he meant to possess and bring back with him to America. A generation earlier, Putnam was already buying Europe by the pound.

Once or twice Putnam was joined on these forays by his new friend and ally of sorts, Henry Stevens, a fellow Yankee booktrader of uncommon bibliographic expertise and commercial book sense who would soon distinguish himself as one of the most successful international book dealers of the nineteenth century.[6] Graduated from Yale in 1843 and possessed of a sharp bibliographical mind honed by experience in dealings with leading American book collectors and libraries, Stevens arrived in London in summer 1845, as he later put it, "a self-appointed missionary, on an antiquarian and historical book-hunting expedition, at my own expense and on my own responsibility, with a few Yankee notions in my head and an ample fortune of nearly forty

sovereigns in my pocket."[7] Supplied with commissions from John
Carter Brown, Henry Murphy, and other collectors back home and possessed of letters of introduction to various bookmen in London, most
notably Antonio Panizzi of the British Museum, Stevens quickly set
about making himself the leading American bookdealer in Europe. To
do so he needed to be in touch with leading local booksellers; one of the
most useful to him in getting established was the man he took to calling
"friend Putnam," whom he might or might not already have known
from earlier days.[8] For his part, Putnam was so thoroughly taken with
Stevens's charm and knowledge that he invited Stevens to stay at
Knickerbocker Cottage and to take up a desk at his office until Stevens
could make his own arrangements. During part of 1846, Stevens occupied the spare bedroom at the Putnams' home, which they gladly
offered him after finally giving up hope that Catherine Hunt Putnam
would accept their longstanding invitation. Routinely, the two men
walked together along Putnam's favorite path in London, which took
them by Regents Park and down Portland Place and Regents Street
to his office. While Putnam was back in the United States in summer
1846 transacting book business related in part to Stevens's connection with the British Museum, Stevens helped out at the office and
accompanied Victorine and the children during part of their annual
vacation to Ramsgate and joined them on their visit to Canterbury
Cathedral.[9]

By that time, though, Stevens was well on his way to making his
own career in the book world and was doing so with such verve that
he soon had more to teach than to learn from a veteran of the trade like
Putnam. Prospects for a career in London were so inviting that within
months of his arrival Stevens was to find, as Putnam had nearly a
decade earlier, that it was possible for an American bookman short on
cash but long on book sense and business acumen to fashion a comfortable niche for himself in the international book trade. And, again as
with Putnam, the general niche that Stevens made for himself was that
primarily of the Yankee bookdealer in Europe, if on the more specialized level of rare books. Disporting his way through the prime book
fields of Europe, Stevens maintained a characteristically nationalistic
élan, one sign of which was the mock-honorific GMB (for Green Mountain Boys) he took to signing after his name. That élan, which he was
adept at displaying or hiding as situations warranted, he typically
exhibited in his correspondence with patriotic clients back home. One

of the most important of them was the American historian Jared Sparks, to whom he expressed his New Year's intention in 1846 to visit the descendant of the royal governor of New York, Edmund Andros, and "yankee" him out of his ancestor's papers and portraits.[10] Judged by his own standards, Stevens was to prove himself the consummate Yankee in the nineteenth-century international book trade.

Andros would not have been the only one "yankee[d]" out of his literary treasures by Henry Stevens. Stevens was an extraordinarily shrewd assessor and salesman of fine books who was every bit the match for publishers, dealers, librarians, and collectors alike. For nearly four decades, Stevens made his career in Europe buying manuscripts and books relating primarily to the Americas and selling them, often at hefty markups, to well-to-do clients on both sides of the ocean. Stevens had initially had no more intention than Putnam of remaining permanently in London, but his role of international book buyer and seller operating as a toll bridge between New World and Old World book traffic proved so successful that he remained there his entire life and built a "book brokerage" business (as Hawthorne called it upon making Stevens's acquaintance in 1856) successful enough to pass on to his son. Shrewd though his business talent was, the basis of his success was as much a matter of culture as of economics.

From the moment of his arrival, Stevens took full advantage of the new market for American "antiquities" (as Putnam did of American "novelties") that was developing in the middle decades of the century. Although preceded by others, such as Obadiah Rich and Putnam, to London's rare books market, he speedily concluded that there was no one in the city, no less in the country, who could match his combination of bibliographical knowledge and business acumen. With extraordinary celerity, he forged professional ties that helped him to push ahead of his rivals; once well set up, he never looked back. Even before his arrival in London, he had made important connections with leading American book collectors, historical societies, and college libraries (especially Harvard, through Jared Sparks), who were taking an unprecedented interest in purchasing materials relating to the Americas, as well as in some cases simply in expanding their general holdings. As the son of the founder of the Vermont Historical Society and as a practiced bibliographer who had paid some of his college debts by working as a copyist for Peter Force, the pioneer collector of Americana, Stevens was intimately aware of the wave of national self-consciousness regarding their history and culture passing over his generation of Americans, which manifested itself, as he stated in one of the catalogues he compiled for clients, in the formation of "the numerous College, Athenaeum, Lyceum, Mercantile, State, Town, Village, and other libraries, more or less public, that are now so rapidly springing up in every part of the United States."[11] No less than Putnam, he was the right person at the right time to profit from that new wealth and self-consciousness by stationing himself as a gatekeeper for the traffic in New World books and manuscripts passing between the two continents.

The necessary location for satisfying that economic and cultural demand, Stevens understood, was in London, where within several months of his arrival he made the one contact that was to put enough sovereigns into his pockets to finance some of his greatest bibliographical ambitions and commercial dealings. That contact was with Antonio Panizzi and the British Museum, the stodgy institution that Panizzi, first as its keeper of printed works and then as its principal librarian, was just then dragging into the modern world and transforming into the model national library of Europe. Within months of their initial meeting, Stevens and Panizzi formed the ultimate bookmen's marriage of convenience: Panizzi offered to make Stevens the museum's exclusive supplier of books relating to the Americas, and Stevens promptly accepted, subject to a 10-percent commission on purchases. Panizzi recognized in Stevens a nonpareil bibliographer-cum-salesman of Americana whom he could use to fill one of the most gaping areas of "deficiency" in the museum's holdings, and Stevens found in Panizzi the most important patron in the English-speaking world—a patron, as luck would have it, just embarked on a massive book-buying campaign funded by an annual appropriation of £10,000. Subsidized by the museum and legitimized by its name, Stevens found himself authorized to deal on a scale that would have been incomprehensible in any earlier era of the book trade, and Panizzi found ways to utilize his talents.

A European liberal interested in the history and culture of the United States, Panizzi had consulted Wiley and Putnam's *American Book Circular* and declared in his 1846 annual report to Parliament that the museum had only 24 of the 160 standard American works in the belles lettres listed there, some of which were held only in corrupted versions published by English reprinters.[12] What Panizzi knew generally, Stevens proceeded to document specifically by poring through the collections of the museum and detailing how limited the American holdings were, totaling fewer than 4,000 books at the time Stevens first gained access to the library. Subsidized by Panizzi's largesse, Stevens moved quickly to fill that paucity, placing large orders for American books through Wiley and Putnam to New York and through William Pickering to Philadelphia. If his own figures are to be trusted, he bought and sold an additional 6,000 volumes for the museum by early 1846, a figure he increased by the tens of thousands during the next generation, turning a marginal collection of Americana into the largest and finest for its time in the world. Not only a book merchant but a bibliophile, Stevens devised a plan as early as 1846 to compile a comprehensive bibliography of American works at the British Museum and approached Putnam about its possible publication. Nothing came of that idea in the short run, although Stevens eventually published in 1866 a *Catalogue of the American Books in the Library of the British Museum.* Indeed, that idea constituted only the first step of Stevens's more sweeping ambition to write the first general descriptive bibliography of books relating to or printed in America to 1700, a work whose historical timing, he believed, was propitious.[13] But Stevens failed to take his *Bibliographia Americana* beyond the planning stage; decades later, after Joseph Sabin launched that project, he came to regret its nonexecution as a wasted opportunity.

Putnam presumably made the acquaintance of Panizzi by the mid-1840s, but there is no evidence that he ever acted directly on his behalf. Putnam made his purchases for the British Museum, rather, through Stevens. In fact, Putnam made his last trip to the United States from London, in summer 1846, at least in part to supply Stevens with books for the museum. Duyckinck reported Putnam as having arrived unannounced in New York that summer and "astonished the town" with news of the book business being done by Wiley and Putnam with Stevens and the British Museum.[14] Putnam spent much of that trip traveling between Washington and northern New England, acting on Stevens's behalf in "ransacking" collections for documents and rare books desired by the museum and bargaining to buy them on the best terms. "I am determined," he wrote Stevens after his arrival, "[the Museum business] shall be done thoroughly and faithfully and as economically as possible—to your credit and my own (to you)."[15] To effect that, he sent out circulars encouraging the individual states (and their U.S. senators) to send their public documents to the museum and visited state capitals from New York to Maine.[16] In Massachusetts and

Connecticut, he hunted up every major librarian and book collector he could find between the Connecticut River valley and the coast and filled much of the shopping list Stevens had entrusted to him at the cheapest available prices.[17]

What Stevens did not know was that Putnam's trip had an additional purpose: to win the agency of the new Smithsonian Institution, which was formally established by Congress that August. Putnam was in Washington early that month, where he spent time lobbying a number of powerful men—President Polk, Secretary of State Buchanan, Daniel Webster, George Perkins Marsh, and Peter Force—to facilitate the exchange of books between the national libraries of the United States and England. At the same time, he lobbied for his own firm. Both Putnam and the New York office wrote to Robert Dunlap, an old acquaintance of Putnam's who was then a U.S. congressman from Maine, with the request that he use his influence with the Smithsonian regents, especially Maine Senator George Evans, to help Wiley and Putnam win the London book agency of the proposed Smithsonian Institution library.[18] That request turned out to be premature, since it took months of political wrangling before the Smithsonian was organized and its individual departments became operational. Not until 1852 was a system of international exchanges established by the Smithsonian, and when that system finally came into being it was Stevens who was designated as its London agent.[19]

Inevitably, the friendly relations between Stevens and Putnam were bound to come into conflict as the balance between their interests shifted from cooperation to outright competition. The focal point of their conflict became the account of James Lenox, the man who by 1846 was each man's chief personal client in the United States. An immensely wealthy New York bibliophile with no immediate family and no profession, Lenox was by then devoting much of his time, energy, and finances to acquiring the greatest private collections of Americana and bibles in the United States. Although committed to no single agent in Europe, Lenox had been using Putnam heavily for European purchases until fall 1845, when Putnam made the mistake—as characteristic of his generosity as of his ingenuity—of mentioning Lenox to Stevens as a possible client for some of the works in American history Stevens had recently purchased. Stevens gratefully followed up on that suggestion, which led to the first in a succession of orders entrusted to him by Lenox. In sending off the earliest of these orders to Lenox,

Stevens, who kept his expenses to a minimum by renting no office of his own, used Wiley and Putnam's facilities in London for collating and shipping, for which service the firm routinely added its own 10-percent commission onto that charged by Stevens.

That arrangement, with the two agents vying for many of the same books and then charging Lenox a double commission, could not continue indefinitely. Which man precipitated its breakup is not clear; Stevens suggested that it was Lenox, concerned not only about the double commission but also about the publicity attaching to his purchases, but it is just as likely that it was actually Stevens. Whoever it was, one thing is certain: by late 1846 Stevens had utterly outmaneuvered Putnam, who lost the battle of Lenox before he was fully aware that a war of the Yankee booksellers was in progress. As the competition for Lenox from late 1846 to early 1847 clearly demonstrated, he was no match for Stevens as either a bibliographer or a businessman. Not only had Stevens, through a series of aggressive purchases, cornered the London market on rare Americana, but he persuasively presented himself to Lenox—in polite but still unmistakably clear terms—as possessing the unique combination of contacts and skills needed to supply him with the choicest bibliographical specimens to be had in Europe.[20]

In fact, the way Stevens presented himself to Lenox, whom he had not yet met, in their ongoing transatlantic correspondence makes for an exquisite study of the clash between gentlemanly and commercial values that was emerging at mid-century (one from which not even Lenox, himself in competition with other gentleman collectors, was exempt). Caught in 1846 within his own web of developing special relationships with three of the greatest book clients of the English-speaking world (Panizzi, Lenox, and John Carter Brown of Providence—all, by no coincidence, avid collectors of Americana), Stevens needed to wheel and deal in order to protect the right to first refusal he dangled before them as favored clients. In tightening the noose around Lenox, whom he was trying to draw into his orbit in 1846, he needed both to show himself to finest advantage and, distasteful though the practice might have been, to show Putnam to least advantage. A fluid and gifted correspondent, Stevens was fully up to the task.[21] Beginning in November 1846, when he was competing with Putnam for the purchase locally of Consul Thomas Aspinwall's superb collection of Americana as well as for a fine private collection in Munich rich in early printed books, Stevens was ready to attack Putnam where he was most vulnerable: as an unnecessary drain on Lenox's pocket:

> I agree with you that you should [not] pay a commission to Messrs. Wiley and Putnam and another to me, on Col. Aspinwall's Library, should you purchase it—The same also in reference to the Magen Library in Munich. Mr. Putnam has not been put to any trouble here about these matters, and as I can just as well ship the books direct to you, I do not see that he can reasonably object to this course. I have several times thought of your paying the double commissions—but as I was led to your correspondence through favor of Mr. Putnam I thought I might be considered as interfering in their business if I said any thing on the subject first. Now that *you* have alluded to it I may with justice say that it is entirely immaterial to me, and as I can just as well send you the books direct as I do Mr. [John Carter] Brown. There is no connection whatever between me and Messrs. Wiley and Putnam—any further than this, that Mr. Putnam has been a *very* kind friend to me since my arrival in England. I would not do any thing that interferes with his business. I confine myself chiefly to rare and costly books and manuscripts, of which he pretends to little knowledge.[22]

With orders he purchased on the Continent for Lenox, he continued, there would be no such problem, since he would be able to send them off directly without going through the facilities of Wiley and Putnam in either London or New York, a mode of operation he adopted by spring 1847 for Continental purchases.

It would be hard to say whether Putnam would have been more taken aback by the intelligence contained in this letter about the Aspinwall Library (which he considered his to buy due to his close personal relations with Aspinwall) or about Lenox. By this time, at least, Putnam was finally sensible of Stevens's encroachment on territory he considered his own, and he attempted to right matters with Lenox in terms that reversed Stevens's advantageous hold on him:

> As I had originally suggested to Mr. Stevens the expediency of sending you a list of some Books on America then in his possession, it may be proper for me to mention that of his recent

purchases I have not had an opportunity of judging with reference to the current market value and would therefore respectfully suggest that although the prices may in most instances be quite as low as any search could obtain the books for, yet this may not be the case with all. I mention this because in two or three instances we had already supplied Mr. Stevens with books which we afterwards found he had subsequently sent to you. I do not, of course, intend, by referring to this, any discredit to Mr. Stevens; but as I am anxious that all the business with which you favor us so liberally, should be attended to in the most economical as well as faithful manner, it might perhaps be useful to you, if your future lists of any works in this department were enclosed, unsealed, to us, enabling us to supply any that we could purchase to better advantage.

I trust you will excuse the liberty I take in making this suggestion, which is done from a good motive.[23]

The cross purposes of these two letters, which reached Lenox within days of each other, might have raised a wry smile from a more genial man. Lenox, though, was anything but amused by the inefficiency of his international transactions and was eager to resolve the matter expeditiously, which he did in mid-1847 when he took Stevens as his European agent. Given Stevens's professional skills and the greater cheapness of books encumbered by a single commission, Lenox would inevitably have made that decision, even without Stevens's strong-armed tactics. In any case, by then Putnam had returned permanently to the United States and thus unilaterally ceded the European field to Stevens.

Before he did, however, he made the most important purchase of his career on Lenox's behalf. In March 1847, Wiley and Putnam represented Lenox at the heralded auction at Sotheby's of the great Wilkes Collection of early printed works, illuminated manuscripts, and first editions of the classics. Attracting many of the leading booksellers in London and a large number of private collectors, the sale took place over an eleven-day period, which by chance coincided with the important book-buying trip (and vacation) that Putnam was making in part for Lenox to France, Italy, and Germany. Before his departure, he had instructed his associate, David Davidson, to bid on the Gutenberg Bible as well as on several other choice bibles for Lenox. For possession of the Gutenberg, Davidson was forced into a spirited competition with

4. Putnam's letter to James Lenox (19 February 1847) announcing the imminent sale of the Wilkes Collection in London, including a fine copy of the "Mazarine" or Gutenberg Bible. (Courtesy Manuscripts and Archives Division, New York Public Library)

another bidder, the great manuscript collector Sir Thomas Phillipps, which began at the extraordinarily high price of £200 and ended with Davidson finally placing the winning bid at £500. Among his other purchases that day were a copy of the first edition of the Bible printed in Paris, a 1476 Biblia Sacra Latina, and a 1470 Biblia Pauperum Germanica (reputed to be one of only two in existence).[24]

Persuading Lenox to accept the Gutenberg at the price of £500 (plus customs and commission) proved to be no easy matter for Putnam. Not only was the previous high price for a Gutenberg only £215, but the sale at Sotheby's had generated a great deal of publicity in both countries, forcing the publicity-shy Lenox into precisely the context for buying that he most disliked. Furthermore, Putnam, who had recently been buying bibles for Lenox off a list of requested items, did not transmit the Sotheby catalogue to Lenox promptly enough to allow Lenox sufficient time to send back purchase instructions. When Lenox balked at the price as excessive, Putnam had no alternative but to offer it (at a 5-percent discount) to Phillipps. Although Phillipps had excitedly bid up to £495 at the sale, his sobered response to Putnam peremptorily ended Putnam's hope: "Sir, as I would not give more than 300 pounds for the 'Mazarine Bible' [as it was familiarly called] in cold blood, there is no chance of my having the Book, and it is right that America should boast of having one copy of it. I am therefore willing to let it go, only hoping that it may not be swallowed up by the Deep Sea."[25] So the matter stood during Putnam's last days in Europe.

His participation in buying and selling in the international market was exciting work, but the most engrossing development for Putnam during the last three years of his residence in England was his fuller and more direct involvement in literary publishing. Beginning in 1845, Wiley and Putnam was making a concerted attempt to join the still small group of major American publishers. Although no match either in size or style of publishing operations to Harper and Brothers or Carey and Hart, it did move up into the second tier of the industry while continuing to rival the Appletons, its nearest model in the American book trade, as a retailer of imported and domestic books in New York. As the firm launched that initiative, Putnam's closely cultivated relations with British publishers and his proximity to the local book trade became valuable assets in the firm's competition with other American publishers for British literary material.

The publishing list of Wiley and Putnam had grown in size and quality during the early 1840s, when the largest number of its works still fell into the category of serious authorship—typically, male, scholarly, and sometimes theological. Among their more substantial titles were John Torrey and Asa Gray's *Flora of North America,* Gray's *Botanical Text-Book,* Edward Robinson's *A Hebrew and English Lexicon of the Old Testament,* Isaac Nordheimer's *Critical Grammar of the Hebrew Language,* James Dana's *A System of Mineralogy,* the English editions of Charles Wilkes's *Narrative of the United States Exploring Expedition* and of John Fremont's *Report of the Exploring Expedition to the Rocky Mountains in the Year 1842,* the important works of Andrew Jackson Downing on landscape gardening and architecture, Charles Lyell's *Travels in North America,* and Mary Howitt's early translation of Hans Christian Andersen's *Wonderful Stories for Children.* At the same time, Putnam also made arrangements, usually with local publishers, for his New York office to publish American editions of a fairly large number of works by British and Continental authors. Among the publishers with whom he made such arrangements were Edward Moxon, John Murray, and Charles Knight, all of whom published heavily in belletristic fields increasingly important to Wiley and Putnam and all men with whom Putnam maintained cordial relations.

The standard arrangement worked out between Wiley in New York and Putnam in London was this: works were generally published through the New York office which, lacking its own facilities, shipped them out to any of a small number of the better independent printing shops in the city. If market conditions and copyright agreements or limitations permitted, sheets of some works by American authors were shipped to Putnam in London, bound, and distributed by him to the local trade. Occasionally, the policy was reversed and works were published by Putnam in London, with sheets sent back to New York for distribution in America. With reprinting as common as it was, Wiley and Putnam only infrequently published works on both sides of the Atlantic.

In 1845 the scale of the firm's publishing operations changed as Wiley and Putnam expanded aggressively into literary publishing. This shift in operations developed rather dramatically and came about through a self-conscious decision made in New York by John Wiley. Although known by his colleagues in the trade (and even by associates in the firm) as a cautious, conservative man and easily underestimated by his critics, Wiley was fully capable of making and executing serious decisions.[26] A half-dozen years before, he had decided to move aggressively into the international book trade; now he committed his firm to an extensive policy of literary publishing that significantly altered the balance between its retail and publishing operations. His decision was based strictly on his reading of marketplace literary economics. Having lived through the cheap publication wars of the early 1840s, by then winding down, and seen the resultant expansion of the supply and demand for printed matter of all sorts, Wiley calculated that the time was opportune to carve out a larger niche in the expanding book publishing sector. His plan was to avoid the ferocious competition taking place at the lower price end of the market, a publishing niche in any case not normally cultivated by Wiley and Putnam, and concentrate on producing books for the firm's customary readership at the middle to upper-middle end of the market. To do this in accordance with the cheapened price and manufacturing standards then established, Wiley hoped to strike a middle-of-the-road compromise by assembling a line of high-quality books addressed to a popular readership, manufacturing them cheaply but handsomely, and selling them at the middling price of between $. 37 ½ and $.50 a volume, with many titles appearing in two-volume formats.

To implement this new policy, he needed an advisor whose range of literary knowledge surpassed his own. Early that year he filled the need smartly in signing an agreement with Evert Duyckinck to become the literary editor of the new Wiley and Putnam Library of Choice Reading, with responsibility to plan and oversee the selection of titles and their promotion for the house. Interestingly enough, Wiley apparently made this decision independently of Putnam, who was at first not aware of his friend's selection to oversee the firm's new initiative: "I am right glad to find that we are engaging the advantage of your valuable judgement in the new 'library,'" he wrote Duyckinck several months after his appointment, "It was quite evident from the first that some one of taste and common sense had had a hand [in] it, but in my very meagre advices respecting home operations, no particulars had been given of the origin, progress or direction of the enterprise."[27] Whatever their differences of business philosophy, strategy, and temperament, Wiley and Putnam were wholly in agreement about the choice of Duyckinck to direct their publishing initiative. It would not take Duyckinck long to demonstrate how wise his selection had been: within weeks of assuming his position, he distinguished himself as the outstanding literary editor then at work in New York.

Duyckinck was well known to both Putnam and Wiley long before their collaboration on the Wiley and Putnam Libraries (1845–47); in fact, the background to their collaboration is a story rich in the print history of the city and nation. As mentioned, Duyckinck and Putnam had a close relationship, dating at least to the late 1830s, a relationship that continued into the next decade as Putnam supplied Duyckinck's fine private library with European books, the several journals he edited in the early 1840s with the latest European literary news, and his friends visiting London with various professional favors. Duyckinck had also presumably known Wiley over roughly the same period, if primarily through his frequent patronage of the Wiley and Putnam bookstore.[28] But it is just as likely that the two men had made each other's acquaintance even earlier, as they were both sons of leading local publishers of the first third of the century. In the more intimate Knickerbocker era of New York publishing and bookselling, the senior Duyckinck and Wiley had collaborated on at least several joint publication projects. By the time their sons renewed the partnership, however, the context of literary publishing had changed so dramatically from local or regional to national dimensions that one of the fundamental operating ambitions of the new alliance was to supply a national market with their works. With Putnam's help they hoped to extend their reach in appropriate cases even to Europe.

Despite their common roots in the Knickerbocker book trade, Wiley and Duyckinck had grown to maturity on significantly different terms. Whereas Wiley had followed his father into the business, Duyckinck had grown up to leisure, having graduated Columbia and found no urgent need to continue on to a career. With no clear professional direction and no ready-made outlet for his talents, Duyckinck had moved more relaxedly through his twenties, traveling, socializing, book collecting, and editing an occasional high-quality journal. During these years, though, his life was never far removed from the bookmaking precinct of Broadway; as he explained about his background to Putnam in 1845, "I had long, whether from infant and boyish years having been passed in my father's bookstore, had an eye on the trade and written many schemes for them on the empty air when Mr Wiley applied to me for council—so the apple had not ripened in a day though it was ready for shaking."[29] The range of acquaintances he formed during the preceding decade with writers, editors, and publishers was exceptionally broad, constituting a potential network of connections that Duyckinck meant to draw upon for distinctly cultural and ideological purposes. Although widely regarded as a genial man, Duyckinck was unyielding in his commitment to American authorship and resolutely opposed to literary piracy, which he saw as the chief impediment to the development of a homegrown literary culture. As early as 1840 he had seen its symbol during a visit to the Harpers' establishment on Cliff Street: "They have a lithograph picture of an empty skull hung up in the counting room, the last relic of a starved author. The brains have been picked out and the man dead long ago."[30] When James Harper, the senior partner, invited him to help the firm skin an author or two, Duyckinck was not the man to be amused.

Why did this gentleman of leisure agree in 1845 to accept Wiley's offer of employment and get involved in the nitty-gritty world of the book trade? Duyckinck certainly did not do it primarily for money, although the Wiley and Putnam salary was a welcome addition to the annual income accruing from his father's estate. Nor did he do it out of affection for Wiley, whom he never particularly liked and at times barely tolerated.[31] Nor out of ignorance, since he was already well acquainted with the rules and personalities of the book trade. The primary basis of his motivation was his longstanding desire to further the cause of authorship and letters in the United States, a commitment that had led him to become an early activist in the movement for international copyright. This was a subject he had no doubt discussed on various occasions with Putnam and other close friends and associates in his house at 20 Clinton Street, an address well known during the 1840s to initiates of his "Young America" literary and political circle. Out of those informal discussions came the initiative, formally approved at the 23 August 1843 meeting organized by Duyckinck and his friend Cornelius Mathews and attended by a group of like-minded men (including Putnam) at the Athenaeum Hotel, to form the American Copyright Club. Putnam, who had recently returned to New York with his family, would spend much of his time that summer and autumn traveling up and down the country from New England to the South, canvassing names for a petition on international copyright that he submitted to Congress in December shortly before his return to England.[32]

But although Putnam and Duyckinck saw eye-to-eye on the connection between international copyright and promotion of American authorship and letters, there was still little more they or their colleagues could do at this time than circulate petitions and make and publish speeches.

Although Putnam returned to his routine in London in late 1843, Duyckinck continued to look for ways to match his ideological commitments to a practical course of action. Early in 1844 he embarked on a campaign to interest a local publisher in a library of contemporary American and European works in the belles lettres that he was hoping to oversee. He approached the Harpers and in all likelihood Wiley and Putnam and other leading New York publishers, but to no avail. Although series publication was fast becoming an accepted practice in both Britain and the United States, his proposal constituted a risky venture that conflicted not only with the existing publishing skepticism toward unknown and unestablished American writers and their relatively expensive, copyrighted works but also with market realities of the early 1840s, the years in which the entire publishing industry oriented itself toward inexpensive books, magazines, and newspapers, and in which cheap European reprints were firmly established as a primary, if risky, source of income for American publishers.

Unable to reach an agreement with any established New York publishers, Duyckinck settled on a small New York bookseller, Isaac S. Platt, who that spring began advertising his plan to bring out the Home Library: "The subscriber proposes to issue under this title,—as centering in Home, and drawing towards it their free, hopeful, manly spirit,—a series of select publications adapted to the best interests of the country. They will be chosen both for their classic merit and their popular character, and will embrace the most varied range of Literature. The plan will include COPYRIGHT WORKS OF AMERICAN AUTHORS, and new works of English writers, to be published by mutual arrangement with them and for their benefit."[33] The advertisement listed as in preparation works by William Cullen Bryant, William Gilmore Simms, William A. Jones, Joel T. Headley, and Elizabeth Barrett, which were to be issued in separate prose and poetry series. The obvious discrepancy between the grandiose vision of the series and its marginal production revealed how improbable Duyckinck's collaboration with Platt was. Only two works, those by Bryant and Headley, were ever issued in the Home Library, and they came out in the simplest pamphlet form, cheaply and unattractively printed and sold at the minimal price of $.12 ½. Within months, Platt abandoned the Library, which must have pushed him beyond his means and left him with little prospect of compensation for his expenses.[34]

The failure with Platt did not deter Duyckinck for long. If he had learned nothing else from working with Platt, he must have come away with the understanding that a viable scheme for series publication required a scale of business organization and concentration of resources far beyond the capacity of a small publisher. But his fundamental ambition remained unchanged. Early the next year he indited his ideas about the future of American letters in a strongly worded article published in the newly founded *American Whig Review,* in which he asserted that "the opening of a new department of literature by native authors may be as well worth talking about as the acquisition of Texas—with this little difference in the subject matter of the two, that while one is an enlargement of the freedom of the mind, the other is a question of the slavery of the body."[35] Confidently shrugging off the era of cheap reprints of uncopyrighted foreign literature by unscrupulous American publishers as a thing of the past, he declared a new era of cultural cooperation at hand in which "union among authors, bringing together the force of their aggregate works, would create a sentiment, a feeling in their behalf, a voice to which book sellers would be compelled to listen. The *taboo* of the American author in the booksellers' stores in Broadway, Cliff, Chestnut and Washington streets must be broken."[36]

He might already have begun to move beyond rhetoric to action. Either by the time he wrote this article or within weeks of its appearance, Duyckinck had blazed his own path to Broadway by concluding an agreement with Wiley and Putnam, the publisher of the *Whig Review,* for a more ambitious version of essentially the same idea he had begun the year before with Platt. In writing the advertisement announcing the forthcoming Wiley and Putnam Library of Choice Reading, a mixture of original and reprinted works in the belles lettres to be brought out in series format, Duyckinck foregrounded his and Wiley's conviction that the cheap publication war had cleared the way for their initiative: "It has shown the extent of the reading public in the country, and the policy of supplying that public with books at low prices proportioned to the extent. Books in the United States must hereafter be cheap. To reconcile the utmost possible cheapness with a proper attention to the literary and mechanical execution of the books published, will be the aim of the publishers in the present series."[37]

By late February 1845, a deal between Duyckinck and Wiley was struck and terms set down, Duyckinck to serve as series literary editor with operating power to choose titles for the Library, solicit contributions, and use his numerous connections to promote the new works; and Wiley and Putnam to issue them in attractive but inexpensive fashion in New York (and in selected cases in London). By the time they reached that agreement or very shortly thereafter, Duyckinck presumably persuaded Wiley to separate the planned titles into two distinct series: the Library of Choice Reading to issue foreign works, most but not all contemporary and many to be paid for via arrangements made with their original publisher or author; and the Library of American Books to issue American-authored works only, many of which were to be original and all of which were to be paid for on a royalties or lump sum basis.[38] The idea of a separate American series was one close to Duyckinck's heart; for nearly a decade he had wished to offer worthy American writers (among whom he had Hawthorne, Emerson, and his old friend Cornelius Mathews originally in mind) access to the broad Anglo-American readership. But for Wiley and Putnam the overall venture was a risky commercial proposition, committing it not only to a scale of publication previously beyond its means but in the American Library to a type of series publication with no clear precedent in the trade, which had been generally more interested in cheap, uncopyrighted foreign works than in copyrighted American works.

The production of the two Libraries marked the culmination of Wiley and Putnam's book publishing activities. Although the house continued to issue a broad variety of other titles, the Libraries quickly established themselves by spring 1845 at the center of its publishing activities. Their production proved to be a major challenge that involved Duyckinck, Wiley, and Putnam in a far-flung enterprise that would have been impossible for them or, for that matter, any other American publisher their size even a few years before. Understood in the broadest terms, it was a transcontinental affair requiring the combined and coordinated activity of their New York and London offices, as well as of the literary and commercial talents and structures of their respective continents. Its chain of operations spanned the United States and Britain: Duyckinck in New York handling the selection of titles, correspondence with authors, and promotion of works; Wiley and his staff in New York keeping the accounts and attending to the production of the works, which were handled by several of the leading local printers and binders; literary professionals, such as Robert Balmanno, John O'Sullivan, and James Russell Lowell, in New York and other cities being asked to make contacts and connections with prospective authors; and Putnam in London, acting primarily as Duyckinck's main operative in the field, making contacts with authors and publishers for advance rights to books, scouring the papers for announcements of new works, and shipping such materials as quickly as possible to New York for publication in advance of possible reprinters. Meanwhile, the two offices coordinated the shipping, printing, publishing, and selling of the Libraries in their respective centers.

At the same time, the production of the Libraries was as much a cultural as a professional bookmaking challenge. During the years of their appearance, 1845–47, the Libraries were the central event in American literary publishing, the most ambitious attempt to date to circulate high-quality, contemporary works among the American reading public. The central figure in their creation, production, and promotion was clearly Duyckinck, who by the time the Library of Choice Reading began to appear in March and the Library of American Books in June had made himself a force to be reckoned with in the New York literary world. With a major publisher supporting his ideas and committing its resources to his plan, an extensive network of personal and professional connections among writers and editors, and literary editorial control over the prestigious *Democratic Review* and New York *Morning News* and influence with numerous periodical editors in New York and elsewhere, Duyckinck had achieved a situation of editorial influence unprecedented in American literary history. Drawing on his broad personal knowledge of contemporary letters and his wide network of contacts among authors, editors, and publishers, he cast his net widely for contributions to the Libraries, assembling for Wiley and Putnam the most impressive list of literary works of any American publisher of the 1840s. In time, his American series included works by Melville, Hawthorne, Poe, Caroline Kirkland, Margaret Fuller, and William Gilmore Simms; his European series, various contemporary works by Carlyle, Dickens, Thackeray, Leigh Hunt, Thomas Hood, William Hazlitt, and other leading writers. Then in the Wiley and Putnam Foreign Library, a slightly later venture that he oversaw and that he and his brother George helped to finance, he brought out the first American editions of Goethe's *Dichtung und Wahrheit* and Cellini's *Vita.*

5. Wiley and Putnam store and office, 161 Broadway. (Courtesy John Wiley and Sons)

Duyckinck performed his editorial work for Wiley and Putnam out of the firm's storefront on Broadway, where he soon found his quarters insufficient to his needs. He was therefore happy to hear in autumn 1845 that Wiley was taking over the upstairs of the building and thinking of converting one of its second-floor rooms into a "literary room."[39] Wiley perhaps remembered the way his father had received his authors in the "den" at the back of the Wall Street store and hoped to duplicate that service for his own firm. But author-editor-publisher relations were hardly then what they had been in Charles Wiley's time, and in any case Duyckinck had in mind an editorial policy far more ideologically driven than that held by either of the Wileys. At a time when his fellow editors had taken to styling their offices as the "inner sanctum," Duyckinck was well aware of the secularization of authority and the raised status that it gave to the belles lettres in his generation. For an American Victorian like Duyckinck, his position marked the opportunity of a lifetime to instill good through letters, and with the Wiley and Putnam apparatus behind him he was determined to do precisely that.

A clubbish man, Duyckinck liked to discuss his plans for the Libraries with his close circle of friends, two of whom, William A. Jones and Cornelius Mathews, he hoped to enlist as contributors to the American Library. Among publishers, his closest confidant was Putnam, whom he counted among his allies in the cultural work that he meant the Libraries, especially the Library of American Books, to do. He was therefore pleased when Putnam enthusiastically expressed his approval of the scope and plan of the project and his pride at having his name associated with it. Duyckinck responded in turn by sharing with him his operating philosophy. The key criterion for him, he stated, perhaps in response to Putnam's use of the term, was "the area of freedom" in the selection of titles; Duyckinck assured Putnam that for the Library of Choice Reading he had

> taken care to sweep a broad boundary line for the "Library" to include all that was good. When you see that the series includes the pick of Murray's, Moxon's, Chapman's, Pickering's publications, books of different classes and others besides you will say that the "area of freedom" is sufficiently large. I only wish that this "area of freedom" like our political one had not a black spot in it. What slavery is to the one pillaged copyrights are to the other. Yet this is a great improvement on former dispensations.

The mental rights of authors are religiously preserved not a word or letter being mutilated, good editions are printed; an unusual class of good books are brought into vogue and a common corrupt class driven out and more than ever is paid to the author. So far good. The copyright law would make all sound.[40]

What he stated here he was to state elsewhere: for Duyckinck the freedom to choose on these terms from the pick of European works for the Library of Choice Reading and to create his own corpus of texts for the American series was crucial. After earlier failures in persuading New York publishers, most notably the Harpers, to pursue his desired publishing strategy of combined nationalism, taste, and morality, Duyckinck now felt himself authorized by his agreement with Wiley and Putnam to pursue his goals systematically. He was so worked up by the prospects before him that he was unable to close a seven-page letter to Putnam full of news about titles going into production without adding the sentiment that there were not enough hours in the day to communicate "the thousand things" he wished to tell Putnam.[41] Beneath the various details and specifics of their ongoing dialogue, though, lay broad ideological concerns about the necessity of delivering "good" and "serious" reading matter to the broadened readership of their generation. The press was not unaware of this mission; a number of newspapers and magazines in New York applauded the advent of the series and gave generally favorable reviews to many of the books as they came off the press. One reviewer even noticed the advent of the Library of Choice Reading in terms that Duyckinck himself might have used: "We regard the starting of this series, in the cheap yet beautiful form in which they are issued, as a new era in our publishing history. Publishers are school teachers, and the books they print and circulate, the lessons they teach.... Books educate the people, and publishers are responsible for the mental and moral training they impart."[42] Although Wiley and Putnam would have demurred from the reviewer's dismissal of the morality of the profit motive, they clearly accepted the underlying basis of Duyckinck's motive.

Excitement about the venture was keen among all its key operators, who launched the series on an accelerated publication schedule in order to lift the Libraries off the ground as quickly as possible. From the first, Wiley and Putnam conceived of and advertised the individual titles as parts of an ongoing series, a marketing strategy that was already common among American publishers. The firm issued the works uniformly in 16mo format, each work containing separate title pages for its particular Library and for the work itself. For promotional purposes, it tipped advertising sheets for one or both Libraries, as well for other Wiley and Putnam titles, into many of the volumes. Adopting the motto of "books which are books," Wiley and Putnam clearly saw and promoted the Libraries as providing the American reading public an alternative to the popularized literature then common but attempted to keep prices for the volumes cheap, normally in the $.37 ½ to $.50 range. Furthermore, to maximize pricing flexibility, the publishers brought out the works both in paper and in cloth covers. A sign of their ideological origin, paperbound copies of works from the Library of American Books had printed on their front covers the maxim of the American Copyright Club.

Just a few months after launching the Library of Choice Reading, Duyckinck and Wiley envisioned it as stretching to fifty volumes or more. They just as quickly decided to protect the intended works by announcing many of them in the press prior to actual publication. That strategy, as Duyckinck explained to his brother, was designed as a preemptive strike against possible incursions from local competition: "This may point out a few good books to others but even if others print Wiley will have the privilege to publish[,] which the 'courtesy of the trade' will not allow him if the announcement is made elsewhere first."[43] Had Wiley and Putnam been operating in a commercial sphere populated by "gentlemen," that strategy might have been an effective one for the Library of Choice Reading, which was necessarily published in the United States without the benefit of copyright protection for either author or publisher. But in the real world of mid-century publishing, a policy that generally worked with such "courtesy-bound" publishers as the Appletons provided little or no insurance against the printing of competing editions by such "discourteous" publishers as the Harpers and smaller firms doing business chiefly off of cheap reprints.[44] In particular, Wiley and Putnam had good reason to beware of the Harpers, who quite justifiably accused Putnam, who as their agent in England was charged with overseeing their interests and sending them suitable books for reprinting, of double-dealing by redirecting material from them to his own firm. Alerted to these bad feelings, Duyckinck forewarned Putnam in early 1846 to beware of an open break between "Broadway and Cliff St." and to prepare for their possible retaliation against Wiley and Putnam.[45] The broader danger, though, was more purely an economic one: some of the more commercially attractive titles in the Library, even with their relatively cheap prices, were bound to become fair game for American pirates able and motivated to undersell Wiley and Putnam.

For the opening number of the Library of Choice Reading, Duyckinck chose to bring out the first American edition of Alexander William Kinglake's *Eothen*. That work, which quickly gained an enduring reputation as one of the most distinguished travel books of its era, was initially so uncertain a proposition in England that it was passed over by John Murray and other leading publishers. In America, meanwhile, its authorship was so much a mystery that some newspapers initially ascribed it to Richard Milnes; even Duyckinck was originally uncertain about its authorship.[46] That book was soon followed by a half dozen new titles, including the first American editions of William Hazlitt's *Table Talk,* Leigh Hunt's *Imagination and Fancy,* and Thomas Love Peacock's *Headlong Hall.* With those works the tone and character of the series were quickly established: works primarily of fiction, poetry, criticism, and travel written by authors, mostly English in origin, who combined "seriousness' with wit or charm. Putnam requested that Duyckinck avoid "not only all silly or bad books, but all heavy ones," but that advice was presumably gratuitous; Duyckinck had already reached the same conclusion: heaviness or any other quality likely to frighten off the general audience projected for the series was to be avoided at all costs.[47]

With Putnam promising to be "wide awake" at his London outpost for new titles and with his own feelers extended in all directions, Duyckinck was well positioned to get the pick of the works he wished for the Library. During the several years of their collaboration in the Libraries, Duyckinck and Putnam tossed a variety of names back and forth across the ocean: Dickens, Thackeray, Carlyle, Lamb, Keats, Hugo, Hazlitt, Browning, Tupper. Many made their appearance in the Library—some with their (or their publisher's) consent, others without. The working understanding between the two men was that contemporary European authors (or their publishers) were to be approached and compensated whenever possible or practical, although in practice intent and act did not always meet. For all their ambitions and aspirations to do justice to their authors and to make a profit for their Libraries, the ability of Putnam and Duyckinck to shake hands across the "unsociable ocean," as Duyckinck styled it, was far from unlimited.

I have already detailed the complicated dealings that Putnam had during this period with Carlyle, several of whose works were issued in the Library of Choice Reading; that arrangement was only one of many that Putnam made on behalf of the Library, although it would be difficult to determine what percentage of the whole list was actually paid for. Certainly, in the case of works from earlier eras, such as Duyckinck's beloved Izaak Walton and Oliver Goldsmith, or from the Continent, such as the autobiographies of Cellini and Goethe, there was no need to make formal arrangements. The situation, though, with regard to contemporary British authors was another matter, and Putnam's letters indicate that among the authors whose works he paid for were Hazlitt, Hood, Tupper, Lamb, and Keats.

Of them, the case of Hood is particularly interesting because Putnam and Duyckinck each came to see Hood as a classic case of the precariousness of authors' rights in their day. By the time the Library of Choice Reading was launched in March 1845, both men were aware of Hood's financial problems and failing health (he died that June), and both wished to compensate him for various of his writings, which they regarded as valuable literary property.[48] Later that year Putnam paid Mrs. Hood the standard sum of £10 as payment for the two-volume edition of her husband's poems selected by Duyckinck for inclusion in the Library of Choice Reading and stated his wish that Moxon, who was issuing a simultaneous English edition, would compensate her fairly by local standards.[49] But *Poems* was actually the second of Hood's works issued in 1845 by Wiley and Putnam: that summer the firm published a two-volume edition of his *Prose and Verse* as one of the earlier titles in the Library of Choice Reading. Whether Putnam paid either the family or Moxon for the right to print it one can only guess; given his relations with Moxon and his affection for Hood, he probably did.

Prose and Verse was one of the more fascinating bibliographic specimens in the Library, a model inside and out of the vagaries of international copyright. The Wiley and Putnam edition carried a statement of copyright deposit supposedly taken out in the publisher's name in the New York City district courthouse, but that act seems to have been a bluff designed to scare off competition. Not only was there no legal basis for doing so but there is no record in the nineteenth-century copyright ledgers of any such deposit. At the head of its text the firm printed an anonymous editor's preface dated 1 July 1845, and composed presumably by Duyckinck, which decried "the injustice of a system by which Hood was deprived of the least participation in the profits of his own works in America." It also went beyond Hood's individual misfortune to make a broader indictment of a cultural system in which all parties were losers: "The foreign author confessedly is injured; the American author (where the system allows such a person to exist at all) is at a disadvantage at every turn; the bookselling interest is deprived of that security of property, based upon right, which is essential to give honor and dignity to trade; and the public are not the gainers."

The text itself contained a small selection from Hood's poetry and a variety of his essays, including his witty "Copyright and Copywrong" letters originally published in the *Athenaeum*.[50] The conformity between the position taken in them on authorship and copyright and Duyckinck's editorial stance was in many ways considerable. Both subscribed to a view of authorship "as a grand moral engine, capable of advancing the spiritual as well as the temporal interests of mankind" and Hood's corresponding contention that copyright protection was in the mutual interest of the individual author and the nation. But this common ideological premise, once put into practice, broke down into divergent transatlantic interpretations. In the last of his letters, written five years after the earlier ones and during a period of heightened agitation in England regarding the necessity of international copyright protection, Hood took aim at the international scope of authorship and piracy. Having identified American reprinting of English works as progressing at "steam celerity," Hood could not restrain himself from addressing American "Publicans and Sinners" forthrightly about their obligation as citizens of the modern republic of letters to hold the line between English "types" and American "antetypes." This was, of course, precisely the kind of Old World cultural nationalism that moved Putnam to acts, such as *American Facts*, designed to redress Hood's victim/victimizer formulation, as well as his collateral charge that thanks to widespread piracy Americans were so busy reading European books that they created none of their own. The latter claim must have been particularly irritating to Duyckinck because Hood made it by attributing that position to—of all people—Duyckinck's comrade-in-arms Cornelius Mathews. This was a charge that men such as Putnam and Duyckinck could least tolerate when it was made with a British accent.

The counterproof to that contention, Duyckinck and Putnam both knew, was in their own Library of American Books, which first appeared in June but had been in the planning stage ever since Wiley and Duyckinck made their agreement. In a circular letter dated 1 March, Duyckinck had begun the task of advertising the two Libraries to the public and, particularly in the case of the Library of American Books, had immediately followed up by sending off letters of solicitation to prospective authors. During the next period of months, he conducted an editorial correspondence on behalf of the firm with Emerson, Hawthorne, Longfellow, Lowell, Simms, Whittier, Poe, Thoreau, Fuller, Caroline Kirkland, Frances Osgood, Elizabeth Lummis Ellet, and James Hall about possible contributions to the Library—some at their initiative but most at his own.

Although not all of these writers entered the series and not all of those who did contributed first-rate works to it, it is clear that Duyckinck was pursuing a coherent vision of American letters closely attuned to the rising, self-consciously culturally nationalistic generation of the 1840s. The most salient criterion of his editorial policy for the Library, of course, was his insistence—a novelty in American letters in 1845—that inclusion in the series be limited to American writers. Although himself a staunch New Yorker operating at a time when local and regional jealousies were nearly as pervasive with respect to culture as to politics, Duyckinck nevertheless built his authorial corps for the Library of American Books according to a national plan. Contributors came from all parts of the country: New England, the Middle Atlantic states, the South, and the West.[51] More significantly, many of the works published in the Library reciprocated aspects of his vision of American letters and authorship in the age of incipient mass publishing and readership. Some did so directly by addressing the current absorption of the United States with itself—its history, geography, and folklore. Among the writers who contributed such works to the series were William Gilmore Simms, Caroline Kirkland, and James Hall. But even works seemingly most removed from a direct concern with the United States, such as the South Sea or European travel books contributed by Melville, Taylor, and Joel Headley, were clearly addressed to American readers and formulated according to American ideological or cultural constructs, which is one reason why they were three of the most popular writers of the 1840s. For like reason, the correspondence of view between Duyckinck and his authors was the result less of his doing than of shared conditions that bound author, editor, publisher, and reader alike into a common framework for cultural discourse.

By March Duyckinck was energetically overseeing management

of the American as well as of the European series: lining up authors, soliciting manuscripts, suggesting book topics, stroking egos, appealing to friends to appeal to their friends—in short, carefully cultivating a cadre of the best writers in the country and dealing with each in the way best assured to supply his Library with first-rate titles. As a rule, his editorial touch was masterly—informed, literate, tolerant, but when necessary aggressive. Emerson, to take an interesting case, he approached as nothing less than a project. Although Emerson was the rare author with whom he was not on personal terms, Duyckinck considered him one of the most original, attractive writers in the country. He was therefore willing to go to extraordinary lengths to sign Emerson to a contract, suggesting to him a medley of possible projects: an Emerson-supervised edition of selections from Walter Savage Landor (to be introduced, Duyckinck insisted, by the 1841 Emerson assessment of Landor that he had read and admired in the *Dial*); a volume of Emerson's essays; a book version of Emerson's lectures on "Representative Men" that Wiley had seen advertised in the local paper; and perhaps most eagerly, a first volume of Emerson poems. When Emerson countered each of these proposals with objections, Duyckinck quickly submitted his counterproposals, angling to overcome Emerson's reservations and to ease his anxiety. Wiley and Putnam, he informed Emerson, adhered to higher standards of protecting authorial integrity than were common in the industry; Wiley and Putnam, he assured him, would gladly sacrifice English publication, despite its own London operations, if Emerson feared a negative effect on his chances of securing dual copyright; and Wiley and Putnam, he promised, would guarantee the fairest terms of royalties that financial conditions permitted. For the much-desired volume of poems, he resorted to flattery: "If you will trust your Poems in New York Messrs W & P will give you any advantages in their power in mode of printing, advertising, etc. I should like greatly to see their imprint on the book. A genuine new book from an American author is not so common a thing as to be relinquished lightly by any one who desires the reputation of publishing true books."[52] A few weeks later, he wrote again to offer specific terms for the proposed volume of poems: Wiley and Putnam to pay royalties of $.06 ($.08 is crossed out in his draft) per copy for six years' printing rights and to guarantee a minimum sale of 2,500 copies, or, if Emerson preferred, a half-profits arrangement.[53] But, in the end, all Duyckinck's feints and arguments were to no avail. Unwilling to accede to Duyckinck's assertion that "New York is the true publishing center" and perhaps left suspicious by the Carlyle negotiations, Emerson continued to market his works through Boston publishers, his decision to do so causing one of the most serious failures Duyckinck was to experience as Wiley and Putnam editor.[54]

With Hawthorne, Duyckinck had better success.[55] Whereas with Emerson, Duyckinck had had to coax and importune a reluctant, guarded author, with the more amenable Hawthorne, eager to break out of his restricted audience and aware that the best chance to do so was through a major New York house, Duyckinck needed only to make overtures and to offer suggestions. The correspondence was further facilitated by the fact that he was on personal terms with Hawthorne, grounds that allowed Duyckinck to swap baby stories with him and to remind him of the fact that his wife and Putnam were cousins. First, he arranged for Hawthorne's editorship of Horatio Bridge's *Journal of an African Cruiser,* which made its appearance as the first volume in the Library of American Books, then quickly moved to persuade Hawthorne to contribute his own work to the series, although the resulting two-volume work, *Mosses from an Old Manse,* was not published in the Library for a full year after their agreement. Its long delay resulted from Hawthorne's difficulty in composing its introductory "The Old Manse," an autobiographical sketch that dramatized the dilemma Hawthorne felt in coming out as an author before the reading public of his day. Not willing to let go of a major author, Duyckinck also prodded Hawthorne to undertake other projects for Wiley and Putnam, including a history of New England witchcraft that he knew Hawthorne well qualified to write but that Hawthorne refused to take on.

Once connected into the New England literary circle, Duyckinck sought to widen the periphery of contributions to the Library by writing to authors he knew personally or through reputation. Lowell, he learned, was willing to publish a book of poems but was unable to escape a commitment to another publisher, and Longfellow, it turned out, had nothing suitable for the American series. But three other leading New England authors were decidedly interested. One was John Greenleaf Whittier, whose "New England Supernaturalism" Duyckinck had enjoyed reading in the 1843 *Democratic Review.* In summer 1845 he invited Whittier to contribute a longer version of that serial to the Wiley and Putnam Library, provided that Whittier could expand it into a full-length book.[56] Duyckinck had originally offered 10-percent royalties on the retail price and only later specified that this figure applied only after expenses had been paid, a condition made necessary by the risk inherent in publishing a work not entirely new.[57] That deal turned out to be far from satisfactory. With business extremely "dull" in summer 1846, the publication of *The Supernaturalism of New England* was delayed for months, and when it was finally issued as a slim volume the following January, its $.25 price allowed little margin for profit for either Whittier or Wiley and Putnam. Another interested author was Henry David Thoreau, who took the initiative in offering his first book manuscript *A Week on the Concord and Merrimack Rivers* unsolicited to Duyckinck, who according to Emerson "gave a favorable opinion of it" to Wiley. But Wiley was less sanguine about its commercial appeal and offered only an author's risk basis for its inclusion in the Library.[58] Expecting he could do better elsewhere, Thoreau chose to keep looking.

Margaret Fuller was also interested in appearing in the Library of American Books, although her dealings with the firm proved complicated. Duyckinck had admired her literary columns in the New York *Tribune* and was eager to see a collection of those pieces assembled in book form in the Library. Fuller apparently first learned about his interest in the project from their mutual acquaintance Elizabeth Ellet and wrote Duyckinck to test the veracity of that report: "I should be glad if this [publication scheme] took place under your auspices, for I have thought from what I observed that your ideas, as to movements in the literary world, are what I truly respect."[59] Several months later, however, she was saying something quite different about the literary judgment of John Wiley, who demanded that she, as he also demanded that summer that Melville, eliminate unorthodox remarks he considered offensive to conventional taste. Fuller attempted to use Duyckinck as a buffer, although apparently without much success. She was further disappointed when Wiley obliged her to cut back her intended broad coverage of Western letters to comply with the Library's standard page count, and she said as much in the book's preface: "I regret omitting some pieces explanatory of foreign authors, that would have more interest now than when those authors become, as I hope they will, familiar friends to the youth of my country." When *Papers on Literature and Art* finally appeared in the two-volume format typical of most titles in the series, she had mixed emotions: Wiley had cut its length—and, she believed, the range of her subjects—to suit the demands of the printer. But even in its scaled-down and censored form, the book gave a more concentrated demonstration of her critical powers than could her scattered pieces in the *Dial* and the *Tribune,* and its appearance in the Library helped to spread her critical reputation in her own time. Perhaps the most interesting of its articles was the one on "American Literature" written for the series, an essay whose typically blunt Fulleresque opening, "Some thinkers may object to this essay, that we are about to write of that which has, as yet, no existence," has a fine irony when read in the context of its publication.[60]

Another author whom Duyckinck was eager to include in the American series was Poe, whose path he occasionally crossed in New York. Poe's situation in 1845 was anomalous. After years of frustrated ambitions, he had achieved a major literary success early in the year with the publication, in Wiley and Putnam's *Whig Review,* of "The Raven," (whose popularity had led the New York literary journalist Charles Frederick Briggs to report back to James Russell Lowell in Cambridge soon after its publication: "Every body has been raven mad about his last poem").[61] Still riding the momentum created by that success, Poe responded positively when Duyckinck invited him in March to contribute a collection of his short fiction to the Wiley and Putnam Library. With Duyckinck selecting the tales in the volume and Poe at least initially quietly acquiescing in his choices, Poe saw his *Tales* published as one of the earliest titles in the Library and to generally favorable reviews. Its critical success soon led Duyckinck and Wiley to propose to Poe a volume of his verse, an area in which the Library was thin. The result was the publication later that year of *The Raven, and Other Poems,* which Poe prefaced with a note stating his satisfaction at seeing his work published in uncorrupted texts and expressing his aesthetic judgment: "With me poetry has been not a purpose, but a passion." Both volumes attracted considerable press attention not only in the United States but in England, where Putnam reissued them from their New York sheets fitted with a cancel title page. What attention they did get in Britain was due in large part to the exertions of Putnam, who used his contacts to get the books noticed in the London press. He even prevailed upon the firm's prized author, Martin Farquhar Tupper, to write a review of Poe's *Tales,* for which Putnam gave him a set of the Library of American Books.[62] Although the profits to Poe were small, the two books gave him the best hearing in Britain and the United

States he got during his lifetime and did so in well-edited volumes whose contents included many of his best works.

Duyckinck was also in contact with the other leading Southern writer of the antebellum generation, William Gilmore Simms. Duyckinck's relationship with Simms was a long and cordial one conducted through the mails when Simms was home in South Carolina and through personal visits when Simms traveled up North. For many years Duyckinck served Simms as a literary agent and did his best to place his works with New York publishers, from whom Simms often felt himself geographically remote. A writer of fine critical and imaginative abilities and of strong sentiments about the state of American letters, as Duyckinck clearly realized, Simms was a strong candidate for inclusion in Duyckinck's circle of cultural nationalists. At the same time, Simms's admiration for Duyckinck's editorial talents was evident, and so too was his recognition of Duyckinck's literary influence: "You are now in a situation to do a real service to American Literature, by opening certain fountains to the public taste which will equally please and purify."[63] Like Hawthorne, Simms was a writer ambitious to establish his reputation as a literary professional both regionally and nationally and for years had sought to overcome the disadvantage of conducting his career from a position of isolation and distance from New York ("the true publishing city").[64] In agreeing with Duyckinck to publish two of his books in New York with Wiley and Putnam, Simms made an arrangement that served the personal and professional interests of all parties well.

The initiative for the deal came from Simms. Soon after receiving notice of the plan of the Library, Simms suggested to Duyckinck the possibility of including a volume of his tales. Duyckinck responded positively, and that became the basis of *The Wigwam and the Cabin*.[65] Although the tales were originally printed in magazines, their appearance as a book gave not only a wider distribution to their contents but also a more concentrated form to their pictures of the life and lore of the Old South. Meanwhile, Putnam attempted to place the manuscript with a London publisher, although without success.[66] Even before that volume was out, Simms suggested a follow-up edition of his critical pieces, which Wiley and Putnam brought out in separately printed volumes in 1846 and 1847 as *Views and Reviews in American Literature, History and Fiction*, one of the finest critical assessments of its topic in the decade. In particular, the impressive first volume with its essays on "Americanism in literature," American history for the purposes of art, Native American art, and Daniel Boone nicely complemented one of the underlying goals of the Wiley and Putnam Library: to open up the native grounds and resources of the United States to literary culture.

Two other authors who extended the reach of the Library were James Hall and Caroline Kirkland, who contributed two relatively early works on the American West. Even before the Library's inception, the Wiley and Putnam publishing list addressed the mounting popular interest in the life and lore of the new territories. The firm had published numerous travelogues of the West throughout the decade, as well as firsthand accounts of the scenery and fighting in the Mexican-American War. To correlate the program of the Library to the current wave of popular interest in the West was therefore a natural move for Duyckinck, who eagerly cultivated relations with Hall and Kirkland. He knew Kirkland personally and even helped her get established in New York literary circles after her husband's death. Putnam also knew her and in time would grow to admire both her and her work. In fact, during Putnam's brief stay in New York in August 1846, the two men visited her at her home in Roslyn, probably to discuss her contribution to the Library.[67] By contrast, Duyckinck knew Hall only through the mails, although his literary reputation was already fairly well established. Both Hall and Kirkland were transplanted Easterners who had lived on the Western frontier (Hall in Ohio, Kirkland in Michigan) and transformed their impressions of those regions into short sketches and tales oriented at least in part to the audience back East. By the mid-forties, Kirkland had returned East and was trying to make her career as a New York City literary journalist, one of the few women of the time to became the editor of a general magazine. Admittedly, neither Hall's *The Wilderness and the War Path* nor Kirkland's *Western Clearings* represents its author at his or her best; both are little more than compilations of mostly earlier work. Nor did Duyckinck help matters: he (or Wiley), taking a editor's (or publisher's) prerogative, decided to bind the two works together as a single number of the Library. That decision infuriated Hall, who protested to the publisher against having his work coupled with what he considered the work of an interloper.[68] That pairing of works was not unique; other titles in the series wound up being bound with mates no less odd.

While activity connected with the Library of American Books naturally centered in New York, Putnam watched its progress with great
interest from London, writing periodically to express his satisfaction
with Duyckinck's editorial management and to exchange views with
him on the two Libraries and bits of literary and social gossip. Putnam
was, however, directly responsible for one title in the Library of American Books: *Typee,* Melville's first novel. Initially the most unknown
author in the Library, Melville had been unable to place this work
with the Harpers in New York in late spring or early summer 1845 and
had sent it on to London with his brother Gansvoort, newly appointed
as secretary to the American Legation. After lengthy negotiations,
Gansvoort reached an agreement for its publication in England with
John Murray, who wished to bring it out in his Home and Colonial
Library of travel books. Meanwhile, the more pressing desire of the
brothers to see the book published in America remained unsatisfied.
Then one day in early January 1846, Gansvoort Melville walked over to
the American Literary Agency in the company of Washington Irving to
make the acquaintance of Putnam, presumably at Irving's suggestion.
The next day an interested Putnam saw the first batch of proof sheets,
which he found so entertaining that he skipped church that weekend to
continue reading the proof to its end (the same story Wiley later found
too heterodox to appear unrevised in the Library). Determined to accept
the story for the Library of American Books and to issue it in New York
as soon as possible, Putnam agreed to pay all production expenses and
offered Gansvoort the generous choice between half profits or 12 ½-
percent royalties on sales. The two men quickly worked out the details
of the agreement, speed being necessary to satisfy their wish to see the
book published in New York as soon after the London edition as possible in order to protect both copyrights.[69] Within several weeks of their
deal, a full set of corrected proof sheets was received by Putnam and
sent by him to New York on the steamer of 4 February. With it he sent a
letter to Duyckinck stating his strong endorsement of the book: "from
what I read of this it is sure to 'take,' to a satisfactory extent, if indeed it
does not prove as good a hit as Dana's Life before the Mast."[70]

Typee did turn out to be a minor "hit" for Melville and for Wiley
and Putnam upon its publication in New York, although it gradually
became clear to both parties that the book was generating more publicity than profits.[71] Ironically, as the only work in the Library of American
Books contracted for originally in England with an English publisher, it

was the only one that was completely out of Putnam's hands after its publication. He did, at least, send it back to America with a puff in the firm's newsletter and an endorsement of its self-proclaimed "unvarnished truth": "Mr. Murray will bring out here, simultaneously with the New York edition, a curious and very interesting book, called "Typee; or, A Peep at Polynesian Life," being a narrative of a residence at the Marquesas, by Herman Melville, of New York. This is no fiction, but a veritable picture of life among the cannibals, from actual observation; and the narrative, at least the one hundred pages I have read, is worthy of Robinson Crusoe in style and in interest, with the additional advantage of being a simple record of facts."[72]

His early assessment of the prospects for the American Library was characteristically optimistic. Upon first hearing of it, he wrote Duyckinck: "I hope the American Series will succeed as well as the reprints. I shall do my best to push it before the 'candid British public.'"[73] No doubt he did; at year's end he reported to Duyckinck that the market for their books was strong: "The American series goes well here—particularly the cruiser [Horatio Bridge's *Journal of an African Cruiser,* edited by Hawthorne]—we shall want 200 at least of all the vols.—and I hope 500 for this market—indeed there ought to be one or two thousand sold here."[74] It would certainly have helped that he succeeded in getting many of the books in the series widely reviewed in the English press. But whether he managed to sell Bridge's *African Cruiser* or any of the other titles in the series in more than the hundreds, if that, is unverifiable in the absence of his firm's records.[75] The likelihood is that he did not. Had they drawn strong interest, they might well have been candidates for reprinters.

How popular were the Wiley and Putnam Libraries? Because the company's financial books have not survived, I can venture only a tentative response. A half century after the fact George Haven Putnam stated, "the publication as a whole produced a deficiency instead of a profit" as part of his general thesis that Duyckinck was aiming over the head of the mid-century reading public.[76] That assessment seems to me unduly harsh; although they were undoubtedly not a major commercial success, I would guess that the Libraries paid for themselves with probably a small profit to spare. Even if aiming at the upper part of the contemporary reading audience, Wiley and Putnam concentrated its offerings in the popular belletristic areas of travel writing and fiction, avoided with few exceptions the usually unprofitable genre of poetry, capitalized on many of the best-known names of the time, and marketed the works widely.

But the younger Putnam was not entirely mistaken in his conclusion. It seems clear in retrospect that the Wiley and Putnam Libraries occupied a publishing niche too narrow to guarantee significant commercial success, lying between the Scylla and Charybdis of mid-nineteenth century publishing. On one side they were hemmed in by the specter of quality; as stated rhetorically by the *Democratic Review,* the works "might be good, but if so they were too good—too good to sell."[77] On the other side they were hemmed in by the specter of popularity; should the works prove to be a hit with the public, the publishers faced the likelihood of having the foreign books reprinted and sold more cheaply, a challenge they could meet only by dropping their own prices and thus driving their already low profit margins beneath the "bottom line." To take the case of a writer whose fiction would have been an obvious choice for the Library of Choice Reading were there not absolute certainty that other publishers would "print on" it, Wiley and Putnam undertook the publication of Dickens's *Dombey and Son* in fall 1846, bringing it out in illustrated monthly numbers priced at $.12 ½ each. The firm did not dare, however, to publish its own two-volume edition of the novel in the Library, knowing that no sooner would it appear than cheaper editions would be for sale on the streets and through the mails.

It is even more difficult to figure their profitability in Britain and on the European continent, which, notwithstanding Putnam's ambitions, were never more than secondary markets for most Wiley and Putnam works. Even there the room for maneuvering was tight. Putnam had no intention of challenging the British publishers with Wiley and Putnam editions of the works of European authors. Practically speaking, therefore, he was limited to publishing the works of American authors, yet even with these he seldom operated with a free hand. Early in 1846, for instance, he wrote to Duyckinck to warn him that the Wiley and Putnam Library of Choice Reading (here used as the generic name for the two series together) was about to face the same danger in England that Wiley and Putnam reprints sometimes faced in New York. The culprit was the London publisher David Bogue, who had come out with his own Library of Choice Reading and who was finding his library "imitated to a 'T' by H. S. Bohn," with the result that "there is an uncivil war between Fleet St. and York St. as well as on the Thames."[78]

Individual titles from the Library of American Books, however, seem to have been largely immune to English reprinting. Putnam typically imported sheets from New York, then had a London title page inserted and the books bound before being sold from the American Literary Agency as well as through the London trade. But such titles as he was selling in 1845–47 did not normally invite much attention.[79]

The Wiley and Putnam Libraries were a publishing event whose impact would be registered more in the future than in its own time. G. P. Putnam's Sons must have recognized this fact in deciding to bring some of the titles back to life under its own imprint nearly half a century later. By that time many of the works were in the public domain. Whether the senior Putnam had a clear sense of the Libraries' literary or literary-historical importance is uncertain. More likely they were primarily a source of pride that merged with, and eventually became subsumed by, subsequent projects taken on by a dynamic young publisher quickly moving ahead to new challenges.

Notes

1. GPP printed the following announcement in some of the advertising brochures tipped into the back of books issued through the London office: "Mr. G. P. Putnam respectfully invites all those interested, to make free use, at any time, of the various sources of *Information Respecting the United States,* Literary, Political, Commercial, and for the use of Travellers, which are made accessible, at the American Literary Agency of Wiley and Putnam, New York; No. 6, Waterloo Place, Regent Street, London."

2. Some of the paintings he displayed at the American Literary Agency were on their way through his house to the 1845 Exhibition of the Royal Academy; among the works were paintings by Jasper Cropsey, Henry Inman, and Asher Durand. GHP, *George Palmer Putnam,* 2:278n.

3. Bayard Taylor, *Views A-foot* (New York: Wiley and Putnam, 1846), 376. Later editions of the book gave a fuller description of Taylor's stay in London, including more details of his relations there not only with GPP but with the American companion who went unnamed in the first edition, Henry Stevens.

4. The story of GPP's possession of Doughty's pictures is a complicated one. In November 1845, Doughty was in desperate need of funds and applied to GPP for a loan of £30, offering as collateral several of his paintings. Although GPP informed Doughty that making such loans controverted his usual policy and furthermore that he was himself then short of funds, he agreed to make an exception. The following April, Doughty, still in need of money and anxious to leave the country, attempted to sell the paintings to him for £50 pounds, but GPP refused.

So the matter stood for another year until GPP, not hearing from Doughty and not knowing where he lived, decided to sell two of them to the American Art Union in New

York (to whose forerunner, the Apollo Association, he had been appointed an honorary secretary in 1842). In December 1847, Doughty contacted him in New York and accused him of selling them without his permission and at a price ($50) so far below their value as to injure his professional reputation. He even took out an ad in the 6 December New York *Herald* protesting the sale of his paintings by second parties to the Art Union but not identifying GPP by name. For the time being, at least, GPP retained the largest of the three paintings in his home. Doughty to GPP, 23 April 1846; Doughty to GPP, 2 December 1847; GPP to Doughty, 3 December [1847]; Doughty to GPP, 5 December 1847—all in GPP-P.

Doughty was not the only American painter then abroad in need of funds. GPP had been alerted a few years earlier to expect Henry Inman to call on him and possibly to ask for a loan; F. W. Edmonds to GPP, 14 May 1844; GPP-P.

5. So few college archives contain information about library acquisitions dating back to the antebellum era that it is difficult to estimate the volume of business done for them by Wiley and Putnam, which held many college accounts during GPP's decade in England.

In the case of South Carolina College (the forerunner of the University of South Carolina), the surviving records indicate that the college bought heavily from Wiley and Putnam, one 1845 transaction alone amounting to $1,000. That transaction occurred during the years immediately after the college had committed itself to expanding the holdings of its newly built South Caroliniana Library, the first freestanding college library in the United States. In addition to ordering both journals and books published in Europe and America, the college had a standing order for a set of Wiley and Putnam's Library of Choice Reading. A check paid by the college for $1,000 was acknowledged in the letter from Wiley and Putnam to President Robert Henry, 22 July 1845; University Archives, University of South Carolina.

6. The best source on Stevens is Wyman W. Parker, *Henry Stevens of Vermont* (Amsterdam: N. Israel, 1963).

7. Henry Stevens, *Recollections of James Lenox,* ed. Victor Hugo Paltsits (New York: New York Public Library, 1951), 12.

8. They had not only numerous acquaintances in common but also a mutual interest in GPP's distant relative General Israel Putnam, whose biography Stevens was intent on writing.

9. Victorine Haven Putnam to GPP, 2 August 1846; HP-LC.

10. Stevens to Sparks, 1 January 1846; Houghton Library, Harvard University.

11. Stevens, *Catalogue of My English Library* (London: C. Whittingham, 1853), vi.

12. Philip John Weimerskirch, "Antonio Panizzi and the British Museum Library," *AB Bookman's Weekly* 67, no. 1 (5 January 1981): 64.

13. Parker, *Henry Stevens,* 116–20.

14. Evert Duyckinck to George Duyckinck, 28 July 1846; D-NYPI.

15. GPP to Stevens, 1 August 1846; Henry Stevens Papers, University of Vermont.

16. A copy of the letter accompanying the circular (but not the circular itself) addressed to the secretaries of the individual states and dated 26 July 1846 is in the Henry Stevens Collection, University Library, UCLA.

17. GPP to Stevens, 13 August 1846; Henry Stevens Papers, University of Vermont.

18. The letters were printed in GHP, *George Palmer Putnam,* 2:411–13.

19. Parker, *Henry Stevens,* 146.

20. In particular, his long autobiographical letter of 14 November 1846 is a model of salesmanship; the Stevens-Lenox correspondence (including various letters from GPP to Lenox, as though symbolically, interspersed) is in JL-NYPL.

21. Even as a correspondent Stevens was GPP's superior. Stevens's letters to Lenox are generally long, detailed, bibliographically rich documents—the product of deep study and long and careful composition. GPP's, by contrast, are briefer, more casually written reports—the product of a man in a rush who had many additional letters to write.

22. Stevens to Lenox, 14 November 1846; JL-NYPL.

23. GPP to Lenox, 2 November 1846; JL-NYPL.

24. An annotated copy of the *Catalogue of the Valuable Library of an Eminent Collector* [John Wilkes] giving the names and prices of successful bidders is in the general collections of the British Library.

25. Quoted in A. N. L. Munby, *The Formation of the Phillipps Library,* 2 vols, 4 nos. (Cambridge: Cambridge University Press, 1954–56), no. 4, p. 24.

26. At just about the time of the firm's initiative, GPP received a letter from Robert Balmanno, a collaborator of the firm, sounding him out on the possibility of the London publication by Wiley and Putnam of a small, illustrated book of his reminiscences. Why if he lived in New York did he ask GPP: "I ask the question of you, because Mr. Wiley is so timid and indecisive that I do not like to ask him. His own Brother says you are the man to go ahead!" Balmanno to GPP, 30 March 1845; GPP-P.

27. GPP to Duyckinck, 19 May 1845; D-NYPL.

28. A stack of his checks made out to Wiley and Putnam is in D-NYPL.

29. Duyckinck to GPP, 29 November 1845; D-NYPL.

30. Evert Duyckinck to George Duyckinck, 14 January 1840; D-NYPL.

31. Their relationship was never a particularly cordial one. Wiley was an occasional object of satire among the congregants in the den of Duyckinck's Clinton Place home. One night in 1843, for instance, his name came up in conversation among Duyckinck, bookseller Charles Welford, and Cornelius Mathews: "There were two things said of Wiley that were rather hard Heaven forgive us—Welford compared his clean, leathery physiognomy to Carlyle's description of Robespierre, something about a cold fishy submarine—and the other was, What does John Wiley do for amusement. Oh the profanity! He eats Graham bread and for a spice goes to a Prayer meeting!" Duyckinck to Thomas Delf, 5 November 1843; D-NYPL.

32. GPP exhausted himself that fall traveling around the country and meeting with members of the book trade. He mentioned in *American Facts* that during his travels he "personally procured the signatures of ninty-seven [sic] of the principal publishers, printers, and bookbinders, in the American cities, to a petition to Congress 'in favor of international copyright'" (84). With his usual sense of addressing readers on both shores, he sent an advance copy of his petition to the *Athenaeum,* where it appeared 28 October 1843. That petition got no further in Congress than did dozens of others during GPP's lifetime.

33. This advertisement ran in the New York *Tribune,* 30 March 1844; and in *Wiley and Putnam's Literary News-Letter* 3 (April 1844): 199–200. Platt is not even mentioned in John Tebbel's *A History of Book Publishing in the United States* or for that matter in any of the other extended accounts of American publishing, nor is he listed in any New York City directory except that of 1842–43, where he appears as "Isaac S. Platt, publisher."

34. For a fuller account of the Library, see George Goodspeed, "The Home Library," *Papers of the Bibliographical Society of America* 42 (1948): 110–18.

35. Duyckinck, "Literary Prospects of 1845," *American Whig Review* 1 (February 1845): 146.

36. Ibid., 150.

37. "New Literary Announcements," New York *Morning News,* 18 March 1845. Numerous reviewers of the Wiley and Putnam Libraries praised them for their combination of high-quality content, presentable appearance, and inexpensive pricing. A typical

instance was the puff given the Library of Choice Reading in the *Broadway Journal:* "If the days of 'cheap and nasty' literature are not ended, we have proof before us that the day of cheap and elegant literature has dawned. Wiley and Putnam's Library of Choice Reading strongly recommends itself by its novel elegance of form, and a tempting lowness of price. The work must succeed."

The firm's approval of this statement is clear from the fact that it excerpted this paragraph and reprinted it along with a long string of blurbs as an advertisement for the Library of Choice Reading; in *Wiley and Putnam's Literary News-Letter* 4 (May 1845): 320. The author of this praise was probably Poe.

38. A copy of the circular (dated 1 March) that Duyckinck wrote to announce the two Libraries is in D-NYPL. That copy belonged to William Jones, a literary critic and Duyckinck intimate whose work Duyckinck planned to and did include in the Library of American Books.

39. As the operations of the firm grew more specialized, so did the configuration of its work space. Wiley had rented a building on John Street several years earlier to handle the wholesale inventory and operations of the firm. Then, when he took over the whole of the building on 161 Broadway, he had an area of the ground floor compartmentalized as his own office. Duyckinck to GPP, 29 October 1845; GPP-P.

40. Duyckinck to GPP, 29 November 1845; GPP-P. Ironically, this letter also communicated word to GPP of the safe arrival in New York of the copy of Carlyle's *Cromwell* that he had purchased for £10 from Chapman and Hall and that would precipitate the dispute with Carlyle.

41. Duyckinck to GPP, 29 October 1845; GPP-P.

42. The possibility exists that Duyckinck wrote this review himself or that it was written at his initiative because it appeared in a journal then published by Wiley and Putnam. Although Duyckinck was outspokenly opposed to the corrupted standards of mid-century reviewing, he was as much a participant in them as were many of the people he scorned; "Books Which Are Books," *American Whig Review* 1 (May 1845): 521.

43. Evert Duyckinck to George Duyckinck, 16 May 1845; D-NYPL.

44. One case in which courtesy of the trade did take effect occurred in spring 1845 when Appleton's, which had been advertising a forthcoming edition of Leigh Hunt's *Imagination and Fancy* in the April issue of its *Literary Bulletin,* aborted its publication plans in deference to Wiley and Putnam.

45. Duyckinck to GPP, 7 February 1846; GPP-P.

46. GPP, who thought that "there could scarcely have been a better pioneer" than *Eothen* with which to lead off the series, informed Duyckinck that the author was "a young man by the name of *Kingley.*" GPP to Duyckinck, 19 May 1845; D-NYPL.

47. Ibid.

48. For GPP, whose name was to be connected with the publication of Hood for many years, that evaluation was no doubt a combination of sentiment and calculation.

49. GPP to Duyckinck, 1 November 1845; D-NYPL.

50. The first three of the letters were published consecutively in the *Athenaeum* on 15, 22, and 29 April 1837; the last two, on 11 and 18 June 1842.

51. This point was typically lost on critics, who criticized him for his excessive loyalty to Cornelius Mathews (whose *Big Abel and the Little Manhattan* he included in the Library of American Books).

52. Duyckinck to Emerson, 20 September 1845; D-NYPL.

53. Duyckinck to Emerson, 7 October 1845; D-NYPL.

54. Ibid.

55. Duyckinck's regard for Hawthorne's talent was longstanding. As early as 1841

he had written of him: "Of the American writers destined to live, he is the most original, the one least indebted to foreign models or literary precedents of any kind, and as the reward of his genius he is the least known to the public"; "Nathaniel Hawthorne," *Arcturus* 1 (May 1841): 330. His belief that Hawthorne was suffering from undeserved neglect was shared by Margaret Fuller, who stated in the book she published in the Library of American Books: "Under the auspices of Wiley and Putnam, Hawthorne will have a chance to collect all his own public about him, and that be felt which before was only a rumor." "American Literature," *Papers on Literature and Art* (1846; repr. New York: AMS Press, 1972), 144.

56. Duyckinck to Whittier, 26 August 1845; D-NYPL.

57. Wiley and Putnam to Whittier, 17 March 1846; Essex Institute (Salem, Mass.).

58. Emerson to William Henry Furness, 6 August 1847; in *Records of a Lifelong Friendship, 1807–1882: Ralph Waldo Emerson and William Henry Furness,* ed. Horace Howard Furness (Boston: Houghton Mifflin, 1910), 61. For Thoreau's publication ambitions for the *Week,* see Richard Lebeaux, *Thoreau's Seasons* (Amherst: University of Massachusetts Press, 1984), 59–62.

59. Fuller to Duyckinck, 2 February 1846; in Robert N. Hudspeth, ed., *The Letters of Margaret Fuller,* 6 vols. (Ithaca: Cornell University Press, 1983–94), 4:182–84.

60. Several months after the publication of *Papers on Literature and Art,* Fuller, who had crossed the Atlantic just weeks in advance of the book, wrote GPP from Paris to request that he send her copies of "American Literature" and of *Woman in the Nineteenth Century* for possible translation into French periodicals. Fuller to GPP, 28 November 1846 [she mistakenly wrote 1836]; GPP-P. The only known portion of this letter before the purchase of the Putnam Collection by Princeton University in the early 1990s was that reprinted in GHP, *George Palmer Putnam,* 2:264.

61. Briggs to Lowell; quoted in Dwight Thomas and David K. Jackson, eds., *The Poe Log* (Boston: G. K. Hall, 1987), 514.

62. GPP to Evert Duyckinck, 3 December 1845; D-NYPL.

63. Simms to Duyckinck, 25 June 1845; in *The Letters of William Gilmore Simms,* ed. Mary C. Simms Oliphant, Alfred Taylor Odell, and T. C. Duncan Eaves, 6 vols. (Columbia: University of South Carolina Press, 1952–82), 2:77.

64. Simms's despair over the difficulties involved in managing his career would become so intense that by 1847, despite his staunchly regional sympathies, he was considering moving north to be near the major publishers; see his letters to the Philadelphia publishers Carey and Hart and to John Henry Hammond of 14 December 1847 and 24 December 1847; in ibid., 2:382–83, 385–86.

65. See his letters to Duyckinck of 15 March, 10 April, and 6 June 1845; in ibid., 2:43–44, 54–56, 66–67.

66. GPP to Evert Duyckinck, 1 November 1845; D-NYPL.

67. Evert Duyckinck to George Duyckinck, 20 August 1846; D-NYPL.

68. "I beg you," he wrote Wiley and Putnam, "not to inflict so great an injury upon me, and so great a disgrace upon my book. The Western Clearings is a wretched imposition—a vile piece of humbug. If the authoress ever was in the West, she has failed to convey the slightest idea of the country or its people." Quoted in Randolph C. Randall, *James Hall: Spokesman of the New West* (Columbus: Ohio State University Press, 1964), 276.

69. Much of the information concerning the deal struck between Wiley and Putnam and Melville, as well as financial records of the production and sale of *Typee* and copies of the copyright deposit, can be found in the Melville Collection, Houghton Library, Harvard University. A large portion of it is excerpted by Jay Leyda in *The Melville Log,* 2 vols. (New York: Gordian Press, 1969), 1:202–4.

70. GPP to Duyckinck, 2 February 1846; D-NYPL.

71. The book was widely and vociferously reviewed in the American press and succeeded in launching Melville as a professional author. Its sales, however, disappointed the Melvilles' expectations. Wiley and Putnam sold about 6,000 copies of their edition during the two and a half years in which they published it, with the profits of $1,465 split equally according to the half profits arrangement the Melvilles had opted for. On the printing history of *Typee*, see Leon Howard's Historical Note, in Harrison Hayford, Hershel Parker, and G. Thomas Tanselle, eds., *Typee* (Evanston: Northwestern University Press, 1968), 295–96.

72. *Wiley and Putnam's Literary News-Letter* 5 (March 1846): 17.

73. GPP to Duyckinck, 19 May 1845; D-NYPL.

74. GPP to Duyckinck, 2 December 1845; D-NYPL.

75. One title from the Library whose English sales are known is the John Murray edition of *Typee*, which sold more than 4,000 copies during its first two years (Hayford, et al., eds., *Typee*, 296). But because Murray published that work in his popular Home and Colonial Library, which had its own established channels of distribution, such statistics do not provide a fair basis for comparison.

76. GHP, *George Palmer Putnam*, 1:269–70.

77. "Notices of New Books," *Democratic Review* 18 (March 1846): 238.

78. GPP to Duyckinck, 2 February 1846; D-NYPL.

79. Virtually the only surviving evidence on foreign sales consists of an undated, unaddressed note that offers any of the titles in the Library of Choice Reading at discounts of 40–60 percent for orders in the hundreds, as well as a suggestion that the Paris agent of the firm, Hector Bossange, might not himself take large orders but that he might induce some other Parisian publisher to do so or even issue them under his own imprint. Attached to this note is a set of printed sheets (dated 15 March 1846) listing the contents of the Wiley and Putnam Libraries and other series and giving the prices at which the individual books were offered to the trade; D-NYPL.

London, Rome, and Back Home to New York

After a decade in London as a bookseller and a half-dozen years as a family man, Putnam was ready by winter 1847 to move back to New York. Victorine's desire to return was, if anything, even stronger; she had left the city a sheltered daughter barely into her womanhood and was ready to return to her friends and relatives an experienced, well-traveled wife and mother. The subject of a permanent return must have been often raised between them in the years following their family visit in 1844, but the decision to act on their desire would not have been feasible had not business considerations reinforced their personal sentiments. That once-remote possibility grew more likely in 1846 as the subject of expenses developed into an irritant between Wiley in New York and Putnam in London that left Putnam having to justify his living and operating expenses to his tighter-fisted partner. To complicate matters, the firm's central position as an importer of books into the United States was facing intensifying competition. By mid-decade, the Appletons and Bartlett and Welford had squeezed their way into territory previously occupied primarily by Wiley and Putnam, and such firms as Harper and Brothers and Ticknor's had released Putnam as their overseas book agent once they found themselves vying repeatedly with Wiley and Putnam for first American rights to British and Continental titles. By spring or summer 1846 Wiley was asking Putnam to spend more time in America than in England, and Putnam returned to England in late August seriously considering or perhaps even acceding to that altered arrangement.[1] Certainly no later than the beginning of the new year Putnam reached the decision to leave the London house open but to return permanently with his family to the United States, from where he could make periodic trips across the Atlantic as business circumstances required. What Putnam could not then foresee was that the firm he would be representing on his nearly annual transatlantic excursions would be not Wiley and Putnam but G. P. Putnam.

Before leaving London, the Putnams planned a farewell pleasure tour of the Continent. They had traveled together through the British Isles when they first arrived in 1841, but now, three children later and with another expected in the summer, they planned a more ambitious, ten-week circuit of the Continent. For the first part of the trip, they traveled with a small group of American companions that included two men identified only as Drs. R. and W., who engaged in a verbal battle of the ancients and moderns during their trip to Italy, with Putnam playing bemused intermediary, and the family's sharp-witted friend and Putnam's erstwhile coworker and cotraveler Henry Stevens—his presence a sign that Putnam intended this as not purely a pleasure trip.[2] In addition to this congenial group, Putnam had the constant company of his pocket ledger, into which he jotted notes meant to facilitate organizing his experiences and impressions into a travelogue, as he had done after his 1836 excursion.[3]

The timing and duration of the trip were no doubt planned backward from the family's planned departure from London in late May. The Putnam party left London 22 February by train on the four-hour journey to Folkestone, ate lunch at a hotel near the station, and then made a smooth, two-and-one-half-hour channel crossing to Boulogne on a steamer far superior to the one Putnam had taken on his maiden crossing in 1836. One thing he fondly remembered as unchanged during the intervening decade: the apple girl on the French side, a woman now, who sold fruit and songs to travelers passing through the station. The next morning, the party began the long trip to Paris, first riding by coach as far as Amiens (a foodless trip that left Putnam thinking of his conductor as "sans le lait de bienfaisance humaine"), then transferring to the railroad for the twenty-five-mile-per-hour ride down to Paris, where they arrived the next morning at 5:30.

Putnam spent the next three days making business calls on local publishers and booksellers, most likely hunting books for clients and for the New York and London stores and making arrangements for the orderly continuation of business relations after his departure. His most important call was presumably made at the home of the Libri family, which was organizing a sale of its superb private library later that spring, a sale at which Putnam meant to make purchases for James Lenox. The books, however, were not yet ready for public inspection— or so Putnam and no doubt the rest of his rivals were led to believe. Neither he nor Hector Bossange, his professional friend and local agent whom he had asked to evaluate various items in the collection for him, was to get through the door that week. The sole exception was Stevens, who was also interested in the sale as the representative of the British Museum and who accordingly had been dispatched with a special letter of introduction from Panizzi to Count Libri that gained him a private audience and several days to scrutinize the collection.[4] While Putnam attended to his affairs those first few days in Paris, Victorine visited various of the city's tourist attractions. During the free days that followed, Putnam joined her for tours of some of the city's leading art museums and galleries, painting and sculpture long being one of their chief common pleasures. After a week in Paris, they continued south across France with few intervening stops, traveling by coach from Paris to Lyons, by boat from Lyons down the Rhône to Avignon, and transferring again to coach for the ride to Marseilles, their point of embarkation for the cruise to Italy.

Already initiated into the Mediterranean custom of bargaining and having set out from London so short of funds that he needed to make the best deal wherever possible, Putnam booked passage at half the proffered price for Victorine and himself on the English ship *Tiger*, bound around the coast of Italy for Naples.[5] Around noon on the clear, bright day of 13 March, they began the first leg of their passage across the Mediterranean, stopping first at Genoa, where they spent several pleasant days touring the city's streets, churches, and university and where Putnam paid a business call at the Palazzo Durazzo. The building was splendid, but he was there to see not the house but its young aristocratic owner, who, Putnam later wrote, "preferring horses, etc., to books, has offered his library for sale, although he is rich and does not want the money: it contains a choice collection of rare books, Aldine editions, MSS, etc."[6] These, at least, were Putnam's words to the general reader; in point of fact, Putnam was at the Marquis's house primarily at the service of Lenox, who had agreed to pay his expenses to those cities where Putnam made purchases for him.[7] Putnam and Lenox had been corresponding since the previous autumn about the purchase of specified items, especially bibles, in the Durazzo Collection but without the obligation on Lenox, a scrupulously choosy purchaser, of buying the entire collection. By early winter, Putnam hoped that he had worked out an arrangement acceptable to Lenox by setting up an agreement with the London booksellers John Payne and Henry Foss (of the firm of "Pain & Fuss," as nicknamed a generation earlier by Charles Lamb) according to which they were to purchase the entire collection and then separate out the choice—and, therefore, costly—Lenox selections for resale to him.[8] Putnam and his English partners were unable to complete their business then, however, and Putnam was obliged to return through Genoa on the way back north. Knowing he would return that way, he used the Genoa post office as his mailing address; a sign of how busy he typically was, more than one hundred letters were awaiting him when he doubled back there in mid-April.

When they returned to the *Tiger,* the Putnams found several new passengers on board, one of whom was already well known to Putnam both personally and professionally: Margaret Fuller. Before leaving New York for Europe the previous summer she had been busy preparing the final text of *Papers on Literature and Art* for publication in the Wiley and Putnam Library of American Books. The sheets of the New York edition, in fact, reached England just weeks after she arrived there in August.[9] So, for that matter, did Putnam, just returned from his exhausting summer of book canvassing up and down the Atlantic coast. If Fuller was still smarting from her frustrating encounter with Wiley, she had no reason to be angry with Putnam, to whom she had asked a letter of introduction from Duyckinck on the eve of her departure from New York.[10] If they had not crossed each other's paths that summer in New York, as they apparently did not, they unquestionably did meet at least several times in London. Fuller probably first met Putnam at the American Literary Agency, where the London edition of her book was on sale and was attracting attention in the British press, and she probably stopped there again to pick up copies of several of her books before going on to Paris in mid-November. She also had a chance to meet Victorine, her hostess one pleasant evening for dinner at Knickerbocker Cottage.[11] Then, on the eve of Fuller's departure for France, Putnam saw her at the birthday celebration of Mazzini's Italian Free School and heard her give an impassioned speech, with Mazzini present, in favor of Italian independence.[12] Several weeks after arriving in Paris ("the city of pleasures," as she described it), Fuller wrote Putnam to request that he send her five copies each of *Papers on Literature and Art* and of *Woman in the Nineteenth Century,* which she hoped to distribute to her advantage in Paris as she had already disbursed the copies she had brought with her from London.[13]

Putnam and Fuller might well have coordinated their meeting in Genoa, a strategic stopping point for both of them. While Putnam was transacting his business for Lenox, Fuller was there serving as an emissary for Mazzini and making the acquaintance of Mazzini's mother, who mistook Fuller as his paramour. Fuller and her traveling companions (Rebecca and Marcus Spring and their nine-year-old son) had followed the same itinerary as the Putnam party from Paris, but had preceded them to Genoa by a matter of days. Whatever the exact circumstances, the meeting of the two parties was unquestionably a fortuitous one. Putnam, a genial but traditionally sociable man, probably saw Fuller as an attractive traveling companion primarily for Victorine, but he also shared with her a wide variety of literary, cultural, and political interests (the last including an acquaintance with Mazzini, an occasional visitor to Knickerbocker Cottage). Furthermore, the circumstances surrounding their reunion were seemingly favorable for the deepening of their relationship; Putnam was as earnest a pilgrim in Italy in his way as Fuller was a passionate one in hers.

All told, the two groups of Americans made a congenial, English-speaking traveling party, and they remained together after they had journeyed down the coast to Naples and back up toward Rome. Together they experienced the most exciting moment, at least for the Putnams, of the entire European trip, which occurred the night of 19 March, a calm, star-lit evening when passengers on board the *Tiger* were jarred out of sleep or conversation by its collision with a French government steamer bound west from Naples. No one on board the *Tiger* was seriously injured nor was the vessel truly endangered, but it was incapacitated and Putnam was forced to transfer his party to the *Ville de Marseilles*—the ship, ironically, that he had initially rejected in Marseilles harbor.[14] The rest of the cruise to Naples passed without incident.

The party spent a busy week touring in southern Italy—Naples, Pompeii, Salerno, Vesuvius. The weather was gorgeous and Fuller, for one, reacted viscerally to her experience during these delightful spring days: "Here at Naples I have found my Italy."[15] Although himself susceptible to the romantic lore of the past, Putnam could never quite reconcile the Italian present with the Italian past, no less lose his own identity in his surroundings. This barrier to self-immersion in Italy became evident, for instance, during one of the highlights of the week: the ascent of Mount Vesuvius. An arduous climb even in the cool season, the mountain tested not only their physical but also their cultural dexterity. On their approach to the mountain, Putnam observed, his group passed "a party of ladies and young misses ascending Vesuvius in very gay silks and satins, fit for a botanical fete," which eventually realized its mistake and turned back. Resolved to be more pragmatic, the Putnam party allowed its guide, an Italian with the unlikely name of Joseph Lewis, to bargain with the crowd of local chairmen to carry the pregnant Victorine up the mountain. What followed was a drawn-out dumb show that eventuated in a compromise price being reached and the whole party safely making the first and safer summit of the volcano, where it philosophized on *buono-mano* and received a fitting memento of the hike: American coins dipped and encrusted in lava (Putnam's comment: a "safe investment of species").

From Naples, they made the long anticipated, overland trip to Rome, whose prospect stirred even Putnam to excitement. Having written ahead to ask his friend Thomas Crawford, an American sculptor residing and working in Rome, to find Victorine and him rooms at the Hôtel d'Angleterre, Putnam was disappointed to find not only it but the various other large European hotels filled to capacity and soon learned the reason: the approach of Holy Week.[16] They eventually found accommodations (at twice the normal price), separate from Fuller and the rest of their party, and spent most of their time in Rome on their own. One night, however, when Victorine felt too ill to go out, Putnam invited Fuller in her place to attend a private performance of Rossini's *Stabat Mater* at the Palazzo del Corso—the two of them apparently taken by their hosts for a married couple.

The irony was perhaps greater than Putnam then understood:

he and Fuller were about to go their separate ways. Even before he and Victorine left Rome, Fuller had made her initial acquaintance of Giovanni Ossoli, a meeting that Putnam years later claimed to have witnessed in St. Peter's Square, and begun the profound transformation from American tourist to initiated activist that carried her far beyond Putnam's scope of understanding and sympathy.[17] Shortly after Putnam returned to New York and updated him about their common friend, Duyckinck noted in his diary on 7 July that Putnam had recounted to him the story (told by Fuller herself in a dispatch printed in the New York *Tribune* on 13 November 1846) of how one September 1846 afternoon she had gotten separated from her companion and found herself seriously lost overnight on Ben Lomond in Scotland. That story Duyckinck labeled a "pendant" to the other Fuller story of misadventure told by Putnam (into which Putnam only long after the fact would be able to insert Ossoli) and recorded by Duyckinck in his diary: "Her loss by day among thirty thousand people in St. Peters. Within the precincts of the sanctuary it is said she received very singular suggestions from the young men of Rome which may afford instructive notes to a future edition of *Woman in the Nineteenth Century*."[18] Although it is impossible to determine whether that salacious interpretation was Putnam's or Duyckinck's, it certainly seems likely that the footloose path Fuller was by then tracking was not one Putnam could have recognized as a model of true womanhood—at least not until years later, when the four-year-old daughter he had left behind in London with her nanny introduced an alternative model of woman in the nineteenth century into the Putnam household (about which, more later).

The two weeks the Putnams spent in Rome were filled with the usual tourist activities common to American visitors of the time: tours of as many churches, museums, and ruins as could be packed into the day; visits to resident Americans; walks through the streets of the city by day and concerts by night; strolls through studios. An exciting prospect under normal circumstances, their stay in Rome was enlivened by the visibility of the new liberal pope (Pius IX), whom many Americans and Italians alike saw wishfully as a reformer, and the heightened atmosphere surrounding the holiday season. In many regards, in those two weeks Putnam proved himself to be a perfect American tourist—imbued, if anything, with an even greater hunger for Old World sights, sensations, and experiences than his fellow nationals. Too energetic for his wife to keep pace, he took time to go off on his own, with or without his "Murray" in hand, to explore the city and to check off the famous paintings on his list of approved works of art. Some of those moments and activities were indicative. He went, for instance, to visit the studios of notable resident artists, enjoying especially the studio of Thomas Crawford, whom he thought a genius and with whom he dined one evening at Cafe Greco, wondering at the attraction to artists of such small, dingy cafes where strong coffee was served in (childlike) demitasses. One evening he paid a visit to Anna Jameson, whom he had met by chance a few days earlier at St. Peter's and whose acquaintance he had originally made during his first visit to England. He also paid his respects to the artistic dead, walking through the Protestant cemetery to see the tombs of, among others, Keats and Shelley. He walked along the Appian Way, noting that its surface was "about as even as last year's pavement in Broadway." And he took every opportunity in Rome, as in many of the cities they visited, to hunt out the great collections of books and manuscripts; he was particularly impressed by the Vatican Library, which he took in more with the eye of a businessman than of a bibliophile.

In Rome, as everywhere he traveled, he tried to stay in touch with news from home. He was an inveterate reader of newspapers; Fuller had known her man when, in the letter she wrote from Paris the previous autumn requesting copies of her books, she had asked him to pass on the latest news from America. In Pisa he had the chance to read up on the latest news in a copy of *Galignani's Messenger,* which filled for its readership the niche occupied in recent decades by the *International Herald Tribune;* in Rome he occasionally stopped by Monaldini's (as later in Florence at Florian's and in Munich at the local public reading room) to read their copies of *Galignani's,* the weekly *Roman Advertiser* ("somewhat cramped in its freedom of opinion"), London *Times,* or whatever other English-language newspaper was available. They kept him informed about both what he could not see with his own eyes and sometimes what he could see but not understand. For example, he had attended the papal Easter benediction in St. Peter's Square, standing among a crowd of tens of thousands and straining to hear the pope's words. It was one of the finest sights of his life, he remarked, but he was unable to make out a single word until he read the English translation in the next issue of the *Roman Advertiser.* As for news about the larger world, he learned through a copy of *Galignani's* read several weeks later in Florence about the event then commanding attention back home: "Another Yankee victory in Mexico was the best piece of news, and would have been better yet, if one had been sure that it was right there should be any fighting there at all." But if he tried to keep himself in touch with one form of expression, he was manifestly out of touch with another. While Fuller was carrying papers for Mazzini and breathing the visionary spirit of Mickiewicz, Putnam, though vicariously sympathetic to the spread of political freedom through Europe, had little to say in his notes about the stirrings in Rome and in other cities throughout Europe that he passed through that spring. His primary attention was plainly directed elsewhere.

After a memorable stay in Rome, the longest of their trip, and with time and funds running low, the Putnams took leave of their traveling companions, some of whom had been with them from London, and headed via Siena to Florence. There Putnam, like Fuller and countless other Americans, made the obligatory visit to the studio of Hiram Powers, enthusing over the replica of the *Greek Slave* ("For my own part, I would sooner have either Powers's Eve or Greek Slave, than the Venus de [sic] Medici"), which Powers was then working on, as would thousands of their countrymen when a finished replica was shipped that summer to America.[19] Riding one fine spring morning up into the surrounding hills and looking down onto the Arno Valley and the domed city, with the thick yellow Italian sunlight beaming down and rows of olive groves and vineyards lining the surrounding hills, he declared Florence the "fairest" city in Europe. By this point, he and his wife were outright Italophiles; she, in fact, more talented than he in languages, would take up the study of Italian with the intent of being able to speak it during their next visit. That return visit did not take place, however, until the 1880s, by which time Putnam was dead and her companions were several of their grown daughters.[20]

Their stay in Florence could be only a brief one, as were those that followed in Milan, Venice, and Verona. The date for their final departure from London looming, the Putnams were feeling the press of time by late April. That fact, however, fails to explain the crisscrossing itinerary they followed on their way back to England. Their return itinerary took them, after weeks of continuous southern sun and warmth, first laterally to Genoa and Verona, and then longitudinally north via a hard, overland climb over the Tyrolean Alps made even less inviting by the damp and chill of Germany, a country and culture entirely less appealing to the Putnams than their counterparts in the Latin south.

From Germany the Putnams continued quickly across the Low Countries, whose sights and scenery were already as familiar to him as those in Italy had proven novel, and across the channel to England. The most plausible explanation for this itinerary is that for this part of the trip Putnam was following the line of business rather than of pleasure. Although he had been visiting libraries regularly during the first half of the trip, for example, the Vatican in Rome and the Ambrosian in Milan, he seems to have chosen cities, such as Genoa, Munich, and Stuttgart, for the return leg that possessed collections of rare books of immediate interest to him—or, more precisely, to Lenox. In Munich, where they arrived in the early morning hours exhausted after jolting, consecutive overnight carriage rides, he was off with only a few hours of rest to visit the palatial Royal Library, a library immensely strong, as he knew, in bibles and the rare European library "willing to part with its duplicates." He returned bright and early the next morning "by appointment," no doubt ready to buy. He did not mention, however, whether he also went to see the Magens library, whose distinguished collection of Aldines, Elzevirs, and bibles corresponded nicely to Lenox's collecting interests. Had he done so, he would have been wasting his time; Stevens preceded him there by weeks, having parted from the Putnams in Paris in order to evaluate and report back not only to Panizzi but also to Lenox on that and a number of other choice collections in Germany.

Their stays in German cities—Munich, Stuttgart, Heidelberg, Cologne—were all short and fast-paced, the last leaving only a thirty-hour voyage between them and London. If the sights of northern Europe were aesthetically and culturally less appealing to Putnam than those of the south, the superior technological development of northern roads, buildings, and railways registered favorably on his American sensibility. He and Victorine were particularly relieved to find the transportation improved after having suffered during their southern travels due to the only partial completion of railway lines. At one point along the line running between Pisa and Florence, Putnam had noted with pride the use of an American-made locomotive driving their train: "American enterprise," he commented, "is excursive." That spirit of enterprise, as admirable as it was familiar, that he thought so lacking in the south he found in abundance in the north, where he noted approvingly the size of the Royal Library of Munich, the city's handsome modern buildings and wide roads, and the fine printing facility and trans-European influence of Stuttgart's *Allegemeine Zeitung* ("the

Times of Germany"). Outside of the German states he noted also with approval the modern industry of Liège (the "Pittsburgh of the continent—picturesquely situated, populous and busy—romance and chivalry have given way to iron foundries and steam engines") and of Ghent (a city he characterized as "modern, active, thriving, and 'go-ahead,'" the Old World analogue to his type-seeking mind of Utica or Buffalo). So, despite the miserable weather that settled over them in Germany, the Putnams happily sped along their way across Germany and the Low Countries, with quick railway nods over the shoulder to cities visited on previous trips, and over the channel back home.

They arrived back in London on 6 May, with Putnam stocked full not only with memories but with a running account of them in his notebook. With his characteristic self-deprecation, he dismissed the importance of those notes once they reached the stage of publication. Unable to launch into the expected sublime over his first look at St. Peter's, he had characteristically written that his pen "was only intended for names and dates, bald as an index" and added in consequence, "I will note names and things not thoughts." That was a serious understatement actually of the quality of his writing ability and the acuity of his sensibility. He might not have had the fluency or sophistication of his friend Bayard Taylor, whose *Views A-foot* had been put to press in New York by Wiley and Putnam just months before and had made a strong popular impression (as a kind of forerunner of the post–World War Two genre of "Europe on— $ a day"). In spite of writing with his usual haste and habitual subordination of himself (the normal unit of expression being the headless, faceless phrase rather than the usual "I"-centered sentence common in travelogue writing), Putnam managed to convey a breezy, discerning impression of his experiences in Europe and a coherent overview that a man of his background, ideas, and values took of the world. Sounding like a Jamesian protagonist standing on foreign ground, Putnam articulated precisely and lucidly the overriding impression he had of the Old World he both admired and distrusted and of his own identity as an American in Europe: related but alien, democratic but superior, simple but cultured, respectful but untraditional, pleasure loving but frugal. Simultaneous with but finally opposed to the travels of Margaret Fuller and the uses to which she put them, Putnam's excursion of 1847 and his published account went only as far and deep as he cared to explore the environment in which he had spent one of the most important decades of his life.

Putnam's last weeks in London were busy with the nonstop preparations for departure. At work he had to catch up with the heavy volume of business that had accumulated during his absence and to ready the London office for his departure. He had decided sometime in the weeks preceding his trip to the Continent to give up Wiley and Putnam's expensive Waterloo offices for simpler quarters in Paternoster Row; that move took place in Putnam's absence. No doubt another cost-cutting act, he also let go of at least one longtime employee.[21] About the same time, Putnam decided to turn over management of the office to his senior associate David Davidson, an experienced bookman well known in the trade and to customers. Davidson was a young American who had been with Wiley and Putnam since 1841 and had risen through their ranks, eventually joining Putnam in London sometime in the mid-1840s and soon proving his worth. By an ironic stroke of fortune, Wiley and Putnam were indebted to Washington Irving for Davidson's services; Irving had sent the young man from Sunnyside, where he had worked as a hired man who gradually earned Irving's trust and affection, to Broadway in response to a letter from the firm's New York office soliciting his help in filling a vacancy in their retail department.[22] To carry out Davidson's former responsibilities as he took over Putnam's, the firm advertised in the trade paper for a professional book-keeper at a salary of £100. It must have expected long hours of this employee because the advertisement specified that all applicants be under the age of thirty and unmarried.[23] It was Davidson whom Putnam had entrusted in March to represent the firm at the Wilkes sale at Sotheby's, and it was Davidson who now had the unpleasant task of informing Putnam that the Gutenberg Bible he had purchased still remained unclaimed. When Putnam's letter of 17 May offering it to Sir Thomas Phillipps came back just a day or two before his departure with Phillipps's categorical refusal to take it at the offered price, Putnam had no choice but to ship the volume to New York and to hope for the best.

Meanwhile, the family was making its own preparations for the move from Knickerbocker Cottage. Visits were paid to various friends and acquaintances. The house was packed up and possessions readied for the voyage. They decided to travel heavy; valuing their furniture too highly to leave it behind, the Putnams packed up as much as they could afford to transport to America. They also brought back with them their beloved English nurse Isabella Cole, who would remain a member of the Putnam household until her death in 1860. They made their return journey without companions, although as it turned out the high seas were full that spring of well-known Americans and visitors crossing from England to America: Frederick Douglass, his freedom purchased, returning home after his long sojourn in Europe, Alexandre Vattemarre making a return visit this time with tens of thousands of French volumes in his possession designated for American libraries, and James Gordon Bennett returning after setting up a European network of correspondents for his New York *Herald.*

They sailed from Portsmouth on 24 May on board the *Margaret Evans,* the same packet ship that had transported the newlyweds to London in 1841.[24] Their family had grown considerably in the interval; they returned now with three children, Mrs. Cole, a servant, and— quite possibly—the Gutenberg Bible. As on their maiden voyage, they booked passage on a packet rather than a steamer to keep down the cost of transport.[25] The *Margaret Evans* was heavily laden for this particular crossing; it held about forty-eight passengers in cabins and another three hundred down below in steerage. The Putnams not only made up one of the larger parties on the ship but also brought on board far more than their share of freight; the hold contained sixty-five cases marked Wiley and Putnam, nearly all of which were filled with the family furniture.[26] On the passage out of England, they passed a ship on fire, but their own voyage was generally slow and uneventful. By then the nineteenth-century equivalent of a frequent flier, Putnam was on terms of familiarity with both the ship and its captain, circumstances that helped him pass the time relatively freely. But the trip was a laborious and anxious one for Victorine, who under the best of circumstances could barely tolerate ocean traveling but who in this instance was approaching full term; she gave birth to a boy (John Bishop) just four weeks after their arrival in New York on 21 June.

Economy also dictated their decision to locate themselves on Staten Island, a largely rural environment they settled in within days of their arrival and one well situated to meet the Putnams' needs: affordable property; relatively quick and easy access (except in winter) by ferry from the neighborhood of their home to lower Manhattan; and open spaces, beaches, and nature trails for the children.[27] Their home was situated at Stapleton on the east side of the island; from the front piazza of their house, which sat a few hundred feet from the water's edge, they had a clear view across the bay stretching from Brooklyn to

Manhattan.[28] Their house was not only reasonably spacious but charming, its overhanging balconies on the south and east filling the rooms on those sides with sun and sea air. They also had the nearby companionship of Victorine's sister Corinna and her husband, who had moved out of the city to a spacious house a few miles down the shore in Clifton. The Bishops kept their own stable behind the house; one of the chief pleasures for the elder Putnam children was riding their horses along the beach. For the five years they lived there, the Putnam children learned to entertain themselves on the island and to form their own tightly knit society, children with parents but also children among themselves, discovering the island to be a delightful place for swimming, boating, riding, gardening, walking, and simply exploring. The location on the island clearly reinforced their parents' progressive ideas of child rearing, allowing the children a maximum of freedom to explore the world physically and intellectually. Their free-spirited ways sometimes upset their aunt, who had a very different ideal from her sister of proper juvenile deportment.[29] All, however, with the children was not fun and games. Aided by Mrs. Cole, Victorine began the practice of home schooling, beginning with her two precocious, eldest children, Mary ("Minnie") and George Haven, to whom she taught not only basic reading, writing, and arithmetic but soon, as they mastered these subjects, music, history, and French. Those lessons gradually spread to include the next children on the family ladder, as the ladder added new rungs at a nearly biennial rate during the next decade.

For people as sociable as the Putnams, however, visits were an important and exciting part of the their routine. Some of their visitors came long distances; George Haven recollected specifically the visits of Susan Warner, Fredrika Bremer, Wendell Phillips, William Talboys (son of the well-known Oxford bookseller, who came to find himself in America and was employed briefly by Putnam at the store), and the Panamanian travel author Joseph Fabens, who brought back with him from one of his voyages a present that the children remembered for years: a pet alligator.[30] A more exotic south-of-the-border visitor at their house was José Antonio Paez, the sometime president, sometime strong man of Venezuela who had received a warm official welcome on arriving in New York in 1850 and a complimentary description in the local newspapers.[31] One visitor not mentioned by George Haven was Andrew Jackson Downing, the leading landscape architect in America and an important Wiley and Putnam author of the 1840s. Another was

Mellen Chamberlain, Putnam's trading partner in autographs, who came down to stay with the family just weeks after they settled on the island.[32]

Occasionally, Putnam brought home with him on the ferry a visitor or friend to pass the night. The most notable were Washington Irving, who asked one day at the store if he might spend the night on Staten Island where he had not been since his army duty in the War of 1812; and his archrival James Fenimore Cooper, who stayed overnight in 1850, a year in which Putnam and Cooper were continuing their collaboration in issuing an edition of some of Cooper's new and old works.[33] More frequent visits came from the family's Staten Island neighbors. By the 1840s the island was home to an unusually interesting and distinguished population. One of those local visitors was Frederick Law Olmsted, who on one visit took part in an amateur theatrical that the Putnams hosted and staged. On this particular occasion, the event that brought down the curtain was the outbreak of a fire in the house.[34] Another frequent visitor was William Emerson, brother of Ralph Waldo. Their most frequent house guests, however, were Putnam's mother and sister Elizabeth, the latter with her children, who generally came for days at a time. If Corinna Bishop was upset by the children's independence and lack of discipline, one can only imagine the reaction of their grandmother, evangelical in temperament and habituated to a more authoritarian set of child-rearing practices.

The Putnams would surely have found the city and country conspicuously changed. The Whig William Harrison had just ended the long Democratic hold on the White House when they left for London in 1841; now they returned to a presidency restored to the Democrats, with whose policies on the tariff, slavery, and the Mexican War Putnam was out of sympathy. On the day that the Putnams docked in New York, President Polk set out from Washington on a political tour of the Northeast, but the Putnams were too busy getting their own lives in order to see him when he passed through New York later that week.[35] Polk's war with Mexico, relayed to newspaper offices around the country via the telegraph, was making news daily, but the Putnams were more preoccupied with getting themselves reconnected to their local environment than concerned about a conflict that remained distant to them, as it did to most Americans. When the next major American war came, however, it would be a completely different matter, intruding into their household and transforming their private lives.

Having been so long away from the city, the Putnams would have seen more clearly than local residents the scale and character of changes remaking New York into a major urban center. The New York *Tribune* reported on 22 June that 4,987 immigrants had entered the city the previous week alone. With its population experiencing uncontrolled growth, the city pushed northward beyond his mother's neighborhood in today's Greenwich Village as stretches of what had been farmland were sold and converted into urban blocks.[36] On one empty lot (today's Bryant Park) the Croton Reservoir was built and became operational by 1842, supplying the city's expanding population with fresh water. A few years earlier Philip Hone had recorded in his diary with only slight exaggeration: "The spirit of pulling down and building up is abroad. The whole of New York is rebuilt about once in ten years."[37] Municipal politics were murkier and nastier than ever. James Harper, the oldest of the brothers with whom Putnam had had (and would yet have) numerous dealings and misdealings, had been elected mayor in 1844 on a nativist, anti-Catholic third-party agenda clearly no more to Putnam's taste than were the publishing policies of his house. Although the local pundit George Templeton Strong proved prophetic in referring to Harper in 1845 as "the immortal Harper, the Mayor that wants to be, but won't be after his present term runs out," Putnam would find his string of successors, if anything, even less palatable.[38] Himself not drawn to direct participation in politics, Putnam was too civic-minded to ignore the goings on in the city. His own involvement, though, was more typically at this time with libraries, historical societies, and museums than municipal politics of the sort that would culminate with Tammany Hall.

The city was also changing for Putnam professionally, although his annual trips and voluminous correspondence had kept him as well informed as a person could be in absentia. Just the same, he had too sharp an eye and too keen a sense of history to have been unaware of the exponential growth that was transforming the small, still generally localized print trade he had first encountered in 1829 into a modern industry. One of the first men in the trade to recognize its potential for transformational growth, an insight underlying his editorship of the *Booksellers' Advertiser* in the mid-thirties, Putnam could see by 1847 that much of the potential was being realized. All sectors of the print industry were growing rapidly. Steam technology, stereotyping, lowered book and newspaper prices were now standard aspects of publishing operations. Large publishing houses—Harper and Brothers, Appleton—

were well established and increasingly doing business on a national and even international scale, while a whole new generation of smaller firms—including his own—was growing to maturity by their side. Penny and two-penny newspapers had become common features of the reconfigured world of American journalism, reaching readers by the tens of thousands and giving the United States the (often begrudging) reputation among Europeans as an international center of print journalism. All in all, the print sector of New York was thriving, and Putnam—the eternal optimist—surely noticed that prospects for continued growth were encouraging.

The first order of business, though, was attending to basics. Putnam arrived back at 161 Broadway at a delicate time in the affairs of his firm, his good friend Duyckinck having been summarily fired in April from the editorship of the *Literary World* by its joint publishers, Wiley (on behalf of Wiley and Putnam) and Daniel Appleton. The dismissal stung Duyckinck. Ever since graduating college, he had yearned to establish a literary weekly of high quality and independent views, an American equivalent of the London *Athenaeum* that might fill what Duyckinck considered the gaping hole at the center of American literary journalism. Duyckinck apparently broached the idea of a Wiley and Putnam-subsidized review to John Wiley in late 1845, but Wiley turned him down without so much as mentioning the idea to Putnam.[39] Then one day in early 1847, Duyckinck was caught by surprise when Wiley, having changed his mind, offered in partnership with Appleton to provide him with money, printing facilities and supplies, and office space for operating a weekly journal.[40] The two publishers agreed to close down their own trade-centered newsletters in deference to Duyckinck's weekly, which they expected to fill that niche and hoped would attract sufficient trade advertising and patronage to pay all or most of their production expenses. The contract was signed on 15 January, and the first issue of the journal appeared on 6 February. From the start, with its intelligent general articles, discerning book and art reviews, foreign literary intelligence (supplied from London by Putnam), extensive publishers' circular of advertisements for new works, and items of local cultural gossip, it proved how good a review in Duyckinck's hands might be.

Within two months, however, it became apparent that Duyckinck's and the publishers' definitions of "independent views" differed sharply. Duyckinck had instinctively involved his controversial friend and crony Cornelius Mathews in his editorial decisions, a move that angered Wiley and infuriated Appleton, who demanded that Duyckinck choose between Mathews and the *Literary World*. When Duyckinck refused to back down and showed no interest in buying the paper from them, they fired him and hired Charles Fenno Hoffman, those editorial changes announced in the 1 and 15 May issues, respectively. Wiley might earlier have acted with greater restraint, but by spring 1847 he had far less need of Duyckinck's good will and services than during the two previous years. Duyckinck had voluntarily ceased to oversee the two major Wiley and Putnam Libraries the previous August or September, at which time he had taken $1,000 payment for his services and left with the expectation that that sum would be augmented by the royalties and interest earned from his and his brother's investment in the Wiley and Putnam Foreign Library.[41] His connection with Wiley, however, continued informally even after the change of editorship, their mutual needs proving stronger than their personal antagonisms.[42]

With Putnam back in the office, Wiley had less need of a hired hand to guide the literary side of the business. That summer, in any case, affairs at the Wiley and Putnam office were relatively quiet. The Wiley and Putnam Libraries, the most ambitious publishing ventures the firm had undertaken, were winding down, and the firm had no significant follow-up initiatives planned. Furthermore, with Putnam now in New York, the firm lacked the direct transatlantic pipeline that had directed so heavy a flow of works from London publishers to the New York office. During his first weeks back in the office, Putnam had numerous other matters to attend to, not the least of which was the process of renewing acquaintance around town with members of the trade. Certainly, one of his most pressing errands was to visit Lenox and to attempt one more time to persuade him to purchase the Gutenberg Bible. This time he succeeded.

The joy (and relief) of selling the Gutenberg, in which the firm had invested a considerable amount of its always short supply of capital, must have been tempered by Putnam's realization that he was losing a lucrative account to Stevens, who lost no time after Putnam's departure in filling his place. In response to the "friendly note" Putnam wrote shortly after settling down in the New York area, inviting Stevens to stay with the family on Staten Island during his expected visit to America and to be treated to Victorine's peaches, Stevens slipped from a return exchange of pleasantries to a fervent self-defense that he had been so rudely and mistrustfully treated at the store by Davidson that he not only avoided going there but also stopped using the London office's exporting services. If that was a violation of the working agreement that the two had negotiated before going off to the Continent, which stipulated that Stevens send whatever books he purchased in Britain for American clients through Wiley and Putnam and credit them their commission, Stevens wished Putnam to know that the true culprit in the affair was not he. "I do not consider that I have violated the agreement," he asserted, pointing out that he had sent approximately £8,000 worth of books to America since his arrival, not £500 worth of which would otherwise have passed through the hands of Wiley and Putnam. Nor was it Putnam, whom he professed he had always found friendly and reasonable, but Davidson—and Davidson alone.[43]

This was hardly the full truth. What he did not say here (although he included it in his biography of Lenox many years later) was that he considered Putnam a bibliographic amateur intruding on territory better left to professionals like himself.[44] Nor did he state how crucial the Lenox account was to his ambitions to center his professional life in London. Putnam's response is unknown, but as a practical matter his options were limited. The relations between the two men had come half circle since 1845; Putnam, who wished to keep his status as Stevens's New York agent, now needed Stevens more than Stevens needed him. Their business relations, however, continued for a period of years after Putnam had established his own business in New York, with Putnam filling that role until the early 1850s, if never to Stevens's satisfaction.[45]

Another matter that followed Putnam to America was the latest flare-up of the long-standing antagonism in Britain toward American publishers for pirating the works of British authors. When he returned from the Continent in May, Putnam had had his attention turned to a series of derogatory remarks in the English press about the professional ethics of American publishers in general and of Wiley and Putnam in particular. The episode was sparked by an article by Leigh Hunt in the London *Atlas,* which *Punch* recast as a sketch of Hunt walking by the American Literary Agency and complaining:

> An English man of letters certainly passes the doors of American booksellers in London with very singular feelings. He knows

they will snatch hold of his book the moment it is published,
sell thousands of copies of it on the other side of the Atlantic
without giving him the benefit of a stiver, and perhaps have the
pleasure of seeing him go by their London windows in the rain,
while they are flourishing in a big house over his head. We
suppose it is all right, and proper, and consistent, and free-
born, and independent, and respectable, and slave-holding, and
lovely, and going-a-head. It is certainly going another man's
head, though with a considerable quantity of their own face
beneath it.[46]

Punch returned to the attack a month later with a comic letter from
Lord Palmerston to his ambassador in Washington authorizing him to
threaten hostilities between the two countries should American piracy
not cease—that article accompanied by a cartoon of an American bookseller dressed as an Indian scalping an English author.[47]

Pressed on his most sensitive nerve, Putnam could not restrain
his impulse to strike back. Within days of returning to London, he sent
a letter to the editor of the *Times* filled with righteous indignation,
reprising the argument he had made in *American Facts* and elsewhere
that unpaid reprinting was not an American but a transatlantic practice, as common in London as in New York. He not only reversed the
British accusation against American publishers but brazenly named
specific British publishers as complicit in this practice (his list included
such well-known publishers as Colburn, Bentley, Tegg, Bohn, and
Routledge but discretely omitted his friends Murray, Chapman, and
Moxon).[48] He also defended himself by informing the British public of
his role in presenting the 1843 petition to Congress advocating international copyright legislation and expressed his regret that the petition stalled in committee. Still unable after his return to New York to
let the matter rest, Putnam took it up again in July in the friendly
pages of the *Literary World,* pointing out that he had been treated
unfairly by the *Times,* whose editor had cut from his letter his regret
that Leigh Hunt, who had initiated this episode of the debate, "had not
benefited by the express sanction which we purchased for our editions
of his recent works" because "if any author deserves honor and reward
it is that delightful essayist." Furthermore, the *Times* editor had cut the
entire paragraph expressing Putnam's continuing commitment to fair
international publishing practices: "We shall continue to advocate legal

protection for the interests of ALL authors, satisfied that *even the people at large will be the gainers by such protection:*—and meanwhile (until that protection is granted), in future, *as heretofore,* whenever a foreign author enables us partially to protect ourselves and him by publication simultaneously with that in Europe, we shall willingly pay him the same proportion of the profits as to an American author—and so, we think, will any other American publisher of standing."[49] Putnam closed by questioning the common argument made by opponents that international copyright would work to the advantage of publishers and authors but to the disadvantage of the reading public; his fundamental conviction then, as always, was that the passage of an international copyright bill would be in the interests of authors, publishers, and the general public alike.

The months of summer and fall passed uneventfully at the office. Wiley and Putnam brought out the final titles in its Libraries, including those in the Foreign Library financed by the Duyckincks. The brothers were particularly eager to see the firm publish the second half of *Dichtung und Warheit* in their Library. Also on hand was what Duyckinck considered "a work of life and insight" by an author known to the firm only as "a Graduate of Oxford."[50] There is no documentation about how Wiley and Putnam came into American rights to *Modern Painters,* but since they had no competition for it, it is possible that Putnam had arranged for it with either Ruskin or his publisher. They also brought out what they advertised as the first American edition of Izaak Walton's *Compleat Angler.* Along with their friendly rivals the Appletons, they continued to import books heavily from England and the Continent via the steamships, their ads for these books as well as their own publications filling numerous columns of the *Literary World.*

It is not at all clear whether Putnam had ever seriously considered striking out on his own during the London years, but in the months following his return to New York the idea gradually took root. Although he could fairly have regarded himself at the time as the most widely experienced bookman in the city, he was still but the junior partner in Wiley and Putnam. Relations between the two men were then, as they had always been, never less than formally correct. Putnam had full respect for Wiley's financial acumen, and Wiley had the highest regard for Putnam's taste and publishing abilities (his "pushing powers," as Duyckinck labeled them).[51] Nevertheless, once installed in the office with a senior partner after years of relative independence, Putnam found the urge to leave Wiley and venture out on his own irresistible. A half-century after their breakup, George Haven Putnam, who knew his father's publishing tendencies better than anyone else, remarked that in many ways Wiley and Putnam were actually well suited to be business partners, that Wiley's temperamental conservatism and financial caution complemented his father's adventurous spirit, literary instinct, and spendthrift tendencies.[52] In late 1847, however, an observation of that sort was the last thing that Putnam wished to hear; with his grand ambition of establishing and operating his own publishing house about to become a reality, he moved decisively toward ending their nearly decade-long partnership.

Toward the end of 1847 he was ready to put his plans into operation. His reputation was such that the announcement of his move quickly attracted attention around Broadway, some curious insiders (such as Charles Welford, a competitor and soon to be a partner with Charles Scribner in the book-importing business) having already speculated on its eventuality. One of the first people informed of Putnam's intentions was, naturally, Duyckinck, who reported to his brother George, then making the grand tour of Europe, on the imminent dissolution of the firm: "It is not yet publicly advertised but goes into effect in a month or so and Putnam starts an independent establishment in one of the new stores alongside of 161 [Broadway]. The Napoleon of the trade must indicate his title by some extraordinary demonstration. I told him I expected to be astonished and he winked at the notion."[53] Duyckinck was no doubt recollecting how Putnam had caught the book sector by storm during his summer 1846 visit when he placed newspaper advertisements for unprecedented numbers of books on behalf of the British Museum, that grand gesture now requiring another.

The actual breakup of the partnership took place in March 1848. The London agency was also discontinued; a notice of dissolution signed in New York on 25 March was published on 1 July in *Publishers' Circular,* the date coinciding with the formal liquidation of the London office. In point of fact, the firm had advertised four of the upstairs rooms at their 12 Paternoster Row office two months earlier as being available for let (or, more likely, sublet).[54] Wiley inherited the firm name in London and New York and immediately resumed operations in smaller rooms in the neighboring Aldine Chambers at 13 Paternoster Row. The separation agreement left Putnam with a half share of Wiley and

6. Original place of business of the firm G. P. Putnam, 155 Broadway, several doors down the street from John Wiley. (Courtesy Manuscripts and Archives Division, New York Public Library)

Putnam's books and stereotype plates but with very little operating capital. Not even a sale of some of the firm's plates and books relieved Putnam's shortage of operating funds, which so insufficiently offset his initial expenses and grand plans that he had to pay the carpenter who built shelves for his new store on three months' credit.[55] To Henry Stevens he described himself as "short as pie crust" a few weeks after opening for business.[56] Other than that initial allotment, his chief asset was his own publishing ability. In winter 1848 that must have seemed to him—and, no doubt, to many in the trade—like a solid foundation on which to erect a publishing house. Putnam was still only thirty-four-years-old, healthy, energetic, and ambitious; he had a nonpareil knowledge of the international book business and a broad acquaintance with its participants on both sides of the Atlantic; he maintained a wide range of contacts among authors, editors, publishers, booksellers, collectors, librarians, and illustrators in the United States and overseas; and he had as clear and compelling a vision of what publishing in the United States could be as any other publisher of his generation. If for the previous decade and longer he had taken upon himself an unofficial role of leadership in the American publishing trade, he was now as ready as he would ever be to oversee a company of his own.

With Wiley exercising his right to keep the old offices, Putnam rented a store just several doors down the street at 155 Broadway and began outfitting it with his share of the old store's stock. An early believer in advertising, Putnam placed frequent advertisements in the local newspapers beginning 2 March and full-page ones in the *Literary World* (at $10 each). By 9 March his store was open for business, its plate glass doors stamped with the title: "Putnam Publisher and Importer." Duyckinck thought the store "the simplest and best in arrangement of any in Broadway—well-lighted, airy and clear as the deck of the Washington."[57] Perhaps he liked it because it carried such a wide selection of titles and was so accommodating to potential customers who wished to look them over. Black walnut bookshelves set on thick matting lined the storefront, and they were stocked with the latest works in the belles lettres and other fields. Armchairs were positioned for casual reading. Furthermore, Duyckinck was proud of the fact that his brother-in-law Frank Panton was employed by Putnam and performing well.

Putnam's immediate idea was to model his own business loosely on that of the old firm: to combine a retail business engaging in the importation and sale of books with a full-scale publishing operation. With so many years invested in international book buying and selling, Putnam was no more willing than many of his peers, including his good friends the Appletons in New York and James T. Fields of Ticknor and Company in Boston, to separate the spheres of publishing and book dealing. His need to remain involved in the international book trade and to keep his connections active in England was so strong that, according to his son, he made a quick return trip to England that spring, the most important outcome of which was that he entered into an agreement with John Chapman, the dynamic young publisher of Carlyle, to serve as his London agent. Putnam had visited Chapman many times at the large building at 142 Strand that served Chapman as both residence and business office, and the two young men, so similar in their energy and ambitiousness, got along well. More important, the connection between the two men made mutual sense, giving each the other half of the transatlantic nexus he desired.[58] For the actual manufacture of his books, Putnam planned to rely on the same high-quality printers and stereotypers employed by the old firm, such as Robert Craighead, John Trow, and T. B. Smith; not until the 1880s, by which time his firm was under the direction of his sons, would the Putnams build their own printing facilities. Although he continued to adhere to the old firm's Anglo-American ideal of a well-made book, Putnam was also eager to utilize the new technologies of bookmaking. He was especially partial to illustration; G. P. Putnam would soon distinguish itself as one of the city's busiest employers of artists and engravers. At the same time, the new company carried the imprint of Putnam's own secular, middle-class, nationalistic taste and values. Freed from the conservatism of Wiley, Putnam immediately loosened himself from the theological circles of Andover and Princeton and re-oriented himself to enter the area of publishing that most suited his sensibility and ideology, the belles lettres.

Duyckinck's hypothesis proved to be an accurate reading of Putnam's mind. Despite operating with shallow pockets, Putnam had deep ambitions, and he made as quick a start as circumstances permitted toward establishing himself as a leading New York literary publisher. He began with a bold and intelligently conceived plan to accomplish that goal: to court a major American writer and to present him to the American public in new, standard dress. The author who suited his purposes best was Washington Irving, the most venerable American writer of the time and one whose works were either out of print in the United States or available only in out-of-date editions. Putnam began his courtship of Irving with the advantage of an intermittent, decade-long acquaintance. He had first met Irving at the 1837 dinner given by the New York Booksellers' Association (where he probably also made the acquaintance of another of his first year's cadre of authors, Poe), and had grown to know him more familiarly when they met in 1842 at the annual dinner of the Literary Fund in London and in autumn 1845 through winter 1846 when they met a number of times at his home and office.[59] That last sequence of meetings followed Putnam's written proposal to Irving in summer 1845 to publish either his new or old works through the New York office.[60] Irving politely declined the offer but not without mentioning the fact that he was preparing a revised edition of his complete works for print and would not forget Putnam's firm when he was ready to enter negotiations for its publication.

Two years later it was Putnam who did not forget that fact. In truth, Irving had long been eager to resuscitate his works but was selective about the conditions under which he would do so. He had been unable to persuade his previous ("mousing") publishers, Blanchard and Lea of Philadelphia, to issue a new edition of his works either in 1842 before he left the country to serve as minister to Spain or in late 1846 after he returned to the United States. Then in January 1847 Wiley and Putnam (but not Putnam himself) had contacted him to offer its publishing services, an offer to which Irving responded encouragingly but noncommittally.[61] No further progress, however, was made in the negotiations with Wiley and Putnam or with any other house over the course of 1847. Then, within weeks of forming his own house, Putnam made the right offer at the right time; the result was that the two men quickly reached a general working agreement for a full-scale revised edition of Irving's works. The prospect of a project so ambitious as to require an initial investment running into the thousands of dollars did not faze Putnam, even though he soon took the precaution to solicit Duyckinck's participation in the new edition on the basis of shared expenses and profits. Always a cautious investor with his inherited funds, Duyckinck, who had had the pick of numerous publishing and editing projects since leaving the *Literary World,* turned him down.[62] With or without outside help, Putnam somehow financed the planned edition, which he enthusiastically advanced toward production well in advance of actually signing a contract. One day in mid-May, Duyckinck encountered Putnam on the street, who excitedly showed him a specimen page of the *Sketch Book* that he was taking to the printer's.[63] Little wonder he was excited: he was about to embark on the largest gamble of his career.

Putnam formally announced the publication of his Irving edition—revised, complete, and uniform—in the 10 June issue of the *Literary World*, even though the contract was not signed until 26 July.[64] Given their personalities and views, perhaps a "gentleman's agreement" was all the two men needed before proceeding to publication, but Putnam was taking no chances. Mindful of the chief external danger to the success of the undertaking, he issued the formal warning to the trade: "Justice both to the author and publisher requires that the importation of foreign editions of Irving's works (or any part of them), which has heretofore been suffered because the American editions were long out of print, should now be *strictly prohibited*. All foreign copies imported or offered for sale hereafter, will be liable to forfeiture, and the vender will incur the usual penalty." The contract authorized Putnam to reprint all of Irving's old works, each one revised by the author, for five years in a uniform duodecimo series as well as in alternative formats. In addition, Putnam was to have the exclusive right to Irving's new works. In return, Putnam was to assume all production expenses and to pay Irving a 12 ½-percent royalty on the retail price of all books sold; furthermore, he was to insure Irving's interest against failure by guaranteeing him minimal revenues ranging on a sliding scale from $1,000 the first year to $2,000 for the last three years.[65] Within months of the publication of the first work, the popularly known *Knickerbocker's History of New York* with which Putnam wisely led off, it became clear that that guarantee would be unnecessary: the two men had a runaway success on their hands. Irving expressed himself in October as surprised by the size of the sales, but at that time it was still too early for them to appreciate the magnitude of their success.[66] In time, Irving was to make both Putnam and himself profits running into the tens of thousands of dollars, Putnam was to make Irving into the first canonized American author, and together they were to form a collaboration that would mark a transformational moment in American literary publishing.

If the agreement with Irving became the foundation on which Putnam built his publishing house, it began as only one part of a larger plan of operations. Putnam launched his business with the intent of presenting

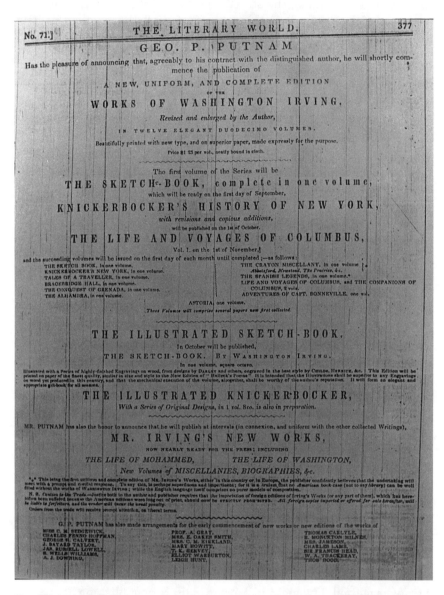

7.   Historic G. P. Putnam advertisement announcing the publication of the Washington Irving edition and plans to publish editions of various other leading Anglo-American authors. (*Literary World,* 10 June 1848; photo by Joseph Golson)

a broad roster of authors to the public; the same advertisement that announced the Irving edition also noted that arrangements had been made for publication of works by Bayard Taylor, Catharine Maria Sedgwick, and Andrew Jackson Downing among American writers; and by Charles Lamb, William Makepeace Thackeray, Thomas Carlyle, Leigh Hunt, and Thomas Hood among British authors.[67] Some of those titles were leftovers from the Wiley and Putnam list, but most were new, as were some of the important titles Putnam published during his first year, including Poe's *Eureka,* James Russell Lowell's *A Fable for Critics,* Francis Parkman's *Oregon Trail,* and the first edition of William Frederick Poole's *An Alphabetical Index to Subjects, Treated in the Reviews, and Other Periodicals, to Which No Indexes Have Been Published.* Each of those last three titles was to prove itself a classic in American letters, and each deserves elaboration.

Putnam owed the good fortune of being offered publication rights to *Poole's Index,* as it became familiarly known in later editions, to the mediation of Henry Stevens. Stevens had met Poole, then an undergraduate at Yale and a librarian of the fraternal society library that Stevens had likewise served, in early 1848 during his American book-buying tour. One skilled bibliographer recognizing another, Stevens quickly saw the utilitarian value of the reference guide that Poole had made to articles in various of the library's journals, and he appreciated the fact that its value might readily extend beyond Yale College. He therefore referred Poole to Putnam, who agreed to finance the production costs and to publish the work in a limited edition of 500 copies— its intended audience, no doubt, libraries and collectors around the country.[68] So small an edition, one smaller by half than Poole had hoped for, suggests that Putnam had something more than profit in mind in accepting it for publication. Most likely, he saw and valued its potential status as a historically important advance in the growth of American bibliography. Putnam should have known: he had devoted so many hours of his youth and early manhood to classifying historical knowledge and to organizing catalogues of books that he would have been among the first to regard *Poole's Index* as a major step forward toward the systematization of information in nineteenth-century America. In putting his imprint on a pioneering guide that was itself both a product of and a response to the proliferation of magazine journalism and to the widening circle of general readers who patronized those journals, Putnam was in effect advancing his own commitment to the centralization not only of the trade but of print culture in America.[69] The need for such a guide was hardly limited to the United States, as a comparable proliferation of print was concurrently occurring in many of the societies of Europe, which explains why Poole's efforts resonated overseas. In Britain, for instance, the editor of the English trade journal *Publishers' Circular* spoke approvingly of it as "an example well worthy imitation on a more extended scale."[70]

By an interesting coincidence, a parallel attempt at the systematization of information was taking place right in Putnam's office. One of his early employees was the pioneering bibliographer Orville Roorbach, who, according to Adolph Growoll, had briefly managed the wholesale department of Wiley and Putnam before joining Putnam after the split and taking a similar position in the new business.[71] Having invested many years of preparation in his project, Roorbach brought out in 1849 his *Bibliotheca Americana*, a compendium of basic publishing information about many thousands of American books. That book appeared with the inscription "For sale by G. P. Putnam" on its title page, although it seems likely that Roorbach was forced to subsidize his own edition. The following year, however, Putnam did publish the thin supplement that Roorbach had assembled. His office was unquestionably the most appropriate address in New York for such a work, and Putnam its most appropriate supplier. Putnam had taken an interest in the forms of literary culture in modern society as early as 1836, when during his initial trip to England he sought out and made the acquaintance of Thomas Hartwell Horne, the erudite historian/bibliographer of print and preprint culture and the author of the pioneering *Introduction to the Study of Bibliography* (1814). Publishing and distributing early bibliographical productions by Poole and Roorbach complemented that early orientation, as well as Putnam's pioneering attempts to bring order to American publishing and letters.

James Russell Lowell's *A Fable for Critics*, published in October, was for Putnam a particularly attractive addition to his list, although, as with Poole, the source of the attraction might not have been primarily financial. It was presumably intended by neither author nor publisher to be a big money maker, appearing in a first edition of probably 1,000 copies, some of which Putnam shipped overseas to John Chapman for sale in England.[72] Just the same, Lowell's work was unusually appealing for Putnam, associating his name not only with one of the brightest young writers in the United States but with the most eloquent spoof of the state of contemporary American letters. *A Fable* coopted Putnam both directly and indirectly; its long, rhymed title page—"Set forth in October, the 21st day, in the year '48, by G. P. Putnam, Broadway"— involved the firm in the act of literary publishing, and its preface implicated Putnam himself in the game of democratic letters by referring poets upset at their exclusion from the poem "to my friend G. P. Putnam, Esquire in Broadway," who would keep the official list of potential inductees to be skewered in future editions of the poem.

Although generally remembered for its sharp insights and barbed witticisms aimed at particular literati, Lowell's primary concern was not with individuals writers at all but with the overall state of contemporary American letters. Ironically deploying an Olympian guise of classical personalities and forms, Lowell incisively analyzed the anti-classical transformation of literary culture caused by modern capitalism and the democratization of print. He was particularly concerned about the development of a print culture in which not one but "a whole flock of Lambs" vied for stature, patronage, and audience and in which (agri)culture was to be measured in terms that conflated quantity and quality:

> By the way, 'tis a fact that displays what profusions
> Of all kinds of greatness bless free institutions,
> . . . .
> With you every year a whole crop is begotten,
> They're as much of a staple as corn or cotton;
> Why, there's scarcely a huddle of log-huts and shanties
> That has not brought forth its own Miltons and Dantes.

If this was the anxious perspective of a patrician democrat like Lowell, it was hardly that of a culturally nationalistic publisher and commercially minded businessman like Putnam, who had fought (and would yet fight) for native authorship and who calculated his own business prospects on its success. A sign of his confidence in the spreading field of American letters, he enthusiastically sent off Lowell's small volume with an accompanying spate of vigorous advertisements to take its place in the market among the new belletristic works of 1848–49.

Another Yankee writer featured in Putnam's early publication list was Francis Parkman, whose *California and Oregon Trail* (which did not become known as the *Oregon Trail* until the 1872 edition) had been serialized in New York's leading literary journal, the *Knickerbocker*, from February 1847 to February 1849. Directly after its serialization, Putnam rushed to issue the work in New York and, by arrangement with John Chapman, in London. *California and Oregon Trail* at first sold briskly, passing through its first printing of 1,000 copies within a month of its publication and going immediately into an all-clothbound second printing of 500 copies. That small printing, Putnam assured Parkman, was occasioned simply by limited supplies of printer's paper and by his own pressed schedule, not by his lack of commitment, and he hoped that it would soon be followed by a third printing of 1,000 additional copies.[73] In subsequent months, however, sales slowed, leaving both men disappointed and looking for ways to reinvigorate interest in the work. Parkman eventually suggested a change of name to which Putnam agreed, advertising the work as *Prairie and Rocky Mountain Life* even before that title was officially adopted for the edition he published in 1851 and binding some copies in leather for sale to district school libraries.[74]

Like a fair number of his deals, this one mixed business with pleasure (the latter, a category that for Putnam typically included family). Putnam had a high regard for both the book and the author, and he and Victorine invited Parkman and his bride to come down to Staten Island.[75] Whether that visit ever took place is unclear, but Parkman did visit him at his Broadway office one day in late 1849 when Putnam was scheduled to dine with Washington Irving, who afterwards remarked that he was disappointed to learn that the man he saw at Putnam's but could not "place" was the author of "that capital book," *California and Oregon Trail*.[76] Putnam's attachment to the work is easily explained; it appealed to his publishing sense as a travelogue on the popular subject of the American West and to his literary taste as a work with a rare combination of sophistication and humor. But in 1850–51, despite its new title, sales trailed off, and Parkman was soon doing his literary business in Boston with the firm of Little, Brown—a pattern Putnam and other New York publishers increasingly faced as Yankee authors who published their early works in New York transferred their allegiance in the 1850s back home to Boston publishers. Putnam's acquaintance with Parkman apparently lagged until 1870, when Parkman inquired about the location of the stereotype plates, and Putnam responded with his usual mood of pleasantry: "I was very glad to see your familiar writing again and it has been a great gratification to Mrs

Putnam (who has pleasant remembrances of our former acquaintance) and to myself to know of your important and successful contributions to History, which have made the name of our former friend 'familiar in our mouths as household words.'"[77]

From the moment he embarked on his independent venture, Putnam set about turning the name of his firm into a household word. At first that meant detaching his personal and professional name from Wiley's. By late June or early July 1848 Putnam had completed arrangements with John Chapman for the handling of his affairs in London and was able to publicize his new London address in his advertisements.[78] But even with the formal separation of his places of business from Wiley's in New York and London, Putnam carried over into his publishing list many of the old Wiley and Putnam titles, such as the works of Carlyle and Hood and the new edition of Ruskin's *Modern Painters*. Wiley followed a similar practice: how else to explain the fact that soon after their breakup he was offering a six-shilling edition in London of his ex-partner's *American Facts*? In all likelihood, their separation agreement gave both men continuing publishing rights for a specified period to the old firm's list, a fallback that Putnam might have needed less than Wiley but that he no doubt needed just the same to begin business with a substantial list. Nevertheless, his publishing instincts led him to familiarize the profession and the nation with his new professional identity as quickly as possible. From 1848 to nearly the end of his career, he did this principally by publicizing the name of his firm as the sole American publisher and distributor of the works of Washington Irving.

Call it a marriage of convenience or a gentleman's agreement, their union of interests in 1848 was as nearly a perfect match as one could then find—indeed, as one could yet have found—between an American author and an American publisher. Their union even contained a poetic logic: Irving had visited the Putnams' Knickerbocker Cottage a few years earlier in London. Although that choice of name possibly pointed back only indirectly through Irving to their common "native" city, there was no coincidence whatsoever when Putnam resumed publishing after the Civil War and issued a Knickerbocker Edition of Irving's works. In fact, by the time Putnam issued his 1848 edition of *Knickerbocker's History of New York,* Irving was not only well aware of the linkage made by his contemporaries between himself and that name place but was willing to capitalize on it in the "Author's Apologia" that introduced the text: "And when I find, after a lapse of nearly forty years, this haphazard production of my youth still cherished among them [the 'descendants of the Dutch worthies']; when I find its very name become a 'household word,' and used to give the home stamp to every thing recommended for popular acceptation, such as Knickerbocker societies; Knickerbocker insurance companies; Knickerbocker steamboats; Knickerbocker omnibuses; Knickerbocker bread, and Knickerbocker tea; and when I find New-Yorkers of Dutch descent priding themselves upon being 'genuine Knickerbockers,' I please myself with the persuasion that I have struck the right chord."[79]

During a publishing relationship between Putnam and Irving that continued as long as Irving lived, and then between Putnam and the Irving estate as long as he lived, the two men manifestly struck the right chord with each other. Putnam found in Irving—both the man and the author—a sensibility remarkably congenial to his own. Like countless people of his generation, he had been a rapt reader of Irving from early maturity and had never ceased to take a visceral pleasure in the charm and grace of Irving's writings. Furthermore, he shared the prevailing opinion that American authorship in the belles lettres began with Irving. By the time of their association, Putnam could not have been unaware that Irving was a living symbol of the triumph of American authorship as much for the general American readership as for himself, his blessing sought by their contemporaries for everything from international copyright protection to career advancement. During his last decade, his fine house (Sunnyside) overlooking the Hudson River became a cultural shrine for tourists, one of the earliest in the United States and the nearest local version of an American Abbotsford. Why this special veneration? A major reason was that Irving was seen as the progenitor and chief practitioner of the Genteel Romanticism— to borrow the term of Adam Sweeting—then in vogue in American culture.[80] By no coincidence, that aesthetic characterized the work of many of Putnam's (and the nation's) most popular writers and writers-to-be of the pre–Civil War period, including Andrew Jackson Downing, Caroline Kirkland, Nathaniel Willis, George William Curtis, Susan Warner, and even Herman Melville. Putnam was too good a reader of contemporary taste and too shrewd a businessman not to know that a potentially huge, ready-made demand existed for a new edition of Irving's works and that his timing could hardly have been better. In placing his imprint on Irving's words, Putnam set himself in the enviable position of putting his wallet where his sensibility was.

The match was no less desirable for Irving. In 1848 he was at the low point in his career, with no new works to show for most of the decade and no publisher willing to meet his terms for publishing a revised edition of the old works. There was good reason for this general reluctance; Irving was a tough bargainer who had made several attempts to persuade his previous publisher, Blanchard and Lea, to issue a new, author-revised edition of his works for $3,000 (later reduced to $2,500) a year for a specified number of years.[81] In all likelihood, not a single established publisher in the country would have had sufficient funds backed by sufficient confidence to finance what must have seemed like not only an extravagant proposition but also one unevenly tilted toward the welfare of the author. Not even as eager a suitor as Putnam would have accepted such terms. Whatever their opening bargaining positions, Irving and Putnam soon reached a far more equitable royalty-based agreement that gave additional incentive to the publisher to promote the edition as aggressively as possible and to the author to wish that a maximum number of copies be sold. That arrangement also proved to be a much more profitable proposition for Irving; his average annual income during the first five-year period was not less than $9,000—a munificent sum for a mid-century writer. That he found Putnam professionally dependable, commercially adept, and personally attractive ensured that his reliance on Putnam would be a long-standing one.

Staking the prestige of his edition on its first titles, Putnam planned to inaugurate the edition with Irving's most popular works, the *Sketch Book* and *Knickerbocker's History,* in that order. But in late July or early August, possibly because Irving's revisions of the former were taking longer than expected, the order of their publication was reversed. On 30 August New York City newspapers announced *Knickerbocker's History* as having been published that day, the *Sketch Book* as due to appear 1 October, and subsequent titles in the edition as set to be published the first day of each successive month—an extraordinarily ambitious schedule for author and publisher to maintain and clear proof of the seriousness with which they jointly undertook the venture. The advertisement in the New York *Commercial Advertiser* (and in the 2 September issue of the *Literary World*) quoted an excerpt from the Boston *Evening Transcript* that must very nearly have approximated Putnam's many-sided ambitions for the volumes: "The typography of this series is all that could be desired. Nothing superior to it has issued from the American press. Irving will be among American classics what Goldsmith is among those of the Fatherland."

As summer passed into autumn, Putnam did everything in his power to establish a special stature for the edition. Although the announced book-a-month schedule proved impossibly ambitious to maintain through the entire publication process, Irving and Putnam did manage to produce a new volume generally by the first of each month for the first half year. During that six-month period, they issued *Knickerbocker's History, Sketch Book, Life and Voyages of Christopher Columbus* (in three volumes appearing over four months punctuated by the publication of *Bracebridge Hall* between the first and second volumes), and *Tales of a Traveller.* Furthermore, Putnam marketed the volumes aggressively. He provided friends in the press, such as Lewis Gaylord Clark of the *Knickerbocker,* advance sheets for early reviews.[82] He advertised the works both singly and collectively in various New York newspapers and magazines and distributed them as quickly as possible to booksellers in the major markets. In Boston, for instance, advertisements for the new edition were placed in city newspapers by early September by such local booksellers as James Munroe, Ticknor and Company, Crosby and Nichols, and B. Perkins and Company. As autumn progressed, volumes of the revised edition reached booksellers from coast to coast, to judge by advertisements appearing in local newspapers.

Always fastidious about the appearance of his books, Putnam had the volumes produced in a wide variety of styles and formats, sizes and bindings. He established as the edition's primary format a uniform clothbound duodecimo, a size large enough to look attractive but small enough to be affordable and popular. In his usual meticulous fashion, he gave careful consideration to the choice of paper and type, with results commented on approvingly by the press. He set the standard price for each volume at $1.25, an affordable price for the middle-to-upper-middle-class readership Putnam saw as the primary audience for the edition. For the same reason, no doubt, he issued all the titles except *Columbus* in a one-volume format, a not-yet-standardized practice in an era when "respectable" publishers still often issued copyrighted prose works in two-volume formats. His ambition was clear: to build up a readership that would buy each volume as it appeared and would end up with a uniform edition of the works. To apply this logic most comprehensively, Putnam also offered the works for consumers and collectors with finer tastes in virtually every binding then available at prices that escalated with the luxury of the material: cloth, cloth extra, sheep extra, half calf, half calf extra, calf extra, calf antique, half morocco, and morocco extra.[83] He also printed an octavo edition of the works and made it available in a similar variety of bindings.

In a bolder initiative that must have been close to his own heart, he also issued an illustrated edition of the volumes. A lifelong enthusiast of nineteenth-century technology applied to bookmaking in all forms but especially with respect to reproductions, Putnam rushed to produce illustrated versions of a number of his firm's works shortly after separating from Wiley. Of them none was as close to his heart or as vital to the financial condition of his firm as the illustrated Irving edition. He recognized the appeal of such works to the already large audience for gift books, an audience mirroring his own sensibility and one to which he oriented a significant part of his list his entire career, as well as potentially to a larger middle-class readership. It seems quite likely that he hit on the idea of the illustrated Irving edition simultaneously with the idea of the revised edition itself; as early as the 10 June 1848 announcement of the Irving edition, he announced illustrated versions of the first two titles. With his usual good sense, he entrusted the primary responsibility for creating the illustrations to F. A. O. Darley, a young artist regarded as the finest illustrator in the United States (and soon to be regarded as having a particular affinity for Irving's idiosyncratic humor). In an early advertisement Putnam made clear his ambition: "It is intended that the illustrations shall be superior to any engravings on wood yet produced in this country."[84] A sign of the regard that Darley's drawings received, not only did they come in for strong praise from reviewers in the press, especially those for the eminently visual *Sketch Book,* but those of "Rip Van Winkle" were put on display at the American Art Union simultaneously with the publication of the book. It is hard to imagine that Putnam, who had strong ties to the Art Union, did not see the exhibit with pride and pleasure.

Sales of the various editions, especially of the standard trade edition, were reportedly brisk. The *Literary World,* by then back in the hands of Duyckinck who was presumably privy to inside information, reported in its 24 February 1849 issue that the *Sketch Book* had sold more than 6,000 copies, but high initial sales figures for it and for subsequent titles in the series tell only a partial story because these books were also meant—and, to judge from their repeated printings and updated editions, proved—to be steady sellers. Putnam brought out frequent new printings through the 1850s and 1860s. Since his contracts with Irving permitted him unlimited use of the stereotype plates during the period of the contract, producing new printings was a relatively low-cost, high-profit operation. Over the years sales figures rose through the thousands into the tens of thousands for most of the individual titles. In 1855, for example, Putnam informed Pierre Irving, the secretary-accountant to his uncle, that he had sold to date about 11,000 copies of the duodecimo edition of *Columbus*.[85] With better-known titles, it seems reasonable to assume that the sales must have been even more encouraging, bringing a fairly steady infusion of cash into the accounts of G. P. Putnam and helping to capitalize other enterprises of the firm.

One of the most interesting projects that Putnam financed with the income from the Irving edition was his revised "author's editions" of selected works by two contemporary American writers: James Fenimore Cooper and Catharine Maria Sedgwick. In bringing out these editions Putnam followed the same logic that he had successfully applied to the Irving undertaking: the authors were popular, esteemed, and active, and their works were not readily available in good editions. Putnam's publishing strategy followed a similar plan of bringing out their works in well-made, uniform hardbound editions—uniform, this time, with each other and also with the Irving edition. Furthermore, he meant to make these editions, like the Irving, available in illustrated as well as standard formats.

Putnam had had some previous professional dealings with both Cooper and Sedgwick during his London years and wasted little time in 1849 in signing them to contracts for revised, selected editions of their earlier works. Well aware of Cooper's literary and popular appeal, he apparently approached him first, although their acquaintance was relatively slight. In late February, Cooper reported to a friend that Putnam had made him an offer to print "a handsome edition of my works, on the same terms as he publishes the works of Irving."[86] Given the publicity and success of his rival's edition, Cooper found Putnam's offer too enticing to reject out of hand, even though he was dissatisfied with Putnam's response to his inquiry about G. P. Putnam's financial resources. Nevertheless, they reached an agreement within days, and Putnam soon proceeded with his plans to initiate the series with *The Spy*, of which, he informed Cooper, he expected to sell 3,000 copies. Although he initially planned to price the work at $1 a volume, it was issued at the $1.25 price of the duodecimo Irving volumes, a logical decision given the fact that the two editions targeted the same market niche.[87] In language resembling that used for the Irving edition, Putnam advertised Cooper's works as "possess[ing] a vitality which will secure a permanent place for them in American Literature" and the value of his own edition as providing those works "a form more permanent and acceptable than that of previous editions."[88] That logic had succeeded wonderfully with Irving; why not also with Cooper?

From the start, Putnam's enthusiasm outpaced Cooper's. He knew that Cooper's name was as commercially valuable with the American reading public as was Irving's, and it seems plausible that he believed that he could work the same marketing magic with Cooper. If he did, he misread the differences between the two authors and, more important, the dissimilar circumstances surrounding the respective editions. Cooper proved to be far less cooperative a partner than Irving had been; from their earliest negotiations he set tough conditions and crowded Putnam's room for maneuvering. The two men proceeded at first on the basis of preliminary agreements, an overall contract not taking effect until 1 January 1850.[89] In addition, in the early stage of their dealings it was Cooper who paid for and controlled the stereotype plates, which he had manufactured in Philadelphia by his longstanding printer John Fagan and proposed to lease to Putnam. But more problematic than having to deal with Cooper on his restrictive terms was having to operate via the complicated publishing history left by a prolific author who had signed away the copyright to many of his works, including the Leatherstocking novels, to earlier publishers. Worse yet, many of those works were still in print. By the time Putnam was set to proceed, he faced the unattractive prospect of seeing his edition appear at roughly the same time that the New York publisher Stringer and Townsend was printing a cheap edition of the works. That new Stringer and Townsend edition of Cooper's novels was out by spring 1850 at $.75 a title, a price Putnam could not hope to match.[90] With advertisements for the Putnam and for the Stringer and Townsend editions appearing in the same issue of the *Literary World,* the two editions must have stood side-by-side in bookstores in New York and around the country.[91] With this kind of competition underselling him at every turn with less fancily produced volumes, Putnam never had a chance to establish the primacy of his edition.

Altogether between 1849 and 1851 Putnam issued thirteen of Cooper's works, including the five Leatherstocking novels and one new novel, *The Ways of the Hour*. He even became recognized as "Cooper's publisher" by the time of Cooper's death in 1851. But that term was something of a sham, Putnam owning neither the plates nor the copyrights of the works he published. Given the problematic circumstances surrounding its publication, the Cooper venture could not have been very profitable to Putnam (or to Cooper), and Putnam lost no time in abandoning it not long after Cooper's death.

Dealing with Sedgwick was a different, more pleasant proposition that mixed personal and professional considerations in Putnam's preferred manner of doing business. He had known her and her family since the late 1830s, when he had represented her interests with London publishers and had chaperoned the family around the city during its London visit. Wiley and Putnam had published *Morals of Manners* in New York and London in 1846, as well as its sequel (*Facts and Fancies for School-Day Reading*) in late 1847 shortly before the partnership ended. Once on his own, Putnam continued to find his warm regard for her reciprocated; her affection for his family was so great and her faith in his professional judgment so strong that he found the way open to engage her in his latest endeavor. As with many of his authors, perhaps especially women, Putnam regularly kept her posted about his family's latest doings. She therefore knew him well enough to connect the name of his son Irving, born in 1852, with his best-selling author, whose works he occasionally sent her as presents.[92]

Beginning in autumn 1849, he issued his own New York and London edition of *Clarence* (the latter in cooperation with his old friend and former Wiley and Putnam employee Thomas Delf, by then set up as an overseas book dealer in London). That work was followed by *Redwood* in April 1850, *A New England Tale* in 1852, and a new edition of *Morals of Manners* in 1854. In addition to this uniform duodecimo series, he also published *Morals of Manners* and *Facts and Fancies* in a less elaborate 16mo edition priced at $.25 or $.50. That cheaper edition was designated primarily for district school libraries, Sedgwick being a favorite nonfiction author for school committees empowered to select titles for classroom use. But soon after he published the trade edition of *Morals of Manners,* severe financial pressures forced Putnam to give up his rights to the Sedgwick edition and to transfer the literary rights and stereotype plates of the novels to the energetic New York publisher J. C. Derby, who was just making his reputation as the flamboyant publisher of Fanny Fern.[93] With that ended their professional connection, although their friendship remained intact until Sedgwick's death.

By the turn of the decade, Putnam could look back with satisfaction on his new professional start. His career was thriving, and so was his family. With four children and another expected and with a growing circle of friends, relatives, and acquaintances on Staten Island and in Manhattan, his family was well installed on a more permanent, more mutually satisfying basis than had been possible in London. A person who had known economic insecurity much of his life, Putnam had better prospects of being able to support his family comfortably than at any previous time, and he had reason to expect better financial times for himself and his business in the years to come. Within a matter of months he had managed not only to turn his fledgling company into a viable publisher but had staked out a position among the leading literary publishers in the city and the nation. With success came a volume of activity he would have to face, in one form or another, for the rest of his life. He was so busy with the daily affairs of his business that the bantering letter his friend Bayard Taylor sent to him in 1849 from California was probably close enough to Putnam's working reality to raise an ironic eyebrow: "Methinks I see you opening it [this letter] at No. 155. You are sitting at your desk behind the screen; twenty-seven manuscripts (17 of them poetry) lie before you; 31 applications by letter are still unread, and 4 authors are waiting outside the screen."[94] With Irving his exclusive "property" for an additional three years and a list that was growing rapidly in size, diversity, and value, Putnam could have looked to the new half century with well-deserved eagerness and confidence. But even he could not have anticipated the major opportunities and perils that lay ahead in the 1850s as he pushed his way into the front rank of American publishers and helped move American publishers generally into the front rank of literary professionals and cultural workers in the society.

Notes

1. Evert Duyckinck to George Duyckinck, 28 July 1846; D-NYPL.

2. Stevens mentioned their trip to the Continent in his letter of 3 May 1847 to Lenox; JL-NYPL. Soon after reaching Paris, Stevens went his own way on what proved to be a book-buying trip so extensive that it helped to set him up in private business.

3. GPP's travelogue was published shortly after his return to New York in Charles Fenno Hoffman's *Literary World* in fifteen weekly installments under the column title of "Foreign Correspondence," 2 (7 August 1847–13 November 1847). GPP then had it bound and distributed privately for friends and family as *A Pocket Memorandum of a Ten Weeks' Journey to Italy and Germany*. That account of the European trip is the primary source for the discussion that follows, unless otherwise noted.

4. Stevens to Lenox, 28 February 1847; JL-NYPL. The sale was delayed until June, by which time GPP was already gone. This might have been a good thing for him because much of Libri's collection was acquired through thievery. See Wyman W. Parker, *Henry Stevens of Vermont* (Amsterdam: N. Israel, 1963), 102–4.

5. GHP passed on the story, no doubt a part of the family folklore, that GPP was so pressed for money in Italy that he had to sell his watch for funds. Although this sounds like legend, GPP had very limited savings during his decade in England and could not easily have afforded the trip without the contribution of James Lenox. GHP, *George Palmer Putnam*, 1:158.

6. *Literary World* 2 (7 August 1847): 17.

7. Sensitive to Lenox's expense-mindedness, GPP tried to assure him from Paris of his strict accountability: "In case the Durazzo purchase is not effected and a similar amount should be ordered from the Libry [*sic*] sale, my expenses to Genoa would not be charged, but be included in the above cost of 10%. I mention this, because my journey to Genoa is made specially in your service, and I should be sorry to charge the expenses without effecting some business to you which would be equivalent." GPP to Lenox, 27 February 1847; JL-NYPL.

Lenox endorsed GPP's letter of 4 January 1847 with a note stating his agreement to pay GPP £30 for his Genoa-related expenses. If GPP was accurate in claiming that the cost of his European trip totaled $700, that single contribution by Lenox (the equivalent of approximately $150) would have covered more than 20 percent of his and his wife's expenses; GHP, *George Palmer Putnam*, 1:158.

8. The collection and the manner of its preferred purchase and disposal were a recurrent subject of discussion in GPP's letters to Lenox of 2 November 1846, 18 November 1846, 4 January 1847, and 19 February 1847; JL-NYPL.

9. As with many of the titles in the Library of American Books, GPP issued his London edition from sheets shipped from New York and bound with a new title page in London. For textual details on the printing history of this edition, see Joel Myerson, *Margaret Fuller: A Descriptive Bibliography* (Pittsburgh: University of Pittsburgh Press, 1978), 24–30.

GPP reprinted favorable remarks on the book from the London *Critic* and *Spectator* in the November 1846 issue of *Wiley and Putnam's Literary News-Letter* (p. 81); the reference there to the *Spectator* as "a wet blanket of a paper" was his habitual way of referring to it.

10. Robert N. Hudspeth, ed., *Letters of Margaret Fuller,* 6 vols. (Ithaca: Cornell University Press, 1983–94), 4:224. GHP claims that Fuller and his father had previously met through his Peabody cousins, a plausible but not necessarily reliable claim; GHP, *George Palmer Putnam*, 1:143.

11. For her letter accepting their dinner invitation, see Hudspeth, ed., *Letters of Margaret Fuller,* 4:234.

12. GPP jotted down his recollection of the evening in a notebook, which GHP incorporated into *George Palmer Putnam,* 2:264–65.

13. Hudspeth, ed., *Letters of Margaret Fuller,* 6:370–71.

14. For Fuller's account of the collision, as reported in one of her letters to the New York *Tribune,* see *"These Sad but Glorious Days,"* ed. Larry J. Reynolds and Susan Belasco Smith (New Haven: Yale University Press, 1991), 130–31.

15. Ibid., 129.

16. Crawford to GPP, 17 March 1847; GPP-P.

17. GPP's well-known version of that story, told nearly twenty-five years after the fact, was meant to be his correction to the account of the first meeting given in the 1869 edition of *Memoirs of Margaret Fuller Ossoli,* 2 vols., ed. R. W. Emerson, W. H. Channing, and J. F. Clarke (New York: Tribune Association, 1869), 2:282–83; GHP, *George Palmer Putnam,* 2:265–66.

But that was actually only his second published version of the story; the first telling—presumably the more authentic version because it was written closer to the actual event and based on notes probably made shortly after the event—occurred only months after the fact when he described his party as departing the Sistine Chapel on 1 April after hearing the Miserere: "Now nearly dark, through a long day, and we had stood in a crowd five hours long. Another concourse had been listening to the same music in St. Peter's, and by mere accident we found Miss **** in tribulation, she having lost her party in the crowd"; *Literary World* 2 (18 September 1847): 156.

18. Donald Yannella and Kathleen Malone Yannella, "Evert A. Duyckinck's Diary: May 29–November 8, 1847," *Studies in the American Renaissance,* ed. Joel Myerson, vol. 2 (Boston: Twayne, 1978), 225.

19. The identical comparison was made that year by Orville Dewey, the Unitarian minister who had officiated at the Putnams' wedding: "There she stands, with a form less voluptuous than the Venus di Medici, but if possible more beautiful to my eye"; *Powers' Statue of the Greek Slave* (New York: R. Craighead, 1847), 19.

20. Ruth Putnam, ed., *Life and Letters of Mary Putnam Jacobi* (New York: G. P. Putnam's Sons, 1925), 20.

21. This man, identifying himself only as "J. D." and claiming that he had worked for Wiley and Putnam for seven years, advertised his services as a warehouse clerk or porter in *Publishers' Circular* 10 (15 March 1847): 123.

22. Ralph M. Aderman, Herbert L. Kleinfield, and Jenifer S. Banks, eds., *Washington Irving: Letters,* 4 vols. (Boston: Twayne, 1978–82), 3:156.

23. *Publishers' Circular* 10 (15 May 1847): 196.

24. GHP, *Memories of My Youth, 1844–1865* (New York: G. P. Putnam's Sons, 1914), 18.

25. The first American ocean mail steamer, *Washington,* was launched that April with the boast that it could deliver mail across the ocean in as little as ten days. That was the duration of the record-breaking crossing of the *Cambria* on the voyage that brought Margaret Fuller to England; Joan von Mehren, *Minerva and the Muse: A Life of Margaret Fuller* (Amherst: University of Massachusetts Press, 1994), 231.

26. See New York *Herald,* 22 June 1847; also, Evert Duyckinck to George Duyckinck, 30 June 1847; D-NYPL.

27. On ferry service, see Charles W. Leng and William T. Davis, *Staten Island and Its People,* 2 vols. (New York: Lewis Historical Publishing, 1930), 2:691–92.

28. GHP, *Memories of My Youth,* 21.

29. Ruth Putnam, ed., *Mary Putnam Jacobi,* 27.

30. GHP, *Memories of My Youth,* 25–26.

31. The visit of Paez to the Putnams' home is mentioned in Leng and Davis, *Staten Island,* 2:942; their source was GHP.

32. Chamberlain to GPP, 7 August 1847; Special Collections, Boston Public Library.

33. On Irving's visit, see GPP, "Recollections of Irving," *Atlantic Monthly* 6 (November 1860): 605; on Cooper's, see James Franklin Beard, ed. *Letters and Journals of James Fenimore Cooper,* 6 vols. (Cambridge: Harvard University Press, 1960–68), 6:238. GPP remembered the combative Cooper as having had an argument with a carman over the right of way as he prepared to board the ferry for the return passage to Manhattan; GHP, *George Palmer Putnam,* 2:250.

34. Laura Wood Roper, *FLO: A Biography of Frederick Law Olmsted* (Baltimore: Johns Hopkins University Press, 1973), 83.

35. GPP was to publish one of the first books on the Polk presidency; Lucien B. Chase, *History of the Polk Administration* (New York: George P. Putnam, 1850). Chase had been a Democratic congressman during those years.

36. One of the people who profited most greatly by the rise in real estate values was James Lenox, much of whose inherited fortune was in mid-Manhattan real estate.

37. Allan Nevins, ed., *The Diary of Philip Hone, 1823–1852,* 2 vols. (New York: Arno Press, 1970), 1:395.

38. Allan Nevins and Milton Halsey Thomas, eds., *The Diary of George Templeton Strong,* 4 vols. (New York: Macmillan, 1952), 1:258.

39. Duyckinck approached the wrong partner. GPP, when finally apprised of the proposal, called it a welcome one for the time and made some suggestions that proved prophetic: "I hope it may yet be practicable for you to agree on a satisfactory and comprehensive plan and bring out such a review as will live. It should (as I humbly think) be equally free from the control of any one book selling house and from the prejudices and partiality of a circle of freinds [*sic*]; in order to create confidence and respect for its literary judgments." GPP to Evert Duyckinck, 2 February 1846; D-NYPL.

40. According to the terms of the contract, Duyckinck was to be paid an annual editorial salary of $500 and to be given an additional $1,000 for payment to contributors. If satisfied after one year, the publishers agreed to extend his contract for a second year and double his salary; Evert Duyckinck to George Duyckinck, 15 January 1847; D-NYPL.

41. Evert Duyckinck to George Duyckinck, 31 August 1846; D-NYPL.

42. Wiley had actually offered to pay Duyckinck the full year's salary when the two sides sat together in May with their lawyers to work out a separation agreement, but Appleton overruled him. Unwilling to risk "ungentlemanly collisions," Duyckinck agreed to take only his first quarter's salary; Evert Duyckinck to George Duyckinck, 14 May 1847; D-NYPL.

43. Stevens to GPP, 18 July 1847; GPP-P.

44. Henry Stevens, *Recollections of James Lenox,* ed. Victor Hugo Paltsits (New York: New York Public Library, 1951), 15.

45. For a discussion of their business dealings during those years, see Ezra Greenspan, "The Battle of the Yankee Booksellers in Europe: George Palmer Putnam, Henry Stevens, and the Fight for Dominance in the International Rare Book Market," *Biblion* 5 (spring 1997): 167–69.

46. "English Authors—American Booksellers," *Punch* 12 (24 April 1847): 178. Speaking in their own voice, the editors compared the practices of American publishers toward English authors to those of American slave owners toward slaves. That choice of metaphor must have further infuriated GPP.

47. "English Authors—American Booksellers," *Punch* 12 (29 May 1847): 235.

48. GPP's letter was dated 15 May and published in the *Times* on 19 May 1847 in a truncated form. It provoked Richard Bentley to respond the following day with his own letter to the *Times* defending his practices and stating that he had paid nearly £15,000 in royalties to three unnamed American authors (presumably, Prescott, Irving, and Cooper). GPP, in turn, answered Bentley after returning to New York with an uncharacteristically ad hominem attack, setting the record straight about Bentley (whose status as "Her Majesty's publisher" he was careful to mention) as a publisher who indeed had been generous to a handful of American writers but who had reprinted the works of other authors without remuneration; *Literary World* 1 (31 July 1847): 611–12.

49. Ibid., 611.

50. Evert Duyckinck to George Duyckinck, 1 June 1847; D-NYPL. Ruskin was published in the United States for many years by Wiley, who apparently retained rights to *Modern Painters* in the Wiley and Putnam separation agreement.

51. Evert Duyckinck to George Duyckinck, 1 June 1847; D-NYPL.

52. GHP, *George Palmer Putnam,* 1:162–63.

53. Evert Duyckinck to George Duyckinck, 13 January 1848; D-NYPL.

54. *Publishers' Circular* 11 (1 May and 1 July 1848): 160; 224.

55. GHP, *George Palmer Putnam,* 1:173.

56. Putnam to Stevens, 13 March 1848; UCLA.

57. Evert Duyckinck to George Duyckinck, 9 March 1848; D-NYPL.

58. Just the year before entering his arrangement with GPP, Chapman had published the English edition of Emerson's *Poems* (the same work that Duyckinck had labored without success to land in the Library of American Books), and he apparently had ambitions to turn his house into a major depot for the sale of American works as well as publisher of selected American titles. According to the full-page advertisement in which he announced his connection with GPP to the trade, he had set aside an entire room for the display of his American stock. In short, he not only partially filled GPP's place in the London trade but offered himself as a convenient proxy; *Publishers' Circular* 11 (15 December 1848): 409.

59. The Putnams hosted Irving several times during winter 1845–46 at Knickerbocker Cottage, and GPP met him on various occasions as well at the American Literary Agency (as on the day that Irving had escorted Gansvoort Melville to GPP's office with the manuscript of *Typee*).

60. Irving's answer is published in GHP, *George Palmer Putnam,* 1:138–40. That letter makes clear that Irving had been approached in March by the New York office, presumably by Duyckinck on behalf of the Library of American Books.

61. Aderman et al., eds., *Irving Letters,* 4:111.

62. Evert Duyckinck to George Duyckinck, 15 May 1848; D-NYPL.

63. Ibid.

64. Pierre Irving, ed., *Life and Letters of Washington Irving,* 4 vols. (New York: G. P. Putnam, 1862–64), 4:40.

65. For the terms of their contract, see Pierre Irving, ed., *Washington Irving,* 4:40–42.

66. Alderman et al., eds., *Irving Letters,* 4:184.

67. *Literary World* 3 (10 June 1848): 377.

68. Parker, *Henry Stevens,* 110.

69. William Landram Williamson, "William Frederick Poole and the Modern Library Movement," (Ph.D. diss., University of Chicago, 1959), 39.

70. "Literary News," *Publishers' Circular* 11 (1 September 1848): 285.

71. Adolph Growoll, *Book Trade Bibliography in the United States in the Nineteenth Century* (New York: Burt Franklin, n.d.), xix, xl.

72. GPP was also secondarily involved with the publication of Lowell's major work of 1848, *The Biglow Papers.* Lowell's friend Charles Frederick Briggs, who lived in New York and was close to New York publishing matters, stated the proposed terms for the publication of *The Biglow Papers* after conferring with GPP: "Putnam says that you may put his name into 100 copies for his London agency and 500 for New York, if you would like for him to attend to the sale and distribution here." That Lowell did favor this arrangement is confirmed by the fact that some surviving copies carry either GPP's New York or his agent John Chapman's London imprint after the Cambridge imprint of the primary publisher, George Nichols. See Jacob Blanck and Michael Winship, comps., *Bibliography of American Literature,* 9 vols. (New Haven: Yale University Press, 1955–91), 6:30.

73. GPP to Francis Parkman, 30 March 1849; Parkman Collection, Massachusetts Historical Society.

74. GPP to Francis Parkman, 26 November 1851; Parkman Collection, Massachusetts Historical Society.

75. Ibid.

76. GPP to Francis Parkman, 3 January 1850; Parkman Collection, Massachusetts Historical Society.

77. GPP to Francis Parkman, 12 March 1870; Parkman Collection, Massachusetts Historical Society.

78. The earliest advertisement of the new location of his London connection was in the New York *Commercial Advertiser* (24 June 1848), followed by one in the New York *Tribune* (28 June 1848).

79. Washington Irving, *History of New York* (New York: George P. Putnam, 1849), xiii–xiv.

80. Adam W. Sweeting, *Reading Houses and Building Books: Andrew Jackson Downing and the Architecture of Popular American Literature, 1835–1855* (Hanover, N.H.: University Press of New England, 1996), 9.

81. For a good summary of Irving's negotiations with publishers during the 1840s, see the introduction to Michael L. Black and Nancy B. Black, eds., *A History of New York,* (Boston: Twayne, 1984), xliv–xlvi.

82. "Editor's Table," *Knickerbocker* 32 (October 1848): 377.

83. Edwin T. Bowden, comp., *Washington Irving: Bibliography* (Boston: Twayne, 1989), 189–90.

84. *Literary World* 3 (14 October 1848): 742.

85. Pierre Irving, ed., *Washington Irving,* 4:189.

86. Beard, ed., *James Fenimore Cooper,* 6:9. Cooper felt scorn for Irving, with whose name his own was typically paired but whose work he considered inferior. That attitude of disdain was well known; nevertheless, GPP, a natural mediator, thought to take the opportunity one day in 1849 or 1850 when the two men both happened to be in his office to bring them together and watched with pleasure as they struck up an animated conversation; GHP, *George Palmer Putnam,* 2:46–47.

87. Beard, ed., *James Fenimore Cooper,* 6:12.

88. *Literary World* 4 (5 May 1849): 401.

89. That is, if GPP accepted the terms of the draft proposal submitted to him by Cooper, which is printed in GHP, *George Palmer Putnam,* 1:245–46. The original is preserved in GPP-P.

90. Beard, ed., *James Fenimore Cooper,* 6:4.

91. *Literary World* 6 (13 April 1850): 381, 384.

92. Sedgwick to GPP, 11 December 1854, GPP-P.

93. Information on the transfer of the stereotype plates of *Clarence, New England Tale,* and *Redwood* to Derby and of *Morals of Manners* and *Facts and Fancies* to Evans and Dickenson can be found in the letter of Charles Sedgwick to GPP, 12 December 1854, GPP-P.

94. This letter of 30 September 1849 is published in John Richie Schultz, ed., *The Unpublished Letters of Bayard Taylor in the Huntington Library* (San Marino, Calif.: Huntington Library, 1937), 24.

CHAPTER 8

Publishing American Arts and Letters, 1850–1852

As Putnam walked up Broadway from the ferry slip to his office each day, his eye would have been caught by names. Signs advertising offices, stores, and services appeared on all levels of buildings along lower Broadway in an early stage of the more cluttered display of proprietary names typical of twentieth-century cities. That display was fine with him; he had none of the reservation harbored by shopkeepers imagined and real, such as Hawthorne's Hepzibah Pyncheon or the young John Ruskin, about public display or commercial advertisement. His own sign, displayed prominently on the front of his store, was as much a badge of pride with him as was the "G. P. Putnam" stamped on title pages and even on the national consciousness. In this regard, he was accepting the ideology and following the lead of other large New York publishers, such as the Harpers and Appletons, who had successfully established their personal/corporate presence in mid-century America. Although Putnam could not himself imitate the in-house joke of Harper and Brothers in which each brother identified himself as "Harper" and relegated the others to the impersonal corporate half of the company name, the underlying logic of his enterprise was the same: like them Putnam sought to equate and have others equate his own good name with that of his firm, an interchange of personal character and economics—his word as good as his bond.

In a related development, society was engaged in displaying its fast-developing cultural categories via lists of names, the primary registry of which could be found by 1850 in the new agencies of print. By no coincidence, this formative generation of publishing, authorship, and letters was one given over to conspicuous attempts by Americans to collect and display its finest works, as one compiler after the next (including such Putnam friends and collaborators as Rufus Griswold, Evert Duyckinck, S. Austin Allibone, and later Edmund Stedman) attempted to define the authors and anthologize the works identifiable as "indicative" of the nation, its culture, and its ideals. By the later 1840s and early 1850s, newspapers and magazines routinely communicated accepted lists of American names—names of geographical locations, writers, painters, editors, and publishers that fit the emerging categories of culture. Furthermore, each category had its subcategories; authors, for example, by gender and genre; painters, by region and style. Fully aware of this development, Putnam began in the early 1850s to publish works that combined what he and his coworkers considered the best of letters with the best of painting. Meanwhile, at the highest level of ingenuity and imagination, such writers as Melville in *Moby-Dick* and Whitman in *Leaves of Grass* surveyed the cultural, economic, sociological, regional, and national categories of their time, devising catalogues that challenged and reinvented the terms of sociocultural organization. And at the more common level of middle-class discourse, journalists, ministers, and editors performed a similar function in public settings ranging from newspaper and magazine articles to speeches and sermons.

Putnam was himself a keeper of cultural lists of a related sort. Some time in the late 1830s, he began what grew over the next two decades into one of the larger autograph collections of his generation.[1] As a publisher and bookseller who did virtually all his communication by letter and who had a network of professional connections and clients stretching across the United States and Europe, he saw the names of leading writers, editors, diplomats, educators, and intellectuals pass over his desk as a matter of course each year by the hundreds. The private act of amassing his collection nicely complemented the public list-making work he did as an annalist of his profession and culture. The impulse that found its expression directly in *American Facts* and indirectly in the publication of works by Poole and Roorbach likewise entered into Putnam's recognition of the value of the "names" that he could reach out, as it were, and gather into his collection.

That this impulse did not derive simply from private avarice is clear. Putnam was as generous to a fault as a collector as he was as a publisher. He gladly traded autographs with correspondents on two continents, and although there were names that he unquestionably coveted, such as that of his kinsman Israel Putnam, he generally gave away more than he received. One of his earliest trading partners was Mellen Chamberlain, a recent graduate of Dartmouth College and an enthusiastic collector who many years later served as the librarian of the fledgling Boston Public Library, the institution to which he later bequeathed his prized autograph collection. One day in 1844, Putnam wrote Chamberlain from his London office to thank him for the receipt of a parcel of names and added: "I can hardly imagine a collector imbued with the monopolizing spirit which necessarily characterizes that portion of mankind, parting with such treasures as magnanimously and gracefully as you have done. I assure you your memory will be embalmed in connection with my American collection."[2] That remark characterized him as well as it did Chamberlain, as he went about building his cherished collection in private and via trades.

Although hardly unique, Putnam's collection was identifiably his, and as such it provides a window on his personal and professional taste. A compendium basically of Anglo-Americana, it contained nearly 1,400 items, mostly letters with a smattering of manuscripts and autographed books. Numerous letters included portraits of their authors. Its range was impressive, including many of the leading authors, statesmen, academics, scientists, and intellectuals of Britain and America, especially from the last century. More broadly understood, Putnam's collecting impulse was part of a widespread cultural development taking place around him in the United States; at a time when a magazine writer noted, "the Collector is abroad," Putnam was one of the growing group that the writer labeled "autographomaniacs."[3] Although he left no commentary on his collecting logic, I think it reasonable to assume that his thinking corresponded closely to that of his contemporaries, who typically sought to identify and separate out the leading figures (normally men) in the emerging cultural, intellectual, political, and economic categories of that era—a logic already present, for that matter, in his publishing list. Indeed, the men and women whose autographs he collected were precisely the people whose works he wished to put into general circulation under the G. P. Putnam imprint.

By one of the remarkable literary professional ironies of their time, Putnam was engaged in a free-flowing trade in "names" with his good friend and genial competitor James T. Fields, then the junior partner of the fast-growing Boston literary publishing house of Ticknor and Company (to become Ticknor, Reed and Fields in 1848, and Ticknor and Fields in 1854). Fields, too, was from his twenties a collector of names, although he entered the field—as he did publishing—later than Putnam and as a result found himself in the 1840s with a network of connections far more circumscribed than Putnam's. The earliest known surviving letter between them is an 1843 thank you note in which Fields expressed his appreciation for Putnam's generosity, apologizing for the fact that he was himself "autographically poor" and stating his wish that "[Noah] Webster [had] added many more expressions synonymous with gratitude to his last edition."[4] On his wish list at the time were the autographs of Thomas Carlyle, G. P. R. James, Mary Howitt, Felicia Hemans, and above all Charles Lamb ("I will have it if I steal it").[5] Always happy to please his friend, Putnam sent him then and for years afterward as many names as he could supply, gladly taking in return Fields's more New-England-centered contributions. Even after Putnam had returned to "this side of the salt water," the dynamics of their exchange continued seemingly unaltered, with names passing back and forth freely between New York and Boston.

Although their professional camaraderie persisted the length of their careers, the publishing and cultural scene around them was changing dramatically in the years following Putnam's return to America. By 1850 the list of American and European authors in publishing demand was growing rapidly, and as the decade progressed Putnam (and New York generally) increasingly came into competition with Fields (and Boston generally) for publishing rights to those authors. Although the trend was not yet plainly evident, the balance especially in the belles lettres would soon shift to Fields's advantage. Whereas Fields had wished out loud to Putnam in 1846 that he "had a new world of autographs to conquer," within a few years they and their entire profession would be engaged in a simultaneously cooperative/competitive enterprise to form and conquer the new world of American letters fast rising around them.[6] The story of his participation in that joint enterprise— for so Putnam, a true believer in and keeper of the publishing trust, invariably saw it—would become the central theme of his professional life in the 1850s.

On the eve of the new decade there appeared a lead article in the *Literary World* that must have captured Putnam's attention. Written by Frederick Saunders, a well-placed figure in the trade who had worked for the Harpers and would soon be working for Putnam, it provided a brief overview of contemporary publishing in Europe and the United States. Although informative and knowledgeable, his survey would have been familiar not only to literary professionals but to many of the general readers of the journal. It consisted largely of names of publishers and gave corresponding lists and figures of literary production, royalty payments, and periodical circulation—all organized around the theme of "the progressive advancement of literary enterprise."[7] Saunders's interpretation was the typically whiggish one of his day: in the aftermath of the invention of the steam press, "the affluent resources of genius and the literary wealth of the world have been rendered universally accessible.... The Press is like the caloric of nature—it overspreads and circulates throughout the whole social system. With this numerical increase of books has been a corresponding increase of authors and readers." In spite of a rather churlish contempt for the simultaneous increase of "pseudo-authorship," he looked optimistically to the future advance of letters, closing with a nod toward the expansion of the press in "the great West."

Another article that would have interested Putnam that winter was the reprinted testimony on the status of American libraries given by Henry Stevens to the library committee of the House of Commons.[8] Stevens noted the conspicuous lack of large concentrations of print materials, by European standards, in the United States but also remarked at length on the extraordinarily large number of public collections, a roll call of which included "the congress library, the state libraries, the college and university libraries, libraries of mechanics' associations, mercantile and apprentice libraries, libraries of learned societies, joint-stock and subscription libraries, town, city, village, and municipal libraries, church or congregational libraries, academy libraries, common school libraries, and Sunday school libraries." What made this development possible, he noted, were two interrelated factors: the spread of universal literacy throughout the society, which underlay the proliferation of libraries; and the economics of American publishing, which was predicated on a large, relatively inexpensive supply of print products addressed to a large, broad-based audience.

Putnam knew the views of both men well and undoubtedly shared their underlying faith in the vitality and expansion of print culture and print-based institutions. Saunders had even included Putnam in his scenario of progress by describing him as the American publisher who "bid fair to elevate the standard of bibliographic taste among us by his numerous and splendid issues"—a position that Putnam would have occupied with pride. Such expansive views as those articulated by Saunders and Stevens, which might have been considered farsighted even a decade before, were rapidly becoming commonplace among American literary professionals. By 1850 he was maneuvering his house into position to render his early vision of cultural progress a print reality.

All told, the early 1850s were exciting, growing years for Putnam and his firm. His initiative of two years earlier was showing unmistakable signs of progress. The distance he had come can be judged by comparing the status of his firm with that of his former partner. Since their breakup, Wiley had taken his reorganized company in an opposite direction from Putnam's. He had signed few new authors and launched few publishing initiatives, preferring instead to exploit his backlist and to highlight his retail and trade bookselling operation. By 1850, his firm's volume of business was sharply reduced compared to the Wiley and Putnam years, and its future was unsure. Early that year during a visit in New York City, James Fenimore Cooper reported to his family the rumor that he had just heard: "Wiley has failed. It is said that Putnam's rivalry has done him much harm."[9] That report, as John Hammond Moore states in his house history of John Wiley and Sons, was probably false and in any case oblivious to the different strategy that Wiley, always more conservative and pragmatic than Putnam, devised for keeping his business going: cutting down the risk of failure by publishing primarily from his backlist while increasing the prospects for revenues by making alliances with out-of-town firms to serve as their main distribution point in New York.[10] That strategy proved sound enough to keep his business solvent through the hard times of the Civil War, after which the younger generation of both Wileys and Putnams charted new paths that carried their family-owned firms to greater size and prosperity than they had known under the direction of their fathers.

By contrast, Putnam was moving full speed ahead with unabated energy, confidence, and ambition. Continually attempting to increase his publishing list, he utilized his resources on all ends, consolidating his hold on old works while searching for new authors and works and devising new schemes to publish innovative works likely to prove attractive to the emerging audience for arts and letters. Like Wiley and their peers generally, he became expert at recycling his backlist, a practice expedited by the bookmaking practice by then prevalent in the United States of printing from stereotype plates. He brought out in 1850, for example, a revised edition of his own *The World's Progress,* the first of many under the G. P. Putnam imprint. He also reprinted editions of numerous of his old firm's works, such as the English-language edition of Goethe's autobiography offered originally in the Wiley and Putnam Foreign Library. To stave off the possibility of a copyright fight, Putnam announced that the supposedly new John Oxenford translation used in Henry Bohn's London edition had been transposed in large measure from the Parke Godwin translation used in his edition and that the importation of Bohn's edition into the United States was therefore illegal.[11] Another reissue, this time from the Wiley and Putnam Library of American Books, was *Mosses from an Old Manse,* which was timed to appear in summer 1850 to take advantage of the publicity surrounding the publication of *The Scarlet Letter.* These were only a few of the holdover Wiley and Putnam titles that Putnam reissued, which included works by Andrew Jackson Downing, Bayard Taylor, Thomas Carlyle, Charles Dickens, Thomas Hood, and dozens of other writers whom he believed still likely to attract readers. Altogether these works filled a substantial part of the early G. P. Putnam list.

Putnam also attempted to improve his leverage over his list by packaging and distributing works in ways designed to maximize their sale. Years of experience in dealing with buyers, suppliers, and rival publishers had taught him many of the marketing tricks of the trade, to which he added variations of his own. One strategy he favored was to package his authors in common formats, the works of like with like (Caroline Gilman with Catharine Sedgwick; Fredrika Bremer with James Fenimore Cooper, who in turn had been paired with Irving), and to advertise them accordingly. Another characteristically—and, for contemporaries, recognizably—Putnam touch was to offer a higher-priced, illustrated line of works to parallel that of his regular trade editions. Especially around the holiday season Putnam liked to advertise a full run of his illustrated editions, which typically began with Irving but included most of his better-selling writers in the belles lettres. Alternately, he attempted to align selected works with a lower market stratum, offering some of his publications in cheaper formats to make them attractive to thrift-seeking individual and institutional buyers. Sometimes he did this by choice; other times, to combat the editions of competitors who undersold his trade editions.

Like many mid-century publishers in the United States and Britain, he organized works from his publishing list into a variety of series and libraries with the intent of encouraging collective buying. He perhaps had in mind the Harpers' marketing success with various series designed for newly organized or expanding public school systems when he began in 1850 to market several series of Putnam's District School Library, each of which contained twelve volumes from his list priced collectively at $6. The logic of that undertaking was as obvious as the spread of public schools around the country and the laws requiring school districts to purchase books for their libraries. Putnam, however, never pursued the educational sector of the market as aggressively as he did the general trade. Similar to the District School Library in most regards except audience was Putnam's Choice Library, which grouped a variety of his books into attractively priced units and marketed them to general readers.[12]

The following year he announced plans to initiate publication of an American edition of the National Illustrated Library, a British monthly series of volumes heavily illustrated with wood engravings, bound in cloth, and offered to subscribers at a cheap price.[13] The idea of the library, as stated in its promotional blurbs, was to offer high-quality books in reprint editions priced low enough to combine "cheapness" with "excellence," an idea that correlated nicely with Putnam's general publishing philosophy. He was in London, in fact, as the first volumes were being issued, but for some unknown reason, despite advertising that project for several months following his return, he abandoned it before publishing the first number.

A far more ambitious and successful venture that he did carry out was the inexpensive packaging of his firm's books that he began marketing in 1852 as Putnam's Semi-Monthly Library. This Library was another attempt by Putnam to encourage serial sales of his firm's publications, this time organized around a kind of loose subscription policy aimed at reaching an audience he advertised as comprising "six millions of readers in the United States."[14] Subscribers received twenty-four works of imagination or nonfiction by well-known writers (Dickens, Hood, Olmsted) at $.25 for each volume or $5 for an annual subscription (paid in advance). The price for these 300-page volumes, Putnam claimed, was so low that "a very large sale only can make it remunerative," but he was willing to gamble that the public would favor his "library" quality edition over the cheaply printed and bound, double-columned editions typically sold at that price. Just the same, he hedged his bet by also offering a more expensive clothbound edition of the books at $.40 per volume or $9 for the whole series.[15] He published titles for the series through 1853 and advertised it heavily for several years. During that period it received widespread complimentary reviews in the press for its concept and execution, but it seems unlikely that the series returned Putnam the kind of public favor he most wished because he abandoned it after 1853.

Another initiative along these lines was Putnam's Railway Classics, begun in 1851 and kept in print for many years.[16] Modeled, ironically, on the thriving railway library of the arch-pirate George Routledge, who had inaugurated it in 1849 with an unauthorized edition of Cooper's *The Pilot* (a work that Putnam himself reissued that year in his author's edition), it was an attempt to bring books and other print material to the newest center of marketing opportunity: bookstalls at railway depots. Putnam knew the phenomenon well; he generally traveled by train when business took him away from New York City, as it often did, and therefore understood the opportunity afforded publishers to adapt their products and make them readily available to a new mode of readership. With a line of books easily adaptable to the kind and circumstances of reading afforded by train travel, Putnam was well positioned to cater to this audience.[17] He did so, however, on a scale far more limited and on a publishing basis far more restrained than Routledge, whose railway library ran into the dozens of volumes each year and drew from a wide range of pirated texts. By contrast, Putnam confined himself primarily to issuing cheaper editions of the works of his own authors. After beginning with selections drawn from Thomas Hood and Dickens's periodical *Household Words,* he gradually concentrated the series around works by such favorite Putnam authors as Washington Irving and George William Curtis and compilations of pieces drawn from the pages of *Putnam's Monthly.* Such works might have been heavier reading than one typically finds at twentieth-century transportation depots, but they obviously suited the taste of Putnam's era; he kept many of these popular, inexpensive books—not to mention, the series itself—in print through the 1850s and 1860s. But that fact does not mean that these "Railway Classics," as he called them, existed in a simple, uncomplicated relation to their times. The drawing adorning the paper-cover volumes of the series gave an unwittingly conflicted expression of the sociocultural bounds in which these books were read: it presented an idyllic, leisure-time landscape with a well-dressed couple strolling in the foreground along the thin sliver of sand passing between the lake on one side and a railroad track on the other—a summer pastoral except for the fact that a train was rounding the bend and approaching them.

That picture nicely characterized the audience to which Putnam was directing his publishing list. As a generality, even in these early years of his career his professional compass pointed upward rather than downward in response to his attraction to an upper-end market niche characterized not only by increasing leisure and disposable income but "discriminating taste." Over the course of the next two decades, with the growing stratification of the publishing profession and of letters, he would identify himself increasingly with the camp of "respectable" publishers. In fact, his dealings with less reputable publishers and authors seem to have been few. One of the few documented instances is a request he received from Edward Judson (pseudonym of Ned Buntline), soon to become one of the country's premier dime novelists, to publish his story "The Moose Hunter of Maine" in the pages of *Putnam's Monthly.* Judson insisted that he had been "legitimate" in his earlier years as a writer for the *Knickerbocker* and the New York *Tribune* before he turned to the writing of "trash" and that he now wished "to leave a better reputation than 'yellow covers' can give me."[18] Putnam and his editors were apparently not impressed.

At the same time that he developed these schemes for improving the distribution and marketing of works already on his list, he explored ways to form connections with additional authors to expand his offerings. In the early 1850s he expanded on his efforts of the previous decade to establish himself as the preeminent publisher of works written by the leading literary authors of the previous generation. One such author whom he clearly yearned to add to his list was William Cullen Bryant, a fellow New Yorker whom he had known for years and whose respect he had as much as Bryant accorded to any publisher. The only Bryant work that Putnam brought out at this time, however, was the relatively minor *Letters of a Traveller* (1850). But this fact did not prevent Putnam from devising a colophon for his firm that identified it with the first group of imaginative writers to be presented as "standardized" in the United States: Cooper, Irving, and Bryant.[19] That colophon, which appeared on the title page of numerous G. P. Putnam publications in the early 1850s, pictured the globe enwrapped in a banner featuring the names of these writers in large letters and "GPP" stamped onto its tail—a more accurate symbol, actually, of his aspirations and pretenses than of reality. For a time in 1851, he even offered for sale separately or together new crayon sketches of each of the three authors engraved on steel and produced in a uniform style.[20]

A different measure of his large-scale ambition for both his firm and the trade was the important project on which he worked in 1850, perhaps in concert with Roorbach: a compilation of books for the trade that he published that year as *Catalogue of Foreign and American Books* (alternately known as *Putnam's Book-Buyer's Manual*). A nearly 200-page listing of mostly contemporary works offered for sale by his firm, he originally advertised it as available to the trade for free, then thought better of the time and resources committed to it and priced it at $.25 in paper and $.75 in half cloth. Although not as comprehensive as Roorbach's *Bibliotheca Americana,* it had the important professional virtue of organizing its holdings alphabetically by subject area and listing current prices, which would have made it a work of considerable utility to the trade generally as well as a convenient guide to buyers of both his own firm's publications and its retail holdings. One documented instance of its usefulness was the means to which Charles Lanman put it in 1852 when asked by the Spanish minister to Washington for advice on how to build "a miscellaneous library"; his response was to write for a copy of the *Catalogue.*[21] It proved so useful that Putnam reissued it through most of the decade at several year intervals with updated addenda.[22]

During the early 1850s Putnam published a wide variety of works by the leading writers of the time, but he was never so fixed on the idea of individual talent as to exclude corporate works or to relegate them to secondary status. The most comprehensive corporate work he issued in the early 1850s was *Putnam's Home Cyclopedia.* Planned as early as 1851, it came out in six volumes over the period 1852–53, each volume a thick duodecimo uniformly bound, titled, and formatted. The model for them and the first volume in the series was the new edition he published in 1852 of his own *The World's Progress* (most recently issued in 1850 but now renamed the *Hand-Book of Chronology* to blend in with the other volumes of the series), with its contents grouped as encyclopedia entries and organized alphabetically.[23] Although he advertised the six works as "each complete in itself" and offered them for sale both individually and collectively, he clearly saw the *Home Cyclopedia* as one continuous series and advertised it as such on the series title page that preceded individual title pages: "These six volumes [listed above] are intended to comprise a comprehensive view of the whole circle of human knowledge—in other words, to form a General Cyclopedia in a portable shape, for Family Libraries, for Teachers, and School Libraries, and for the general reader." As such, the *Home Cyclopedia* carried Putnam's personal and ideological signature in presenting itself as a potentially standard reference work conveniently offering systematized knowledge to the general reader.

Of the dozens of new titles he issued each year in the early 1850s, the large majority were in the belles lettres. Among them there were two popular areas of particular concentration, although not singled out by him as such: travel literature and women's fiction and nonfiction. Putnam had been paying them close attention ever since his earliest association with John Wiley. His connection with travel writing was especially tight; not only had he traveled widely and written several travelogues himself but the form and conventions of the genre corresponded to his own middle-class, patriotic values and assumptions. For similar reasons, they spoke to a generation of American readers interested in the larger world but not necessarily willing to have their basic assumptions about themselves, their society, and the rest of the world unduly upset.

The typical Putnam traveler journeyed into the unknown robust, inquisitive, and quietly superior. That traveler cut a figure like that of Bayard Taylor, his most popular travel writer during the twenty-five years of their professional association, who trekked confidently across Europe on modest funds or bravely fended off bandits in the Southwest, rather than that of the middle-aged Melville, a lost soul wandering the Judaean Hills in search of faith and identity. Not surprisingly, many of the authors whose travelogues he published Putnam counted among his personal friends. Taylor (after whom he named one of his sons) was his single best-selling author and closest friend in this regard, but there were others as well: George William Curtis (nicknamed the "Howadji" for his travels to Arabia and soon after to be invited to join the editorial team of *Putnam's Monthly*), Washington Irving (in both his New and Old World books), Frederick Saunders, Francis Hawks, Benjamin Silliman, and Frederick Law Olmsted. Although their works covered much of the globe, their ethnographic compass typically pointed back home. A different kind of high-profile travel project that Putnam published during this period was an edition of Charles Wilkes's five-volume *Narrative of the United States Exploring Expedition,* his record of one of the most important scientific expeditions of the century.[24] In addition Putnam published various works by officials of the American Ethnological Society in New York, among whose members he had numerous friends and acquaintances.

If anything, however, his most important travelogues during these years came from England. In the 1840s, he had published American editions of important books by George Borrow and Alexander William Kinglake. Then in the early 1850s, he published the two path-breaking works in Assyriology by Austen Henry Layard, *Nineveh and Its Remains* and *Discoveries in the Ruins of Nineveh and Babylon.* During his 1839 expedition to Asia Minor, Layard had first spotted what five years later would become the site of his great excavation. As he recalled his discovery years later: "I saw for the first time the great mound of Nimrud rising against the clear evening sky.... The impression that it made upon me was one never to be forgotten."[25] Out of his subsequent excavations came one of the great archaeological treasure mounds of his time, which, transported with great excitement to England, passed into the collections of the British Museum and increased public interest in and knowledge of one of the least-known major civilizations of the ancient world.

Layard was not only a premier archaeologist of his generation but also a superb travel writer; his accounts of his expeditions to Mesopotamia were immensely popular with the reading public on both sides of the Atlantic. He published those works with Putnam's old friend John Murray, the leading travel publisher in England. In 1849 Putnam arranged with Murray for an American edition of the account of the first expedition, *Nineveh and Its Remains.* That work proved so successful that Putnam put it through successive printings during the next five years and published it in various formats: one and two volume, abridged and unabridged, lavishly and simply illustrated editions. By 1852, he was advertising the work as having sold 12,000 copies (13,000, on the title page of one printing that year). Building on the success of that work, he lost no time announcing in October 1851 a new agreement with Murray for the simultaneous transatlantic publication of the follow-up volume, *Discoveries in the Ruins of Nineveh and Babylon,* although the work was not ready and would not be printed until 1853.[26] This time, however, his publishing luck ran out. With interest in and expectations for the new volume running high, his authorized edition had been in circulation for only a few months before it was met by a competing edition issued by the Harpers. Putnam responded by bringing out a less expensive edition stripped of some of the maps and diagrams printed in the original, then in frustration took to the local papers to publicize the Harpers' unethical dealing in the matter: "Messrs. Putnam and Co. consider that common courtesy and justice, and even the more doubtful custom of the American trade, entitle them to expect exemption from a rivalry as uncalled for as it is ungenerous and discreditable to any respectable business man."[27] Such actions availed him no better then than they had on other such occasions; eventually he ceded the book and Layard to the competition.

Popular and profitable as were the travelogues of Layard and Taylor, Putnam found a source of true fortune in 1850 in what must then have seemed an unlikely place. Commercially successful fiction by female authors was hardly unknown to Putnam, who after all was putting his new edition of Sedgwick into print that year. But he was caught by surprise when a first novel by an unknown writer provided him with his first taste of a runaway best-seller. The story of how the manuscript of Susan Warner's *The Wide, Wide World* made its way onto Putnam's list is as good as most legends, which is what that account probably is: as told by George Haven Putnam, who got it from Susan's sister Anna Warner and other sources decades after the fact, his grandmother came upon the manuscript at their house and noted qualities in it that had evaded professional readers and publishers. Warner's father had first shown the manuscript to several publishers, and only after receiving a succession of rejections did he take it to Putnam's, where an in-house reader gave it an ambivalent reading.[28] Perhaps it took one woman of deep religious conviction to appreciate the sensibility of another, but that seems unlikely, especially in the case of a book that would soon grip the minds of tens of thousands of its readers. Warner's own explanation—and the assumptions on which it was based—was also interesting: "I never can guess what made Mr. Putnam take it in. Unless that he who had so many dear children of his own, felt something of the pathos there was about it all; the girl's pained effort, in her father's hand."[29] But that explanation seems equally dubious, a woman's misreading of a businessman's intentions. Whatever his exact motivation, Putnam was either sufficiently impressed by the book or, at least, sufficiently excited by its publishing prospects to invite its author to stay with his family that autumn on Staten Island while she was reading through the proof—a nice gesture but hardly a typical one even for a man as open-handed with his generosity as Putnam. In fact, she stayed with the family for three weeks as the printer's proofs slowly made their way back to the house, then was invited but declined to return to their house for a second extended stay to read the proofs of volume 2.

The Wide, Wide World was first announced in early November as one among a handful of works soon to be issued by G. P. Putnam's. Registered for copyright on 14 December and delivered to Warner three days later, it was out just barely in time for the holiday season, although its timing proved far less important to its success than Putnam had thought.[30] Although hardly the overnight success that *Uncle Tom's Cabin* would soon prove to be, it generated a delayed excitement in taking gradual hold of the reading public. Within two months the modest first printing of 750 copies was sold out and a new one issued, a process that Putnam had to repeat with increasing frequency more times that year and the next than he had ever done with any of his previous publications. The extent of its sales clearly caught him off guard. He advertised it rather lightly for months, and one contemporary report has him at first refusing a telegraphed order for 50 copies.[31] Once it caught on, however, it quickly became the best selling book on his list. Whereas he was accustomed with "hits" to expect sales running into the unit of thousands, with *The Wide, Wide World* he was mistaken by a factor of ten. His miscalculation was understandable: no previous American novel had sold in such quantities. By chance, however, just as the sales of *The Wide, Wide World* began pushing into the tens of thousands, *Uncle Tom's Cabin* (1852), which had generated considerable advance interest during its passage through serial publication, raced off to book sales that within a year registered yet another digital increment beyond those of *The Wide, Wide World*. On top of those publishing "events," the publication and best-seller status of *The Lamplighter* were not far behind. The conclusion drawn by numerous contemporaries, including publishers who sometimes knew better, was simple: it was a new era for publishing and letters. With *Harper's Monthly,* founded only in 1850, taking magazine sales for the first time into the hundreds of thousands and Robert Bonner's *New York Ledger* a few years later doing the same for story papers, publishers quickly began conceiving of a mass market unforeseeable just a decade before.

The Wide, Wide World was more than a sales marker along the road of American literary publishing; it was a literary creation that generated extraordinarily powerful responses from its readers. Its story of an unprotected girl separated from her parents and forced to make her way alone through the world clearly resonated with the reading public. According to a reviewer in the New York *Times,* "The truth is that one book like this is not produced in an age"; to another in the Newark *Advertiser,* it was "the most valuable work of the kind I have ever read. It is capable of doing more good than any book, other than the Bible."[32] No critic has stated this point as powerfully as Jane Tompkins, who has called it "the Ur-text of the nineteenth-century United States."[33] For her the harrowing, desperate situation of Ellen Montgomery in the novel corresponded physically, psychologically, and emotionally to that of Warner as well as innumerable Victorian women, a claim commensurate with numerous documented instances of individuals reading this novel (and other domestic fictions like it). One such instance, quite possibly the first, took place within the Putnam home circle, where family readings were a commonplace and where *The Wide, Wide World* was read in part or in its entirety before it reached print. This unusually rich instance of antebellum reading presents a fascinating ensemble of a female author, her male publisher, her solicitous hostess, and their children assembled in the Putnams' Staten Island home around a domestic fiction, which was not only read but proofread as the manuscript went into production in fall 1850. Moreover, it invites a discussion not only of Warner's dealings with Putnam and his family but more generally of the complicated gender relations between women authors and male publishers of that era.

In April 1851, Putnam responded to a letter Warner had recently sent him inquiring about the sales of her novel and the possibilities of her pursuing a career as a professional writer. She had good reason to ask: she had written her novel and lived the previous years of her life under duress. The impulse that had driven Warner to write was most immediately her father's—and, therefore, her family's—financial exigency. In this regard, her family situation was roughly comparable in its downward socioeconomic mobility to that of numerous other writers of the time (for example, Hawthorne, Emerson, Alcott, Whitman, Poe, and Melville), but the very terms of her novel, especially the characterization of young, unprotected Ellen Montgomery, attested to the degree to which such a situation was more complicated for a woman than for a man. Her solicitation of Putnam's professional opinion about her prospects was therefore a matter of intense concern to her—she who would "thank God for it all" when she saw its success—and it is not difficult to imagine the anxiety she must have suffered as she waited for his response. When it came, though, it was mildly encouraging; it communicated the fact that the first printing was nearly sold out and a second ordered and gently offered the following professional advice: "I should not dare to offer even suggestions, touching the difference between pens and needles,—but it is fair to say that many have chosen the pen with less warrant and encouragement."[34] Although the distinction between pens and needles originated with Warner, it was certainly one with which Putnam was himself comfortable; in fact, it reflected the actual configuration of his household on many a night as he wrote and Victorine knitted.[35] On a broader level, it reflected his personal preferences in dealing with female authors; ever since his earliest relations with such writers as Sigourney, Sedgwick, and Jameson, he preferred to operate in situations that narrowed the gap between the needle and the pen but without undermining the legitimacy of the gap in the first place.

That Warner was, in this sense, a "comfortable" author for Putnam to deal with seems clear. He could recommend her to Victorine as warmly as a model of femine deportment as he had Sedgwick during the period of their transatlantic engagement. Victorine would have seen as much for herself: Warner was a thoroughly accommodating guest during her residence with the family in late September to early October 1850. The physical territory was familiar to her, as she had recently spent some time visiting on Staten Island with an old friend (during which she continued to work away at *The Wide, Wide World*), but she was wary to intrude on the less familiar territory of the Putnams' domestic arrangements. She spent the weeks of her visit in a state of prolonged deference—deference to Putnam as an authority on the business of getting her book to the printer and public, and deference to

Victorine as materfamilias of a large, bustling, and admirable household. Deference—or, at least, surface deference—seems to have been an established habit with her by this time in her life; it was certainly her mode of behavior while her manuscript passed from composition to production. Once the novel was done, she had deferred to her father in its placement with a publisher. It was he, a published author himself, who shopped the bundled manuscript among the publishing houses of New York, and it was presumably he who negotiated the terms of publication and perhaps even signed the contract with Putnam. So, too, in her dealings with Putnam, she followed his professionally informed lead in turning the manuscript into a published book, quite possibly even accepting his advice to cut the last chapter of the manuscript from the finished version.[36] She was not even aware of the fact that he meant to stereotype the work until she had been with him for more than a week. Even then, it took a question from Victorine to solicit the information that Warner was reluctant to ask for herself. Years later, after having made a worldwide reputation for herself and written numerous books, Susan Warner was still generally ignorant about the basic facts of domestic and international copyright.[37]

Warner apparently found the weeks of her stay in the Stapleton cottage fascinating. She had come down from the family home on Constitution Island, near West Point, directly to the Broadway store, where she was introduced to Putnam and Victorine and installed in one of the big armchairs behind the screen blocking off the store's work area from the "snuggery," as Warner called it. There, while waiting for Putnam to finish his day's work before their departure for the ferry, she inspected two works that Putnam thought might be of interest to her: an illustrated edition of Susan Cooper's *Rural Hours,* a book that was surprising both Putnam and the Coopers by its popularity, and a fancy edition of *Pilgrim's Progress* that Putnam had been given as a present in England. He also left with her a first bundle of proofs, but she preferred to postpone its inspection to the privacy of their house. He later returned after having located a third ticket for that evening's Jenny Lind concert (one of the hottest tickets in the city that year), which necessitated their quick departure for the ferry in anticipation of the return trip that evening.

In the days that followed, Warner quickly, quietly blended into the family routine, while trying her best to retain her privacy—an impossibility, she was to find, in a household through which five young children moved by day and numerous visitors by evening. From her first day with them, Warner found herself unprepared for the intense sociability of the Putnams, who frequently hosted friends, neighbors, and family and generally kept them—and her—to later hours than she was accustomed to. They invited her to join them on their rounds of the islands, occasional trips to Manhattan, and home entertainments, even to play the piano for their guests. When Victorine was away or indisposed, Putnam asked Warner to perform the female ritual of hosting the daily tea, a custom they brought back from England along with many of the outfittings of their house. All in all, they so fully included her in their routines and activities around the clock that she found it a chore simply to keep up with the purpose of her visit, the reading of the proofs.

In spite of that frustration and her general wariness about obtruding her presence on a busy household, she generally enjoyed her time with the family. She plainly admired both Victorine and Putnam and the way they conducted their family relations, and she approved of their model of home education. Before long she fell into a routine of her own, watching the family going through its daily activities, chatting with Victorine and the children, joining the family for visits to and from the Bishops and their friends, playing the piano, reading through the pile of books, magazines, and newspapers that Putnam typically brought home each evening from the office—all the while working her way through the proofs. Studiously though she read through them by day and sometimes even late into the night, she found herself making but slow progress, barely completing the small bundles of proof that Putnam brought back each day from the city. After three weeks, she had read through only the first of the two projected volumes.

Her novel (whose title was advertised in its pre-publication form as *The Wide, Wide World, as a Child found it*) attests eloquently to her fascination with children, a fascination that had much room for play during her visit. Her relations with the Putnam children were good enough that the two eldest would be invited several years later to pay a return visit to the Warners on Constitution Island. Of the children, it was the oldest, the precocious eight-year-old Mary, who seems to have taken particularly to her, and probably she to Mary. From their first introduction, Mary was delighted to meet the author of "Robinson Crusoe's Farmyard," a children's work recently published by her father that she knew through a family reading.[38] From that moment on, she seems to have thought of Warner as filling the exalted category of storyteller. In return, Mary, literate and sophisticated beyond her years, freely volunteered to her new friend the information that her elders believed that she too would grow up to be an author (in fact, she would be published in the *Atlantic Monthly* within a decade). Although neither of them yet realized it, they already had a second text in common. One day in Warner's presence, Mary asked her mother when the children would next hear "the story of Ellen," a chapter of which she had heard and been entranced by during a family reading.[39]

That request no doubt took Warner by surprise, since she had done her best during the visit to hide her professional side from all but the senior Putnams. No Jenny Lind, Warner was so uncomfortable with the public status of authorship that she sought to retain her privacy by insisting that the pseudonym Elizabeth Wetherell (the name of her great-grandmother) be printed on the book.[40] And so it was as Elizabeth Wetherell, not Susan Warner, that she became a household name on both sides of the Atlantic, although her true name soon grew to be a matter of common knowledge.

She was still presenting herself to the world as Elizabeth Wetherell when she followed up *The Wide, Wide World* with *Queechy* in 1852. Putnam was nearly as eager as she to see the new novel in print. Although he apparently did not think it as good as he now considered *The Wide, Wide World* (an opinion shared with and perhaps borrowed in part from his daughter, who called it "interesting" but less "absorbing" than its predecessor), he knew a publishing opportunity when he saw it.[41] He therefore advertised the new novel both before and after its publication far more aggressively than he had *The Wide, Wide World* and tried to do so in such a way as to set it in the latter's wake, a tactic that anticipated and perhaps magnified critics' tendency to read the new novel in the context of the earlier one. With so much advance publicity running before it and the magical name and reputation of its author surrounding it, Putnam brought out the largest first printing he had ever authorized of a book: 7,000 copies of the long novel in its two-volume format.[42] Not surprisingly, *Queechy* got off to a very fast start, with numerous reviews and heavy sales (Putnam advertising it as having passed 70,000 copies by 1853). Furthermore, Putnam and Warner had high enough expectations after *The Wide, Wide World* to take the precaution of arranging for prior English publication with the religious publisher James Nisbet and Co. of London, even though the state of copyright protection for American writers in England was then unstable at best. Leading American works were being pirated as a matter of course; *Queechy* would soon have the empty honor of joining their ranks.[43] Warner was so popular in England, in fact, that she became one of the prime American targets of piracy; *Publishers' Circular* reported in early 1853 that "cheap editions of Miss Warner's popular and characteristic American Tale *[The Wide, Wide World]* are making their appearance in all directions, outvying one another in price and appearance, but entirely regardless of the interests of the author, or those with whom she had entered into arrangements."[44]

Another important new female client whom Putnam published at mid-century was the Swedish novelist and memoirist Fredrika Bremer. Her works were among the most popular of any contemporary writer in America, and she filled the emerging antebellum role of author/celebrity nearly as well as did Dickens during his American tour of 1842. By contrast with Warner, she was so much a public figure as an author and lecturer that the captain of a ship sailing for Charleston refused to take her on board when he found out her identity for fear that she might expose him in print as Dickens and Trollope had done to various people in publishing travelogues of their American excursions.[45] Putnam had made her acquaintance at the Newburgh, New York, home of their common friend Andrew Jackson Downing, where the subject of a new edition of her works was first raised.[46] Although Bremer had been published through the 1840s by the Harpers, she did not hesitate to enter into negotiations with Putnam, nor he with her. The deal they discussed centered on the republication of two of her most popular novels, *The Home* and *The Neighbours,* with Putnam to pay her (as the Harpers did not) a royalty on all copies sold.[47] That deal was perhaps finalized during the brief visit that she made to the Putnams on Staten Island in late October 1849, where she enjoyed being part of the domestic atmosphere and seeing the autumn colors at their peak.[48] After showing her around the island, Putnam took her back to New York on the ferry and left her with the Spring family of Brooklyn, already known to him as Margaret Fuller's companions during their Italian tour in 1847. Knowing the sales potential of his new author, Putnam lost no time in getting her works ready for print by the beginning of 1850 as the latest addition to his series of "revised author's editions."[49] For her part, Bremer was happy to announce—and Putnam to print—her pleasure at their deal in the preface she wrote for that new edition: "Among the many agreeable things which have met me on my arrival in the United States of America, I count as one the proposal of Mr. Putnam to give a new edition of my works, on conditions which cannot but be agreeable to me, since they offer me the privileges of a native author."[50]

Such deals were not likely to make Putnam any friends on Cliff Street (the familiar metonym for the Harpers' offices). Sure enough, a brief but nasty publishing war broke out between the two houses in early 1851, one that in many regards anticipated the Layard incident of 1853.[51] The Harpers' retaliation came indirectly: they announced their intention to print an edition of George Borrow's autobiographical *Lavengro,* a highly attractive work that Putnam had announced his house as ready to publish in an authorized joint Anglo-American edition arranged between John Murray and himself from the author's proof sheets.[52] Professing disbelief in their advertisement and ignorance at their desire to injure him, Putnam tried several times to warn them off and inquired the cause of their aggression. Fletcher Harper, who plainly considered Putnam's position ingenuous and responded to each of Putnam's complaints with a list of his own, made it clear that he and his brothers fully intended to defend their "invaded rights" but never explicitly stated that his firm had taken Borrow hostage in return for Putnam's presumed expropriation of Bremer. In response, Putnam, a true believer in "courtesy of the trade," the extralegal arrangement between publishers by which the legal vacuum left by the lack of international copyright protection was replaced by a system of prior announcement enforceable only by gentlemanly cooperation, appealed to their sense of trade "equity and usage." That plea failing, he took a more aggressive course of action: he threatened, first, to expose the Harpers to the court of public appeal, then, when they persisted, actually published an exposé of the affair in the pages of the *Literary World,* printing excerpts from the letters that had passed between the two houses into the public record and adding his editorial judgment that "the trade" would recognize that his edition actually aided the sales of the Harpers' cheaper edition.[53] He even accompanied Bremer to Cliff Street in an attempt to work out their differences with the Harpers in person. Their response, according to the well-known version of the story recounted decades later by George Haven Putnam, was simply: "Courtesy is courtesy and business is business."[54] Even if possibly apocryphal, that response neatly captured a fundamental difference between the two sides in publishing philosophy, if not always in practice. Finally, after receiving no satisfaction with these means of moral suasion, he reverted to its economic counterpart, advertising his edition of *Lavengro* as the only complete one on the American market, a point that the Harpers contested privately to him by letter and publicly in their edition, which not only was complete but a good deal cheaper than his.

That Bremer was one of the authors caught in the masculine tug-of-war between two powerful New York publishers is distinctly ironic, since she exemplified in her work and reputation the virtues of home and hearth. Despite her high-profile status as a lecturer (whose tour around the country had been arranged in part by Putnam), few writers of the age invoked the virtues of female domesticity more lavishly than she. In the introduction she wrote for the Putnam edition of *The Neighbours,* for example, she explicitly equated the fate of the nation with the status of its women, and implicitly with the active good that women could perform for "home-life" by the penetration of their literary works into the domestic circle.[55] Similarly, when she came to publish her important book of New World memoirs, she gave it the significant title of *Homes of the New World.* The Harpers, it soon became clear, were as uninterested in her ideology as interested in her economic worth, setting their "house" against her "home" by promoting their old edition of the work and selling it at a fraction of the price of Putnam's fancier library edition. Not surprisingly, it did considerable damage to Putnam's, which brought in far less revenue for author and publisher than Putnam had hoped and anticipated. In the end, his experience with Bremer replicated the experience he had with numerous other European authors he had reprinted in America: his more expensive editions generally proved handicapped in the competition against cheaper editions brought out by rival firms. Although Putnam would have been the last to admit it, this was one more instance in which the laws of the market clashed with and won out over the sentiments of friendship and good will.

Putnam's dealings with Warner, Bremer, and Sedgwick in the early 1850s represented only a small portion of his dealings with female authors of the period. Like many of his peers, Putnam was well aware of the rising popularity of "lady writers," especially in the belles lettres, and gave them a prominent place on his publishing list. Their prominence among his literary authors there seems to conform to the conclusion that Michael Winship has drawn about the relative importance of female authors in the list of Ticknor and Fields in Boston, a house similar to G. P. Putnam's in size and orientation. Women filled a more important niche in the belles lettres section of Putnam's list in that decade than in the previous one, if still a relatively small part of the total list and revenue of the firm (although it seems likely that due to Warner's runaway popularity female authors generated a larger percentage of G. P. Putnam's revenues than of Ticknor and Fields's).[56] In bringing their works before the public, Putnam felt no conflict between his personal ideology and business considerations; the two manifestly supported each other. He found all three of these authors both personally and literarily sympathetic (indeed, Victorine mentioned to Warner that her husband considered Sedgwick "a piece of perfection").[57] The thought that the act of publication via industrialized processes situated within the capitalistic marketplace might have violated the spirit of their work seems not to have crossed his mind.

He must have had similar feelings about many other female writers who appeared on his list in the early 1850s, including Susan Fenimore Cooper, Anne Lynch, Caroline Kirkland, Caroline Gilman, Emma Willard, and Elizabeth Ellet. (Lynch and Kirkland, in fact, were not only professional clients but friends.) Their works tended by and large to the upper half of the audience typically addressed by Putnam's books. More often than works by men, theirs were gift books finely produced and lavishly illustrated. One example was Ellet's *Family Pictures of the Bible,* an expensively designed book whose purpose was to present the Bible as "the best instructor of families," a lesson Ellet feared was becoming obscured in an increasingly secular age.[58] Similarly, Kirkland edited for Putnam *The Book of Home Beauty* (sometimes promoted as *The Home Book of Beauty*), a fancy gift book that was advertised jointly with and published at roughly the same time as *The Home Book of the Picturesque.*[59] It contained twelve expensively produced portraits of American "ladies" and was widely regarded as one of the most lavishly manufactured works of its day, though not universally held in high regard. Putnam claimed to have spent $10,000 on its production, a sum that he seems unlikely to have made back in sales. He would soon have an additional reason to question his decision to publish it: it caused a mild controversy as critics branded it an indecorous use of women's faces in the public sphere.[60]

More popular in its day and more interesting reading today than either of these gift books was Susan Cooper's *Rural Hours,* a fine work of nonfiction that gives a view of the natural world in many ways analogous to Thoreau's *Walden* but that outsold it many times over in the

1850s. Written in the form of a journal, it plays her stream of thoughts over a full cycle of the natural year, offering observations about the environment, wildlife, Native Americans, local people, and ponds. Just as her work might well have appealed to a more leisure-bound, female audience than Thoreau's, so Cooper took and practiced a view of authorship far more guarded and cautionary than Thoreau. More like Warner in this regard, she preferred to protect her identity by having "by a Lady" printed on the title page (even though she gave a hint by dedicating the book to "the author of *The Deerslayer*"). Furthermore, she claimed to offer her book only with "reluctance" to the public, opining that the proper outlet for such observations was the privacy of the fireside shared with family and friends. Once published, however, the book surprised everyone by the extent of its success. Its fast sales left her father, as obstreperous in his dealings on her behalf as on his own, muttering about the bad bargain he had made for her: Putnam to receive five years' printing rights in return for assuming production costs and paying Susan 12 ½-percent royalties once the first 1,000 copies were sold to offset its manufacturing expenses.[61] To the Philadelphia publisher George Graham, he complained, "When I let Putnam have 'Rural Hours,' I did not [know what I was selling], or he should not have got it for twice what he pays."[62] In the last literary letter he ever wrote, he was still expressing pride in his daughter's achievement; he described *Rural Hours* to their English publisher Richard Bentley as "the best American book you have published in ten years" and as one that already placed "its author in the foremost ranks of American literature," even as he bemoaned its lost sales potentials overseas due to piracy.[63]

At the price of 12 ½-percent royalties Putnam had undoubtedly made a good deal, one that got better as the book went through its first and second printings that year. He soon made the decision to bring out a fancy illustrated edition, containing twenty-one pictures of flowers and birds and priced from $5 to $9, depending on the quality of the binding (one copy of which he presumably showed Warner during her first visit to his office). He also lost no time in carrying on negotiations with Susan Cooper to issue her next work, a novel (*The Shield*) that he advertised heavily for several years, although it was apparently never completed. Instead, he issued her edited volume, *The Rhyme and Reason of Country Life*. By that time, a relationship that began primarily in deference to her father had developed into one of respect for her as a talented, profitable author in her own right.

During his initial dealings with Susan Cooper, Putnam was conducting separate, unrelated discussions with her father, hardly his easiest client but unquestionably one of his most "esteemed"—a value that went a long way with Putnam. Never the person to back away from a fight or a lawsuit and as different in temperament from Putnam as Irving had proven his like, Cooper ironically had become widely recognized by 1850 as a "Putnam author," although Putnam's rights to his works were tenuous at best. During 1850 the two men discussed plans for publishing Cooper's next work, a social history of New York City to be called *The Towns of Manhattan,* and probably reached a formal agreement during Cooper's overnight visit on Staten Island in November 1850.[64] The proposed work should have been inordinately attractive to Putnam, who had recently published E. Palmer Belden's slim history *New-York: Past, Present, and Future,* but who would surely have regarded Cooper's planned work as entirely a more attractive publication. In fact, it would have had special significance to him not only as the work of a major author but also as a potentially pioneering synthetic urban history organized around its reading of the city as fated to grow into a metropolitan center and international commercial emporium. That reading of New York corresponded nicely to Putnam's own experience of the city and to his pride as an adopted son given to identifying his publishing house with New York's preeminence as a cultural and publishing center.

Cooper advanced through the manuscript quickly the following spring and summer despite an illness that eventually compelled him to dictate the work to his daughter Charlotte. Through sheer force of will, he proceeded far enough by July to send Putnam the introduction and first eight chapters for printing but soon afterwards lapsed into complete incapacity and died in September.[65] Undeterred by Cooper's death, Putnam and Susan Cooper attempted to salvage the work for publication. Plagued from the start, however, by Cooper's illness, the work encountered a succession of obstacles. First, the conclusion of the introduction was misplaced in Putnam's office and eventually given up as lost. Then, communication between Putnam and Susan over the form of the volume became strained, as his patience was worn thin by her requests for changes. Finally, a fire at the printing shop where the work was to be produced destroyed the majority of the manuscript already drafted, as well as plates manufactured from it.[66] Notwithstanding

Susan Cooper's continuing desire to work with the manuscript still in her possession, the work was never published in their time.

Despite the failure of that project, Putnam did memorialize Cooper in a different way. Assuming the banner of "Cooper's publisher" and responding to the general desire to commemorate him as a pioneering American author, Putnam organized testimonials in New York at City Hall in September within days of his death, at the New-York Historical Society the following month, and at Metropolitan Hall the following February. In addition, he preserved the memory of those events as well as the tributes that poured in by mail by compiling and publishing a *Memorial of James Fenimore Cooper.*[67] The initiative to produce a testimonial for the public record was as fitting a gesture as was the volume itself. Cooper had occupied a prominent place on the national stage for three decades, one, ironically, that none of the writers (including Hawthorne, Melville, Emerson, Longfellow, Simms, Prescott, Parkman, and Dana) whose letters of tribute were published in the *Memorial* could reasonably expect in their time to fill. A reflection of Cooper's standing, the contents of the volume included letters and speeches by men not only in letters but also in politics (Daniel Webster and Charles Sumner) and the ministry (Francis Hawks and George Bethune)—the distance between the fields not yet prohibitive. That memorial proved to be the only one actually completed after Cooper's death; plans to erect a physical marker were discussed for several years but failed to reach execution.

Putnam also had bolder, farther-sighted publishing ideas for the new decade. One of the most interesting was taking shape during the first weeks of 1850, when he wrote to the president of the American Art Union in New York to request the temporary loan of various landscape paintings currently on display.[68] His intent, he explained, was to publish at his own cost an elaborate demonstration of American achievement in painting, the first of his many attempts to pay tribute to the arts in the United States. Figuring the work to himself preliminarily as *The Book of American Art,* he conceived of the volume as matching letter press texts to engravings made from the work of the leading contemporary American painters on display that year at the Art Union—from which he specifically requested Thomas Cole's *The Dream of Arcadia.* The kind of project that he typically wished executed on the highest level of contemporary bookmaking, he planned to spare no expense in its production and to print it in a large format somewhere between octavo and folio. Should the book prove acceptable to the Art Union and popular with the public, he proposed turning the idea into an annual publication.

The idea was seemingly as timely as it was bold. The Art Union, as Putnam well knew, was the most important mid-century institution in the country for the patronage and popularization of American art and one whose mission paralleled in important ways the ideological orientation of his publishing house. The Art Union was then at the peak of its influence and popularity in the art world not only of New York but of the nation. It claimed a membership of nearly 19,000 members; operated a gallery of its own on Broadway stocked with new works, particularly in landscape, purchased from American painters; and distributed those paintings to its members via an annual lottery.[69] Art Union shows were regularly reviewed in the local newspaper and magazine press, and the organization for a time issued its own *Bulletin*. Moreover, not only the Art Union, in whose management Bryant was involved, but the entire New York art world was then engaged in unusually close relations with the local literary world. Just the year before, one of the primary supporters of the Art Union, Jonathan Sturges, had commissioned a painting by Asher B. Durand commemorating the friendship of Bryant and Thomas Cole, recently deceased. That immediately celebrated landscape *Kindred Spirits* (1849) set the recognizable figures of Cole and Bryant on a rock ledge overlooking a Catskills waterfall with Cole drawing his friend's attention (and that of the viewing public) via his pointed brush toward the pastoral background as the proper subject for American art and literature. Even in the unlikely case that Putnam did not see the painting when it was exhibited at the National Academy of Design, he had already internalized a similar message as he proceeded with his plans to execute his joint art and letters project. Given the fact that he had cultivated a personal and professional network of relations nearly as extensive in the arts as in letters, it was a project that he was unusually well qualified to carry out.

The planned publication was well calculated to bring Putnam a combined civic and entrepreneurial pride. It bound his cultural nationalism with his publisher's instincts for what might sell, his belief in the maturity of American creative endeavor with his confidence that there existed a readership sufficiently large and prosperous to justify expensive, elaborate publications of the sort he was planning. He stated this belief explicitly in his "Publisher's Notice," in which he called his book "an experiment, to ascertain how far the taste of our people may warrant the production of home-manufactured presentation-books, and how far we can successfully compete with those from abroad." He continued: "Whether the volume shows any progress, however, in American book-making, must be left to the public decision. If that tribunal affords the needful encouragement, this may be followed by future volumes of similar import, but more worthy of the artists and of the country."[70] Such a work was guaranteed to bear the Putnam imprint in the way that most appealed to Putnam: the American publisher as public servant and cultural activist. That the "notice," which concluded with his signed initials placed beneath what might readily be construed as his publishing ideology, could so easily slip into the collective first person testifies to the ease with which Putnam identified his publishing function with the needs of the nation.

When the Art Union apparently refused his request, Putnam persisted on his own with a variation of his original plan. He announced it formally as early as September 1851 in the new trade journal as *Home Book of the Picturesque* and issued it as a "presentation book" in time for the fall holiday season of Christmas 1851.[71] A small quarto priced at $7, it was one of the most expensive books that he published that year and the kind of project on whose production he characteristically invested inordinate amounts not only of capital but of time and energy. In the end, the adherence to high standards of quality showed: *Home Book* was one of the most elaborately produced books of American art published in its time. It set texts drawn from well-known American writers to thirteen engravings of landscape paintings drawn primarily from New York and New England scenes. Putnam selected the paintings from the work of the leading New York painters of that time—Cole, Durand, Frederick Church, John Kensett, Jasper Cropsey, and others—many of whom were personally known to him. So, for that matter, were many of the authors, most of whom had published longer works at one time or another with his firm (including James Fenimore and Susan Fenimore Cooper, Irving, Bryant, and Taylor). Putnam dedicated the volume to Durand, the most revered painter of his time and the president of the National Academy of Design, as "an initiating suggestion for popularizing some of the characteristics of American landscape and American art." If that dedication reflected Putnam's own thinking, the volume also bore Putnam's personality more slyly in its frontispiece engraving, which displayed a panoramic view of New York harbor from Staten Island such as the Putnams might have seen from their house at Stapleton.

Was *Home Book* a success? No financial records of its sales have survived, and so one can only hazard a guess as to its profitability. That it continued to be printed for many years after its initial press run in 1851 suggests that it found a substantial readership, although Putnam was never able to capitalize on his originating impulse and continue the project on a periodic basis. But there were also noneconomic measures of success by which he would presumably have evaluated the project. One was American bookmaking standards, which he hoped to raise to a level equal to that of European gift books. In this regard, too, his success was mixed. The engravings, he admitted in his "notice," were too small to do justice to the originals, even though the book succeeded in bringing technological advances in engraving into the art of bookmaking. Another was the standard of cultural achievement, about which he expressed himself more fully pleased. What he did not state—because he did not discern—was that on a deeper cultural level his book was the product and proof of a gaping incongruity between the theme and the mode of production of his entire culture, an incongruity that might have been apparent to a more complex-minded person, such as Cooper or Thoreau, than it was to him.

Home Book was only one of the many presentation books brought out by Putnam in the early years of his company. His publishing list always carried a substantial investment in illustrated works intended for the upper reaches of the middle-class audience, especially in the heavy book-buying season of the holidays. Another planned gift book was one that never reached production but is particularly revealing of Putnam's mode of thinking and operating. It has survived simply as a jotting of ideas in Putnam's hand on a single leaf of paper, which might have been directed to himself or perhaps to someone else.[72] The volume he had in mind was a companion or follow-up of sorts to *Home Book,* a quarto or large octavo gift book intended for Christmas 1852 and tentatively titled *A New Art-Union: or, Old World Pencils and New World Pens.* Putnam might not have had all the details worked out, but—true publisher that he was—he did have his publisher's imprint scrawled beneath the preliminary title. He envisioned the project as a volume to be issued in parts or perhaps simply in bound form and to include reproductions of fifty to one hundred European paintings "of the highest eminence" to be accompanied by selections from "the best American authors." Always alert to the latest technological developments in bookmaking, he pondered the possibility of combining colored lithographs "done by the new process of printing in water colours" with etchings and woodcuts.

The most likely reason he abandoned that project was that he was committing himself to production of another gift book, *Homes of American Authors,* scheduled for Christmas 1852. It proved one of the most ambitious projects his firm embarked on that year, its numerous, intricate production details to occupy his time and attention for months. It was presumably inspired in part by *Homes and Haunts of the Most Eminent British Poets* by his London friend William Howitt, but its content and formulation clearly reflected Putnam's own culturally nationalistic views.[73] Early on he tried to interest George William Curtis in overseeing the book's preparation and composition, but Curtis declined, offering instead to contribute individual sketches.[74] Putnam therefore took primary responsibility for the book into his own hands, with secondary help from Frederick Saunders and Charles Frederick Briggs.

Production of the volume was long and tedious; it involved extensive correspondence and face-to-face dealings with authors willing to write original sketches of each of the volume's seventeen selected "American authors" and their residences. Likewise, it required his oversight of the various artists and engravers assigned the task of providing high-quality reproductions of their residences and facsimiles of pages of their manuscript work—not to mention the sometimes delicate negotiations with the subjects for their permission. To take one example, Putnam exchanged letters over a period of months stretching through spring and summer 1852 with William Prescott, who owned three houses, about such matters as the selection of houses for the volume's illustration (they eventually included all three), instructions on getting sketches of the houses made, and biographical details to be incorporated into the sketch.[75] Overlapping that correspondence was the one he conducted with George Hillard, who agreed to write the sketch of his friend on the condition that his own name be withheld ("My aims and views are now exclusively professional and I do not desire, at present, to come before the public in any literary aspect whatever"), a position Hillard later recanted in frustration once his name was revealed in the Boston newspapers.[76] Then there were practical matters to be worked out between Putnam and Hillard: coordination of visits with Prescott, consideration of whether or not to use details provided by Prescott to Putnam in the sketch, mailing of drawings to New York, length and timing of submission, amount of compensation.

His dealings with Prescott and Hillard were replicated many times over with the volume's other authors. Meanwhile, Putnam also supervised the time-consuming task of coordinating the complicated production details with engravers and printers in New York. One interesting variation on what must have been for him a well-worn procedure was his decision to rely on daguerreotypes of Cooper's and Webster's houses to serve as the reproductive originals for his engravers. That decision required a word of assurance to his readers, who, as Putnam assured them, would be seeing reproductions "not less authentic" than the engravings more conventionally made from sketches and paintings.[77]

The volume was ready and printed as planned in time for the holiday book-buying season. Its underlying idea—one might as readily call it the credo—was stated expressly by Putnam in his preface: "Although there are no Abbotsfords, which have been reared from the earnings of the pen, among our authors' homes, yet we feel a degree of pride in showing our countrymen how comfortably housed many of their favorite authors are, in spite of the imputed neglect with which native talent has been treated. Authorship in America, notwithstanding the want of an international copy-right which has been so sorely felt by literary laborers, has at last become a profession which men may live by."[78] With the intent, then, to produce a book that would serve as testimony to the fact of (remunerative) American authorship, Putnam gathered together two carefully selected teams of American authors: the primary ones to serve as subjects (not to mention, as object lessons) and a secondary one to compose their biographical sketches. Many of the primary authors he chose had professional dealings with his firm: Irving (of course), Cooper, Bryant, Sedgwick, Simms, Hawthorne, Lowell, and John Pendleton Kennedy; others, such as Emerson, Longfellow, and Prescott, were well known to him, if not then house authors. The selection was not easy; Putnam apologized publicly in his preface for the exclusion of equally deserving authors but promised that this would be only the first in a two-volume series.[79] He might nearly have based a second volume on his secondary authors (Bryant being the only crossover), who represented in their own right a partial demonstration of the book's basic proposition; three of them—Charles Frederick Briggs, George William Curtis, and Parke Godwin—would soon gather with him to plan the beginnings of *Putnam's Monthly,* and the remainder (Caroline Kirkland, Henry Tuckerman, George Hillard, Edward Everett Hale, Rufus Griswold, George Washington Greene, and George Washington Peck) were also well-known, widely respected literary professionals.[80]

Conceived and executed in the politest tones of the day, *Homes of American Authors* conveyed a good mood of national consensus; as far as its authors were concerned, not even Lowell could anger the residents of the South, Simms those of the North, or Webster (who died weeks before its publication) his opponents across regional and political lines. Poverty and class division were unknown; racial, religious, and ethnic strife, nonexistent; the struggles of authors for a livelihood or conflicts between them and publishers or readers, unspoken. Nestled in such stately dwellings as Sunnyside, Elmwood, Woodlands, Otsego Hall, Cragie House, and the Old Manse (which seemed deeded by right of imagination to Hawthorne), America's authors, the reader was to understand, were well provided for and their status as citizens of the republic of letters secure. Even the engravings contributed to the mood of peace and prosperity, showing off the houses to good effect as temples set out on rural or restricted grounds "sequestered" from the strife and conflict of the modern city and marketplace. One person who immediately saw the value of the work as Putnam wished it to be seen was his like-minded friend and trading partner James Fields, who put in his order for an early shipment of twenty-five copies in cloth and ten in morocco with the declaration: "I shall make it a speciality to sell a good many. I do not know of a book so captivating to the eye and heart of an American."[81] Another person to whom he was proud to show it was Thackeray, to whom he inscribed a copy on 29 November.[82]

Attractive though the book was ideologically and aesthetically to Putnam, it was not necessarily as good a business proposition as he had hoped. It left him divided against himself, one part wishing to proceed with a follow-up volume, the other fretting about the tight margin he had left himself for profits after its costly production.[83] In winter 1853 he had discussions with Nathaniel Willis, then in summer with Jared Sparks, about their inclusion in such a volume but then decided in each case to postpone the work until the next publishing season, citing difficulties finding "a *suitable* selection of homes" to the former and the press of his firm's involvement in the new Crystal Palace to the latter.

The more likely explanation is that he had lost faith in the work's financial viability; in the end, economics won out over pride.[84]

In publications such as these, Putnam typically sought to publish from his favorite, habitual position of unanimity. Such clashes as he periodically had with the Harpers and the various professional frustrations that invariably came his way did little to shake his fundamental faith in his calling. If anything, with the passage of the years and the growth of his firm and the whole American publishing industry toward maturity, he felt an increasing sense of professional camaraderie and a need on occasion to speak publicly on behalf of the trade. One moment that he did occurred in mid-1852, when he took upon himself the challenge of responding to the hard-hitting complaint made in a letter to the editor of the *Literary World* by Jotham Carhart about the imbalance in the relations between authors and publishers: "Authors, instead of riding on the backs of publishers, are ridden by them, and the old fable of the man and the pony is daily illustrated before our eyes. . . . Authors must be asses—if, with the whole power of the press in their hands, they allow themselves to be used after this fashion."[85] As a result, he claimed, publishers lived in stone mansions on Fifth Avenue while authors more typically lived as "tenants-at-pleasure in various boarding-houses, or chance lodgers at third-rate hotels."

Provoked into a response perhaps the same day he read this letter, Putnam retorted with a public apologia for the entire profession.[86] He was offended, in part, by the factual ignorance of Carhart's assertion. As counterproof, he freely offered up his own domestic situation as one more truly representative of the living arrangements of American publishers: "Although I may boast that some of our best and most popular authors are on my list, my experience of publishing has so far left me no margin for 'free-stone': and, as a comparatively successful business of five years has effected so little beyond ordinary expenses, I am afraid the mansion will not be ready this year." At the time, of course, he could just as readily have argued the other side of the proposition and used his firm's forthcoming *Homes of American Authors* as proof of authorial affluence, but he chose not to. Perhaps he refrained because his fundamental complaint was less with Carhart's ignorance than with his underlying premise that authors and publishers were natural rivals, not allies, in the dissemination of the written word among the reading public. That premise struck at the very basis of Putnam's faith in the collective mission of American publishing—of publisher with publisher, and publisher with author. He therefore insisted that he spoke for all American publishers—"from the Harpers to Mr. John Smith in Arkansas"—in declaring that he, for one, would readily share his net profits with his authors, while cautioning that the percentage of works in which profits could be shared was much greater than that that returned only losses.

The following year, a event occurred that demonstrated his unshakable professional camaraderie. He was in Washington the week before Christmas when he heard of the catastrophic fire that had completely destroyed the Harpers' Cliff Street offices and factory, the finest printing-publishing facility in the United States. In spite of his bruising fights with them over market share and professional differences over a wide range of issues, including the international copyright question that was his primary reason for then being in the capital, Putnam lost no time in sending them his sympathies. He went on to acknowledge their past differences but appealed for future cooperation and mutual respect: "Anything else than cordial good will and friendly relations between myself and all engaged in the trade, and especially those at the head of the trade, is deeply repugnant to my feeling." As with Putnam, it clearly was.[87]

By chance, waiting for him on his return home was a letter from a friend and occasional contributor to *Putnam's Monthly,* Erastus W. Ellsworth, who took a very different view of the fire and mistakenly assumed that Putnam would also: "And now if one were to remark to you that Harper and Brother's had at length been overtaken by a righteous retribution, would you not acquiesce in the sentiment as a striking and impressive one;—and would you not think of that providence as a discriminating providence which permitted that lighted match to drop into 'Harper and Brother's' camphene instead of your own? Would you not?—In confidence?—Ha?"[88] Although Ellsworth severely misjudged Putnam's views, not to mention his disposition, he was not entirely mistaken in his imputation about conflicts between publishers any more than Carhart was about conflicts between authors and publishers. Despite Putnam's protestations and self-assurance, both men located fault lines in literary professional relations that would become more pronounced and more frequently identified in the last third of the century.

The early 1850s were all-round growing times for Putnam. His family was expanding, bustling, and thriving. By 1852, when he was thirty-eight and Victorine twenty-eight, they had six children, half of whom had been born in Staten Island (John Bishop in their newly purchased cottage within weeks of their arrival in America in 1847, Amy in 1850, and Irving in 1852). At the same time, the elder children were beginning to display intelligence and talent at home, going outside the house for the first time to study in the religious school overseen by their local pastor, Alexander Mercer.

Meanwhile his business was growing apace. As he headed toward the end of his first half-decade in business as G. P. Putnam in late 1852, Putnam could take pleasure in the fact that he had succeeded in attracting some of the leading writers of both the past and the present generation to his fast-growing house. In Susan Warner, he had one bestseller established and a second apparently on the way. He employed at various times some of the leading professionals in his field—Orville Roorbach, Frederick Saunders, Charles Briggs—and would soon bring in a new group of talented young men to help him manage the literary side of his business. With prospects rosy for the future, he decided that year to solidify the commercial side of the business by taking a partner, John Leslie, into the company for the first time and accordingly renaming it G. P. Putnam and Company. Putnam had known Leslie, a New York City businessman, at least since the late 1840s, when they had jointly held the property on Broadway that Duyckinck rented for the offices of the *Literary World;* it is possible that Leslie was an employee of the firm for several years before he became a partner.[89] No doubt he brought a much-needed supply of capital into the business, as well as expertise in managing the firm's books. The publishing side remained strictly Putnam's affair.

Several highlights of these first years of the new decade deserve mention. In spring 1851, Putnam managed to combine business with family to their mutual profit by taking George Haven with him on his nearly annual trip to London. His primary reason for bringing Haven, who had been badly scalded in a domestic accident, was to restore his health, but Putnam was also particularly close to his oldest son and enjoyed the chance of introducing him to professional colleagues and of reintroducing him to family friends left behind. He had no foreknowledge of the fact that his young son, whose only citizenship at the time was English, would repeat this crossing as head of G. P. Putnam's

Sons on so regular a basis for fifty years that one could tell the season by his comings and goings to and from England. Father and son booked passage on the side-wheeled steamer *Franklin* of the German American line, sailing from New York on 30 May and reaching England by mid-June.[90] Crossing the Narrows on its way out to sea, the ship passed within easy viewing distance of the Putnams' Stapleton home, from which the other children waved handkerchiefs as the ship moved across their line of sight.[91]

The main purpose of the trip for Putnam was to coordinate relations and make deals with his partners in the English book trade, especially John Murray and Thomas Delf (the latter having replaced Chapman as his London agent). He had good reason to meet with his British colleagues in 1851, since he was not only searching for new works for publication in the United States but also hoping to improve arrangements for those Putnam works that were published in England by formal agreement. With the state of international copyright extremely unsettled in England, many Putnam books were being pirated by the aggressive new generation of publishers, especially George Routledge and Henry Bohn, each of whom in scanning the list of forthcoming American works in the *Literary World* had targeted Putnam's publishing list for works to add to their cheap libraries.[92]

Particularly vulnerable at the time were the works of Irving, which were nearly as desirable a publication in England as in the United States. Hoping to do his best for Irving, Putnam had contracted with John Murray in 1848 for the publication of the author's revised edition in England, but their arrangement was soon subjected to the typical stresses of transatlantic publishing. The Irving edition was soon snagged on the uneven border between American and English publishing conditions and regulations. Whereas Putnam was motivated to produce the books as fast as possible at home in order to sustain momentum for the entire series, Murray complained that his firm needed "breathing time" between titles: "The public are taken too suddenly and cannot understand an author writing at such speed."[93] More seriously, while Putnam was kept busy coordinating the printing, proofing, advertising, and marketing schedule for the work on his side of the Atlantic, Murray not only needed but demanded that he be given a minimal lead time in getting his edition into print in advance of Putnam's lest he lose his claim to English copyright protection.

When Putnam arrived in London in 1851, Murray was in the midst of court proceedings against Bohn and Routledge to protect his American publications, especially the works of Irving, from unauthorized republication. He had requested an affidavit from Putnam in January 1850 certifying the date of his American publication of Irving's *Mahomet and His Successors,* which Murray could then use in a suit he was planning to bring against the London pirates. Bohn and Routledge had seldom been more than a few months behind him in issuing their competing editions, as sure enough they were in 1850 in printing their own editions of *Mahomet.*[94] Within months Murray sought an injunction against the Irving (and Melville) reprints issued by Bohn and Routledge and sued for damages. The result was a long, complicated suit that was a year old when Putnam came to Albemarle Street to discuss it and other matters with Murray. He would then have heard from Murray the good news that in the related case of *Boosey* v. *Jefferys* the Court of Errors had recently upheld the right of foreign authors to seek British copyright protection. He would also have heard, however, that that ruling was insufficient in and of itself to end Murray's problems with the pirates. In fact, one of the problems Murray had encountered in prosecuting his case had inadvertently been caused by Putnam, who Bohn claimed (no doubt correctly) had sold copies of various works in the revised edition of Irving's works to his agents Delf and Chapman for resale in England. Frustrated by the twists and turns of the case and worried about his mounting legal costs, Murray finally decided several months after his meeting with Putnam to sell Bohn his rights to most of the titles in the Irving edition for £2,000.[95]

As always during his overseas trips, Putnam also took time for pleasure. He and Haven visited some of their friends, and he was able to leave Haven with a family to which the Putnams had been particularly close. He himself attended an amateur performance of a play by Bulwer in which Dickens, Jerrold, and Charles Knight acted; heard Thackeray lecture on the poets of Queen Anne's time; and took part in a meeting on the international copyright question chaired by Bulwer. But the special treat for father and son was the recently opened Crystal Palace in Hyde Park, which was being widely touted in the transatlantic press as one of the wonders of the modern world. It not only held Putnam's interest, it transfixed him. As he reported back to a New York newspaper, he stood before "that last and biggest of the world's wonders" in rapt fascination, and he made repeated visits to it during their short trip.[96]

His fascination with "that wonderful structure of glass and iron" was widely shared; its rapid-fire construction on a once vacant lot aroused a sense of amazement perhaps best articulated by Dickens: "Two parties in London relying on the accuracy and goodwill of a single ironmaster, the owners of a single glass-works in Birmingham and of one master-carpenter in London, bound themselves for a certain sum of money, and in a few months, to cover eighteen acres with a building upwards of a third of a mile long."[97] Inside those acres and within the iron, steel, and glass structure were housed the products of the world's economy and imagination—including, Putnam noted, a small display of his firm's books.[98] In regarding what he considered an overpowering monument to "progress" and "industry," Putnam stood solidly with the middle class, safely insulated from the attacks on the Great Exhibition as fact and symbol by critics on the left such as Marx and the right such as Dostoevsky. He stood, for that matter, directly in line with many of his colleagues and friends in the publishing profession in London, where one publisher after another put into operation schemes of various sorts—books, catalogues, guides, prints—to profit from this monument to capitalism. Putnam became so entranced with it that he brought home with him that summer not only mementos of the building to share with family and friends but powerful memories that in time affected his publishing plans when New York decided to follow London's model in hoisting its own Crystal Palace above the city.[99]

A second highlight, one motivated by his desire to be closer to the center of New York publishing and printing activity, was his removal of his offices in spring 1852 from 155 Broadway to 10 Park Place, a block of handsome structures running between Columbia College and City Hall Park. Before making the move, he sold off his entire retail stock at auction. The sale took place ten consecutive evenings at the auction houses of Lyman and Rawdon and of John Keese, with Putnam advertising as particularly attractive the Abbotsford edition of the Waverly novels and the Cadell edition of Scott's life and work, Bohn's Classical Library, Pickering's edition of Milton, the folio plates of Layard's *Ruins of Nineveh,* and prints of the London Crystal Palace and other spectacles.[100] In dispensing with his stock, he brought a new supply of much-needed capital into his business. Confusion surrounding the move kept his doors shut for the first two weeks of May and sent prospective shoppers looking for him at Park Row, one of the new centers for booksellers (to which John Wiley, among others, had relocated).

Later that year, probably in October or November, Putnam also made a domestic move.[101] After five generally happy years on Staten Island, he purchased a house at 92 East Sixteenth Street, the attractive residential neighborhood that his peripatetic family favored whenever it chose to live in Manhattan during the next two decades. The account he had provided that summer for Carhart's edification about the state of his personal affairs was apparently only partially true; the new house was a large, handsome brick structure, which Putnam had finely furnished in advance of their move (Mary recalled in particular the green velvet wallpaper chosen for the first floor reception rooms).[102] According to their son's memory of the event, Putnam presented the move to Victorine as a surprise, having purchased and outfitted the house without her knowledge and then taken her to see it under the pretense of visiting prospective houses.[103] In that decision as in most matters relating to their family life and living arrangements, she deferred to his judgment implicitly.

Living in the city had clear advantages for the entire family, although the children could not then be persuaded of the fact. Playing in the adjoining Stuyvesant Square was a poor substitute for the open fields and beaches that they had previously taken as their extended home territory, and they were hardly used to any adults, no less policemen, patrolling their playgrounds. But the city offered children and parents alike broader social, cultural, and educational possibilities than could their isolated home on Staten Island, a fact of increasing importance as the older children approached the time when they would move out of home to institutional schooling. Sure enough, not long after the move their parents began making more formal arrangements for their education. One outcome was that Mary was placed with her father's friend and client Francis Hawks for instruction in Latin; the deal was apparently a convenient way for Putnam to allow Hawks to return a financial debt. It is just as plausible, however, that the most immediate reason for the move was Putnam's need to be closer to his business, whose expansion was putting increasing pressure on his time and energy. Particularly pressing was the new monthly magazine he decided either that summer or autumn to launch, a decision whose timing coincided so nearly with that of the family move that the two might well have been interrelated. Both, in turn, were related to the larger world of Manhattan, which now for the first time became the center of Putnam's activities both personally and professionally.

Notes

1. I have seen printed catalogues of its contents ("A Private Collection of Autograph Letters, Documents, and Curiosities") at the American Antiquarian Society and the Library of Congress (GPP Collection).

2. GPP to Mellen Chamberlain, 25 October 1844; Rare Books and Manuscripts, Boston Public Library.

3. "Autographomania," *Overland Monthly* 3 (October 1869): 342. For a scintillating cultural reading of this phenomenon and more broadly of orthography in America, see Tamara Plakins Thornton, *Handwriting in America: A Cultural History* (New Haven: Yale University Press, 1996), esp. 78–88.

4. Fields to GPP, 23 November 1843; GPP-P.

5. By a curious eventuality, Fields came into a Lamb autograph fifteen years later when he purchased one at the 1858 sale of GPP's collection; see the copy of "Private Collection" in the GPP Collection, Library of Congress, which has Fields's name pencilled in the margins by GPP (p. 8).

6. Fields to GPP, 7 July 1846; GPP-P.

7. "The Publishing Business," *Literary World* 6 (5 January 1850): 11–13.

8. "The Public Libraries of America," *Literary World* 6 (3 March 1850): 195–97.

9. James Franklin Beard, ed. *Letters and Journals of James Fenimore Cooper,* 6 vols. (Cambridge: Harvard University Press, 1960–68), 6:155.

10. John Hammond Moore, *Wiley: One Hundred and Seventy-five Years of Publishing* (New York: John Wiley and Sons, 1982), 54–60.

11. GPP ran the following warning in his announcement of the work: "In consequence of portions of this work having been incorporated into the London Edition of *Goethe's Autobiography,* published in Bohn's Standard Library, the sale of that work will therefore be prohibited in this country, it being an infringement of the copyright"; *Literary World* 6 (1 June 1850): 553.

12. See *Norton's Literary Gazette* 1 (15 December 1851): 108.

13. See his advertisement for it in the *Literary World* 8 (3 May 1851): 363. Although such a project fit his publishing style and interests, I have found no other evidence that GPP ever made a substantial investment in this venture.

The announcement of the English edition appeared in *Publishers' Circular* 14 (15 March 1851): 107. After GPP gave up on the project, the London edition was imported into the United States by the well-known auction firm of Bangs, Brother and Company; see the *Literary World* 10 (20 March 1852): 215.

14. *Literary World* 10 (7 February 1852): 112.

15. *Norton's Literary Gazette* 1 (15 February 1852): 40, and (15 June 1852): 104.

16. The earliest mention I have found for Putnam's Railway Library is in *Norton's Literary Gazette* 1 (15 November 1851): 88.

17. He was not far in advance of his competition. Charles Norton advertised his own line of railway books just a month after GPP; New York *Tribune,* 22 December 1851, 1.

18. Judson to GPP, 16 December [n.y., but in context presumably 1853 or 1854]; GPP-P.

19. I deliberately use "standardized" to reflect nineteenth-century terminology rather than the anachronistic "canonized," which more generally represents twentieth-century academic terminology.

When Evert Duyckinck, admittedly a New York "nationalist," compiled his portrait gallery of illustrious Americans who "have more than others helped to make America what it is to-day," he included among his century's imaginative writers only Bryant,

Irving, Cooper, and Longfellow (and only Joel Barlow among earlier writers); *National Portrait Gallery of Eminent American,* 2 vols. (New York: Johnson, Fry and Company, 1862–64), 1:vii.

20. See GPP's advertisement in *Norton's Literary Gazette* 1 (15 November 1851): 88.

21. Lanman to "Sir," 27 September 1852; GPP-P.

22. It is still useful today to contemporary historians as a general guide to books available to antebellum book buyers, as well as to works of writers canonized today but then more fluidly situated in local taste, circumstance, and consumption.

23. The six volumes appeared in the following order: (1) GPP, *Hand-Book of Chronology and History* (1852); (2) George Ripley and Bayard Taylor, *Hand-Book of Literature and the Fine Arts* (1852); (3) Thomas Antisell, *Hand-Book of the Useful Arts* (1852); (4) Parke Godwin, *Hand-Book of Universal Biography* (1852); T. Carey Callicot, *Hand-Book of Universal Geography* (1853); and (6) Samuel St. John, *Hand-Book of Science.* I have been unable to determine whether St. John, whose popular *Elements of Geology* was kept in print by GPP right through the 1850s and 1860s, ever completed his volume; no copy of it is listed in the National Union Catalogue, but it was advertised for sale by GPP.

24. For an account of the complicated printing history of the expedition, see Daniel C. Haskell, *The United States Exploring Expedition and Its Publications* (New York: Greenwood Press, 1968).

25. Quoted in *Nineveh and Its Remains,* ed. H. W. F. Saggs (London: Routledge and Kegan Paul, 1970), 18.

26. The announcement appeared in the *Literary World* 9 (4 October 1851): 273. It is possible that GPP knew that the book was far from ready for publication and was simply protecting a valuable prospect by way of prior announcement, a standard procedure in matters of courtesy of the trade.

27. *Literary World* 12 (18 June 1853): 490.

28. For Warner's version, see her elder sister's biography; Anna B. Warner, *Susan Warner* (New York: G. P. Putnam's Sons, 1909), 283.

29. Ibid., 262.

30. The discussion of the publication history of *The Wide, Wide World* and of Warner's relations with the Putnams is based primarily on the following sources: Anna B. Warner's *Susan Warner,* a rich source of information on the two families and their relations; reviews and advertisements in the periodical press, especially in the *Literary World* and *Norton's Literary Gazette;* the Warner entry in the *Bibliography of American Literature;* the various family biographies and autobiographies by GHP and Ruth Putnam; Edward Halsey Foster, *Susan and Anna Warner* (Boston: Twayne, n.d.); and recent feminist scholarship on Warner, especially Susan S. Williams's "Widening the Word: Susan Warner, Her Readers, and the Assumption of Authorship," *American Quarterly* 42 (December 1990): 565–86; and Jane Tompkins's afterword to her reprint edition of *The Wide, Wide World* (New York: Feminist Press, 1987), 584–608.

31. *Literary World* 12 (5 February 1853): 110.

32. Both reviews are quoted in Anna B. Warner, *Susan Warner,* 344. The *Advertiser* review was excerpted by GPP in advertisements for the book; see, e.g., his blurb in the *Literary World* 10 (29 May 1852): 370. He also sent a copy of this review to Warner; Anna B. Warner, *Susan Warner,* 349.

33. Tompkins, ed., *Wide, Wide World,* 585.

34. Anna B. Warner, *Susan Warner,* 346. She unfortunately excised the remainder of this important letter, whose original is lost.

35. For a fine illustration of an analogous scene (1852) of a boy writing into his copybook while a girl sews standing by his side, see Thornton, *Handwriting in America,* 56.

36. Tompkins, ed., *Wide, Wide World,* viii.

37. Her views are primarily known from the answers she gave to a questionnaire sent out by *Publishers' Weekly* in 1872 to solicit information about domestic and international copyright. To the question, "Can you suggest any desirable changes in the domestic copyright law," she responded: "I do not understand the present condition or needs of the same." She apparently elected not to mail the questionnaire back; it survives at the Constitution Island Association. For the text of her responses, see Mabel Baker, *Light in the Morning: Memories of Susan and Anna Warner* (West Point, N.Y.: Constitution Island Association Press, 1978), 90–91.

38. The work recast the novel as a story book accompanied by a pack of playing cards (twenty-four cards to a pack, colored by the Warner sisters for an additional fee).

39. The chapter in question concerned a little African American girl and was cut before publication; Anna B. Warner, *Susan Warner,* 296.

40. Ibid., 323.

41. I take these details from Warner's journals; Jane Weiss, ed., "'Many Things Take My Time': The Journals of Susan Warner" (Ph.D. diss., City University of New York, 1995), 287.

42. *Literary World* 10 (24 April 1852): 302. Warner was at GPP's store as *Queechy* was about to be sent out to advance customers and reported on the preparations to her sister: "It is published tomorrow. Five thousand, Mr. P. told me yesterday, are in boxes, to be sent or already I suppose sent off, to orders. A greater start than any book ever had out of his store." Anna B. Warner, *Susan Warner,* 352.

43. On the overseas arrangement for *Queechy,* see the advertisement in the *Literary World* 10 (17 April 1852): 274. Nisbet would subsequently issue a number of her later works in England.

44. *Publishers' Circular* 16 (16 February 1853): 81. Sampson Low, Jr., son of the publisher of the *Circular,* took a personal interest in the state of Anglo-American literary trade, in which his firm was becoming one of the most important English dealers in the mid-1850s. During his autumn 1852 trip to the United States, he bought the English rights to numerous American works, including GPP's *Homes of American Authors.* He came out to Warner's home at Constitution Island in October and paid her £20 for the rights to a small printing of *The Wide, Wide World,* but he failed to persuade her to sell him rights to a new work; Anna B. Warner, *Susan Warner,* 364, 367–68.

45. Fredrika Bremer, *The Homes of the New World,* trans. Mary Howitt, 2 vols. (New York: Harper and Brothers, 1853), 1:250.

46. GHP, *George Palmer Putnam,* 2:289.

47. It seems likely that GPP had in mind the publication of other works by her, as well. He advertised his intent in 1851 to publish her *American Letters* (probably an early title for what became *Homes of the New World*) in *Norton's Literary Gazette* 1 (15 November 1851): 88.

48. Bremer, *Homes of the New World,* 1:64–67.

49. Epes Sargent placed a blurb for the "exquisite" Putnam edition of *The Neighbours* that must have pleased him greatly: "Mr. Putnam will beat the English publishers by and by in the tasteful style of his books. He has introduced a new era in American book publishing." Sargent to GPP, 10 December 1849; GPP-P.

50. Fredrika Bremer, "Author's Preface," *The Neighbours* (New York: George P. Putnam, 1850), vii.

51. The originals of the letters that passed between the two houses are in GPP-P.

52. See, e.g., the advertisement for this long-delayed work in the *Literary World* 8 (8 February 1851): 114.

53. *Literary World* 8 (22 February 1851): 157.

54. GHP, *George Palmer Putnam,* 1:252.

55. "And if ever a nation shall deserve to present to the world a new and higher face of home-life, it must be that people in which woman is treated with the highest regard and true chivalry—where she is permitted to become all that nature intended her to be." Bremer, *Neighbours,* x.

56. Michael Winship, *American Literary Publishing in the Mid-Nineteenth Century: The Business of Ticknor and Fields* (New York: Cambridge University Press, 1996), 67–69.

57. Anna B. Warner, *Susan Warner,* 293

58. *Family Pictures from the Bible* (New York: G. P. Putnam, 1849), 2.

59. See, for instance, the joint advertisement for these two gift books in the New York *Tribune,* 10 December 1851.

60. A letter of 21 November 1851 by GPP (although not in his hand) discussing the attacks made on the book and the unsolicited defense put up on his behalf by the editors of the New York *Evening Post* is in GHP-C (scrapbook, p. 128).

61. Beard, ed., *James Fenimore Cooper,* 6:95–96.

62. Ibid., 214.

63. Ibid., 282.

64. Ibid., 204.

65. The best source on the compositional and publishing history of *Towns of Manhattan* is James F. Beard, Jr., "The First History of Greater New York," *New-York Historical Society Quarterly* 37 (April 1953): 109–45.

66. I take most of the details for the discussion of *Towns of Manhattan* from the exchange of letters between the two Coopers and GPP in the James Fenimore Cooper Collection, Beinecke Library, Yale University; and from Beard, "Greater New York," 113–16.

The fire that destroyed the manuscript and plates of *Towns of Manhattan* then in Putnam's possession presumably destroyed not his office, as Beard thought possible, but his printer's. For one thing, there is no documentation of a fire at Putnam's office during 1851–52. For another, fires at printing shops, which used highly flammable materials, were extremely common in the nineteenth century. More specifically, the approximate date of the fire alluded to in the Cooper-GPP file corresponds to the fire that destroyed the printing establishment of Robert Craighead, one of the two Manhattan printing houses most frequently patronized by GPP. Craighead advertised his business as reopened in *Literary World* 10 (7 February 1852): 97.

67. *Memorial of James Fenimore Cooper* (New York: G. P. Putnam, 1852). GPP's role in organizing the volume was unquestionably altruistic, but he also took the opportunity at the back of the volume to insert a one-page advertisement for his firm's twelve-volume edition of Cooper's selected works, as well as its editions of Susan Cooper's *Rural Hours* and *The Shield* (never actually completed) and of Charlotte Fenimore Cooper's translation of Ida Pfeiffer's *A Journey to Iceland.*

68. GPP to President and Committee of the American Art Union, 14 January 1850; GPP-P.

69. John K. Howat, "A Climate for Landscape Painters," in *American Paradise: The World of the Hudson River School,* ed. John K. Howat (New York: Metropolitan Museum of Art, 1987), 53–54.

70. *Home Book of the Picturesque: or American Scenery, Art, and Literature* (New York: G. P. Putnam, 1852).

71. The copy owned by the New York Public Library was inscribed on Christmas 1851 by William Cullen Bryant to his wife.

72. The sheet is in GPP-P. It was bound as the last page in one of the folio albums in which Princeton University received the collection.

73. GPP made the comparison to Howitt's book explicitly in a letter to Ralph Waldo Emerson in which he solicited Emerson's inclusion in the volume; GPP to Emerson, 7 April 1852; Houghton Library, Harvard University.

74. Curtis to GPP, n.d. [but presumably 1852]; George W. Curtis file, Clifton Walker Barrett Collection, Alderman Library, University of Virginia.

75. The correspondence between GPP and both William Prescott and George Hillard is in the William Prescott file, Barrett Collection, Alderman Library, University of Virginia.

76. Hillard to GPP, 21 June 1852 and 24 July 1852; Barrett Collection, Alderman Library, University of Virginia.

77. *Homes of American Authors* (New York: G. P. Putnam and Company, 1853), iv.

78. Ibid., iv.

79. Ibid., iii–iv.

80. GPP paid Kirkland $25 for her article on Bryant, which must have been the standard payment he made to contributors; GPP to Kirkland, 15 August 1852; GPP-P.

81. Fields to GPP, 12 November 1852; GPP-P.

82. That copy is in the Berg Collection, New York Public Library.

83. GPP to George William Curtis, 14 August 1852; GPP-P.

84. GPP to Willis, 28 February 1853; GPP-P; GPP to Sparks, 8 July 1853; Jared Sparks Collection, Houghton Library, Harvard University.

85. "Free-Stone for Authors," *Literary World* 10 (22 May 1852): 363.

86. "'Free-Stone'—Authors—Publishers," *Literary World* 10 (5 June 1852): 395–96.

87. GPP to Harper and Brothers, 14 December 1853; GPP-P.

88. Ellsworth to GPP, 20 December 1853; GPP-P.

89. Duyckinck's account books for the late 1840s have multiple entries for rents paid to GPP and Leslie; D-NYPL. The claim that Leslie was already then working for GPP rests on his signature on a letter from the firm to Caroline Kirkland, 1 November [1849]; Kroch Library, Cornell University.

90. GHP, *Memories of My Youth, 1844–1865* (New York: G. P. Putnam's Sons, 1914), 28–9.

91. Victorine Haven Putnam to GPP, 3 June [1851]; HP-LC.

92. See, for instance, the list of titles in Bohn's Shilling Series and Routledge's Popular Library from July 1850; both series are dominated by the works of Irving; James J. Barnes, *Authors, Publishers and Politicians: The Quest for an Anglo-American Copyright Agreement, 1815–1854* (London: Routledge and Kegan Paul, 1974), 156–57.

93. Robert Cooke (of John Murray) to GPP, 29 August 1849; GPP-P (box 11, scrapbook, p. 25).

94. Robert Cooke to GPP, 25 January 1850; GPP-P (box 11, scrapbook, p. 25). One wonders how GPP reacted to Murray's request because he had in fact already issued the first volume of *Mahomet and His Successors* in December (a fact that Bohn turned to his advantage by mentioning it in an advertisement for his unauthorized edition of the work). Murray persisted in bringing out the work, although he might have withheld royalties to Irving, as he had threatened to do. On the various editions of the work in New York and London, see Edwin T. Bowden, comp., *Washington Irving: Bibliography* (Boston: Twayne, 1989), 464–71.

95. For a detailed account of the whole affair, see Barnes, *Authors, Publishers and Politicians,* 155–65. Although extraordinarily meticulous, Barnes is mistaken on one

point. Murray planned to institute legal proceedings before the mutual depredations practiced by Bohn and Routledge against each other following reprinting in February 1850 of Emerson's *Representative Men.* Murray was "almost prepared" to take legal action by 25 January 1850 when his firm requested of GPP the above-mentioned affidavit.

96. "A Flying Trip to the Glass-House, etc.," New York *Evening Post.* An undated clipping of the article is in GPP-P (box 11, scrapbook).

97. Dickens, *Household Words,* quoted in Eric de Mare, *London 1851: The Year of the Great Exhibition* (London: J. M. Dent, 1973), n.p.

98. "Flying Trip to the Glass-House, etc."; in GPP-P.

99. One of those Crystal Palace mementos he gave to the local workman who had rescued Mary from drowning that summer. Ruth Putnam, ed., *Life and Letters of Mary Putnam Jacobi* (New York: G. P. Putnam's Sons, 1925), 25–26.

100. I take the details of his move primarily from his advertisements in the *Literary World* 10 (10 April 1852): 272, and in the New York *Tribune,* 13 and 23 April and 14 May 1852.

101. The Putnams were living on Staten Island at least until September 1852, when Susan Warner accompanied GPP to the island to pick up Mary and George Haven to take them with her to her home; Anna B. Warner, *Susan Warner,* 361.

102. Mary Putnam [Jacobi] autobiography; Mary Putnam Jacobi Papers, Schlesinger Library, Radcliffe College.

103. GHP, *George Palmer Putnam,* 355–56.

CHAPTER 9

Putnam's Monthly and "the Putnam Public"

With the Putnams' move to Manhattan came a dramatic change in their social relations. Shortly after moving into their new home, they began entertaining formally on a scale not previously possible for them. Their "weekly soirees of the lions, tigers, and tamer animals, male and female," as Putnam called their Tuesday evenings, soon became an informal social and cultural institution in the life of the city, which until then had few venues for bringing together literary and artistic people for conversation and socializing.[1] Friendly people with an easy, accommodating social style, the Putnams opened their doors by invitation to many of the cultural elite of the city and to visitors from near and afar. In a puckish mood the day of the initial soiree, Mary put up a sign on the front door, "Nobody admitted who cannot talk," but there was not much danger of that happening with the kinds of guests that they typically hosted, who included William Cullen Bryant, Evert Duyckinck, Frederick Law Olmsted, Bayard Taylor, Francis Hawks, Henry Tuckerman, Caroline Kirkland, Charles Anthon, Susan and Anna Warner, George Ripley, and Anne Lynch. Likewise, out-of-town friends visiting the city, such as James Russell Lowell, Catharine Maria Sedgwick, John Pendleton Kennedy, George Sumner, Asa Gray (of Harvard), and

Benjamin Silliman (of Yale), occasionally dropped in for one of their parties.[2] One of their most distant visitors was Thackeray, who spent at least one evening with them during his American excursion of 1852–53.[3] Another distinguished-looking visitor around that time was Eleazar Williams, about whom there was much discussion in the United States in early 1853 about whether his origins were in France or in an American Indian cabin. A particularly vivid reminiscence of those evenings was recorded by Anna Warner, who had taken rooms for the winter of 1852–53 with her sister and father just blocks from the Putnams' house. She remembered the parties as "the very pleasantest assemblies to which we ever went," where the talk was good and smart and ranged over the major domestic and international topics of the day, where the guest list included the finest literary and artistic society the city could boast, and where the latest novelties were on display (Putnam one day showing photographs, then "an absolutely new thing," and another day a Chinese newspaper mailed to him from California).[4] There were limits, however, to the range of their social relations, their set of friends occupying a level a full rung below the haute monde that George William Curtis would soon satirize in *The Potiphar Papers* and Edith Wharton retrospectively in *The Age of Innocence*. As Curtis had Mr. Potiphar complain in one of the installments serialized in *Putnam's Monthly,* "When Pearl-Street comes to Park Place, Park Place must run for its life to Thirtieth-street."[5] That remark would have come in for a good laugh by the Putnam staff at 10 Park Place.

By no coincidence, many of the Putnams' visitors were contributors to the new magazine Putnam was planning to launch. Three of their more regular visitors, in fact, were the editors-to-be of the planned publication, Charles Frederick Briggs, Parke Godwin, and Curtis; and the connection between Putnam's move to New York, his evening parties, and his new magazine must have been calculated. Even without a successful outcome to Cooper's *The Towns of Manhattan,* Putnam's publishing identity was firmly associated by 1852 with his adopted city, an association that also marked his magazine beginning with the publication in its second number of the first of Clarence Cook's "New York Daguerreotyped" sketches and continuing as long as he owned the magazine.[6] Although he advertised *Putnam's* as "an American Magazine—Original and National" and intended to draw on writers from around the country, the center of his publishing network was clearly located in New York. So, for that matter, was the market placement of the magazine, which Putnam gradually positioned to fill a void in the periodical sector of the city as well as of the nation.

The character and format of *Putnam's Monthly* emerged over the course of autumn 1852 from the collaborative thinking of Putnam and his editorial "triumvirate" (as they liked to call themselves). Although his son has claimed that Putnam was contemplating the publication of a literary magazine during their 1851 trip to England, the actual impulse behind *Putnam's Monthly* as it emerged in 1852–53 apparently originated with its founding editor, Charles Frederick Briggs. Briggs was one of the most experienced newspaper and magazine journalists in New York, with extensive prior stints in editing the *Broadway Journal* and *Holden's Dollar Magazine;* by 1852 he was eager to return to periodical work and ambitious to do so on a new magazine organized along high-quality, culturally nationalistic lines.[7] The obvious address in New York to which to take that ambition was Putnam, with whom he had worked on *Homes of American Authors* and earlier works. Briggs undoubtedly knew New York City addresses well; as plans for the new magazine went forward that autumn, he was publishing a series of sketches, "Walks among the New-York Poor," in the New York *Times* that explored the city's neglected neighborhoods.[8] But his journalistic eye and sensibility, like Putnam's, were turned primarily toward the upper socioeconomic strata, and the two men shared a variety of ideas and ideals whose chief instrumentality was the literary magazine they both hungered to bring out.

Putnam's desire to publish such a magazine was keen. He already had nearly two decades' experience importing, retailing, and editing journals of various sorts. As recently as 1850–51 he had played middleman to the American editions of *Revue des deux Mondes* and Dickens's *Household Words.* More important, he had watched since 1850, along with many of his peers, the astounding success that his competitors, the Harpers, were having with their monthly magazine. If, as seems likely, his eye was tracking the upward trajectory of *Harper's Monthly* rather than the more common downward trajectory of such competitors or imitators as Stringer and Townsend's *International,* Putnam was a shrewd enough publisher to foresee a timely opportunity to position a new, alternately fashioned magazine laterally from *Harper's Monthly* in an unoccupied space of the periodical market. So if and when Briggs came to him with a proposition or an idea, Putnam would have been uncommonly receptive and eager to put it into practice. Conditions were then unusually good for publishing schemes, but literary economics was not the sole basis of his planning. He was also motivated by the prospect of publishing a magazine whose outlines corresponded as directly to the character and mission of his firm as *Harper's Monthly* did to its. As *Harper's Monthly* had made its mark as primarily a magazine of reprinted fiction and relatively numerous illustrations, so *Putnam's Monthly,* as he and his editors were conceiving it, would make its as being explicitly the voice of American authorship and the magazine for readers of serious as well as entertaining letters. That there was a sufficient authorship and audience to sustain such a venture Putnam was so confident in autumn 1852 that he was willing to stake the prosperity of his publishing house and the credibility of his name.

These were some of the general thoughts and calculations that emerged during intense discussions conducted, first, between Putnam and Victorine at their house with the three designated editors, as well as with Caroline Kirkland (herself an experienced journal editor) and their old friend George Sumner; and, later, in a follow-up meeting between the four chief operators held at a deserted house on Park Place targeted for conversion to a store. Relations between Putnam and his editors were both personally and professionally cordial, centered on a core of shared political, cultural, and social values and reinforced by mutual respect. Although Putnam meant to play an active role in the overall promotion and distribution of the magazine, he planned to leave the general editorial management and responsibility for its day-to-day operations primarily to the generally like-minded professionals he hired as editors.

In choosing Briggs, Curtis, and Godwin to conduct the magazine, he could hardly have associated himself with three more talented journalists then active in New York City. Briggs, the oldest and most seasoned of the three, was a man of consummate literary magazine experience and of wide professional connections in New England and New York.[9] Furthermore, he wielded one of the sharpest wits and most cutting pens among literary journalists of his generation. Curtis, designated to be the literary editor, was a writer and editor endowed with a golden touch for the culture of middle-class letters, a talent he would immediately demonstrate in penning numerous of the wittiest sketches contributed to the pages of *Putnam's,* including *The Potiphar Papers* and *Prue and I.* Despite his youth, he was even better connected than Briggs to the literary community of their native New England, the area with the largest concentration of writers in the country. On top of these professional talents, he appealed to Putnam as a man after his own heart, as smooth and genial as Briggs could be rough and brash (the admiration was mutual; Curtis liked and respected Putnam, whom he once called "the most gentlemanly of publishers").[10] Godwin, who was known to Putnam through both the New York *Evening Post* and the fine volume he had edited for *Putnam's Home Cyclopedia,* was involved in planning the magazine but played a less central role than Briggs and Curtis in its operation through the first half year. But beginning with the second volume, the force of his personality and views began to mark the magazine more fully, and from that time Godwin distinguished himself in his contributions to *Putnam's* as one of the most forceful political writers in the country. He stated himself so forthrightly on the slavery issue, in fact, that his views roiled the already choppy waters the magazine had to navigate in reaching all sections of the country.

Taken together, the three men were journalists and writers of experience and distinction, advocates of a more or less common politics of antislavery reform, and outspoken proponents of cultural national-ism and international copyright—a combination of attributes that could only have bound them to the views and opinions of Putnam. Further-more, since they were all to be contributing editors, Putnam was able to count on them to provide a substantial part of the copy of the maga-zine—a tremendous advantage, as time would show, because they wrote many of the magazine's best pieces and in the process injected into it a spirited, sophisticated tone that set a standard for the entire magazine. With their talents and personalities nicely matched, they presented the most powerful editorial team in Manhattan.

Preparations for the January publication of the first issue pro-ceeded through the fall. Some time probably late in September, Putnam drafted a circular letter that he sent to dozens, perhaps hundreds, of American writers to announce his plans for the magazine and to solicit their patronage and contributions. Putnam had previously taken ad-vantage of special occasions to speak his mind as an American pub-lisher, but this time, recognizing his planned magazine as the literary and publishing opportunity of a lifetime, he sounded as ringing a call for American letters as had yet been made by an American publisher:

> We take the liberty of informing you of our intention to publish an Original periodical of a character different from any now in

existence, and, as it is our wish to have the best talent of the country to aid us in the undertaking, to solicit your assistance as a contributor.

We propose to publish *monthly* a work which shall combine the popular character of a Magazine, with the higher and graver aims of a Quarterly Review, but to preserve in all its departments an independent and elevated tone; and to make it as essentially an organ of American thought as possible.

The want of such a publication, we believe, has long been felt in this Country, and it is only after mature consideration, and on the advice of some of the most eminent literary and scientific men of the Union who have offered us their aid, that we have determined on the attempt to supply this want. We believe that the facilities connected with an established publishing business will enable us to place the work at once on a high footing, and beyond ordinary contingencies.[11]

Positive responses to his circular and his request for permission to cite them for promotional purposes came from nearly one hundred authors, whose names he immediately listed as potential contributors in his general advertisement for the magazine (although he steadfastly refused to print authors' names inside the magazine itself). That list, which included Emerson, Hawthorne, Thoreau, Longfellow, Simms, Warner, Sedgwick, and Cooper, was itself partial proof of the fact of American authorship, which Putnam was counting upon.[12] Emerson's response typified the deep vein of national pride that Putnam was tapping into: "Nothing could be more agreeable to me than the establishment of an American Magazine of a truly elevated and independent tone."[13] Such sentiments were important to him in reaffirming the belief not only that he was acting on the most honorable grounds but that he was occupying them on behalf of the leading writers of his time.

Putnam also took great care to see to the manufacture and distribution of the magazine on a level that would meet his high standards of printmaking. He chose John Trow as printer and arranged for the use of new type and good paper—his standard in this regard, as in others, probably *Blackwood's,* the most highly regarded general magazine of the era. To ensure that *Putnam's* would have a transatlantic publication, as the best British journals did, he met some time in late October or November with the London publisher Sampson Low, who

No. 1.   25 Cents.

Putnam's
Monthly

January,

1853.

NEW-YORK:
G. P. PUTNAM & COMPANY,
10 PARK PLACE.
LONDON:—Sampson Low, Son & Co.

Entered according to Act of Congress in the year 1853, by G. P. PUTNAM & Co., in the Clerk's Office of the District Court for the Southern District of New-York.

LONGFELLOW

8.   Sketch drawn by William Thackeray on the cover of his copy of the inaugural issue of *Putnam's Monthly*. The three figures (Longfellow, at right; Curtis, at bottom center; and a black field worker, at top center) are his. (Courtesy Berg Collection, New York Public Library)

was visiting New York with the intent of making arrangements with American publishers and authors for English rights to their works, and arranged with him for the "simultaneous" publication of *Putnam's* in England.[14] To ensure an immediately ample subscription, Putnam followed the practice common in the volatile periodical market of purchasing the subscription list of the recently disbanded *Whig Review,* a first measure toward building a much wider base of patronage for his magazine.[15] By late December, all was in readiness for the appearance of the first issue of the magazine, which Putnam optimistically brought out in a series of printings that totaled 20,000 copies.[16] His hope was that his "great experiment," as he proudly described it to Bayard Taylor, would take New York by storm the way that Thackeray was then doing.[17]

The magazine was issued in a large octavo format with pea green covers—the color with which it would be popularly identified. It sold for the usual price of American monthlies, $.25 an issue or $3 a year (postage added), and ran to 120 pages of double-columned print. Within weeks, reviews of the magazine appeared in newspapers around the country, a sign that *Putnam's* was reaching readers nationwide, although its circulation, like its authorship, was undoubtedly concentrated in the cities of the Northeast.[18] Many of the reviews responded approvingly to the editorial line that Briggs took in the January issue: "It is because we are confident that neither Greece nor Guinea can offer the American reader a richer variety of instruction and amusement in every kind, than the country whose pulses throb with his, and whose every interest is his own, that this Magazine presents itself to-day.... To an American eye, life in New-York, for instance, offers more, and more interesting, aspects, than life in London or Paris."[19] Briggs also made clear in his opening remarks his strategic intent to position the magazine between the traditional spheres of quarterly reviews and popular monthly magazines as a periodical that would be simultaneously serious and amusing, instructive and entertaining—the same basic position that Duyckinck had struck in the various Wiley and Putnam Libraries and that Putnam had taken throughout his career. This was the guiding editorial policy that Putnam stated, for instance, in responding to the proposed submissions on public policy of James Gillespie Birney, leading abolitionist and former presidential candidate: "Of course in a popular magazine like ours we can only mix such articles as these occasionally with lighter matter, for after all people expect to be entertained and amused rather more than they care to be instructed by what they read in a magazine."[20]

The high quality of *Putnam's* was readily apparent to readers from the first issue—and with good reason. The editors had clearly commanded the best magazine talent in the country and located the national pulse at various pressure points: Longfellow and Lowell contributed poems that would have met Putnam's standard of "national" poetry; Thoreau, the "what I got by going to Canada was a cold" opening segment of *An Excursion to Canada;* the travel writer Richard Kimball, a timely article on Cuba, whose possible annexation by the United States as a future slave state was then a topic of heated debate conducted along sectional lines; Fitz-James O'Brien, the first installment in a series on "Our Young Authors" that began with Donald Mitchell but got no further than Melville in the February number; Francis Hawks, a reminiscence of the recently deceased, best-selling travel writer John Stephens; Mrs. Rebecca Hicks, a serialized novel called *Virginia* (no doubt intended to attract Southern readers); and Horace Greeley, a piece on spiritualism, one of the hot topics of the day. Curtis and Briggs filled a fair amount of the copy themselves. Curtis published six or seven pieces, including a humorous society sketch called "Andrew Cranberry, Attorney-at-Law" that set the tone for much of the subsequent fiction in the magazine (as well as implicitly located the magazine in the periodical market away from the quarterlies by referring to the *North American Review* as "the best of sedatives"). Briggs contributed, among other matters, several smart pieces on American authorship: one, entitled "The Homes of American Authors," that drew attention to Putnam's recent gift book ("confessedly the book of the year") and confirmed its ideas; and the other, a sharply stated article entitled "Uncle Tomitudes" that commented not simply on the unprecedented popularity of Stowe's novel but on the new conditions that underlay the growth of modern literary culture generally: "Such a phenomenon as its present popularity could have happened only in the present wondrous age. It required all the aid of our new machinery to produce the phenomenon: our steam-presses, steam-ships, steam-carriages, iron roads, electric telegraphs, and universal peace among the reading nations of the earth."[21] What he did not say but plainly hoped was that a related logic would propel his magazine to a comparable periodical fate.

That was an unlikely goal, however, for a magazine such as *Putnam's* whose editorial policy set standards too high to allow it any

realistic chance to achieve the six-digit circulation of *Harper's* or
Godey's. Parke Godwin said as much with his typical directness in
setting out the editorial goal of producing "a first-class periodical": "It
was never our purpose to issue a monthly exclusively for milliners; we
had no ambition to institute a monopoly manufacture of love-tales and
sing-song verses.... No! we had other conceptions of the variety, the
importance, the dignity, and the destiny of literature. Our thought, in
establishing this enterprise, was, and it still is, that literature is the full
and free expression of the nation's mind, not in belles lettres alone, nor
in art alone, nor in science alone, but in all these, combined with politics
and religion."[22] That point of view unquestionably expressed the opinion of the collective management team, as well as of most of the contributors, whose identification with the goals of the magazine was a
recurring theme in correspondence with Putnam and Briggs.

Given the lay of the periodical landscape in the mid-1850s, to
maintain such a view was implicitly to set *Putnam's* against the model
of *Harper's*. That inevitable contrast was maintained editorially in formal silence during the years Putnam operated the magazine; not until
1857, by which time the magazine was out of his hands, would the editors' true assessment of *Harper's* as "a repository of pleasant, various
reading, of sprightly chit-chat, and safe, vague, and dull disquisitions
upon a few public questions" be spoken aloud in print.[23] Nevertheless,
the cultural clash between the two monthlies was widely recognized at
the time and was occasionally spoken aloud by some of their contributors and correspondents. The literary agent for Antioch College Library,
for instance, wrote Putnam shortly after seeing the first issue of *Putnam's*, which he immediately "conceive[d] ... a rival of Harper's Magazine," and explained that he had taken it upon himself to state the
superiority of the former to the latter in newspaper notices in Ohio
and North Carolina.[24] Henry James, Sr., answered Putnam's circular
by inviting a contrast between the promise of the not yet published
Putnam's and the disappointing quality of *Harper's* ("a mere stale and
dishonest hash").[25] The magazine publisher George Graham drew a
similarly invidious comparison in wishing Putnam success, even if he
had his own selfish reasons for doing so: "The success of 'Putnam's
Monthly' is the salvation of 'Graham' for it will stop the prevailing opinion in the trade and among the public that Harper is to master us all.
This I confess I at one time feared, and fear it no longer,—if Putnam
triumphs. I am *too poor* to fight them."[26] Graham was hardly alone; no

other American publisher had the resources or the journalistic formula to match the Harpers in the monthly periodical market. Of course, it was never Putnam's intent or expectation to match them but simply to set up operations on their flank.

As matters developed, there was ample room at least in the short run in the periodical market for both *Harper's* and *Putnam's*. In the succeeding months of 1853, the quality of the magazine held firm, and so did its sales, with a printing base beginning in January around 20,000 copies, rising to 22,500–25,000 in February, and increasing yet again at its peak to about 35,000 copies that summer—a solid and profitable circulation, if hardly one to put the fear of Mammon into the editors of *Harper's*.[27] Given the likelihood that the average copy of an antebellum magazine such as *Putnam's,* which appealed to both men and women and quickly earned a prominent status, had multiple readers, the actual audience of the magazine was unquestionably much higher, although the advertised figure of 150,000 readers given in 1854 seems inflated.[28] Even at the time that Putnam was forced to give up the magazine in early 1855, it was still running a profit. Furthermore, its reputation remained strong throughout the period, both publicly in the press and privately in correspondence with the editor or publisher and in the remarks of writers.

The editors of *Putnam's* unquestionably had as deep a talent pool and as broad a reservoir of good will on which to draw as any American magazine had yet enjoyed. Occasional statements in the magazine indicated that the "editorial sanctum" was often awash in submissions, and editorial decisions were frequently slow, sometimes frustrating and confusing would-be authors. So, too, did the fact that at some point during the first year the editors responded to the volume of contributions by assigning numbers to incoming manuscripts and requesting that authors facilitate correspondence by using those numbers. The correspondence file with the editor reveals that authors came from all parts of the country, with the South and West well represented. But the most common and valued contributors, those who could be relied on for repeated and high-quality submissions, were primarily Northeasterners, men and (less often) women experienced in the world of professional journalism. Briggs handled most of the editorial correspondence and made most of the editorial decisions, but management lines in the office were often flexible and occasionally slack. While this pattern might have had something to do with Briggs's difficulty in keeping up with the volume of work (nearly one thousand submissions in the first year alone), it also seems likely that the three editors operated on the basis of a loose arrangement by which each one was individually responsible for soliciting his own contributions, as well as evaluating and editing those already submitted. Those tasks were laborious enough to keep them all—if Briggs most especially—busy through the monthly editorial cycle, as well as from month to month.

Putnam also was deeply involved in the management of the magazine. Despite the fact that he was already pressed for time by the responsibilities of running his expanding business, he was not the kind of publisher to keep his hands off the literary affairs of the magazine.[29] One major task that he arrogated to himself was to initiate contact with some of the most desirable writers in the country. It was Putnam, for instance, who solicited Hawthorne in February 1853 as a possible contributor in a letter that showed far more care and effort than he took in his normally breathless correspondence. Part of Putnam's reason for writing was to pay Hawthorne his royalties for the new Putnam edition of *Mosses from an Old Manse,* a measly sum, he was forced to admit, compared to the sums Hawthorne was earning from his Boston publishers for his recent success with *The Scarlet Letter* and *The House of the Seven Gables.* His primary motivation, however, was to make his own sales pitch, encouraging Hawthorne to serialize his next romance in *Putnam's* prior to its book publication. In return for such an arrangement Putnam was prepared to offer "the *highest rate* of payment promptly in cash," as well as the transatlantic copyright "secured beyond contingency" via their arrangements with Sampson Low.[30] It was also Putnam who formally contacted and subsequently conducted most of the correspondence with Longfellow, not only the most popular poet but also one of the most "magazinish" writers in the country. That relationship of suitor and suited was played out by the two men in gentlemanly terms and eventuated in mutually satisfactory results, with Longfellow frequently submitting poems that he implicitly knew would be accepted and Putnam gladly paying him the highest fees given to any poet in the magazine. For Longfellow's "beautiful" "The Two Angels," for instance, Putnam cheerfully paid $50 and added his sentiment: "We feel proud of being the medium of introducing such a gem to the tens of thousands who will admire and appreciate it."[31] Likewise, he handled the correspondence with many other writers with whom he had previously had professional dealings, including Melville, Francis Lieber, Asa Gray, and Maximilian Schele de Vere.

Payment for all accepted pieces was not only the standard operating policy of the magazine but also a matter of principle.[32] Although magazines like *Putnam's* could expect submissions to come from a range of writers running from seasoned professionals to outright novices—indeed, Briggs and his successor followed the pattern of many of their peers in periodically instructing potential contributors in the basics of editorial policy and submission formalities—Putnam insisted on treating all authors as professionals.[33] He had wisely forborne specifying terms of payment in his circular except to say that "we expect to pay as liberally as the nature of the work will allow," an intent that became his standard operating policy. With writers of Longfellow's or Hawthorne's caliber and desirability, there was no standing pay scale; they could have asked for any reasonable sum with the expectation of its being met. After his first poem was printed, Longfellow typically received $50 for each subsequent poem, the same sum generally paid for Lowell's poems before a fiasco erupted over his discontinued "Our Own." The norm of payment, however, was $3 a printed page for prose pieces and $10 to $25 for poems depending upon their length—figures that Putnam sometimes proffered apologetically as being less than he would have paid his authors had the economics of publication permitted. In practice, however, those figures were subject to negotiation by better-known writers. Francis Lieber, for instance, was able to negotiate that standard fee up to $5 a page.[34] So did Melville, who regularly received that sum from *Putnam's* and whose aggregate payment from the magazine for the eighteen months during which his submissions coincided with Putnam's ownership amounted to $674.50 (the equivalent, perhaps, of half of an upper-end, annual editorial salary).[35] In a few amusing instances, authors did not wait to be offered a fee. James Avis Bartley of Virginia, for instance, sent a poem called "The Curse of Washington" for which he expected "the sum of *one thousand dollars*" to be sent to him "without immediate delay."[36] Ellen Ludlow of Otswego, New York, volunteered her services to *Putnam's* as a regular contributor "with all due humility and a high respect for the character of the Magazine" in return for an annual salary of $300. The alternative, she warned, was that she would offer her poems to the Harpers, whom a friend had assured her "will take all my offerings."[37] But Bartley and Ludlow were exceptional not only in their expectations but also in their posture; most writers were content—and some even ecstatic—simply to see their work in print and to receive whatever payment was offered.

The governing opinion at 10 Park Place was that *Putnam's* printed the highest level of periodical literature that the United States had yet seen, an opinion that had wide currency around the country and even overseas. Public testimony to that effect appeared in dozens of newspapers and magazines around the country, and sometimes reappeared in *Putnam's* ads. Undoubtedly, a fair number of those puffs were paid for; the Putnam office frequently received offers from editors around the country offering to trade (favorable) notice of *Putnam's* in their columns in return for subscriptions, books, or professional favors—editorial business conducted as usual in the 1850s. But remarks by respected writers, editors, and publishers and candid comments in correspondence with the editor repeat that verdict so frequently that it is difficult to contest the conclusion that *Putnam's* commanded unparalleled respect among its contemporaries. Even in England, the magazine was widely reputed the finest American publication of its type and was sometimes compared favorably with its British counterparts.

A similar opinion has been common among twentieth-century literary historians, a judgment that seems borne out by a close reading of the magazine: during the twenty-eight months that Putnam published the magazine, *Putnam's* consistently printed the highest quality of articles in the country's periodical history.[38] Some of the imaginative fiction and poetry remains interesting, engaging, even noteworthy today. One of the most frequent and respected contributors was Melville, then in a transitional phase of his career between book and periodical publication, whose "Bartleby, the Scrivener," "The Lightning-Rod Man," *The Encantadas,* and *Israel Potter* first appeared in *Putnam's* (and "Benito Cereno" shortly after Putnam gave it up). James Russell Lowell, one of Briggs's closest friends, was a frequent contributor, his finest pieces published in the magazine being "A Moosehead Journal" and "Fireside Travels." Thoreau published several installments of *An Excursion to Canada* (and then *Cape Cod* in the post-Putnam period). Longfellow contributed frequently and published several of his most popular poems, including "The Jewish Graveyard in Newport" and "My Lost Youth," in the magazine. Three of the wittiest serials of the 1850s all made their appearance in the magazine: Curtis's *The Potiphar Papers* and *Prue and I,* and Frederic Cozzens's *Sparrowgrass Papers.*

So did one of the best novels of the time, *Wensley*, written by Edmund Quincy expressly for the magazine. The magazine also printed a wide variety of shorter tales and sketches by some of the best feuilletonists in the country, including Curtis, Nathaniel Willis, and Fitz-James O'Brien.

The nonfiction, though understandably less well known today, was equally good. Clarence Cook's fine series on Manhattan, "New York Daguerreotyped," was a thoroughly incisive history of the city, and William Swinton's "Rambles over the Realms of Verbs and Substantives," a series that Walt Whitman later helped to turn into a book, was intelligent and provocative. Several pieces on Russia and the "Eastern Question," a subject of considerable interest in the United States during the Crimean War, were extraordinarily insightful, if sometimes sneeringly hostile.[39] No number of the journal appeared without at least one travelogue, some of which were memorable. The editors were especially successful in enlisting the finest group of travel writers in the country, including Bayard Taylor, Richard Kimball, Charles Dudley Warner, Caroline Kirkland, Thoreau, Curtis, and George Calvert; their coverage encompassed Japan (a major new focal point of interest to the country and to G. P. Putnam and Company since Admiral Perry's expedition), Cuba, Hawaii, Haiti, Mexico, the Middle East, India, Russia, the major cities of Europe, and Canada, as well as the United States from coast to coast. At their best, as in Warner's fine "Salt Lake and the New Saratoga," these travel sketches combined sharp reportage on the strange and familiar, wit, and entertainment in a language formulated to speak to the American middle class.[40]

Book, theater, and art reviews were a regular feature and written chiefly by some of the best reviewers of the time, and often with as much sophistication as one encounters in antebellum American criticism. Most of them were combined at the end of each issue as "Editorial Notes," on which Curtis, Briggs, and Godwin all worked regularly, with frequent help from Charles Dana, George Ripley, and Richard Grant White. Their reviews here and sometimes in separate pieces covered such works as *Walden, Uncle Tom's Cabin,* the novels of Dickens, the Brontës, and Thackeray, the histories of Bancroft and Alison, the works of Lowell and Melville, the controversial Collier second folio of Shakespeare, Lermontov's *A Hero of Our Time,* as well as whatever works or issues were then coming up for discussion in literary circles. Naturally, a favorite theme of the reviewers was the state of American letters, a concern to which Briggs in particular paid close attention and on whose behalf he made a number of calls. One interesting instance was an 1854 review, presumably his, of the earnest attempt by Elbert H. Smith to write an original American epic, *Ma-Ka-Tai-Me-She-Kia-Kiak; or, Black Hawk and Scenes in the West*. Squirming to find the proper vocabulary with which to describe the "discursive freedom" that Smith brought to his poem by contrasting it with the situations of Virgil, Milton, and Alexander Smith, the reviewer stated his enthusiasm for the project by calling it "the most remarkable epic poem of the age."[41] In an article characterized more by its casual bigotry than its critical acumen, the contributor J. J. Trux identified a different location for "the advent of the coming poet who is to take away from America the sin and the shame of never having produced an epic, or a lyric, commensurate with Niagara and the Rocky Mountains": black minstrelsy.[42] Later that year, Charles Dana contributed one of the most discerning reviews of the first edition of *Leaves of Grass;* Briggs's response to Whitman's verse is unfortunately unknown.[43] In addition, Briggs kept a watchful eye on other matters relating to the state of mid-century American letters, such as the proliferation of novels by women writers and the prospects for copyright (which seemed bright in the early days of the magazine but dimmed by late spring). Although he liked and admired Stowe for *Uncle Tom's Cabin,* he had reservations about Fanny Fern and sentimental writing generally. About copyright he had no reservations whatsoever; like Putnam, he saw it as directly in the interest of American writers that their works be protected overseas and be circulated on equal terms domestically with the works of foreign authors.

Some favoritism was naturally shown to G. P. Putnam and Company books, which were reviewed far out of proportion to their numbers in general circulation but which did not invariably receive uncritical treatment. In addition, George P. Keese reviewed the New York theater, and Briggs kept a close eye on the institutions of American art—sometimes a jaundiced one, as when he commented on the monotony of shows at the National Academy of Design: "There is still the 'Landscape—Durand.' The same birch tree, the same yellow sky, the same amiable cattle, the same mild trees and quiet water.... It would be a curious study to examine all the catalogues of the Academy, and see how nearly the whole of the twenty-eight pamphlets are alike."[44] His fundamental criticism of the New York art scene was also practical: what New York most needed was a permanent exhibition hall. Putnam must have agreed, although it would be nearly two decades before the efforts of like-minded people would result in the opening of the Metropolitan Museum of Art.

Putnam's authors and editors did not hesitate to address the major social, political, and cultural issues of the day: annexation of new territories into the Union; the future of slavery; the rights of women; the effect of the accelerating pace of technology on patterns of thought, belief, and behavior; the "national character" as expressed in letters, politics, and manners; and international copyright. No one spoke more powerfully and directly on the various issues of the day than did Godwin, whose outspoken *Putnam's* articles on slavery and the territories were influential in the formulation in 1856 of the Republican Party platform. In his slashing attacks on the institution of slavery, misuse of public patronage, and arrant ineptitude in the White House, Godwin injected a venom not common into the normal decorum that governed discourse by editors and writers alike in the magazine. He was not alone, however, in stating strong opinions in the magazine. In fact, strongly expressed views on one side of an issue sometimes occasioned equally strongly expressed counterviews.

One such debate began when Henry James, Sr., published a ferocious attack on "the woman's movement" and its leaders as "furnish[ing] another and a striking commentary upon woman's incapacity as a legislator or leader in human affairs."[45] One writer soon intoned the belief, although probably not in response to James, that "those who are laboring for the rights of Woman would obtain their object by a far shorter road, if they could be persuaded to concentrate the zeal and talent they possess on the great ark of Female Education, the true remedy for the 'wrongs of woman.'"[46] But a plainly offended Caroline Kirkland, responding to James and to other men who drew a restrictive "sphere" around women, took a more aggressive line in satirizing "the American ideal woman" as typically portrayed in magazines: "She was born to be the humble contributor to man, to bear with his tempers, follow his fortunes, humor his whims, cater for his wants, watch over his illnesses, bring up his children, economize his means, promote his very enjoyments,—be wholly lost and swallowed up in him while he lived ..." Her conclusion: "Few of our lady friends, we may venture to say, would be prominent in desiring to become ideals on these terms."[47] The debate was still alive a year later when a presumably female correspondent, reversing the chauvinistic jargon and defending her sex as truly the "strong-minded," made roaring fun of James's hopeless attempts to type women. If James was correct, she said, men might just as well restrict their conversations with women to the weather and child rearing.[48]

By the same token, the editors did not intend to steer clear of topical matters, preferring to operate as much as possible on the premise that quality and popularity were reconcilable. Carrying out that policy sometimes meant publishing poems and stories of a more melodramatic or insipid character than they were comfortable with. Even *Putnam's* had its share of stories and poems whose sole reason for being was to decide the marital state of their heroines. And sometimes it meant publishing articles on subjects that were problematic. In one instance—one of the most revealing moments of the way the editors judged their readers' taste—they swallowed their reservations and accepted for publication "Have We a Bourbon among Us?" an article that they knew from the start was risky, especially for a fledgling magazine in its second month of publication.[49] They were soon glad they did, for the article provoked a sensational interest with the reading public. Recounting a spotting of the Dauphin in New York prior to the one Mark Twain recorded along the banks of the Mississippi River, the article was an early manifestation of American fascination with royalty, and the prompt, vocal response indicated that it had hit home. Marshaled into respectability by an introductory letter from the respected Francis Hawks attesting to the good character of its author (Rev. John Hanson), the good faith of its subject (Eleazar Williams, an Episcopalian minister and longtime Indian missionary), and the authenticity of the documents relating to the presumed Dauphin, the article made a long, suppositious argument on behalf of the proposition that the Rev. Eleazar Williams, recently returned to civilization from the woods, was the long lost Louis XVII.

Early on Putnam must have asked himself whether the undertaking was worth the effort and risk. Just days before publication, Hanson, angry because he considered the article so "materially altered" since passing through proof, wished it returned or, if actually printed, threatened that he would disown it publicly.[50] With the article already stereotyped and printed, Putnam was unprepared to back down, and he quickly sent off to Hanson a response that contained a strange weave of not always interlocking arguments. First, he defended his decision to cut several pages, noting that Hanson had himself thought to omit those pages as irrelevant to the piece, while also pointing out he had been compelled to cut several pages from the preceding article as well in order to keep that entire number of *Putnam's* from overrunning its page limit. He then switched to a financial argument: his investment in the article was considerable—$300 for the stereotyping and printing and $130 for the engraving of Williams that accompanied the text and his expenses in New York. Further on he stood on his authority as publisher: "I can only say that for the contents of the magazine I alone am held responsible: and as in addition to the question of judgement I have to provide for the cost and take all pecuniary risk, I ought not to be expected to act directly contrary to my own judgement." But, most likely, his most genuine motivation was the one that he adduced almost casually near the end of his letter: that the omitted pages were objectionable "as committing the magazine more to an advocacy of the Bourbons than seems to me desirable." After all, it had been only a few years since Putnam had befriended Louis Napoleon and hosted a number of other European revolutionary refugees at his London home, and long after the failure of the revolutions of 1848 he continued to feel an almost instinctive sympathy with the liberal opponents of the ancien régime. But with all these points adduced, he closed in his usual conciliatory fashion, assuring Hanson that his good will was a "far greater consideration with me than any supposed or expected profit in this matter."[51]

Putnam had good reason to be squeamish about the article, which for all its show of facts, documentation, and logical reasoning maintained an improbable thesis that might well expose the good name of his magazine to public ridicule. For every Hawks who accepted the argument, there were friends who advised him to keep his distance from it (as, for instance, did George Sumner, who warned Putnam late that year against publishing a book-length version of Hanson's "cock and bull story").[52] Making calm decisions was not easy when questions swirled about the affair: Was Williams the son of Marie Antoinette or of a Native American woman (whose affidavit attesting to the facts of his birth at Caughnawaga, New York, became a part of the public record)? Was a clergyman capable of fabricating such a story? Did his features look French or Indian? Putnam's measured response was to take the middle ground: to print the story but to dissociate *Putnam's* from partiality to either side. Instead, he positioned the magazine in the role of neutral caretaker, vouching for the good character and faith of the author and subject and stepping aside to allow them to use the medium of *Putnam's* to present their case. But while that was going on, Putnam made private inquiries. He began no doubt with getting to know Williams, whom he offered to host at his house; when Williams declined, the Putnams invited him and Hanson to several of their Tuesday evening parties (at one of which George Haven recalled also meeting Thackeray).[53] After the story was published, Putnam made formal inquiries with Hanson's sources, whose responses did nothing to dissuade him from continuing to promote the story, especially as it was meeting with great interest. He printed a sequel by Hanson in April, and, with controversy still in the air, a partial rejoinder of sorts in July.[54] Finally, Putnam agreed to publish Hanson's full treatment of the affair, which appeared in early 1854.[55] By that time, the Hanson thesis had provoked widespread interest and sometimes even partisan responses from readers, writers, politicians, and diplomats across the United States and even in Europe.

That affair brought a quick surge in circulation to *Putnam's,* but it was only a small incident in the broad editorial policy of keeping *Putnam's* topical and making it a consistently interesting, engaging magazine. Published and private reports and reviews confirm that the editors generally succeeded. Even today, a casual read through *Putnam's* might well persuade the reader of good times, smiling faces, and general unanimity. Congeniality seemed to be the official editorial tone of the magazine. In a pleasant, if not altogether accurate, public remark made in the post–Civil War reincarnation of *Putnam's,* Briggs stated his idea of the implied readership of the magazine: "The model subscriber to a magazine, in fact, has a personal interest in the work; is a species of partner in the enterprise; has a community of interest with others, and enjoys a welcome sense of continuity, of a pleasure which ends not with the hour, but has a promise of renewal from month to month."[56]

On the surface, this statement about editorial-readerly community was unquestionably genuine. There was, no doubt, much talk and probably rough consensus at 10 Park Place about "Maga." and the "Putnam Public," as they conceived them. In addressing their audience, as the editors often did outwardly in the editorial style common in antebellum America, they spoke with an extraordinary degree of presumed camaraderie and self-consciousness, which, in turn, was often matched by an analogous attitude among the magazine's authors. Talk by editors and contributors within the pages of the magazine often pointed self-reflexively backward and inward into the circle of editors and readers. With a regularity that could only have warmed a publisher's heart, both authors and editors repeatedly praised and publicized the magazine. It was one of the editors (probably Briggs) who announced, for instance, that "the demand for *Putnam's Monthly* surpasses the power of machinery to supply it, unless it is begun betimes, so that what comes to you in the autumn, has parted from us in the summer."[57] Frederick Cozzens drew attention to its power of mediacy when he had Mr. Sparrowgrass assure his wife that, although he didn't know the answer to her question about local New York place names, he knew how to find the answer: "I will make it a public matter through the pages of *Putnam.*"[58] Caroline Kirkland also foregrounded the disseminating power of *Putnam's* as a medium in beginning her article on George Washington, "But our Monthly travels as on the wings of the wind; and modest and unassuming as it is, wins easy way into parlors and workshops, ships and factories, wherever our tongue is spoken."[59] And Edmund Quincy, who accepted Briggs's request in writing his fine novel *Wensley* expressly for serial publication in *Putnam's,* had his narrator refer to his audience explicity as the "Putnam public" and implicitly operate on the assumption that author, narrator, and reader would be meeting through the mediacy of that magazine.[60] Such talk and posturing on this self-consciously culturally nationalistic magazine, ranging from pride to bluster, was based on the presumption of an underlying harmony of interests between authors and editors, publisher and readers, and, the most encompassing of categories, Americans and Americans—their common ground being located somewhere within the office at 10 Park Place or inside the covers of *Putnam's.*

This was, of course, a myth—the myth of the "neutral ground," to use the term by which one correspondent irked by a Godwin article protested the magazine's failure to maintain its self-advertised position of editorial independence.[61] Even before the first issue of the magazine went to press, word of its imminent arrival sparked a controversy. Upon receiving an announcement from Putnam about the planned magazine, the Boston literary journal *To-day* responded by wishing him good luck but adding the hope that *Putnam's* surmount all local or regional prejudices: "We hope, that, whoever may be entrusted with the conduct of this new American magazine will have really a whole American heart, and will not allow its pages to be disfigured by any of those local prejudices which have heretofore almost invariably characterized journals of literary pretension emanating from the city of New York." No sooner was that wish printed than the *Southern Literary Messenger* angrily aimed a retort at *To-day* and New Englanders generally that its readers might just as well expect "Mrs. Harriet Beecher Stowe [to lay] down the law of Love to One's Neighbour."[62] That exchange of shots over the head of the as yet unborn *Putnam's* was to prove a portent.

In truth, a magazine like *Putnam's* could not help but occupy a social, political, and cultural setting that was as much an emerging battle zone as was American society in the 1850s. The editors at *Putnam's* tried to avoid this unpleasant truth and developed strategies to overcome it. Just the same, fault lines crisscrossed beneath the grounds on which editorial policy was made. To take several important instances— the editors devoted disproportionate attention to New York City, quietly slighting the other cities of the country, if without the smug provincialism characteristic of the *Knickerbocker.* Perhaps they silently assumed that a consensus about New York as the national center had by then developed and that what was said of New York would therefore have a broad currency commensurate with their stated desire to be a national magazine. Even as they did, their peers around the country complained about the lack of a comparably high-quality magazine in their own cities. In the case of Boston, Frank Underwood, a *Putnam's* contributor, did something about that perceived omission by leading a successful effort that resulted in 1857 in the founding of the *Atlantic Monthly.*[63] To take another instance—although the *Putnam's* editors must have known from personal experience how precarious was the economic life of American authors, they did not seriously entertain doubts publicly about the presumed reciprocity of authorial and publishing interests in the order of cultural production. In one of the most ironic cases of an author drawing attention to the magazine, Fitz-James O'Brien—the same O'Brien who just a few years later staged his own one-man strike against the Harpers by parading outside their office wearing a sandwich board that bore the message: "One of Harper's authors. I am starving"—wrote a story for *Putnam's* about a writer who muses over his multiple possibilities: "I have four servants (in blue liveries) waiting respectfully at the end of the spacious and richly furnished apartment in which I am sitting, in order to carry this article, page by page, to the editors of Putnam's Monthly. If he don't take it, I'll offer it to Harper, for I want the mo—— that is to say, I am anxious that the public should have the benefit of my—acquaintance's experience."[64]

More troubling yet, *Putnam's* editors and authors acted and pos-
tured as though they spoke in the name of the entire nation, but they
did so on the basis of a set of assumptions that in the 1850s was becoming increasingly difficult to maintain unquestioningly: the superiority
of the Anglo-Saxon "race" to all others and of whites to blacks, of the
Christian (and preferably Protestant) religion to the non-Christian, of
the native-born inhabitant to the immigrant, and of the middle class
to all others. In reality, however, even within the pages of the magazine, hot debates sometimes flared up over matters of current national
interest, such as slavery and women's rights, which in turn reflected
the lack of unanimity in the society at large. Godwin's contributions in
particular became a flash point for debate, arousing strong antagonism
among many—and probably most—of the magazine's Southern readers. Strongly worded protests about the views of Godwin and others
reached 10 Park Place in the form of letters to the editor and printed
notices in the press.

Rather than dodge the issue, Briggs chose to face it directly in
1854, devoting "A Special Editorial Note for the People South of Mason
and Dixon's Line" to his counterstatement. Taking the argumentative
high road, he insisted that, even though seven-eights of *Putnam's* readership lived in the North, the magazine's "sole aim is to publish the best
literary productions which the country can afford; and whether they
come from Maine or Missouri, Vermont or Virginia, is a matter of not
the slightest weight in deciding on their availability." In general, however, he took no cognizance of the possibility that neither *Putnam's* nor
any other magazine could then achieve his stated goal of "properly represent[ing] the whole Union."[65] How difficult that task actually was
should have been suggested to him when he agreed to print a formal,
Southern response to Godwin's "Our Parties and Politics" late in 1854,
which beginning with its epigraph ("Audi alterem partem") and continuing through its long argument took systematic issue not only with the
major antislavery claims against the South but also implicitly with the
consensus editorial view of the magazine.[66] This antagonism toward
Putnam's was by then a commonplace in Southern journalism. A writer
in the Richmond *Enquirer,* for example, expressed pleasure in late 1854
at hearing from local booksellers "that Putnam's is rapidly vanishing
from the market."[67] By that time, the damage had been done; the editor
of the *Southern Literary Messenger* was merely stating the obvious
when he asserted in early 1855 that *Putnam's* had "recently outraged

the entire slaveholding portion of the Union by lending itself to the extremist views of the abolitionists," a view repeated in different terms by a contributor to *DeBow's* who identified and dismissed *Putnam's* in 1856 as "the leading Review of the Black Republican party."[68] Little wonder that George Palmer Putnam's cousin S. M. Newton encountered sectional resistance in 1854 when trying to gather subscriptions in Texas; that must have been increasingly the experience of the magazine's southern agents as the editors took a more outspokenly ideological stance.[69]

This failure of editorial vision was as much Putnam's as his editors', whose broad cultural and political myopia he shared. Not surprisingly, he proved himself no more able than Briggs to see that the pleasant prospect of a community of Putnam readers meeting through the agency of a national magazine was a chimera. Much as he desired to publish pieces of a "national character," he failed to discern possible splits in the neatly reciprocal relationship he was envisioning between author, publisher, and audience.[70] This was hardly the first time that Putnam allowed his habitual preference for unanimity to blind him to the widespread presence of division and conflict in his society. That preference had characterized his thinking and behavior ever since he entered the New York professional world in the 1830s, but it became increasingly unrealistic as the divisive pressures within the United States grew during the 1850s.

A related failure proved, if anything, even more problematic in the case of Briggs, a temperamental individual who had little of Putnam's personal serenity and habitual optimism. The incongruity between ideology and reality complicated his role as *Putnam's* editor, where he vacillated between seeing his editorial relations with the Putnam readership as a collaboration and as a confrontation. The lack of a consistent editorial philosophy was apparent numerous times in 1853–54, but for convenience I wish to focus on his dealings with two of the magazine's most important contributors as an abbreviated way of discussing the breakdown encountered by *Putnam's* in seeking consensus.

One was Edmund Quincy, a man whom he knew in January 1853 only by reputation and through common friends, especially James Russell Lowell, but whom he quickly befriended and adopted as a confidant once they began their collaboration on getting *Wensley* into print.[71] Briggs was delighted both with Quincy's sophisticated but accessible regional story and with Quincy, on whom he wished to bestow the magazine's highest honor by offering to include him—voluntarily or not, he joked—in a group daguerreotype of "a party of Putnamites" tentatively scheduled to be printed in the January 1854 issue.[72] Dealing with Quincy turned out to be one thing; dealing with the Putnam reading public, quite another. Although Briggs prided himself on his ability to read public taste and issue a magazine designed to please it, he was hardly at peace with the public he dutifully served, which he sometimes thought of as a "monster" guided by capricious taste. He experienced this lesson during the run of *Wensley* when, he confidentially noted in a letter to Quincy, the "Putnam public" approved enthusiastically of such popularized fare as *Evangeline* and Tupper's *Proverbial Philosophy* but rejected a long poem ("Our Own") written by Lowell for the magazine that he personally thought "superlatively good."[73] At the risk of damaging his relationship with Lowell, he stopped its serial publication in midcourse. Early on in their collaboration, he warned Quincy, himself no novice at contemporary journalism, "It is a capricious public, and manifests, at times, a mortifying lack of taste," a valuation particularly ironic when applied to a novel such as *Wensley* that inscribed friendly author-reader relations into its text.[74] Fortunately for Briggs, the fickle public liked *Wensley,* sparing him the dilemma he experienced with Lowell of facing up to the disjunction between his preferences and those of the reading public and of regarding with a more critical eye the strained connection between *Putnam's,* the reading public, and contemporary American society.

Briggs also found himself caught in an editorial bind in his dealings with Melville, whom he and Putnam both held in high regard. They not only customarily paid him at their highest rate of remuneration but printed his work as frequently as that of any other fiction writer other than Curtis and featured him in February 1853 as the second subject in the series "Our Young Authors." Nevertheless, in May 1854 Briggs found it necessary to reject Melville's latest contribution, "The Two Temples." The reason, he apologized to Melville, was popular morality: "My editorial experience compels me to be very cautious in offending the religious sensibilities of the public, and the moral of the Two Temples would array against us the whole power of the pulpit, to say nothing of Brown, and the congregation of Grace Church."[75] A sign that the two men had discussed the matter, Putnam followed up Briggs's letter a day later with one of his own, expressing his fear of offending "our Church readers" but also offering the consolation of requesting permission to include "your head as one of our series of portraits" in the magazine.[76]

Although Briggs and Putnam could not accept that story, they gladly published all the other numerous stories and serials that Melville offered. The first one was "Bartleby, the Scrivener. A Story of Wall-Street" (to call it by its full magazine name), which appeared as a two-part serial in November and December 1853 and concluded directly after the final installment of *Wensley*. Its appearance in *Putnam's* was not without ironies that would surely have been more apparent to Melville than to Briggs or Putnam. Just the year before, he had published his scathing novel *Pierre,* which contained some of the most bitter complaints and denunciations in its time about the forms and institutions of antebellum literary culture—even as it necessarily issued through them. In composing it Melville had drawn deeply on his own disillusioning experiences in the American literary marketplace, putting his title character, an aspirant author, through a series of bruising dealings with a variety of those institutions, including the "Gazelle Magazine," "Captain Kidd Monthly," Zadockprattsville lyceum, and "Wonder and Wen," publishers. Not surprisingly, *Pierre* was received with a corresponding contempt in the American press in summer and autumn 1852 that amounted to the most wholly hostile treatment any of his novels had yet received. Well aware of its downward course in writing his overview of Melville's career for the February 1853 issue of *Putnam's,* Fitz-James O'Brien had explicitly warned that Melville "totters on the edge of a precipice, over which all his hard-earned fame may tumble with such another weight as *Pierre* attached to it."[77] It was at this downward trajectory in his career that *Putnam's* management came into formal contact with Melville, who had meanwhile begun the process of remaking himself into a writer of shorter works for the magazine public.

If in the twentieth century "Bartleby" has been generally seen as another Melvillian boulder rolled down onto the reading public, it is clear that Briggs and Putnam did not see it that way. Nor in all likelihood did the Putnam public. Given the context of its periodical publication and its employment of literary sentimental conventions, it is more likely that the readers of *Putnam's* interpreted "Bartleby" in terms accepting of the literary and social status quo rather than subscribed to twentieth-century views of the story as Melville's embittered, subversive meditation on authorship and property rights in America. Far from reading rich symbolic meaning into its dead letters, walls, and partitions, the Putnam public presumably found in it the same magazinish qualities of geniality, mirth, and pathos that recommended *Wensley* and dozens of other stories to them. Briggs himself clearly took pride in offering it to the public, even alerting Quincy to be on the watch for its imminent publication, and it is hard to imagine that Putnam did not share his enthusiasm.[78]

It quickly attracted wide notice; the Duyckincks made public what was already an open secret by revealing Melville's authorship days after the concluding segment had been published.[79] But the most fitting evidence of its magazine popularity and sentimentalized interpretation was its recycling a half-year later in Curtis's *Prue and I,* serialized in *Putnam's,* in which the narrator meditates about a retiring office clerk named Titbottom: "Before I knew him, I used sometimes to meet him with a man whom I was afterwards told was Bartleby, the scrivener. Even then it seemed to me that they rather clubbed their loneliness than made society for each other. Recently I have not seen Bartleby; but Titbottom seems no more solitary because he is alone."[80] If Curtis was ascribing to Bartleby a popular, sentimental interpretation that he could freely assume a commonplace, his contemporaries turned that reading back upon him during the 1850s by frequently pairing him with Melville.[81] So, for that matter, did Curtis's colleagues at *Putnam's,* who saw the two of them, and Quincy as well, as their kind of writer and wished to enshrine all three in the magazine's illustrated "Valhalla." Melville, whose distancing from norms and rules of literary deportment was already well underway, was not willing to join such a literary club. But even though he might have identified Briggs as being on the other side of the antebellum cultural divide separating "truth" from "popularity," in reality Briggs encountered many of the same problems as editor of *Putnam's* in trying to span the gap he too perceived between popularity and truth.

Running the magazine undoubtedly brought Putnam both pleasure and profit, but it also brought him his share of aggravation and strain. Authors, engravers, and printers had to be engaged, supervised, and paid for their services. Deadlines had to be met, letters answered, rejections (dozens each month) sent out. In addition, he also had to maintain harmony in the editorial sanctum. Fortunately, the three editors got along reasonably well and divided their chores to everyone's satisfaction. One reason they did was that they did not try to crowd their persons or egos into the editor's space all at once. Briggs alone worked regularly in the office, with Curtis generally on the road making visits, traveling, lecturing, or vacationing, and Godwin typically spending his time at home in Roslyn or at the downtown office of the *Evening Post*. Curtis and Godwin did much of their work as contributors, editors, and proofreaders from places outside the office. Another factor that helped to keep the peace was the largely unquestioned status as leader that Briggs enjoyed as chief editor. Curtis, who had the ability but lacked the tenacity to play that role, sometimes disagreed with Briggs's taste or judgment on specific matters, but he generally trusted his expertise and never challenged his authority.

This does not mean, however, that everything proceeded smoothly in the office. Briggs was not an easy man to get along with; his good friend Lowell once referred to him as "you mock-crustaceous Briggs," but not everyone could see the "sweet sensitive soul" beneath the tough shell.[82] Fortunately for all involved with the magazine, Briggs did not often upset his colleagues, who learned to live with what Curtis called his "crotchets."[83] When an occasional disagreement did arise, as when Curtis disparaged the innovation Briggs made to the editorial columns in summer 1854 ("the 'Editor at Large' I dislike as much as any article I have ever seen in the Mag.—and you can bite my head off for saying so, if you choose)," there was sufficient mutual respect and broad agreement among the men to preempt the possibility that any of them would lose his head over such incidents.[84] Moreover, Putnam was an expert at keeping his editors in line and his magazine on course.

Putnam's relations with all three men were good during their period of collaboration and remained cordial for many years thereafter.[85] Just the same, crises arose with each of the men that demanded his personal attention and soothing touch. How often he needed to intervene one can only guess on the basis of the surviving correspondence. Midway through the first year, for instance, he reassured Curtis that his services were not only a desired but a necessary part of the magazine's existence. Far from agreeing to accept Curtis's "resignation," Putnam wished him to know how high an esteem he had for him and his pen and how willing he would be to accommodate Curtis's health and schedule in any practical way he could.[86] No doubt he did just that, as he probably had no choice with an author so widely admired by the public and so keenly desirable to literary publishers in New York and New England. By 1854 Putnam was increasingly forced to share Curtis with the Harpers, who had published his first book and who persuaded him to share the "Editor's Easy Chair" at *Harper's Monthly* with "Ik Marvel."

With Godwin, Putnam faced a somewhat different set of problems, if one no less urgently in need of a soothing presence. Less sure of his talents and less consistent in his behavior, Godwin needed to be coaxed and coddled by Putnam, who accommodated him to whatever extent possible. In summer 1854, for example, as Godwin was working his way through an important and timely essay, "Our Parties and Politics," he wrote Putnam to explain that the article, though drafted, did not yet meet his "satisfaction" and that he therefore preferred not to rush it into print. Because the August number was already filled, he suggested delaying publication until the September issue.[87] When he sent his article in shortly afterward, he requested that it be placed at the "Head" of the number, a place not simply of honor but, more important for him, of visibility of a sort likely to attract the attention of lyceum directors filling their speakers' rosters for that winter's lecture circuit.[88] Putnam, who was himself intermittently involved in arranging lecture schedules on behalf of individuals and organizations, knew that logic well and acceded to the request, although he was predisposed in any case to open each issue with his strongest article. More important, Putnam stood behind Godwin whenever his articles generated controversy, as strongly worded essays on current politics inevitably did in the factionalized atmosphere of the 1850s. Beginning with his attack on Franklin Pierce in the September 1853 *Putnam's,* Godwin did not hesitate to hurl invectives across the usually polite columns of the magazine.[89] He was hardly unaware of this fact, confessing to Putnam at one point, "My convictions are so decided that I find it impossible to express my self in a way, which will not give offense."[90] By the time he directed his attention to sectional issues, he touched raw nerves in the South that immediately generated powerful reactions against him and the magazine; Putnam, however, made no effort to restrain him.

Curiously, of his dealings with the three editors, it is most difficult to discern Putnam's relations with Briggs. Working together on a daily basis presumably eliminated the need for communication in writing, leaving little record of the terms or character of their collaboration. To all appearances, it was a friendly one, with no report of personal conflicts or clash of views having survived. But sometime in spring or early summer 1854, their professional relations seem to have quickly unraveled. The primary cause was reports that reached Putnam about Briggs's editorial irresponsibility. Overworked in editing not only *Putnam's* but also a weekly newspaper, Briggs was apparently falling further and further behind a responsible timetable. To take an extreme case—the Boston writer Frank Underwood complained in early 1855 that receipt of his article was formally acknowledged fifteen months after he sent it; he feared that his grandchildren would see it in print before he did.[91]

Underwood could not have known that by the time of his complaint Putnam, who had heard similar complaints from others, had already dismissed Briggs. Putnam was presumably ready to make a change as early as May, when he offered the editorship to Curtis, who refused it, and then possibly even considered assuming much of the editorial burden himself.[92] By October he had heard enough. He confidentially mentioned the matter to Frederic Beecher Perkins, a respected *Putnam's* contributor and formerly general adviser to the parent company then living in Hartford, and offered him employment at the magazine. Whether he meant Perkins to replace Briggs as editor or simply to serve as an all-around amanuensis was unclear to Perkins at the time and is still not easily answered.[93] In all likelihood, Putnam assumed much of the decision-making function himself and left the secretarial work and some of the screening of manuscripts to Perkins and to Curtis and Godwin, whose responsibilities and status were at least formally unaffected by the departure of Briggs. In most regards, the magazine appeared outwardly unchanged, and *Putnam's* readers, who in any case had never been informed of the chief editor's identity, would have discerned no major editorial changes in reading the magazine. James Fields, who was apprised by Putnam of the change in October, thought it might actually work for the better that Putnam had taken "exclusive and conclusive" charge: "Go ahead and prosper! There is no reason why you should not conduct matters with the assistance of the two noble youths, Curtis and Godwin, good fellows both and men of genius."[94]

In truth, however, the situation at *Putnam's* was altered in autumn 1854 not only by the departure of Briggs but even more seriously by the first major financial crisis (about which more in chapter 10) faced by G. P. Putnam and Company, a crisis so critical that Putnam was forced by the severely diminished state of his firm's capital to make choices between various projects and to reduce payments to authors. Even Longfellow, from whom he continued to request contributions, was advised that during these "hard times" his previous fee might temporarily be too high for Putnam to meet.[95] Although reluctant to lose a magazine on which he had invested so much time and energy and in which he took such pride, Putnam elected in early 1855 to sell it and began looking for prospective buyers. In late January, he offered it to Bayard Taylor, who was growing affluent from the combination of royalties paid him by Putnam and large fees earned on the lecture circuit. Putnam described *Putnam's* to him as "capable of yielding a handsome income" and as likely to do so under a new organization more capable than he then was of giving it ample time and attention, but Taylor rejected his proposal.[96] Putnam then offered the magazine to his former employee Joshua Dix, who had recently gone out on his own and was publishing an American edition of *Household Words* before entering into partnership on 1 March with Arthur Edwards as Dix and Edwards, book and magazine publishers.[97] The sale of the magazine by Putnam to the new firm took place formally in March; the price asked and the price received, according to Putnam, was $11,000, a nice final profit to go with the profits he had been making from individual issues.[98]

The transfer of *Putnam's* to Dix and Edwards transpired with so little attendant publicity that many literary professionals in New York, no less in the rest of the country, were at first unaware of the transaction. Emerson had obviously not heard even half a year later, when he sent Putnam the controversial article by Delia Bacon concerning the authorship of Shakespeare's plays that appeared in *Putnam's* the following year.[99] But the fact of the transfer was not a secret; a notice stating the basic details appeared in the pages of the New York *Tribune* in late March and another in late April, the latter presumably to coincide with the publication of the first issue of the magazine under Dix and Edwards's control.[100] That issue (and those that followed) emerged little changed outwardly or inwardly, with Curtis and Godwin retained as editors and joined by Frederick Law Olmsted and the basic format left intact. Nor was there significant alteration in its title, tone, content, price, or quality. Not even the address of the magazine had changed, Dix and Edwards operating out of rooms in the same Park Place building as G. P. Putnam and Company. All in all, the intent of the new editorial and publishing team was clearly to continue the successful formula of their predecessors. They had good reason to do so; the magazine had been quite profitable for Putnam, as it would be for them during most of the two years that they controlled it.[101] But their serious mismanagement of their business, which left the active partners scheming against each other and the silent partner Olmsted representing their interests in England with vague instructions and little idea about how to proceed, eventually drove the magazine into a decline in both its contents and its profitability.[102]

For Putnam, the sale of the magazine represented the loss of one of the most attractive parts of his overall operations. Its loss must have hurt; once his publishing house was restored to a modicum of profitability and scale after the Civil War, he did not hesitate to resuscitate the magazine. At the time of his divestiture, however, he had little time to mourn its loss. He still had a sizable publishing house to run and projects to carry out, not only for his own firm but for the entire industry, which he went about accomplishing with his usual energy and optimism right up until the more serious financial crisis of 1857 threatened him with the loss of more than just his magazine.

Notes

1. GPP to Taylor, 9 December 1852; BT-C.

2. GHP mentions some of the visitors in *George Palmer Putnam,* 1:360–64; the remainder I have culled from various sources. On Mary's sign, see Anna B. Warner, *Susan Warner* (New York: G. P. Putnam's Sons, 1909), 373.

3. GPP had rushed to present him shortly after his arrival in New York with an offer to publish a volume of his lectures, but Thackeray politely declined his "generous offer" in favor of the Harpers', whose $1,000 honorarium must have been more generous than GPP could afford to offer; Gordon N. Ray, ed., *The Letters and Private Papers of William Makepeace Thackeray,* 4 vols. (Cambridge: Harvard University Press, 1945–46), 3:130–31.

4. Anna B. Warner, *Susan Warner,* 373.

5. "A Meditation by Paul Potiphar, Esq.," *Putnam's Monthly* 1 (June 1853): 655.

6. GPP also announced plans to publish "New York Daguerreotyped" as a book but it was never finished; his advertisement for it ran in the *Literary World* 12 (12 February 1853): 134. The complicated relations between GPP and Cook over the planned work can be seen in their correspondence in GPP-P.

7. The basis for the claim that the idea for *Putnam's Monthly* originated with Briggs comes from the open letter that Curtis sent to Briggs and that Briggs incorporated in his introduction to the second series of the renamed magazine; *Putnam's Magazine* 1 (January 1868): 5. There is no evidence confirming or refuting that assertion, but the

claim probably is factually correct, if of limited significance. On GPP's earlier thoughts about starting a magazine, see GHP, *George Palmer Putnam,* 1:354.

8. The articles began on 11 October 1852 and continued intermittently into November. Although signed "CLB," they were undoubtedly Briggs's.

9. GPP must have known Briggs at least as early as 1847–48, when Briggs oversaw the publication of *A Fable for Critics* for his good friend Lowell. In a fine token of his affection and appreciation for Briggs, Lowell dedicated the second edition of the poem to Briggs and assigned him the copyright. Briggs also helped GPP during summer 1852 with the production of *Homes of American Authors,* a book that had an obvious connection, whether directly or indirectly, with the founding of *Putnam's Monthly.* The best source of information on Briggs, although somewhat unreliable about his management of *Putnam's,* is Bette Statsky Weidman, "Charles Frederick Briggs: A Biography" (Ph.D. diss., Columbia University, 1968).

10. Curtis to Charles Eliot Norton, 10 June 1852; Houghton Library, Harvard University.

11. I have seen copies of this circular at D-NYPL, GPP-P, and the James Russell Lowell Collection in Houghton Library, Harvard University.

12. *Literary World* 11 (27 November 1852): 338.

13. The letter is unpublished; the original is pasted into the scrapbook in GPP-P (box 11).

14. Ads for the English edition of *Putnam's Monthly* appeared in Sampson Low's *Publishers' Circular* 16 (1 January 1853): 8, and (17 January 1853): 31.

15. Frank Luther Mott, *A History of American Magazines,* 5 vols. (Cambridge: Harvard University Press, 1930–68), 2:420.

One Western contributor and subscriber to the *Whig Review* wrote GPP about the time of the merger to offer "to add a western feature to your truly American work" and to inquire whether his subscription would automatically carry over or whether he would need to send payment for a new subscription; Robert W. McKenney to G. P. Putnam and Company, 20 January 1853; GPP-P.

16. That figure was mentioned both by the editor of the *Literary World* 12 (15 January 1853): 52; and by Briggs in a letter to Lowell; quoted in Mott, *American Magazines,* 2:426.

17. GPP to Taylor, 9 December 1852; BT-C.

18. This pattern of national authorship and readership, but with a concentration in the Northeast, is also reflected in the correspondence file for the magazine (or, at least, that portion of it preserved in GPP-P).

19. "Introductory," *Putnam's Monthly* 1 (January 1853): 1.

20. GPP to Birney, 30 November 1854; James Gillespie Birney Papers, Clements Library, University of Michigan.

21. "Uncle Tomitudes," *Putnam's Monthly* 1 (January 1853): 98.

22. "American Despotisms," *Putnam's Monthly* 4 (November 1854): 531.

23. "*Harper's Monthly* and *Weekly,*" *Putnam's Monthly* 9 (March 1857): 296.

24. Isaac Watters to GPP, 2 February 1853; GPP-P. A clipping containing his notice accompanies his letter.

25. Quoted by GHP, *George Palmer Putnam,* 1:294.

26. Graham to GPP, 25 October 1853; GPP-P.

27. These circulation figures are based on various sources, including the confidential statements made by Briggs to Lowell for the January issue, by GPP to Hawthorne (22,250) and by Briggs to Edmund Quincy for the February issue, and by Briggs to Quincy for the June issue (35,000). See, respectively, Briggs to Lowell, 23 January 1853, Houghton

Library, Harvard University; GPP to Hawthorne, 10 February 1853; GPP-P (printed in GHP, *George Palmer Putnam,* 1:374); Briggs to Quincy, 1 June 1853, Quincy Collection, Massachusetts Historical Society. GPP advertised a printing of 35,000 copies of the June 1853 number in the *Albion* 12 (4 June 1853): 275, and retrospectively claimed that the standard printing of the magazine ran between 30,000 and 35,000 copies; "Rough Notes of Thirty Years in the Trade," *American Publishers' Circular and Literary Gazette* 1, octavo series (15 August 1863): 291.

28. *Albion* 13 (10 June 1854): 276.

29. GPP announced in his "Publishers' Notice" at the end of the second volume that *Putnam's* had received 980 submissions its first year, of which it had been able to publish only 10 percent.

30. The original letter is in GPP-P; GHP published it, with slight errors of transcription, in *George Palmer Putnam,* 1:371–72.

31. GPP to Longfellow, 6 April 1854; Houghton Library, Harvard University.

32. The New England journalist Frank Underwood was one writer who explicitly reciprocated this philosophy: "I suppose that if an article is worth publishing at all, it is worth paying for; and I trust that you will not consider me mercenary in putting the 'price' foremost"; Underwood to G. P. Putnam and Company, 7 March 1853; GPP-P.

33. The policy of encouraging authorship unquestionably bore results. One novice, for example, clipped off the instructions to authors that appeared on the cover of *Putnam's* and attached it to the top of his letter to the editor in recognition of his/her appreciation of the editor as "the best promoter and encourager of American magazine writers"; F. B. to Editor, 17 February 1854; GPP-P.

34. Lieber to Putnam, 25 March 1853; GPP-P.

35. Merton M. Sealts, Historical Note, *The Piazza Tales and Other Prose Pieces, 1839–1860,* vol. 9 of *The Writings of Herman Melville,* ed. Harrison Hayford, Alma A. MacDougall, G. Thomas Tanselle, et al. (Evanston: Northwestern University Press, 1987), 484, 493.

36. James Avis Bartley to Editor of *Putnam's Monthly,* 14 September 1854; GPP-P. A month later, he was willing to let the management "say what you can afford to pay for the poem"; Bartley to Editor of *Putnam's Monthly,* 14 October 1854; GPP-P.

37. Ellen Ludlow to "Messrs. Putnam," October 1853; GPP-P.

38. The most authoritative opinion in this regard has been that of Mott, *American Magazines,* 2:426.

39. See, e.g., Parke Godwin's "What We Have to Do with the Eastern Question," *Putnam's Monthly* 3 (May 1854): 514–22.

40. "Salt Lake and the New Saratoga," *Putnam's Monthly* 2 (September 1853): 260–64.

41. "American Epics," *Putnam's Monthly* 3 (June 1854): 639–48.

42. "Negro Minstrelsy—Ancient and Modern," *Putnam's Monthly* 5 (January 1855): 74.

43. "Editorial Notes," *Putnam's Monthly* 6 (September 1855): 321–23.

44. "Editorial Notes," *Putnam's Monthly* 1 (June 1853): 701. Briggs's sarcasm upset the Duyckincks, who considered it "an extreme one-sided view and that not always the best side"; *Literary World* 12 (4 June 1853): 461.

45. "The Woman's Movement," *Putnam's Monthly* 1 (March 1853): 279. Although it is impossible to infer the editor's opinion of James's view, there can be no doubt that James was held in high esteem in the *Putnam's* office; the editor asserted that there were "few better writers as to style than Henry James" and referred to him as "the ablest rhetorician in this country[,] one whose rhetoric is not a mere vehicle of display, but the

graceful and proper expression of his profound thought and his deeply poetical and religious nature." "Editorial Notes," *Putnam's Monthly* 3 (March 1854): 334, 336.

46. "Educational Institutions of New-York," *Putnam's Monthly* 2 (July 1853): 4.

47. "The American Ideal Woman," *Putnam's Monthly* 2 (November 1853): 527–28.

48. "The Proper Sphere of Men," *Putnam's Monthly* 4 (September 1854): 305–6. The possibility exists that the letter was a joke played by the editor or in collaboration with him, since it was signed "Oomansfere, Centre Village" and mistakenly dated June 1852.

49. "Have We a Bourbon among Us?" *Putnam's Monthly* 1 (February 1853): 194–217.

50. Hanson to GPP, 14 January 1853; GPP-P.

51. GPP to John Hanson, n.d.; GPP-P.

52. Sumner to GPP, Christmas 1853; GPP-P.

53. GHP, *George Palmer Putnam,* 1:302–5.

54. "The Bourbon Question," *Putnam's Monthly* 1 (April 1853): 442–62; "Letter from V. Le Ray de Chaumont," *Putnam's Monthly* 2 (July 1853): 117–20.

55. *The Lost Prince* (New York: G. P. Putnam and Company, 1854). The copy of this book in the collections of Thomas Cooper Library at the University of South Carolina is that of Hamilton Fish, then junior senator from New York and one of Hanson's public supporters.

56. *Putnam's Magazine* 1 (January 1868): 122.

57. "Editorial Notes," *Putnam's Monthly* 4 (September 1854): 338.

58. "Living in the Country," *Putnam's Monthly* 4 (December 1854): 622.

59. Kirkland, "Washington's Early Days," *Putnam's Monthly* 3 (January 1854): 1.

60. *Putnam's Monthly* 2 (December 1853): 608.

61. "Editorial Notes," *Putnam's Monthly* 5 (January 1855): 102.

62. An excerpt from the notice in *To-day* was printed together with a response in the "Editor's Table," *Southern Literary Messenger* 18 (December 1852): 756.

63. *The Atlantic Monthly* not only replaced *Putnam's Monthly* as the leading literary magazine in the country but took an initial step in that direction by purchasing the subscription list of the by then defunct *Putnam's Monthly.*

64. "Hard-Up," *Putnam's Monthly* 4 (July 1854): 50. On O'Brien's one-man strike, see Eugene Exman, *The House of Harper: One Hundred and Fifty Years of Publishing* (New York: Harper and Row, 1967), 72.

65. *Putnam's Monthly* 3 (March 1854): 344.

66. "Our Parties and Politics: A Southerner's View of the Subject," *Putnam's Monthly* 4 (December 1854): 633–49.

67. Quoted in "Putnam's Monthly," *Liberator* 24 (8 December 1854): 193.

68. "Editor's Table," *Southern Literary Messenger* 21 (January 1855): 59; "The Relative Political Status of the North and the South," *De Bow's* 22 (February 1857): 129. (The author signed himself "Python" and dated the postscript containing the cited words 29 December 1856.)

69. Newton to GPP, 3 December 1854; GPP-P.

70. This was the term he used, for example, in requesting a submission from Longfellow; GPP to Longfellow, 9 November 1854; Houghton Library, Harvard University.

71. For a more comprehensive discussion of their collaboration, see Ezra Greenspan, "Addressing or Redressing the Magazine Audience: Edmund Quincy's *Wensley,*" in *Periodical Literature in Nineteenth-Century America,* ed. Kenneth M. Price and Susan Belasco Smith (Charlottesville: University Press of Virginia, 1995), 133–49.

72. Briggs to Quincy, 2 October 1853; Quincy Family Collection, Massachusetts Historical Society. No such daguerreotype was ever printed.

73. Briggs to Quincy, undated (but presumably September 1853); Quincy Family Collection, Massachusetts Historical Society.

74. Briggs to Quincy, 13 June 1853; Quincy Family Collection, Massachusetts Historical Society.

75. Lynn Horth, ed., *Correspondence,* vol. 14 of *The Writings of Herman Melville* (Evanston: Northwestern University Press, 1993), 636.

76. Ibid., 637.

77. "Our Young Authors—Melville," *Putnam's Monthly* 1 (February 1853): 164.

78. Briggs to Quincy, 2 October 1853; Quincy Family Collection, Massachusetts Historical Society.

79. "Literature, Books of the Week, Etc.," *Literary World* 13 (3 December 1853): 295.

80. "Sea from Shore," *Putnam's Monthly* 4 (July 1854): 47. Barton Levi St. Armand was the first person to note this point of conjunction between Melville and Curtis; "Curtis's 'Bartleby': An Unrecorded Melville Reference," *Papers of the Bibliographical Society of America* 71 (April-June 1977): 219–20.

81. One person who did was Fitz-James O'Brien, himself one of the leading feuilletonists of the decade, who analyzed their respective statures as American writers; "Our Authors and Authorship. Melville and Curtis," *Putnam's Monthly* 9 (April 1857): 384–93.

82. Lowell to Briggs, 8 February 1854; Houghton Library, Harvard University.

83. Curtis to Charles Eliot Norton, 28 May 1853; Houghton Library, Harvard University.

84. Curtis to Briggs, 26 August 1854; Berg Collection, New York Public Library.

85. GPP, "Rough Notes," 291.

86. For GPP's letter to Curtis and the latter's response, see GHP, *George Palmer Putnam,* 1:314–16.

87. Godwin to GPP, n.d. (but, given its inquiry about whether the July *Putnam's Monthly* was out yet, probably a few days or a week before 1 July 1854); GPP-P.

88. "Considering the *amount* that I have written for Maga, (if not the quality) I ought to come away the earliest contributor." Godwin to GPP, n.d.; GPP-P.

89. "Our New President," *Putnam's Monthly* 2 (September 1853): 301–10.

90. Godwin to GPP, n.d.; GPP-P.

91. Underwood to "Sir," 6 January 1855; GPP-P.

92. Curtis to Charles Eliot Norton, 24 May 1854; Houghton Library, Harvard University; Curtis to Parke Godwin, 6 July 1854; Bryant Collection, New York Public Library.

93. GPP's letters to Perkins have not survived, but the situation at *Putnam's* can be roughly inferred from Perkins's response; Perkins to GPP, 14 October and 6 November 1854; GPP-P.

94. Fields to GPP, 7 November 1854; GPP-P.

95. GPP to Longfellow, 28 November 1854; Houghton Library, Harvard University.

96. GPP to Taylor, 26 January 1855; BT-C; Taylor to GPP, 24 February 1855; GPP-P.

97. Dix had run the retail and importing operations of G. P. Putnam for a few years. At the time of his decision to go into partnership with Edwards, GPP wrote him a strong letter of recommendation assuring Edwards of Dix's competence and character; GPP to Edwards, 1 February 1855; Houghton Library, Harvard University.

98. GPP, "Rough Notes," 291.

99. Emerson to GPP, 19 October 1855; Houghton Library, Harvard University.

100. New York *Tribune,* 29 March 1855, 1, and 26 April 1855, 1.

101. On the date of their first issue, see Arthur Edwards to Joshua Dix, 25 March 1857; Houghton Library, Harvard University. Edwards, who handled the financial side of the business, reported that *Putnam's* had earned the company net profits of $4,486

during May–December 1855, $5,908 during January–May of 1856, and $3,600 during June 1856–February 1857. They were printing 21,000 copies and selling about 19,000 during their first year of operation, but sales were down to approximately 14,000 copies during December 1856–February 1857. Corresponding figures for profits under GPP's management have not survived, but it seems likely that the magazine's greater circulation yielded larger profits.

102. The best sources of information about Dix and Edwards, as well as about the history of *Putnam's Monthly* during the period it was under their control, are the George William Curtis and Frederick Law Olmsted files at Houghton Library, Harvard University.

Years of Boom and Bust, 1853–1857

Twin towers dominated Putnam's professional thinking and planning from late 1852 to early 1855. While working to bring *Putnam's Monthly* into existence and to assure its success, he was also preparing to maneuver his firm into position to become the official publisher of the New York World's Fair (the Exhibition of the Industry of All Nations, as it was formally called). The Exhibition was to be held in mid-1853 at the newly constructed Crystal Palace, one of the great architectural enterprises of mid-century New York. The model for the ambitious publishing venture Putnam envisioned, as was often the case, came from England, where the opening of the original Crystal Palace at Hyde Park had generated unprecedented national and international interest. While the daily and weekly newspapers in London were filled for months with news about the Crystal Palace and its Exhibition, enterprising book and periodical publishers, many of them well known to Putnam, rushed to produce books and magazines featuring various aspects of the event. That process had begun by the time of his brief visit in 1851 and accelerated in the months that followed, with many of the publications reaching the United States. At least two of them influenced Putnam's plans directly: the lavishly illustrated folio serial brought out by John

Tallis, *Tallis's History and Description of the Crystal Palace and the Exhibition of the World's Industry in 1851,* and the *Illustrated Catalogue of the Great Exhibition of 1851* issued by the *London Art Journal* (whose editor Samuel Carter Hall was an old friend).[1]

If on one level Putnam saw a promising business opportunity in undertaking his own Exhibition-related publishing ventures, on another level he was responding to his deep-seated faith in the combined forces of technology, capitalism, and progress—all united under the aegis of American nationhood. A close approximation of this ideological blend was the iconographic engraving that his firm had manufactured and presumably intended to print as the frontispiece of one of its Crystal Palace publications.[2] That engraving connected the contemporary Crystal Palace to an overarching historical narrative of American "progress" (to use one of the terms most frequently associated with the building and its exhibits). Its two horizontal lintels formed a frame for a central portrait; the upper one depicted the setting of the New York Crystal Palace as seen from the outside, with a crowd gathered on the surrounding grounds, while the bottom one portrayed the arrival of the first Anglo-European settlers on North American shores and their greeting by the native inhabitants. Filling the central frame was the figure of Columbia, crowned "America" and seated next to an American eagle holding in its beak a banner inscribed with the lettering of the New York Crystal Palace. Both figures presided over and above symbols of contemporary art and labor.

For Putnam the citizen (and for hundreds of thousands of his fellow citizens), the Exhibition of Industry promised to display modernity on a scale never before seen in the Americas. For Putnam the publisher, it offered a chance to combine a unique cultural and historical event with a rare economic opportunity and to present it to his fellow citizens/consumers in an act of disinterested patriotism. As early as November 1852, even as he was putting together the apparatus of *Putnam's Monthly,* he submitted his initial proposal to the committee responsible for overseeing the erection and management of the Crystal Palace that he be appointed its official publisher. His terms were these: first, that his firm be granted the "exclusive" right to print two different kinds of publications, the Exhibition catalogue in plain and illustrated editions and an illustrated serial devoted to the various subjects of the Exhibition; and, second, that it be granted the right to sell these publications within the building as well as through the normal agencies of

9.　Engraving designed for G. P. Putnam and Company's Crystal Palace publication depicting Columbia presiding over symbols of contemporary American art and labor. (Courtesy Princeton University Library)

the trade. In a real stroke of publishing acumen, he also requested that the illustrated serial be produced by a "steamprinting press of great power" set up and operated on the Exhibition floor. In return for these privileges, he pledged to pay the Exhibition 10 percent of gross sales on the catalogues and half profits after expenses on the serial.[3] Several weeks later, he offered a modified plan of remuneration for the proposed publications, offering to pay either 12 ½-percent royalties on all copies sold (the sum, he pointed out, that he paid on "the works of Irving, Cooper and our best writers") or a straight half-profits arrangement payable after the return of production expenses.[4]

Once he reached terms with the Exhibition organizers, Putnam lost no time in protecting his investment by announcing his plans and even printing the committee's letter of authorization in the local papers.[5] He then contacted Benjamin Silliman, Jr., an eminent scientist and the head of the mineralogy, mining, and chemistry departments of the Exhibition, and offered him the general editorship of the planned illustrated journal at a salary of $1,300, out of which Silliman was to pay his contributors.[6] Silliman eventually accepted the assignment but only after renegotiating terms: permission to hire Charles Goodrich as his associate editor, a salary for himself of $1,000, and presumably funds with which to pay Goodrich and contributors.[7] The two men soon reached terms not only on these matters but on the kind of serial they wished to produce, one that presented a "permanent record"—as well as constituting an exemplary specimen—of the artistic and technological forces bringing social, economic, and cultural advancement to the United States.[8] The text was to present assessments, as nearly authoritative as possible, of the "progress" of art, science, and industry in modern America and Europe as represented at the Exhibition and would be accompanied by more than five hundred wood engravings executed at the highest level of expertise then available in the United States.

If publicity alone were sufficient to guarantee the success of a publishing venture, Putnam had good reason to believe that he was embarking on one of the most promising enterprises of his career. While he was making his arrangements in winter and spring 1853 for his various Exhibition-related publications, the Crystal Palace and the Exhibition were the subject of widespread publicity and discussion, and their formal opening was anticipated as likely to be one of the great spectacles of the year. But the opening ceremony was delayed by the extraordinarily complicated logistics involved in coordinating the construction of the building and arranging for the collection and display of goods, machines, and artwork from various parts of the world. When the ceremony was finally held on 14 July, the building was still incomplete, many exhibits not yet installed, and unopened crates and boxes scattered through much of the building. In the days and hours preceding the formal opening, workmen by the hundreds—carpenters, masons, smiths, painters—labored frantically to prepare and decorate the building for the inaugural ceremony, which was scheduled to be held in the presence of President Franklin Pierce and several of his senior cabinet officers. Coming north specifically for the occasion, Pierce had arrived in New York earlier that day after a triumphant public journey via Baltimore and Philadelphia. A crowd estimated at ten thousand people was admitted to the Palace that morning, its ranks supposedly limited to exhibitors, official visitors, and season ticket holders. Meanwhile, many of the people denied tickets gathered outside. It is hard to imagine that Putnam, who had urgent proprietary as well as personal reasons to be there, was not among those making a first tour of the interior while awaiting the arrival of the president. He would have had much to occupy him during those intervening hours, part of which he must have spent inspecting his firm's office inside the Crystal Palace, which oversaw the sales of its publications at various parts of the Exhibition.[9] He would have been pleased to note that the first copies of his duodecimo Exhibition *Catalogue* and of the first number of his *Illustrated Record* were on display and available for sale.[10] So was a collection of his most attractively printed and bound books, which were presented in an ornately carved oak bookcase manufactured by the local firm of Bulkley and Herter and prominently positioned near the printing presses.[11] True to his leanings, Putnam had singled out for that display a variety of works in the belles lettres by American authors.[12]

As he stood under one of the tallest domes ever built in the United States and awaited the festivities, Putnam might well have felt confident about the chances for success of the Crystal Palace and of his own investment in it. A creation financed entirely by and through the private sector, the building was nonetheless one of the largest, architecturally most advanced structures ever erected in the United States, if only a fraction the size and capacity of its Hyde Park prototype. Its plan chosen as part of an architectural competition, the Crystal Palace was a curious mix of religious and secular, traditional and modern elements. Built primarily of cast iron and glass, it was designed on the principle of a Greek cross, whose long aisles met in a large rotunda surmounted by the glass dome and overhung along their lengths by clerestory windows. The site selected for the building was the four-square-block area known as Reservoir Square bounded by Fortieth and Forty-Second Streets, and by Sixth Avenue and the Croton Reservoir.

10.   Exterior view of New York Crystal Palace, site of the Exhibition of the Industry of All Nations; lithography of Nagel and Weingaertner. (Courtesy Eno Collection, New York Public Library)

In January 1852 the municipality of New York granted a five-year lease on the land to the organizers, then in March the state legislature issued a charter authorizing them under the name of the Association for the Exhibition of the Industry of All Nations to offer a stock subscription for the purpose of raising operating funds of $300,000 (soon expanded to $500,000) to meet construction and management costs. Although proud to showcase their wares under an American roof, the directors of the Association quickly went about soliciting contributions from around the world as well as from across the country, the "world" (which in this case spanned only North America, Europe, and a scattering of British colonial possessions) being allotted more than twice the exhibition space reserved for the United States. Due to poor planning and difficult logistics, not much of the rest of the world turned out for the opening ceremony, but American dignitaries were there by the hundreds, including members of Congress, generals, chaplains, college presidents, and civic leaders. Also present was a large press delegation made up chiefly of local journalists.

The crowd was forewarned to be in the building no later than 8:00 A.M., leaving the organizers more than ample time before the scheduled 1:00 ceremony for placement of dignitaries on the two platforms set up in the northern nave, orchestra rehearsal, and various last-minute details. It was the president, it turned out, caught downtown in a thunderstorm, who arrived late, leaving the pent-up crowd anxious and restless before he reached the building at 2:00 (Secretary of War Jefferson Davis came even later). With the bands playing "Hail, Columbia," "Yankee Doodle," and other patriotic tunes, Pierce was escorted to his seat of honor on the speakers' podium. From then on, at least, matters proceeded smoothly. As the large municipal police contingent posted around the building kept order over the large crowd gathered outside, the ceremony of prayers, speeches, responses, and musical performances went largely according to plan. The Episcopalian bishop of New York Jonathan Mayhew Wainwright opened the ceremony with an invocation well suited to the occasion in which he offered thanks to God the Creator for the material abundance bestowed on the nation and asked protection for the "manifestations of skill, genius, enterprise, and industry" on display before the gathering.[13] He was followed by Theodore Sedgwick, the president of the Association, who formally welcomed the guests gathered together from overseas and across the United States. Sedgwick then directed his various nationalistic remarks to President Pierce, from whom he sought "the seal of national approbation" for the enterprise while proudly noting that the building was the product entirely of private investment—private enterprise at the service of the proposition that "our objects were public, and our aims national." Sedgwick concluded by formally requesting a response from Pierce, who, though plainly fatigued, after a musical interlude gave a brief, apparently spontaneous speech thanking the organizers for "strength-ening and perpetuating the blessed union." His remarks were enthusi-astically received by the public and greeted at its conclusion with "six tremendous cheers" rather than the three requested by Sedgwick (according to the New York *Times* and *Tribune*). Followed by music and fanfare, the brief ceremony then ended, and the Exhibition was formally considered open, although the doors were not opened to the general public until the next day.

Public commentary on the festivities, Crystal Palace, and Exhibi-tion continued for days. Most but not all reports were laudatory. An interesting dissent came from Horace Greeley's *Tribune* (and presum-ably from Greeley himself), whose reporter grumbled the next day about the organizers' failure to do proper homage at the ceremony to labor. That point was taken up several days later by one of the most eloquent men in the city, Rev. Edwin Chapin, in a sermon on the moral signifi-cance of the Crystal Palace preached at his Broadway church and later published in the New York *Times*.[14] Chapin linked the meaning of the ceremony directly to the biblical text (Psalms 8:6) around which he built his sermon: "Thou madest him to have dominion over the works of thy hands." These words, he proclaimed, were "the expression of that grand, impressive ceremony, with its dignitaries and its multitudes, with its banners and towering plumes, with its fervent prayers, and its choral hallelujahs swelling over all. It was a recognition of the mission of Man upon the earth, and an appeal to God for the legitimacy of Labor." Acknowledging the complaint of the *Tribune* that the ceremony had failed to represent labor fairly, Chapin added that the proper dominion of man as exhibited in the Exhibition, rightly understood, embraced both labor and labor-saving machinery, both the worker and the work of his hands. Meant unambiguously, Chapin's commentary might have been construed more ironically after the death of ten workers at their jobs that summer rebuilding the English Crystal Palace at Sydenham.

Chapin's message was one whose seamless formulation of labor and enterprise would have appealed to Putnam, who readily entered into the spirit of celebration that surrounded the Exhibition. Although uninvolved formally in the opening ceremony, Putnam was well repre-sented symbolically and practically beyond the exhibit of his books. In accordance with his earliest request, prominently located in the build-ing's main aisle were two modern, steam-powered printing presses (one for the letterpress and the other for the illustrations), positioned there expressly to produce his company's *Illustrated Record* in sight of the viewing public. Two workers were hired to feed them paper, and issues of both the *Illustrated Record* and *Catalogue* were sold right from the floor to visitors walking through the building. Within days of the opening ceremony, the production of the two publications became an item of public attention, a matter widely noticed and commented on in the press.[15] The *Illustrated Record* itself commented on its own visibility: "This *Record* is printed upon two power presses, in the building of the Exhibition, moved by steam power supplied by engines, whose duty it is to drive the machinery of the mechanical department. Thousands of visitors will thus be able to see, probably for the first time, the rapid movements of these seemingly intelligent operatives, whose one sole requirement appears to be an insatiable appetite for fair white paper."[16] Even the choice of workers to feed paper to the presses became a public concern; as soon as the building opened, an anonymously written letter to the editor of the New York *Tribune* raised the issue of whether it was proper for women, who typically performed this function at printing houses, to carry it out in the open expanse of the Crystal Palace.[17]

The most obvious measure of the seriousness that Putnam attached to his Exhibition publications was the extraordinary investment he made in their production: $40,000 in the *Illustrated Record* alone (a sum he publicized widely).[18] That sum was an extravagant expenditure for his still undercapitalized company, an outlay perhaps twice the total investment he had made in *Putnam's Monthly* and one not even remotely proportionate to any of his previous publishing projects. It was an understatement to note, as he did in the *Record* itself, that its investment of time and capital, "if devoted to other objects, would certainly have produced a much greater pecuniary return."[19] Why then such an investment? The primary answer seems to have been his impression that it combined national service with professional advantage. In the "Publishers' Notice" that he appended to the volume— this being another publishing opportunity too special to be passed over without a Putnam professional credo—he made clear his belief that the volume was inside and out a paragon of American enterprise. It was the product of American engravers (80 percent, he proudly noted, from New York), writers, editors, printers, papermakers, and type casters all united in the service of the greatest display of modernity ever hosted in the United States; and it was a work designed to reach the broad American reading public. He could hardly have worn his pride in the *Illustrated Record* more visibly: "In truth, it is a copiously and beautifully illustrated Encyclopedia of Manufactures and the Fine and Useful Arts; uniting to a brief but comprehensive history of each particular subject up to the date of publication, the theoretical and critical views of distinguished gentlemen who have made those subjects their special study. We are not aware that any other work of the kind can be mentioned which gives so much valuable information and expensive illustration at so low a price. We confidently assert that when the expense of its production is considered, no similar book excels it in cheapness. We have aimed to place it within the reach of all classes."[20] At the same time, his optimism about the venture matched his pride in its national worth; the trial figure for the printing run of the *Catalogue* that he suggested to the Association for their approval was 100,000 copies.[21] That for the *Illustrated Record* must have been nearly as large. Much as he was investing his hopes and his money in these ventures, he was also anticipating what he considered "the collateral advantage" of publicity that sales at and on the subject of the Exhibition would bring to the full run of his publications.[22]

Early on, when expectations for the Crystal Palace were running high and predictions for its success were commonplace, Putnam's hopes for the success of his publications must have seemed reasonable. Many other people undoubtedly saw the Crystal Palace and Exhibition in ideological terms similar to his. In one instance that nearly replicated Putnam's publishing logic, a reviewer for the *Illustrated Magazine of Art* told readers that the *Illustrated Record,* serialized at $.25 for each of its thirteen double issues, was priced low enough to put it "within the reach of every family in the land. And shall any American family be without it?"[23] Furthermore, numerous individuals backed their belief in the venture with their capital. As time went on and the novelty of the Crystal Palace wore off, however, it became clear that hopes and predictions for the success of the Crystal Palace were a delusion for its thousands of moral supporters, and a bad investment for its hundreds of shareholders. The price of the stock began to tumble in the days immediately following the opening ceremony, losing one-seventh of its value within the first half-week and never recovering as attendance and receipts lagged far behind projections. The special turnstiles imported from England, similar to those used to count visitors at the entrances of the Hyde Park Crystal Palace, rarely registered more than 10 to 15 percent of their maximum capacity of 20,000.

The Exhibition was plagued with problems from the beginning. The delays in opening the building and then in displaying its full range of exhibits got it off to a bad start from which it never recovered. Attracting overseas exhibits to New York in sufficient numbers to justify the floor allocation proved difficult. Furthermore, the organizers had underestimated how inconvenient the building's location, so far to the north of the population center of Manhattan, might be. Existing transportation lines did not carry passengers that far uptown; as a result, many people found themselves dropped off far from Reservoir Square and left with an arduous walk. Proposals mindful of the working class to keep the building open on Sunday and to maintain low entrance fees made little difference. As the months of 1853 went by, the financial condition of the enterprise became so grave that proposals for its reorganization, even its closure, were discussed. In an act of desperation, the stockholders and directors appealed to P. T. Barnum, whom they elected first a director and shortly afterward president of the Association, to restore life to what even Barnum thought of as "a corpse long before I touched it."[24]

The measure that had worked once to quicken interest in the project was resorted to a second time, and the reinauguration of the Crystal Palace was held with pomp and ceremony on 4 May 1854. Barnum led the formal procession, with his fellow directors falling in behind him "two deep" (as the New York *Times* reported the next day, unaware that skeptics, by then numerous, might read into those words an unintended double entendre). Speeches as optimistic and wishful as those made the year before were delivered by a new set of speakers, including Barnum, Horace Greeley, Parke Godwin, and Henry Ward Beecher. A gold medal (or its $1,000 equivalent in cash) was offered to the outstanding accomplishment in both invention and art displayed during the previous year at the Exhibition, and ten $100 medals to other outstanding achievements in those fields. The end result of these and other promotions, however, was the same: a quick burst of interest and then a long falling off. Gradually, the Association slid into bankruptcy.

Putnam was one of the people whose losses could be measured in dollars: $20,000 on the *Illustrated Record,* a huge figure both in absolute and comparative terms on his initial $40,000 investment).[25] That investment proved to be one of his single worst professional mistakes, a misjudgment symptomatic of his occasional tendency, as his son later noted, to be guilty of an "overestimate of the literary standard of the

American community and [a] miscalculation as to the number of Americans who could be depended upon to read the higher class of literature."[26] How soon he realized this mistake is an interesting question. He certainly did by spring or summer 1854, when caught in a severe credit squeeze endangering his operations he appealed to the Association for its permission to auction off stereotype plates and printed copies of unspecified Crystal Palace publications. Not surprisingly, he was denied permission, as in other ways he found his maneuverability limited by his status as contractor to the Association.[27] But even before seeking this solution, with so much of his operating capital invested in the project and printed stock piling up beyond the modest numbers sold to subscribers and purchasers at the Exhibition, Putnam had tried a variety of imaginative ways to market his publications, especially the *Illustrated Record.* He had offered it in double serial numbers at the monthly price of *Putnam's Monthly,* as a bound volume, and in combination with other G. P. Putnam publications.[28] These marketing stratagems eventually resulted in the sale of the entire edition but only when offered at sharply reduced prices. His own recollection was that he wound up selling off 12,000 of the 15,000 copies at trade prices and auctioning off the rest "at 'a song'" at the New York trade sale of September 1855.

Nearly as serious as was his direct loss were the indirect losses Putnam suffered by his investment in the Crystal Palace fiasco. His publishing list of 1853–54 was filled with books and pamphlets related to the Exhibition in addition to the "authorized" publications produced on the spot. In all likelihood, those works were also financial losers. More important, the heavy concentration of his resources of time, money, energy, and attention in those projects, not to mention in *Putnam's Monthly,* must have distracted him from pursuing alternative projects. A close look at his publishing list reveals a slackening of the gains he had made in his first half-dozen years. During the period he was preoccupied with *Putnam's Monthly* and the *Illustrated Record,* he signed up few new authors of distinction, printed fewer new titles than in preceding years, and enjoyed no runaway successes. Bad enough in itself, his publishing position was also weakening comparatively. For the first time since he had gone into business for himself, he was losing ground to his competitors. As the market for the belles lettres was expanding around him, so was his competition in New York, Boston, Philadelphia, and even in the West. Not only were the Appletons and Harpers thriving in his neighborhood but new firms run by Charles Scribner, J. C. Derby, and others were vying for many of the same authors and properties that were desirable to Putnam. At the same time, the center of literary publishing was moving from New York to Boston as more and more established authors were signed by such Boston firms as Phillips, Sampson and Company; John Jewett; Little and Brown; and especially Ticknor and Fields.

Despite these developments, to all outward (and perhaps even inward) appearances G. P. Putnam and Company was thriving in 1853–54, as Putnam continued to pursue the expansionist policies he had followed since 1848. Even with so many resources tied up in the *Illustrated Record* and *Putnam's Monthly,* he continued to offer a fairly wide range of new publications in 1853–54 in addition to those linked directly to the Exhibition and a broad, diverse backlist that had accumulated from as far back as his Wiley and Putnam days. Putnam also tried to get a small number of new projects into print. In 1853 he had considered publishing a sequel to *Homes of American Authors* (see chapter 9) before rejecting that plan and instead, in an analogous act of national "service," bringing out a successor volume, *Homes of American Statesmen,* that celebrated "the homes of the men to whom we owe our own."[29] That gift book was completed in time to appear on his Christmas 1853 list. Imitative in layout and ideology of the earlier volume, *Homes of American Statesmen* was original in one significant regard: it was the first American book to reproduce a photograph (or, more precisely, a daguerreotype) directly into its pages, in this case its frontispiece.[30]

Patriotic gift books of this sort were attractive to Putnam, but their financial importance to his firm was clearly secondary to that of the works of his chief authors: Irving, Warner, and Taylor. In the 1850s Irving remained Putnam's main cash cow (as Putnam remained Irving's). Relations between the men were respectful and congenial, if at no time truly close; Putnam knew better than to venture across the gap of age and status, and Irving did not invite him to do so. But Putnam's reverence for Irving—it was nothing less—continued unabated the full span of their relationship. A person who habitually showered friends and clients with gifts, Putnam enjoyed favoring Irving with tokens of his regard—books, writing supplies, engravings, fruit—and Irving returned the gestures with his own, the most important, of course, being new works and extended rights to the old ones. At some unspecified date in

the late 1850s, they exchanged reciprocal, symbolic presents. On notic-
ing the clutter and disorder of Irving's private library during one of his
periodic visits to Sunnyside, Putnam not only rearranged and systematized the books and papers but made a mental note to send Irving a
modern writing desk with drawers for ordering his papers. In return
Irving made him a present of the old writing table where he had written his most recent works, which Putnam proudly kept at home for the
rest of his life.[31] Another Irving token that he kept with pride was a
letter of thanks acknowledging Putnam's 1852 Christmas present for
the Irving family. Irving used that occasion to express his broad appreciation for Putnam and to single out their relationship as one of the
most special of his life: "I take pleasure in expressing the great satisfaction I have derived, throughout all our intercourse, from your amiable, obliging and honorable conduct. Indeed I never had dealings with
any man, whether in the way of business or friendship more perfectly
free from any alloy."[32] Special as that sentiment was to Putnam personally, it soon passed beyond their private relationship and into societal
folklore when it was published after Irving's death and later cited as
proof of the mutual trust between American publisher and author.[33]
In short, Putnam's contemporaries were as willing as he to elevate
Irving to a level above the marketplace and onto the mantelpiece and to
sentimentalize his reputation as father figure to American letters, a
judgment that had the secondary result of elevating Putnam by way of
association.

   Throughout the decade, Putnam persisted in bringing out Irving's
old works in various sizes and formats; the frequency of these editions
was a sign of Irving's continuing popularity and Putnam's success in
profiting from it. In spring 1855 Putnam alerted purchasers that the
author's revised edition, begun in 1848, was then complete at fifteen
volumes and that they could therefore make suitable arrangements for
its binding and storage. Eager to cultivate the next set of purchases, he
simultaneously announced the inception of a "second series" of Irving's
works.[34] This was sound business policy, although it does raise the
question of whether Putnam had yet sensed that his most profitable
author was well past his prime. Whatever his private opinion, he did
what any commercially minded publisher would do: he encouraged and
abetted his most popular author to capitalize on his fame by preparing
new works for publication. In the first two years of their collaboration,
Putnam had published several "new" works by Irving (*Oliver Goldsmith:*

A Biography and *Mahomet and His Successors*) as part of the collected edition. Then in 1855, he successfully persuaded Irving to pull various uncollected essays out of his desk and prepare them for publication as *Wolfert's Roost* (1855), which he published as the first work in the new series.[35]

Putnam's highest ambition, however, was to see Irving write the one genuinely new work that he had left in him: a biography of George Washington. Putnam was well aware of the potential of a full-scale biography of the nation's chief icon by its chief writer, although he could have foreseen no better than Irving that it would not only take nearly the last decade of his life to complete but consume him in the process. Irving had begun work on the project as early as the late 1840s but failed to make much progress. Nor did he for much of the first half of the 1850s, by which time the project had become a personal obsession, a quest strangely at variance, as Stanley T. Williams has noted, with the role of idler-denizen of Sunnyside that he preferred to play.[36] That public image of Irving was as remote from truth as was Hawthorne's self-cultivated reputation as recluse and man of obscurity. Irving had always possessed a sharp sense of reputation, status, and literary economics even as he cultivated his privacy-loving image, and his professional drive did not dull with age or with the developments transforming the American literary culture of the 1840s and 1850s. In his sixties and seventies that drive became centered on the Washington biography. At one point the mounting pressure brought on by his slow progress carried Irving as nearly as he ever came to an open display of anger at Putnam; when Putnam enthusiastically advertised the projected three-volume *Washington* in early 1855 as due to be ready by year's end, Irving quickly wrote him: "I have authorized no such statement— Neither have I authorized your previous advertisements that the second volume would be published in August and the third in October. I wish you would make no promises on my behalf but such as I distinctly warrant."[37] Work—often feverish and all-consuming—on the project, which stretched to five volumes, was to preoccupy him until nearly the final months of his life.

Another writer with whom Putnam was readily identified in the mid-1850s and for many years thereafter was Taylor (an identification internalized in the most personal fashion when Putnam named a son after him, as he already had after Irving). With Taylor, however, the relations were so personal as often to render indistinguishable the line between friendship and business. The connection between the men stretched unbrokenly from their time together at the American Literary Agency in London right up until Putnam's death a generation later (on which occasion Taylor was to tell George Haven that he had always thought of his father "as a dear and near friend, not a business associate").[38] Their regard was mutual; each saw the other as representing the highest ideals of his profession. Putnam, for his part, singled out Taylor early on as one of the premier writers of his generation; once formed, his opinion never changed. For this reason, he also singled him out as an author whose works he wished—and, later, planned—to keep together under his own imprint.

Taylor was a publisher's dream: an author who wrote books that were both reputable and popular and who was able to produce them on a fairly consistent and frequent basis. Whereas a "hit" brought quick delight, Putnam always preferred a work or an author who brought in "permanent" returns. Taylor's first work, *Views A-foot,* was just such a book, one that remained popular and reputable and sold well through the 1850s and 1860s, going through more than twenty printings in its first decade and justifying the production of new plates and a new edition in 1855.[39] In the meanwhile, Taylor published other travelogues with Putnam whose contents spanned much of the globe (including *Eldorado, A Journey to Central Africa, The Lands of the Saracen,* and *A Visit to India, China, and Japan*). Terms between the men during the pre-1857 period were fairly uniform: Putnam paid all production expenses and gave Taylor 12 ½-percent royalties on all books sold, a figure slightly better than the 10 percent ($100 per 1,000 copies sold after expenses) that Taylor received from Wiley as a literary novice for the original *Views A-foot* in the Wiley and Putnam Library of American Books.[40] The Taylor-Putnam collaboration was generally limited, however, to his travel literature. After publishing his first volume of poems with Putnam, Taylor solicited and received Putnam's permission to publish subsequent volumes with "the all-potent imprint of Ticknor, Reed and Fields," the acknowledged national leader in the field.[41] Neither man then saw the potential for an eventual bidding war for all of Taylor's works.

His dealings with Taylor brought Putnam more pleasure than did his relations with any other author; they very nearly approximated his ideal of author-publisher relations. The term that best described those relations was "collaboration," as Putnam might have defined it—two people working together in consultation and harmony toward a common goal of producing "good" and "serious" books that provided their readers with entertainment and knowledge, and their author and publisher with profits. By contrast with his dealings with Irving, Putnam could and did express himself freely with Taylor, a man of his own generation with whom he shared not only large parts of his home and professional life but also much of his own cultural vocabulary. Whether it meant discussing business deals, the latest news in the city, or national events, the two men found a breadth of shared references and common assumptions for filling in the "entre nous," as the popular phrase went.

The two men collaborated on a wide variety of projects, which included not only travelogues but also occasional and edited works such as the *Hand-Book of Literature* ("hack work," as Taylor thought of it, done for the money) that he coedited for *Putnam's Home Cyclopedia*. It was typically Putnam who initiated this and other projects such as gift books and literary collections in which he involved Taylor over the years; such works drew on their common appreciation of and devotion to middle-class taste. So did Taylor's numerous travelogues, which must have found in Putnam a broad acceptance of the kinds of ethnocentrically based sociological, anthropological, and cultural judgments that informed the work of most nineteenth-century travel writers conversant and comfortable with the prevailing conventions of the genre. No less than Taylor, Putnam saw the world with America at its center and other countries sliding to the margins according to their distance from American standards. Not surprisingly, those works passed smoothly from Taylor to Putnam and from manuscript to print. No record survives of substantive disagreements between the two men or requests for major editorial changes; the usual procedure, soon a routine, was that Taylor wrote and prepared his manuscripts for publication (sometimes at Putnam's urging), and Putnam quickly put them to press and brought them out at the appropriate time (sometimes in consultation with Taylor).

During the mid-1850s Putnam could also count on substantial profits from the sales of Susan Warner's novels, which continued to sell well then and even retained some popularity through the remainder of the century. A summer 1852 advertisement announced the cumulative sale to date of 75,000 volumes of *The Wide, Wide World* and *Queechy*, and their sales showed no sign of slowing.[42] Those sales, however, did not enrich the author or completely solve her family's exigencies.

Warner and her family struggled throughout the decade to pay off the debts incurred years before by her father's extravagant purchase of Constitution Island. Until the first royalties check came in, the family lacked sufficient firewood or food to get through the winter of 1849–50 in comfort. Their situation eased somewhat in the early and mid-1850s, when Putnam was paying her royalties that probably ran annually into the thousands of dollars, even if the report printed by an unidentified newspaper that Putnam had paid them $10,000 above the contracted royalties was nothing but a rumor.[43] For his part, Putnam did not hesitate to make advertising capital out of his dealings with Warner. In February 1853, for example, he tried to induce Hawthorne to publish with him by mentioning that he had recently paid Warner $4,500 royalties for the sales of her work over a six-month period.[44]

For a time in the mid-1850s, Putnam served as publisher to the whole Warner family. Perhaps wishing to strengthen his good relations with the sisters, Putnam published their father's *The Liberties of America* in 1853.[45] But his primary concern was with the sisters, who had begun their careers collaboratively with him before the publication of *The Wide, Wide World* as joint authors of *Robinson Crusoe's Farmyard* and who continued that pattern of separate and joint publishing with him. They did so precisely at a time when the sales of novels by women had caught the attention of both the reading public and the entire publishing trade. With such names as Harriet Beecher Stowe, Maria A. Cummins, E. D. E. N. Southworth, Catharine Maria Sedgwick, Fanny Fern, and Grace Greenwood linked with Susan Warner's in the minds of American readers and publishers, Putnam must have been keenly aware of the commercial importance to himself of Warner's fame. In fact, he used every means at his disposal to capitalize on and promote Susan's popularity, as J. C. Derby was doing with Fern and John Jewett (among others) with Stowe. While *The Wide, Wide World* and *Queechy* continued to be fast sellers on the market, Putnam published additional works related and unrelated to the sisters. He published, for instance, a musical book called *Lyrics from The Wide, Wide World* (1853) that adapted excerpts of Warner's text to songs for voice and piano written by Charles W. Glover. He also published Anna's first solo novel, *Dollars and Cents* (written under the pseudonym of Amy Lathrop), a popular work not only in the United States but in England, where it become a target for frequent reprinting.

These were relatively minor ventures, however, when weighed against Putnam's and the sisters' expectations, which had grown immeasurably on both sides since the time shortly after the publication of *The Wide, Wide World* when Susan had timidly asked Putnam to assess her professional viability. More nearly fulfilling his expectations, in all likelihood, was the juvenile series called "Ellen Montgomery's Book Shelf" that the sisters began with *Mr. Rutherford's Children,* published in 1853. Cleverly designed to capitalize on the success of *The Wide, Wide World,* its organizing logic was based on the transitive principle that a reading public that had identified with Ellen would also take an interest in her favorite books. With "Elizabeth Wetherell" promising to continue the series as long as the public showed interest, even if that meant until the entire shelf of Ellen's books had been published, the series was well designed to cater to the length and breadth of its audience's patronage.[46] Putnam worked hard to promote and sell each book, as it came out, both as an individual title and as part of a series, publishing them all with a series title page and in a common format. They apparently sold well, if hardly as well as Susan's first two novels. An advertisement in early 1855 for *Carl Krinken,* which had been published only the year before, listed its sales as over 12,000 copies.[47] The "Book Shelf" continued to appear through the decade before ending with the publication of its fifth volume, *Hard Maple,* in 1859. By that time Putnam was no longer the Warners' publisher nor were they writing the kind of domestic fiction that interested him, the sisters having turned their attention primarily to religion and given their works to the firm of Robert Carter, one of New York's leading publishers of religious fiction and nonfiction. But their personal relations with Putnam and Victorine remained warm, and the two families stayed in touch until the end of Putnam's life.

Although he devoted much of his time and attention in 1853 to overseeing *Putnam's Monthly* and his Crystal Palace publications, Putnam was concurrently involved that year and through the mid-1850s in a much broader array of professional activities involving both his firm and his profession. Early that year the unresolved status of international copyright resurfaced with renewed urgency. It became a subject of discussion in the press as rumors began to circulate that Secretary of State Edward Everett and British Minister John Fiennes Crampton had been negotiating a binational copyright treaty. That news excited Putnam, who had agitated for more than a dozen years for the fundamental principle of reciprocal protection to domestic and foreign authors wherever their works were published. Over those years Putnam had done his best to articulate his position to legislators, publishers, authors, and the reading public on innumerable occasions and in innumerable formats, including Capitol Hill, trade meetings, and newspapers and journals controlled by friends or himself. His circle of acquaintances in this work was wide, including many of the best-placed people in major committees of Congress, educational institutions, the print and publishing trades, and the ranks of authors and editors. But for all the time spent and trips made to generate support for his views, he had seldom realized much more than the pride of righteous action tempered by the frustration of repeated setbacks. Resilient as ever, however, he found his hopes revitalized in early 1853 when word of binational negotiations spread through the American print media.

Putnam had an inside source about the progress of the negotiations in Everett, his one-time inspiration and longtime professional colleague, who wrote him in February or early March to request a list of American works reprinted in England. Putnam had known Everett at least since the early 1840s, when Everett was American ambassador to England, and the two men had met on numerous social occasions at each other's residences and places of work. Putnam had kept him informed of his work on *American Facts* and other projects related to the cross-cultural relations between England and America, and the two men no doubt continued to confer from time to time over the intervening years about strategies to further their common goals. Putnam had compiled lists of the sort Everett requested in 1853 so many times since the late 1830s that he could have recited from memory many of the approximately 850 works on the list that he sent to him (and leaked to the press). Everett's response, however, was disheartening. Having moved from the Department of State on 4 March to his new office as senator from Massachusetts, he wrote Putnam that after conferring with colleagues he had concluded that the time was unpropitious for any new initiative. The Senate, he was finding, was then preoccupied with other issues, and in any case opponents had already prejudiced many members against the idea. His only recommendation was that Putnam use the power of his magazine to influence opinion—gratuitous advice since Putnam and Briggs were already presenting their case in *Putnam's Monthly.*[48]

Probably just a few days before receiving Everett's discouraging report, Putnam was caught off guard when the respected Philadelphia publisher Abraham Hart challenged him in the course of the March New York trade sale to debate the issue, then on the minds of many in the trade as one likely to reset guidelines for their profession, and to do so right then and there before their colleagues. Holding in his hand a London-manufactured, Putnam-imprinted copy of Layard's *Discoveries in the Ruins of Nineveh and Babylon* that was offered for sale by G. P. Putnam and Company in the United States, Hart inquired why the United States should approve legislation protecting works such as that printed in London but intended for sale in New York and other American cities. Putnam's formal response is unknown, but it is clear that he felt himself ill equipped to debate Hart on the spot, a point he reiterated when the two carried their exchange of views into print in the form of public letters sent for publication to the unofficial book trade paper, *Norton's Literary Gazette and Publishers' Circular.*[49] One reason for his refusal was personality; a diffident man even in private settings, Putnam knew his limitations as a speaker and foresaw that he would be at a disadvantage to Hart in a public forum.[50] Another was the peculiarity of Putnam's rhetorical style; his habitual mode of assuming or seeking consensus and of arguing on the basis of prima facie assertions was an inappropriate one for capturing the minds of an industry gathered in public and divided over an issue likely to regulate the terms and conduct of its dealings. By contrast, Putnam had few peers among his colleagues in expressing his views in print, where he was far more likely to employ his habitual manner to rhetorical advantage.

The debate in *Norton's* matched two of the most respected, knowledgeable men in the trade, each man well able to articulate his position. Although both men professed to be friends of American authors, readers, and manufacturers, the clear divisions in their views reflected fault lines between these perceived constituencies. At the time of their debate, the most basic expression of the positions commonly taken by their peers was the equivocating one recently articulated by the editor of *Norton's:* "If cheap books wrong the writers, dear books would wrong the readers."[51] Putnam did not typically state propositions in the form of simple dichotomies, and this was one that he would have denied out of hand. He clearly believed that he could and did speak on behalf not only of publishers and readers but of authors (Hart specifically recognizing him as having the "honor" of being "the peculiar and particular champion of the rights of authors"). His aim in engaging Hart—and, through Hart, the entire profession—in public dialogue was to move beyond a position already well known to the trade to an exposition of ideas whose aim was explicitly to "remove, as far as possible, certain illogical mystifications which have been connected with the supposed effect of an International Copyright."

Those mystifications centered on widely held beliefs (often recited by politicians) that both the American manufacturing sector and the American reading public would suffer from the modified economics of publishing in the proposed new era of international copyright. These assertions, Putnam argued, were false as regarded both producers and consumers. There were two reasons why the many people employed in the manufacturing sector—including printers, binders, papermakers, typesetters—would not be losers, as was commonly argued, in a economy based on liberalized trading practices and regulated by reciprocal author rights. First, American manufacturers produced books more cheaply than did the British and therefore could compete advantageously against foreign competition in an open market. Second, the imbalance between books imported to and exported from the United States had righted itself so dramatically in the past two decades that the domestic bookmaking sector had little to fear from open doors. He pointed out that Hart's example of his firm's importation of Layard's *Discoveries in the Ruins of Nineveh and Babylon,* a book too expensive to be reprinted profitably and therefore brought out by Putnam in the American market from sheets imported from John Murray, was the exception that proved the rule. Moreover, he parried Hart's accusation by proceeding to name the many instances in which he and other publishers exported their sheets or plates to England for reprinting (as, for instance, he had exported sheets or plates of various Irving editions and other works to Murray and other English publishers). If there was a real threat to the bookmaking crafts, he asserted in an argument unusual for the time, it came from a different source: the unhealthy working conditions common in the poorly ventilated printing offices and binderies of the country. Neither in this debate nor at any time did Putnam risk angering those workers or their employers by denying the necessity of a "home manufacturing" clause in any possible international copyright agreement. As for the common "bugbear of high prices as a necessary consequence of copyright," Putnam argued that the new economics of author protection would not significantly affect the historical progress made in the nineteenth century toward cheaply produced and sold print products. Under the proposed copyright conditions he predicted a rise in prices of only 10 percent, and he anticipated that consumers would gratefully pay that "tax," just as he—and, he assumed, Hart and the rest of the trade—would gladly see authors duly rewarded for their intellectual labor.

In short, he forecast that international copyright, far from undermining the economics of literary production and consumption, would strengthen them and lead to a period of mutual prosperity for all parties to letters:

> The American mode of making *books for the people—books at MODERATE PRICES for general circulation—will not only yield the English author the most profitable returns, but it will give employment and protection to the very large number of men and women engaged in the manufacture of books in this country;* in the paper mills, the type-foundries, the printing-offices, and the binderies. Thus the author will be paid on each side of the Atlantic; industry protected in its proper place; the publisher enabled to manufacture books in a respectable and economical manner, free from the petty rivalries resulting from the present unsound state of things; and the reading public will be supplied with fairly-printed books, which yield the author his equitable per centage, without any essential addition to the price.[52]

As though this prospect were not itself a sufficient justification for copyright advocacy, he also argued—"insinuated" may be the more accurate term—that international copyright would put the entire publishing industry on the more ethical basis to which its proprietors all wished to see it elevated. This was the crux of Putnam's position: all literary professionals were as one and thus to be addressed not just as peers but as partners engaged in a common endeavor.

Hart found himself hard pressed to answer a string of arguments made with such broad-minded geniality and optimism that they threatened to coopt him to their vision of professional camaraderie. Rather than try to take Putnam on directly, he asserted what was common to their positions: a desire to see authors fairly compensated, a respect for home manufactures, and a commitment to protect the current pricing norms (and, through them, their common position as publishers of high-quality, middle-class books). He claimed that he did not oppose the principle of international copyright per se, only the means proposed for its adoption by treaty rather than by Congressional reform of the Copyright Act. Beyond those general observations, however, he was clearly far less sanguine than Putnam about the prospects for mutual amity and prosperity. For one thing, he insisted more unequivocally than Putnam that American manufacturers be protected against their overseas rivals and that one way of doing so was to link the right of foreigners to gain American copyrights for their works to the printing of those works in the United States (a winning argument with print-making professionals that eventually became incorporated into the copyright treaty signed by the United States in 1891). For another, he expressed his outrage at the behavior of authors in labeling publishers as "pirates," "robbers," and "thieves." Furthermore, he foresaw little chance that authors and publishers would ever meet on mutually supportive grounds as long as their relations contained the inherently oppositional principle by which publishers necessarily rejected manuscripts they were unwilling or unable to print. All in all, he was clearly less dissatisfied with the current practices of reprinting and trade courtesy and more cautious about granting foreign authors protection of an "unrestricted" nature.

At the March trade sale Hart rightly challenged the statement that Putnam had sent through the press that his views on the proposed copyright treaty represented the opinions of 95 percent of his peers, a claim Hart vociferously disputed a second time in *Norton's*. He knew very well as a resident of Philadelphia, which had a particularly large concentration of copyright opponents, that the claim was an arrant exaggeration. He was no doubt aware that opponents of the proposed treaty stretched across the country and included not only most of the book manufacturing sector but also some of the largest publishers in America, most notably the two great firms of Carey (and its various successors, with one of which he was affiliated) and Harper's—the two houses that had turned the reprinting of foreign fiction into a major source of American enterprise. Those firms would not support any legal change that endangered their right to reprint popular and profitable European works, which was after all a basis of their livelihood. The Harpers were particularly staunch defenders of the status quo, although they played a quiet role in the 1853 debate. When solicited the previous summer by President Fillmore for their opinions on the proposed international treaty, they had responded in slyly equivocal fashion:

> We have carefully considered the subject of an international copyright, to which our attention was called by your letter of the 9th inst. The great importance of such an arrangement, as that which it is proposed to make by treaty with Great Britain, becomes more and more manifest the more the subject is considered. But although our experience and observation have led us to form opinions more or less definite upon it, we have concluded, in consequence of our close relations with all the parties to be affected by it,—with the authors of England and this country on the one hand, by whom its enactment is mainly sought, and with the industrial interests and the reading public of the United States on the other, by whom its operation would be largely felt,—to abstain from taking any steps to influence the action of our Government in regard to it.[53]

They knew, as Hart no doubt did, that as defenders of the status quo they had the strategic advantage and that a debate in the papers was not likely to have a dramatic effect in deciding the issue either way. Events soon justified their confidence. Interesting as it might have been, the 1853 Putnam-Hart debate did little more than restate positional lines already well known to the trade. In the weeks that followed, their peers would learn—as Putnam already had from Everett—that Congress was not predisposed to debate, much less legislate, the issue in its current session and that the status quo would therefore hold at least into the near future.

That fall Putnam, then approaching his fortieth birthday, was invited to receive an honorary master of arts degree from Bowdoin College, one of several he had to date received. Notice of the decision was sent to him by Bowdoin College president Leonard Woods—the same man whom Putnam had taken in hand in 1845 during his European tour preparatory to assuming the presidency. It is not clear that Putnam actually attended the ceremony; no record of his presence survives in either the Brunswick paper or college records. Whether he attended or not, it is easy to suppose that the occasion brought him back to his earliest memories. For years he had looked forward to his trips to New England, which business often required; such trips were an opportunity, when time permitted, not only to meet with professional friends and colleagues but also to visit and tighten ties with Putnam and Palmer cousins scattered across the region. A return to Brunswick and reception of an honorary degree from his hometown college would likely have marked a significant moment in his life. Although Putnam made light of the honorary degrees he received, they probably meant more to him than he was willing to admit. Certainly nothing more sharply upset the balance of his normally genial poise than the occasional anxiety attacks that entered his dealings with men whose formal learning made him aware of the limitations of his own primary school education. In truth, however, it was not until his own children, heirs to a more leisurely, comfortable youth, grew to maturity and attended such schools as Harvard, Cornell, Amherst, Göttingen, and the Sorbonne that the family educational circle would be rounded. Putnam was to experience that advantage only vicariously.

If 1853 was the year in which Putnam launched two of his most important publishing initiatives, 1854 was to prove the most fateful year in his career since going into business for himself. The year started promisingly enough. *Putnam's Monthly* was flourishing, the Exhibition publications still seemed a viable investment, and the overall business seemed to be prospering. Meanwhile his family was flourishing in its Manhattan home, the latest in the string of residences that the semi-itinerant Putnams had occupied since their initial housekeeping in London. Never fully reconciled to living in the city, the family was excited to learn that it was about to make another move.[54] Sometime that winter or spring Putnam accepted a good offer for the Sixteenth Street house and in turn bought a large house in the village of Yonkers, whose title he assigned to Victorine in what might have been a blind precaution against possible financial hard times. The house occupied a large, open tract of land about a mile north of the town center and stood on high ground commanding a view overlooking the Hudson River valley. Despite the distance from his downtown office, Manhattan was reasonably accessible either via the Harlem River railroad or by boat; a water lover since childhood, Putnam preferred the latter especially during the summer, when he typically took the "Republican" boat to work.

The move was keenly satisfying for the whole family, the charms of small town living more than compensating for the loss of New York society. The house was capacious enough to accommodate not only the large, still expanding family but their numerous guests. Surrounding the house were spacious grounds containing fruit trees, vegetable garden, chicken house, and stable. Since riding was a passion with Victorine, Putnam took care to keep the stable occupied and well managed. He was, however, a notoriously poor judge of horse flesh, a fact well known in the family and then nationally (if anonymously) disseminated once their neighbor Frederick Cozzens saw a specimen of that acumen and turned it into the "I have bought me a horse!" strand of *The Sparrowgrass Papers* serialized in *Putnam's Monthly*.[55]

Putnam was no more able to compartmentalize his publishing responsibilities during these years than he had in the past. If anything, residing in the small town provided him with even more of the public-spirited, civic challenges he always relished, even though business affairs in the city continued to press upon his time and energy. During the three years the family lived in Yonkers, he played a leading role in organizing a local library and oversaw the operations of the local lyceum, which brought to Yonkers (and often to the Putnam home) such friends and acquaintances as Horace Greeley, Wendell Phillips, Henry Ward Beecher, Theodore Tilton, George William Curtis, George Bethune, Edwin Chapin, and Edward Everett Hale. Many of these men were also political allies, an increasingly important consideration with Putnam as, with sectional issues such as the future status of Kansas impinging on his consciousness, he was drawn into groups that would soon play an instrumental role in forming the Republican Party. Putnam himself played a leading role in managing the activities of the local Fremont committee during the 1856 federal election, organizing speakers and printing and circulating campaign literature and broadsides.

It was still possible, however, to maintain politically neutral relations, as the Putnams did with the new set of local friends they made in these years. Like them, these new friends, whatever their origins, typically had frames of reference extending beyond their locality. The Putnams also tightened their established ties with old friends already resident in their vicinity, such as Cozzens, who lived just on the other side of the city center, fellow publisher J. C. Derby, and Washington Irving (Sunnyside was less than ten miles up the river). George Haven recalled in particular the numerous occasions when the family nag and its successors were harnessed for the trip up to Sunnyside.[56]

If the departure from city to village living pleased their parents, it delighted the children, who still took the open stretches of Staten Island as their standard of the good life. Their preference for their new rural environs was immediate, although it could hardly have been like the experience their father had known growing up in small-town Maine. Common to father and children, though, was the gap they all felt between city and country living, a feeling that they shared with many Americans of their time. One person who understood it well was their urbane friend and neighbor Cozzens, who astutely captured the peculiar flavor of antebellum country living in *The Sparrowgrass Papers* (originally published as "Living in the Country" in *Putnam's Monthly*). That work presupposed that its primarily urban audience would readily identify with the "Sparrowgrassii" in seeing such activities as keeping horses and gardening as recreational activities and country living as a return rather than a point of origin.

Although already double schooled in city and country living, the older Putnam children were still young enough to take to the idea of country living with less irony and purer enthusiasm than their parents, finding that the open spaces around their house accorded well with the freedom of exploration that had been a basic part of their upbringing. Like their father in Maine, the children enjoyed a wide variety of outdoor activities. Favorite pastimes included skating and sledding by winter; bathing, fishing, and playing ball by summer. Exploring the area was a pleasure to be enjoyed in all seasons, the Hudson River being an especially attractive place for their adventures (George Haven remembered during one long cold spell crossing over the frozen river to the Palisades on the New Jersey side). They also played along the banks and fished the Saw Mill River, which with increasing commercialism and growing population was fast losing the associations common among an earlier generation that still called it by its historic name of Nepperhan.

As the older Putnam children grew into their second decades, however, they graduated to more serious activities. Some of the changes were initiated by their parents, some by themselves. While home schooling continued for the younger children, Mary and Haven were sent off to more formal programs of study in the area, as well as given private lessons (including instruction in chess, a game taught to Haven by Frederick Beecher Perkins). From this time on, they attended separate schools, a decision that Mary doubly resented since her parents' specific choice for her was an all-girls school. The children were also expected to join their parents in attending the local Episcopalian church—the choice of denomination another of the family's itinerant rituals often linked to their current place of residence. Their parents had always been regular attenders of Sabbath and holiday services and true believers, but they were unusually open-minded for their time about adherence to particular denominational dogmas. Putnam in particular had often made it a practice to attend different kinds of religious services when he was traveling.

With children as intelligent and headstrong as Mary and Haven, however, much of the direction was internal. As early as her Staten Island years, Mary was attempting to blaze her own path to independence. One day, for example, she shocked her mother by announcing her intention of dissecting a large rat that she had found outside in a barn (the act, she later noted facetiously, with which she began her medical career).[57] Some of her bolder forays met the stiff resistance of her mother, who occasionally relegated her to a week of solitary confinement in her room. During her Yonkers years, she took the lead among her friends in organizing a debating circle, which considered such current events as racial relations, the treatment of Indians, and women's rights. She also edited for that group a newspaper, much of whose first (and only) issue she wrote herself. Her struggle for independence, however, had its emotional price. As her twelfth birthday approached in summer 1854, she lamented the imminent loss of her youth: "The stiff hedge of decorum binds me in. I am expected to cut off my childish things, to become a woman, while my heart is yet young, and why?"[58] During this period, finding a path to womanhood was proving more difficult for her than was finding a path to manhood for Haven, whose transition through adolescence was eased by his acceptance of and smooth relations with his father. During their second year in Yonkers, he was handed responsibility for the vegetable garden and paid for his work. He also occasionally accompanied his father to the office, which might have been held up to him as a possible professional destination. Furthermore, he seems not to have had even the usual adolescent quarrels with his father's beliefs and practices.

Mary, by contrast, found no straight paths to maturity available for a person of her ideas, views, and sex. The two models of womanhood offered her by her family, her mother's and her grandmother's, both proved problematic. On the one hand, she could not accept the domestic model that her young mother, only a half generation older than she, accepted cheerfully and willingly. Disinclined at any time in her life to adopt the idea of divided spheres, Mary preferred even in adolescence to associate with boys in recreational and intellectual activities and to contest established bases of authority. When it came time to assist their mother in taking partial responsibility for tending to the younger children, it was more often not she but the next daughter in line, Edith, who served as domestic helper. On the other hand, Mary could no more accept the old-time religious synthesis of Catherine Hunt Putnam (or, for that matter, the evangelical one of Susan Warner, at whose house she had begun to read and think seriously about sin and salvation).[59] For a time in late 1854, she exchanged long, thoughtful letters about religion with her grandmother, who found in Mary's passionate mind and sensibility an opportunity for proselytizing that she had never found in her son (although in what could only have been an act of filial devotion he did publish that year a volume of her commentaries on Genesis).[60] Although granddaughter and grandmother opened a dialogue on the subjects of faith and the Christian good life, subjects that would preoccupy her throughout her teenage years, Mary would eventually seek her life answers in science and find their practical applications in the new social activism of the last quarter of the nineteenth century.

That early turning point in her life coincided with a turning point in her father's professional affairs. The miscalculation he had made in contracting his services and linking his operations so heavily to the Crystal Palace had cost his business dearly, leaving Putnam for much of 1854 operating on a straitened margin of financial maneuverability. The losses from the Crystal Palace fiasco might well have been a factor, if not necessarily the primary one, in his repeated attempts to raise money that spring and summer. First, he sold large quantities of his publications and some sets of stereotype plates at the spring trade sale.[61] Then, in what must have been a related move, he abandoned the retail side of his operation, in the process giving up some of the rooms at 10 Park Place that he had previously rented. The sale of his entire retail stock, advertised for weeks in advance throughout New York newspapers, took place the afternoons and evenings of 9–11 May at the showroom of Bangs, Brother and Company, the city's leading auctioneer.[62] Up for sale were not only one of the widest selections of choice books in the city—one reason that Putnam's stores on Broadway and Park Place had been patronized over the years by such writers as Poe,

Irving, Cooper, Melville, Bryant, Warner, Kirkland, and Duyckinck—but many works in fine English and American bindings, a reflection of Putnam's own taste for well-made books. How much money that sale brought into his coffers is unknown, but the sum was surely a large one, running well into the thousands of dollars. After the sale, he found himself for the first time since entering the book trade a publisher first and foremost with no retail operation. He did continue, however, to operate as a purchasing agent (at a "modest commission") for individual and institutional buyers, a role that he had previously served to offset some of his expenses in traveling overseas.

The income from the sale turned out to be insufficient to solve the firm's liquidity problems. By July or August, Putnam came to realize that his business was in serious danger of being unable to pay its bills. What caused this financial crisis, and why did it persist even after he had twice sold off considerable assets to raise operating funds? It seems unlikely that the losses incurred by his Crystal Palace publications alone could have brought on a crisis of such proportions. Perhaps those publications compounded the cash shortage the firm often faced as Putnam stretched his operating capital, a sizable (and presumably excessive) portion of which he secured by loans, to its limit to keep pace with his plans. Putnam himself attributed this summer 1854 crisis to his carrying of "too much stock and too many responsibilities."[63] An alternative—and no less plausible—explanation is that his partner John Leslie, who kept the accounts, had either seriously mismanaged them or, even worse, actually embezzled funds from the company (as he did in 1857). Putnam had never served as accountant for any of his firms and generally did not keep a close eye on the financial books, an aloofness that would cost him dearly in 1857 and probably already did in 1854. Whatever the actual reason, for the third time in six months Putnam elected to go to the auction house to raise operating funds; this time, however, he had no choice but to put on the block properties that affected the core of his business: his publishing operations. He made this decision peremptorily, circulating his announcement through the trade only days before the sale took place and timing it to coincide with the end of the New York trade sale held in the latter half of August at Bangs, Brother and Company. As he well knew, that large seasonal event, with many of the major booksellers and publishers in the country in attendance, was the single best place for him to raise the funds he needed to pay his creditors. His situation was so dire, with rumors in the trade circulating that G. P. Putnam and Company would be forced to declare bankruptcy, that he resolved to sell off the stereotype plates and printed copies of the majority of the books on his publishing list. As it turned out, the sale of his properties was one of the largest in the history of the American book trade, with bids approaching the initial manufacturing costs of some of his choicest works and Putnam realizing a total revenue of $70,000. In the exchange of money for literary properties, however, many of his most important assets passed out of his hands: *Putnam's Home Cyclopedia* (which included his own *The World's Progress*), *Homes of American Authors, Homes of American Statesmen, Home Book of the Picturesque,* as well as works by Hawthorne, Layard, Sedgwick, Olmsted, Bremer, Bryant, Kirkland, Parkman, Kennedy, Silliman, Susan Cooper, and many others.[64]

That night, to express his thanks to his colleagues, Putnam hosted a trade dinner at the Astor House. It was just the kind of professional occasion that he enjoyed, a night of conviviality among friends and peers; the chief entertainment was provided by James Fields, who recited a humorous poem written for the occasion. In the days that followed the trade sale, salutations poured in from authors, publishers, and family. Fields, one of his closest friends in the profession, wrote to Bayard Taylor soon after returning to Boston: "We all feel sorry for Putnam. So clever and friendly a fellow, so much liked every where must be put on his legs again."[65] His cousin Elizabeth Peabody, who was in the process of getting settled in New Jersey and promised once "regulated" to invite the Putnams to visit her, wrote to commiserate with his reversal: "I was grieved to hear of your troubles but with your reputation and your talents I think adversity will be short lived with you."[66] The successful Philadelphia publisher George W. Childs, another of his closest associates in the trade, wrote him to offer congratulations on the results of the sale and to express his good will: "Without flattery I can say that you occupy the first position in our trade as a publisher and a gentleman."[67] Another friend and an occasional client, George W. Greene, also had words of solace and inspiration for Putnam: "Energy and talent like yours must work their way thro' worse things than this and I hope yet to see the day when you shall be as far above all your brothers of the trade in success as you are in the nobler qualities that deserve it." More important, Greene had a practical suggestion meant to reciprocate the act of kindness that Putnam had done for him during his time of distress: he offered to put Putnam in touch with a former student of his from Brown University who was looking to go into publishing and had $10,000 to invest in the operation.[68] There is no record, however, that Putnam accepted the offer.

The good will of the profession might temporarily have heartened Putnam, but there was no mistaking the sobering fact that the overall damage done to his company was serious and long lasting. In the days and weeks that followed, he scrambled to hold his business together. The single most important task he faced was to meet with his creditors and demonstrate to them that his firm was solvent. Describing himself as "humbled" on the eve of that fateful 15 September meeting, Putnam was able to reach an arrangement for debt extension that seemed to satisfy all sides.[69] The agreement was especially favorable to him, his creditors permitting him to pay back their loans on an interest-free basis and over periods ranging from six to twenty-four months.[70] Little wonder that Putnam emerged from the meeting pleased with the outcome, describing himself—in a revealing term—as "gratifi[ed]" by his treatment.[71] Once that agreement had been worked out, he could turn to his future prospects and reassure his remaining authors that he remained fully able to pursue their interests. Irving, who had good reason to be worried by the rumors about the financial health of his publisher, had sent his nephew Pierre Irving to Manhattan to look over Putnam's account books. Satisfied by Pierre that the situation was manageable, Irving determined to stick by the man who had given his works a new life.[72] So, to Putnam's relief and appreciation, did Taylor and the Warners. Here, for once, Putnam found that loyalty was a two-sided coin of "value" on which he could draw both in the marketplace and in personal relations. Beginning in 1854, he needed that asset more greatly than he could have foreseen.

Putnam survived the crisis with his operations considerably restricted but his spirits generally unaffected. His business affairs continued unabated; he published Taylor's *A Journey to Central Africa* the week following the 15 September meeting, and he pressed on with the publication of *Putnam's Monthly,* whose management he took more directly into his own hands shortly after the retrenchment of his firm. During these weeks, however, he was operating on a much more conservative basis. For the next year at least, Putnam cast a cautious publishing profile more like that of Wiley than that of the "go ahead" publisher he had been through much of his career. During this period his list was dominated more than ever by the works of Irving, Taylor, and Susan and Anna Warner. Fortunately for all concerned, virtually all their works proved to be profitable, and several, beginning with Taylor's *A Journey to Central Africa,* sold in the tens of thousands.

That book—and the two travelogues that soon followed—was the product of Taylor's longest expedition, an around-the-world voyage over the course of 1851–53 that an admiring Putnam described as an act of "putting a girdle round about the earth."[73] Taylor's letters back home had left his publisher salivating as early as Christmas 1852 at the prospect of new publishing ventures: "And what a traveller you are! Ledyard, Park, Stephens, Marco Polo, Sir John Mandeville, Capt. Wilkes, the Howadji, Waghorn, Mellville [*sic*], Layard, Capt. Cook, and (I was going to say) Gulliver himself, all combined into one volume duodecimo, and with large additions into the bargain. What books we shall have when you return!"[74] But first Putnam had to bide his time, since Taylor got no closer to the Western Hemisphere than Gibraltar before reversing direction, heading back east and eventually joining Commodore Perry on his historic trip to Japan.

When he finally got back to America in late 1853, he began work on the segment of the trip that had taken him up the Nile far into the African continent and immersed him in the cultures of various Arab and black African tribes. He had even cut back his hair near to the scalp and donned the local costume in preparation for his initiation into African mysteries; the 1854 Putnam edition of *A Journey to Central Africa* accordingly displayed a Brady daguerreotype of its author dressed in traditional Arab garb.[75] Taylor, however, was no nineteenth-century Lawrence of Arabia; there were distinct limits to his willingness or ability to leave behind his own social and cultural constructs. Early in his experience, he described how he randomly summoned a local "donkey-boy" in Alexandria "Abdallah" and then learned to his surprise that that actually was his name—or so the boy told Taylor and so Taylor believed.[76] The attitude of immunity with which he began his adventures at the mouth of the Nile adhered to him throughout his journey of thousands of miles up and down the river, leaving him largely unchanged when he emerged months later from his extended, initial encounter with Africa. His first act upon his return to Cairo was to dash at full speed from the boat through the city streets, knocking down people as he ran, on his way to the English embassy to collect his accumulated mail from home: "Was not that a sweet repayment for my five months in the heat and silence and mystery of mid-Africa, when I sat by my window, opening on the great square of Cairo, fanned by cool airs from the flowering lemon groves, with the words of home in my ears, and my heart beating a fervent response to the sunset call from the minarets: 'God is great! God is merciful!'"[77] Although he stated early in the book that as he sailed from Alexandria to Cairo America "seemed very dim and distant," as a writer he never lost sight of his home audience or contact with its expectations. That mind-set paid off. The work struck a receptive chord in the United States, where the book sold out its first printing on the day of publication and went quickly through second and third printings.[78]

Putnam lost no time in publishing Taylor's follow-up work, *The Lands of the Saracen,* in time for the holiday season; naturally, he brought it out in an edition uniform with *A Journey to Central Africa.*[79] But he could hardly allow himself to approach this holiday season with the same entrepreneurial zeal with which he had approached recent ones, when he had led off his list with such works as *Home Book of the Picturesque, Homes of American Authors, Homes of American Statesmen,* and the opening issue of *Putnam's Monthly.* In autumn 1854 he had only a handful of new projects scheduled to go into production late that year or early the next, and most of them were the low-risk affairs of well-established Putnam authors.[80] They included Melville's *Israel Potter* (reprinted with few changes from *Putnam's Monthly*), Susan Cooper's *The Rhyme and Reason of Country Life,* Irving's *Wolfert's Roost* (which Putnam advertised in the 12 February *Tribune* as having sold out its first printing on the day of publication), and a new volume of "Ellen Montgomery's Book Shelf." He also had on hand or in preparation new printings or editions of various established works, including novels and juveniles by the Warner sisters, the best-known novels by John Pendleton Kennedy, and new multivolume sets of the works of Oliver Goldsmith and Joseph Addison. And he continued to publish another type of safe sale, one valuable to him for its ability to generate steady income: Asa Gray's studies in botany and James Dana's in mineralogy, as well as a new edition of Cooper's *History of the Navy of the United States of America.* In a day of increasingly flashy advertising strategies, Putnam kept his firm's advertisements for these works relatively low-key (the house key, in general) and spare, using single item ads far more than he had in the past when his list was more expansive and G. P. Putnam ads commonly ran a half or even full page. Terms of publication seem not to have changed. Melville, for instance, received the usual 12 ½-percent royalties that Putnam generally offered his most valued authors, while Taylor and Irving continued on the terms they had been receiving.

The new strategy of pared down offerings and careful management proved successful, gradually restoring stability to Putnam's operations and allowing him to remain a viable publisher. Selling off *Putnam's Monthly* might well have contributed to this goal both financially and strategically, freeing Putnam from the excessive number of obligations on his money and time (although perhaps contracting his ability to re- cruit new authors and retain current ones). With fewer works to attend to, he could devote more time to their marketing and distribution, an aspect of the profession in which he had long excelled and to which he now dedicated a larger proportion of his resources and attention. He also took it upon himself to serve as the supplier of selected publica- tions by other publishers, including a variety of works for Ticknor and Fields and *Putnam's Monthly* for Dix and Edwards, the latter an agree- ment presumably reached at the time of its transfer.

During the first half of 1855, Putnam initiated no major new projects for his firm but concentrated on marketing the works already on its list. He did take the leading role, however, along with several other estab- lished New York publishers, in founding a new trade organization, the New York Book Publishers' Association. The most ambitious attempt in decades to organize the book publishing profession both in the city and in the country and the first since its growth into a modern industry, the Association was envisioned as a means of addressing various prob- lems arising from the decentralized status of the profession. The first discussions began informally in March among Putnam, his old friend William Appleton, and a few other New York publishers; those talks proved successful enough to lead to more formal meetings in subse- quent months, to which the whole book publishing trade was invited. The organizers then took their case to a general meeting at which the assembled publishers approved the planned Association and elected Appleton president, Albert Barnes vice president, Lowell Mason trea- surer, and Putnam secretary (the role he typically accepted in profes- sional organizations). Other early members included such old friends and associates as John Wiley, John Trow, Charles B. Norton, and Henry Ivison. By June most of the New York trade (with the significant excep- tion of the Harpers) had joined. By that time, the Association was ready to take on longstanding concerns about issues of pricing and distribution, which had proven particularly problematic at the major trade sales held regularly in New York, Philadelphia, and Cincinnati. Although very sizable amounts of books, stereotype plates, and stationery were often offered for sale at these events, the terms of exchange—lots often too small to interest big purchasers and a pricing system that allowed publishers to retract their lots if prices bid proved unsatisfactory— often kept away many of the larger companies. The Association leaders therefore decided to put the trade sales directly under their organization's supervision and to provide incentives sufficient to attract larger concentrations of publishers and their products, beginning with the September trade sales that would take place in Philadelphia and New York.[81] Once these preliminary measures were taken, Putnam sent off a circular to the major daily New York City newspapers informing the public of the new organization and advertising "the important and honorable business which [publishers] pursue."[82]

The Association took other steps as well to tighten the workings of the profession. It set up a room designed to serve as both a headquarters and a library and reading room in the Appleton Building on Broadway. Open on a daily basis with Charles Norton appointed as its librarian, the room doubled as a publishers' exhibition and reading room; members of the trade were encouraged to send Norton their latest publications for formal display and possible adoption by visiting booksellers, educators, and librarians. The Association also authorized and supervised the printing of the first independent trade journal in the United States, *American Publishers' Circular and Literary Gazette*. Beginning with its opening issue, *American Publishers' Circular* advertised itself as a central repository of publishers' advertisements, trade sale information, and general print-related stories, the lack of which had been lamented in recent years since the decline of *Norton's Literary Gazette* to little more than an advertising sheet for its proprietor and the closing of the Duyckincks' *Literary World*. Issued weekly, edited professionally, and printed handsomely with a fairly wide distribution, the *Circular* would prove to be the best trade paper the profession had yet seen (and would see before the founding of its successor, *Publishers' Weekly*).

The establishment of the reading room, the new procedures for trade sales, and the founding of *American Publishers' Circular* were all collective decisions taken and acted upon in committee and general meetings. But one further initiative taken early on by the Association seems more identifiably Putnam's alone or primarily: the decision to organize under its auspices an elaborate professional gathering of American authors and publishers to celebrate the rise of American letters.[83] The date chosen was the evening of 27 September, a day timed to coincide with the New York trade sale. The idea of an authors-publishers dinner was not entirely new; Putnam had played a leading role in organizing New York City's previous tribute to authors, the Booksellers' Dinner of 1837 at the City Hotel (an event he fondly remembered for the remainder of his life). But in the years since, "booksellers" had given way to "publishers," and "letters" had taken on shapes and dimensions unforeseen just a few decades before. Mindful of these developments, Putnam wished to stage an elaborate public celebration that would do justice to what he proudly saw as a new era of culture in the United States.

Although he was scheduled to spend part of September on a business trip in New England, he took the primary responsibility for planning the affair and superintending its various details ("and these things make work for some one"). Authorized by the Association to make the necessary preparations and provided with a budget of $4,000 raised primarily from the subscriptions of local publishers, Putnam arranged with Charles Stetson (the "prince of caterers") of the Astor House to provide the food, settings, and music for a sit-down dinner planned for a guest list Putnam expected to exceed six hundred people. He authorized Stetson to make his arrangements "liberally and in the best manner," allotting him $2,000 from his budget for doing so and delegating him full responsibility to attend to all details relating to the food and musical entertainment.[84] It seems likely, however, that Putnam attended to the site selection himself. In contracting to rent the Crystal Palace, he might have assumed that the assemblage would be too large to be hosted comfortably in any of the city's hotels or public halls, or perhaps he simply preferred to stage the dinner in the largely vacant building, which had been officially closed in late 1854 and put up for sale but, until a buyer was found, was rented out for special occasions. Although he was hardly one to pursue a purely personal motive when executing a public cause, he could not have been unaware of the symmetry that returned him on a second memorable occasion to that building, nor would he have been unaware of its importance in his life when he stood under its dome to deliver the most important speech of his life.

Interior View of the New York Crystal Palace for the Exhibition of the Industry of all Nations.
TAKEN ON THE FIRST OF DECEMBER 1853.

11.   Interior view of Crystal Palace, lithography of Nagel and Weingaertner.
(Courtesy Eno Collection, New York Public Library)

In the weeks leading up to the dinner, Putnam also took charge of the formal correspondence, sending out dozens, possibly hundreds, of letters of invitation as well as suggestions to chosen individuals for formal toasts and speeches. The decisions he made and the responses he received tell a great deal about Putnam's and his contemporaries' views of authorship and letters. By the standards of the day, he clearly held to a wide generic definition of both and to a broad idea of the social periphery for letters, inviting not only a wide array of professional authors and members of the trade but congressmen, diplomats, large city mayors, clergymen, college presidents, and newspaper and magazine editors. No doubt, legitimacy was very much on his mind, as he sought to invest authorship, publishing, and letters with the mantle of the highest, most comprehensive authority. His choice of speakers, some of whom he had visited in New York and Boston in the days and weeks preceding the festival, was revealing. They included Senator Charles Sumner, whom Putnam had known for years but less intimately than he knew Sumner's brother George; Judge William Duer (one-time president of Columbia College), Rev. J. Adams (at whose house Putnam visited earlier in the day); William Cullen Bryant; Oliver Wendell Holmes; Rev. Edwin Chapin, who complained privately to Putnam about the topic he was asked to respond to; Rev. Henry Bellows; Edward Everett; and Robert Winthrop (ex-chairman of the Library Committee of the House of Representatives and a strong proponent of international copyright). And, predictably, he asked James Fields to recite a poem written for the occasion.[85]

Inclusive as it must have seemed to him, the catholicity of Putnam's taste had its distinct limits. The guest list was overwhelmingly white, Anglo-Saxon, and Protestant. The only clergymen invited to speak were Protestant, and there were probably few members of other religious groups seated either at the tables set up for the official guests of the Association or in the upstairs galleries relegated to spectators. No Catholic or Jew was invited to speak, and the only identifiable Jew on the invitation list was Abraham Hart, who would otherwise have been present had he not chosen to stay home to observe Sukkot. No identifiable African Americans made his guest list; Putnam overlooked the black author most likely to be invited, Frederick Douglass, whose *My Bondage and My Freedom* was issued the month before by a trade publisher and was currently receiving unusual publicity and registering strong sales.[86] Nor did he invite a number of highly idiosyncratic writers, such as Whitman (whose recently published *Leaves of Grass* received close notice in the current issue of *Putnam's Monthly* and probably had been offered for sale at the just concluded New York trade sale) and Henry David Thoreau (whose *Cape Cod* was currently appearing in *Putnam's*). And although many women writers were included among the guests of the Association and seated at its official tables, not to mention a much larger proportion of women seated in the galleries, Putnam offered none of them the honor of addressing the audience—even in response to the formal toast made to female authorship. In all likelihood, none of these distinctions (except for a formalistic one about gender) probably occurred to him. He did, however, give the evening an added dimension of inclusiveness by treating as public documents to be read aloud at the Crystal Palace and/or printed in the newspapers the congratulatory letters of various writers who were unable to attend in person, including Melville, Emerson, Prescott, Lieber, Mann, and Simms.

The dinner took place in the building's north nave (as had the opening ceremony of the Exhibition two years before), which had been sectioned off and decorated for the occasion. The chief officers of the Association sat with the invited speakers and selected dignitaries at a long table placed on a raised dais toward the center of the room, with a statue of Gutenberg and his printing press positioned opposite the president's place. Six more tables for guests and members of the trade were positioned in front of the dais in parallel lines, while hundreds of spectators sat in the galleries overhead. Portraits of the pioneer publishers Mathew Carey and Daniel Appleton hung from beneath the upper galleries, and gaslights spelled out the motto of the evening: "Honor to Genius."

In both its idea and its actuality, the evening was one of the greatest personal and collective triumphs of Putnam's life. As he looked out from his seat at the speakers' dais onto the assembled audience, he would have seen the largest and most conspicuous gathering to date of American authors and publishers (an observation actually drawn by Appleton in the evening's first speech). In addition, he would have seen much of his professional life gathered around him, with Putnam authors and associates past and present assembled in force: Washington Irving, Bayard Taylor, Susan and Anna Warner, John Pendleton Kennedy, Evert Duyckinck, Erastus Ellsworth, Charles Briggs, Caroline Kirkland, Frederick Perkins, and George W. Greene, to name only

12.   Second page of Putnam's letter to Charles Stetson of the Astor House arranging for the catering of the 27 September 1855 authors-publishers dinner organized by Putnam at the Crystal Palace. (Courtesy Manuscripts and Archives Division, New York Public Library)

those people most directly connected to his fortunes. Also present were men and women who oversaw various of his personal rites of passage: John Frederick Schroeder, who had received him as a teenager and given the necessary affirmation for the publication of *Chronology;* Orville Dewey, who had officiated at the Putnams' wedding, and Lydia Sigourney, who had blessed it; and David Wells, the gifted economist and friend who was soon to become a partner in G. P. Putnam and Company. Victorine, who accompanied the wife of George W. Greene, was presumably seated in the gallery opposite and above the speakers' dais.

The long night of celebration consisted of a multicourse dinner and a long series of speeches, toasts, responses to toasts, and musical interludes. Following the benediction given by Alonzo Potter (Episcopalian bishop of Pennsylvania) and the serving of supper, the official program began with the welcoming speech of William Appleton on behalf of the New York Book Publishers' Association. Appleton spoke of the assemblage as "the genial gathering of kindred spirits" and of the special calling of his profession to serve in "exercising a wholesome guardianship over the literature of the country." He was followed by Putnam who had prepared himself carefully to give the major speech of the night, having written it well in advance, drawn proof from the printer, and sent copies to respected friends (such as Everett) for suggestions.

After various pleasantries, he proceeded to articulate the core ideal of his career: "The interests of the writers and publishers, and sellers of books, in this great and thriving country, are daily growing in magnitude and importance;—and those interests are, or should be, mutual and identical." Drawing on his long years of service to American letters, he recited his meliorist view of American history and culture in considerable detail before as receptive an audience as he was likely to find (he invited much of it). In a setting and occasion made to order, he centered his remarks around a celebration of American cultural accomplishments and of the publishing profession that disseminated them to a literate public. He did this primarily in the form of a roll call, naming the outstanding doers (some present) and deeds in the various fields of the arts, letters, and science and giving their sum total in the language of technology: "Why, sir, the sheets from our book-presses alone, in a single year, would reach nearly twice round the globe; and if we add the periodicals and newspapers, the issues of our presses in about eighteen months would make a belt, two feet wide, printed on both sides, which would stretch from New York to the Moon!" He then closed by reciting the evening's seventeen official toasts: "the Republic of Letters," "American Literature," "Literature and Statesmanship," "Our Lady-Guests and Their Writings," "the Clergy," "Our Men of Science," "the Fine Arts," "the Bench and the Bar," "Institutions of Learning," "the Printing Press," "Editors of the Newspaper Press," "Periodical Literature," "English Literature and Our Guests Who Illustrate It," "the Sister Cities of Boston, Philadelphia, and New York," "the Publishers of Boston," "the Publishers of Philadelphia," and "the Booksellers of the Union."[87]

On a night of seamless harmonies, when previous or current discord between authors and publishers, free market traders and moral guardians, scientists and religionists, proslavery and antislavery activists was forgotten, Putnam was clearly in his element. Although the festivities continued well into the night, he no doubt would have been pleased to preserve their spirit indefinitely. Years later he expressed the thought in public, which must have occurred to him many times in private, that many of the speeches and letters of that night "should be preserved in some permanent shape for future reference, for they were full of good things, and of special interest as illustrative of the progress of American book-making."[88] Although in the past he had published memorial and occasional works honoring particular individuals or events, he did not have the funds himself—assuming that he had the inclination—to publish the documents relating to the Crystal Palace authors-publishers dinner, nor did the Association set him up to do so on its auspices. He did, however, pass on texts of letters and perhaps of speeches to the newspaper press and to the editor of the *American Publishers' Circular*, which covered the event in their next issues. He also preserved the originals of the documents among his private papers. By a curious quirk of fate these documents eventually were given to the New York Public Library, which rose on the ground previously occupied by the Crystal Palace.

With the glow of that night fading, Putnam returned to the business of making a living. He had worked himself into exhaustion earlier in the month, coming down with chills and fever that limited the contacts he had hoped to make during his trip to Newport and Boston, and he was still far from well at the time of the Crystal Palace dinner. He remained so weak in October from a renewed bout of illness following a return trip to Boston that Victorine, who rarely concerned herself with his professional affairs and hardly ever accompanied him on business trips, joined him on a publishing and book selling trip to Indiana and Ohio that he considered too important to be delayed.[89] That trip was probably connected with Bayard Taylor's newest venture, a massive travelogue compendium called *Cyclopaedia of Modern Travel* that Taylor had contracted for with the Cincinnati firm of Moore, Wilstach, and Keys. That ambitious firm had suggested the project to Taylor during his winter 1855 Midwestern lecture tour and proposed to sell the work by subscription.[90] A writer who doubled as an entrepreneur, Taylor placed high hopes on the venture, anticipating that he might earn as much as $10,000 if the publishers fulfilled their promise to set a price of $4 for a work exceeding 900 pages (which Taylor made sure that it did).[91] The proposition also intrigued Putnam, who advised Taylor throughout the negotiations and asked his help in persuading his Cincinnati publishers to grant G. P. Putnam and Company distribution rights under its own imprint to the eastern trade. Effecting that arrangement was a good turn that he advised Taylor would contribute to everyone's interest, a point that he no doubt repeated to the publishers during his own trip.[92] It was not until 1856, however, that the *Cyclopaedia* was published under the proposed scheme, and not until 1857 that Taylor saw his first royalties, which fell far short of projected earnings. Meanwhile, Taylor had the compensation of a steady income from his previous books, which, Putnam reported, "continue to go—not with the spasmodic or steam engine fashion of the quacks, but with a steady sober demand," *Central Africa* having reached 12,000 and *Saracens* 8,000 copies by the end of 1854. At the same time, his newer works published with Putnam and Ticknor and Fields were also reportedly doing well.[93]

As his financial affairs improved over the course of 1855–56, Putnam gradually eased away from the policy of fiscal and publishing conservatism that had helped him to survive his 1854 crisis. With the return of a substantial infusion of income from his core group of steady sellers came an upsurge of his general optimism. Perhaps the strongest expression of it was his pent-up expectation for Irving's long-awaited, multivolume *Washington,* which Putnam frankly thought "ought to bring a fortune to both of us."[94] That prediction, however, proved premature when Irving was unable to finish the project, as planned, in 1855, which limited Putnam's publication options and reduced his volume of sales.

About the same time or perhaps a short while later, Putnam also raised the subject with Irving of a possible autobiography. Putnam had been urged to do so by his new friend S. Austin Allibone, with whom he had become close in 1854–55. Allibone, then hard at work on his monumental *Critical Dictionary of English Literature and British and American Authors,* had initiated the relationship, writing to Putnam to express his appreciation for him as one of the great publishers of their generation ("the Murrays, the Longmans, the Bentleys, the Careys, and the Putnams of modern times").[95] The two men quickly passed from pleasantries to free exchanges of personal and professional views, then to visits to each other's homes. When Allibone came to visit Putnam in Yonkers in June 1855, Putnam took him at his request to meet Irving. Allibone had a pressing reason for the introduction because, as he informed his new friend, he was eager "to write a good literary biography of the most distinguished American now living."[96] Never to carry out that plan, he did write a good sketch of Irving for his *Critical Dictionary,* but by 1856–57 he was importuning Putnam to persuade Irving to do himself what no one else could do as well. As though Putnam was unaware of its commercial value, Allibone reminded him that an Irving autobiography "would make you many thousands of dollars undoubtedly."[97] But Allibone was unaware that Irving was already overwhelmed with the Washington project; no Irving autobiography was ever to get written.

With the gradual restoration of his fiscal stability, Putnam became less dependent on the works of any one or two authors. While Taylor continued to fill his list with new works at a prolific rate and Irving augured good sales into the foreseeable future, Putnam moved toward a renewed diversification of his list during 1855–57. One of his biggest gambles in this context was his purchase at the September 1855 trade sale of the stereotype plates and remaindered stock of the multivolume *Iconographic Encyclopaedia of Science, Literature, and Art.* That monumental work of German origin had originally been published in Leipzig by Brockhaus, then translated and adapted for American readers in an 1851 edition by Spencer Baird, assistant secretary of the Smithsonian Institution.[98] It is not hard to see why it appealed to a publisher of Putnam's character. Furnished with a wealth of all-purpose information for the mid-nineteenth-century general reader, lavishly illustrated, and handsomely presented, the *Iconographic Encyclopaedia* could easily have been mistaken for a G. P. Putnam reference work. Much as he admired such projects intellectually and valued them commercially for their long shelf lives, Putnam did not have even remotely enough funds to initiate the publication of a reference work of this sort, no less the kind of general American encyclopedia that the Appletons would soon launch under the direction of Charles Dana and George Ripley. Given his operating constraints, the acquisition of the *Iconographic Encyclopaedia* ready-made was the next best thing. Furthermore, it was a work, as Baird noted in his introduction, that could be read "as a series of text-books, capable of being used as such, and to which recourse may be had for all the general information required on a given subject."[99] Putnam might well have seen it as a commercially attractive investment for that very reason, since he quickly offered the work to the trade either as a multivolume set or in eleven constituent parts bound and sold as separate volumes.[100]

He also had on hand during 1855–57 several parallel kinds of series publications in the general sciences. One was the set of works generated by the United States Exploring Expedition under Charles Wilkes that Putnam published in 1856–57. Putnam's edition of the *Narrative* of the expedition was a lavish production, issued in a five-volume set or in parts, fully illustrated with line engravings, woodcuts, and steel vignettes.[101] Another—and clearly interrelated—set of publications was the individual works by two of the leading scientist-authors of the time, James Dana of Yale (himself a chief researcher for the expedition) and Asa Gray of Harvard. "Dana on mineralogy" and "Gray on botany" were already not only standard texts but even standard phrases in the book trade of the time.[102] (Dana's *Manual of Mineralogy* was reprinted as recently as 1978.) Both men were longtime Putnam (and, before that, Wiley and Putnam) authors, but now with his slimmed-down commitments Putnam devoted closer attention to the publication and sale of their works.

Gray in particular fit Putnam's category of "author-friends," and his books that of "works of high character."[103] Putnam had known him since his first year in London, when he took Gray to visit the Houses of Parliament and other tourist attractions and shifted the responsibility from Gray to himself of purchasing a set of books for the library of the University of Michigan. An ambitious young scientist at the outset of his career, Gray was already planning at the time to publish his first work with Wiley and Putnam and joked to Putnam about their joint prospect: "As Murray's fame is derived from Byron, so shall you be immortalized and known to all posterity as the publisher of the celebrated Dr. Gray!!!"[104] His prediction came closer to the mark than either man could then have known, as in subsequent years he became a "standardized" American author and Putnam his publisher of choice for nearly two decades. Their relationship was tested, however, in March 1854, when at the New York trade sale Putnam made the nearly instantaneous decision to sell the plates (but not the future rights) of Gray's *Genera of the Plants of the United States.* He also had to stop payment on a company note written to cover his purchase of Gray's botany volumes for the Wilkes expedition.[105] But Putnam never considered giving up Gray as a client. He retained control over the more popular *Botanical Text-Book,* and after the trade sale he moved quickly to repurchase the *Genera.* Furthermore, his first initiative after exiting the September 1854 meeting with his creditors was to encourage Gray to produce a new edition, pledging himself to "make a new and vigorous effort to render this work more profitable" than it had yet been.[106] A year later the two men reached terms on the publication of three works by Gray, for which Putnam leased rights in exchange for paying Gray an annuity.

Another group of new works prominent on Putnam's list belonged to his longtime favorite category of travel literature. For nearly a decade, he had been better established in travel literature than in any other genre, although he never devised a mechanism for taking commercial advantage of that concentration as he had for clusters of works in other genres. The most important new title on his list in that genre was his 1856 edition of Lieutenant Richard Burton's *Personal Narrative of a Pilgrimage to El-Medinah and Meccah.* The first American edition, Putnam's was actually a condensed version of the three-volume London original, which he issued in a one-volume format introduced by Bayard Taylor. That edition of Burton proved popular, although not to the same extent that Layard's works had been, which may be why it remained unchallenged on the American market as long as Putnam retained control of it. He also published several works on Japan—"that double-bolted land," as Melville called it in *Moby-Dick*—that Commodore Perry's much-publicized expedition of 1852–54 was destined to open to the United States. Both books were the product of men who had accompanied Perry. The earlier of the two was *A Visit to India, China, and Japan, in the Year 1853* (1855) by Taylor, who had joined Perry's expedition en route in Shanghai. The other was *Graphic Scenes in the Japan Expedition* (1856) by the expedition's chief artist William Heine, whose book was accompanied by ten color plates. The chief prize, however, in the acquisition of print rights to the expedition went to Appleton's, which published the trade edition of the *Narrative of the Expedition* compiled by Putnam's friend Francis Hawks from the journals of Perry, Taylor, and others.

Putnam also published a fair amount of fiction during this period. The most important new novel on his list was Fredrika Bremer's *Hertha,* which had been promised to him long before but whose publication was delayed until summer 1856. His relations with Bremer had remained good in the years since their previous collaboration, during which time Bremer retained her affection for and loyalty to him. Remembering past battles for her works, Putnam attempted to minimize the risk of competition by printing prepublication advertisements that excerpted her letter authorizing him as her American publisher.[107] Early the next year, he published the first novel, *The Bay Path; a Tale of New England Colonial Life,* of Josiah Holland, then the coeditor of the Springfield *Republican* and soon to be a best-selling novelist (but only after he left Putnam and became a Scribner author). Most of the fiction on Putnam's list, however, came from the already established works of such writers as Irving, Sedgwick, and the Warners, which he sold both in large quantities at trade sales and by various retail combinations. In addition he assembled various of his juvenile works and sold them as parts in Putnam's Story Library, which he issued in 1856–57. During the same period he also resumed active promotion of Putnam's Railway Classics, which likewise drew primarily from the best-known works by Irving.

In early 1856 he made two changes to his company. He relocated the business from Park Place to the upper floor of 321 Broadway, a move that was made in tandem with Dix and Edwards. The rooms were more spacious than his old ones, and the location a bit farther uptown placed him in the current of the general move of the trade up the avenue. Within a week or so of the move he took David Wells into the firm as a junior partner, adding his investment of $10,000 to the general operating funds of the company and his various books to the firm's list.[108] But Wells turned out to be as comically ill-fitted for the profession as Theodore Roosevelt would be for the company in the 1880s, and by mutual consent with Putnam he withdrew himself and his investment from the company in January 1857.

Busy as he was restructuring and revitalizing his business after its near collapse in 1854, Putnam remained as much a good citizen of the profession as he had been in years past. Having accrued by then more than two decades of experience and the broad respect of his peers, he was widely recognized in and out of the trade as one of its senior figures and its most knowledgeable spokesman. After playing the role of cofounder of the New York Book Publishers' Association, he remained the most active member of its executive committee, to which he was annually reelected. Other than day-to-day affairs, his concerns were primarily with three matters: the trade journal, trade sales, and international copyright. He had been eager to see the establishment of an independent trade journal and supported the *American Publishers' Circular* with both his advertisements and his influence. He was less satisfied, however, with the state of the trade sales, which even under the direction of the Association failed to attract the support of the entire profession, the Harpers and a fair number of other houses holding out and staging their own sales at a separate location. As had been his practice before they had come under the supervision of the Association, Putnam supported the trade sales with large invoices of his firm's publications.[109] He also supported them on a collegial basis, as when he stood up in the middle of the spring 1856 sale in New York to defend the new rules that governed their operations, as well as the other initiatives taken by the organization, as being conducive of the "greatest good of the greatest number."[110]

He also spoke his mind formally about the unsatisfactory state of copyright, which remained an agitated issue in the mid-1850s, with various court cases testing property definitions in matters of translations and dramatic works and trade conflicts flaring over territorial barriers to literary property. Using his position as an officer of the Association, Putnam offered a resolution at its monthly meeting on 12 November 1856, "that in the opinion of this Association it would be highly desirable for the interests of Literature and the Book Trade, that an International Copyright Law should be passed, with such stipulations and restrictions as would secure, mutually, a just and equitable protection to the mechanical interests involved in the question, both here and in Europe."[111] At the next month's meeting, he raised the issue again and was seconded by his fellow officer Lowell Mason, who gave a long speech supporting the resolution.[112] They did not move, however, for a vote on the resolution, which came in for further discussion at meetings well into 1857. Even if the editor of *American Publishers' Circular* was speaking accurately when he claimed that they were eventually able to generate consensus among their colleagues in the organization, the practical value of any such resolution was limited.[113]

It is more likely, however, that the paper's editor was making the same problematic assumption as Putnam and his allies in believing that the Association could and did speak for the entire profession. In truth, an organization that had its headquarters in the home of its president and that was boycotted by the largest member of its trade could no more claim to represent the profession on copyright than it could on trade sales. That fact should have become clear to the Association officers when a group of Boston publishers mobilized to present a petition to the Senate taking an opposing position on the copyright issue or when a competing trade sale was organized by nonmember publishers. Understood in a broader context, such conflicts were actually only one part of a larger struggle in the late-antebellum book industry, as well-intentioned publishers like Putnam and his allies attempted to arrogate authority to themselves over the entire industry. Their easy assumption, however, that they could automatically command the allegiance of publishers outside the Northeast and impose their own middle-class norms on publishers operating outside the "good books" market was bound to come into conflict with the realities of a more heterogeneous population, more varied reading tastes, and a more volatile marketplace than they typically anticipated.

Putnam entered spring 1857 as optimistic about the prospects for his firm as he had been since his reversals in 1854. With business brisk early in the year, he was already making plans for the next two seasons, which were to include new works promised by Taylor, busy as ever turning his latest set of travels into publications (and himself eager as ever to market them), and the fourth volume of Irving's *Washington*. In May, however, he received the news that his friends and neighbors, Dix and Edwards, had closed their doors and declared bankruptcy. That report touched Putnam, who liked Dix and revered Curtis. He was particularly surprised to learn that after their failure Curtis, who at Dix and Edwards had continued his customary policy of working as an editor without assuming a financial stake, agreed to take his chances as an active partner and investor in the reconstituted firm of Miller and Curtis. That prospect left Putnam, who had never had a partner as congenial as he found Curtis, contemplating the thought: "How I shd. have gloried in having such a man for a partner!"[114] Two months later, the thought came back to haunt him when John Leslie drowned during a Fourth of July picnic.[115] Distracted by the loss of his young partner of four years, Putnam was stunned to discover in the days that followed as he began to pore over the account books that Leslie, who had the authority to write his name on company checks and notes, had diverted large sums to personal speculation and had drained the firm of capital. At first Putnam was unsure how serious his situation was. As late as mid-July he was hopeful that he could steer his way through the crisis, although he confessed to Asa Gray how unclear he remained about even the basic facts: "[Leslie] had (unfortunately) so entirely the management of our accounts and finances, that I have not been able to unravel some important matters known only to himself, or to keep engagements which he had made without my knowledge."[116] Ironically, the family's Staten Island pastor, Alexander Mercer, who had apparently invested in the firm through Leslie, had suspected him of wrongdoing for some time and was finding his suspicions confirmed even as Putnam was figuring out the details and extent of the embezzlement.[117]

On 9 July the New York Book Publishers' Association offered a collective resolution lamenting "the sudden and afflicting dispensation which has removed from our number our former associate and friend," and many of its individual members appeared at Leslie's funeral that afternoon. Putnam was no doubt among them, but in the days to follow he anxiously began consolidating his accounts and making good on bills come due.[118] Unlike 1854, however, Putnam was operating under the worst possible financial conditions: a general economic contraction of historic proportions pressed creditors and debtors across the country into one tightened chain of mutual obligation and unforgiveness. The Panic of 1857 ended the prolonged prosperity that the American publishing industry had enjoyed for a decade and a half. Although individual seasons had been slow and individual firms had languished, there had been no sudden, prolonged downturn comparable to that which swept over the trade in the second half of 1857, compelling firm after firm—Fowler and Wells, Dix and Edwards, John P. Jewett—to close their doors and driving the volume of business down precipitously for those firms fortunate enough to survive. Caught in the middle of this squeeze, Putnam found himself by September unable to raise enough funds to pay off those lenders who called in their loans to him. As a result, for the second time in three years, he was forced to assemble his creditors and open his accounts to their inspection. This time, however, he had no recourse but to watch as his business was forced into receivership.

Notes

1. Hall's experience with the *Illustrated Catalogue of the Great Exhibition* might have been a portent. It sold well but did not cover its lavish production costs, seriously undermining Hall's finances; *Dictionary of National Biography* (London: Oxford University Press, 1967–68), 8:972.

2. This illustration passed down inside one of the folio autographs albums assembled by GHP toward the turn of the century and is now part of GPP-P. (It is located with the Crystal Palace correspondence at the end of the "C" file.)

3. GPP to Theodore Sedgwick [president of the Association], 13 November 1852; GPP-P.

4. GPP to Theodore Sedgwick, 1 December [1852]; GPP-P.

5. See, e.g., his announcement in the *Literary World* 12 (12 February 1853): 134.

6. GPP was on good terms with both Benjamin Sillimans, father and son. He had visited them in New Haven numerous times during his business trips to New England. The father was one of the most distinguished and influential scientists in pre–Civil War America. GPP published his travelogue *A Visit to Europe* in 1851 within weeks of the opening of the Crystal Palace.

7. Silliman to GPP, 31 March 1853; GPP-P.

8. The term comes from the editors' preface; B. Silliman, Jr., and C. R. Goodrich, eds., *The World of Science, Art, and Industry Illustrated from Examples in the New-York Exhibition, 1853–54* (New York: G. P. Putnam and Company, 1854), xi. (Subsequently cited by its more familiar name, the *Illustrated Record*.)

9. *Official Catalogue of the New-York Exhibition of the Industry of All Nations* (New York: G. P. Putnam and Company, 1853), 6. (Subsequently cited as *Catalogue*.)

10. *Illustrated Record,* 34. This fact was also mentioned in the *Catalogue,* 33–34.

11. *Illustrated Record,* 67–68.

12. *Catalogue,* 62.

13. The texts of his prayer and the major speeches that followed were printed the next day in the local newspapers; see, for instance, the New York *Tribune,* 15 July 1853, 5; and the New York *Times,* 15 July 1853, 1.

14. New York *Times,* 18 July 1853, 1.

15. See, for instance, the lead article ("Progress of the Exhibition") in the New York *Times,* 21 July 1853, 1.

16. *Illustrated Record,* 7. This fact was also mentioned in the *Catalogue,* 33–34.

17. "Employments for Women," New York *Tribune,* 16 July 1853, 6.

18. He publicized this fact in his advertisements, in the *Illustrated Record,* and even a decade later in his reminiscences. See, respectively, *Albion* 13 (29 April 1854): 203, and *Norton's Literary Gazette and Publishers' Circular,* n.s. 1 (1 March 1854): 128; *Illustrated Record,* v; and "Rough Notes of Thirty Years in the Trade," *American Publishers' Circular and Literary Gazette,* octavo series 1 (1 August 1863): 259.

19. *Illustrated Record,* v.

20. Ibid., vi.

21. GPP to Theodore Sedgwick, 15 February 1853; GPP-P.

22. GPP to Theodore Sedgwick, 1 December [1852]; GPP-P.

23. "The American Crystal Palace," *Illustrated Magazine of Art* 2 (July-December 1853): 259.

24 A. H. Saxon, *P. T. Barnum: The Legend and the Man* (New York: Columbia University Press, 1989), 189.

25. "Rough Notes," 259.

26. GHP, *George Palmer Putnam,* 2:3.

27. P. T. Barnum to GPP, n.d.; GPP-P.

28. One way he tried to sell off his edition was to publish the *Illustrated Record* in a uniformly illustrated edition with the *Catalogue* of the Exhibition and with his firm's *A Day in the Crystal Palace.* Alternatively, he paired the *Illustrated Record* with his firm's *Annotated Catalogue* and sold them together for $5. Yet another ploy was to offer it in combination with other of his publications, the most obvious pairing being with *Putnam's Monthly,* a work he could reasonably see as addressed to a comparable audience of cultured, nationalistic readers. As early as November 1853, Putnam was offering to sell bound copies of the magazine for the following year together with unbound copies of the *Illustrated Record* for $5, a sharp discount from the normal individual prices of $3 unbound or ($4 bound) for *Putnam's Monthly* and $4.50 for the bound *Illustrated Record* (upon its publication the following spring). As late as spring 1854, he was also offering it in a single bound volume together with his firm's new *Science, Fine Art, and Mechanism Illustrated* for $6.50, the latter also bound and sold separately at $3.50. This information comes primarily from advertisements that ran during 1853–54 in *Norton's Literary Gazette and Publishers' Circular,* the *Albion,* and the New York *Tribune.*

29. *Homes of American Statesmen* (New York: G. P. Putnam and Company, 1853), iii.

30. Ibid., iv.

31. GPP, "Washington Irving," *Harper's Weekly* 15 (27 May 1871): 495.

32. Ralph M. Aderman, Herbert L. Kleinfield, and Jenifer S. Banks, eds., *Washington Irving: Letters,* 4 vols. (Boston: Twayne, 1978–82), 4:344.

33. Edited versions of the letter were published by Pierre Irving, ed., *The Life and Letters of Washington Irving,* 4 vols. (New York: G. P. Putnam, 1862–64), 4:120–21; and J. C. Derby, *Fifty Years among Authors, Books and Publishers* (New York: W. Carleton and Company, 1884), 308. GHP reproduced a slightly edited facsimile of the letter in his *Authors and Publishers: A Manual of Suggestions for Beginners in Literature* (New York: G. P. Putnam's Sons, 1883), 9–11.

34. See his advertisement, *Norton's Literary Gazette and Publishers' Circular* n.s. 2 (2 April 1855): 146.

35. GPP, "Washington Irving," 495.

36. Stanley T. Williams, *The Life of Washington Irving,* 2 vols. (New York: Oxford University Press, 1935), 2:218–19.

37. Aderman, et al., eds., *Letters,* 4:530–31.

38. GHP, *George Palmer Putnam,* 2:379.

39. On this stage of its printing history, see Jacob Blanck and Michael Winship, comps., *Bibliography of American Literature,* 9 vols. (New Haven: Yale University Press, 1955–91), 8:150–51.

40. Taylor to J. B. Phillips, 16 October 1846; Pierpont Morgan Library.

41. Marie Hansen-Taylor and Horace E. Scudder, eds., *Life and Letters of Bayard Taylor,* 2 vols. (Boston: Houghton, Mifflin and Company, 1885), 1:208.

42. *Norton's Literary Gazette and Publishers' Circular* 2 (15 August 1852): 164.

43. Anna B. Warner, *Susan Warner* (New York: G. P. Putnam's Sons, 1909), 351.

44. GHP, *George Palmer Putnam,* 374.

45. Henry Whiting Warner had actually previously published *An Inquiry into the Moral and Religious Character of the American Government* with Wiley and Putnam (1838).

46. "The Story of Ellen Montgomery's Bookshelf," *Mr. Rutherford's Children* (New York: G. P. Putnam and Company, 1854), 5–7.

47. The copy of *Wolfert's Roost* (New York: G. P. Putnam and Company, 1855) at the American Antiquarian Society has this advertisement. It was placed in an advertising catalogue for the firm's works dated February 1855 and tipped into the back of the book.

48. Everett's letter of 25 March 1853, saved by GPP and now contained in GPP-P, is published in GHP, *George Palmer Putnam,* 2:261.

49. The letters of GPP and of Hart appear, respectively, in *Norton's Literary Gazette and Publishers' Circular* 3 (15 April 1853): 62–64; and (15 June 1853): 99. The following discussion of their views is based primarily on these texts.

50. When called on a few years later to address the profession at the Boston trade sale on behalf of the New York contingent, GPP began his remarks by claiming that his peers were unfortunate "to be represented by the one least able to speak for them—the one whose oratorial abilities are not yet developed." He thought well enough of his remarks, however, to pass them on for publication in the Boston newspapers; GPP-P (box 11, scrapbook, p. 41).

51. "International Copyright," *Norton's Literary Gazette and Publishers' Circular* 3 (15 February 1853): 18.

52. *Norton's Literary Gazette and Publishers' Circular* 3 (15 April 1853): 62.

53. Their letter was published only after it became public knowledge that the Senate had chosen to postpone consideration of the proposed treaty; *Literary World* 12 (2 April 1853): 268–69.

54. The sketch that follows is drawn primarily from family memoirs, especially GHP, *George Palmer Putnam,* 1:364–65, 385–99; GHP, *Memories of My Youth, 1844–1865* (New York: G. P. Putnam's Sons, 1914), 46–55; and Ruth Putnam, ed., *Life and Letters of Mary Putnam Jacobi* (New York: G. P. Putnam's Sons, 1925), 34–43. GHP is mistaken in dating the move as having occurred in 1855; *George Palmer Putnam,* 1:364.

55. The series ran through volume 6 (July-December 1855).

56. GHP, *George Palmer Putnam,* 1:399.

57. Autobiographical sketch; Mary Putnam Jacobi Papers, Schlesinger Library, Radcliffe College (p. 5).

58. Ruth Putnam, ed., *Mary Putnam Jacobi,* 35.

59. Ibid., 36.

60. Catherine Hunt Putnam, *The Book of Genesis, by Moses* (New York: G. P. Putnam and Company, 1854).

61. A list of purchasers is given in *Norton's Literary Gazette and Publishers' Circular,* n.s. 1 (1 May 1854): 215.

62. For the date of the sale, see the New York *Times,* 9 May 1854, 1; *Norton's Literary Gazette and Publishers' Circular,* n.s. 1 (15 April 1854): 185 and (1 May 1854): 215. One of his friends (presumably either Godwin or Bryant) at the New York *Evening Post* took the initiative to put in a good word for Putnam; New York *Evening Post,* 11 May 1854, 2.

George L. McKay lists a unique copy of the auction catalogue as in the possession of the New York Public Library, but that copy is unlocatable and presumably lost; *American Book Auction Catalogues, 1713–1934: A Union List* (New York: New York Public Library, 1937), 84.

63. GPP, "Rough Notes of Thirty Years in the Trade," *American Publishers' Circular and Literary Gazette* octavo series 1 (15 August 1863): 290.

64. Ibid., 290.

65. Fields to Taylor, 22 September 1854; Huntington Library.
66. Peabody to GPP, 4 October [1854]; GPP-P.
67. Childs to GPP, 3 October 1854; GPP-P.
68. Greene to GPP, 11 September 1854 and 26 September 1854; GPP-P.
69. GPP to Asa Gray, 13 September 1854; Gray Herbarium Archives, Harvard University. He signed the letter, "your humbled friend."
70. GPP to Asa Gray, 22 September 1854; Gray Herbarium Archives, Harvard University.
71. Ibid.
72. The information about GPP's meeting with creditors comes from Irving's letter of 5 October 1854 to John P. Kennedy, another worried GPP author; Aderman, et al., eds., *Letters,* 4:501–02.
73. GPP to Taylor, 9 December 1852; BT-C.
74. Ibid.
75. Hansen-Taylor and Scudder, eds., *Bayard Taylor,* 1:221.
76. Bayard Taylor, *A Journey to Central Africa; or, Life and Landscapes from Egypt to the Negro Kingdoms of the White Nile* (New York: G. P. Putnam and Company, 1854), 19.
77. Ibid., 521.
78. GPP advertised the book as having sold 10,000 copies its first ten days on the market; New York *Tribune,* 14 October 1854, 1. Although that figure might well have been inflated, the book undoubtedly had an exceptionally high advance and early sale, reports of Taylor's adventures having circulated widely through his letters published in the *Tribune* and through word of mouth.
79. GPP announced it as "now ready" in his advertisement of 7 December 1854 in the New York *Tribune.*
80. See, for instance, his Christmas ad that ran in the New York *Tribune* beginning on 21 December. The one exception was his last Exhibition-related publication, *The Crystalotype,* an expensive, technologically sophisticated gift book that included the five hundred engravings used in the *Exhibition Record* supplemented by twelve new "sun pictures" (i.e., photographs). He printed it in a quarto, leather-bound edition of one hundred copies. This information comes from the Putnam ads in the New York *Tribune,* 14 December 1854, 1, and 21 December 1854, 1. No copies of this book are reported extant.
81. The printed copy of the trade sale regulations that GPP sent to J. D. B. DeBow (inscribed with a handwritten clarification) survives in the DeBow Collection, Perkins Library, Duke University. As Association secretary, GPP presumably sent out such broadsides to publishers around the country.
82. A trial draft of the circular replete with crossings out survives in GPP's hand in GHP-C (scrapbook, p. 129).
83. Several recent books have discussed the centrality of this event in antebellum culture: Susan Coultrap-McQuin, *Doing Literary Business: American Women Writers in the Nineteenth Century* (Chapel Hill: University of North Carolina Press, 1990), 28, 39, 47; Ronald J. Zboray, *A Fictive People: Antebellum Economic Development and the American Reading Public* (New York: Oxford University Press, 1993), 3–6; Ezra Greenspan, *Walt Whitman and the American Reader* (New York: Cambridge University Press, 1990), 3–7.
84. GPP to Stetson, 14 August 1855; GPP-NYPL. GPP mentioned a budget of $2,500 to Stetson but later (and, no doubt, more accurately) estimated the figure to be $4,000; "Rough Notes of Thirty Years in the Trade," *American Publishers' Circular and Literary Gazette,* octavo series 1 (1 August 1863), 258.
This letter is bound up with the surviving official correspondence of the Crystal

Palace dinner in two bound albums (in GPP-NYPL). GPP presumably so valued the event that he preserved its correspondence.

85. Their letters to GPP are in the Crystal Palace albums, GPP-NYPL.

86. Its publishers Miller, Orton and Mulligan ran high-visibility advertisements for the book and claimed that it had sold 5,000 copies in its first two days in print; see, e.g., their advertisement in the New York *Tribune,* 21 August 1855, 1.

87. *American Publishers' Circular and Literary Gazette* 1 (29 September 1855): 67–69.

88. "Rough Notes of Thirty Years in the Trade" *American Publishers' Circular and Literary Gazette,* octavo series 1 (1 August 1863), 258.

89. John Leslie to Asa Gray, 20 October 1855; Gray Herbarium Archives, Harvard University.

90. Taylor to GPP, 20 January 1855; GPP-P.

91. Hansen-Taylor and Scudder, eds., *Bayard Taylor,* 1:316.

92. GPP to Taylor, 9 March 1855; BT-C.

93. Ibid.

94. Ibid.

95. Allibone to GPP, 29 September 1854; GPP-P.

96. Allibone to GPP, 9 June 1855; GPP-P.

97. Allibone to GPP, 8 June 1857; GPP-P.

98. GPP had been an agent for the publications of the Institution in the early 1850s. See his letter to Spencer Baird, 16 April 1851; Smithsonian Institution Archives.

99. Spencer Baird, ed. and trans., *Iconographic Encyclopaedia of Science, Literature, and Art* (New York: Rudolph Garrigue, 1851), 1:iii.

100. For details, see his advertisement in *American Publishers' Circular and Literary Gazette* 1 (10 November 1855): 161.

101. In his advertisement for the *Narrative,* he spoke of the volumes as produced in a manner "equal, if not superior, to anything of the kind ever produced in any country." *American Publishers' Circular and Literary Gazette* 2 (3 May 1856): 270.

102. John Hammond Moore, *Wiley: One Hundred and Seventy-five Years of Publishing* (New York: John Wiley and Sons, 1982), 237.

103. GPP used these terms in his letters to Gray of 14 March 1854 and 24 April 1854; Gray Herbarium Archives, Harvard University.

104. Jane Loring Gray, ed., *Letters of Asa Gray,* 2 vols. (Boston: Houghton, Mifflin, and Company, 1893), 1:266.

105. A. Hunter Dupree, *Asa Gray, 1810–1888* (Cambridge: Harvard University Press, 1959), 195.

106. GPP to Gray, 22 September 1854; Gray Herbarium Archives, Harvard University.

107. Her letter to GPP was dated 2 May 1855, and his advertisements for the work, with her letter excerpted, soon followed; see *American Publishers' Circular and Literary Gazette* 1 (1 September 1855): 9.

She stated her commitment to GPP in the dedication of the novel (to Andrew Jackson Downing): "In now giving my Hertha in the hands of Mr. George P. Putnam, I am conscious that I intrust to him the work, which, of all my writings, has the deepest root in my own life and consciousness,—a work which sacred duty commanded me to write."

108. GHP, *George Palmer Putnam,* 2:78–79.

109. At the March 1856 auction, for instance, his firm sold 5,340 volumes of Irving's works, 3,500 volumes of Cooper's, and 2,100 of Taylor's. *American Publishers' Circular and Literary Gazette* 2 (5 April 1856): 205.

110. He could claim to speak disinterestedly because his own firm had drawn one of

the worst placements (106 out of 110) for its products in the new lottery system adopted by the Publishers' Association for determining the order of sales. Ibid.

111. *American Publishers' Circular and Literary Gazette* 2 (22 November 1856): 713.

112. *American Publishers' Circular and Literary Gazette* 2 (13 December 1856): 769. For the text of Mason's speech, see *American Publishers' Circular and Literary Gazette* 2 (20 December 1856): 793–94.

113. *American Publishers' Circular and Literary Gazette* 3 (24 January 1857): 49.

114. GPP to Taylor, 5 May 1857; BT-C.

115. Mary Putnam Jacobi speculated (quite plausibly) years after the fact that Leslie committed suicide; autobiographical sketch, Mary Putnam Jacobi Papers, Schlesinger Library, Radcliffe College (p. 15).

116. GPP to Gray, 16 July 1857; Gray Herbarium Archives, Harvard University.

117. GHP, *George Palmer Putnam*, 2:18–19.

118. *American Publishers' Circular and Literary Gazette* 3 (18 July 1857): 451.

CHAPTER 11

Print, Public Service, and the Civil War

"Business was not" was the way the trade paper described commercial conditions that fall.[1] Exaggeration for most, that assessment very nearly became literal truth for Putnam. After having operated on his own for nearly a decade and established his reputation as one of the leading figures in the trade, he faced the prospect of losing his business and of not having the means to begin a new one. By the time that he met formally with his creditors, Putnam realized that the worst scenario was unavoidable: he had no alternative but to declare bankruptcy. In going through that process, he had the good fortune of being assigned a receiver—Lowell Mason—who was a longtime professional acquaintance and fellow officer of the Publishers' Association. He could reasonably have expected that Mason would do whatever was possible to persuade creditors that it was in everyone's interest to arrange a settlement that permitted Putnam to resume business operations as soon as possible, if only as a means to pay back loans. This was precisely what Mason did. One personal item was spared at least for the time being: Putnam's treasured autograph collection, which had come home with him from London and grown thicker over the following decade. But a year later even that would follow most of his business properties to the auction block.[2]

Mary recalled the events of that summer as constituting "the great misfortune of my father's life," and George Haven remembered their father as having aged considerably over the course of the summer.[3] It is not hard to understand their impressions: Putnam was forced to confront the prospect of beginning his career over at age forty-three and having to do so with heavy debts and few offsetting assets. The situation was hard enough in itself, but he also had to shoulder mounting family responsibilities as father to eight children (Ruth having been born the previous year in Yonkers). One reason he was able to bear that burden as well as he did was that he had the solid support of his family. Mary carried away from that period the image of her mother consoling him the day he returned from the office with the awful news: "It was an illustration of the beautiful little sketch of Washington Irving called 'The Wife'" (not for nothing did the Putnam children read their father's favorite client).[4] In the days and weeks that followed, Victorine kept the household running smoothly and the atmosphere cheerful, and the elder children did what they could to ease the burden; Haven even clerked and ran messages downtown. Just the same, the crisis could not but overshadow the entire family, and it soon did in the most visible way. Although the title to the Yonkers house was not attachable because in Victorine's name, she nevertheless insisted—and Putnam agreed—that as a matter of honor it be put up for sale and some of the proceeds used to reimburse creditors. No time was lost in putting that wish into action; the sale took place in September and brought in $12,500. Meanwhile, Putnam bought a large but less expensive house in the lightly settled Melrose area of the Bronx, where the family moved in October. A gangly, two-story structure of many rooms spaced in seemingly arbitrary fashion and surmounted by a cupola, their "Melrose chateau" or "beehive," as they privately referred to it, defied aesthetics but served the family well for the three years the Putnams lived in it. Surrounded by seven acres of mostly primary growth woodland, the children made the most of their new situation, although for the first year the family could not afford to maintain a horse in their stable as they had enjoyed doing during more prosperous times.

Putnam had little time to enjoy the new house; his most immediate concern was to revitalize his business. Soon after emerging from bankruptcy, he reported his business to Taylor as "happily adjusted" and himself ("considering the crash of big houses now going on") as "fortunate."[5] That quick expression of hopefulness might have placed him in the same optimists' club as the flamboyant P. T. Barnum, a man otherwise his temperamental opposite who the year before had emerged from bankruptcy with the declaration: "All praise to Him for permitting me always to look upon the bright side of things."[6] So did Putnam, but his September forecast to Taylor on his operating situation proved premature: the task of restoring his business was to prove a much more complicated, prolonged undertaking than he had anticipated.

Following the conclusion of the bankruptcy arrangement, he was back in operation once again as simply G. P. Putnam, with no partner. He was doing business, however, in those first months on a wobbly basis with few visible resources, most of his former properties having been sold at the executor's auction and sizable debts still remaining that he then had more intentions than resources for repaying (he would still be making good on them well into the Civil War).[7] But as after the crisis of 1854, so in 1857 he retained one critical asset for rebuilding his business: his special relationship with Washington Irving. There are two differing versions of how that relationship continued, although they agree on the crucial fact of a renewed partnership. Pierre Irving recounted publicly a few years after the fact that Mason had offered the plates of Irving's works at auction and that it was Irving himself who purchased them. Rather than sell them to any of a number of eager publishers, Irving then offered them back to Putnam, who though unable to buy them outright agreed instead to lease them from Irving until he could raise enough money to return to their previous terms.[8] In his own account of the deal, Putnam explained to Bayard Taylor at the time that he had simply sold the plates (as well as some of the stock) directly to Irving in return for the $18,000 he owed him and that he had then leased the plates back.[9] Whichever account is accurate, the common result was that the productive circuit between Irving and Putnam remained unbroken and that Putnam found himself reinstalled that fall as the supplier of Irving's works to the market. With the fifth volume of *Life of Washington,* the one that would complete not only the biography but also Irving's collected works, still in progress, the continuity of that connection was precious to Putnam (and to Irving).

This was virtually the same arrangement that Putnam sought to reach with Taylor, whose interests he self-consciously saw as intertwined with those of Irving. Settling Taylor's account turned out to be a bit more complicated, however, because Putnam, in payment of a $6,000 debt, had transferred to David Wells, his previous partner, temporary ownership of Taylor's plates, with the written understanding that the plates be returned to Putnam on settlement of the debt. Putnam now interceded with Taylor, absent on an extended trip to Europe, to buy them back himself upon his return and to follow Irving's example by leasing them to Putnam. That arrangement, he tried to persuade Taylor, would work to their mutual advantage. Drawing on their long friendship, he also stated that his commitment to their success had been redoubled since his recent failure: "You will be assured therefore that I appreciate and value the excellence of your books— and that my ambition—after all the troubles and anxieties of 25 years as a publisher will be satisfied if I can provide a moderate support for my family in the humbler capacity of steward and publishing agent for Washington Irving and Bayard Taylor." Optimistic and faithful as always, he predicted that Taylor's works already in print "will continue to be classical scores of years hence."[10] Taylor was at the time in no position to make that decision, since he was connected to the world of American letters during his travels only via Putnam and Charles Dana, his executor; however, after returning to the United States in October 1858, he did accede to Putnam's terms.

So, for the period stretching from autumn 1857 until the outbreak of the Civil War, Putnam did business primarily in the capacity of "agent" for Irving and Taylor. That arrangement soon proved to be broadly beneficial to all three men. For the writers, it meant in effect having the nearly exclusive services of one person overseeing the production and distribution of their works, a provision that might well have formed part of their contractual agreement with Putnam. That their agent was not only one of the most adept book trade advertisers and marketers in the country but also a man who had every motivation for pursuing their interest as his own could only have sweetened the arrangement for them. For Putnam, the arrangement amounted to nothing less than a renewed lease on life as a literary professional. Furthermore, it augured a future with reduced risks and investments, on one side of the ledger, and unusually good prospects of long-term profits, on the other—all in all, as safe a deal as the volatile profession of publishing permitted a person with little capital. Although the new circumstances necessitated of him a radical shift of professional identity from publisher to agent, Putnam seems to have made the adjustment with remarkably little regret and no self-pity. The cheerful expression he showed to Taylor in 1857 remained the one he continued to present in his professional dealings during the succeeding years. As he told his old client Captain Wilkes of the United States Exploring Expedition in 1859, "I am at present engaged almost exclusively in the management of Irving's and Taylor's works—their continued popularity providing almost as much business detail as I can well attend to—a comfortable consideration when (not one but) a dozen have to get their bread and butter out of mere agency commissions."[11]

During the years leading up to the Civil War, Putnam gave their works a degree of attention that might well have been the envy of the trade. He oversaw not only the passage of the manuscripts into production and distribution but also the accounting, filing reports regularly with Taylor and Irving. With reduced demands on his attention and increased incentive to shift responsibilities from others to himself, he was able to operate during this period with a slimmer staff and reduced costs. His longstanding employees, W. W. Piggott and W. G. King, went into business on their own in May 1858, as had many of Putnam's former employees, and the company moved that same year into small offices at 506 Broadway (opposite the St. Nicholas Hotel). Then in May 1859, he transferred his offices to 115 Nassau Street, a strategic move made in order to situate himself in the same building as Sheldon and Company, one of the leading schoolbook and religious publishers and jobbers in the country and a firm with what was for the time a highly developed system of national distribution through the countryside as well as in cities. The lack of such a national network had long been a source of irritation for Putnam, as for his colleagues generally. It was one thing for him to have a standing agreement with a company like Ticknor and Fields, which pledged itself in 1858 "to assist by all means in our power in the circulation of your books, they being of that class which we like to sell"; it was quite another actually to get his books to all parts of the country.[12] To redress that problem, Putnam had arranged with Sheldon and Company as early as February 1859 to handle the distribution of his books, the agreement to take effect as of May 1, leaving him hopeful that it would give him improved prospects of reaching "a new market in many places."[13] Upon being apprised of the new arrangements, Taylor quickly agreed that it could be a change only for the better over Putnam's "present plan of having a few general agents, [which] cuts off many of the booksellers in smaller havens, and curtails the sales."[14] The timing of the move was important, with Irving's fifth and last volume of *Life of George Washington* then in press.

Although he published an occasional work during these years by established clients (such as George W. Greene, Henry Tuckerman, and Captain Wilkes), Putnam devoted himself primarily to the publication of the new works and the distribution of the established works of Irving and Taylor. Even with the continuing economic slowdown, the market for both was still strong. Lowell Mason had managed to sell 1,200 volumes of Irving at the fall 1858 trade sale alone, but Putnam more than tripled that figure in selling 4,000 volumes at the spring 1860 trade sale. He continued to use the venues of trade sales for selling off large lots of Irving's books, a practice that included the trade sales in Philadelphia and Boston as well as in New York. He had no intention, however, of limiting his efforts to market his best-selling author only through the trade, with its limited distribution and large discounts. Instead, he developed a multifaceted system of getting Irving's works to the widest possible audience. Besides the bulk sales of lots to booksellers and publishers through the trade sales, he also sold the books via subscription. Although he had been pursuing this method of distribution for years, he intensified his efforts in 1859–60 once he was in a position to market Irving's "complete" works, hiring agents around the country to hunt up subscriptions from potential readers remote from or unlikely to buy from established bookstores, as well as to penetrate more deeply into urban markets. It is possible to speak with some authority about how this method of sales was handled, since a surviving "dummy" of his 1860 "National edition" of *The Sketch Book* has been preserved.[15] This particular copy had been offered through the subscription office of S. McHenry, Walnut Street, Philadelphia. His canvasser brought in the names of forty subscribers from the Philadelphia area, beginning with that of the well-known author George Boker, obviously a lure to impress and attract other people. Available only through subscription, the edition was offered on a monthly basis over twenty-one months, each volume to be bound in boards and illustrated with steel and wood engravings and to be priced at $1.50 payable to the agent on delivery. For this particular edition, the subscriber could accept the works (with or without the *Life of George Washington*) in either sixteen or twenty-one volumes.

Putnam had correctly foreseen in early 1859 that the completion of *Life of George Washington* would give "a new start" to the sale of Irving's complete works.[16] He must also have privately entertained the thought that the death of the septuagenarian author would give a further impetus to sales and elevate Irving's literary status. When it occurred later that year, it nevertheless came to Putnam as a great personal shock; the loss of a man he thought of as a "national benefactor" marked an era in his own life and, in his opinion, in the cultural life of the United States.[17] Putnam was among the hundreds of mourners at the funeral held that late Indian summer day—a "Washington-Irving-day," he noted—at Sleepy Hollow, where Irving was buried in the family plot, but Putnam chose not to speak on that occasion nor at the Irving commemoration held the following April at the Academy of Music.[18] He did arrange, however, to have a large number of tickets to the New-York Historical Society's Irving birthday celebration held 3 April 1860 set aside and given to publishers in town attending the trade sale ("for if booksellers are not interested in Irving who is?").[19] Putnam had his chance to memorialize Irving publicly later that year in the more congenial print medium of the *Atlantic Monthly,* where he paid his proper homage and did his part in inducting Irving into the national pantheon of writers and national heroes.[20]

As a practical matter, however, he also took quick steps to assure that his own connection with Irving would continue beyond the grave. It seems unlikely that the subject of posthumous literary arrangements ever came up between the two men, but within several months of Irving's death Putnam raised the subject with Pierre Irving, his uncle's secretary and now his literary executor. The two men soon reached agreement not only for a renewal of the previous Putnam-Irving contract but also for the publication of a full-scale Irving biography, to be prepared by Pierre from the trove of papers and manuscripts left behind by his uncle. Aware of the historical and commercial appeal of the proposed work, the first major literary biography of any American writer and one befitting Irving's unique status as a "standard" American author, Putnam announced it as early as spring 1860 and planned to bring it out in a format uniform with Irving's own works.[21]

Putnam saw to it that that planned work would have no lack of recognizable company on retail and family bookshelves around the country. Spurred on first by the completion of Irving's works and then by his death, Putnam issued an outpouring of Irving editions over the course of 1859–61 unprecedented for an American writer: the Sunnyside edition of the complete works (available through retail) and the

National edition of the complete works (through subscription); the Mount Vernon, Popular, Sunnyside, and Library editions of *Life of Washington,* not to mention the other editions (and their quarto, octavo, and duodecimo formats and multiple possible bindings) that he had brought out in earlier years and the popular Irving titles that he continued to sell from his 1857 Railway Classics series. Following Irving's death, Putnam intensified his longstanding practice of aggressively encouraging purchasers to buy not only particular titles but all of Irving's works and to do so in uniform series. For those purchasers who had assembled their Irving collections over the years, the latter practice proved to be a problem, as Putnam himself acknowledged after the publication of the fifth volume of *Life of George Washington.* Despite his efforts to choose easily replicable patterns of binding, not all sets could be precisely matched as binders' materials changed over the years.[22]

Demand for those editions must have been strong; Putnam's accounts book for Irving showed payments to the estate during the twelve-month period following Irving's death totaling nearly $11,800 (and $22,300 for the period 1859–64).[23] What all these editions and the aggressive marketing that got them to readers amounted to was Putnam's attempt to establish Irving as a "classic" American author— the first American to be given this honorific status. Others would soon follow, as Putnam's colleagues in the trade adopted similar marketing strategies for their leading writers, resulting in a common institutional practice by postbellum literary publishers of demarcating particular contemporary American and foreign authors for special treatment, whether in distinct bindings, in full-scale editions, or both.

Handling Taylor was a related but slightly different proposition, since Taylor lacked Irving's stature even as he continued to produce new, popular works at a rate matched by few writers of his quality. Putnam considered him to be a writer of "classic" books and expected that he would continue to produce such works at a rapid clip into the foreseeable future. Although duly deferential toward his friend, Putnam could speak more freely with him and initiate suggestions more openly than he had been able to do with the reserved Irving. In the mock-serious tone he often took with his close friends, Putnam had urged him shortly before his company's 1857 crash, "Take care of yourself, for the sake [of] your country and your 1,000,000 of readers—and (especially) of your publisher!"[24] After the crash, there was a new urgency to his communications, although their publishing relationship remained as much and perhaps even more than ever a collaborative endeavor, with Putnam advising (and sometimes badgering) Taylor about publication timing, offering suggestions about new projects, and arranging mechanisms to expedite the reading of proof. Putnam also knew that he had in Taylor an author who was willing to engage in promotional activities. When Taylor's lecturing schedule took him to the Midwest, for example, Putnam asked him to meet with local booksellers and encourage them to buy and display his works. In one specific instance he even requested that Taylor follow up on his own attempt to persuade the Ohio superintendent of schools to adopt Taylor's and Irving's works for the state curriculum—this at a time when Putnam was working to get their works adopted by the school libraries of various Midwestern states.[25] That ambition was a major reason why Putnam counseled Taylor to adopt discretion and omit a paragraph from the manuscript of his newest work that expressed "sacred fury" ("especially considering that all the school libraries and all the families sooner or later are to have these books for the rising generation").[26] He gave the same advice a few years later when Taylor turned to the writing of fiction, cautioning him against an attachment to "isms" that could only endanger his good relations with the reading public.[27]

Despite the altered dynamics of their dealings, their relationship continued to be a generally productive and friendly one during these years. Even as Putnam was still attempting to emerge from the worst of his troubles in autumn 1857, he rejoiced to hear that Taylor had married during his most recent travels in Europe. Putnam was one of the "select eight" (others included George William Curtis, Nathaniel Parker Willis, and Charles Dana) who celebrated the marriage at a dinner held in Taylor's absence at Delmonico's.[28] He was happy to see Taylor enter the "home circle"—as he and the rest of his family called it—and hoped that the expanding Taylor and Putnam home circles would soon overlap. No doubt, he had professional as well as personal motivation for this sentiment, but the affection between the two men was genuine, although it apparently did not find its counterpart between their wives. In subsequent years, he and Victorine urged the Taylors to visit them whenever in New York and kept them updated about the health and doings of their children (especially Taylor's namesake).

As the decade reached its close, Putnam found his professional standing as agent/publisher solidifying, if not fully settled. The works of Irving and Taylor continued to sell well and put his affairs for a time on a fairly stable basis. Just the same, his resources were so limited that he continued to operate his business as a fiscal balancing act, with outlays and debt reimbursements at times threatening to outweigh capital and income. In the days approaching the 1860 general election, for instance, he reported himself to Taylor as "very dry," with a large royalty payment coming due to the Irving estate and sales then running relatively slow. At the time, he believed (mistakenly) that his liquidity would again flow once "the timid people get over their big scare" and accepted the fact of Lincoln's election.[29] A further complication that year was the coincidence that Taylor was also strapped for cash to pay mounting family bills, a necessity that led him to draw more freely on his account than Putnam could afford. In all likelihood, Putnam did not help matters; despite his long experience at juggling accounts, he occasionally made fiscal errors. More than once he embarrassed himself and probably infuriated Taylor by writing him notes that failed to clear the bank. Clearheaded and dexterous though he was with respect to other aspects of his profession, Putnam continued to demonstrate little skill at accounting, a subject that remained for him more an art than a science. His various attempts to explain to Taylor his latest experiments in bookkeeping would hardly have reassured his friend that he had the slightest expertise at double-entry bookkeeping.[30]

By the late 1850s, the Putnam parents faced the novel prospect of dealing with children rapidly advancing toward maturity—and doing so more quickly than their parents were at first prepared to recognize.[31] If he had not already given the matter serious thought, the shock of 1857 led Putnam for perhaps the first time to consider seriously the long-term educational and professional training of his children. In a family in which the children tended to bond as birth pairs, Mary and Haven were already approaching the stage at which the possibility of higher education needed to be weighed, and Edith and Bishop were not far behind. A fitting symbol of their relations and paths, Mary and Haven took the Harlem River train together weekday mornings from their local Melrose station into the city, then separated to walk to their respective schools. Mary's represented a break with the family's long-established practice of private schooling, a habit no doubt inherited from two generations of Palmer women who had given their mature working years to operating their own schools in communities across New England and New York. She owed that decision, ironically, to her grandmother, now retired but still knowledgeable about local schools, who strongly recommended a new public school setting up on Twelfth Street. Despite Putnam's initial resistance to the idea of a public school for his children, he was sufficiently impressed during his visit to this school to break with the family tradition and enroll his daughter.

Because of the unsystematic nature of her previous schooling, she was initially placed in a low class, but she quickly closed the gap between herself and her peers and then moved up to her own age group, finally graduating among the top students of her class. She was far from satisfied, however, with having completed the full curriculum normally prescribed for girls of her class; she wished, rather, to continue her studies on a higher, professional level, although she was not certain until the early 1860s of her specific orientation. Whether around this time she ever seriously considered for herself—or her father for her—a career as a writer is an interesting question, authorship being in his eyes as acceptable a career for women of her background as her eventual choice of medicine was not. As early as age nine or ten, Mary was recording her philosophical musings in an exercise book; one into which she incorporated Longfellow's popular "A Psalm of Life" survives from 1852.[32] The following year she jotted down this typical entry of self-observation: "I am getting to write better than usual, and shall try to continue to write good, though [in an unexplained reference] Papa's life was saved by his writing bad."[33] Seven years later, teenage Mary was writing "good" enough to compose a clever story, "Found and Lost," that so impressed her father that he decided to submit it to James Fields for publication in Ticknor and Fields's *Atlantic Monthly*. Fields accepted it and published it in the April issue, which also included Whitman's "Bardic Symbols" (later renamed "As I Ebb'd with the Ocean of Life").[34] By chance, Putnam's good friend S. Austin Allibone, himself an ardent admirer of Mary, was entertaining William Ticknor in the library of his Philadelphia home when Putnam's letter announcing the publication arrived.[35] When the actual check came, Putnam took special pleasure in cashing it and paying Mary her author's fee in gold coins.

Meanwhile, Haven attended the private school on Twenty-Third Street run by his father's friend John MacMullen (one-time librarian of the New York Society Library). Due to his father's financial constraints, an arrangement was worked out for tuition to be waived in return for Haven's services as aide and later, once he had demonstrated his competence, as teacher. During his second winter at MacMullen's school,

Haven was assigned to teach a group of students his own age, a task that forced him to scramble simply to keep ahead of the assignments. From there he graduated to the well-known Columbia preparatory school kept by the scholar and writer Charles Anthon. It is hard to imagine that his father did not also have some acquaintance with Anthon, who for years had been a New York educational institution. An enormously prolific and successful author, Anthon had written enough books and sold enough copies of them to constitute an entire department at Harper and Brother's, but he also taught Greek and Latin at the college while preparing the rising generation of college-bound boys in the classics at the Columbia Grammar School. Haven was one of the hundreds of aspirants who passed through his books or personal instruction on their way to a course of higher studies. Intellectually nimble and dedicated, he distinguished himself as one of the top students in his class each of the two sessions he spent with Anthon, excelled in the college matriculation examinations, and considered himself ready by the end of spring 1860 to move on that fall with his classmates to Columbia College.

By the year of that fateful election, the elder Putnam children were also graduating from the Putnam home school of civic affairs and proceeding to the rambunctious world of national politics. Given the charged atmosphere of the times and the fact that they grew up in an activist home, through which social, religious, educational, and political leaders frequently passed and occasionally stayed overnight and in which the elder children were encouraged to participate in family discussions, it was predictable that Mary and Haven developed strongly held views on the issues of the day. They both by that time ascribed to their parents' liberal, antislavery views, but they did so in different ways. Mary was the more original thinker and active reformer of the two but had less of a ready-made outlet for the expression of her opinions. Once she moved out of the house and put distance between her parents and herself, she would find ways to overcome that limitation. Meanwhile, Haven adopted many of his father's causes as his own. Most immediately, that meant becoming active alongside him in party politics. Putnam had been a busy supporter of the Republican Party since its organization and performed various services for it in the years leading up to the 1860 election, primarily on the community level. Occasionally he involved Haven in them.

The most memorable occasion was the night of 27 February, when they went together to Cooper Union, one of the largest meeting halls in the country, to hear the long-awaited New York City address of Abraham Lincoln. Although a Seward Republican at the time, as were most of his friends, Putnam had been on the speakers' committee of the Young Men's Central Republican Union that had invited Lincoln to give a "political lecture" in the city, and he took advantage of his position to situate his son toward the corner of the speaker's platform, itself crowded with local dignitaries eager to see the much talked about but still largely unknown Westerner. From his oblique angle, Haven commanded an unobstructed view of Lincoln and of William Cullen Bryant, who introduced him to an eager, if initially skeptical, audience. No doubt surprising an audience that expected to witness a display of homespun wit and folklore, Lincoln captivated it that night by delivering a tightly reasoned, eloquently restrained speech on the issue of slavery in the territories, excited reports of which circulated the next day through the New York press and subsequently across the country. To take one example of the reaction, the New York *Tribune,* which would scold Lincoln during the Civil War for the timidity of his policies, printed his speech in its entirety from proofs corrected later that night by Lincoln himself in its offices and called it "one of the happiest and most convincing political arguments ever made in this City."[36] Many people in attendance, including the Putnams, walked away from the hall with the impression that they had just taken part in an historic occasion. The glow of that night remained with Haven for decades; he even published an edition of the speech, by then not readily available in print, in the early-twentieth-century biography he wrote of Lincoln.[37] But neither father nor son, who at the time was not an American citizen, had the slightest premonition that the events of that election season would change the course of their lives.

A few months later, Putnam addressed one of the most politically motivated letters of his life to James Chesnut, U.S. senator from South Carolina (although less known today than his wife, the Civil War diarist Mary Boykin Chesnut).[38] Normally decorous in his social intercourse, Putnam apologized for intruding himself ("an unimportant and inconsequential individual ... engaged in trade, and not in statesmanship") on Chesnut with only the slightest previous acquaintance but reminded him that they had met twenty years before in London, when they had passed a brief but pleasant time together. His reason for addressing him now in an unsolicited letter, he explained, was that he had recently seen Chesnut's name attached in the papers to so slashing an attack against Charles Sumner ("a gentleman and a scholar") that he wondered whether that James Chesnut could possibly be "identical with the courteous and accomplished gentleman" he retained fond memories of. In similarly polite terms, Putnam proceeded to inform Chesnut that his own antislavery views accorded with those of "many thousands of the calmest[,] wisest, and most sincerely patriotic *statesmen* now living in this country," not to mention 10–15 million of their fellow Americans. He was himself, he protested, no abolitionist and prided himself on having "many good—excellent—respected—friends at the south who are slaveholders." On this occasion, however, that demurral must have been lost on Chesnut, who would hardly have been prepared to hear Putnam's follow-up assertion that slavery might be acceptable to some in the South but was viewed generally in the United States as "a national *evil*—an unmitigated *curse*."

A line of address that must have infuriated Chesnut, one of the most unyielding supporters of slavery in the country, it apparently struck the ingenuous Putnam as entirely prudent and reasonable. In expressing himself to Chesnut as finding himself in "honest amazement" that Southern politicians did not understand Northern sentiment, Putnam clearly either did not remember very well or had not accurately taken the measure of his correspondent. There is no record that Chesnut ever took the time to respond to Putnam directly; five months later, however, he did indirectly to Putnam and to people of similar views when he resigned his Senate seat in protest against Lincoln's election and subsequently was present to receive Col. Anderson's surrender at Fort Sumter. Putnam's well-intentioned but provocative act was, in fact, an exemplary demonstration of the attitude that George Haven Putnam described years later as characteristic of the ingenuity of his father, a man "so upright and unselfish that it was difficult for him to realize the possibility of any one being activated by motives that were not upright and unselfish, [who] would say of men whose actions appeared dutiful—'that he did not understand them,' 'that there was doubtless some explanation that was not evident,' but it seemed impossible for him to form a really harsh judgment."[39] With such gaping ingenuity, Putnam was unprepared for the quick series of events following the November election that brought on secession and war. In this regard, however, he had mass company.

The election and its aftermath affected every aspect of the Putnam home circle, which even before the disintegration of the union and the outbreak of war was losing its coherence as the oldest children pursued their separate interests. By 1860 Mary was pressuring her parents for permission to continue her studies. After graduating from the Twelfth Street school, she had occupied herself with various activities, including teaching both inside and outside her home. Her strong desire, however, was to pursue a course of scientific studies with the eventual goal of becoming a physician. With this intent in mind, she enrolled at New York's College of Pharmacy, the best option for her in the city if not a fully satisfactory one, and began a period of intermittent studies that would be interrupted during the early Civil War years by family and social exigencies. She took that initial step in career training not only without her parents' support but to a large extent in opposition to their wishes. For them, their eldest daughter's career choice clashed with their ideal of "feminine character," a belief it took them much of the decade to modify, if never to give up completely.[40] Putnam's opposition was, if anything, stronger than Victorine's. In early 1861 he expressed his reservations explicitly in asking her to postpone her schooling in favor of helping out at home: "I really and deliberately think that you owe more to your mother and the younger children than you do to any one else or to any other plans or enterprise, however worthy and important. I think you may be of immense use in relieving and cheering your mother and that she will need your aid at home."[41] Whatever money he saved, he promised, he would put into her account for her future use, but the real issue for him seems to have been less economy than principle. Just the same, he did not attempt then or later to interpose his authority between her and her career goals. Persuasion, not dictation, was his and the family's style; in any case, Mary was so strong-minded that dictation would surely have proven counterproductive.

Torn between conflicting demands, she did for a short while accommodate his request, although she then returned to her studies and graduated from the College of Pharmacy in 1863. That same year she quietly made her formal break with the Baptist Church, the sustaining faith of her grandmother (and, at that period, of her father), writing her pastor that she found herself "a total disbeliever in the distinctive tenets of the technically called orthodox system of divinity."[42] Her heart by that time was set on service to medicine, and later that year she got reluctant permission from her father to continue her professional education in Philadelphia at the Female Medical College of Pennsylvania in what he persisted in deprecating as "the repulsive pursuit ... of Medical Science." While reminding her how proud he was of her achievement, he could not restrain himself from offering his most urgent paternal advice: "But *don't* let yourself be absorbed and gobbled up in that branch of the animal kingdom ordinarily called strong-minded women! *Don't* let them intensify your self-will and independence for they are strong enough already. *Don't* be congealed or fossilized into a hard, tenacious, unbending personification of intellectual conceit, however strongly fortified you feel sure that you are."[43] Little wonder that the emotional as well as physical distance between the two increased during the last decade of his life, as he found himself unable to comprehend her desire for independence or to reconcile her accomplishments with those of the women writers, such as Sedgwick, Sigourney, and Warner, he most admired.

During the same period, Haven was also beginning to move increasingly outside of the family circle, although neither he nor his parents could have anticipated how quickly circumstances would project him into an orbit of his own. During his summer 1859 vacation from school, he took what might have been his first job outside the house when he went to work on one of the crews carrying out the plans for the new Central Park designed by Frederick Law Olmsted, the Putnams' former Staten Island neighbor. The family's designated gardener since its Yonkers years, Haven had developed a taste for working in the out-of-doors and perhaps was already beginning to think of a career in forestry, his career preference before he enlisted as well as when he came out of the Union Army in 1865. His parents were well acquainted with Olmsted, but it is unknown whether Haven owed the job to their initiative or to his own.[44] Nor is it expressly known how Putnam, who had enjoyed taking his oldest children on Sunday walks through the classical spaces of Regents Park, would have reacted to Olmsted's visionary plan to remake central Manhattan into a new kind of park organized along more fluid, decentralized lines. Though men of the same generation, Putnam had a less flexible, accepting attitude than Olmsted toward the social and demographic dynamics transforming New York City into a metropolitan center.

The following summer, after completing his college preparatory studies with Anthon, Haven made a long walking tour of New England with his school friend Cabot Jackson Russell. It gave him a chance to see much of the countryside, which he was deeply attracted to, as well as to visit many of his paternal cousins. Although he was scheduled to begin studies at Columbia shortly after his return, that plan had to be postponed because of periodic bouts of an eye disorder he had begun experiencing earlier that year. The continuing severity of his ailment so alarmed his parents that they decided in consultation with the family doctor, once all normal treatment had proven ineffective, to adopt the not uncommon plan of sending him overseas for extended exposure to salt water and treatment by a leading European specialist. So just weeks before the general election, he set sail for Europe on a trip that, no one could have foreseen, was to last for nearly two years.

He sailed as the only passenger on board a Maine-chartered brig out of New York harbor. His father had chosen it primarily for its cheapness, the forty-dollar fare only a fraction of what a steam-powered packet would have cost. Haven's course of action, short of medical treatment, was left so broadly undetermined that his father supplied him with letters of introduction to friends in both England and France. It was a good thing he did because their old family physician in London, Dr. Newton, referred Haven to a local eye doctor who, after putting him through a two-week course of treatment that failed to provide relief, referred him in turn to a specialist in Paris. Without waiting for further instructions from home, Haven made the crossing and arrived in Paris, where he found quarters with George Trow, the son of the New York printer with whom his father had been doing business for nearly thirty years. The younger Trow, who at the time had no more intention than did Haven of following his father into the family business, was enjoying a student's life in the city and proved a good host and guide for a teenage compatriot short on funds and lacking a working knowledge of the language. While undergoing treatment, Haven underwent a quick course in French and began joining his friend in attending classes at the Sorbonne and getting a taste of the city. Much as he enjoyed his time there, his vision remained so impaired that he could barely apply himself to learning to read French.

In March 1861 he took the advice of his French doctor and traveled to Berlin for treatment by the leading oculist in Europe, Baron von Graefe. His sojourn in the German states was meant to last only as long as his period of treatment but actually continued for more than a year. Like Henry Adams, who preceded him to Berlin by a few years and who studied at the university, he found the city dull and provincial, especially after his exposure to Paris. With his vision improving, he offered to return home that first summer, but his father rejected his offer, arguing that he was still too young to do military service (he would not turn eighteen until the following spring) and that since the conflict in any case was likely to be short-lived he might as well make the most of his opportunities abroad. While undergoing von Graefe's prescribed treatment, which included a recommendation that he spend as much time as possible out of doors, he managed to work off a curiosity to see Europe that approximated his father's wanderjahr of 1836. That summer he took an extended walking tour through parts of central Europe that left him on his own for long periods, although he did look up Bayard Taylor's wife and family at her parents' home in Gotha. Most of the time, however, he spent on his own or with traveling companions whom he picked up for stretches along the way. In many ways a sheltered American teenager of his generation, he had the most exciting experience of his walking tour during the day he spent on his own in Prague, where he walked with pleasure through the exotic Jewish Quarter and eventually found himself wandering through its ancient graveyard. With dark falling, he suddenly realized that he had gotten locked in the cemetery and, feeling himself in the unaccustomed situation of an alien, forced his way out in panic through a bordering house and quickly made his way to the locked gate, where, persuading the guard that he was a Christian rather than a "Hebrew," he crossed back into the city's open sector.

Combining the advice of the Taylor family with what he had heard from others about the relative merits of German universities, he decided not to return to Berlin but to enroll at the University of Göttingen and pursue a course of scientific studies preparatory to advanced study in forestry. His months at Göttingen were intellectually lively, but like his Americans classmates he found himself unable to separate life in a German university from life back home, especially as reports, many grossly inaccurate, began to cross the ocean and filter down through layers of European ignorance to the students. Years later he bemusedly recalled the conversation he had had with an Orientalist on the faculty who approached him as an expert on America and asked for help in reconciling the breadth of the fighting with the limited geography of the battlefields. Not until the professor took him to a map did Haven understand that the scholar believed the warring parties to be North and South America and the battlefield to be Panama.[45] As the conflict stretched on, he also encountered a polarization of opinions among the different nationalities of students, Austrians, Prussians, and some Bavarians and Saxons siding with the Northerners versus Britons and citizens of most other German states with the Southerners. One day the antagonisms exploded into an international brawl that ended with the imprisonment of some of the combatants.[46]

Following the end of the year's studies in summer 1862, Haven renewed his request to return home, his eyes now largely restored to full use. By that time his father was eager not only to receive him back home but to enlist him in his business.[47] The day he landed in New York, Putnam proudly took him along on his visit up Broadway to the Maine regiment whose lodging and feeding he was then overseeing. They then took the train up to the family's current place of residence, the fishing village at Five Mile River Landing (later, through Putnam's initiative, renamed Rowayton) on the Connecticut shore of Long Island Sound. Since selling their "chateau," the family had migrated for brief periods to homes in New Jersey and Manhattan, before buying the house overlooking the water in which the core of the family would live until 1867. Once reinstalled at home, Haven quickly absorbed the surrounding war spirit and asked his father for permission to join the army, a request that Putnam could hardly refuse since it made Haven, in effect, the Putnam family representative in the Union Army. After a few weeks of relaxation and spoiling, father and son returned to the city and made their way to the headquarters of a regiment about which Putnam had heard good things, which was then being organized through the auspices of the Young Men's Christian Association. Both father and son satisfied with what they saw of the men, Haven enlisted as a noncommissioned soldier, rejecting his father's offer to intervene with the governor to get him a lieutenancy. A few days later, he joined his unit, the New York 176th Volunteers, and began a long training period at Jamaica, while the unit accumulated enough recruits to become ready for active duty. Stationed there through the fall months, he enjoyed Sunday visits from his family, during one of which he made the acquaintance of his sister Edith's good friend Rebecca Shepard, who caught his eye then and with whom he would subsequently enter into a serious relationship. Finally in December, the unit shipped out on the only vessels available, two New Bedford whale boats, to join the army under General Banks instructed to move up the Mississippi River from New Orleans.

Putnam must have watched the training and dispatch of his oldest son with mixed feelings of pride, admiration, apprehension, and possibly even envy. The coming of the war had forced him to reconsider his own position as a family man, citizen, and publisher. Within weeks of the firing of shots on Fort Sumter, he had written Taylor, "But for my infantry regiment at home, I should have been off for the wars myself before this."[48] In truth, even the mere thought was little more than wishful thinking; it is hard to imagine what Putnam, then forty-seven, gentle in nature, and lacking even his father's skill at pigeon shooting, would have been able to contribute to a fighting army. He immediately proved himself adept, however, at serving city and country in ways more congenial to his talent for organization, communication, and dissemination. As recruitment of soldiers began on a local basis, he became involved in the organization of troops in New York City, helping to secure food and lodging for the new regiments. Then, as regiments began to reach the city from points north, he extended his help to them as well, exerting himself with special pride to lodge and equip troops from Maine passing through the city. He continued to keep track of their activities and location through the war.

His thinking during the first months of the war had been as simplistic and abstract as that of most of his fellow citizens, an unqualified bravado filled with high-minded aspersions toward "treason" and long-range threats directed at "Jeff Davis." During the initial stage of the "rebellion," he maintained the unexamined certainty, his section's as much as his own, that the conflict would be resolved cleanly and quickly as soon as the Union army exerted its overwhelmingly superior power. On this basis he rejected his initial son's request to return home, in early summer 1861. That conviction waned with the passage of time, beginning with the trip he made to Washington, D.C., in July 1861, a trip that coincided with the first major battle of the war. During a stay originally meant to last only a few days, he unexpectedly succeeded in procuring a pass through a senator of his acquaintance and got his first and only personal view of the battlefield. Along with several friends, spectators as much as he of a conflict in which the age-old dividing line between civilians and combatants did not always hold, he witnessed the aftermath of the battle at Bull Run that took place on Sunday, 21 July, between the Army of the Potomac of Irvin McDowell and the combined Southern armies of Pierre G. T. Beauregard and Joseph E. Johnston. What he saw and soon thereafter reported back north in the newspapers and the *Knickerbocker Magazine* was enough to complicate, if not erode, his untested confidence in Union superiority.[49]

He published his account largely to counter and correct the impression given by the well-known correspondent for the London *Times*, William Russell, and others that the Union forces had been badly beaten and their ranks thrown back into panicked disarray toward Washington. Putnam had seen no such one-sided outcome to the battle or disorderly flight and, mindful as he habitually was of the power of the print medium, he lost no time upon his return to New York doing his best to reverse the damage done to public morale by Russell, who was widely disliked by Northerners for his pro-Confederate reportage. Perhaps his account did some minor good at the time, with portions reprinted in newspapers from Washington to Boston; today its chief value consists as much in its expression of his and his generation's unrealistic attitudes and expectations as in the accuracy of its eye-witness testimony. Written in his habitually genial first-person style and guided by his usual upstanding assumptions, it has more in common with his European travelogues of the 1830s and 1840s than with the new documentary reportage being done by the cameramen and artists who followed the Union forces into battle and recorded the carnage of the battlefield. (Mathew Brady boasted many years later that he had taken several equipment-filled carriages that day to Bull Run, although no images survive to corroborate him.) In strict fairness, though, to the unprecedented nature of the situation he faced, it should be pointed out that the tone and content of Putnam's reportage corresponded closely to the gay expectations entertained by the hundreds of civilians—congressmen, journalists, Washingtonians, and simple curiosity seekers—who traveled by carriage, buggy, and horse toward Centreville, Virginia, to see their army, composed heavily of volunteers serving only months-long enlistments, defeat the enemy and clear the way for the eighty-mile march to Richmond. Armed with wine and brandy, opera glasses, and picnic lunches, many of them were less prepared than Putnam to witness the first battle of a new era of warfare or afterwards to appreciate what they had seen or heard.[50]

While waiting that sun-filled Saturday of 20 July for his pass to be authorized, Putnam spent a full day touring, conversing, and observing. In the morning, he had a good-humored conversation with Adam Gurowski outside Willard's Hotel, bantering with the expatriate Pole about the relative merits of American and European armies, then stopped by the White House (where John Hay informed him that Lincoln was out) and by the Treasury (where he did meet Secretary Salmon Chase) to pay his respects. That afternoon, he drove with several companions along the southern bank of the Potomac ("worthy in its amplitude if not in its depth, of being the national river") and visited a number of local landmarks, including the mostly deserted plantation of Robert E. Lee ("a picture of dilapidated aristocracy ... [that] seemed to symbolise old Virginia herself, as needing an infusion of Yankee energy and thrift"). By the time he returned to the city, his pass was ready.

Awake and on the road early the next morning and not unmindful of the irony of its being the Sabbath, Putnam took the boat with his three friends to Alexandria, then boarded the 9:00 train filled with a primarily German-American New York regiment also en route via the Orange and Alexandria Railroad to Fairfax Station. Disembarking and moving ahead of the regiment on foot, they decided to adopt the precaution of triangulating their way to the battleground by walking first northeast to Fairfax Courthouse, a station on the main road between Washington, D.C., and Centreville, and then southwest along that highway rather than making a direct line for Centreville through possibly partisan-filled woods. The scenery along the way, Putnam remarked, would have been "picturesque" had it not been for "the rather frequent annoyance of carrion by the wayside." At Fairfax Courthouse, Putnam and his young Rhode Island companion H. H. Tilley went on ahead of their two companions and, with the sounds of guns growing louder and the day growing hotter, slowly made their way toward Centreville.[51] As they passed through various encampments and lines of troops, they met two of their peacetime acquaintances now in uniform, one a publisher known to Putnam from trade sales wearing the insignia of a captain in his Michigan regiment and the other a foot soldier in a Rhode Island regiment pointed out by Tilley to Putnam as a cousin of his old friend George W. Greene. Continuing west through the mid-afternoon hours, they got within about a mile of Centreville but not within viewing range of the actual fighting when they stopped to take note of the turmoil they could by then hear taking place over the hill to their west. What they then witnessed was the immediate aftereffects of the day's combat, as various civilians (including Russell) and troops rushed by them in retreat, imparting conflicting news of the battle. They also saw the largest group of those troops met by a rearguard Union regiment, guns pointed at the fleeing soldiers to reverse their flight, that had been moving quickly down the highway from Vienna toward Centreville and unexpectedly found itself called on to stem the retreat.

That location was as far west as Putnam and Tilley got that day. Removing the contents of their haversack and positioning themselves by a well, the two men served water and what little food they had left for several hours to soldiers returning from the fighting in various degrees of fatigue and health. Around sundown they retreated with an army wagon toward Fairfax Courthouse to pass the night, collecting pieces of information and trying to make sense of the swirling rumors about the Northern retreat. Finding an inn for the night, they took dinner and then conversed until 11:00 before retiring to sleep, the thought never occurring to them that day that they might have been in imminent danger.

Putnam awakened his friend the next morning at 1:30 A.M. to begin the long walk back toward Alexandria, their destination being the 7:00 A.M. boat across the Potomac to the capital. Rain had begun to fall by the time they reached the boat, turning a somber day even grayer, but they encountered few signs of hysteria and reached the city without incident. Always curious about things and apparently unfatigued by the uninterrupted pace he had kept the previous day and a half, Putnam walked over to the Capitol to view the daily work of the Congress, which he intently observed as it debated a proposal to prohibit the return of fugitive slaves by Union soldiers to their masters. His particular villain, that day and every day, was John Breckinridge, the Copperhead senator from Kentucky who led the opposition to the proposed legislation. Putnam then caught the 2:00 train north via Baltimore (a city dangerous for Northerners to pass through just several months before) and Philadelphia, where he made an overnight stop before boarding the morning train and continuing on to New York.

The Civil War had as great an impact on Putnam's professional life as on his family life, although the result in both regards was to prove unpredictable. Even before the outbreak of the war, business conditions in the country had grown destabilized, and merchants like Putnam foresaw that actual fighting might well mean the loss of their Southern market and the renunciation of Southern debts. Once hostilities developed into secession, the impact on the book trade was quick and powerful, slowing the production and sale of most kinds of books and periodicals throughout the war years and increasing their prices substantially (although, of course, giving impetus to the composition and sales of books and periodicals about the war). Although Putnam suffered the same economic effects as his colleagues, the heightened nationalism brought on by the war, combined with his somewhat improved financial condition, seems paradoxically to have revitalized his career as a publisher.

The national events of 1860–61 caught Putnam at a particularly nostalgic moment in his life. At the last New York trade sale before the 1860 election, he had addressed his colleagues briefly, talking about the changing technology of bookmaking over his lifetime and about the history of his dealings with various authors, especially Washington Irving, of whose works, he mentioned, he had to date sold 700,000 volumes.[52] The following week at the Philadelphia trade sale, he had projected that mood onto an unprepared Moses Thomas, the aging publisher of the original edition of the *Sketch Book,* who was caught by surprise when Putnam asked him publicly to recount his memories of Irving to their colleagues.[53] A reporter for the New York *World* covering the earlier trade sale noted at the time, "Mr. Putnam's thirty years in the publishing world, here and in London, would doubtless afford a fund of curious and entertaining information, which should in some way be recorded and preserved."[54] That remark was so close to Putnam's own thinking that it seems likely that Putnam had conferred with the reporter about his plans to write a book of professional memoirs (preliminarily called "Thirty Years Notes"). Not even the beginning of full-scale fighting seems to have dissuaded him from pursuing his desire to tell the story of his times. A few months after he returned from Bull Run, he sounded out some of his closest professional associates, including James Fields and George W. Childs, about his project. Fields urged him strongly against the idea, protesting that he was still too young to publish a volume that might do damage to his "good name."[55] Childs, by contrast, encouraged him to persevere in the project, which he anticipated would become "the booksellers' Bible."[56] Whatever determined his final decision—the intensifying war, the unexpected turn of his career, unfavorable literary economics prospects, or simply the overwhelming press of affairs—Putnam never wrote what would certainly have been the premier publishing chronicle of his generation. The closest he came—and the next best thing—was the informal, intermittent series of articles he published in the trade paper in summer 1863 as "Rough Notes of Thirty Years in the Trade."

More than at any other period of his life, Putnam practiced his profession during the war years in the joint capacity of publisher/citizen. Never too busy in earlier years to devote large amounts of his time and energy to acts of citizenship, Putnam gave so freely of himself to public service after Lincoln's election that his personal and professional roles became virtually indistinguishable. After the outbreak of fighting, he redoubled his commitment to public service, playing an important civic role not only, as mentioned, in recruiting and lodging troops on their way to battle but also in collecting books and food for their sustenance in the field and medicine and other supplies for their recuperation. Much of this aspect of his Civil War public service came via his position of leadership in such recently organized wartime organizations as the Union League Club of New York, the United States Sanitary Commission, the Metropolitan Fair Association, and the Loyal National League. Working through the auspices of these organizations, he solicited or contributed books, autographs, and other memorabilia to be distributed to troops, used to raise wartime funds, or mailed to people of influence in the United States and across the ocean to recruit them to active support of the Union. His main agency in this last regard was the Loyal Publication Society, which he founded and oversaw as a means of distributing printed material—books, tracts, polemics—in support of the war effort. In one particular act of largesse, he and his friend Henry Tuckerman gathered through the society a large collection of books in Americana from fellow publishers to be entrusted to the English scholar Goldwin Smith (future professor at Cornell University) for deposit at the new library at University College, Oxford. There, as Smith wrote, they might fulfill their purpose of "diffusing a knowledge of American literature and character."[57]

Although some of his colleagues grew discouraged by economic conditions and many houses went out of business, Putnam retained his characteristically upbeat publishing outlook throughout the war years. In early 1862 he published a notice to the trade, "I venture to suggest that a constant though moderate supply of such books as are really of *permanent value,* as well as of *immediate interest* and *attraction,* will prove both safe and politic and profitable, even though the war is not yet ended—as in good time it will be, and truth and justice are sure to triumph."[58] His actions matched his rhetoric: he pursued a cautiously activist publishing schedule based on the production of works he considered of "permanent value" right up to mid-1864, when he temporarily retired from the profession to devote more time to government service.

He entered the period with his finances consolidated and his list tightly configured around Irving and Taylor. Sales of Irving's works in particular remained strong even during the war years, with Putnam repeatedly selling several thousand copies at trade sales alone and continuing to print and market them as aggressively as in years past. He not only kept the market stocked with various editions of Irving, refreshing them periodically with new printings, but added to them. The most elaborate single addition was his Artists' Edition of the *Sketch Book* (1863), a work that demonstrated among other things how hard it was for Putnam even in wartime to check his predisposition to spend extravagantly on cherished projects. He reportedly spent $20,000 in producing this extraordinarily fancy edition of his single most valuable title, its huge expenses owing to his decision to issue the book with 120 illustrations designed by the leading artists of the country, to print it on superfine paper, and to engage the leading binder in the city, Mathews, to cover it in high-quality leather. The presswork alone was reportedly done at ten times the normal expense.[59] Lacking the capital to finance the edition entirely by himself, he offered a partnership to Henry Holt, a recent Yale graduate whom he had recently met; it was with this project that Holt began his distinguished career as a New York publisher.[60]

One wonders whether Putnam was speaking factually or wishfully when he stated in his introduction to the volume: "An intelligent and discriminating taste for this manner of illustration, and for general excellence in the art of book-making, is rapidly increasing in our community, even in this period of national discipline; and the publisher of this volume has endeavored to place it a step in advance, to meet the purer and severer requirements of popular demand."[61] Whether the popular demand matched the Putnam demand was not a question that Putnam was asking openly, but he had the good sense, at least, to double up on what was likely to be the most popular part of his investment by printing a separate volume called *The Hudson Legends* from the sheets and illustrations of "Rip Van Winkle" and "The Legend of Sleepy Hollow." Fortunately for the partners, the Artists' Edition went through several print runs and in time perhaps proved mildly profitable.

About the same time, Putnam was also completing the publication of Pierre Irving's multivolume Irving biography (*Life and Letters of Washington Irving,* 1862–64) with which Putnam had long planned to consummate his Irving edition. With the second of the four volumes only weeks out on the market, he called the work in 1862 "the most notable book of the season," and he rushed the two remaining volumes into print as soon as they were ready, then printed the whole work as a set.[62] Naturally, he sold the work in multiple formats to match and complement the various editions then available of Irving's collected works. Because he found himself too pressed by multiple professional and civic responsibilities to see that work, as well as the Artists' Edition of the *Sketch Book* and other new titles of 1863, through production and to advertise them throughout the country, he passed on the bulk of those jobs to J. C. Derby, one of the most inventive and energetic book promoters in the profession. For those services he paid Derby a 5-percent commission on sales.[63] But Putnam still did his best to use his contacts with friends to get favorable notice for his books. One such friend was James Fields, who offered to open up the pages of the *Atlantic* to a friendly review of the Irving biography, to whose composition Putnam enlisted another longtime friend Evert Duyckinck.[64] Duyckinck, however, missed the press deadline and the article never appeared in the magazine.

Until 1863 all the works in the Irving editions were produced in New York, as had been almost all Putnam's publications since his return from London except for a small number of imports. That year, however, he entered into an initial agreement with Henry Houghton for a new "blue and gold" edition of the *Sketch Book* to be produced at the Riverside Press in Cambridge. That new edition was no doubt meant to match the already famous blue and gold editions of Ticknor and Fields, the Boston firm with which Putnam (presumably not coincidentally) had entered into a joint marketing agreement in their respective cities. That agreement gave Putnam the improved access to markets that he perennially sought, but it also opened up dangers of a new sort, as he learned when he came upon an advertisement he interpreted to state that the Blue and Gold *Sketch Book* was a Ticknor and Field publication. He immediately objected to Fields, who quickly moved to allay his concern in pointing out by return mail that "everybody will understand, unless insane, that we issue the B. and G. Ed. with your name on the title page first and ours following, that G. P. P. has put the sale of this particular work into the hands of T. and F. because T. and F. issues so many B. and Gold books."[65] During this same period Putnam was also marketing Irving's works in England, where he had entered into an arrangement for their sale with his sometimes partner of earlier years, Richard Bentley.[66]

Putnam likewise kept Taylor's works before the public in various editions, although never with the degree of success he experienced with Irving's works. Always looking for new ways to present his core writers, Putnam initiated a new subscription edition (the Caxton) of Taylor's collected travels over the course of 1861–62, which he presumably meant to complement the National Edition of Irving's works. Such an ambitious venture taken in the midst of the war would have surprised many in the trade, as Putnam was well aware, but to him it made good marketing sense, being a companion not only to the Irving but to the Thomas Hood series he was then selling. Soon after the Caxton edition was issued, however, Putnam came to realize that it had been a serious mistake; it never returned production expenses. For that matter, sales of nearly all of Taylor's early works decreased during the war. In letter after letter, Putnam was forced to report to Taylor that his books were not selling as fast as they both had hoped, a refrain so common that Taylor must have come to dread its predictability. But as usual, Putnam continually held out to Taylor the expectation of imminent improvements. During the long, gloomy year of 1862, for example, he saw a breakthrough moment in Lincoln's long-awaited decision to issue the Emancipation Proclamation ("the glorious new declaration of independence"), which Putnam interpreted as a harbinger of better times for the United States and improved conditions for publishers and authors. The day after Lincoln's declaration of intent, Putnam forecast "a greatly improved demand for books" by 1 November.[67] Events would show that he was seriously mistaken; no election, proclamation, battle, or campaign short of total Union victory was to change book trade conditions seriously for the better.

Despite the depressed market conditions, Taylor continued to produce his prose works at his usually prolific rate and Putnam to issue them apace throughout the war years. That process continued even after Taylor was posted in 1862 to the American legation in St. Petersburg. Although discouraged by his declining royalties and occasionally dissatisfied with his image as "the prince of modern travelers" that Putnam capitalized on for advertising purposes, Taylor continued to rely heavily on Putnam's judgment. He needed to do so in the early 1860s, in particular, as he branched out into fiction with the first of three projected novels, *Hannah Thurston*. He held out such high expectations for that novel, whose incomplete manuscript he took with him to St. Petersburg, that he claimed he would be disappointed if it sold fewer than 20,000 copies.[68]

For his part, Putnam, who had his own reasons for impatiently awaiting its completion, also anticipated—correctly, this time—that it might be an unusually strong seller. What he did not expect was its dedication to him. A recent visit to London and a drive from Regent Street to Waterloo Place had reminded Taylor of the circumstances of their first meeting; now, seventeen years later, Taylor declared in the book's dedication that Putnam remained "the faithful friend, the man of unblemished honor and unselfish ambition, to whom the author's interests were never secondary to his own."[69] Putnam responded in a letter with his own appreciation for Taylor, holding up their cordial relations as proof of his faith that antagonism between authors and publishers was "impolitic and absurd."[70] For the time, at least, their relationship remained creatively collaborative, with frank suggestions passing between them about the timing of new works and editions, the effect of national elections on sales of fiction, the importance of titles, and the viability of a Canadian residential "dodge" by Taylor to establish British copyright for the purpose of protecting the overseas sales of his works by Sampson Low (residence being a requirement for British copyright following the 1854 *Boosey* v. *Jefferys* judgment).[71]

Whereas for most publishers the Civil War marked a period of business contraction, for Putnam it ushered in a period of gradual expansion, during which he capitalized on the surplus revenues from the sale of works by Irving and Taylor and from recent nonpublishing income to embark on new ventures. One such project brought him back to his earliest act of publication, now nearly thirty years behind him, as he prepared a new edition of his still valuable first book, now called *The World's Progress,* by updating it to 1861 (or, to use his historical end marker, "to the inauguration of Lincoln"). The following year he published Richard Kimball's new business novel *Undercurrents of Wall Street* with a personal endorsement that presumably drew on his own experience: "The Publisher believes this to be not only the most vivid and skilful but the most truthful picture of the ups and downs of mercantile life, especially in New York, which has ever been attempted."[72] He also reissued some of his company's earlier works. The majority of the new works he published during this period, however, related directly or indirectly to the Civil War.

Politicized as he had become in 1860–61, he had quickly responded to the outbreak of war by forming a partnership, kept separate from his position as agent to Irving and Taylor, with the talented journalist Frank Moore to issue various war-related works. The most significant product of their collaboration was the serial archive, the *Rebellion Record,* which quickly established its value as one of the most important and original publications of and about the Civil War. It was also one of the first, Putnam advertising the first number two weeks after the surrender of Fort Sumter.[73] Issued on a weekly basis, the *Record* was designed as an illustrated print compendium of disparate materials relating to the conflict, including speeches, resolutions, newspaper articles, maps, poems, and songs from both North and South presented in mostly chronological sequence and accompanied by engravings of notable participants. Edited ostensibly, as Moore stated in the inaugural issue, on the principle of "entire impartiality," the *Record* proclaimed its owners' ambition as being to provide "in a digested and systematic shape, a comprehensive history of this struggle; sifting fact from fiction and rumor; presenting the poetical and picturesque aspects, the notable and characteristic incidents, separated from the grave and more important documents."[74] In their attempt to keep the *Record* as nearly comprehensive as possible, Moore and Putnam also issued a *Supplement* that included material that had originally passed them by, such as the historic exchange of public letters between Greeley and Lincoln in August 1862, in which Lincoln eloquently defended his policies against Greeley's abolitionist "Prayer of Twenty Millions" with an open letter stating his overriding attachment to the Union: "If I could save the Union without freeing any slave I would do it, and if I could save it by freeing all the slaves I would do it; and if I could save it by freeing some and leaving others alone I would also do that."[75] The virtue of the *Record,* however, was not in its parts but in its totality—or, more particularly, in the ongoing accumulation of war-related materials it presented week by week, month by month, finally year by year to the attention of a reading public inescapably presented with news of the war.

Contemporary reaction was widespread in the North and generally positive; a particularly insightful review in the New York *Journal of Commerce* commented on the way that the new wealth of information afforded by modern print was making coverage of the Civil War a fundamentally different reality from that of the American Revolution and even more recent wars. Like Putnam and Moore, the reporter had few doubts about the accuracy and objectivity of the coverage: "As the war goes on, it daguerreotypes itself on the pages of the 'Record,' every feature standing out clear and distinct. All the movements of those who stand behind the scenes and direct the drama are visible to the eye from the remarkable collocation which is effected in these pages. Causes and effects are brought close together, and none can be so blind as not to see the connection."[76] His faith, like theirs, was in the power of print to bring the conflict home to the American public with a directness, clarity, and objectivity not possible in previous conflicts.

That faith, of course, today seems exaggerated after innumerable twentieth-century wars broadcast through contemporary media have communicated among other lessons the distinct limits of editorial objectivity and the textured nature of mediacy itself. But even in its own time such limits should have been visible to many of the readers of the *Record,* which boasted an editorial policy of "entire impartiality" even as it delivered itself to the public on a weekly basis in conspicuously red, white, and blue paper covers portraying a thirty-four-star flag and communicated an editorial message hardly mistakable for its aggressive pro-Unionism. The *Record* had other limitations, as well. For all its vaunted comprehensiveness, it lacked the immediacy of effect that was fast becoming available to war coverage as journalists, photographers, and artists accompanying the armies transmitted images of the conflict through the print, telegraphic, and photographic media to the public. At least at the outset, not only did Moore and Putnam not anticipate the kind of media event the war would become, but they so lacked perspective on the character and duration of the conflict that they did not foresee that had they continued publishing at the initial weekly rate, by war's end their serial would fill library shelves. This lack of foresight may also explain their corresponding failure to realize that in time increasing bulk would generate decreasing novelty and falling sales.

Moore handled the editing, Putnam the publishing responsibilities; in all likelihood, they shared the financial risks and profits in three equal portions with their third partner Charles T. Evans, the former head of Putnam's subscription and canvassing department who had gone into business on his own. The three men remained partners in the venture until 15 December 1863, when Evans sold his one-third interest to Henry Holt.[77] Presumably as a precaution Putnam kept the *Record* and other joint publishing ventures with Moore separate from the affairs of his publishing firm, although all Putnam titles emanated from the same 532 Broadway office from January 1861 to April 1863, then for the next year from his new office on the upper floor of the building at 441 Broadway situated next door to the Appletons. During the three years he was connected with the *Record,* he marketed it much as he did many of his earlier serial publications, offering it for sale in various formats (weekly, monthly, bound volumes) and distributing them through his own agency and Evans's, as well as through local news dealers and the trade.

Although he unquestionably took it on as a commercial venture and kept it only as long as it remained commercially attractive, Putnam also saw the *Record* as an effective means of promoting the cause of the Union both domestically and internationally. To this end, he organized a group of prominent New Yorkers to contribute to a fund he oversaw for supplying copies of the *Record* to fifty-five influential people and libraries in Europe, as well as to American editors. He also composed and printed a circular to accompany these presentation copies in which he stated his and his committee's belief "that the comprehensive collection of documentary materials for history which this work contains, will be useful in conveying just views and accurate information in regard to all aspects of the great struggle in which our nation is engaged."[78] Among the Europeans to whom he mailed presentation copies were Queen Victoria, Tzar Alexander II, Napoleon III, and King Victor Emmanuel II, as well as such makers of opinion as John Bright, John Stuart Mill, George Eliot, Harriet Martineau, Ferdinand Freiligrath, and various other journalists and authors throughout Europe.[79] In disseminating these volumes as well as various of the pamphlets issued by the Loyal Publication Society, Putnam saw himself as performing his civilian duty in helping the North to win the battle over foreign opinion, whose bearing on the actual conduct of the war he was keenly aware of. At the same time, his attempt to influence European leaders and intellectuals via print was another manifestation of his decades-long mission to address—to his mind, redress—European ignorance of or hostility to the United States. Given his mind-set, replies such as that of Harriet Martineau must have heartened him: "I am journalist, reviewer, magazine-writer,—anything to get in a word in rebuke in refutation of the partisans of the South who take advantage of the prevalent ignorance of the details of American affairs. Your gift is of the greatest use in supplying me with a firm ground of facts on all occasions."[80] Gratified by such support, he chose to put her response and those of other recipients, such as John Stuart Mill, into the public record by publishing them as pamphlet no. 70 of the Loyal Publication Society.[81]

In addition to the *Rebellion Record,* Putnam collaborated with Moore during the war on a variety of patriotic publications, chiefly collections of war sermons, poems, and songs. What he earned from the sale of those works, even when combined with the sales drawn from the rest of his publishing list, however, was unequal to the income he earned from 1862 to 1866 as the United States revenue collector for the Eighth District of New York. He had been nominated for that lucrative position by a group of politically influential friends, including William Cullen Bryant and David Wells, who successfully made the case for his candidacy with Secretary of Treasury Chase and President Lincoln.[82] That move for a mid-nineteenth-century man of letters was hardly unusual, a time when it was still possible for Putnam and his contemporaries to invoke the idea of "the republic of letters" and to see the spheres of letters and public duty as interlocking. He was certainly no stranger to the commonplace reality of men of letters moving into public service; he had associated for a decade in London with members of the American legation and in subsequent years in Washington with members of Congress, and he had many predecessors among his circle of friends, acquaintances, and clients who had preceded him in making a similar move, including Washington Irving, George Bancroft, Edward Everett, Nathaniel Hawthorne, Horace Mann, Theodore Fay, Frederick Law Olmsted, and Horace Greeley (who, though home in New York during the Civil War, was widely caricatured and ridiculed as the puppet master who moved Lincoln forward and backward). The same year that Putnam accepted his appointment, Bayard Taylor was angling, with Putnam's support, for the ministry in St. Petersburg, although he was ultimately to get a lesser post.[83]

The position that Putnam received carried an amplified importance to the federal government during wartime. His awareness of this fact would have been sufficient reason alone for Putnam to take his responsibility with due seriousness. He had another good reason, as well: the position carried lucrative rewards for him personally. The district that he oversaw, bounded laterally by the Hudson River and Fifth Avenue and longitudinally by Eighteenth and Forty-Second Streets, was the wealthiest in the country, no incidental consideration for him given the fact that his compensation was calculated on the basis not of a fixed salary but of commissions linked to his collections. Furthermore, as the growing length and cost of the war drove the government to impose a number of new taxes, including an income tax, his own revenue grew apace. Taylor rightly considered it a golden opportunity for his friend, as he believed the Russian appointment would be for him: "The times have tried us all pretty severely, and it is a great satisfaction to know that you are now tolerably secure."[84] The position was anything but a sinecure, however; it became Putnam's primary professional responsibility during his four years in office, taking precedence over his publishing accounts. Furthermore, he gradually developed the ambition to conduct his office on a higher degree of professionalism than that on which civil service positions were customarily administered.

For the first two years he kept two offices and worked two full-time jobs (in addition to his spiraling volunteer work). During that period he spent extensive amounts of time not only at his collector's office at 921 Broadway and at his publishing office at 441 Broadway, but also at the Loyal Publication Society headquarters at 863 Broadway, whose publications he continued to oversee. The price was physical exhaustion, early days in various locations around town often stretching into long nights spent at the collector's office with his clerks writing letters and receipts. But in 1864, he sold out his interest (as Holt did his) in the *Rebellion Record* to the New York publisher David Van Nostrand, a specialist in military publications who paid them $12,000.[85] George Haven Putnam later claimed that Moore, who remained editor and part-proprietor, had been drawing expenses on the joint account dishonestly, a charge that he no doubt picked up directly from his father; if accurate, Putnam had again chosen his business partner unwisely.[86]

In any case Putnam had more on his mind at the time than his ventures with Moore. That spring Putnam, just recently turned fifty years old, made a decision of more sweeping consequence to his publishing career in entering into an agreement to expand the printing connection he had established the previous year with Henry Houghton, who had recently gone into partnership with Melancthon Hurd as the New York-Boston firm of Hurd and Houghton. As of 1 August 1864, Putnam authorized them to take temporary control over the manufacture and sale of his entire publication list.[87] He closed his office and referred clients down the street to theirs at 401 Broadway. Why he chose Hurd and Houghton to represent his interests is not clear. He had known Hurd, who had worked for Sheldon and Company until his partnership with Houghton, for years, but it is more likely that Putnam's attraction was to Houghton, whose Riverside Press was one of the leading facilities in the country and who gave him marketing advantages through Boston not previously available to him. Then, too, he might have been attracted to Houghton by the fact that books produced at Riverside Press, as he pointed out to Taylor about his own, would carry the "éclat" of one of the most distinguished commercial presses in the United States.[88]

So in August 1864, for the first time since he came to New York in 1829, Putnam was largely, if not quite entirely, removed from the book business. Despite his improved income, precious little went into savings or into plans for future business operations. Instead, he chose to use much of his income to pay his creditors from 1857 the difference between the 60 percent mandated by the agreement and the 100 percent he felt obligated by honor to return. He also used some of it to settle his family more comfortably than it had been since leaving Melrose in 1861, establishing a pattern of dual summer/winter residences—summers at various locations from the New Jersey side of the Palisades near Fort Lee to the southern Connecticut shore, winters at the house he bought at 107 East Seventeenth Street (which in 1863 he rented out for a year to the actor Edwin Booth, whose acquaintance he had first made in London). The primary family home for much of the 1860s was the cottage at Five Mile River Landing, which Putnam was renting when Haven returned from Europe in July 1862 and then purchased in 1864. That location was too far from Manhattan for commuting, so Putnam took a room in the city and returned home primarily on weekends. Meanwhile, the Putnam household was changing internally. As older children began to move out, new ones entered: Kingman Nott born in 1859, and Herbert in 1861, the ninth and tenth of the Putnam children (and the last to reach maturity).

Putnam and his family became more fully immersed in the war as the years of fighting dragged on. His early confidence in the swift and certain success of the Union army gave way to a toughened support of the war effort and of Lincoln's administration. That support was tested most severely in 1864. Early that year he joined a group of prominent New Yorkers in addressing a petition to the National Executive

Committee of the Republican Party, requesting that the national convention be postponed from June until September to allow time for the prosecution of the war to take precedence over internal acrimony.[89] As often before, he was involved in a gentlemanly project anything but consonant with the surrounding turmoil.

By the time the acrimonious presidential campaign of 1864 was in full swing, two of the Putnam children were living south of the Mason-Dixon line and making their contributions to the war effort. Haven, who had originally enlisted for but a year, reenlisted for the duration of the war, served with his unit in four Southern states and on several fronts, and rose through the ranks by war's end to major. Much as he disliked army life at the time ("I have never been a soldier by taste or choice, and have never been able to feel that my experience in the army was anything more than an episode in my real life's work," he protested directly after his release), his service period turned out to be the most memorable time of his life; he would proudly carry the nickname of "the Major" to the end of his long life in 1930.[90] He saw areas of the country new to him and came into close contact with people foreign to his own experience, such as immigrants, laborers, and freed slaves (for whom he displayed far less sympathy than did his two eldest sisters). He fell ill for a period with malaria in Louisiana, spent a night in the field with an uninvited poisonous snake in his sleeping bag, saw action in both Louisiana and Virginia, fell prisoner to Confederate forces twice, and took part in the early policing that accompanied the end of hostilities and the beginning of Reconstruction in Georgia. Barely twenty-one at war's end, he emerged from its experience having seen full displays of both the worst and the best in human nature. And, like his father, he came away from the Civil War with a strengthened and concretized appreciation of the overriding ideal of national unity, one that both father and son valued then and later above considerations of national, regional, or ethnic diversity.

During the period of his illness in June 1863, Mary came down to the field to nurse him back to health. The initiative to make the long, dangerous trip to New Orleans without escort was hers, although she had gotten her parents' consent (they being less suited to execute the mission themselves). After locating his unit in a remote part of the state and looking after him until he recovered, she returned for a while to New Orleans, where she had made friends, before coming home. That fall she resumed her medical training, this time in Philadelphia at the

Female Medical College of Pennsylvania. She quickly completed her few remaining courses and received her medical degree in April, her father losing no time despite his ambivalence in proudly supplying her with her first set of professional cards.[91] During the remainder of that year, she did clinical work in Philadelphia, New York, and Boston, where she worked with the pioneer physician Marie Zakrzewska at the New England Hospital for Women and Children.

Then in December 1864 she discontinued her medical work in New York to go south on a second nursing mission, this time to Virginia to look after Edith, who had been working for several months in Norfolk as a volunteer teacher with freed slaves. After several years of shouldering much of the responsibility for teaching her younger brothers and sisters, Edith had found herself presented with an opportunity to do some good outside the "home circle" when she was asked to join a group of women being sent by the Freedmen's Bureau to teach school in Norfolk. In all likelihood, she was inspired to take this step by the presence in her family since late 1863 of the young black woman (known in the family as Sarah Contraband) whom Mary had befriended in New Orleans and brought back to the family home at Five Mile River Landing. Secured by the Union army and regarded as a haven for "contrabands," Norfolk had grown into a center for educational, religious, and economic training of the ex-slaves; dozens of schools had been organized in the town and vicinity by dozens of organizations, one even on the estate of Governor Wise.[92] But the task awaiting the volunteers was immense. It had been bluntly stated that summer by Lucy Chase, one of the most dedicated Northern aid workers active not only in the city but in the entire South: "Next to driving the colored people into the country, Genl. [Benjamin] Butler desires to drive them upon their feet."[93] Monumental in itself, the task was complicated by local hostility, poor working conditions, lack of books and other educational material, and limited understanding between blacks and whites. As matters turned out, Edith's actual service was brief and her contribution modest. While working long hours to teach basic literacy skills to three generations of African Americans, she contracted typhoid fever in November and remained too weak through the rest of the year either to teach or to travel home. Mary, who probably arrived a day or two before Christmas, stayed with her until she had regained enough strength to travel and then escorted her home to Five Mile River Landing in January or February 1865.[94]

Although relieved to have Edith safely home, the family passed an agonizing fall and winter waiting for news of Haven. Putnam traveled to Washington as soon as he heard that Haven had been reported missing in the 19 October battle of Cedar Creek and waited several weeks to hear word of his fate. In the weeks that followed, he sent out inquiries in all directions, even across Dixie, and enlisted numerous friends in government, the military, and private life in hopes of locating him. In what must have been only one of many such investigations, his prewar acquaintance from Columbia, South Carolina, James Carter, searched the prisoner lists across the state for mention of Haven's name. He found none, but he did use the opportunity to send back to Putnam a piece of his mind: "It is indeed mortifying to me to see the sons of my contemporaries, engaged in a war of invasion on my country, and sanctioning by their presence the most stupendous policy which the world has ever saw." [95]

Once Putnam learned that Haven had been taken prisoner and sent to Libby Prison, he established a close contact with the military command and the War Department in his desire to see his son released, reaching as high as the commanding Union officer for prisoner exchanges, General Ethan Allan Hitchcock.[96] Despite high-level assurances that the government was actively involved, Putnam and his family must have gone through the worst winter of their lives. The letter of acknowledgment from headquarters meant to reassure him that "everything was being done" was mistakenly addressed to Haven, and Putnam's original worries intensified when for months he received no word of or from his son.[97] Then after he learned that Haven had been sent to Libby, Putnam received no word for weeks that he had been transferred to Danville Prison. He did not find out until their reunion near war's end that Haven had been held in Richmond for only two weeks before his transfer to Danville, where he lived through the winter of 1864–65 in a tiny room he called a "pig-sty" and spent several hours each day "skirmishing" (as the Northern prisoners took to calling one of their chief daily activities) with the vermin that infested the prisoners.[98]

Putnam's situation of awaiting news about a son held prisoner of war was, of course, a common one in the last days of the war. In fact, he had been in touch throughout the war with other parents concerned about the fate of their sons. In the first or second year of the war, for instance, he had communicated with the father of Cabot Jackson

Russell, Haven's walking companion of 1860, who was taken captive early in the war. He no doubt heard soon after the battle that Russell fell in the disastrous 1863 assault on Fort Wagner along with his commander Colonel Robert Gould Shaw and many of the other men of the largely African American 54th Massachusetts (the Putnams would remember that battle and publish a firsthand account of it in *Putnam's Magazine,* full of complimentary references to Russell, in 1869).[99] Then during the dismal fall of 1864, Putnam learned that his onetime professional associate and longtime acquaintance Frederick Saunders was also awaiting news of the whereabouts of his son. By chance, Frank Saunders and Haven Putnam were both at Danville during the last months of the war, where they made each other's acquaintance, as Frank mentioned in a letter to his father.[100]

The highest hope of parents that winter throughout the country, North and South, was that a prisoner exchange could be effected. Such exchanges had been arranged in the first years of the war but had then ceased, with Lincoln refusing to accede to Southern demands that slaves-turned-Union soldiers be excluded from exchanges and Grant arguing against them as being a strategic advantage to the undermanned Confederate army. But with political pressure building in 1864 as reports of horrible conditions reached the North, Northern leaders relented and the trades resumed in the last months of the war. No doubt aware of the improved chances for success, Henry Holt advised Putnam in January 1865 of a well-born Southern second lieutenant held in Fort Delaware who he thought would make a good trading partner for Haven; the young man's influential Charleston family had previously made such an arrangement for his brother and held up hopes of repeating it for him.[101] By that time, Putnam was already in communication with a Confederate officer held at Fort Donald in Delaware who was also eager to be Haven's partner in a trade. Neither special exchange, however, seems to have been effected.

When Haven was finally freed on 3 March, it was as part of a general prisoner exchange. He arrived the previous day by train at Richmond and then walked unescorted across town to the prearranged gathering place at Libby Prison (into which he had to ask this time to be admitted). During that surreal excursion across Richmond, he managed to get a good look at the city that tens of thousands of eager Union troops, as well as Lincoln himself, were still weeks away from seeing from the inside. The next day he and his fellow freed prisoners were transported on a truce boat via Norfolk to Annapolis for decontamination and medical treatment. On landing, he sent his father the telegram with the news for which the Putnams had been waiting for months. Several days later, he was safely home, his health so good, in fact, that after a month of recuperation he was able to rejoin his unit, repositioned to North Carolina, in the field.

What with the overwhelming strain of household worries, the portentous election campaign of 1864, and the long-anticipated assault on Richmond, Putnam experienced abrupt mood swings during the last half-year of the war, which he categorized in his mind as the period between the reelection and the assassination of Lincoln. If he had entertained thoughts as late as 1863 of joining the army, he understood by the election of 1864 that the one irreplaceable person in the Union was the unconventional-looking man whom he had first seen that February 1860 night at Cooper Union and who had grown so greatly in stature as to have become fixed in his mind as a national savior. As a result, he was deeply shaken by the assassination. The younger Putnam children remembered the occasion as the first time they had ever seen adults, no less their parents, cry.[102] For Putnam, the assassination was "a fearful calamity to this country," but he nevertheless believed that the country would come through the current "'age of sensations'" whole and renewed. He correctly foresaw, however, that Reconstruction would proceed more sternly in the absence of "our great though tender-hearted President." With good reason, he wished out loud: "God grant that Andrew Johnson may be equal to his task"; it could not have occurred to him at the time that that benediction might encompass not only the clemency-seeking leaders of the Confederacy but also himself in his capacity as a federal office holder.[103]

One other shock, this one of a more personal nature, hit the family that month. Just days before war's end, Mary announced to her parents that she had become engaged to her former instructor at the New York College of Pharmacy, Ferdinand Mayer. Although her mother had accepted her father at age sixteen, her parents were caught completely by surprise by the engagement, Victorine describing her husband as "dumb-founded" by the news and herself as "disturbed at the thought of the broken circle."[104] Mary's siblings were no more accepting of the perceived impending breakup of the family circle; Haven reported to a friend: "My selfishness ... has met with a sad shock lately. My eldest sister Minnie, a fellow student of mine, one of the dearest girls in the world, and one whom I had always considered as my special property, is going to be married.—I suppose it is the way of the world, but it is a great disappointment to me."[105] Until that moment the parents apparently no more saw their nearly twenty-three-year-old daughter in the role of wife than they saw Mayer, a German-born Jew and well-regarded chemist, as a suitable marriage partner. In the end, neither did Mary. Although Mayer was older and far better-established professionally than she, characteristics that undoubtedly attracted him to her in the first place, she gradually became aware that she had mistaken their relative strength and independence. She admitted as much to her father in asking for his intervention just weeks before the date set for the wedding: "But I am not sure that his intellect or character are as strong as mine. . . . I influence him a great deal, he scarcely influences me at all, in a word, I can manage him, and that makes him far less interesting than if he, by superior power, controlled and magnetized me."[106] Although not used to being asked to intercede on behalf of his independent-minded daughter, he responded immediately and the engagement soon came to an end.

Life returned to normal in the months following the armistice, which had little immediate impact on either of Putnam's positions. He continued to spend most of his day at the collector's office uptown on Broadway, sometimes finding time late in the afternoons to check in at the office of Hurd and Houghton and engage in shoptalk and keep watch over his clients' accounts. Despite his pre-armistice predictions, business remained slow and unpromising after the war's end. One thing that did change, however, was the composition of his collector's office, into which he drew his son as deputy collector shortly after Haven was released from the army. The thought of bringing Haven into business was not new to Putnam; he had considered employing his son alongside himself several times during the war and had even made inquiries in 1863 and 1864 about getting him a discharge, although nothing came of them. For his part, Haven still had thoughts at the time of his discharge in June 1865 of resuming his studies, whether in Göttingen or elsewhere, in hopes of eventually joining the ranks of the rising generation of young scientific professionals with whom he had associated on two continents. But he quickly agreed—not entirely un-reluctantly—to postpone that goal at his father's request that he come work for a year in the collector's office, and by July he was installed in his new position.[107]

In actuality, he was to last in the office as long as his father did. Appointed under Lincoln, Putnam was fired under Johnson. The immediate cause of his dismissal was his principled refusal to pay the apportionment expected of all government appointees to support the president. Like the husband of his cousin Sophia Peabody Hawthorne, who had also described the feeling of being fired from a government position as decapitation and taken his injured pride to the court of public opinion, Putnam did not hesitate to dramatize and publicize the incident. He lost no time after his dismissal that fall in publishing a defense of his conduct in the local press and in sending out circulars giving the texts of letters defending his conduct by the secretary of the Treasury and the commissioner of the Internal Revenue.[108] As he reported the matter several years later in the New York press, "on the very day that President Johnson dismissed me for the crime of not supporting his 'policy,' and refusing to pay $500 for the 'Johnson club,' I sent to Washington the last dollar of more than twenty millions ($20,000,000), which I had collected and paid over in careful uniformity to the law of the department."[109] Although justified by his own standards, his behavior in the matter was politically ingenuous. Putnam might have been a devoted and trustworthy government servant, but he was anything but a loyal Johnson supporter; he disagreed strongly with Johnson's policies, an antagonism that he made public in 1866 a few months after his dismissal in compiling a pamphlet for the Union League Club taking sides with the Republican Congress against the president in the battle over Reconstruction.[110]

He had widespread support for his self-defense among colleagues in the publishing trade and no doubt won the minds of some of the growing number of people in New York and elsewhere critical of Johnson's policies. But if a public show of support always registered as meaningful with Putnam, it did nothing to fill the void in salary and time left by the dismissal. Given these circumstances, it was inevitable that Putnam would choose to resuscitate his publishing business. That decision was made within weeks of his dismissal and was advertised on 1 December, the same day that his return was formally greeted in the trade paper: "That excellent man, liberal gentleman, and experienced publisher, George P. Putnam, has ascended again from the place of office-holder, which he condescended to fill, to the honorable position of a member of the trade."[111] He speedily made the necessary arrangements with Hurd and Houghton for the return of his literary properties and opened his doors for business directly after New Year's Day, 1867. When he did, he faced the public with his affairs changed in one fundamental way: as the senior member in the reconfigured firm of G. P. Putnam and Son, he was finally able to operate in tandem with the talented, trustworthy partner that he had lacked ever since splitting up with John Wiley.

Notes

1. *American Publishers' Circular and Literary Gazette* 3 (7 November 1857): 693.

2. His autograph collection was put up for auction at Bangs, Merwin and Company beginning on 13 December 1858. Copies of the auction catalogue are at the American Antiquarian Society and at the Library of Congress (GPP Collection).

3. GHP, *George Palmer Putnam,* 2:5; autobiographical sketch; Mary Putnam Jacobi Papers, Schlesinger Library, Radcliffe College.

4. Autobiographical sketch; Mary Putnam Jacobi Papers, Schlesinger Library, Radcliffe College.

5. GPP to Taylor, 25 September 1857; BT-C.

6. A. H. Saxon, ed., *Selected Letters of P. T. Barnum* (New York: Columbia University Press, 1983), xviii.

7. The sale of GPP's properties by Mason at the spring 1858 trade sale alone brought in $16,000, more than 10 percent of the total sales generated that week; *American Publishers' Circular and Literary Gazette* 4 (17 April 1858): 186.

8. Pierre Irving, ed., *Life and Letters of Washington Irving,* 4 vols. (New York: G. P. Putnam, 1862–64), 4:237–38.

9. GPP to Taylor, 13 January 1858; BT-C.

10. Ibid.

11. GPP to Wilkes, 12 July 1859; Wilkes Family Papers, Perkins Library, Duke University.

12. Ticknor and Fields to GPP, 10 August 1858; letter books (MS Am 2030.2 [57]), Ticknor and Fields Papers, Houghton Library, Harvard University. I owe thanks to Jeffrey Groves for turning my attention to this letter.

13. GPP to Taylor, 16 February 1859; BT-C. Also, see advertisements about the new relationship placed by GPP in *American Publishers' Circular and Literary Gazette* 5 (7 May 1859): 223 (and by Sheldon and Company in the same issue, 226).

14. Taylor to GPP, 19 February 1859; GPP-P (box 11, scrapbook, p. 32).

15. Irving Family Papers, Rare Books and Manuscripts Division, New York Public Library.

16. GPP to Taylor, 25 January 1859; BT-C.

17. He used the term in "Recollections of Irving," *Atlantic Monthly* 6 (November 1860): 610.

18. Ibid., 610.

19. GPP to George Henry Moore, 30 March 1860; New-York Historical Society.

20. GPP, "Recollections of Irving," 601–12.

21. *American Publishers' Circular and Literary Gazette* 6 (24 March 1860): 148.

22. *American Publishers' Circular and Literary Gazette* 5 (18 June 1859): 296.

23. GPP kept a special notebook for the Irving account in the late 1850s, which he apparently transmitted to Pierre Irving after his uncle's death; Irving Family Papers, Rare Books and Manuscripts Division, New York Public Library (box 17).

24. GPP to Taylor, 5 May 1857; BT-C.

25. GPP to Taylor, 25 January 1859; BT-C.

26. GPP to Taylor, 1 July 1859; BT-C.

27. In responding to GPP's anxiety about unconventionalisms in the novel, Taylor stated, "You make the popular mistake, in speaking of my 'tilt' against them. I do no such thing: some of my characters do, it is true, but *my own views* are nowhere expressed in the book." Taylor to GPP, 18 September 1863; GPP-P (box 11, scrapbook, p. 33).

28. GPP to Taylor, 16 November 1857; BT-C.

29. GPP to Taylor, 30 October 1860; BT-C.

30. The subject came up between them repeatedly. For a vivid example of his accounting "system," see GPP to Taylor, 7 June 1859; BT-C.

31. The following sketch draws heavily on his children's volumes of memoirs, especially GHP, *George Palmer Putnam;* GHP, *Memories of My Youth, 1844–1865* (New York: G. P. Putnam's Sons, 1914); and Ruth Putnam, ed., *Life and Letters of Mary Putnam Jacobi* (New York: G. P. Putnam's Sons, 1925).

32. Mary Putnam Jacobi Papers, Schlesinger Library, Radcliffe College.

33. Her entries appear in the back pages of a ledger her mother had kept in London from 1843–47 and then brought back to the United States and that Mary must afterwards have claimed as her own copybook; HP-LC.

34. [Mary Putnam], "Found and Lost," *Atlantic Monthly* 5 (April 1860): 391–407. She also successfully placed a second story the next year: "Hair-Chains," *Atlantic Monthly* 8 (November 1861): 534–49.

35. Allibone to GPP, 26 March 1860; GPP-P.

36. New York *Tribune,* 28 February 1862, 4.

37. GHP, *Abraham Lincoln: The People's Leader in the Struggle for National Existence* (New York: G. P. Putnam's Sons, 1909).

38. This curious letter of 8 June 1860 survives in a draft written in an unidentifiable hand but signed unmistakably at its end by GPP; GPP-NYPL.

39. GHP to John Hart Morgan, 18 January 1873; Kroch Library, Cornell University.

40. Ruth Putnam, ed., *Mary Putnam Jacobi,* 67.

41. Ibid., p. 61.

42. Ibid., 58.

43. Ibid., 67.

44. Olmsted had long held a high opinion of GPP, whom he described in a letter to his father "as the most liberal and honest of all the publishers or at least is so esteemed by authors." Olmsted to his father [front page missing but conjecturally dated on letter as late 1850]; Frederick Law Olmsted Papers, Library of Congress.

45. GHP, *Memories of My Youth,* 189–90.

46. Ibid., 193–94.

47. GHP to James Hart Morgan, 30 September 1862; Kroch Library, Cornell University.

48. GPP to Taylor, 23 April 1861; BT-C.

49. "Before and After the Battle: A Day and Night in 'Dixie,'" *Knickerbocker* 58 (September 1861): 1–21. That account was widely reprinted, including in *Rebellion Record* 2 (1862): 59–60 (in "Documents" section) and 20–23 (in "Poetry" section); and in GHP, *George Palmer Putnam,* 2:123–53.

50. Fleeing civilians actually contributed to the post-battle breakdown of discipline in Union ranks by clogging the road eastward that the army needed for its own retreat.

51. One of them wrote GPP shortly after returning home to find out how he had managed after their separation, then a second time a month later to thank him for the current issue of the *Rebellion Record* and to state his agreement that "Mr. Russell over *shot* the mark in giving his description of the retreat." C. T. Greenleaf to GPP, 26 July and 29 August [1861]; Special Collections, Dartmouth College Library, Dartmouth College.

52. *American Publishers' Circular and Literary Gazette* 6 (22 September 1860): 483.

53. *American Publishers' Circular and Literary Gazette* 6 (29 September 1860): 498.

54. Quoted in *American Publishers' Circular and Literary Gazette* 6 (22 September 1860): 483.

55. Fields to GPP, 30 September 1861; GPP-P.

56. Childs's letter of 21 September 1861 is in GPP-P; it is reprinted in GHP, *George Palmer Putnam,* 2:165.

57. See *American Literary Gazette and Publishers' Circular* octavo series 4 (15 December 1864): 109, and octavo series 4 (15 March 1865): 263. Smith's letter of acknowledgment was printed in *American Literary Gazette and Publishers' Circular* octavo series 5 (15 June 1865): 73.

58. *American Publishers' Circular and Literary Gazette* 8 (February 1862): 19.

59. *American Literary Gazette and Publishers' Circular* octavo series 4 (15 December 1864): 109–10.

60. Henry Holt, *Garrulities of an Octogenarian Editor* (Boston: Houghton Mifflin, 1923), 95.

61. "Publisher's Notice," *Sketch Book* (New York: G. P. Putnam, 1864), 3.

62. GPP to Bayard Taylor, 23 September 1862; BT-C.

63. GPP to Bayard Taylor, 30 June 1863; BT-C.

64. GPP to Duyckinck, 21 April 1862; GPP-NYPL.

65. Fields to GPP, 4 September 1863; GPP-P (box 11, scrapbook).

66. The two men had had transatlantic professional dealings ever since GPP had gone into business on his own, but that practice ended in the early 1850s when Bentley came to see the publication of American books as too risky an investment. But after soliciting GPP in 1860 to renew their relationship, Bentley had resumed an occasional partnership with GPP on a reduced scale.

67. GPP to Taylor, 23 September 1862; BT-C.

68. Taylor to GPP, 18 September 1863; GPP-P (box 11, scrapbook).

69. Taylor, *Hannah Thurston* (New York: G. P. Putnam, 1862), 3–4.

70. GPP's letter is printed in Marie Hansen-Taylor and Horace E. Scudder, eds., *Life and Letters of Bayard Taylor,* 2 vols. (Boston: Houghton, Mifflin and Company, 1885), 2:416. The original letter is in BT-C.

71. Simon Nowell-Smith, *International Copyright Law and the Publisher in the Reign of Queen Victoria* (Oxford: Oxford University Press, 1968), 37–40.

72. *American Publishers' Circular and Literary Gazette* 8 (February 1862): 19.

73. *American Publishers' Circular and Literary Gazette* 7 (27 April 1861): 153.

74. *Rebellion Record* 1 (1861), iii.

75. The initial exchange took place in the newspapers: Greeley's first and second letters in the New York *Tribune,* 20 and 25 August 1862; Lincoln's response originally in the Washington *National Intelligencer,* 23 August 1862, then reprinted in both the New York *Tribune* and the New York *Times,* 25 August 1862. GPP and Moore reprinted all

three letters in the *Rebellion Record: Supplement* (New York: G. P. Putnam, Henry Holt, 1864), 480–83 (in "Documents" section).

76. Reprinted in *American Publishers' Circular and Literary Gazette,* octavo series 1 (1 April 1863): 49.

77. For information on Evans, see "Sketches of the Publishers: George P. Putnam," *Round Table* 3 (17 February 1866): 106.

78. The circular is in GPP-NYPL.

79. Some of the return correspondence is in GPP-NYPL.

80. Martineau to GPP, 19 June 1863; GPP-NYPL.

81. *Letters from Europe Touching the American Contest* (New York: Loyal Publication Society, 1864).

82. He felt a particular debt to Bryant, whom he thanked profusely for his effort while awaiting the outcome of his application: "Even though the outcome in question may not be effected, I cannot help feeling richer and stronger, with such words in my possession, from authority so high and so greatly respected." GPP to Bryant, 7 August 1862; Bryant-Godwin Papers, Rare Books and Manuscripts Division, New York Public Library.

83. On being apprised of Taylor's chances, GPP immediately wrote to well-connected friends, such as Bryant and George Bancroft, to advise them of the "necessity" of Taylor's appointment. GPP himself unhesitatingly considered his friend better qualified for the post than were "nine out of ten of the class [of] politicians who are usually selected for these missions." GPP to Taylor, 1 December 1862; BT-C.

84. Taylor to GPP, 18 October 1862; GPP-P (box 11, scrapbook).

85. "Sketches of the Publishers," 106.

86. GHP, *George Palmer Putnam,* 2:163–64.

87. According to the memorandum of agreement, Hurd and Houghton were to receive 15-percent commission fees on their sales of Putnam's works; Ellen Ballou, *The Building of the House: Houghton Mifflin's Formative Years* (Boston: Houghton Mifflin, 1970), 68.

88. GPP to Taylor, 15 July 1864; BT-C.

89. A manuscript copy of the petition, dated 25 March 1864, is in the collections of the New-York Historical Society. The first of the several dozen signers was Bryant; GPP was third.

90. GHP to Henry Rose Hinckley, 22 May 1865; GHP-C (box 3).

91. Ruth Putnam, ed., *Mary Putnam Jacobi,* 70.

92. Henry Lee Swint, *The Northern Teacher in the South, 1862–1870* (New York: Octagon, 1967), 62.

93. Quoted in Henry L. Swint, ed., *Dear Ones at Home: Letters from Contraband Camps* (Nashville: Vanderbilt University Press, 1966), 128.

94. Mary presumably left home within several days of writing a letter to the editor of the New York *Times,* as did five other progressive women. She and her allies protested the antifeminist claims contained in a letter printed in the *Times* on 18 December by "a Mother of the Old School" and defended the necessity and ability of women to serve as medical professionals. The six letters were printed in the *Times* on Christmas day, as Victorine Putnam informed her daughter in a letter she wrote her that day and addressed to Norfolk. The letters were unsigned by proper name; Mary's was probably the one signed "One Who Claims To Be a Physician"; Ruth Putnam, ed., *Mary Putnam Jacobi,* 72.

95. Carter to GPP, 7 December 1864; Special Collections, Dartmouth College Library, Dartmouth College.

96. Hitchcock wrote GPP on 22 January 1865 to explain the latest circumstances

concerning prisoner exchanges and the prospects for his son's release; Special Collections, Dartmouth College Library, Dartmouth College.

97. Henry Bennett to "G. H. Putnam," 18 December 1864; Special Collections, Dartmouth College Library, Dartmouth College.

98. I take these details about GHP's incarceration from his letter to Henry Rose Hinckley, 7 March 1865; GHP-C (box 3). Hinckley was a friend from Massachusetts with whom GHP had spent considerable time in Paris and Berlin.

99. His father wrote to thank GPP for the "kind notice" of his son he had printed in the New York *Evening Post;* William C. Russell to GPP, n.d.; Special Collections, Dartmouth College Library, Dartmouth College. The survivors' account of the decimation of the 54th Massachusetts was told by J. M. W. Appleton, "That Night at Fort Wagner," *Putnam's Magazine* 4 (July 1869): 9–16.

100. Frederick Saunders, Jr., to GPP, 20 January 1865; Special Collections, Dartmouth College Library, Dartmouth College.

101. Henry Holt to GPP, 20 January 1864 (Holt misdated the year, which was actually 1865); Special Collections, Dartmouth College Library, Dartmouth College.

102. Ruth Putnam, ed., *Mary Putnam Jacobi,* 77.

103. GPP to Taylor, 18 April 1865; BT-C.

104. Ruth Putnam, ed., *Mary Putnam Jacobi,* 75–76.

105. GHP to unnamed correspondent, n.d. (but, in context, clearly datable to April 1865); GHP-C.

106. Ruth Putnam, ed., *Mary Putnam Jacobi,* 80.

107. GHP to [Henry Rose Hinckley], 22 June 1865; GHP-C.

108. Copies of the two letters (8 October and 22 October 1866) from the secretary of treasury, Hugh McCulloch, to GPP are in GPP-P (box 11, scrapbook). Although McCulloch defended GPP's "character as an officer or gentleman," he was also careful to defend President Johnson's prerogative to discharge government employees on "the principle of rotation."

109. A clipping of this letter to the editor of the New York *Evening Mail* (probably from 23 May 1870) is in GPP-NYPL.

110. GPP, comp. and ed., *The Real Questions Before the Country* (New York: John Trow, 1866).

111. *American Literary Gazette and Publishers' Circular,* octavo series 8 (1 December 1866): 91.

G. P. Putnam and Sons (and Daughters), 1867–1872

In summer 1866, Putnam drew up a schedule of his properties; then in the year's closing days he added to it his last will and testament.[1] His decision to take that latter step might have been prompted by the loss of his government position, or perhaps, though still in good health and robust spirits at age fifty-two, he was simply taking account of "the uncertainty of life," of which he had already had his share, to make provision for his wife and children. One day in summer 1869 the wisdom of his precaution was made more immediate when, while inspecting a building under construction where he was considering renting rooms, Putnam was knocked to his feet and pinned down by a falling crane, somehow loosened from its mooring on top of the building. Although badly bruised and left lame for a short time, he suffered no lasting physical injury.[2] Nor did the accident affect the thinking underlying his will, which, left unmodified, remained a strictly family affair, a document addressed to family members according to their internalized categories of wife, older four children, and younger six children. In its simplest aspect it was designed to take account of their future needs by arranging for the transfer of all his property to them.

By his loose reckoning his estate at the time consisted of $26,480 worth of literary properties (mostly in stereotype plates and bound and unbound books); $2,000 worth of manuscripts, paintings, and collections of letters; $11,000 worth of Connecticut real estate ($8,000 for the house at Five Mile River Landing and $3,000 for a house in Darien purchased in March 1865); and $2,500 worth of household goods. The only other major item was his life insurance premiums, collectable by his wife and worth $16,000 at his death. All in all it was not a very large estate, as he acknowledged, especially for a man who had been engaged in a high-powered business career stretching over three decades. He had no regrets about that fact, however, for two reasons. First, he believed that the true legacy of his estate consisted more in "the excellent material training" the children received from the family—older from mother and younger from older—than in any money or goods they might receive from him. Second, he saw in George Haven—and at this time, only in George Haven—his successor, putting his special blessing on his talented oldest son: "I feel it to be my special duty and pleasure to make extra exertion and extra provision to aid him in forming and pursuing his own plans for life, whether professional or otherwise, should he at any time need temporarily or permanently any means belonging to the family—but it is my hope and desire that he will adopt and continue the book-publishing business, in which I have gained, over many drawbacks, a creditable reputation and support."[3] He also took specific cognizance of his second son, John Bishop, who had replaced Haven as the family gardener and fix-it-man before going on to Pennsylvania Agricultural College for a course of studies in the new scientific approach to agriculture, one that might have pleased his paternal grandfather. At this time Putnam was fully reconciled to the likelihood that Bishop would continue to go his separate way professionally and wished to reward him for the "excellent qualities, and his steady and earnest industry in the pursuit which he seems to have chosen" by assigning to him the house in Darien.

He also more briefly singled out his daughters Mary and Edith, expressing his esteem for them and assigning them "such portion as my executors [Victorine and George Haven] may deem to be proper and suitable, according to their circumstances and those of the family." There was apparently never any serious thought by either father or daughters that they would follow Haven or any other sons into the business. Edith was at the time occupied largely with teaching and raising chickens and lived in the Darien house. In the next decade she would resume her studies, receiving her bachelor's degree in 1878 from Cornell University, a school with which her father and oldest brother had close ties through Goldwin Smith.[4] Then as later, Edith was less of a concern to her parents than was Mary, who was carrying her career ambition in a new direction. Convinced that she had exhausted the possibilities of medical education in the United States but unsatisfied with the extent of her training, she followed the international example of her older female contemporaries, Emily Blackwell, Marie Zakrzewska, and Lucy Sewall, by deciding to pursue her studies in Europe. After making inquiries at various places, she decided to take the ambitious step of applying for admission to l'École de Médicine at the Sorbonne. The process went slowly, her application running up against a barrier of not only gender considerations but concern about her formal preparation, which necessitated months of preliminary studies in Paris before she could be officially considered for admission. In time, with persistence and patience, she succeeded in securing admission and in so doing became the first woman accepted to classes at the Sorbonne's medical school. Putnam watched the process for years with ambivalence. Although he consented to her decision to embark for Paris and offered whatever financial support he could afford, in truth he continued to find her the most ungraspable of his children. For that matter, his ambivalence was matched by hers; much as she adored her family, she undoubtedly needed to keep a broad distance—even an ocean—between them in order to establish her life on her own terms. She maintained that distance for five years, although she remained in touch through long letters and occasional visits by relatives and common friends. By the time she returned home permanently in 1871, much would have happened to transform all their lives.

When Mary left for Paris, her father was still holding his Internal Revenue position, as well as operating a small painting gallery he had opened earlier that year at 661 Broadway in the building previously occupied by the National Academy of Design. Late that year, Putnam hosted the annual exhibition of the Artists' Fund Society. After he lost his collectorship, however, he had no choice but to make quick plans to resume his publishing career. He opened G. P. Putnam and Son for business in 1867 in the same building that housed his gallery. It was located in a section of the city still undeveloped when Putnam had entered the employ of Wiley and Long nearly thirty years before down on lower Broadway, the trade having moved with the flow of the commercial tide northward up the island. After three decades of experience, which had taken him to nearly a dozen locations along a several miles' stretch up the avenue, Putnam now found himself one of the most senior members of the profession. Whatever pride he took in that status, however, he was forced to carry on his affairs with only the barest minimum of operating funds. Some of the original capital invested in the business came from the savings, such as they were, that his son had been able to accumulate from his army salary; the majority, presumably, from whatever savings Putnam had been able to set aside during the years of his collectorship. He also considered himself owed $9,500 by the government for unpaid commissions at the time of his firing but sensibly held out little hope that he would soon be paid because his compensation was entangled in the collections of his successors in a system of codependence made worse by rampant bureaucratic incompetence and corruption.[5] Perhaps Putnam also managed to attract an investor or two, but if so they were silent partners included neither in the company name nor in the historical record.

Little wonder, then, that the refrain of the Putnams' correspondence with Haven during the half-dozen years of their collaboration in the reestablished company concerned the scarcity and insufficiency of operating funds. "I don't know where publishers' profits are to come from," Haven complained at one point in exasperation, and he, in particular, chafed under their restricted circumstances. They also affected Haven's personal life in ways both simple and complex, causing him to forego such simple pleasures as weekend trips and forcing him to postpone his plans to marry his fiancée, Rebecca Shepard.[6] He also felt compelled to deny his own professional ambitions for the firm; as he confessed to one of his closest friends toward the close of the second year's operations, "I do believe I could run a business beautifully with a proper margin of capital.— I have some magnificent theories on the matter, but this grinding along, touch and go, every now and then bumping against the bottom of ones [sic] resources, is dreadfully harassing."[7] As the one responsible for handling the accounts, Haven had good reason to complain, since the fiscal reality he faced was one of rising production costs, weak demand, and tight profit margins. That combination, exacerbated by the lack of a capital reserve, not only limited the firm's maneuverability but periodically threatened its very solvency during its first decade of activity. As late as 1875, there were occasional moments when Haven could not be sure that the firm would still be conducting its affairs the following week.[8]

Worse yet, the Putnams operated at a serious competitive disadvantage against the growing number of firms in and outside the city better endowed than theirs. In a sketch of post-war New York City, one of the sharper-eyed contributors to *Putnam's Magazine* described the new financial conditions of the city as follows: "Here, too, all tends to greater and greater concentration, and businesses cannot now be begun without fortunes, which thirty years ago men were content to end with."[9] That might have been an exaggeration, but it made a point that the Putnams would have understood immediately. Prices for the raw supplies of book manufacturing had gone up substantially as a result of wartime inflation, authors' compensation had more than doubled, and the overall cost of doing business was correspondingly higher than it had been before the war. Appleton, Harper, and Scribner all commanded financial and literary resources far greater than his, as did Lippincott's in Philadelphia and Fields and Osgood (successor to Ticknor and Fields) in Boston; and even recently founded firms, such as George Carleton's in the city and Roberts Brothers in Boston, had connections with the younger generation of writers that might have reminded Putnam more of his operations in the years following his separation from Wiley than in his current situation. Ten or twenty years before he had known the leading young writers as a matter of course; now he had far less contact with the generation of writers coming of age in the 1860s, such as Mark Twain, William Dean Howells, Henry James, Jr., Louisa May Alcott, Rebecca Harding Davis, Artemus Ward, or—perhaps the most commercially attractive young writer— Bret Harte. But even with limitations on his operating ability, Putnam still had his good name, which continued to command respect both with authors, artists, and editors, and with bankers, suppliers, and print craftsmen. During the first years of partnership with his son, they had to depend on that name and the network of connections built around it over three decades to reestablish the firm's place in the domestic and Anglo-American book trade.

The division of responsibilities at G. P. Putnam and Son corresponded to their respective strengths. Putnam handled the publishing and manufacturing side of the business; Haven, the financial and bookkeeping side, with gradually increasing attention to relations with authors as his two brothers entered the business and relieved him of some of his earlier burden. Putnam expressed himself early on as delighted with the talents of his son: "Haven is A. 1. as a business man and is my mainstay[:] cashier—book keeper—salesman, correspondence clerk etc."[10] Able to depend primarily on each other, they kept their office staff to a minimum to limit expenses. Whereas the Harpers and Appletons owned and operated large manufacturing and office facilities employing many dozens of workers, the Putnams resumed business in 1867 by occupying only the upper floor of a small storefront and employing a staff of three full-time people, Henry Van Siclen as trade department head and two family acquaintances as general clerks. Of the various professional advisers and clients who passed frequently through their rooms, perhaps only Frederic Beecher Perkins, who had helped to edit the original *Putnam's Monthly* in its final months, was on salary.[11] With so little help, even the general routine of business affairs kept father and son busy to the limit of their ability to function; within months Haven had picked up his father's signature habit of writing "in haste." Before long, with expanding commitments and an increasing volume of business, they found themselves unable to function without additional help, which came at least in part from within the family; John Bishop was recalled from his studies in Pennsylvania to join the firm in 1867 and Irving (the third oldest of the brothers) from Amherst College in 1872.

During that first year the volume of their affairs was fairly considerable for a "new" firm. As in 1848, Putnam launched his business with ambitious plans. As he had built his first business on Washington Irving, so two decades later and a million copies of his works sold he still carried Irving on his masthead and marketed him as his main asset. Putnam had by then regained ownership of the Irving plates by paying a surcharge (normally of $.09 per copy) over and above the royalty payments he regularly made to the estate. Upon resuming business he immediately offered Irving's works in the various editions and texts (including condensed versions of the longest ones) that he had marketed earlier in the decade, as well as in the Hurd and Houghton Riverside Edition. He had reached a five-year agreement with Pierre Irving to continue their mutually profitable arrangement, one that Putnam wished passed down to Haven in the event of his own death.[12] Assuring that continuation was more a matter of insurance than sentiment. Putnam had experienced an unpleasant scare (and, no doubt, outrage) in the closing months of the war when he learned that James

Fields, by then senior partner in Ticknor and Fields following Ticknor's death the previous year, was making overtures to the Irving family to acquire publishing rights to Irving's works. Too busy to come down to New York to explain matters in person, Fields assured "friend Putnam" by letter that he had no such intent: "You have known me long enough to determine whether I am capable of undertaking any project of so mean a nature as that laid to our charge."[13] As far as is known, that was the end of that affair, although it was not the last time that Fields made an incursion into Putnam's territory.

Putnam would undoubtedly have liked to replicate with Taylor an arrangement similar to the one he had with the Irving estate, but he was in no position to do so because he had been unable to purchase back the plates of Taylor's works. The next best thing, he took back publication of Taylor's works from Hurd and Houghton and hoped to continue their post-1857 terms. As with Irving's works, he hoped to maintain the G. P. Putnam relationship with Taylor not only into the foreseeable future but beyond his own time into Haven's. Not surprisingly, he featured Taylor prominently on the initial G. P. Putnam and Son lists, with the Caxton and cheaper editions out in fresh impressions, and he published Taylor's newest work, *Colorado,* shortly after resuming business. That work was well into production at the Riverside Press when Putnam and Son opened its doors, although formal publication was delayed until February while Putnam attempted to stir up interest out West by sending off advertising circulars to booksellers from the Rocky Mountains to California. As he was then doing with Irving's works, Putnam attempted to sell Taylor's both by subscription and through the retail trade. He was to have scant success in either regard, however, with *Colorado,* whose slow sales proved a disappointment to both author and publisher.[14]

Publishing Taylor's new work was the exception to the norm that first year. To minimize the inherent risks of underwriting new works, Putnam filled out his list for the most part by drawing on not only his two main standbys but also other established authors and texts previously connected with his business. Not the least among them was his own standard reference book *The World's Progress,* which he brought out that fall in a new edition updated to 1867. He also printed new versions of other older titles, some dating to the 1840s: Bastiat's *Sophisms of the Protective Policy* (which he had issued long before the Civil War, collaboratively with the Charleston bookseller John Russell), W. S.

Mayo's travel novel, *Kaloolah,* which went back to the days of Wiley and Putnam; Hood's works; St. John's textbook *Elements of Geology;* and Klipstein's textbook *A Grammar of the Anglo-Saxon Language.* In a less expensive category, he also renewed publication of the Putnam Railway Classics as $.75 paperbacks, beginning with Irving's *Tales of a Traveller* and continuing with four attractive collections drawn from *Putnam's Monthly:* "Maga" Stories, "Maga" Social Papers, "Maga" Excursion Papers, and "Maga" Papers on Paris.

Putnam was also planning a limited number of new initiatives, some probably right from the inception of business. Two were textbooks (in astronomy and geography) by his friend and client of many years before, Theodore Fay, with whom he apparently hoped to replicate the success he had enjoyed with Asa Gray. Both author and publisher entertained particularly high expectations for the geography project, which included a textbook and atlas designed for use in high schools that Fay hoped would be adopted as a standard part of American high school curricula. Haven at the time thought the geography text "superior to anything before heard of," but sales were so slack that the book probably never met even its production expenses—an early lesson for Haven in the gambles of his new profession.[15]

Several of their most interesting publications that first year were in the fine arts, still one of Putnam's major personal and professional interests. He had been one of the leading publishers of art books in the country during the 1850s, and he returned to publishing in 1867 apparently intent on recapturing that position. This ambition was facilitated by longstanding friendships with many of the city's leading artists, such as Asher B. Durand, Daniel Huntington, John Kensett, and Sanford Gifford. Furthermore, Putnam was involved in early postwar efforts to found an art museum in New York, one that would do justice to the city's aspirations to be the artistic center of the nation. His interest in publishing art books was therefore no more coincidental than was his firm's location in the old National Academy of Design building, where he kept open his art gallery for a period of months even after he and Haven had initiated their publishing operations.

The most important of the publications he put to press that year was unquestionably *Book of the Artists: American Artist Life* by Henry Tuckerman, a friend and client for many years. The product of many years of research and the outgrowth of several of Tuckerman's antebellum works, *Book of the Artists* was the most ambitious attempt of its generation to write what Tuckerman called "a Biographical History of American Art."[16] It is not hard to imagine the attraction that such a project had for Putnam, who like Tuckerman saw the quality of American life as closely connected to the quality of its culture. Putnam's faith in the arts, which clearly overlapped his faith in print, came through conspicuously in his publisher's statement, where he called *Book of the Artists* "a candid and comprehensive survey of the Progress of Art in the United States." The "publishers," he continued, had prevailed upon Tuckerman to undertake the work in the "faith" that such a project "appeared to be an essential want in our literature, and a theme which cannot fail to be emphatically interesting and acceptable, not merely to those more directly connected with Art, professionally and as collectors, but also to the many thousands of intelligent people who can appreciate and enjoy good pictures, although they may not have means to buy them."[17] By that logic, if people could not afford to buy the originals, they could afford this particular book—a logic that typified the way Putnam attempted to place the "intelligent people" of the United States in relation to the arts and letters with himself as their grateful intermediary.

Few contemporaries could equal Tuckerman's knowledge of the history of the arts in the United States. A longtime student of the American art scene and an acquaintance of many of its leading practitioners and collectors, he was, as his book made clear, widely informed about American art history right up to the contemporary moment. Broadly inclusive of earlier generations of American artists, his book also contained brief sketches of the newer generation of artists, such as Winslow Homer (singled out for *Prisoners from the Front*), James McNeill Whistler (singled out for *The White Girl,* described at secondhand from a murky review), and Martin Johnson Heade (whose first initials he reversed). But if he knew at first or secondhand about the latest work being done by American artists, it was clear that the locus of Tuckerman's values and views was in an earlier generation's veneration of the "American school" of landscape, genre, and portraiture. That perspective was no longer unchallenged in 1867. At a time when discussion of the arts increasingly divided along an east-west, New World–Old World axis, Tuckerman took the (now) conservative path of native favoritism that Putnam also followed in the postbellum years. Tuckerman's introductory survey of the history of painting in America was itself one of the most cogent cultural statements of its kind and an exemplary nativist statement in the postwar debate on American arts and letters then being carried on by, among others, James Jackson Jarves, Henry James, William Dean Howells, and Mark Twain. In it Tuckerman made clear his belief in "true artist-feeling" as one of the great goods in any "civilized" society and as a safeguard as well as expression of America's national genius. He was plainly uncomfortable, however, about the actual place of the arts in modern, democratic America ("our practical and busy land") generally, and in New York specifically, "the third metropolis of the civilized world" but an international emporium still without a major art museum.

Putnam undoubtedly shared many of Tuckerman's views about the value of the arts in America and his specific desire to see New York do critical and institutional justice to them. But he could hardly have followed him in setting the spirit of commerce in opposition to that of art, a division that seemed oddly out of place in a book containing a pioneering listing of private art collections in the United States, many of which were formed and owned by the class of businessmen and professionals that was increasingly challenging the "Four Hundred" as the leading art patrons in New York. To have insisted on that dichotomy for Putnam would not only have undermined his position as a publisher, but upset his basic faith in the power of commerce to do social and cultural good. His handling of Tuckerman's book was a case in point; with his usual blend of entrepreneurial energy and cultural pride, he advertised *Book of the Artists* as a landmark work and brought it out that fall in several formats, one a regular trade edition and the other a more expensive subscription-only edition of 150 copies printed on large paper. To make the latter edition especially attractive, he offered it jointly with a *Portfolio of Photographic Portraits of Eminent Artists*.[18]

A venture of a completely different sort materialized for the Putnams in summer 1867 when they were invited to become the exclusive suppliers of English-language textbooks to the then-westernizing Empire of Japan.[19] They owed this opportunity, one of the most attractive publication deals offered to any American publisher in the nineteenth century, to Putnam's friendship with the Japanese ambassador to the United States, Arinori Mori, whom he had met through Secretary of State Seward and for whom he had done a professional service that left Mori well disposed to him. One day in July or August, the Japanese minister of education, Ono Tomogoro, who had crossed the Pacific to supervise the purchase of the books and had been referred to G. P. Putnam and Son by Mori and Seward, came to the Putnam office at 661 Broadway to explain his country's new curricular needs and to negotiate terms for the first shipment of texts. Within a few weeks the Putnams assembled a curriculum from the works of the leading educational publishers in New York and sent off a sample shipment of books by steamer to Japan. To their surprise, the titles were accepted sight unseen and the $20,000 invoice paid by the government in advance of the books' arrival in Tokyo.

To serve as his liaison for future deliveries in what was designed to be a continuing partnership between his firm and the Japanese government, Putnam dispatched John Bishop to Yokohama via San Francisco early in September; with him went the financial hopes of the new firm. Word of his mission circulated not only through the profession but through newspapers around the country; within days of his sailing, one of the Boston cousins wrote the family for details after reading the news in the local papers.[20] But no sooner did the Putnams' door to fortune open than it closed, the first shipment being also the last. They apparently had little or no knowledge at the time that Bishop departed of the severity of the civil disturbances then occurring against the government of the shogun, which were already disrupting normal life in Japan. By the time Bishop reached Yokohama in January 1868, the country was engaged in a civil war. Although access to Tokyo was strictly forbidden to foreigners, he insisted on traveling there despite the risk, arriving in the city only to learn that the officials to whom he had letters of introduction had either resigned or committed suicide and that the books shipped from New York had arrived safely but subsequently sat unopened in a local warehouse. They apparently never left their crates.[21]

Compelled to carry a pistol and to travel under the protection of armed guards, Bishop eventually grasped the severity of conditions and concluded that the conflict was likely to last far longer than he was prepared to stay. He therefore reluctantly gave up his mission and returned home to deliver the bad news, which, given the slowness and unreliability of the transhemispheric mails, might not have preceded him to New York. Whether or not he then realized it, he had witnessed a historic reconfiguration of Japanese politics, which culminated later that year with the overthrow of the government of the shogunate, which had been in power since the early seventeenth century, and the abandonment of many of its policies, including the refashioning of the curriculum and schools according to Minister Tomogoro's model.

The dream of easy money in summer 1867 was first vivid for Putnam just as another dream came to life: the resumption of *Putnam's Monthly*. The prospect of reviving the magazine had been dancing before his eyes from the moment that he had returned to publishing in January, but he was not immediately ready to commit himself or his resources to its publication. Before taking that step, he conferred widely with friends and colleagues in the profession about the advisability of that plan. Great as the temptation was, he was still undecided in June, when he informed Bayard Taylor, once again overseas, that he was weighing "urgent suggestions" to resume *Putnam's* but that they were impractical "unless somebody chooses to invest *money* which *we* have not to invest."[22] That somebody, in effect, was presumably the shogun of Japan.[23] By August, with his head racing to keep up with his heart, Putnam made up his mind to resume publication of the magazine as of the New Year.[24] Once decided, he let his enthusiasm run free; as he told Taylor, one of the writers he was most eager to enlist as a main contributor, "As to material, we shall recieve [sic] *20 times* as much as we can use—but I am ambitious to do *a big thing* and have nothing but the best. We want to excel all that has been done. Excelsior is the word."[25]

More dispassionately put, the word should have been "gamble." Although the original *Putnam's* had turned out to be a profitable venture and was remembered by many of its former readers as a cultural landmark, Putnam was too experienced a literary professional to have been unaware that the odds of repeating its success were against him. In fact, given the more crowded company he would be keeping, the odds of either a financial or a cultural success were far more heavily against him in 1867 than they had been in 1852. This time he had to face not only the still overarching competition of *Harper's Monthly* (now backed by *Harper's Weekly*) but also that of the well-established *Atlantic Monthly,* a magazine that had filled the niche created by the first *Putnam's* and whose operators had, as Putnam did not, existing connections with many of the leading periodical authors in the country. To make matters worse, there was competition from other magazines already in the field, such as *Lippincott's,* the *Galaxy,* and the *Nation,* as well as leading English magazines reprinted in America and their American "eclectic" cousins. Well aware of the periodical lay of the land, a reviewer for the *Nation*, a journal admired by Putnam and his associates but considered by them "sour" due to its unceremoniously outspoken views, was simply being honest in forecasting a tough road ahead for the new magazine, commenting upon hearing of its planned resumption that competition for writers was already tight and upon seeing its first issue that "in general, our standard of excellence in periodical literature has risen, and the old *Putnam's,* if it were to appear now, might seem less good than before."[26]

That observer was right on both counts. Late to mobilize and surrounded by look-alike magazines, Putnam could hardly count on the novelty and cultural support he had enjoyed in 1852–53, when he had brought something timely and novel to American magazine journalism. Furthermore, he was well aware how high a target he had set for his magazine with its predecessor: "When I look back over the 1st vol. of the old series it is marvelous to find how good that was and how hard it is to beat, or even to approach it—But we mean to try."[27] With good reason he publicly invoked his old favorite Oliver Goldsmith in describing the venture as having been activated by "a knack at hoping."[28] If Putnam was a past master at hoping, so, at least for the time being, was the tougher-minded Charles Frederick Briggs, back for a second round as editor, who noted in the opening issue, "There may be too many physicians and too many lawyers in a community; but the evil, if it exist, of too many publishers or of too many publications will soon correct itself by the infallible agencies of the economy of trade."[29] As 1868 approached, Briggs and Putnam grew eager to take their chances in the "magazine mania" of the time, confident that they had the good will from the past and the right combination of people and ideas in the present to make a success of their venture.

Preparations for a strong beginning proceeded rapidly through autumn 1867. As he had fifteen years before, Putnam sent advertising circulars to leading writers and editors around the country, hoping to lure as much as possible of the nation's established talent to his magazine. By November he was listing in his advertisements a corps of contributors dominated by names from his past—Melville, Bryant, Taylor, Curtis, Duyckinck, Lieber, and Ripley (most of whom would contribute only rarely, if at all)—and promising that the magazine would be "a National Publication, supported by the Best Writers, in each department, in every section of the country."[30] By the eve of the inaugural number's appearance, he had lined up dozens of submissions for future issues and clearly considered himself ready to sustain the magazine into the indefinite future.[31] Meanwhile, he was also attending to the collateral task of gathering subscriptions. He had advertised in September for "500 agents for profitable books of the highest character. Ladies can do well."[32] Perhaps that call was only for subscription books on his list; however, by the time the new magazine's first issue was set to appear, Putnam was advertising for 1,000 agents to comb the country collecting subscriptions expressly for it.[33]

The first issue of *Putnam's Magazine* (as distinguished from *Putnam's Monthly*) was out by mid-December, an attractively printed publication looking much like its predecessor in its pea-green covers. Due to the inflation caused by the war, it was priced at $.35 an issue or $4 a year, a figure about one-third higher than 1850s prices but comparable to that of its competition. Its press run is unknown, but it seems reasonable to assume that Putnam would have aimed no lower than to duplicate the 20,000-copy combined printing of the first issue of *Putnam's Monthly*. Its opening article was so fitting as to be symbolic; written by Briggs, "The Old and the New: A Retrospect and a Prospect" turned out to be less a self-styled "gossipy little prelude" than a prophetically accurate self-analysis that looked back to its predecessor and forward to its aspirations. Aided by a letter from Curtis that he incorporated into his piece, Briggs surveyed the birth and maturation of the original *Putnam's* and the writers who had contributed to its success, noting sadly that many of them—including Kirkland, Thoreau, Hawks, O'Brien, even the Bourbon prince and his scribe, to name just a few of its most prominent contributors—were by then dead, and others grown silent ("And where, let us ask, is Herman Melville? Has that copious and imaginative author, who contributed so many brilliant articles to the *Monthly,* let fall his pen just where its use might have been so remunerative to himself, and so satisfactory to the public?"). By contrast with 1853, however, Briggs's editorial message now seemed conservative; taste, he fatuously claimed, had not changed in the interim, and what had served the magazine once would serve it equally well fifteen years later: good fiction serials and unsparingly honest political articles, both of which he was confident he would be able to solicit.[34]

To read the next article, however, Van Buren Denslow's "Thirteen Years of the Nation, 1854–67," was to be presented with an account of how much actually had changed over that period. That article looked back explicitly to Parke Godwin's still well-known "Our Parties and Politics" from the September 1854 *Putnam's,* itself a reaction to fast-changing times and events, and tracked the course of the nation from Godwin's day through civil war and social revolution. With its view of two separate societies founded on opposing principles of free and slave labor now struggling to integrate themselves into the first true union in modern times, Denslow's article forecast an era of American history that, wherever it might finally lead, would inevitably depart from the societal model of the past. His own opinions about the new era were clear, and they undoubtedly carried the endorsement of Putnam and the editorial staff in enthusiastically supporting Congressional plans for Reconstruction based on the principle of universal male suffrage. Perhaps more than any other article, that sober-minded, outspokenly opinionated opening essay set the tone, content, and character of the new *Putnam's,* which idealistically heralded the coming of a more prosperous, more equitable society. So, at least, the world looked from the doorstep of 661 Broadway on the eve of 1868; whether the editors of the magazine were still so cheery about national prospects in 1870 was to be quite another question.

The strategy of the magazine, as set down by Putnam in his publisher's statement at the end of the first volume, was to balance the qualities of a monthly magazine with those of a quarterly review—that is, to position it, like its predecessor, in the magic zone between serious and entertaining reading.[35] With a magazine subtitled "Original Papers on Literature, Science, Art, and National Interests," that was a delicate balancing act as likely to risk mutual exclusiveness as to achieve the desired breadth. Hoping to reach an audience across geographic lines, Putnam clearly meant to return *Putnam's* to the kind of representativeness he had sought in the antebellum years. In all likelihood, this was why he turned to Briggs a second time to serve as his senior editor. It is possible that he initially entertained reuniting the entire editorial "triumvirate," but if he did he would have found Curtis and Godwin unavailable because of their prior commitments to *Harper's Weekly* and the New York *Evening Post,* respectively. Instead, he brought in Denslow from the New York *Tribune* to run a regular department on current affairs, Edmund Stedman to do book reviews, and Henry Tuckerman and S. S. Conant (at various times) to cover the fine arts. He also eventually persuaded Bayard Taylor to contribute a long column on arts and letters overseas.

Briggs was immediately proven correct: *Putnam's* continued its predecessor's policy of expressing its views frankly on matters of society and polity, trusting that there existed an audience of serious, like-minded readers to follow its lead and to help it reach what Putnam called a "broad, generous nationality." It addressed the most important issues of its tumultuous times, its earliest numbers coinciding with the constitutional crisis that culminated in the impeachment of President Johnson—no favorite of either Putnam or his editors. The once "Black Republican" magazine of the mid-1850s was reborn in 1868 more in the form of "true blue" Republican, as it attempted to remain loyal to what it considered the party's social, political, and economic ideals. It came out in support of a variety of principles: universal male suffrage; increased educational opportunities for all Americans, including women and blacks; separation of church and state; encouragement of industrial development; centralized currency; patronage of the arts at the municipal level; and international copyright. Most of these goals *Putnam's* confidently associated early on with the Republican Party and its leadership, but with the passage of time its initial enthusiasm for Grant the candidate changed to disillusionment with Grant the president as old sources of corruption went unaddressed and new scandals broke out.

More crucial to the magazine than party politics per se, however, were social issues, especially those relating to the composition of American society. If the editors began their tenure with the view that by fighting a civil war the country had earned a mandate to carry on social and economic change, they gradually shifted their position to one centered on the subsequent fight to preserve a national union they considered worthy of the name, a reorientation that might have led some to wonder whether the new *Putnam's* was in the vanguard or the rearguard of its times. The editors published numerous pieces and editorial columns on pressing social issues. One was the place of women in the society. Clarence Cook captured the character of that issue in editorializing, "Turn which way we will in these days, there stands the woman-question confronting us."[36] That observation was clearly supported by the incessant treatment the issue received in the magazine, which, though generally sympathetic to the idea of "women's rights," nevertheless published broadly conflicting articles on what the proper place of women should be in the home, the workplace, and the voting box. An even more pressing issue—one that often seemed to pinch a raw nerve—

was the status of the church in society. Although the editors were un-questioningly and aggressively pro-Christian and pro-Protestant, they launched themselves into the local Catholic-Protestant controversy with a degree of vituperation reminiscent of the antebellum debate over nativism. This time, however, their own insecurity showed as they vented their outrage at the new ascendancy of Catholics and Catholi-cism in New York City, a Catholicism they saw as spreading into the schools and City Hall.

Putnam was presumably as active in both the editorial and the financial management of the second series as he had been of the first, and the general taste and views expressed by the new team of editors unquestionably reflected his own. He had been seriously frustrated by his own experience in and with the federal bureaucracy, and the early years of the Grant administration did nothing to encourage him to expect change. Had he lived long enough, he would surely have sup-ported the cause of civil service reform, whose leaders included not only numerous of his long-term associates, such as Curtis and Bryant, but also members of his family, including his two eldest children. He was, however, both less bitter than some of his colleagues and more cheerful about the prospects for a national union across geographical and reli-gious lines.

A more immediate source of anxiety for Putnam was his maga-zine's unrelieved gravity, which led him and his editors to look for ways to lighten its tone and contents. They sought to duplicate the minor success they had achieved in the first number of the new series with William D. O'Connor's well-timed Christmas story, "The Carpenter," which was reviewed widely and favorably, as was Briggs's opening sketch.[37] There were few comparable successes, however, in the three years that Putnam published the magazine. He did publish several humorous stories by Elizabeth Stoddard that contained some of the best qualities of *The Morgesons,* but it is likely that Putnam considered her husband Richard, who served for a period as an assistant editor, the more important contributor to the magazine.[38] Late in 1868 Putnam advertised that "contributions are also expected from 'Mark Twain' and other 'tragic' writers," but if he actually made an overture to Twain he never succeeded in getting a contribution from him or for that matter from any of the leading humorists of the time.[39] Overall, the quality of the fiction and poetry published in *Putnam's* was decidedly inferior to that not only in the *Atlantic* but also in the first series of *Putnam's.*

Whereas its predecessor had generated outstanding and popular serials later issued as books, such as *Israel Potter, The Potiphar Papers, Prue and I, Cape Cod, Wensley,* and *The Sparrowgrass Papers,* Putnam was forced to settle on obviously inferior serials for his new magazine, a double loss to him because it also reduced the chance to republish serial titles as good books. Worse yet, the magazine was not only top heavy in content but back heavy in format, with so much space given over to regular editorial departments, none of which could be called sprightly and most of which were too lengthy or dull to hold the reader's interest, that the magazine's sag grew more pronounced with time.

Putnam and his team of revolving editors never found the golden touch that they had exercised in the 1850s. The magazine got off to a slow start and never really found its place. Midway through publication of the magazine's first volume, Putnam confided to a friend that the work was hard: "It is a harder machine to run than you would imagine—I have been presumptuous in supposing that I could do it."[40] That same month he declared that he had no ambition of overtaking *Harper's Monthly* or the *Atlantic* and midway through the second volume that "we are not yet *rich* and the Mag. is not yet making money"— as wish or actuality, both statements remained true to the end of its life.[41]

Frank Luther Mott identified the central problem of the magazine succinctly: "It lacked Curtis."[42] More broadly speaking, the new magazine lacked the light touch and charm that not only Curtis but Lowell, Kirkland, Melville (in most of his stories), Quincy, and Charles Dudley Warner had given its predecessor. Its last editor, Parke Godwin, tried to finesse the issue in declaring that "the proper function of a Magazine is to amuse as well as to instruct, or, rather, is to instruct by means of amusement"—a strange comment to come from a man whose favored genre had been and remained the jeremiad, as in his major contribution to the second series, "Our Political Degeneracy—Its Causes and Remedies."[43] But the failure of *Putnam's* to amuse the reading public neither began nor ended with Godwin. Throughout its life the magazine both sounded heavy in tone and content and looked it. Whereas most of his competitors were willing to follow the popular trend in American magazine journalism by generously setting illustrations alongside letterpress, Putnam insisted on keeping his virtually unrelieved by illustrations. Twenty years later, illustrations were so standard a part of magazine journalism that William Dean Howells, former editor of the unillustrated *Atlantic Monthly* (1871–81) and soon-to-be editor of the heavily illustrated *Harper's Monthly,* gave a laughing nod at their indispensability in *A Hazard of New Fortunes* when he brought together a literary editor and business manager to plan their new periodical:

> "Going to have illustrations?"
>
> "My dear boy! What are you giving me? Do I look like the sort of lunatic who would start a thing in the twilight of the nineteenth century *without* illustrations? *Come* off!"[44]

Heaviness was not the only problem with *Putnam's Magazine;* it also suffered from a seemingly willful backwardness. Algernon Tassin pinpointed this trait in writing about it (and about Melville and Irving, whom he associated with the magazine) from his vantage point in the early twentieth century: "For *Putnam's* in spite of its new and progressive idea of handling public questions, had upon it the large shadow of Irving. (It even counseled Melville to read his Addison! Not that Melville didn't need advice, heavens knows; but it would be difficult to devise for his staccato temper a more ludicrous misfit than the undulating Addisonian phrase.) And there was much of the conscious Knickerbocker superiority and deliberate Knickerbocker exclusiveness about it."[45] Even to some of its contemporaries, *Putnam's* gave the impression of belonging to an earlier era, an impression the editors unintentionally reinforced in taking the magazine's first series as their frequent frame of reference and in habitually referring to their readership as people of "taste," "education," or "judgment." This situation was not exclusive to *Putnam's.* The *Atlantic* would also soon be struggling to retain its market niche, falling precipitously from a circulation high of 50,000 copies in 1869 to below 20,000 copies for most of the 1870s.[46] But given his ethos and ideology, there would have been more sorrow than consolation for Putnam in the changing patterns of taste and culture that swept both magazines—and the literary elites that produced and consumed them—increasingly to the margins in the 1870s during the second era of cheap books and periodicals that began months after his death.

Putnam's failed not for lack of effort; the editors never stopped trying to locate the best talent, but they did so with limited success. They even sought to exploit one of their old audience favorites, but "The Last of the Bourbon Story" proved to be just that.[47] Well aware of the problems his editors were having finding first-rate material, Putnam worked various strategies from the publisher's end to address the dilemma of a limited readership and restricted capital. In July 1868 he purchased the *Northern Monthly* and merged it with *Putnam's*. With matters even graver the next year, he attempted in November 1869 to form a group of investors, whose stockholders included Bryant, to share expenses and profits with him.[48] He was so confident that he had succeeded that he advertised the forthcoming January 1870 number as being published by the Putnam Magazine Company.[49] That deal, however, was never consummated, leaving Putnam no recourse but to continue publication on the old terms.

Circulation figures are extremely hard to come by; the most nearly reliable source is George Haven Putnam, who though deferring the management of *Putnam's* to his father kept its accounts. He stated its circulation as averaging 12,000–15,000 copies, a range that, if correct, signaled a weak and unsatisfactory magazine circulation for that time.[50] Moreover, after the Japanese deal fell through, the funds for operating the magazine could have come only from the already strained general resources of the company. Given these circumstances, not even a man as hopeful or committed as Putnam could have maintained the magazine indefinitely.

During its last year *Putnam's Magazine* was clearly a failing proposition. Its size was scaled back, the heavy-handed Parke Godwin, then on leave from the *Evening Post,* was installed in April as managing editor, and its quality diminished. By summer or early fall 1870, Putnam saw no alternative but to look for the most financially advantageous exit he could find. His best option was the offer of his friend and colleague of many years, Charles Scribner, whose expanding house was eager to follow the trend in postbellum publishing by establishing its own in-house monthly magazine. Unable to hide his disappointment, Putnam broke the news of the impending deal to Godwin shortly after his "delicate negotiation" with Scribner had ended in August; even then he did not cease justifying their endeavor: "We have not been throwing Pearls to swine—of course—but we don't find enough customers for sober literature alone—People must have pictures and sensations— and amusement—and so we 'give in' to those."[51]

The new arrangement took effect in November, the last month that *Putnam's* was issued in the nineteenth century, and it required Putnam to throw his support for a year behind the new magazine (to which he contributed an article, as did his daughter although not necessarily out of loyalty to him).[52] It could only have been painful for him to see not only the end of his dream but in effect its transferral to a man—Josiah Holland, Scribner's designated editor—for whom he had little personal or professional esteem. Nor could it have been easy for him to see how quickly Holland, by then one of the most popular writers in the country, brought *Scribner's* to a much greater national circulation by adopting a formula for magazine popularity that Putnam had failed or more likely simply refused to practice. The wonder is that he emerged from the experience as little embittered as he did.

Losing the magazine at least had the compensation of freeing him to devote more of his time and attention to the firm's general publishing operations. During the half-dozen years in which father and son(s) worked collaboratively, G. P. Putnam and Son (or Sons, after Bishop was made a partner in 1870) went through a process of cautiously expanding its list. A few of the new titles on the firm's list during the years 1868–70 came from articles or serials printed in the magazine, such as Mary Clemmer Ames's *Eirene; A Woman's Right,* Maximilian Schele de Vere's *Wonders of the Deep,* and—distinctly the best of the group—George Kennan's *Tent-Life in Siberia.* One more piece that passed from the magazine into book publication grew out of the magazine's fixation with the Catholic-Protestant controversy, the "reformed" French priest Father Hyacinthe's *The Family and the Church.* That work was edited and prepared for publication by the energetic American polemicist Leonard Bacon, who also translated and edited a volume of Father Hyacinthe's sermons for the firm.[53] But the vast majority of its titles then and later adhered to the miscellaneous list that had long typified Putnam's publications.

One of the more attractive writers published by Putnam during this time was William Dean Howells, whose *No Love Lost* was issued in 1869. But that was only a marginal publication for the fast-rising Howells, and it was a sign of the times that he was already falling into the orbit of James Fields. For that matter, Putnam published relatively little original fiction and almost no original poetry, preferring to concentrate his resources on such genres as travelogues, art books, semischolarly studies in art and literary history, reference works, and reprints. If anything, the Putnam list was oriented more than ever toward the "discriminating" reader. Among the more interesting titles on the Putnam list during these years were two significant biographies: a slightly expurgated version of the London edition of *The Life of John James Audubon* (1869) and Henry Tuckerman's *The Life of John Pendleton Kennedy* (1871). The list also included an 1871 edition of Horace Mann's *Lectures and Annual Reports on Education.* In summer 1870 Putnam capitalized on interest in the just deceased Dickens to produce a rather hastily written study by Frederic Beecher Perkins called *Charles Dickens: A Sketch of His Life and Works.*

Perhaps the largest and certainly the most profitable category of publications came from works and authors previously handled by Putnam. He reissued Susan Fenimore Cooper's *Rural Hours* with a new introduction in 1868. The next year he brought out Bryant's *Letters from the East* and a new edition of *Letters of a Traveller,* as well as of several of his best-known poems illustrated by William Linton, the leading wood engraver of his generation. Another writer from the past he now served was the recently deceased John Pendleton Kennedy, whose best antebellum novels as well as scattered works left in manuscript Putnam brought out in a new edition in 1872. That edition seems to have been commissioned by Kennedy from the grave; his will left $5,000 and instructions for its preparation.[54] Putnam also brought out what he hoped would become a popular work in his friend Benson J. Lossing's *History of England,* a subject that was then so much a topic of interest as to be almost a genre unto itself.[55] He was also in contact once again with Susan Warner, although George Haven's claim that they published editions of several of her works at this time seems premature by a half-dozen years.[56] What Putnam was actually in touch with her about was her family's copy of a Gilbert Stuart portrait of George Washington, which she wished Putnam to sell, presumably, to relieve their renewed shortage of money. But no such sale ever took place, and the portrait eventually passed down through Anna Warner to the library at West Point.[57]

Putnam's most important accounts from the past, of course, remained those of Irving and Taylor, although both went through changes during this period. Putnam continued to handle Irving as befit his status as the best-selling writer on his list, keeping multiple editions of his works before the public during these years, at one time as many as five: the Knickerbocker, Riverside, People's, Sunnyside, and the new Jefferson editions. In 1869 he altered his arrangement for the manufacture and distribution of the works by contracting with the fast-growing Philadelphia house of Lippincott's for their joint management in the hope that Irving might thereby reach a wider audience.[58] He also found ways to incorporate pieces of Irving's writings along with those of other Knickerbocker and post-Knickerbocker writers in the kind of artistic gift books, such as *The Sunnyside Book* (1871), that he had always favored, to such an extent that they became a signature production of his house. For that particular project he mined his company's literary archives for suitable selections not only from Irving but also from the two series of *Putnam's* (including pieces by Bryant, Curtis, Howells, O'Connor, Taylor, and R. Stoddard) and supplemented them with paintings, drawings, and engravings by leading American artists. The result was one of the most handsome gift books of the year.

Putnam also hoped for comparable success with Taylor, whose prose works—in the term of his will—were meant to be "perpetually" renewable both to the public and to his firm. No sooner had Putnam signed his will, however, than that wish was put to the test of the postbellum marketplace. With authors as commercially attractive as Irving and Taylor, it was only a matter of time before other publishers tried to maneuver them away from Putnam toward their own houses. Putnam was well insured with respect to Irving by his special relationship with both Pierre Irving and the family legacy, and he probably assumed that he was equally well insured with respect to Taylor by their longstanding collaboration. If he did, he was mistaken. When the "seduction" of Taylor came in the late 1860s, Putnam was caught largely unprepared and forced to fight not only for the preservation of that account but, given the identification of his name with Taylor's, for the reputation of his firm as a viable publisher of leading American writers.

It constituted one of the most interesting triangles of the decade in American letters: Putnam, Taylor, and their mutual friend James Fields. In what amounted to one of the longest enduring connections in contemporary American letters, Putnam had by then been publishing Taylor for twenty years and counted him among his closest friends and clients, as both men did Fields over the identical period. Ever since Taylor had taken ownership of his plates from Putnam, the arrangement between them had called for Putnam to pay him a set royalty for the sale of each book at an agreed on rate (usually $.20-.25 per volume in the inflationary war years), which was subject to occasional negotiation and revision according to market conditions and individual necessities. But Taylor grew increasingly dissatisfied over the course of the mid-1860s with the remuneration he was receiving from Putnam, which proved insufficient to maintain his family in style on their Cedarcroft estate. Caught between rising expectations and falling income, Taylor was forced to confront the unpleasant reality, which he resented as unbefitting his status as an established author, that he would have to supplement his writer's income by a lecturer's or editor's salary.[59] Embittered by that prospect, Taylor had no patience for the irony emerging from his professional life: the young man who had originally made his reputation by recounting the story of how he had reduced the expenses of the grand tour to a scale that made such a trip accessible to the many had developed such expensive habits in the intervening two decades that he was forced to engage in the literary/journalistic equivalent of hard labor in order to maintain his family's manor—a manor for which he wished a reputation, like that of Irving's Sunnyside, as a literary shrine lifted above the grime and sweat of capitalistic toil. As his royalties payments steadily declined during the war years, along with the sales of his books, Taylor became painfully aware that the gap between his means and ends was widening.

He was therefore ready by 1866–67 to listen to the blandishments of Fields, not only one of his closest professional friends but a fellow poet—as they both thought—and the publisher of his numerous volumes of poetry, the genre that was as surely for Taylor as for Poe a "passion." Long before Taylor had embarked on his translation of Faust and the writing of his "major" poetry, Frederick Law Olmsted had astutely measured him as a poet at heart: "Taylor," he wrote in 1855 after meeting him at the office of *Putnam's Monthly*, "is exceedingly sensitive of his reputation as a poet and ... hates to be called a traveller."[60] This self-image gave Fields access to a side of Taylor unavailable to Putnam, an advantage, of course, powerfully reinforced by his superior assets. Fields was already paying Taylor as much as $20 a page for contributions to the *Atlantic Monthly* when in September 1866 he offered him $5,000 for rights to publish his next novel, first as a serial in the *Atlantic* and then as a book, cautioning him "to keep this a 'secret.'"[61] With Taylor's attention fully engaged, Fields proceeded in the following months to offer to take over the publication of all of his prose writings, presumably putting him on an annuity basis of payment similar to that which his house had offered a number of other leading writers in its large and growing list of American writers. That prospect was enticing to Taylor as more nearly approximating his vision of the artistic life than anything Putnam had been able to offer and as reversing the downward slide of his literary income.

Unable to postpone indefinitely the unpleasant conversation he knew he would have to have with his old friend, Taylor discussed the situation with Putnam in late 1867, comparing the arrangement that the two currently had with the one that Fields was proposing. Putnam's reaction, he reported back to Fields's partner, James Osgood, was "frank, manly and friendly, as I knew he would be."[62] Putnam admitted to him that he could not match Fields's offer of guaranteeing a stipulated sum (the arrangement, ironically, that Putnam had himself pioneered in his original 1848 agreement with Irving, as Taylor was well aware), but he asked for a year in which to make intermediate plans.[63] Taylor could not but assent to that request, even becoming in 1868 a contributing editor to *Putnam's Magazine*. The period of temporizing continued for several years, during which Putnam awaited the completion of Taylor's long promised *By-ways of Europe* and kept the old arrangement in place even as sales of Taylor's works continued to fall. In 1869 Putnam renewed his request for an additional year's grace, promising to reward Taylor by initiating the publication during that period of a cheaper edition (the Household) of his works that he promised Taylor would bring in expanded sales and royalties.[64] Finally, late that year, Fields ended the affair. The person who had initiated the idea of the transfer of Taylor's literary property, he now summarily withdrew his offer and recommended to Taylor a policy of conciliation: "Let me say here, privately, that on Putnam's account, I am content. I do feel very warmly toward my old friend and yours, and I am sure it is just as well that you should not be sundered. I trust he will never consider me as in any way interfering with his business matters. A better man than G.P.P., I do not know, and I would go far to serve him, if it were in my power."[65]

The conclusion of this affair was not without its ironies. Fields no doubt considered his final actions as motivated by principle, but a more accurate judgment is that they were guided primarily by his general disenchantment with the changing terms of his profession. Although he was at decade's end outwardly more successful than ever, the central figure in Anglo-American literary publishing, Fields was utterly worn out, having suffered in the immediately preceding years from bruising dealings with various of his old clients who he felt had violated their friendship and loyalty to him. By late 1869 or early 1870, just as the negotiations with Taylor were approaching the point of decision, he had drawn the conclusion that there was "a new era opening before me" that he, for one, found uncongenial to his style and practice.[66] As the Taylor episode revealed, however, there was another version of events, and one quite different, if no less unflattering to Fields, from the one that the disenchanted writer Gail Hamilton had been telling clients of the firm about Fields's penny-pinching methods. Putnam, however, would have been the last person to discuss the matter in public, which is the most likely reason why his reaction to Fields's incursion passed unrecorded. On the contrary, his personal and professional ethos was so deeply and unshakably ingrained that one could safely assume that the two men would continue their amicable dealings to the end of their professional days. In actuality, that end was already imminent, since within a matter of months Fields retired from the profession.

Putnam, by contrast, had lost little of his love for the trade, even though he plainly believed that the conditions for publishing were far less attractive than they had been in the two decades preceding the war. "The whole aspect of publishing," he commiserated with Taylor in 1870 after having just read his friend's remarks on the subject in the New York *Tribune,* "is changed for the worse—as far as I can judge. 20 years ago there was far more bargaining and life in the book-market. Then we scarcely dreamed of smaller edns. than 1500 to 5,000—now we print *250* as often as a larger no. at a time."[67] That belief had no discernible effect on his professional activity or his commitment to the profession, which he now represented in various capacities as one of its most senior members and to which he now wished to see his sons commit themselves.

One sign of his own recommitment was that Putnam resumed his earlier practice of making frequent transatlantic excursions, which had been interrupted by the downturn of his publishing fortunes in the mid-fifties. Doing so was a practical necessity for a publisher intent on remaining in the front ranks of belletristic publishers in a society whose literary taste, like his own, remained staunchly Anglocentric. Even before he went overseas in early 1869, he had sent Haven the previous year as the representative of the firm, while he attended to matters at home.[68] Provided with numerous letters of introduction to his father's former friends and current "correspondents" in the trade, Haven made the acquaintance of many of the leading publishers in the city, including John Murray, Sampson Low, Henry Bohn, and Richard Bentley, as well as the generation of their descendants.[69] Although the

Putnams were in no position to challenge such firms as Ticknor and Fields and Harper and Brothers for the works of the leading European writers, Haven's trip would prove to be more successful than either father or son could then appreciate. As Haven quickly perceived, the Putnam name still exerted considerable influence with British publishers, opening doors and allowing him access that few other twenty-four-year-olds could expect. In the years following his father's death, he was to remake the name wholly as his own, reestablishing the London branch of the house and cultivating relations with British publishers and authors so successfully that under his direction G. P. Putnam's Sons played a role in transatlantic publishing as substantial as that once played by Wiley and Putnam.

Putnam's trip of 1869 registered on him as nothing less than a life experience, one that repeatedly brought back memories of his first impressions of London and Paris in 1836. To judge from the pace he kept during his several months overseas, he had lost little of the prodigious store of curiosity, enthusiasm, or sheer energy that he had possessed when still in his own twenties—even now with his twenty-six-year-old daughter living in Paris. He sampled every available means of transportation, habitually with an eye to the technological gains made over the past. He took note of generational changes in urban architecture, advertising, consumption, and religious practice. He renewed his acquaintance with both the "official" tourist places (St. Paul's, Westminister Abbey, and Parliament) and places personally meaningful to him (Waterloo Place, Regents Park, Paternoster Row). He made a point of traveling to see the Crystal Palace ("magnifique") relocated at Sydenham.[70] He returned to see the neighborhood in St. John's Wood in which the family had lived and retraced his favorite path through the city, the one he had taken many times with Henry Stevens by his side, from Regents Park down past Portland Place (home to the offices of Richard Bentley) and Regent Street to Waterloo Place ("the center of London grandeur"). He visited the art museums, taking special interest in the expanding South Kensington Museum (later renamed the Victoria and Albert) that he considered a model for the kind of museum he hoped to see built back home. He attended a wide variety of houses of worship, sometimes doubling up on Sundays by attending both morning and evening services. He garnered a ticket from the secretary of the American Legation and sat in Speaker's Gallery and heard Gladstone, whom he also heard in the House of Commons. He dined frequently with

professional colleagues, old friends, and new acquaintances. He paid
calls on as many old friends as he had time for, as well as some people
previously known to him only through correspondence, such as John
Bright (with whom he chatted at his home while the brother of David
Livingstone waited politely below). Other old friends, such as Mary and
William Howitt, he simply lacked the time to see.

If in his first years in Europe he had inveterately practiced the
mental exercise of comparing and contrasting Old and New Worlds,
now he found himself turning that habit toward past and present. It
began with the crossing; he made the trip in but nine days in a ship that
was larger and faster than any he who had once been an expert on the
subject had previously known. Wherever he went during his weeks
in London and Paris, it seems, he came upon landmarks that caused
him to look backward and forward. In Paris, he saw a city radically
transformed ("Hausmanized," he called it) since his previous visit into
an imperial capital, with its "miles and miles of broad, palace-lined,
asphaltum-paved streets, newly built where narrow lanes and uncouth
rookeries only existed at the time of your last visit."[71] In London his
impressions were more personal. He had first seen Queen Victoria,
then a seventeen-year-old princess, one night at a musical festival at
Exeter Hall, then later at Buckingham Palace as a young queen walking arm in arm with Prince Albert; now Albert was dead and she was
the longest reigning monarch in Europe. Or, to take an example closer
to his own experience, he remembered George Routledge when the
latter occupied a stall at Leicester Square and conducted business buying and selling job lots; now Routledge was one of the richest publishers
in the city, with warehouses needed to store the works issued from one
of the prized publishing lists in the English-speaking world. Of all the
changes he took note of, what perhaps impressed him most was the revolution he perceived as having occurred since his last visit in the economics of English literary culture. His hosts, he increasingly believed,
now practiced the "American plan" of literary production, bringing out
books, magazines, and newspapers so inexpensively that they had surpassed the Americans at their own antebellum innovations in lowering
prices and popularizing print culture.

One subject that he failed to examine comparatively was himself;
had he done so, even with all the changes that had taken place in his
life, he might have noticed an underlying core similarity. Despite the
swirl of change around him and in his own life circumstances, Putnam

remained remarkably unchanged as a literary professional. One sign was that, just as he had done with several of his earlier trips, so he turned this one into a matter of public record. He was already setting it down on paper during the return leg of his voyage and had it published shortly after his return in *Putnam's Magazine*.[72] Infused with his unvarying professional faith, that narrative differentiated little between publishers, politicians, and authors: all were actors in the public sphere, and all as such deserved roles in the account of his trip that he addressed to the *Putnam's* readership.

The primary purpose of his trip, of course, was to renew his connections with overseas publishers in the hopes of positioning his firm to receive American rights to their works. He therefore spent much of his time in London making the rounds of the major publishing houses of the city, some of whose senior members he had known for two or even three decades: Murray, Nisbet, Trubner, Longman, Routledge, Low, Macmillan, Smith and Elder, Hotten, and Bell and Daldy. He also paid visits to the home of a number of authors, including Wilkie Collins, Charles Reade, and Anne Thackeray (whose father's monument he had visited at Poet's Corner). During his visit with Collins, he apparently made a serious appeal to receive American rights for his next novel, but, as he was soon to learn, his ability to attract a successful British novelist in 1869 was hardly what it had been in the Wiley and Putnam days when he enjoyed a fairly free reign.[73]

Just the same, he must have been successful in conducting his business, because he repeated these trips in each of the remaining years of his life. If unable to compete for the works of the leading overseas authors, Putnam was resourceful enough to know that he could compete for alternative kinds of works. In fact, a substantial number of his publications in the years 1869–72 came through arrangements made during or after his trips. One was a set of science textbooks popular in Great Britain that Putnam arranged with the Scottish publisher William Collins to reprint in the United States. Putnam had scant success, however, in duplicating Collins's success in British schools with those in the United States, which even in the antebellum generation had been drawing away from their earlier dependence on foreign textbooks.[74] In a similar kind of deal, he reached an arrangement with Alexander Murray and Son of London to bring out in New York their series of reprints of standard authors.[75] Pricing it to undersell competing editions and marketing it in 1870–71 as Putnam's Popular Histories, he included in it such works as Gibbon's *The Decline and Fall of the Roman Empire,* Hume's *History of England,* Smith's *The Wealth of Nations,* and Pepys's *Diary,* as well as more contemporary titles.

He also issued several other sets of series on his own during his last two years. One was the Knickerbocker Edition of Standard Poets, including volumes of Collins, Gray, Goldsmith, Pope, and Coleridge. To his old personal "standard poet" Thomas Hood he devoted a fancier Artists' Edition as a gift book for Christmas 1871 (a work that he naturally issued in an edition uniform with the still-in-print Artists' Edition of the *Sketch-Book).* Late that year he also began the publication of Putnam's Handy-Book Series, a series of housebook manuals whose most interesting title was his own contribution, *The Best Reading,* the latest of the popular guides to various aspects of the book trade and general knowledge he had been compiling for decades. This one was a practical how-to guide to the purchase of "good books" addressed to private and institutional book buyers.

In 1870 Putnam moved his company offices uptown one more time, settling early that year into more spacious rooms in the new building at the corner of Twenty-third Street and Fourth Avenue occupied just a few months before by the Young Men's Christian Association. The move to the Association Building pushed his publishing office for the first time up above Washington Square and placed it closer to the attractive new commercial area near Madison Square, a location then especially advantageous to the firm since the Putnams also decided to reopen the retail operations that had been discontinued since the mid-1850s. The Putnam bookstore, in subsequent decades to become one of the best in the city under the management of Irving Putnam, at that time handled a wide range of the books of established publishers around the country, as well as the choice imports that Putnam or Haven either purchased in person during their overseas trips or ordered through catalogues. Putnam had stocked up particularly heavily on rare books and fine illustrated edition during his 1871 trip to London, and such works subsequently became a special branch of their business.[76] What distinguished their bookstore, however, from its competitors were the specialty items that Putnam delighted in personally and offered to his wealthier clientele, such as Japanese artwork, work boxes, and ornaments; art reproductions produced by the latest processes (such as oleographic facsimiles of oil paintings, which Putnam sold bound and unbound, in singles and in sets); and fancy domestic and imported stationery and cards; as well as the domestic and imported art books that were a staple of the store.

His civic duty in the last years of his life did not end with his self-styled decapitation by President Johnson in 1866. One sign that he retained his head and that it was still turned toward public service came the following year. On the evening of 3 March 1867, the young Western journalist Mark Twain attended the regular meeting of the Century Association as a one-time guest at its ornate club house on Fifteenth Street. His impression of that "most unspeakably respectable Club in the United States," as reported back to the *Alta California,* was memorable: "It was storming like everything, and I thought there would necessarily be a small attendance, but this was not the case; the reading and supper rooms were crowded, and with the distinguished artists, authors, and amateurs of New York. I averaged the heads, and they went three sizes larger than the style of heads I have been accustomed to. In one of the smaller rooms they averaged best—thirteen heads out of the twenty-seven present were what I choose to call prodigious."[77] One of the heads present that evening belonged to "Putnam, the publisher," who had taken pleasure in the camaraderie of the Century Association since his election in 1859.[78]

In actuality, Putnam was at the time an active member not only of the Century but also of the Union League Club, to which he had been elected shortly after its founding in 1863. Membership in those exclusive clubs, which consisted of the leading New York men in the professions, business, politics, and arts, was important for him not only as a social forum but also as a base of operations for pursuing acts of civic duty. Although perhaps more comfortable in the more artistically centered Century Association, he had played a more active role in the Union League Club, which had been the base of operations for his Loyal Publication Society during the war. Then in the late 1860s, it became the primary setting for what developed into the single most meaningful public mission of his later years, which culminated in the historic meeting held on the night of 23 November 1869 in its new Madison Square club house. The single item on the agenda that night was the proposal "to found an institute and museum of art" for the city of New York.[79]

As chairman of the club's committee on art and the leading publisher of art books in the city, Putnam was not only well positioned but strongly motivated to play a leading role in addressing what was increasingly a major embarrassment to civic leaders. During the several preceding years there had been serious discussion locally about the possibility of founding a museum to house and display a permanent art collection. Henry Tuckerman, for instance, had presented such a proposal in 1867 virtually as an ideological manifesto in *Book of the Artists:* "New York is nobly supplied with Hospitals and Libraries, but she lacks one Institution essential to a great civilized metropolis—a permanent free Gallery of Art."[80] The practical work of solicitation and organization was already underway in 1868, carried out primarily through the auspices of the Union League Club and its committee on art. At the November 1869 meeting, a gathering of three hundred people held as an open forum with reporters present to publicize its proceedings, the decision was taken to proceed with plans to found a museum for the city. To put that resolution into practice, a general supervisory committee of fifty men was elected, which in turn designated a thirteen-man subcommittee, chaired by Putnam, to conduct the actual conceptualization, planning, and site selection of the museum.

The work proceeded slowly and unevenly in the following months, progress retarded by intellectual and personality conflicts between committee members. Given his low-keyed personality and accommodating manner, not to mention the neutralizing fact that he had no money to commit to the undertaking, Putnam was often called on to mediate between the strong-minded, strong-tempered men on his committee, whom Haven once characterized as "centrifugal atoms" on seeing them emerge from meetings at the Putnam offices.[81] But, with time, the hard work of determining the character of the institution, drawing up by-laws for its governance, raising funds, renting quarters, and buying art works got done. In April 1870 the state of New York chartered the new institution as the Metropolitan Museum of Art, by which time John Taylor Johnston had been chosen its first president and twenty-six others (including Putnam) named to its board of officers.[82] Over the next year, quickened progress was made: money was raised, a strong beginning collection formed, and temporary quarters taken in a rented brownstone at 681 Fifth Avenue. The Metropolitan Museum opened to the public in this building on 22 February 1872, with Putnam recently appointed as its first honorary superintendent.[83] Plans were already under discussion to strengthen the collection and to build a new home for the museum far up Fifth Avenue on land designated for that purpose by the commissioners of Central Park. But during its first year of operations, the museum remained in its cramped, rented quarters and operated with a skeletal staff under the most limited conditions. On some days, Putnam pressed himself into service and functioned as the only usher present on the premises.

The other major focus of his public service was his rededication to the still unresolved status of international copyright. For three decades "next year," as his son noted, was the term in Putnam's lexicon for the year in which reciprocal protection of literary property beyond national borders was finally to become a reality.[84] The Civil War and its aftermath had submerged the movement under more pressing matters, but by the late 1860s Putnam was once again fully involved. He was the leading figure among the group of men who met at the Fifth Avenue Hotel on the night of 30 January 1868 to plan a course of action.[85] The meeting culminated in the appointment of a committee, chaired by him, that was authorized to call a second meeting several months later for the purpose of forming a combined authors and publishers advocacy group, the International Copyright Association. Before that meeting took place, the committee adopted the preliminary strategy of writing to Senator Charles Sumner to ask his advice about the path more likely to bring eventual success: a negotiated treaty or a Congressional bill. Sumner was not optimistic about the chances for a treaty, the path unsuccessfully explored in 1853 when Everett had negotiated one with his British counterpart in Washington that then failed to get through Congress. He also warned them more generally that the timing for any initiative might not be propitious, with presidential elections nearing and bad postwar sentiments toward England still strong. But even before Sumner's letter reached the committee, they learned that Representative John D. Baldwin of Massachusetts, the chairman of the House of Representatives Library Committee, had introduced his own international copyright bill, which was read twice on the floor of the House on 21 February.

Thinking the time therefore ripe for an initiative, Putnam sent out a circular ("Justice to Authors and Artists") from his office in early March formally announcing that the organizational meeting would take place on 9 April. With the circular he also sent a memorial for the collection of signatures to be sent to Congress to support Baldwin's bill. The April meeting took place in the rooms of the New-York Historical Society, Putnam presiding. He read from a selection of the numerous letters sent by men unable to attend and introduced the evening's main speakers, William Cullen Bryant, Horace Greeley, S. Iraenus Prime, Francis Lieber, and Samuel Osgood. Feelings ran strong, with the speeches of Bryant and Prime repeatedly interrupted by applause and the resolutions drafted by Putnam's committee setting out fundamental principles unanimously approved. Speaker after speaker recited reasons that international copyright would do good to what were presented as the interrelated causes of authorship, dissemination of letters, and national honor. Rev. William R. Williams even provided a scriptural defense (1 Corinthians 9:11) of the measure by invoking the tenet of the rightness of payment by student to teacher. By the end of the evening, the International Copyright Association had come into being, support for Baldwin's bill voiced, and officers chosen (Bryant as president, a group of leading writers as vice presidents, and a group of publishers including Putnam as officers of the executive committee).

During that evening of good feelings, there was little opposition. One old nemesis, James Harper, returned Putnam's courtesies with his own, communicated indirectly by letter through his nephew, in declining the invitation to attend. Another, Henry Carey, the ideological leader of the anticopyright publishers ("Caryatides," in James Fields's dismissive term) also failed to attend, although he asked for copies of the resolutions to mail to friends in order that they might see what they were up against.[86] His influence, nevertheless, was perceptible. It surfaced, first, when Putnam read the confident statement from his letter: "As regards the decision at which our people must arrive, I have no fears whatsoever, provided only that they be enabled to see both sides of the question."[87] And it surfaced even more powerfully in the speech of Prime, who associated Carey's opposition to the right to literary property with the socialist opposition to property generally and quoted at length one of Carey's most powerful—and infuriating—attacks on their position:

> The day has passed in this country, for the recognition of either perpetuity or universality of literary *rights*. The wealthy Carolinian, anxious that books might be high in price, and knowing full well that monopoly privileges were opposed to freedom, gladly co-operated with Eastern authors and publishers, antislavery as they professed to be. The enfranchised black, on the contrary, desires that books may be cheap, and to that end he and his representatives shall be found in all the future co-operating with the people of the Centre and the West in maintaining

the doctrine that literary *privileges* exist in virtue of grants from the people who own the materials out of which books are made; that those privileges have been perhaps already too far extended; that there exists not even a shadow of reason for any further extension; and that to grant what now is asked would be a positive wrong to the many millions of consumers, as well as an obstacle to be now placed in the road towards civilization.[88]

That passage must have touched a sore spot of progressive men like Putnam, who were still close enough to the Civil War to take personal umbrage at an argument that savaged their class and regional assumptions. But on that night and in that forum, at least, Carey's voice was drowned out by the chorus of supporters gathered to bring the issue to a successful outcome.

The night was a throwback for Putnam to some of his earliest connections in the movement, reuniting him with two of his closest collaborators in Bryant and Lieber.[89] It must also have been a vivid reminder of the celebratory Crystal Palace authors and publishers dinner he had organized in 1855; it recombined in a new way the unity of interests that had been the organizing theme that night. Little wonder that Putnam and his committee considered their meeting a historic moment in an honorable cause: "It is not probable that so valuable a presentation of the grounds upon which an International Copyright Law is claimed to be the right of authors and publishers everywhere, will ever again be made."[90] And little wonder that he worked through that month with renewed energy. Just days before the meeting, he received a letter from Baldwin requesting his help in redressing the balance of petitions reaching Congress from copyright opponents; Baldwin was especially interested in his aid in influencing the opinion of one swing vote on his Library Committee belonging to a representative who, in Baldwin's words, had "what phrenologists would call 'an excessive development of the organ of approbativeness.'"[91] Putnam's response was, as usual, to disseminate information. He immediately worked with Edmund Stedman to print the meeting's proceedings, the text of Bryant's speech, and excerpts from the most useful of the letters he had received.[92]

Once again, however, his optimism proved premature. Baldwin's initiative died that year in Congress, as would another in 1871. Seemingly beyond frustration, Putnam was back in Washington again the following year, just a few weeks before his death, to meet with members of the Judiciary Committee in the hope of correcting what he considered the most serious injustice in the domain of American letters. At no time in his life did he seriously doubt the rightness of either his conviction or his action. In truth, however, he seems never fully to have understood that he did not speak on behalf of the entire profession on this issue any more than he did on trade sales and other disputed matters. As in earlier years, there remained many established houses intent on profiting from free use of foreign literary material, a group that would be led by the 1870s by a new generation of publishers similarly inclined, including many who operated on a lower socioeconomic stratum than the Appletons, Scribners, and Putnams. Nor did Putnam take account of the profusion of interests that overwhelmed his position and that of his loyal followers when the issue of international copyright reached the floor of Congress.

The year 1869 was a year of life cycles for Putnam, although neither he nor his friends and relatives could have suspected that he was himself entering the last stage of life. In January his mother died at the age of seventy-seven following a brief period of decline and illness; the coroner labeled the cause of death a combination of "general debility" and "cardiac effusion."[93] Although transported far from her roots in early republican America, Catherine Hunt Putnam had remained to the end of her life a powerful force in both her family and community. Even in fast-changing, materialistic times she retained a coherent sense of divine service that was not always comprehensible to the younger generation of New York-raised Putnams. According to a family story, Haven once said of her: "To this particular servant of His, the Lord seems to have spoken in no uncertain tone and in a way not to be misunderstood."[94] His brothers probably were just as irreverent; at this time they were showing more interest in the new crazes of intercollegiate football and competitive sculling than in the issues that mattered most to her. Putnam himself had greater reverence for her; despite their temperamental differences, he had remained consistently devoted to her, the only parent he had known for most of his life. The last surviving member of her generation of Palmers, she was also the last direct link to his New England past, to which he retained a sense of connection. If never able to sympathize with her crusading spirit, he respectfully published her occasional writings, helped with her finances, and shared in her attachment to the extended Palmer family.

13.   George Palmer Putnam in 1870, age fifty-six. (Photo by Joseph Golson)

At the time of her death, she was being cared for in the Twenty-third Street home of her children Elizabeth and Isaac Smith, with whom she had lived since giving up teaching and selling her own home in the 1840s. Until her final months she had remained active outside the house in missionary work—and, no doubt, within the household as well. Putnam seems never to have expressed his sentiments about her in any surviving form, but fortunately at least Mary, always one of her favorites, did. From her distant perspective in Paris she came to a shrewd appreciation of her grandmother as a woman of overriding strength and weakness: "Her conflicts were all mental, and sufficiently terrific, it must be confessed. A singular, a unique character,—and most rare in her entire ignorance of herself. I think that was really astonishing especially in a person who devoted so much time to self-analysis and introspection. But an intense, disinterested, devoted life!"[95] In its more secularized form, that life of disinterested devotion was her lasting legacy to both her son and her granddaughter.

At the time of the funeral, Victorine was pregnant with the couple's eleventh child, Sidney Mason, a sickly baby born prematurely in May who survived barely beyond his first year. His birth was followed by the wedding of Rebecca Shepard and Haven in June. Shortly after his mother's death and before the expected birth and marriage, Putnam had made his memorable 1869 trip to England and France. Its purpose was not all business and sightseeing; its personal highlight was his several days' visit in Paris with Mary. A joyful reunion for both, it was not without its incongruous moments, the result of differing viewpoints grown no closer with time. Putnam had written ahead to inform Mary of his plans to arrive in the city the evening of 9 March and to go directly to his rooms at the Grand Hotel, designating the next afternoon for their meeting at her lodgings near the Luxembourg Gardens. But Mary had no intention of delaying a reunion after a separation already of nearly three years' duration. She was at the hotel hours ahead of his midnight arrival to greet him, appearing there, as she wrote her mother, "to the horror of the affectionate parent," who—she should have known—would have "some kink about impropriety in my coming to the Grand Hotel alone etc."[96]

Mary saw him with a new clarity after their long separation. Perhaps still carrying a mental image from the visit paid her the previous year by Aunt Elizabeth Peabody, who had unsuccessfully attempted to persuade Victorine to join her on her European trip, she transmitted the following sketch of her father back to the home circle: "I find father looking quite well,—just the same, indeed, in regard to bodily appearance, but his manner,—always so calm, now seems almost supernaturally calm and quiet, and disengaged. He impresses me almost as something ethereal. The sweet, vague, gentle nature, in which he and Elizabeth Peabody are so profoundly akin, seems to me more manifest than ever because freed from the least cause for irritability or even excitement. As Haven says, he is a blessed man,—I do not think I exaggerate my feelings, in saying, a holy man."[97] Meant, no doubt, as high praise, this was also faint irony. Idealist to idealist, adored daughter to adored father, they valued each other's character, took pleasure in each other's company, but invariably strained each other's patience. During their few days together Putnam took her to the home of the son and daughter-in-law of his oldest Parisian friends, the Bossanges, for dinner, but she found them insufferably bourgeois ("I am not accustomed to this kind of people,—and I may add, don't mean to be. Life is too short for mere comfort").[98] He took her to breakfast with American acquaintances of the family who were fellow guests at the Grand Hotel; she found them pretentious and off-putting. Nor, by the same token, was he favorably taken with the dinginess of her living quarters on the Left Bank; nothing in his background or views prepared him for that European student style of living. They could agree, at least, about the charm and character of Mary's roommate, a Mlle. Collin, and about the merits of the Réclus family, French Protestants of learning and refinement and soon to prove themselves patriots of unusual political courage.[99]

Father and daughter had a great deal to catch up on. Putnam no doubt heard much about her professional accomplishments; she was by then one of the most highly regarded students in her program and was making steady progress advancing through the series of examinations leading up to the thesis and degree. To help finance her living expenses, she had employed the literary gift her father had long admired (and probably still valued above her scientific skills). She had contributed letters for a period, first to the New Orleans *Times,* then, at Parke Godwin's request, to the New York *Evening Post.* After publication of *Putnam's* resumed, she became one of its more frequent contributors; the last of her six articles, a firsthand report on the declaration of the French Republic, was printed in the last issue of the magazine.[100] Putnam would also have asked her for word about what he and the family most wished to know: when she was coming home. She, for her part, would have heard from him about what she most longed for: family news. Although she was in communication at various times with members of her family, they were dispersing in so many individual directions that it was impossible to keep up with all their latest activities. She was concerned about many things: the health of her pregnant "little" mother, to whom she sometimes played not only nurse and doctor but also parent; the well-being of Amy, the family pet whose illness had recently occasioned Victorine to spend a southern winter with her; the career plans of Edith, whose mind and education she wished to see filled out through a grand tour while she herself was still in Paris to enjoy her company; and the growth in mind and body of Herbert, who was only five when she left home. Never a voluble man, Putnam must have been hard pressed to supply all the news she hungered for, a difficulty under any circumstances but an impossibility during as brief a stay as he was making. Before leaving Paris, he bought her—nice sign of his mixed sentiments—both a microscope and a new dress, two things that she badly needed.[101]

Mary found herself disappointed and homesick after his departure. She had tried (too) hard to please him and felt that she had succeeded poorly, but she was also too intelligent not to recognize the universality of that pattern among adult children and parents. Rather than feeling reconnected to the family by his visit, she felt the distance more intensely than at any time in the preceding three years. But, as luck would have it, an opportunity presented itself in early June for her to serve as a medical escort to an invalid on her way home from France to Boston. With time for preparations short, Mary departed without so much as sending word ahead to inform the family of her arrival. Instead, upon landing in New York she simply presented herself unannounced at the store, startling her father and brothers. She then accompanied her patient directly to Boston, immediately turning around and taking a train to the station closest to the family's Five Mile River Landing home. Her father was there to meet her at the station, "running," she noted with pleasure, "to meet me as if you were a boy let loose from school."[102] Entering the family house, she found her mother seated with the month-old baby on her lap, a picture that remained with her for life. The reunion, however, was short-lived. A few days later she joined her father and elder siblings on the trip to Dorchester, Massachusetts, for Haven's wedding, then returned with them to the family house to spend the few remaining days of her brief visit before returning directly to France to complete her studies. At the time, she anticipated she would receive her degree in little more than one additional year.

Shortly after her return to Paris in summer 1869, she read in the newspapers about the accident that had nearly killed her father in September but was relieved to hear from her mother about his recovery. She did not see him the next year but she did see Haven, who represented the firm that year in England before crossing the Channel to spend time with her. Her affection for him was as strong as ever ("I always feel that Haven is my twin and part of me and that I do not complete myself until he is along side").[103] It must have felt like old times to be alone together, although now they met as adults and with Paris as the setting of their reacquaintance. He no doubt conveyed the family's wishes that she return home as soon as possible, and they separated with the expectation that she would be done with her studies and on her way back before the next winter. But within days of his departure, the Franco-Prussian War broke out and, as the city came under siege and the school went into suspension, her plans changed dramatically.

She chose to remain in Paris through the first siege and to persist in her studies despite all the surrounding disruptions and deprivations. She worked through the terrible winter of 1870–71, trying to keep her mind focused on her work. Despite delays caused by the continuing political instability in the city, she managed to advance her work toward completion by early 1871, although she had to wait for the reopening of the school to take her degree. She had just finished her fifth and final set of examinations when her father arrived in England in July 1871. As soon as she received word from him that he had reached London, she wrote him on 21 July to invite him to the crowning moment of her studies. Three days later she stood dressed in the unisex robe given to students by the institution to defend her thesis publicly before four examiners from the Medical Faculty and an audience of students and doctors estimated by *Le Figaro* as numbering three hundred.[104] The only disappointment was that that audience did not include her father, who might have received her message too late to see her receive the highest grade possible ("parfaitement satisfait"). It is just as plausible, however, that what actually held him back was some presumably unconscious reservation about her career.

When he finally arrived a week later, he found her in no mood to celebrate her personal triumph. Nor, it seems, was he. One reason was that, however well-meaning were their intentions toward each other,

her recent experience living through the siege and identifying with the French had touched her in ways that an outsider could not possibly understand. There was also a more specifically private reason; she had informed her parents only shortly before Putnam's departure from home that she had entered into and now recently broken off an engagement to a French medical student of Jewish background.[105] Her feelings for him were deeper and the pain of disappointment sharper than they had been four years before during her engagement to Mayer. Arriving in Paris shortly after the breakup, Putnam no doubt found his own position anomalous and himself excluded a second time from his daughter's private world. During their few days together she refused to discuss the affair. Only after his departure would she raise the subject, which she did in a letter directed to him in London. She apologized for his having found her—recycling his term—"a mysterious personage" but defended her right not to disturb his peace of mind by something she still felt too painful to discuss.[106] The real issue, she explained, was not an incompatibility for her between "marriage and professional duties" but an irreconcilability between her and her friend over their homelands that neither was willing to compromise.[107]

In short, his brief visit that summer touched the rawest nerves in their relationship. Had father and daughter followed their original plans of making the passage back home together, they might have had time and circumstance to work out their disagreements and reduce the distance between themselves. But Putnam had already given his consent to her request to stay on in Paris a few additional weeks to take on an important medical case recently offered to her, and so he preceded her back to America. Neither of them could have known that that would have been the last opportunity they would have to spend prolonged time alone together. More than thirty years later, when she was herself suffering from advanced brain cancer, she would look back on that missed opportunity with special regret.

During the last few years of his life, the family continued its itinerant pattern, with Putnam spending most of his time in various rented quarters not far from his office, while the nucleus of his family remained in Connecticut with Victorine, who claimed that the city "always does depress me."[108] Some of the older children were by then living outside the house, including Haven, whose professional reason for doing so became also a personal necessity when he finally married Rebecca

Shepard in June 1869. Putnam lived with them in the early months of their marriage in rented rooms on Twenty-eighth Street. In 1870 they all moved into more luxurious quarters in what has often been called the first—it was actually the second—apartment building in the United States, the Stuyvesant Building at 142 East Eighteenth Street designed by Richard Morris Hunt, Putnam's fellow committeeman from the Union League Club.[109] In spite of the prevailing association of apartment buildings with "French" living arrangements, the Stuyvesant Building (or French Flats, as it was accordingly called) attracted a high-class clientele, which in its early years included Bayard Taylor, the painter Worthington Whittredge, the publisher William Conant Church, and the architect Calvert Vaux. All four of its bottom floors were divided into four large, well-lit and -ventilated flats, each with its own bathroom, kitchen, dumbwaiter, and living and sleeping rooms; the top floor, which was designed for artists, accommodated four high-ceilinged studio apartments under the mansard roof. Rents ranged from $1,000 to $1,500 a year depending on proximity to the ground, as was typical in walk-ups.[110] That building would soon start a trend; by the time that William Dean Howells's March family in *A Hazard of New Fortunes* began their (now famous) search for suitable housing in 1880s New York City, apartment-style living was a popular option for middle-class families.

In 1871 the family was reunited in a house taken in the neighborhood of Stuyvesant Square at 328 East Fifteenth Street, a familiar area as the family had already lived at various locations on East Sixteenth, Seventeenth, and Eighteenth Streets; it was to be Putnam's last home.[111] The location placed him within reasonably close walking distance of his office and situated the family in a neighborhood filled with such longstanding literary friends as Bryant, the Stoddards, Richard Watson Gilder, and Mary Mapes Dodge. The new house became the site of a family reunion of sorts, bringing together for the first time in years both parents with the oldest as well as most of the youngest children. Haven and Beckie moved in with them because they were unable to afford their own lodgings. And, as of September 1871, the household also included Mary, who decided to carry on a private practice while also accepting Emily Blackwell's offer to teach at the New York Medical College. Once installed in the new house, she set up her medical practice in the basement dining room, Putnam himself hanging her shingle outside the house.[112] In March 1871, with the birth of Haven and Beckie's first child Bertha, the first member of the third generation entered the Putnam household—a compensation for Victorine, no doubt, for the loss of her own baby the year before.

A sign of his advancing years, Putnam's last two years, 1871–72, were filled with deaths. In March 1871 he lost one of his favorite cousins, Sophia Peabody Hawthorne. His pleasure in her company went back to the years of his apprenticeship in Boston, when he had paid occasional visits to the Peabody home in Salem. During the intervening half century, however, he had actually had much more contact with her older sister Elizabeth, for whom he had been an overseas agent during his London years and done odd professional favors ever since. Likewise, the family saw much more of her than of Sophia, since the unmarried Elizabeth frequently stayed with the Putnams when visiting in New York and even when in Massachusetts maintained closer relations with both parents and children. But Putnam remained more attached to Sophia, and by the late 1860s he had a new reason to renew his relations with her. In an ironic turnabout, after years of unsuccessfully seeking to become her husband's publisher, Putnam became hers following her highly publicized disagreement with Fields over royalty payments due the Hawthorne estate. Putnam had published several of her English travel sketches in *Putnam's Magazine* and in 1869 he published the longer book version of her travels as *Notes in England and Italy* (as well as several of her son Julian's poems and sketches in the magazine).

Putnam also lost two old-time professional friends late that year. In August came the death of Charles Scribner, who went back nearly as far as he to the days when the city publishers were clustered around City Hall Park and before that even further down Broadway. They had been professional, if not truly social, friends for many years, having tracked parallel careers in literary publishing and the transatlantic booktrade before their magazines affairs brought them into collaboration in 1870–71. Another event that had brought them together, if only for a few days, was a fire in 1867 at the Winter Garden Theater that threatened the Broadway block where both men's stores were located. As the flames approached Putnam's store, he and his staff shuttled whatever was portable across the street to the store of Scribner, who had opened its doors as a haven to Putnam.[113] It was Putnam who delivered the formal remarks, as he was increasingly called to do at such occasions, at the honorary meeting of the trade that was held later that year in Scribner's memory. Obviously moved by the occasion, Putnam gave a heartfelt eulogy in which he held up Scribner's career as a model for the profession and his death as a loss not only for the profession but for the nation: "For is not the nation itself influenced for its best welfare by the books which our late friend has been the means of scattering broadcast over the country?"[114]

Then, a week before Christmas, came the death of Henry Tuckerman, one of Putnam's most regular and familiar if not most profitable authors. The two men had worked together on various books and on both series of *Putnam's,* and they shared a commitment to the artistic life of the city and nation, which both saw as significantly advanced by the founding of the Metropolitan Museum. Tuckerman tragically did not live to attend the official opening. He was desperately ill in the final months of 1871 as he bravely worked on the posthumous edition of the works of John Pendleton Kennedy being published by Putnam; the last letter he wrote was to Putnam to declare his wish to cede all royalty payments owed him for the edition.

Eighteen seventy-two was a busy year in Putnam's life. Affairs and duties at the Metropolitan Museum, many self-imposed, occupied numerous of his "free" hours, crowding the normally long working day he habitually kept at his own office. In a loosely related responsibility, he also agreed to serve as a judge for American entries to the Vienna Exhibition scheduled to open in spring 1873. Meanwhile, he had no lack of duties in the office; by 1872 the firm's expanding publishing list included more titles than it had handled since his bankruptcy in 1857. One of the new titles issued that year, Taylor's *Beauty and the Beast,* gave Putnam an unusual kind of headache. He had apparently sent out an advertisement for it in which the provisional subtitle "Novellettes" was erased and changed to "Tales of Home." The printer, however, read through the erasure, conflated the subtitles, and printed them as "Toilettes"—a mistake that angered Taylor and embarrassed Putnam.[115] But that was the least of his troubles. Business was slow throughout the year, an early sign of the even harder times to come in 1873. With their firm's income sharply limited and its expenses relatively inelastic, the Putnams operated through the year on the most tenuous financial terms, with Haven occasionally forced to time the writing of checks to anticipated income. Whether father and son ever discussed the possibility that the firm might fail, a prospect that unquestionably weighed on Haven, is unknown, but it seems clear that Putnam was seriously troubled by business problems. Although he made his usual business trip to England that summer, his letters home revealed him as unusually troubled, a change apparently observed by his family.[116]

Shortly after his return, he and Victorine made the formal acquaintance of Mary's new fiancé, the pioneering German-Jewish physician Abraham Jacobi (1830–1919). By then widely regarded as the outstanding pediatrician in the United States, Jacobi had had to struggle to establish himself professionally during his early years in America after fleeing Germany as a political prisoner in 1853. He met Mary for the first time at the 4 December 1871 meeting of the New York County Medical Society, of which he was president. She was to be formally admitted to membership that day, only the second woman to receive that honor, and he adapted part of his formal remarks specifically to her, speaking of the receptivity of the society to all people regardless of gender and race.[117] Their relationship developed quickly. In Jacobi, Mary finally found her proper match, a man of broad horizons, strong principles, independent character, and unsurpassed medical knowledge. She had once complained to her mother from Paris: "it is my destiny . . . to be sought after by spoony men."[118] She was probably correct: her expanded life experience and independent views made it difficult for her to find a suitable mate in her generation of American men. It was hardly a coincidence, therefore, that each time she had fallen in love it had been with a foreign national (and not just that but with an exotic— a Jew—even within the category of foreign national). By summer she and Jacobi had entered into a formal engagement. To mark the event Jacobi invited Mary with her parents to dinner at his large house on West Thirty-fourth Street, the only time Putnam saw the house where his daughter would live most of the remainder of her life. Although Jacobi was hardly the kind of man that Putnam would have chosen as his son-in-law, this time at least he was able to respect her choice.

In fall 1872 Putnam watched with interest as Horace Greeley, his friend of many years, challenged Grant for the presidency. Although nearly temperamental opposites, Greeley and Putnam had taken career journeys that in important ways tracked parallel routes. Both sons of northern New England, each had come to New York City in time to participate in the early stages of the explosion of the print-related industries of the city and had risen to local and national prominence on the wings of their professions. Putnam had maintained close contacts over the years not only with various of the editors of the *Tribune* but with

Greeley himself, who was a fellow clubman at the Union League and coworker for international copyright. Now he watched as Greeley launched himself into one of the most self-destructive campaigns in American presidential history; Greeley would lose not only the race but his health and sanity. Days after the election he wryly placed a note in the *Tribune* that he was resuming its editorship after "embarking in another line of business six months ago."[119] Three weeks later he was dead. If Putnam was in town at the time, it is likely that he attended the funeral activities on 4 December and perhaps even the burial at Greenwood Cemetery. If so, it was the first of four trips he made to the cemetery that month.

Putnam's last week was one of almost unrelieved mental pain, although he himself seemed spared from physical discomfort. Whether or not he felt close enough to take Greeley's death to heart, that of Bishop's wife Hattie in childbirth hit him personally. Both she and the baby (their first) died in their Newark, New Jersey, home on the evening of Friday, 13 December, leaving Bishop distraught and the family stunned. The next day Putnam heard that his old friend the landscape painter John Kensett had died. One of Putnam's dearest associates in the world of New York City art, Kensett had been involved with him most recently as comembers of the executive committee of the Metropolitan Museum.[120] On Monday the sixteenth, Putnam attended Hattie's funeral in New Jersey. Two days later, he attended Kensett's, which took place at the Presbyterian Church at Fifth Avenue and Nineteenth Street. Many of the leading artists in the country were there to honor Kensett, as well as many of his friends from the Union League Club and Century Association.[121] The strain showed on Putnam; he returned from the Kensett funeral feeling tired and showing incipient signs of bronchitis, although the family at the time saw no reason to be alarmed.[122]

Inclement conditions gripped much of the eastern third of the country the next two days, as the city experienced New York City winter weather at its worst. Snow showers alternated with rain on Thursday, and Friday the twentieth dawned wet and muggy, before turning colder that night as snow fell and streets iced. Putnam was in the store most of that day, one of the last shopping days before the holidays. About 5:00 P.M. he was proudly showing a ministerial friend a copy of his firm's latest gift book, the *Gallery of Landscape Painters*, which G. P. Putnam and Sons had issued for the 1872 holiday season.

A lavishly prepared folio edition illustrated with steel engravings, it presented the work of some of America's leading landscape painters, even though in truth both the contents and the method of their illustration were soon to become antiquated. As he held the book in his hands, he suddenly slumped over, falling to the floor. Haven and Irving were soon by his side, and with help from others nearby lifted him onto a table. A doctors was called for but arrived too late: Putnam had died in Haven's arms. The cause of death, according to the coroner's report, was "disease of the heart"—presumably a massive heart attack.[123]

The funeral took place on Monday, 23 December, at the Baptist Church, corner of Madison Avenue and Thirty-first Street. The faith of his mother, it also became his in his later years, during which he had been one of the leading members of his congregation. His pallbearers represented various of the way stations of his life: John Wiley, William Cullen Bryant, Daniel Huntington, Henry Holt, John Sargent, Sanford Gifford, John Taylor Johnston, and Vincent Colyer.[124] Giving an international flavor to the large crowd that filled the church was the presence of the Japanese consul. The burial followed at Woodlawn Cemetery, the new nonsectarian burial ground located in a section of the Bronx that would have been familiar to the family from their residence the previous decade in Melrose. Why the family made that decision is not clear; it could not have been family tradition because Woodlawn had been laid out only a decade before and his mother was buried in Brooklyn. Woodlawn, however, was regarded as one of the most handsome "rural" cemeteries in the country and was rapidly becoming a favorite burial site of leading New Yorkers by the time of Putnam's death.

Amidst the gloom of that week came an act of professional kindness that reciprocated in spirit and act the many good deeds Putnam had done for numerous of his colleagues, not to mention for the trade itself. With the sons in mourning at home, professional colleagues (one of whom was Wiley), well aware of the family's financial exigencies, kept open the Putnam bookstore through the holidays, the most important book retailing days of the year.[125] That aid perhaps offered short-term relief, which must have helped because Putnam had left no capital for reinvestment in the cash-starved business, only life insurance policies whose premiums Victorine signed over to the business.

In the days and weeks that followed, tributes were printed in newspapers and magazines around the country. Both in private and public some paired the deaths of Putnam and Greeley, although few were then aware of the extent to which not only their lives but their respective spheres as book and newspaper publishers had been interwoven for nearly half a century. In early January, the New York book publishing trade passed a set of resolutions honoring Putnam that it sent out to newspapers for publication.[126] But the most eloquent—not to mention, knowing—of the tributes following his death was that of Mary, who, true to her family's gift for the written word, committed it to paper and had it printed anonymously. It closed by way of comparison with Irving:

> Irving has a national fame which will last, at least for a while; that of his friend, in the hurry of events, and in the urgent proportion of other things, must be sooner forgotten. It is for that very reason that I, as one of his nearest and dearest friends, have tried to gather up into an imperfect portrait these few traits of a man that I loved, not merely from habit and association, but because his character has always impressed me as winning and touching and lovely. He was nearly always inadequate fully to express himself; who is not that is worth the expression? He lacked grace and presence, so that his real depth and force were frequently concealed or misunderstood. But when these had once been felt, they were not easily forgotten. Nor, in a world thronged at once with louder merit and with vices yet more loud, can pass unprized and unmissed this life, which, though so energetic in action, possessed its greatest power in silence; and which, though so vivacious in worldly activity, yet through singleness of purpose and sincerity of belief ever kept itself at heart unspotted from the world.[127]

* * *

In a letter to the Putnams congratulating them on Mary's public success in defending her thesis in 1871, George William Curtis made an observation that would prove prophetic: "In your boys and girls how happily you will both re-live!"[128] Putnam died too early to see the prediction come true, but Victorine, who died in 1891, lived long enough to see at least some of the achievements of their children. She could have done so with pride: she had raised one of the most accomplished families in nineteenth-century America.[129]

The three eldest boys changed the name of the firm directly after their father's death to G. P. Putnam's Sons, the name under which they combined their talents, ambitions, and finances in rebuilding the family company. Haven reported to Bayard Taylor just days after his father's death that they had inherited little else from their father besides his "good name" and the company infrastructure, but he had confidence in his own abilities and believed that he had taken on much of the burden of running the company even before his father's death. The first years were as hard as the preceding ones. They had to survive the Panic of 1873, then several more years of precarious finances. As in years past, the main problem was fiscal: the business was badly undercapitalized, a problem that at one point in the 1880s brought into the firm the unlikely figure of Theodore Roosevelt as a junior partner.

In the years and decades that followed their father's death, the three brothers built the foundations of a successful business by putting it on a more solid publishing and financial basis than at any time under their father. Men of a different generation, they systematized the production and management of the company more fully than he had ever been able—perhaps ever thought—to do. With Haven running the publishing side, Bishop the manufacturing, and Irving the retailing, they were able to coordinate its various activities more smoothly than in years past. One key to their operations was that they managed to control the cost of manufacturing their works more efficiently than in an earlier era, particularly after Bishop oversaw the building of the firm's Knickerbocker bookmaking plant in the 1880s. Another was that Haven was a far better business man than his father. If less of a visionary, he was a man of outstanding talent and leadership ability and one of the most intelligent and literate publishers of his generation (as well as its nearest approximation to his father's many-sided role as trade organizer, unofficial annalist, and international copyright advocate). He was also one of its most scholarly figures, the author of numerous books, including *Authors and Their Public in Ancient Times* and *Books and Their Makers During the Middle Ages.* More to the point, he was a perceptive reader of his times who steered the company's publications generally toward history, science, and education, fields that matured in postbellum America alongside a far more high-school- and college-educated populace than his father had known—a populace that Henry James would bemusedly call "the most schoolhoused of peoples."[130] Although he and his brothers catered to the middle- to upper-middle-class audience that had been their father's chosen public, they learned the lesson of overreaching long before it was recited anecdotally to them in 1907 by a family friend, who repeated loosely from memory what he had heard more than three decades before from Horace Greeley: "The publisher is only a business man, and as such he must keep close to the market, cater to the popular demand. He must not yield to sentiment, has no duty. The public will not brook any manners in him except those of a servant! I can not give him verbatim. 'It is a pity it is so,' he said. 'George Putnam tried to lead the public, but did it at his cost: it did not thank him.'"[131]

Coordinating to a degree never achieved by their father the manufacturing and selling of their books, their packaging in a wide variety of popular series, and the workings of the New York and (reestablished) London offices, the brothers built a business that became one of the pillars of mainstream American publishing during the last generation of the nineteenth and the first generation of the twentieth centuries. They ensured its continuity by reorganizing it formally as a family-owned and -operated business. Their planning proved successful: they remained in business together as G. P. Putnam's Sons for nearly fifty years, Bishop dying in 1916, but Haven and Irving continuing to oversee the business until their deaths in 1930 and 1931. Although Bishop's talented son, George Palmer Putnam, (1887–1950) entered the business for a time, he left G. P. Putnam's Sons to pursue other ventures and the family lost control over the house shortly after the demise of the second generation.

The business was in effect a gentlemen's only affair; the sisters' only role was as silent partners whose holdings of company stock were invested and reinvested, with their permission, in the firm. The most talented of them, Mary and Ruth, found other paths for their work.

In the years following her return to New York from Paris, Mary earned a reputation as the outstanding woman physician of her generation in the United States. A medical writer as well as a practitioner, she found her written voice in the dozens of articles she published on matters of pediatrics, pathology, neurology, and medical training. A woman with a strong social conscience, she labored not only medically but also politically for a variety of causes, including the training of women doctors, female suffrage, and primary education. Although strikingly a woman of her own time, she also resembled generations of Palmer and Putnam women before her in the last regard, practicing her ideas about primary education on her daughter and publishing the results as *Physiological Notes on Primary Education and the Study of Language* (1889).[132]

Ruth Putnam graduated from Cornell University in 1878 and devoted her life to study, thought, and writing. She published nearly as many books as her eldest brother—most with G. P. Putnam's Sons, for which she did extensive service—but her range was narrower and her interests more focused. Her central topic was the history of the Netherlands, whose leading student she became in the United States in the generation after John Lothrop Motley. That interest included the early history of the Dutch in New York, a fitting legacy—and, presumably, an inherited one—from her father's Knickerbocker connections, especially Washington Irving.

The youngest of the children to survive, Herbert (1862–1954), undoubtedly knew his father least well but carried his devoted concern about books and the public sector to a higher level than was possible in Putnam's time. Educated at Harvard (largely at the expense of Corinna and John Bishop), he trained for the law but soon found his metier in the emerging profession of librarianship. Early in his career he served as librarian of the Minneapolis and Boston public libraries; he then moved on in 1899 to his major position as librarian of Congress. Half a century earlier, his father had watched with pride as Panizzi built up the collections of the British Library, then a generation before had regarded with approval the bravery of family friend Elie Réclus, who had stood guard as head of the Bibliothèque nationale and protected its collections from looting during the 1871 siege. To have seen the United States, which had historically lagged behind European countries, follow those countries in erecting a true national library (something that the Library of Congress had not been during his time) and the Jefferson Building to house it would have brought Putnam pride. So, too, would the knowledge that it was his son who oversaw its growth and modernization during his forty-year tenure as librarian.[133] By the time Herbert left office in 1939, his father's century-old dream of building a national culture had its official monument and storehouse.

Notes

1. HP-LC. It was signed by GPP on 1 November 1866; by his witnesses, 12 January 1867. It passed down through his youngest son Herbert and through Herbert's

descendants to the Library of Congress. It presumably remained in force at least through 1869, since the clause pertaining to the support of Catherine Hunt Putnam, who died that year, is crossed out. Whether it still held sway in 1872 when GPP died suddenly with no previous history of illness is unknowable; the New York City Surrogate's Court contains a GPP file for his will, but my inquiry found the file empty.

2. GHP, *George Palmer Putnam,* 2:354; GPP to Bayard Taylor, 13 September 1869; BT-C. A variant but probably less reliable account of the accident was given in the trade journal, where it was reported that GPP was hit by a dumbwaiter that fell from the third floor during his visit inside what might have been the same building; *American Literary Gazette and Publishers' Circular,* octavo series 13 (1 September 1869): 249.

3. HP-LC.

4. Her diploma is in HP-LC (container 30).

5. GPP to Bayard Taylor, 11 January 1867; BT-C.

6. GHP to Bayard Taylor, 4 March 1869; BT-C.

7. GHP to John Hart Morgan, 6 December 1868; Kroch Library, Cornell University.

8. For example, he wrote his mother one day that summer, following a period when business had been much slower than usual and revenues from the trade sale just a fraction of expectations, that if he had not succeeded in securing a $2,000 loan late the previous evening he was going to suspend payment that day; GHP to Victorine Haven Putnam, 30 July 1875; HP-LC.

9. Charles W. Elliott, "Life in Great Cities," *Putnam's Magazine* 1 (January 1868): 98.

10. GPP to Bayard Taylor, 7 June 1867; BT-C.

11. For details on the office staff, see GHP, *George Palmer Putnam,* 2:200.

12. This wish is expressed in his last will and testament; HP-LC.

13. Fields to GPP, 7 January 1865; GPP-P.

14. He reported to Taylor that he had sold only 2,000 copies after the first year; GPP to Taylor, 27 March 1868; BT-C.

15. GHP to Victorine Haven Putnam, 16 October 1866; HP-LC (container 5). Years later he took a completely different view of the matter; GHP, *George Palmer Putnam,* 2:341–42.

16. Henry T. Tuckerman, *Book of the Artists: American Artist Life* (New York: G. P. Putnam and Son, 1867), ix.

17. Ibid., vii.

18. That same season, GPP supplemented the publication of art works on his list by also bringing out *A Landscape Book,* an updated version of his 1852 *Home Book of the Picturesque.* In spite of the fact that the new edition was filled out with several additional essays, it remained as much as its predecessor an expression of the antebellum romantic landscape aesthetic.

19. The sole source known to me for information about the arrangement between G. P. Putnam and Son and the government of Japan is GHP, *George Palmer Putnam,* 2:305–20, on which I have necessarily drawn heavily in composing this sketch. I have also drawn on standard histories of modern Japan, as well as on the three private letters sent by John Bishop Putnam in Japan to his family that were thought interesting enough by his father (as indeed they were) to be printed in *Putnam's Magazine*: "Familiar Letters from Japan," *Putnam's Magazine* 1 (May 1868): 631–35; "A New Yorker in Japan," *Putnam's Magazine* 1 (June 1868): 758–62; and "A Visit to Yedo," *Putnam's Magazine* 2 (July 1868): 103–6. The letters unfortunately contain no details about the firm's business arrangement; GPP presumably edited them out.

20. E. C. Bates to Victorine Amy Putnam, 10 September 1867; HP-LC (container 5).

21. His son's inability to execute the company enterprise actually elevated his status in GPP's eyes. With Bishop waiting in limbo in San Francisco for instructions about where to go next, GPP lost no time in recalling him to the family and family business: "He waits at San Francisco for Barnes' instructions, thinking they might want him to go to Oregon or Sandwich Islands. He sends an excellent letter to Barnes and makes the best of his failure which is certainly no fault of his. The War smashed every chance of success for months to come if not for years. The poor fellow is mortified that he didn't succeed but he has no cause for it—He has shown uncommon business ability. I have telegraphed him to come home at once—for we want him with us." GPP to Victorine Haven Putnam, 21 April 1868; HP-LC.

22. GPP to Taylor, 7 June 1867; BT-C.

23. Both undertakings were mentioned in the same announcement in the trade journal, although not formally linked there; *American Literary Gazette and Publishers' Circular*, octavo series 9 (2 September 1867): 233.

24. He advertised its appearance as early as 21 August 1867 in the New York *Tribune*, (p. 6), then in the *Nation* 4 (29 August 1867): 178.

25. GPP to Taylor, 24 August 1867; BT-C.

26. *Nation* 4 (29 August 1867): 164; and 4 (12 December 1867): 472.

27. GPP to Bayard Taylor, 27 March 1868; BT-C.

28. "The First Volume," *Putnam's Magazine* 1 (January-June 1867), iii.

29. "Monthly Chronicle," *Putnam's Magazine* 1 (January 1868): 122.

30. *American Literary Gazette and Publishers' Circular*, octavo series 10 (15 November 1867): 63.

31. GPP advertised a long list of articles and serials set to appear in future issues of *Putnam's Magazine*, although a sizable minority were never published in its pages; *Nation* 4 (5 December 1867): 463.

32. New York *Tribune*, 3 September 1867, 6.

33. *Nation* 4 (5 December 1867): 463.

34. The erroneousness of that view was patently clear to one of his successors as editor, who spoke of the "tremendous history" the country had experienced since the appearance of the first series of *Putnam's Monthly;* "Editorial Notes," *Putnam's Magazine* 5 (April 1870): 501. It would also be proven inaccurate by the events in Western Europe, where the Franco-Prussian War upset the balance of power in the magazine's closing days.

35. "First Volume," iv.

36. "Table-Talk," *Putnam's Magazine* 3 (January 1869): 123.

37. One of the most interesting reviews was that of the *Nation*, which immediately noted and commented on the story's coded reference to Whitman: "Mr. Walt Whitman is the chief figure in it—chief in the author's intention—and is glorified as the grand incarnation of friendliness and brotherliness—to which we do not say No, for he may be that; that would have formed a part of any description of him which we might have made. Certainly he seems to have impressed more than one man with a great affection for him. But all this making men fall on his neck, and 'kiss him on the mouth,' and lean, fainting, in his embrace, and shrink from the holiness of his aspect, and so on—albeit he is disguised as 'The Carpenter,' and the men are imaginary men—is an offence, and offensive enough to justify the word 'disgusting' above written." *Nation* 4 (12 December 1867): 472.

38. The Stoddards were neighbors and social friends of the Putnams during the years of the second *Putnam's*, but it seems likely that the relationship was maintained primarily by the men.

39. New York *Tribune*, 14 November 1868.

40. GPP to S. A. Allibone, 20 March 1868; Barrett Collection, Alderman Library, University of Virginia.

41. GPP to Bayard Taylor, 27 March 1868; BT-C; GPP to Taylor, 5 October 1868; BT-C.

42. Frank Luther Mott, *A History of American Magazines,* 5 vols. (Cambridge: Harvard University Press, 1930–68), 2:429.

43. "Note by Mr. Godwin," *Putnam's Magazine* 5 (March 1870): 384.

44. The novel was originally published in 1890; repr. New York: Meridian, 1994, 13.

45. This article was the seventh in a perceptive series by Tassin called "The Magazine in America"; "*Putnam's* and the New Journals of Opinion," *Bookman* 42 (September 1915): 67.

46. Ellery Sedgwick, *The Atlantic Monthly, 1857–1909* (Amherst: University of Massachusetts Press, 1994), 127.

47. In the "Monthly Chronicle" that month, the writer (probably GPP) recounted some of the facts about the publication of the original article in *Putnam's Monthly* and added the further point of information that he had received through Williams' executor a dress believed to be that of Marie Antoinette, which the executor wished him to sell in order to pay "some of the debts of his late majesty"; *Putnam's Magazine* 2 (July 1868): 127.

48. *Nation* 9 (25 November 1869): 463.

49. *Nation* 9 (16 December 1869): 545; New York *Tribune,* 18 December 1869.

50. GHP, *George Palmer Putnam,* 2:206. Mott (or his printer) made an inadvertent slip in estimating the circulation of the second series of *Putnam's* as 1,500; Mott, *American Magazines,* 2:430.

51. GPP to Godwin, 27 August 1870; Bryant-Godwin Papers, Rare Books and Manuscripts Division, New York Public Library.

52. GPP, "London Revisited," *Scribner's Monthly* 3 (December 1871): 191–98.

53. *Discourses on Various Occasions by the Reverend Father Hyacinthe* (New York: G. P. Putnam and Son, 1869).

54. Part of the will is printed in Henry T. Tuckerman, *The Life of John Pendleton Kennedy* (New York: G. P. Putnam and Sons, 1871), 483–84.

55. While still waiting to see the printed work, GHP wrote Lossing that he and his father were "looking forward hopefully to the *history.* Our traveller, who has just started out to take orders in the West, takes with him some proof-sheets, with which to announce the work." GHP to Lossing, 9 February 1871; Special Collections, Vassar College Library, Vassar College.

56. GHP, *George Palmer Putnam,* 2:350. According to the *Bibliography of American Literature,* Warner did not publish editions of those works (*Wych Hazel, The Gold of Chickaree,* and *Diana*) until 1876–77; Jacob Blanck and Michael Winship, comps., *Bibliography of American Literature,* 9 vols. (New Haven: Yale University Press, 1955–91), 8:512–13.

57. I am indebted for this information to Jane Weiss, the editor of Susan Warner's journals.

58. GPP to Bayard Taylor, 8 September 1869; BT-C.

59. On his financial arrangement with GPP in the mid-1860s, see Marie Hansen-Taylor and Horace E. Scudder, eds., *Life and Letters of Bayard Taylor,* 2 vols. (Boston: Houghton, Mifflin and Company, 1885), 2:429.

60. Olmsted to his father, 13 July 1855; Frederick Law Olmsted Papers, Library of Congress.

61. Fields to Taylor, 13 September 1866; Huntington Library.

62. Taylor to James Osgood, 23 October 1867; Huntington Library.

63. Taylor to James Osgood, 30 October 1867; Huntington Library.

64. GPP to Taylor, 27 October 1869 and 30 November 1869; BT-C.

65. Fields to Taylor, 29 December 1869; Huntington Library.

66. Quoted in W. S. Tryon, *Parnassus Corner: A Life of James T. Fields, Publisher to the Victorians* (Boston: Houghton Mifflin, 1963), 349.

67. GPP to Taylor, 5 August 1870; BT-C.

68. GHP was mistaken in claiming that his father traveled to England in 1867; GHP, *George Palmer Putnam,* 2:331.

69. For an account of his trip, see GHP, *Memories of a Publisher* (New York: G. P. Putnam's Sons, 1915), 44–59.

70. GPP to Victorine Haven Putnam, 2 March 1869; in Joel Myerson, "George Palmer Putnam: Literary London in 1869," *Manuscripts* 38 (spring 1986): 156.

71. GPP, "Some Things in London and Paris—1836–1869," *Putnam's Magazine* 3 (June 1869): 733–43; reprinted in GHP, *George Palmer Putnam,* 2:219–48. Most of the details in the following section come from this source.

72. GPP wrote a friend shortly after his return from this "immensely enjoy[able]" trip: "The pages in the magazine were the literal pencillings in a memo. book which I made in two or three mornings on board the steamer—as much for my own satisfaction as anybody's." GPP to John Jay Smith, 24 May 1869; Library Company of Philadelphia.

73. Collins, who had previously published in the United States primarily with Harper and Brothers, was apparently willing to play the field in 1869. He sent the identical offer of terms and synopsis of his projected novel to GPP, Harper, and Appleton, the work to go to the highest bidder. Collins to GPP, 10 August 1869; GPP-P.

74. GHP, *George Palmer Putnam,* 2:351–52.

75. *American Literary Gazette and Publishers' Circular,* octavo series 16 (1 November 1870): 4.

76. *American Literary Gazette and Publishers' Circular,* octavo series 18 (1 November 1871): 5.

77. Twain quoted in *The Century, 1847–1946* (New York: The Century Association, 1947), 27.

78. He was nominated that year by his friend, the artist Daniel Huntington, and elected to membership; D. Seymour (club president) to GPP, 5 February 1859; GPP-P. In 1870 he became a member of its committee on literature; I owe this information to the Century Association's curator, Jonathan P. Harding.

79. Will Irwin, Earl Chapin May, and Joseph Hotchkiss, *A History of the Union League Club of New York City* (New York: Dodd, Mead, 1955), 88. The following sketch of the founding of the Metropolitan Museum of Art is based primarily on *A History of the Union League Club,* 85–92; Leo Lerman, *The Museum: One Hundred Years and the Metropolitan Museum of Art* (New York: Viking, 1969), 11–21; GHP, *George Palmer Putnam,* 2:324–31; and reports in contemporary New York newspapers and magazines.

80. Tuckerman, *Book of the Artists,* 11.

81. GHP, *George Palmer Putnam,* 2:325–27.

82. Lerman, *Museum,* 16.

83. On his appointment, see *Publishers' and Stationers' Weekly Trade Circular,* n.s. 1 (25 January 1872): 44.

84. GHP, *Memories of a Publisher,* 45.

85. The following discussion is based primarily on the important manuscript volume recently transferred from the Law Library to the Division of Manuscripts, Library of Congress (currently designated MMC 3588, George Palmer Putnam Papers). In late 1930 this made-up volume was donated to LC by R. R. Bowker, who presumably inherited

it from the recently deceased GHP or received it via his family. Its contents include the printed pamphlet *International Copyright Association* (New York: International Copyright Association, 1868), about fifteen of the perhaps several hundred letters written to GPP (or to association secretary James Parton) by authors and publishers unable to attend the meeting and bound into the volume, the text of the second edition of Henry Carey's *Letters on International Copyright,* and—incongruously—the 1858 printed auction catalogue of GPP's autograph collection, including pencillings in of prices received for each item. I owe thanks to Alice Birney for making special provisions for me to inspect this work (hereafter cited as ICA-LC).

86. Fields to GPP, 7 April 1868; in ICA-LC.

87. *Letters on International Copyright,* 12; in ICA-LC.

88. *Letters on International Copyright,* 19–20; in ICA-LC.

89. He was to issue Bryant's speech as a pamphlet, as he had that of Lieber and others a generation earlier. Its imprint gives the publisher as the International Copyright Association, but its address was Putnam's building.

90. *International Copyright Association;* in ICA-LC.

91. Baldwin to GPP, 1 April 1868; in ICA-LC.

92. Stedman to GPP, 26 April 1868; in ICA-LC.

93. Death certificate, New York Department of Records and Information Services, Municipal Archives.

94. Rhoda Truax, *The Doctors Jacobi* (Boston: Little, Brown, 1952), 95.

95. Ruth Putnam, ed., *Life and Letters of Mary Putnam Jacobi* (New York: G. P. Putnam's Sons, 1925), 203.

96. Ibid., 207.

97. Ibid., 207.

98. Ibid., 208.

99. GPP would send the ticket he was offered to attend the opening of the Suez Canal later that year to Émile Réclus, who made the trip and witnessed the ceremony, then filed an account of it that was translated by Mary Putnam and published as a lead article in the magazine; "Our Trip to Egypt," *Putnam's Magazine* 5 (March 1870): 328–43.

100. "The Fourth of September in Paris: Familiar Letter from a Young American," *Putnam's Magazine* 6 (November 1870): 553–60.

101. Ruth Putnam, ed., *Mary Putnam Jacobi,* 212.

102. Ibid., 236.

103. Ibid., 250.

104. For excerpts from the newspapers, see ibid., 288–89.

105. Only his last initial ("M") survived in the family record; Truax, *The Doctors Jacobi,* 100, 261n3; Ruth Putnam, ed., *Mary Putnam Jacobi,* 282.

106. Ruth Putnam, ed., *Mary Putnam Jacobi,* 292–93.

107. Ibid., 293.

108. Victorine Haven Putnam to Amy Putnam Pinckney, [1870]; HP-LC.

109. Union League Club of New York, *Report of Executive Committee,* January 1866, 4.

110. Sources for this sketch are Gwendolyn Wright, *Building the Dream: A Social History of Housing in America* (New York: Pantheon, 1981), 136–37; Sarah Bradford Landau, "Richard Morris Hunt: Architectural Innovator and Father of a 'Distinctive' American School," in Susan R. Stein, ed., *The Architecture of Richard Morris Hunt* (Chicago: University of Chicago Press, 1986), 61–4; Paul R. Baker, *Richard Morris Hunt* (Cambridge: MIT Press, 1980), 204–8; Charles Lockwood, *Manhattan Moves Uptown* (Boston: Houghton Mifflin, 1976), 294; and Allan Nevins, *The Evening Post: A Century of Journalism* (New York: Boni and Liveright, 1922), 368.

111. On the location of previous Putnam family homes, Victorine Haven Putnam to Amy Putnam Pinckney, 14 July [1870]; HP-LC.

112. Ruth Putnam, ed., *Mary Putnam Jacobi,* 310.

113. GHP, *George Palmer Putnam,* 2:332.

114. "In Memoriam," *Scribner's Monthly* 3 (November 1871): 110.

115. GPP to Taylor, 16 April 1872; BT-C.

116. Ruth Putnam, ed., *Mary Putnam Jacobi,* 312.

117. Ibid., 301–3.

118. Truax, *Doctors Jacobi,* 70.

119. Glydon G. Van Deusen, *Horace Greeley: Nineteenth-Century Crusader* (New York: Hill and Wang, 1964), 421.

120. GPP and Kensett were memorialized together at the 4 January 1873 meeting of the museum's trustees; New York *Times,* 9 January 1873.

121. "An Artist's Funeral," New York *Tribune,* 19 December 1872, 2. GHP was mistaken in claiming that his father attended Kensett's funeral the morning of his own death. There was actually a two-day interval; GHP, *George Palmer Putnam,* 2:359.

122. GHP to Bayard Taylor, 31 December 1872; BT-C.

123. Death certificate, New York Department of Records and Information Services, Municipal Archives.

124. *Publishers' and Stationers' Weekly Trade Circular,* n.s. 2 (26 December 1872): 698.

125. The others were Henry Holt, Andrew Armstrong, and Alfred Houghton. "Card," New York *Tribune,* 23 December 1872.

126. *Publishers' Weekly* 3 (16 January 1873): 42.

127. GHP reprinted her memorial sketch at the end of *George Palmer Putnam,* 2:393–407.

128. Quoted in Ruth Putnam, ed., *Mary Putnam Jacobi,* 288.

129. At least three of the children—George Haven, Mary, and Herbert—deserve full-scale biographies.

130. James made the remark during his return visit to the United States in 1904–5 after an absence of nearly a generation. It appeared in his series on "The Speech of American Women," which was originally published in *Harper's Bazar* (November 1906–February 1907); repr. *The Speech and Manners of American Women,* ed. Inez Martinez (Lancaster, Pa.: Lancaster House, 1973), 24.

131. Las Casas L. Dean to G. P. Putnam's Sons, 16 November 1907; GHP-C (scrapbook, p. 102).

132. Carol B. Gartner, Mary Putnam Jacobi entry in Lina Mainiero, ed., *American Women Writers: A Critical Reference Guide from Colonial Times to the Present* (New York: Ungar, 1979), 381.

133. On his mission of transforming the Library of Congress into the national library of the United States, see Jane Aikin Rosenberg, *The Nation's Great Library: Herbert Putnam and the Library of Congress, 1899–1939* (Urbana: University of Illinois Press, 1993).

Index

Index

Index

Graham's Magazine, 294
Grant, Ulysses S., 419, 444, 474
Gray, Asa, 285, 297, 357, 374, 436
  Botanical Text-Book, 159, 370
  Flora of North America, 159
  *Genera of the Plants of the United
    States*, 370
  relations with Putnam, 369–70
  sudden sale of *Genera* by G. P. Putnam
    at 1854 New York trade sale, 370
Gray, Thomas, 458
Greeley, Horace, 42, 123, 293, 330, 333,
  349, 413, 462, 474–75, 479
  death, 475
  exchange of letters with Lincoln, 410
  linkage with Putnam by contempo-
    raries, 477
  "Prayer of Twenty Millions," 410
Greene, George Washington, 271, 354–55,
  363, 365, 386, 402
Greenwood Cemetery, 475
Greenwood, Grace, 340
Griffin, Joseph, 18, 19–20, 57 n. 33, 77
Griswold, Rufus, 240, 271
Growoll, Adolph, 46
Grund, Francis, 118
Guizot, François, 96, 101–2 n. 35
Gulliver, John, 22
Gulliver, John Putnam (cousin), 24, 86,
  100 n. 3
Gulliver, Sally Putnam, 22, 24
Gurowski, Adam, 401
Gutenberg Bible, 202, 203
  purchase by Wiley and Putnam, 156–58
  sale to Lenox, 208
Gutenberg, Johann, 363

Hale, Edward Everett, 271, 349
Hall, James, 174, 188 n. 68
  The Wilderness and the War Path, 180
Hall, Samuel Carter, 324, 375 n. 1
Hamilton, Gail, unflattering view of
  Fields, 454
Hancock, John, 6
Hansen-Taylor, Marie, 389, 398
Hanson, John, 442
  "Have We a Bourbon Among Us?" 302–4
Harper and Brothers, 51, 61, 66, 67, 73,
  74, 81 nn. 5 and 7, 118, 121, 127, 128,
  131, 141 nn. 48 and 49, 141–42 n. 51,

158, 162, 163, 170, 181, 206, 239, 243,
  246, 252, 259, 272, 287, 295, 297, 306,
  316 n. 3, 358, 372, 392, 433, 434, 455,
  484 n. 73
  beginning as New York City printers, 35
  Bremer affair, 260–61
  Borrow affair, 260–61
  fire at Cliff Street plant (1852), 273
  role in copyright debate of 1853,
    346–47, 377 n. 53
Harper, Fletcher, dispute with Putnam
  over Bremer and Borrow, 260
Harper, James, 61, 162, 206, 462
Harper's Family Library, 41, 81 n. 7
Harper's Monthly, 41, 288, 295, 440, 446,
  447
  contrasted with *Putnam's Monthly*, 294
  "Editor's Easy Chair," 312
  as model of success in periodical pub-
    lishing, 287
Harper's Weekly, 440, 443
Harrison, William Henry, 98, 99, 103, 205
Hart, Abraham, 362
  debate with Putnam about interna-
    tional copyright, 343–47
Harte, Bret, 433
Harvard College, 2, 4, 348, 480
Hawks, Francis, 68, 251, 278, 285, 293,
  302, 303, 371, 442
Hawthorne, Julian, 472
Hawthorne, Nathaniel, 2, 3, 11, 135, 150,
  165, 166, 174, 179, 182, 187–88 n. 55,
  255, 270, 271, 290, 297, 337, 340, 354,
  413, 422, 472
  appearance in Library of American
    Books, 176
  The House of the Seven Gables, 239, 296
  Mosses from an Old Manse, 176, 245, 296
  The Scarlet Letter, 245, 296
  solicitation to contribute serial novel to
    Putnam's Monthly, 296
  Twice-Told Tales, 68
Hawthorne, Sophia Peabody (cousin), 2,
  422
  Notes in England and Italy, 472
Hay, John, 402
Hazlitt, William, 166, 172
  Table Talk, 171
Heade, Martin Johnson, 437
Headley, Joel T., 163, 174

493